China

A Historical and Cultural Dictionary

China

A Historical and Cultural Dictionary

Edited by

Michael Dillon

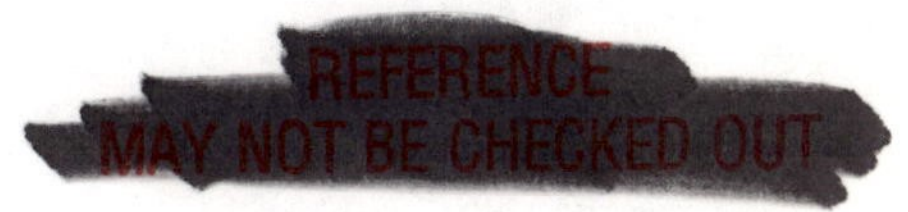

CURZON

Durham East Asia Series

First published in 1998
by Curzon Press
15 The Quadrant, Richmond
Surrey, TW9 1BP

Typeset by LaserScript Ltd, Mitcham, Surrey
Printed in Great Britain by Biddles Ltd., Guildford and King's Lynn

British Library Cataloguing in Publication Data
A catalogue record for this book is available from the British Library

ISBN 0–7007–0438–8 Hbk
ISBN 0–7007–0439–6 Pbk

INTRODUCTION

In 1979, I was rash enough to put together on my own a *Dictionary of Chinese History* (London: Frank Cass, 1979), which I described as a guide to "personalities, events, ideas and institutions in China from earliest times right up to the present day." In the Preface to that book, I explained that:

> It is not encyclopaedic, as that would be impossible in a work of this size and probably beyond the competence of any single author. Rather it is an attempt to provide a quick and easy reference to the names and terms which occur most frequently in English-language works on China and which can usefully be explained in a few hundred words.

This new reference book is not a reworking of that earlier volume, although inevitably it covers many of the same events, personalities and ideas which appear time and again in accounts of Chinese history and the essential factual information in some entries is of necessity broadly similar. It is still not encyclopaedic, but its scope is much wider. The entries have been written by seven main contributors whose sinological interests range in time from antiquity to the People's Republic and in subject matter from art, archaeology, philosophy, political thought and literature to sociology, politics and ethnicity in addition to conventional narrative history and who regularly work from Chinese language sources.

Entries have been selected on the basis of their potential interest to the general and specialist reader. It was not found possible to arrive at an objective list of the most important entries. The individual contributors, working on the basis of an initial list of headwords, have selected the entries they felt were most important in their own fields. In spite of the range of expertise and interests of the contributors, this work, like its predecessor, does not claim to be comprehensive. Even in a reference volume of this size, there may be entries that some readers will be surprised to see included and omissions that may appear equally eccentric. Biographical entries present a particular dilemma. Anyone familiar with the standard English-language biographical dictionaries now available for the Song, Ming and Qing dynasties and the Republican and Communist periods of 20th century China, to say nothing of the biographical material in dynastic and local histories in Chinese, will be aware of the vast amount of material available. Rather than attempt to summarise the contents of these biographies, the authors of the present work have tried to concentrate on the most familiar, the most commonly occurring and historically most significant names.

Where appropriate, suggestions for further reading have been attached to entries. The entries are not a summary of these works and do not necessarily represent the views of the authors cited, as the intention has been, as far as possible, to give a generally acceptable account of historical events, while indicating significant controversies. Reference works and more general historical texts have been suggested in the Bibliography at the end of the book.

The contributors are:

Sarah Dauncey
Michael Dillon
Caroline Mason
Keith Pratt
Johannes Reckel
Don Starr
Zhong Hong

ROMANISATION, CROSS-REFERENCES AND CHINESE CHARACTERS

The ***Hanyu pinyin*** 漢語拼音 system of romanising Chinese characters has been used throughout this book. Although the relative merits of different systems continue to be discussed, most books and journals in the last forty years have moved to this system. It has the merit of simplicity, avoiding the hyphens and diacritical marks of its main rival the Wade-Giles system, for which see the entry on **Romanisation** in the main body of the dictionary. Spellings in the older Post-office system have also been avoided, wherever possible – even where those spellings have become well-established.

So, Sun Yat-sen appears as Sun Yixian, Chiang Kai-shek is Jiang Jieshi, Peking is Beijing and Canton is Guangzhou, although the older spellings are given a cross-reference and alternative spellings have been supplied where necessary, for example in the names of politicians on Taiwan. Cross-references appear in **bold type**. Some names which appear very frequently and the names of most dynasties have not been cross-referenced.

Chinese characters have been included where it was thought helpful or appropriate. After long deliberation it was decided that they should all be traditional long-form characters *fantizi* 繁體字 rather than the simplified *jiantizi* 簡體字 which are the standard forms that have been used in the People's Republic of China since the 1950s. It may look strange to see CCP terms written in *fantizi*, especially when used alongside *Hanyu pinyin* romanisation, but to have included both forms would have been unwieldy. It is hoped that these characters might be useful for readers educated in Chinese or another East Asian language, but who are not familiar with *Hanyu pinyin*.

ACKNOWLEDGEMENTS

I am very grateful to the other contributors for providing their entries at a time when so many other tasks were competing for them, to Christina Bridgwater for typing, editing, liaison with the publishers and general administrative support; to Joyce Dillon for typing and editorial assistance; to Dr Marjorie Dryburgh for generating the initial list of headwords, and to Caroline Mason for meticulous proof-reading and copy-editing of the manuscript and many suggestions. Wu Daming's assistance in solving computer problems was invaluable. Zhong Hong's careful checking has prevented mistakes with Chinese characters. Any errors are, of course, the responsibilities of the authors and the editor.

Michael Dillon
Durham
October 1997

A CHENG (Ah Cheng) 阿城 (1949–)
The pen name of writer Zhong Acheng 鐘阿城 who came to prominence in the mid 1980s with the publication of his short novel *The King of Chess* in 1984 followed by *The King of Trees* and *The King of Children* (both 1985). The last was made into an acclaimed film by Chen Kaige in 1986. Ah Cheng was born into a privileged Beijing family which was rocked by the **Anti-Rightist Movement** and the **Cultural Revolution**. Like most other educated youths Ah Cheng was sent down to the countryside as part of the Cultural Revolution and spent most of his decade of exile (he returned to Beijing in 1979) in the minority area of Xishuangbanna, in the far south west near the border with Laos. His cultured family background and knowledge of traditional literature and philosophy led him to develop skills as a storyteller in Xishuangbanna to supplement his income. He also developed artistic skills (producing a well-known sketch of Zhou Enlai during the anti-Gang of Four protests of 1976, later published in the first issue of the literary journal *Today*) and on the strength of that returned to Beijing as an art editor. In 1986 he went to the USA and settled in California. His stories, on the theme of educated youth in the Cultural and post-Cultural Revolution period, are noted for their Daoist influence, their respect for traditional cultural values and, although less overtly dissident than the works of many of his peers, their rejection of the voluntarist excesses of Maoism in favour of a gentler, more spiritual and more ecological existence.
AH CHENG, *Three Kings*, trans. and introd. by Bonnie MCDOUGALL (Collins Harvill, 1990).

A Q (Ah Q) 阿Q
The anti-hero of **Lu Xun**'s most famous story, *A Q zheng zhuan* 阿Q正傳 The True Story of Ah Q', whose name has become a synonym for the self-deluding, cowardly bully. Ah Q is said to epitomise what Lu Xun saw as the worst traits of the Chinese of his period; he is oppressed by those richer and stronger than himself and suffers a series of ignominious defeats which he deludes himself into regarding as victories. He in turn attempts to bully the weak and sexually harass the female, greedy for status but stumbling uncomprehendingly to his eventual execution.
LU XUN, *Diary of a Madman and other Stories,* trans. William LYELL (University of Hawaii Press, 1990); Leo Ou-fan LEE, *Voices from the Iron House: A Study of Lu Xun* (Indiana University Press, 1989).

ABACUS *Suanpan* 算盤 'counting frame'
A device on which calculations based on the decimal system are performed. The use of the abacus was recorded in China in the early years of the Ming dynasty. It consists of an oblong frame of wood, which has a bar running lengthwise. Through this transverse bar at right angles are inserted a number of parallel wires (either 9, 11 or 15) having moveable balls on them, five on the lower side and two on the upper side of the bar. Each of the five on the first wire counts singly, but each of the two balls counts as five, i.e. when both are drawn to the dividing line they stand for ten. The next wire to the left will similarly deal with tens and the next with hundreds. As the abacus was considered easy to learn to use and calculations on it were very rapid, it became popular in China in the

Ming period and was introduced to Japan and South-east Asian countries around the 17th century. The abacus is still taught in China as part of the standard school curriculum, and is used regularly in everyday life by older people.

ABAHAI (1592–1643)
Manchu leader and eighth son of **Nurhachi.** On the death of his father he was just one of eight **Banner** princes but gradually became the pre-eminent Manchu noble. He raided Korea, the territory controlled by the Mongols of present-day Inner Mongolia and northern China between 1629 and 1638. In the Manchu capital of Mukden, he developed a style of government that was based in part on the Ming court and was a predominantly civil administration rather than the military administration of the old Manchu Banner system. The government incorporated Mongol and Chinese officials as well as Manchus and became the model for the Manchu-Mongol-Chinese administration that governed China under the Qing dynasty. Abahai was reponsible for abandoning the variety of ethnic terms used in the Manchu homeland including **Jurchen** and from 1635 Manchu became the only acceptable name. He renamed his empire the Qing ("pure") in 1636 and proclaimed himself emperor with the intention of overthrowing and replacing the Ming dynasty. He launched an invasion of north China in 1640 and also brought the Amur region of northern Manchuria under his control, but died before he could realise his ambition of conquering China.

ABAOJI (872–926)
Khitan chieftain who established the supremacy of the Yelu clan among the nomad tribes of the North-east and founded the Liao dynasty, taking the title of Emperor Taizu in 907 AD.

ABORIGINES
The indigenous population of China, many of them speakers of languages related to the Malay-Polynesian group, whe gradually came under the control of the **Han** ethnic group as it expanded from its Yellow River origins. They are now officially referred to as **National Minorities,** but the name is still sometimes used for the non-Chinese population of the central mountain belt of **Taiwan.**

ACADEMIA SINICA
Founded in 1928 as part of the Sino-Western cooperative movement for scientific research that established the Institute for Prehistoric Research, the Geological Survey, the Rockefeller Medical Institute and the Free Chinese University. Scientists associated with it who were active in the early exploration of archaeological sites around **Anyang** included Dong Zuobin, Sven **Hedin,** and Xia Nai. From 1928–38 archaeological work was under the direction of Professor Li Ji. See also **Bronze age**, **Neolithic Period**, **Oracle Bones**.

ACADEMIES *shuyuan* 書院 'book gardens', or libraries.
Private centres of academic study where independent discussion of philosophical and political ideas could be maintained free of government control. First established by scholars in the Song dynasty, they reached their

peak of influence in the Ming. Because of their outspoken opposition to maladministration and **eunuch** corruption three attempts were made to suppress them, in 1537/8, 1579 (see **Zhang Zhuzheng**), and 1625 (see **Wei Zhongxian**). They survived into the Qing, when their role was much diminished.

John MESKILL, *Academies in Ming China* (University of Arizona Press, 1982).

See also **Academy of Painting**, **Donglin Academy**, **Hanlin Academy**, **Imperial Academy**, **Schools**.

ACADEMY OF PAINTING ***Hua yuan*** **畫院**

Semi-bureaucratic institution drawing on the professional painters at court, competent in a wide variety of painting types and styles. There is little information about such official painting academies before the Song dynasty, though in the Tang period certain painters were summoned to court and undertook special official commissions. The Song Academy of Painting, officially founded in 984, was a subdivision of the **Hanlin Academy** of Letters. It sought to enlist as members the leading artists of the day, who worked in a style of painting that met with official approval. The tradition of direct imperial patronage culminated in Emperor **Huizong** of the Northern Song. He kept tight control over the painters in the Academy, handing out the subjects to be painted and setting examinations as though the painters were candidates for administrative posts. Successful painters were given a number of Court ranks. In this way the emperor could establish and enforce certain standards and principles of painting. The imposition of a rigid orthodoxy in the Song academy laid the foundation for the decorative and realistic "palace styles" which were to govern court taste until the 20th century. The development of the court academy also fostered the ambition of the scholar- artists to free painting from the stigma of its being a craft skill, which in turn promoted the development of **literati painting**. There was no official imperial painting academy in the Yuan and Ming dynasties. During the Qing dynasty there was an Academy of Painting under the **Qianlong** emperor.

F. WEN and M. FU, *Sung and Yuan Paintings*, (New York, Metropolitan Museum of Art, 1973); W.C. FONG, *Beyond Representation: Chinese Painting and Calligraphy, 8th–14th Century* (Yale University Press, 1992).

AFRO-ASIAN CONFERENCE see **BANDUNG CONFERENCE**

AGRICULTURAL PRODUCERS CO-OPERATIVES ***Nongye shengchan hezuoshe*** **農業生產合作社**

Unit of rural administration created during the **collectivisation** of agriculture in the early 1950s. **Mutual aid teams** created during the campaign for **Land Reform** were gradually amalgamated to form cooperative farming units usually based on existing villages. The first APCs were established in 1954 but most were created during the **High Tide of Socialism in the Countryside** in 1955–6, by the end of which more than 90% of households were designated as members of APCs. They were planned as an interim stage on the way to full collectivisation and the peasant members derived their income both from wages for their labour and rent for land they had owned since Land Reform. See also **Higher Producers' Cooperatives** and **Communes.**

AGUDA (1068–1123)
Jurchen leader of the Wanyan clan from the middle and lower Sungari region who challenged **Khitan** Liao supremacy over Manchuria and northern China, adopted the title of Emperor Taizu in 1115, captured the Liao dynasty's Supreme Capital at **Jehol** (1120–1) and went on to establish the **Jin** ("Golden") dynasty in 1122. See also **Huizong , Song Dynasty.**

AH CHENG see A CHENG

AH Q see A Q

AI QING 艾青 (1910–1995)
Leftist poet influenced by European modernists, especially the Belgian poet Verhaeren (1855–1916). Jiang Haicheng 蔣海澄 (he adopted the pen name Ai Qing in 1933) was born into a landlord family in Zhejiang, but was raised until the age of five in a poor peasant family; the poem which first brought him recognition as a poet was a eulogy to the woman who brought him up *Dayanhe – wo de baomu* 大堰河－我的保姆 'Dayanhe – my wetnurse' (1933). After middle school he went to study fine art at West Lake Art College in 1928 but the following year decided to go to Paris on a work-study programme. Whilst studying art in Paris from 1929–32 he took up poetry and was attracted to modernism and symbolism, particularly the works of Verhaeren, Rimbaud, Whitman and Mayakovsky. After his return to China he joined the League of Left-wing Artists in Shanghai in 1932 but was arrested and imprisoned from 1932–5 by the Guomindang for political subversion. Ai Qing published his first poetry collection under the title *Dayanhe* in 1936. During the anti-Japanese war he was initially in Chongqing but, with the encouragement of **Zhou Enlai**, moved to **Yan'an** in 1941. Two poems from 1941 illustrate where his loyalties lay: *Wo de fuqin* 我的父親 'My father' written after the death of his father is a renunciation of his feudal, exploitative family (in marked contrast to his attitude towards his wet-nurse) while *Mao Zedong* 毛澤東 is a personality cult type paean to Mao. In spite of the apparent political correctness of his poems, his theoretical essay *Shi lun* 詩論 'On poetry' (1940) showed a commitment to professional literary standards which resulted in his being included in the 1942 Yan'an rectification campaign (see **Yan'an Forum on Literature and Art**) and targeted for severe criticism in the 1958 **Anti-Rightist Movement.** It was 1975 before he was allowed to return to Beijing from exile in Xinjiang and 1979 before he was rehabilitated and allowed to resume his literary career. His highly political poetry is characterised by its populism, romanticism and sentimentality. He wrote of the suffering of the poor, their exploitation, his love of China, patriotism, sacrifice, the cruelty of warfare, all in plain understandable language which appealed to a mass audience.

AI QING, *Selected Poems* ed. Eugene Chen EOYANG (Beijing: Foreign Languages Press, and Indiana University Press, 1982).

AIDI 哀帝, HAN EMPEROR (Liu Xin 劉欣, 26–1 BC, r. 7–1 BC)
Grandson of Emperor **Yuandi**. His short reign saw intense political rivalry involving members of powerful families with imperial connections, his

homosexual favourite Dong Xian, and officials whose views on political reforms were linked to their belief in the validity of either the Old or the New Text editions of the Confucian Classics (see ***Guwen***). Under Aidi it was the former, generally more reactionary than their opponents, who were able to push through a number of reform measures. Some involved the structure of the government and the role of its senior officials, some were designed to reduce state expenditure, and included the closure of the **Music Bureau.** But the Emperor's early death enabled the Wang family, much favoured under his predecessor **Chengdi,** to stage a come-back, and paved the way for **Wang Mang's** usurpation of the throne. See also **Han Dynasty, Liu Xin**

Michael LOEWE, *Crisis and Conflict in Han China* (George Allen and Unwin Ltd., 1974).

AIGUN, TREATY OF (1858)

Signed by Russia and China to agree the boundary between the two in the Amur River area. Land on the left bank of the Amur was recognised as Russian and that on the right bank as Chinese downstream as far as the Ussuri river. Land between the Ussuri and the sea was not assigned under this treaty but was acquired by Russia under the terms of the Supplementary Treaty of Peking signed in November 1860 after the Western attacks on Peking. This treaty was considered by the Chinese to have been one of the **Unequal Treaties** and its provisions were never accepted. The Amur border has been a disputed area since and was the scene of fighting between Soviet and Chinese troops in 1969 during the **Sino-Soviet Dispute.**

AISIN GIORO

The family name of the leading Manchu lineage which provided the emperors of the final dynasty of imperial China, the Qing dynasty. The last emperor was Aisin Gioro **Puyi**.

ALBANIA

China's only ally during its period of isolation in the 1960s. Although China and Albania appear to have little in common in size, location or culture, Albania, ruled by a Communist Party from 1946 to 1991 and led by Enver Hoxha for much of that time, appeared to be China's only partner in the Communist world during the **Sino-Soviet dispute.** In the early 1960s as the dispute evolved, the USSR frequently attacked Albanian policies as a proxy for developments in China with which it disagreed.

ALCOCK CONVENTION (1869)

The agreement that resulted from negotiations on revisions to the **Treaty of Tianjin** of 1858. Named after Sir Rutherford Alcock, British Consul in Shanghai and subsequently Minister (Ambassador) in Beijing, the convention provided for the establishment of a Chinese consulate in Hong Kong, increases in the customs duty to be paid on imported opium and silk and restrictions on the most favoured nation concept to the disadvantage of the British. These terms were opposed strenuously by British commercial interests and the ratification of the Convention never took place. Chinese anger at this led to an upsurge of xenophobia during which the **Tianjin Massacre** of 1870 took place.

All China Federation of Trades Unions

The state-controlled Trades Union organisation established in the early years of the People's Republic. Independent trades unions were not allowed to operate and the ACFTU functioned mainly as a conduit for information passing between the CCP and the labour force and as a provider of welfare benefits.

Altan Khan (1507–82)

The leader of a Mongol resurgence in the middle of the sixteenth century. Altan Khan, also known as Anda Khan, was the grandson of Dayan Khan, a Mongol leader of the late fifteenth century. Altan Khan's forces attacked the area that is today Shanxi province and threatened the Ming dynasty's capital city Beijing in spite of the complex of defence works built by the government. Thousands of civilians were massacred or taken prisoner, cattle and horses were driven away and farmland and buildings were destroyed over a wide area. After laying siege to Beijing in 1550, Altan Khan secured an agreement with the Ming court that allowed for horse fairs to be held at Datong in Shanxi and Xuanhua to the north-west of the capital. With the support of Chinese sympathisers, he occupied a substantial part of Shanxi and the old Mongol capital of Karakorum in present-day Mongolia in 1552. Continued expansion gave his forces control over the area that corresponds to the present-day Qinghai province in 1559–60 and over the Kyrgyz and Kazakh tribes of Central Asia in 1572 and eventually Tibet in 1573–8. In 1570, he came to a peace agreement with the Ming emperor and was referred to by the Chinese as a vassal. Altan Khan was converted to the Yellow sect of Tibetan Buddhism by the third reincarnation of Tsong-kha-pa, the sect's founder. It was Altan Khan who bestowed on the incarnate lama the title of **Dalai Lama**.

Altishahr

Southern Xinjiang (*Nanjiang* 南疆) or the cities of that region which lie between the Kunlun mountains and the Taklamakan Desert. The name means "six cities" in the Uyghur language of that region and refers to Kashghar, Khotan, Yarkand and other oasis towns. Precisely which six towns are referred to is not entirely clear.

Amban

Qing dynasty officials appointed in pairs to represent the Chinese government in **Tibet,** to offer advice to the Tibetan government, and to maintain a small Chinese military garrison in **Lhasa**. The post was created in 1728 and was of symbolic rather than real value in relation to the notion of Chinese imperial authority. Amban were involved in Tibetan politics but had little success in imposing Chinese control over Lhasa.

L. Petech, *China and Tibet in the early 18th Century* (Leiden: E.J. Brill, 1950); H. Richardson, *Tibet and its History* (London: Shambala Publications, 2nd. edition, 1984).

Amherst, William Pitt (1773–1857)

Leader of the first major British diplomatic mission to China after the failure of the **Macartney Embassy**. Amherst who had been Governor of India was charged with expanding trade with China and extending diplomatic representation. He left Portsmouth in southern England on February 8 1816 and sailed directly to the port of Tianjin on the coast near Beijing in order to avoid the obstacles that Macartney had encountered in Guangzhou (Canton). The mission arrived on August 13, but the Jiaqing emperor was not enthusiastic about receiving an embassy from Britain and the familiar arguments about whether Amherst would perform the ***koutou*** ensued. Although the delegation reached Beijing, an audience with the emperor was not granted and they left for Britain from Guangzhou on January 28 1817, having failed to achieve their objectives. This failure and that of the 1834 **Napier mission** led to frustration among British traders and politicians which were to culminate in the **Opium War**.

Alain PEYREFITTE, *Collision of Two Civilisations* (Harvill Press, 1993).

AMITABHA *AMITOFO* 阿彌陀佛

The Buddha of Infinite Light, ruler over the Pure Land *qingtu* or *tsushita* Western Heaven, and one of the most powerful Buddhas in the eastern canon; believed to be incarnate in **Tibet** as the **Panchen Lama** and served by the Bodhisattva Avalokitesvara (**Guanyin** 觀音 in Chinese, Chenrezi in Tibetan), incarnate as the **Dalai Lama**. Because this sect's requirements of its followers were so simple, principally that they should repeat the phrase "Homage to Amitabha" to gain salvation in the next life, it was the most popular school of **Buddhism**. Pictures of the Western Heaven were a favourite subject for artists, some of the grandest being found among the murals at **Dunhuang**.

AN LUSHAN 安祿山 (703–757)

The Turkic-speaking commander of a Tang frontier army from Yuzhou and Pinglu in central Asia and leader of a catastrophic rebellion against the court of Emperor **Xuanzong** which broke out in 755. His ambitions had been fuelled by the extraordinary favours shown to him by the Emperor's own favourite concubine **Yang Guifei**, which culminated in the royal couple taking him as their adoptive son. Following a rise in **eunuch** influence, a general decline in bureaucratic efficiency, the loss of territory in the South-west to the newly declared state of **Nanzhao** and the disastrous defeat of Tang armies by Arabs at the **Talas River**, An led a military insurrection which began in the region of modern **Beijing**, captured **Luoyang** and drove the court from **Chang'an** towards temporary exile in **Shu** (modern Sichuan). He himself was killed in 757 and with **Uyghur** help the Tang retrieved the throne from his so-called Yan dynasty. The rebellion was put down in 763, but the dynasty's authority had been irretrievably weakened and its fortunes were now past their peak.

The rebellion had cultural as well as political repercussions. When the court fled the capital, many female musicians from the *Jiaofang* (see **Music Bureau**) were dispersed across the country, encouraging the spread of popular entertainment more widely through urban centres. Poets reflected the anguish of the people affected by the fighting, and the great landscape poet **Wang Wei** was himself captured and imprisoned by the rebels. The previous openness to foreign, especially Turkish, influences was replaced by a more guarded revival of Chinese culturalism. It was after the An Lushan rebellion that thinkers and writers such as **Liu Zongyuan** and **Han Yu** began the revival of Confucian ideas and standards which culminated in the formation of **Neo-Confucianism**. See also **Li Linfu** .

E.G. PULLEYBLANK, *The Background to the Rebellion of An Lu-shan* (London: Greenwood Press, 1955).

ANALECTS see *LUNYU*

ANARCHISM *Wuzhengfu zhuyi* 無政府主義

From around 1906, when it was first introduced until the mid-1920s anarchism was the most potent revolutionary force in China. The earliest use of the term for anarchism, *Wu zhengfu zhuyi*, seems to have been around 1903 when articles appeared on Emma Goldman and on anarchist assassinations in the West (a major anarchist strategy from 1890–1901). There was initially much confusion between nihilism *xuwu zhuyi* 虛無主義 and anarchism, but a general sympathy for the oppressed Russians and their use of terrorist methods. This interest was manifested in Wu Yue's 吳樾 attempted assassination of a group of ministers at Beijing station in September 1905. The earliest works introducing socialism to China were translations from the Japanese published by Liang Qichao's Guangzhi shuju 廣智書局 Extension of Knowledge Book Company in Shanghai and the *Xinmin congbao* 新民叢報 'New People's Miscellany' magazine in Yokohama. These tended to be social democrat rather than revolutionary, reflecting Liang's inclinations. Socialism in general seemed more applicable to the industrialised West than to agrarian China. After the Russo-Japanese war and the attempted 1905 revolution in Russia, articles on Kropotkin and anarcho-communism appeared in Japanese socialist publications. The Japanese Socialist leader Kotoku Shusui converted to anarchism after reading Kropotkin's works whilst in prison; he was executed in 1911 for a plot against the Emperor. Anarchist groups developed first among overseas Chinese students in Paris and Tokyo; returning students spread anarchist ideas and by the time of the 1911 revolution young intellectuals were aware of the principal anarchist ideas. **Ba Jin** was one well known Chinese convert to anarchism. What killed off the nascent anarchist movement in China was, as in many other parts of the world, the success of the Bolshevik revolution in Russia,. The anarchists remained significant into the 1930s but were not able to compete with the centralised party structures of the communists and the Guomindang.

Arif DIRLIK, *Anarchism in the Chinese Revolution* (Berkeley: University of California Press, 1991); Robert A. SCALAPINO and George T. YU, *The Chinese Anarchist Movement* (Berkeley: University of California Press, 1980 (rept.)); Peter ZARROW, *Anarchism and Chinese Political Culture* (Columbia University Press, 1990).

ANCESTOR WORSHIP

The origins of this tradition may be found as far back as the neolithic **Yangshao** society. It was already of major importance at the Shang dynasty court, where it was believed that the royal ancestors occupied a place among the feudal hierarchy of spirits on high and could be contacted through the intercession of a shaman. Kinship ties were a vital political weapon to both Shang and Zhou ruling houses as they struggled to extend their authority over a growing feudal empire, and as an element of **filial piety** they became closely connected in early imperial times with the religio-political cult of **Confucianism**. It was the responsibility of the head of the extended family to maintain the sacrifices to the senior male ancestors of the preceding three generations. A room might be set aside in the household where memorial tablets were set up outlining their genealogy and achievements. Ancestor worship thus underpinned the most important socio-economic institution of traditional Chinese society, the Confucian **clan**. The need for a wife to bear sons stemmed not only from their public and economic role in promoting clan interests but from their continuance of the family name and ability to maintain the sacrifices to their ancestors (see **Marriage**). In this way family traditions constituted a form of **immortality**.

Regular rites in honour of imperial ancestors were a major part of court ceremonial, and constituted one of the main elements in the **Rites Controversy** that undermined the Catholic mission to China in the Qing period. (See also **Jesuits**).

H.D.R. BAKER, *Chinese Family and Kinship* (Macmillan Press Ltd., 1979).

ANGLO-CHINESE CONVENTION (Beijing, 1906)

The Chinese had not signed the **Anglo-Tibetan Convention** of 1904, but now advanced their claim to sovereignty over **Tibet** in a ratification of the **Lhasa** treaty which – in the absence of any Tibetan representative – reversed the right of Britain and Tibet to conduct direct negotiations as they had done in Lhasa, indicating that in future the Chinese government must be involved in all matters concerning the administration or territory of Tibet.

ANGLO-RUSSIAN CONVENTION (St Petersburg, 1907)

Concerned to forestall the possibility of Russian influence in **Tibet**, Great Britain here signed an agreement which reversed its former implied recognition of Tibetan independence, specifically acknowledging Chinese suzerainty over Tibet (as it had done in Beijing (Peking) the year before), agreeing that neither Britain nor Russia should conduct negotiations over Tibet except through the Chinese government and that neither should attempt to send resident representatives to **Lhasa**.

ANGLO-TIBETAN CONVENTION (Lhasa,1904)

Concluded by Colonel Younghusband as the outcome of his expeditionary invasion and signed as between the governments of Great Britain and **Tibet**. Though the British acknowledged Chinese suzerainty in Tibet and allowed the presence of the Chinese **Amban** at the signing of the accord, the Amban himself did not recognize it. The principal clauses were the payment of a financial indemnity to Britain of over half a million pounds; the establishment of British trade fairs at **Gyantse**, Gartok and Yatung, and the right of British and Tibetan officials to negotiate further trading conditions; and the rejection of any other foreign presence in Tibet. The last was aimed at Russia, which the British suspected of having political designs on Tibet. The British, on the other hand, claimed the right to occupy the Chumbi Valley until the indemnity had been fully paid and the three trade fairs had been successfully opened. The Convention also fixed the line of the Sikkim-Tibet frontier.

ANHUI CLIQUE

Warlord group, led by **Duan Qirui** from Anhui, which emerged from the split in the **Beiyang Warlord** clique in 1917 and which controlled the government in Beijing (Beiping) in the 1920s. It fought with the Zhili clique and was defeated in 1922.

ANNAM *AN'NAN* 安南

Chinese Protectorate in the northern part of present-day Vietnam. The Chinese name An'nan means Pacification of the South. Disputes over Chinese and French influence in the region led to the **Sino-French War** of 1883–5.

ANTI-COMINTERN PACT

Agreement signed by Germany and Japan on November 25 1936 to cooperate against communism, and later joined by Italy. It provided political support for the Japanese invasion of China in 1937. See **Anti-Japanese War**.

ANTI-CONFUCIAN CAMPAIGN

The campaign to criticise Lin Biao and Confucius (*pi Lin pi Kong* 批林批孔) followed the death of **Lin Biao** and was part of the struggle for ideological control over the Chinese Communist Party that took place after the **Cultural Revolution**. Like many contemporary political campaigns, it was cloaked in the language of the controversies of ancient philosophy. In July 1973, Mao is reported to have claimed that Lin Biao, like the Guomindang was a supporter of the **Confucian** view of the world rather than the **Legalist**, with which he himself identified. The campaign was launched with an article by Yang Rongguo in the *People's Daily* on August 7 1973. The article, entitled "Confucius – a thinker who stubbornly upheld the slave system" (*Kongzi - wangude weihu nuli zhi de sixiangjia* 孔子–頑固的維護奴隸制的思想家) claimed that the Confucian concept of *ren* 仁 "benevolence", was nothing but a mask for his support for a cruel and outdated slave-owning society at a time when feudalism was a new and progressive force. The campaign gathered momentum after the publication of a joint editorial in *People's Daily, Red Flag* and *Liberation Army Daily* on January 1 1974 and took on some of the appearance of the mass campaigns of the Cultural Revolution. In retrospect, it became clear that, although he was never attacked by name, one of the main targets was **Zhou Enlai,** who was re-establishing his power base in the Foreign Ministry and the CCP, and that the campaign had been enthusiastically taken up by **Jiang Qing** and her supporters and gradually redirected against Zhou. It was a political campaign carried out largely through speeches and newspaper articles and had almost ended by the time Zhou died in January 1976.

ANTI-FOREIGNISM

Rising tide of xenophobia at the end of the 19th century in response to increased Western presence in China, and in particular the activities of foreign missionaries. It reached its height during the **Boxer Rising**.

ANTI-IMPERIALISM
Although opposition to imperialist and colonial activities in China is usually associated with the CCP, it was also part of the political platform of the GMD. In the early decades of the 20th century, anti-imperialism manifested itself in popular demonstrations such as the **May Fourth Movement** and the **May Thirtieth Incident**. Treaties signed in Washington and London between the GMD on the one hand and the USA and Britain respectively on the other, provided for the abolition of extraterritorial rights and the return of concessions to China, and were regarded as an important step in the struggle against imperialist control over China.

ANTI-JAPANESE WAR 1937–45 *Kang-Ri zhanzheng* 抗日戰爭 **'The War of Resistance against Japan'.**
China and Japan had been at war in 1894–5, a conflict usually referred to as the **Sino-Japanese War**. The Anti-Japanese War is the name given to that part of the Second World War that was fought on Chinese soil. It began with the **Marco Polo Bridge incident** on July 7 1937 when Japanese troops clashed with Chinese soldiers and used the incident to invade China without a formal declaration of war. In what has been described as the forerunner of Germany's *blitzkrieg* swift and concentrated military thrust, Japanese units overran the northern part of China by October 1937. In August, fighting for control of the Shanghai delta intensified and the city was finally captured in November. Japanese forces marched on the Guomindang's capital city of Nanjing, entering it on December 13. What followed was one of the worst war-crimes committed during the Second World War in Asia – the Rape of Nanjing (see **Nanjing, Rape of**). By the end of 1938, Japanese military units had taken control of all the key population centres of eastern China and the railway lines that linked them. Jiang Jieshi's Guomindang government was forced to retreat and established a temporary capital in Chongqing, a town on the Yangzi River in the south-western province of Sichuan. Resistance by the Guomindang forces was limited, in spite of political and military support from the United States and Britain. In the north-west of China and in smaller **base areas** in other parts of the country, guerilla forces under CCP leadership carried out a variety of resistance operations during which they succeeded in harrying and obstructing the movement of the Japanese army of occupation. After the Japanese attack on the US naval base of Pearl Harbour in Hawai'i on December 7 1941, the conflict in China was linked inextricably with the entry of the United States into the Second World War. The Anti-Japanese War was brought to an end, not by the guerrillas, but by the United States Air Force attacks on Hiroshima and Nagasaki with atomic bombs on August 6 and 9 1945. Japan surrendered unilaterally on August 12, Japanese units in China were gradually demobilised and the CCP and GMD recommenced the struggle for power in the **Civil War**.

James W. MORLEY ed., The China Quagmire: Japan's Expansion on the Asian Continent, 1933–1941, Selected Translations (Columbia University Press, 1983); Marius JANSEN, Japan and China: From War to Peace, 1894–1972 (Rand McNally, 1975); Lincoln LI, The Japanese Army in North China 1937–1941: Problems of Political and Economic Control (Tokyo:Oxford University Press, 1975).

ANTI-REVISIONISM CAMPAIGN ***Fan xiuzheng zhuyi yundong*** **反修正主義運動**
Part of the **Cultural Revolution**. Followers of **Liu Shaoqi** were designated as revisionists *xiuzheng zhuyizhe* 修正主義者 for wishing to apply Marxist principles less rigidly.

ANTI-RIGHTIST MOVEMENT ***Fan youpai yundong*** **反右派運動**
Political campaign and mass movement denouncing mainly intellectuals who were deemed to be "rightists". The campaign began during the **Hundred Flowers** movement which was ostensibly to provide the intelligentsia with the freedom to make constructive criticisms of the policies of the CCP. The key document of the campaign was Mao's speech *On the Correct Handling of Contradictions among the People* at the eleventh session of the Supreme State Conference on February 27 1957 in which he outlined his views on antagonistic and non-antagonistic conflicts in society and the continuing existence of class struggle in socialist China. A revised version of the speech was published in *People's Daily* on June 19 1957, and by then the CCP Central Committee was already committed to a full scale campaign against those alleged to have been rightists, having published its *Directive on Organising Forces to Repulse the Attacks of Rightists* on June 8. In the mass nationwide campaign that followed, as many as 500,000 educated professionals, artists, writers and scientists, including the novelist **Ding Ling** who had won the Stalin prize, were branded as rightists *youpai* 右派 by a movement that had a target of five per cent in each and every work unit. Most of these lost their jobs, were expelled from the CCP and many were exiled to the countryside for re-education through labour. The classification of "rightist" extended to the family of the accused and this brought discrimination in employment and even marriage. Rightist labels remained in place until after Mao Zedong's death.

ANXI 安西
A military protectorate-general established in the seventh century in what is today western Gansu by the Tang imperial court, marking a significant expansion of the influence of Chinese power towards Central Asia.

ANYANG 安陽
An area in northern Henan province, rich in ancient archaeological sites and first explored in the 1920s by the **Academia Sinica**. It was the locality for the greatest concentration of finds dating from the late Shang dynasty. As the last capital and royal domain it was known to its own people as Shang but later referred to as Yin or **Yinxu**. Among the most important locations in this vicinity are those at Xibeigang, where the royal cemetery of the kings who ruled from the city was first discovered in the 1930s, and at nearby Xiaotun, best known for its late **neolithic** grey pottery, its palace foundations, its **oracle bones**, and the tomb of **Fu Hao**.
LI Chi *Anyang* (University of Washington Press, 1977).

ANYUAN COLLIERY STRIKE September 13 1922
An early success for the labour organisation policies of the CCP which had been founded just over a year previously. Strikes in the Anyuan coal mine in

Pingxiang county, Jiangxi and on the Zhuzhou-Pingxiang railway in Hunan involved over 17,000 workers and three key Party leaders, **Liu Shaoqi**, **Li Lisan** and **Mao Zedong** were involved. The strike succeeded in compelling the management to recognise the negotiation rights of the trades union's Worker's Club. A painting of Mao, approaching Anyuan and carrying a rolled-up umbrella, became one of the icons of the **Cultural Revolution**.

AO 隞

The last but one capital of the Shang dynasty, occupied for twenty-six years in the middle of the second millennium BC under Kings Zhong Ding and Wai Ren. It was located within the region of modern Zhengzhou, Henan province, and possibly incorporated the Shang settlement at **Erligang**.

APRIL FIFTH INCIDENT *Siwu shijian* 四五事件

Demonstrations and riots in Tian'anmen square following the death of Zhou Enlai in 1976 which foreshadowed the protests and deaths of June 4 1989. Zhou, Prime Minister and highly regarded by many in China as a moderating influence during the Cultural Revolution died on January 8 and a formal ceremony of mourning was held in the Great Hall of the People on January 15, at which Deng Xiaoping gave the funeral oration. The thousands of people who lined the streets of Beijing as his body was taken to the crematorium at Babaoshan were testimony to the high esteem in which he had been held throughout the Cultural Revolution. In late March and early April around the **Qingming festival** during which families clean the graves of their dead relatives, the commemoration of Zhou Enlai took on the characteristics of a political movement and pamphlets, poetry and articles praising him and attacking Jiang Qing and her supporters began to appear. In Beijing, tens of thousands of people flocked to Tian'anmen square to lay wreaths and recite poems in Zhou's memory, harbingers of the **Democracy Movement** that was to follow the death of **Hu Yaobang** in 1989 and lead to the massacre in and around Tian'anmen Square. The Politburo decided that the actions of the demonstrators were counter-revolutionary and on the night of April 4, police and troops removed the wreaths and poems that had been posted on walls and monuments and arrested some demonstrators. On April 5, the demonstators returned in large numbers and there were clashes with the police during which there were injuries and possibly deaths and police vehicles were burned. After the death of Mao Zedong and the arrest of the **Gang of Four**, who were later accused of repression in the incident, the whole affair was redesignated a revolutionary rather than a counter-revolutionary incident.

ARAB TRADERS

Merchants from the Middle East dominated the Indian Ocean trade with China from the seventh century to the thirteenth century, the period during which China was ruled by the outward-looking Tang dynasty, the Song and the Yuan. Although they are usually referred to as Arab merchants, they may have spoken Arabic or Persian and have been followers of Islam, Nestorian Christianity or Judaism. Although there were Middle Eastern quarters in the Tang capital of **Chang'an**, Arab influence is most notable on the southern and south-eastern coast of China, where trading communities established themselves in areas with privileges very similar to the **extraterritoriality** granted to Westerners in the 19th century. The greatest monument to the Arab presence in China is the collection of inscriptions in Arabic, Persian and Turkish found on the elegantly carved gravestones in the Muslim cemetery in the port city of Quanzhou 泉州 in Fujian province. After the wave of Arab expansion died down in the 13th century, Middle Eastern merchants were replaced in the Indian Ocean trade by the Portuguese, the Spanish and later the Dutch.

ARCHAEOLOGY see *JINSHIXUE*

ARCHERY

Hunting with bows and arrows was a popular pursuit of the nobility from the Shang dynasty onwards, and mounted archery in warfare, using both single-arc bows and crossbows, was greatly facilitated by the invention of the stirrup in the early **Warring States** period. But archery was also a pastime with important ritual connotations performed to music at the court in ancient China. The significance of hitting the target in the context of important religio-social ceremonies may have been linked to the evolution of the centre (***zhong*** 中) as a locus of philosophical symbolism from the Zhou period onwards.
See also **Weapons.**

ARCHITECTURE

The Chinese architectural tradition began in the Yellow earth region of northern China and the principal architectural features have changed little over three thousand years. The basic building material used was not stone but timber. The fundamental structure of Chinese traditional buildings featured large curved overhanging roofs of ceramic tiles, supported by rows of timber columns bound together by horizontal beams. The columns stood on a platform of solid compressed earth, faced with stone or brick, in order to keep the floor of the building above the damp ground. The joints of the wooden columns and beams were mortised and tenoned with the minimum use of nails, allowing a certain amount of movement in the event of an earthquake. The ***dougong*** 斗栱 or wooden brackets, were developed for the junction of the column and beam in order to spread the load. All these parts were made in standardised shapes but varied in size for buildings of differing functions and importance. Buildings in China were considered an integral part of their surroundings and were usually planned on a south-north axis, with the main buildings facing south. The chief buildings of a complex lay one behind the other along this axis, separated by courtyards which were themselves flanked by buildings of minor importance to the east and west. Relatively few early Chinese buildings have survived because of the nature of the material, wood, in which most were built, and the predictable consequences of fire over time. However, pottery models of houses and farmsteads from as early as the Han dynasty do survive and give a good indication of what they looked like. Chinese building forms and structure systems have had a major impact on architecture in other countries of East and South-east Asia.

CHINESE ACADEMY OF ARCHITECTURE, *Ancient Chinese Architecture* (Hong Kong and Beijing, 1982).

Arrow War (1856)

Also known as the second **Opium War**. Conflict between Britain, France and China which developed after Chinese troops in Guangzhou boarded a Chinese ship, the *Arrow* on October 8 1856. The *Arrow* was sailing under a British flag, and when the crew were arrested on suspicion of piracy, Harry Parkes, British Consul in Guangzhou demanded that the Viceroy of Liangguang, Ye Mingchen, release them and apologise for the insult to the British flag. The crew were released but no apology was forthcoming and British warships shelled the city of Guangzhou, destroying thousands of buildings. French forces entered the action in support of the British and both sides demanded compensation from the Chinese. British and American naval forces attacked the defences of Guangzhou and throughout 1857 the town was under siege by British and French troops, finally falling on December 29. Its capture led to the Chinese authorities being obliged to sign the Treaty of Tianjin in 1858. See **Tianjin, Treaty of**.

Art

The definition of art in China has changed through the ages. Music was probably the first of the fine arts to mature to the point where is was recognised as a direct vehicle for self-realisation. The six arts, *liuyi* 六藝, of the Zhou period were music, ritual, archery, charioteering, writing and arithmetic, mastery of which created a well-rounded person. From the Tang dynasty onwards, poetry and calligraphy have been undertaken by scholar-officials as the highest arts. And in later periods, the principal arts were gradually formulated into the four arts, ***siyi*** 四藝 (the lute *qin* 琴, the game of *weiqi* 圍棋, calligraphy and painting) which had to be mastered by a well-educated gentleman.

While the Chinese literate regarded calligraphy and ink painting as the only true liberal visual arts, other arts such as sculpture, textiles, porcelains and enamel work, though much esteemed by Western collectors, were given the lesser status of "artisans' works". See also **Painting, Figure painting, Landscape painting, Music.**

Autonomous regions *Zizhiqu* 自治區

Provincial-level units of local administration introduced in the early years of the **People's Republic of China** to reflect the ethnic differences of certain regions, particularly in northern and western China and to suggest that ethnic minority groups, the **National Minorities**, were allowed a degree of autonomy in the government of their regions. The Xinjiang Uyghur Autonomous Region *Xinjiang Weiwuerzu zizhiqu* 新疆維吾爾族自治區 in the far north-west of China was formally constituted on October 1 1955, the Guangxi Zhuang Autonomous Region *Guangxi Zhuangzu zizhiqu* 廣西壯族自治區 in the south-west on March 5 1958. October 5 1958 saw the establishment of the Ningxia Hui Autonomous Region *Ningxia Huizu zizhiqu* 寧夏回族自治區, and the Tibetan Autonomous Region *Xizang zizhiqu* 西藏自治區 was formally established on September 9 1965. The part of Mongolia which remained within China after Mongolia's independence became the Inner Mongolia Autonomous Region *Nei Menggu Zizhiqu* 内蒙古自治區. At a lower level of local government, there are many autonomous prefectures *zizhizhou* 自治州 and counties *zizhixian* 自治縣 in areas where the ethnic mix is complex. The degree of genuine autonomy has varied and some analysts view the structures as a complete fraud. The ratio of Han Chinese to ethnic minority cadres which has differed from time to time and from region to region is an indication of how much real power lies in the hands of the minorities.

AUTUMN GRAIN see **DOUBLE TAX**

AUTUMN HARVEST UPRISINGS *Qiushou qiyi* 秋收起義 (1927)
Peasant rising in Hunan led by Mao Zedong and **Qu Qiubai** under the orders of the Central Committee of the CCP after the collapse of Guomindang and CCP cooperation following the **Shanghai Coup**. The insurrection was launched on September 9 with units of the National Revolutionary Army, local peasant militias and workers from the Anyuam colliery and achieved some initial successes including the capture of Liling and other county towns and the destruction of sections of the Guangzhou-Hankou railway. However, they were unable to hold on to their gains in the teeth of GMD and local landlord militias and Mao retreated with the remnants of his army to **Jinggangshan** on the borders of Hunan and Jiangxi where they regrouped. Although the uprising failed, Mao's experience of it convinced him of the importance of peasants in China's revolution and influenced his long-term political and military thinking.

BA 巴
A state based on the middle reaches of the **Yangzi** River and the valleys of the Han and Jialing Rivers in modern eastern Sichuan that formed a buffer between the state of **Shu** to the West and **Chu** to the East in the **Warring States** period. Its culture shared some features with that of Shu, although it retained distinctive characteristics such as its boat-shaped coffins. Its geographical position meant that it was more directly involved than Shu in the politics and warfare of the central states. Following the **Qin** state's annexation of Shu in 316 BC Ba also became a commandery, and the resultant control of the Han and Yangzi Rivers was an important part of the Qin strategy leading to the defeat of Chu in 278. **Liu Bang**, founder of the Han dynasty, had previously been enfeoffed by **Xiang Yu** as king of the former territories of Shu and Ba.

S.F. SAGE, *Ancient Sichuan and the Unification of China* (State University of New York Press, 1992).

BA JIN 巴金 **(1904–)**
Pen name of Li Feigan, a prolific modern novelist and anarchist, one of the leading literary figures of twentieth century China. Born into a rich landlord-official family in Sichuan, Ba Jin was brought up in a large extended household traditionally considered the ideal. However, after the death of his beloved mother when he was nine and his father when he was thirteen, Ba Jin came under the control of his despotic grandfather and came to detest the tyranny of Confucian social values. He read **New Culture Movement** literature and the writings of **anarchists** like Kropotkin (his pen-name is taken from the Chinese versions of *Ba*kunin and Kropot*kin*) and joined an anarchist organisation in Chengdu around 1920 (he appears to have remained an anarchist until 1949).

After leaving Chengdu in 1923 he studied in Nanjing for two years, seems to have spent the following two years mainly engaged in anarchist-connected activities (he was greatly affected by the 1925 **May Thirtieth Incident**) and then went to Paris in early 1927 where he was supported by his family on the understanding that he would study at a technical college. However, apart from studying French, his main occupation was reading and translating anarchist works. He wrote his first novel, *Miewang* 滅亡 'Destruction', while he was in France and sent it to a friend in Shanghai who, to Ba Jin's surprise, arranged for it to be published in a leading literary magazine, *Xiaoshuo yuebao* 小說月報 'Short Story Monthly'. The novel was about young revolutionaries in Shanghai; Ba Jin said his motivation was to unburden himself of all the memories. This is true of much of his writing: he describes in heroic terms the tragic lives of young people destroyed by the system, as its victims or its combatants, but in spite of the tragedies his works usually end on a note of hope. Over the following two decades he wrote prolifically, around twenty novels and a similar number of collections of short stories. His most famous novel, *Jia* 家 'Family', is a broadly autobiographical description of the evils and hypocrisy of the traditional family system. He continued to translate anarchist works but at a diminishing rate. His anarchist beliefs, clearly deeply held, set him apart from most left-wing writers who had Communist sympathies, but the support of leading figures like **Lu Xun** and his own enormous popularity ensured that he was tolerated, and when he was writing patriotic works in the war positively welcomed, by the Communist hierarchy. This was not true for the Guomindang whom he had to flee on occasions, as in 1934 when he felt obliged to go to Japan for several months. After 1949 Ba Jin was given high posts in the literary hierarchy but he wrote little of significance and what he did write was politically correct. He later spoke of his guilt at his willingness to denounce fellow writers in the **Anti-Rightist Movement** – doing what was expected of him. He suffered severely in the **Cultural Revolution** but was afterwards restored to high office, including chairmanship of the Chinese Writers' Association.

BA JIN, *The Family*, trans. Sidney Shapiro, intro. Olga Lang (Doubleday Anchor, 1972); Olga LANG, *Pa Chin and His Writings: Chinese Youth between Two Revolutions* (Harvard University Press, 1967).

BACKHOUSE, SIR EDMUND TRELAWNY, 2ND BART. (1873–1944)

A scholar and sinologist, Backhouse was an eccentric best-known during his life-time as the author (with J.O.P. Bland) of *China under the Empress Dowager* (1910) and *Annals and Memoirs of the Court of Peking* (1914). Originally from a prosperous Quaker family in Darlington, he spent much of his life in Beijing, largely in reclusion, and was the donor of several important gifts of Chinese books and manuscripts to the Bodleian Library in Oxford. Since his death, it has been discovered that many of the activities in which he claimed to have been involved (such as the sale of arms from China to Britain in World War I) were largely fantasies and lacked any basis in reality. Doubt has also been cast on the authenticity of the "diary" around which most of *China under the Empress Dowager* was constructed.

Hugh TREVOR-ROPER, *Hermit of Peking* (Penguin, 1978).

BACKYARD FURNACES
Small-scale steel plants set up during the **Great Leap Forward** of 1958 in an attempt to increase steel production rapidly. Most were in the countryside but urban work units also established them. The raw materials were scrap iron, household pots and local supplies of iron ore and labour was provided by people who were normally farmers, factory and office workers, teachers and students. It is generally recognised that the quality of the steel produced was of such low quality that the experiment was a failure, but it was an example of the ability of the CCP to mobilise millions in a political campaign.

BAI CHONGXI 白崇禧 (1893–1986)
Guangxi military officer. He was from an old-established Muslim family in the province and joined the Guomindang (GMD) in 1924 but retained a power base in his home province together with the other members of the so-called Guangxi clique, Li Zongren and Huang Shaohong. He served in the **Northern Expedition** and was the garrison commander in Shanghai who gave the order for the attack on communists and trades unionists on April 12 1927, that later became known as the **Shanghai Coup**. He was Minister of War from 1946–9 and fled to Taiwan when the GMD forces were defeated.

BAI HUA 白樺 (1930–)
Pen name of Chen Youhua 陳佑華, contemporary writer of poems, short stories and film scripts and Communist Party activist. Bai Hua came from Xinyangxing in Henan province. His early years were scarred by Japanese aggression, including the murder of his father, buried alive by the Japanese in 1938. As a teenager, he started writing and taking part in left-wing political activities. He joined the People's Liberation Army in 1947 as an underground propaganda worker in Guomindang areas and took part in the **Huaihai campaign.** Bai Hua formally joined the Party in January 1949. From 1951 he was a full-time writer of a broad range of literary forms including short stories, novels, poems, essays, plays and film scripts. He spent periods of time in ethnic minority areas and his writings were influenced by their culture; for example, the long narrative poem *Kongque* 孔雀, 'Peacock' was based on a Dai minority legend. In 1952 he was appointed head of a PLA creative writing group in Kunming, but was expelled from the army after being labelled a rightist in 1958. After working in a factory he was transferred to Haiyan Film Studios in Shanghai where he started writing film scripts. He returned to the army in 1964. After the Cultural Revolution and the 1978 liberalization he wrote a number of film scripts including the acclaimed *Jinwan xingguang rulan* 今晚星光如藍 'The Stars Gleam More Brightly Tonight', on the lives of soldiers in the Huaihai campaign. The filmscript for *Ku lian* 苦戀 'Unrequited Love' (co-written with Peng Ning) received a more frosty reception and made Bai Hua a major target in the Anti-Spiritual Pollution campaign of the early 1980s.
BAI HUA, *The Remote Country of Women,* trans. Qingyun WU & Thomas BEEBEE (University of Hawaii Press, 1994).

BAI LANG REBELLION (1914)
Predominantly peasant uprising led by Bai Lang 白朗, often known erroneously

as the White Wolf as his name sounded similar to the Chinese for that. On January 11 1914, the rebels took Guangshan in Henan and moved through Shaanxi to Gansu where they linked up with **Hui** Muslim insurgents. They were defeated by government forces at Fuqiang in Gansu on June 2 1914.

Phil BILLINGSLEY, *Bandits in Republican China* (Stanford University Press, 1988).

BAIHUA 白話

The 'vernacular language' of China as opposed to ***wenyan*** 文言, the 'classical language'. In traditional China as a written form *baihua* was mainly confined to 'frivolous' literature (including some of the masterpieces of fiction and drama) and to fringe works, but its use expanded in the late nineteenth century as Christian missionaries and political reformers sought to reach a wider audience. The use of *baihua* became one of the clarion calls of the **New Culture Movement** and by the 1920s it had replaced *wenyan* as the normal written form. See also **Chinese Language**.

Jerry NORMAN, *Chinese* (Cambridge University Press, 1988); John DEFRANCIS, *The Chinese Language: Fact and Fantasy* (University of Hawaii Press, 1984).

BAI JUYI (Po Chu-i) 白居易 (772–846)

One of the most popular and accessible of the Tang poets. Bai Juyi came from a lower bureaucracy background and was born in Xinzheng in present day Henan. He passed his *jinshi* 進士 examination in 799 followed by the *bacui* 拔萃 examination (see **Examination system**) two years later, after which he held a series of relatively minor bureaucratic posts. His career was blighted by a period of exile after he had given his support to his fellow examinee and lifelong friend, Yuan Zhen, and he was never able to achieve what he had hoped for in the political sphere. He wrote poetry from an early age and when he was 17 or 18 had travelled to the capital, Chang'an, where he amazed Gu Kuang with his proficiency. He became a prolific poet leaving almost 3,000 poems in which he favoured the new *yuefu* 樂府 style of long regulated verse pieces. His simple but attractive style made his poetry very popular with people of all backgrounds and spread even as far as Japan where it was quoted in *Genji Monogatari*, the 'Tale of Genji'. Two of his most famous poems are *Changhen ge* 長恨歌 'Song of eternal sorrow' which tells the sad and very romantic story of the Tang emperor Minghuang's love for Yang Guifei and *Pipa xing* 琵琶行 'Song of the Pipa' on the sorrows of a female musician.

Arthur WALEY, *The Life and Times of Po Chu-i* (George Allen and Unwin, 1949).

BAIMAO NÜ 白毛女 'The White-haired Girl'.

An opera in five acts based on a story circulating in CCP-controlled border areas in the early 1940s of a white-haired woman villagers believed to be a ghost. When she was tracked down by local officials they discovered she was the daughter of a poor peasant who had been raped by the local landlord. She had run away to the mountains, given birth to a child and was living off her wits in a mountain cave. The story was turned into the first national opera by He Jingzhi 賀敬之 and Ding Yi 丁易 and performed in Yan'an in 1945. It won the Stalin Prize for Literature in 1951 and enjoyed renewed popularity during the **Cultural Revolution**.

HO Ching-chih and TING Yi *The White-haired Girl*, trans. YANG Hsien-yi and Gladys YANG (Beijing: Foreign Languages Press, 1954).

BAMBOO ANNALS *Zhushu jinian* 竹書紀年
A chronological account of history from ancient times down to the year 298 BC, said to have been buried in the tomb of King Xiang of Wei (died 296). Although edited since its rediscovery in the Jin dynasty and once regarded as a Song dynasty forgery, its early provenance has now been reestablished and its value as a source of information on the Zhou dynasty proven.
E.L. SHAUGHNESSY, "On the Authenticity of the Bamboo Annals", Harvard Journal of Asiatic Studies, 46(1), 1986: 149–180.

BAN BIAO 班彪 **(3–54)**
Father of **Ban Gu**. He began work on the ***Hanshu***, intending it to form a continuation of Sima Qian's ***Shiji***. His principal independent work as a historian was his essay on **kingship**, *Wangming lun* 王命論 'Discussion on the mandate of kings', in which he strongly affirmed the theory of the **Mandate of Heaven** and linked it with the newly restored Later Han dynasty.

BAN CHAO 班超 **(32–102)**
Twin brother of **Ban Zhao**. As a military commander he re-established **Han** Chinese authority over that of the **Xiongnu** in the Western Regions after AD 73 with victories in Khotan and Kashghar. After defeating the Kushan, descendants of the Yuezhi people in Bactria, Ban was appointed Protector General with his capital at Kucha, where he remained until 102.

BAN GU 班固 **(32-92)**
Later Han historian and Poet, author of the **Hanshu** 漢書 *History of the Former Han*. He was the son of historian and scholar Ban Biao 班彪(3-54). Ban Gu was a precocious student who resolved after his father's death to complete the latter's *Shiji houzhuan* 史記后傳, a 65 *juan* former Han dynasty supplement to the ***Shiji*** 史記 *Historical Records* of **Sima Qian**. This became the *Hanshu*, a history of the first half of the Han dynasty, whose modified *Shiji* format became the pattern for later dynastic histories. The **biao** 表 'tables' and *Tian wen zhi* 天文志 'Astronomy Treatise' were completred after Ban Gu's death by his sister **Ban Zhao** 班昭 and Ma Xu 馬續. Ban Gu was initially imprisoned for his temerity in writing dynastic history, but later gained imperial support and enjoyed a distinguished career as a scholar-official, although he never achieved high office. According to some sources he participated in the **White Tiger Hall** discussions on the classics convened by Emperor Zhang in 79 and produced the official account of the proceedings, the *Baihutong* 白虎通. Ban Gu was an accomplished poet, especially of the ***fu*** prose-poem, genre. His well-known *fu* include the *Liang du fu* 兩都賦 "Fu on the two capitals", a description of the slendours of the two cities and a rebuttal of those who wnated the capital restored to Chang'an, and the autobiographical *You tong fu* 幽通賦. Ban Gu was imprisoned as a result of the affair of General Dou Xian 竇憲 and died there.
BAN GU: *Courtier and Commoner in Ancient China: Selections from the "History of the Former Han" by Pan Ku*, trans. Burton WATSON (Columbia University Press, 1974);

XIAO Tong, *Wen Xuan or Selections of Refined Literature, Volume 1: Rhapsodies on Metropolises and Capitals*, translations, annotation and introduction by David R. KNECHGTES (Princeton: Princeton University Press, 1982).

BAN ZHAO 班昭 (AD 41–c.115)
Daughter of Ban Biao; twin sister of **Ban Chao** and sister of **Ban Gu**; early China's most famous female scholar and writer. On her brother's death she completed his work on the ***Hanshu*** and collaborated with the renowned scholar Ma Rong in the study of the **Confucian Classics**, but her best known book was the *Nüjie* 女誡 'Instructions for Women', in which she elaborated on the four womanly virtues identified in the ***Liji***, those of speech, virtue, behaviour and work. See also **Virtuous Women.**

N..L. SWANN, *Pan Chao, Foremost Woman Scholar of China* (New York: Russell, 1960 (1932)).

BANDITS
Banditry was endemic in many periods of Chinese history, both because of the frequent recurrence of natural disasters rendering people unemployed and vagrant, and because of the absence of any formal means for the expression of public opinion contrary to official policy. Those condemned as bandits were sometimes bands of homeless seeking to support themselves in whatever way they could, and sometimes groups of dissidents resisting measures handed down from the capital for implementation by the local **magistrate**. But since taxes were transported from regional centres to the capital in convoys and internal trade earned merchants considerable fortunes, there were also, of course, those tempted into more deliberate lawlessness. Bandits were traditionally associated with the hills, cave hideouts, darkness, secrecy and *yin* 陰; officials, representative of open and legitimate rule, resided openly in walled towns on the plains, and symbolised *yang* 陽. (See ***Yin-Yang***) Since *yang* could not exist without *yin*, and since ordinary people could not really identify with officialdom but could often understand bandit aims, banditry could become glamourised. The Chinese equivalent of the Robin Hood story is found in the popular novel ***Shui hu zhuan***, which tells of an outlaw band waging successful campaigns against corrupt officialdom. Bandit groups were often the instigators of **Peasant rebellions** and the dividing line between bandits and peasant rebels and revolutionaries was always blurred, from earliest times up to and including the formation of the CCP's **Workers and Peasants Red Army.** See also **Secret Societies.**

BANDUNG CONFERENCE (1955)
The Afro-Asian Conference held in Bandung, Indonesia from April 18–24 1955. Representatives attended from twenty-nine Third World countries ranging from pro-Western to pro-Soviet with many non-aligned regimes also taking part. The conference agreed on statements opposing colonialism and promoting economic and cultural cooperation. The Chinese delegation was led by **Zhou Enlai**, who, in addition to addressing the plenary session of the conference, negotiated and signed an agreement on dual nationality which required Indonesian citizens of Chinese ancestry to decide on either Chinese or Indonesian citizenship. Following the conference, the term 'Bandung Spirit' was frequently used to indicate special economic and diplomatic relationships between China and its Asian neighbours.

Banking

Throughout the imperial period, money-changing shops, *qianpu* 錢鋪, were located in market towns, where they were responsible for creating the strings of copper cash that were used in commercial transactions and for relating them to the system of silver coinage in which taxes were payable. In the 18th century, the *qianpu* evolved into the native banks *qianzhuang* 錢莊 which provided credit for merchants and could issue bank notes and make payments in other parts of the country. A specialist branch, the Shanxi or remittance banks, *piaozhuang* 票莊 were able to remit money over great distances.

Andrea McElderny, *Shanghai Old-Style Banks (Chien-chuang) 1800–1935* (University of Michigan Press, 1976).

Banners

The Banner system of organising **Manchu** fighting men was introduced by **Nurhachi** in 1601 as part of his strategy of uniting all the Manchus under a unified command rather than in separate tribal leagues. Companies of troops were grouped under four banners, yellow, white, blue and red, and, as the size of his military force grew, four more banners of the same colour with red borders (or a white border in the case of the red banner) were added. In addition to their military function, the banners also evolved into administrative units encompassing the whole of the Manchu population. Taxation, levying of conscripts and family registration were among their responsibilities. As the size of the population under Nurhachi's control grew, additional banners were created. In 1634, eight Mongol banners were established to include the Manchu's Mongolian allies, and in 1642 eight Chinese banners were inaugurated. Although the Manchus adopted a Chinese form of civil administration once they had established the Qing dynasty in 1644, Manchu bannermen remained an important part of the ruling elite and were garrisoned throughout the country. They played an important role in the expansion of the Qing empire in the early part of the eighteenth century, but as their military role disappeared, the bannerman declined as a group and became inefficient, militarily ineffective and corrupt. When the imperial government needed a strong military backing against internal rebellion and external threats in the nineteenth century, the banner system was unable to provide it.

Pamela Kyle Crossley, *Orphan Warriors : Three Manchu Generations and the End of the Qing World* (Princeton University Press,1990)

Banpocun 半坡村

The best known example of an early **Yangshao** neolithic settlement. The site, outside modern Xi'an, Shaanxi Province, was excavated between 1954 and 1957 and has been radio-carbon dated to c.5,000 BC. The settlement consisted of over forty buildings, the largest – a communal centre – covering c.160 sq. metres, and was surrounded by a defensive ditch up to 6m deep. It was an agricultural community, farming with hoes, hunting, fishing, weaving textiles for clothing, making pottery, and storing grain and seed in jars buried in pits. Over two hundred graves were discovered, indicating a variety of burial practices (single, group, face up, face down, limbs straight, limbs flexed). Heads generally pointed to the west or north-west. The bodies of children were also buried in urns.

Pottery was decorated with primitive and roughly pricked patterns but also with more sophisticated red and black painted designs, especially of fish. Nearly ten thousand tools and utensils were unearthed from the site, including awls, arrowheads, fish hooks, net sinkers, stone knives, adzes and chisels, bowls, jars and basins.

K.C. CHANG, *The Archaeology of Ancient China* (Yale University Press, 4th ed., 1986).

BAOHUANGHUI 保皇會 'Protect the Emperor Society

The organisation set up by the 1898 reformers under **Kang Youwei** to support the **Guangxu Emperor** and act as a focus for the reformist, as opposed to the revolutionary, cause. In April 1898 Kang had set up the short-lived *Bao guo hui* 保國會 in Beijing and Shanghai with the three aims of protecting the nation *bao guo* 保國, protecting the race *bao zhong* 保種 and protecting the culture *bao jiao* 保教. After Kang was forced into exile he set up the *Zhongguo weixin hui* 中國維新會 China Reform Association, initially in Victoria, Canada, as an organisation to channel overseas Chinese support to the reformist cause. At an early meeting supporters suggested changing the name to the *Bao huang hui* in recognition of the Guangxu Emperor's role; the English name remained unchanged. In August 1900 the Society carried out an unsuccessful military uprising to depose the Empress Dowager, **Cixi.** This was the organisation's one and only military venture. Afterwards the Society concentrated on building up a large network of branches among overseas Chinese communities throughout the world, especially North America, which developed very successful educational and commercial activities. However, the Guangxu Emperor's death in 1908 largely removed the Society's raison d'etre and the reformist cause collapsed. See also **Hundred Days Reform**.

Jung-pang LO ed. and trans., *K'ang Yu-wei A Biography and a Symposium* (University of Arizona Press, 1967).

BAOJIA 保甲

A system of local administration and control based upon the ancient **Legalist** and **Confucian** concepts of mutual responsibility and the subordination of the individual to the group. Used in the seventh century and again briefly in the eleventh century as part of **Wang Anshi's** reform measures it was applied most widely and systematically during the Ming and Qing dynasties. A *bao* 保 comprised a thousand households, subdivided into ten *jia* 甲 of ten *pai* 排 each. One *pai* consisted of ten households. Each *pai, jia* and *bao* was under the supervision of a headman (*zhang* 長) who checked that information about the inhabitants within was posted on the door placard of each household, submitted regular reports to superior authorities on the numbers, movements and activities of his population, and raised and trained militia. Members of each unit were responsible for each other's behaviour and for reporting misdemeanours. In the eighteenth century the functions of the *baojia* and ***lijia*** structures merged. Aspects of the system have been revived in the People's Republic in the form of **street committees**. See also **Gentry.**

K.C. HSIAO, *Rural China, Imperial Control in the Nineteenth Century* (University of Washington Press, 1960).

BARBARIANS *YI* 夷, HU 胡

In the Sinocentric world view of the elite of imperial China, those living in or on the periphery of the country who did not speak Chinese and whose culture was not that of the **Han Chinese** were considered to be barbarians. In many cases the difference was between the settled agricultural society of China and pastoral nomads on the plains in the north and west. Many of the major dynasties in China's history have been the result of the conquest of "civilised" Chinese by barbarian invaders, notably the Jin and Liao regimes of northern China and the Mongol Yuan and Manchu Qing dynasties which ruled the whole of the country. Linguistic, social and cultural interchange between Han and non-Han people makes it extremely difficult to demarcate the two in many cases.

BAREFOOT DOCTORS *Chijiao yisheng* 赤脚醫生

Part-time rural paramedical workers, whose role was popularised during the **Cultural Revolution**. The term doctor is a misnomer as most had received only basic first aid and diagnostic training, but they provided simple medical care in parts of the countryside where there was no access to modern hospitals and doctors trained in Western medicine. The barefoot doctor system grew out of the policy of "walking on two legs", which was developed during the **Great Leap Forward** and in which the strategy of developing a modern medical service but also contining the practice of traditional methods such as acupuncture and herbal medicine was outlined.

BASE AREAS *Genjudi* 根據地 OR REVOLUTIONARY BASE AREAS *Geming genjudi* 革命根據地

The collective term for the areas under CCP control before the establishment of the People's Republic of China in 1949. The earliest were at Jinggangshan in 1928–9 and the **Jiangxi Soviet** based at Ruijin from 1931–34. After the **Long March**, the key base area was the Shaanxi-Gansu-Ningxia Border Region with its headquarters at **Yan'an**, but throughout the War of Resistance against Japan there were a number of smaller base areas in both northern and southern China.

***BEI TIE* 碑帖**

Bei and *tie* are two major forms of calligraphic work, which played an essential role in the development of the art and tradition of Chinese **calligraphy**. *Bei* refers to calligraphy copied and engraved on stone from which ink-imprint versions were made and was a method of reproducing examples for study, which became known in China from the third century AD. *Tie* refers to calligraphy on silk or paper in small format, such as letters and comments by early masters. Calligraphy on *tie* was usually circulated in the original and was only engraved on stone if it were an especially prized example. Inscribing on stones was a method of recording events or biographies in Ancient China. Innumerable steles, tablets, tombstones and monuments were erected at different times, many being of great aesthetic as well as historical value. Although stone cutting was the work of artisans (with the only exception being the carving of **seals**), the individual style of the writer of the text was retained and transferred to the stone. Ink rubbings from calligraphy chiselled in stone were widely used for reproducing calligraphy works. The earliest surviving sample of such rubbings comes from the Tang dynasty, when calligraphy by **Wang Xizhi** was cut into stone at the order of the emperor.

Making copies was fundamental to the development of all aspects of the art of writing. The methods of copying were increasingly exploited as the value of the writing of particular individuals came to be recognised. These copies were also useful to rulers wishing to promote one form of writing over another. In this way they developed not only a canonical body of content, but a canonical body of writing forms and styles. The many works of calligraphy in *bei* and *tie* forms have provided the Chinese with a repository of models which are widely treasured and frequently followed.

BEI DAO 北島 (1949–)

Pen name of Zhao Zhenkai, poet and writer. Bei Dao began to write in the early 1970s, during the later stages of the **Cultural Revolution**, which had interrupted his education but which became the stimulus for much of his early work. He became a leader of a group of young poets producing poems known as **menglong shi** 朦朧詩 "misty" or "obscure" poems, a term originally used by their detractors as condemnatory. In late 1978 with friends, he founded a literary magazine called *Jintian* 今天 'Today' publishing "unofficial" literature; this was forced to close down in September 1980. However, by then many of the *Jintian* writers enjoyed considerable literary fame and were being published in official literary journals. Bei Dao was always associated with the democracy movement and after June 1989 found himself exiled in the West where he has since lived and worked. He has produced a substantial body of poetry, much of it with an undercurrent of protest, some short stories and a novel, *Bolang* 波浪 'Waves'.

BEI DAO, *Waves* ed. Bonnie McDougall, trans. Bonnie McDougall and S. Cooke (Heinemann, 1987); Bonnie MCDOUGALL ed. and trans., *Notes from the City of the Sun: Poems by Bei Dao* (Cornell, 1983); BEI DAO, *Forms of Distance*, trans. David Hinton (New York: New Directions, 1994).

BEI ZHILI see **ZHILI**

BEIJING 北京 (PEKING)

Capital city of the last dynasties of the Chinese empire and since 1949 also the capital of the People's Republic of China. Beijing means 'Northern Capital' in the same way that Nanjing means 'southern Capital', the names dating from the twin capital system of the Ming dynasty. It was known as Beiping 北平, 'Northern Peace' during the Republican Nanjing Decade (1928–37) and that name was still officially used in Taiwan for decades after 1949. The city was the southern base of the **Khitan** regime in the tenth century and as Yanjing 燕京 was the capital of the Jin dynasty from 1153 . As Daidu or **Khanbaligh**, it was the winter capital and then the permanent capital of the Mongol Yuan dynasty, and it became the main capital of the Ming dynasty in 1421, relegating Nanjing to the status of second capital as the Yongle emperor moved his court north to counter the renewed Mongol threat. The city was rebuilt around the Imperial Palace, the **Forbidden City**, and this was also used by the court of the Qing dynasty.

BEIJING, CONVENTIONS OF (1860)

Agreements finally resolving the conflict between China and Britain and France after the **Arrow War** which should have been settled by the 1858 **Treaty of Tianjin**. The terms were dictated to **Prince Gong** under duress after troops under the command of Lord Elgin had burned down the Summer Palace, the Yuanmingyuan. The Convention between Britain and China was signed on October 24 and that between France and China on October 25 1860. China agreed to grant foreign powers the right to station diplomats in Beijing, and Tianjin was opened as a treaty port.

BEIJING MAN (*Sinanthropus pekinensis*)

The name popularly given to the skulls and bone fragments of the early hominoid type found in 1921 at **Zhoukoudian**, south-west of **Beijing**, dating from 500,000 years ago in the early palaeolithic age. Bones from around 750,000–800,000 years ago have been discovered at Lantian, Shaanxi province (see **Prehistoric China**). Beijing Man was around five feet tall, erect in posture, and had shovel-shaped incisors as in the modern mongoloid race. His brain capacity was halfway between that of an ape and modern man, and he seems to have been familiar with fire. All surviving bones from Zhoukoudian were lost during the **Anti-Japanese War** (1937–45).

H.L. SHAPIRO, *Peking Man* (George Allen and Unwin, 1976).

BEIJING OPERA

Popular entertainment form relating a limited number of familiar, traditional stories to the accompaniment of music, dance, and acrobatics. Its present form has matured since the mid-18th century, when it was much favoured at the court of the **Qianlong Emperor**, but its history incorporates the love of acrobatics at the Han court and earlier, the masked dances of the Tang period, the rise of popular story telling to musical accompaniment in the Song, and the development of early operatic styles in the Yuan and Ming. It combines colour, excitement, humour, and vocal virtuosity. Scenery is non-existent, props are few, but costumes and masks or facial make-up are gorgeously elaborate and identify the character's role and nature, such as the martial hero, the poor scholar, the corrupt judge, the bandit chief, the clown, the god, the femme fatale, the lion. Stylised movement and gesture indicate stages in the action, and the plot is unveiled in passages of soliloquy or dialogue interspersed with music, singing and action. Dazzling and daring feats of leaping, tumbling and swordsmanship are performed. Percussion features prominently in the accompaniment, and both the bodily control and the falsetto singing voice of the performers require long and physically arduous training. All parts were traditionally played by men, and despite the supposedly lowly status of public entertainers great reputations and fortunes were made by the masters of both female and male parts. See also **Drama, Mei Lanfang, Musical Entertainment**.

J.I. CRUMP, *Chinese Theater in the Days of Khubilai Khan* (University of Arizona Press, 1980); Colin MACKERRAS, *The Rise of the Peking Opera 1770–1870* (Oxford: Clarendon Press, 1972); Colin MACKERRAS, *The Chinese Theater in Modern Times: from 1840 to the Present Day* (Thames and Hudson, 1975).

Beiping see **Beijing**

Beiyang 北洋 Army
Land forces under the control of the **Beiyang Warlords** and commanded at the end of the 19th century by Ronglu, Manchu Governor-General of **Zhili** and supporter of the Empress Dowager **Cixi**.

Beiyang fleet
Navy created by **Li Hongzhang** in 1888 during the period of the **Self-Strengthening Movement**. It was financed from the collection of customs and other taxes in northern China, hence its name which means "Northern Ocean". During the **Sino-Japanese War** of 1894–5, the provincial fleets remained non-combatant and only the Beiyang navy engaged the Japanese. In spite of the size of the fleet, it was comprehensively defeated because of the superior speed and advanced technology of the Japanese vessels.

Beiyang warlords
Military officers loyal to **Yuan Shikai** who were a powerful political force in the early years of the **Republic of China**. In 1917, they feuded and split into the **Anhui Clique** and the **Zhili Clique.**

Bencao Gangmu see **Li Shizhen**

Big Sword Society ***Dadaohui*** **大刀會**
One of the names under which groups of **Boxer** rebels operated in Shandong province during the 1890s. They were notorious for their attacks on Christian missions.

Blooming and Contending
The process by which ideas were supposed to emerge during the **Hundred Flowers Movement**. It is an abbreviation of the slogan "let a hundred flowers bloom and a hundred schools of thought contend" *baihua qifang, baijia zhengming* 百花齊放, 百家爭鳴 and had its origins in the philosophical debates of the **Warring States** period.

Blue Shirts
Organisation of loyal followers of **Jiang Jieshi**. It was created in 1932, but had its roots in the Blue Shirt Society *lanyi she* 藍衣社 founded in 1926 by officers from the **Huangpu Military Academy** opposed to the Communist Party. Although it was opposed to Japanese aggression in China, its anti-Communist activities and name inevitably invited comparison with fascist organisations in Europe at the same time.

Bo Gu 博古
The *nom de guerre* of Qin Bangxian 秦邦憲 who was one of the leading members of the **Twenty-Eight Bolsheviks** who were the majority faction of the CCP during the early 1930s. He was General Secretary of the party from 1931–5 when he was replaced by **Zhang Wentian**. An active Politburo member

during the **Anti-Japanese War**, he died when the aircraft carrying him from Chongqing, where he had been negotiating with the GMD, crashed on its return journey to Yan'an.

Bo Juyi see **Bai Juyi**

Bo Yibo 薄一波 (1908–)

Prominent CCP politician and guerilla leader in Shanxi province during the **Anti-Japanese War**. Bo joined the Central Committee of the CCP in 1945 and became a highly successful career politician in the PRC, rising through party and government posts, particularly in the State Planning and Financial and Economic Commissions.

Bogue, Treaty of the (1843) *Humen tiaoyue* 虎門條約

Treaty signed by Qiying, the Viceroy of Liangjiang and Sir Henry Pottinger, the British Plenipotentiary at Guangzhou. It set out in detail how the provisions of the **Treaty of Nanjing** were to be implemented, including particulars of customs tariffs. The Bogue, which name derives from the Portuguese *Boca Tigre*, is a translation of *Humen* 虎門 Tiger Gate, the name of the main opening of the Pearl River south of Guangzhou.

Bohai

Manchurian kingdom (Parhae in Korean)founded in 698 by a Malgal general on what is now the border between northern Korea and China, by putting together the remnants of the **Koguryo** population defeated by the alliance between the Korean state of **Silla** and the Tang court. It gradually spread throughout Manchuria and was extinguished by Khitan forces in 926.

Adami Norbert, *Bibliography on Parhae: a Mediaeval State in the Far East* (Wiesbaden, 1994); Johannes Reckel, *Bohai – Geschichte und Kultur eines mandschurisch-koreanischen Königreiches der Tang-Zeit* (as vol.5 of Aetas Manjurica) (Wiesbaden, 1993/95);

Bön

Tibetan religious system which pre-dated the seventh-century arrival of **Buddhism** (see **Tibet**). It has been identified as an indigenous form of shamanism and an earlier import from Iran or India, even as an earlier version of Buddhism. Evidence for its rapid assimilation with the Lamaism promoted by King Trisong Detsen comes from documents discovered at **Dunhuang**, but rivalry also continued between the two religions.

Bondservants, imperial *Baoyi* 包衣

Chinese servants of the Qing court, members of families originally captured in Manchuria before 1644. Despite their subject status senior bondservants acquired great authority and wealth within the **Imperial Household Department**, and themselves employed staff of lower grade servitude. See also **Banners.**

Book manufacture

In the period from the Eastern Zhou to the Han, books were written on bamboo or wood slips, known as slip fascicles, and silk. Texts were written vertically from top to bottom on one side of the slips, which were then arranged right to left and bound together with cords. The slips could then be rolled up into a fascicle. Silk books, unlike the clumsy slip fascicles, were soft, light and portable, but much more expensive. Both slips and silk were replaced by **paper** towards the end of the Later Han dynasty. To overcome the problems in the time-consuming process of transcribing books by hand, methods of **printing** were developed. The earliest was in the form of rubbings, where original texts were engraved in stone and rubbings taken from them on paper, allowing the potential for considerable circulation of a single text. The other form of printing was with carved wood blocks, which later evolved into systems using movable type. There exists evidence of simple printing in the eighth century, sophisticated printing in the ninth and a flourishing printing trade by the tenth century. The invention of movable type in the mid-eleventh century did not, however, replace carved woodblock editions in the following centuries. One reason was that the scholar class wanted not just communication but elegance of communication, and movable type could never achieve the balance required of Chinese calligraphy.

In the late Ming period, illustrated books flourished in response to the growing affluence of the merchant class and its developing patronage of the arts. In the evolution of bookbinding methods, from the scroll to butterfly, wrapped-back, and stitched-thread styles, simplicity, convenience and practicality were the major concerns. For a multi-volumed book, the soft volumes were stacked one upon the other and contained within a hard casing which was folded round and secured with bone or ivory toggles.

BOOK OF CHANGES see ***YIJING***

BOOK OF DOCUMENTS see ***SHANGSHU***

BOOK OF FILIAL PIETY see ***XIAOJING***

BOOK OF HISTORY see ***SHANGSHU***

BOOK OF LORD SHANG see ***SHANGJUNSHU***

BOOK OF RITES see ***LIJI***

BOOK OF RITUAL see ***LIJI***

BOOK OF SONGS see ***SHIJING***

BORODIN, MIKHAIL MARKOVICH (1884–1951)

Soviet diplomat sent to China after the agreement signed by Sun Yixian and Adolph Joffe to help Sun reorganise the Guomindang. Borodin, whose original name was Michael Gruesenberg, was born in Lithuania in 1884 and lived in the USA between 1907 and 1917. From 1919 he worked for the **Comintern**. He arrived in China in 1923 with General Galen who was responsible for creating an effective GMD military force, and was accompanied by forty other Soviet advisers. Borodin was the architect of the programme of the remodelled GMD and of the first **United Front** with the CCP. Political and strategic differences within the new GMD led to attacks on him by the GMD right wing and he was finally forced to return to Russia on July 27 1927 after losing the battle to permit members of the CCP to remain within the GMD. He continued to work in propaganda and journalism in the Soviet Union and headed the Soviet Information Bureau from 1941–9. His replacement as Comintern adviser in China was M.N. Roy

Dan JACOBS, *Borodin: Stalin's Man in China* (Harvard University Press, 1981).

BOURGEOISIE see **CLASSES**

BOXER RISING (1899–1901) ***Yihetuan yundong*** **義和團運動**

A period of major unrest in northern China at the end of the nineteenth century, mainly associated with the secret society the Yihequan 義和拳 "The Fists of Righteousness and Harmony", popularly known as the Boxers. China was in crisis. Defeat in the **Sino-Japanese War** was followed by the **Hundred Days Reform**, an elite movement which questioned the very basis of imperial rule. To many Chinese in the countryside, the parlous state into which the country had fallen – economic depression, famine and banditry – was due simply to the presence of foreigners. A wave of xenophobia spread throughout the villages, in many cases supported by the local **gentry** who feared and resented the way that Christianity appeared to be undermining the Confucianism that formed the basis for their control of the population. All foreign poducts were suspect as well as the foreigners themselves and foreign-owned businesses, factories and railways and foreign currency in circulation all came in for criticism.

In 1898 the Yellow River burst its banks and caused disastrous flooding. Sichuan, Jiangsu, Jiangxi and Anhui provinces were all badly affected, but the greatest catastrophe was in Shandong. To superstitious rural Chinese, this was proof positive that the foreigners had been interfering with nature.

The Yihequan were an offshoot of the **Eight Trigrams** sect which was part of the **White Lotus** tradition of millenarian **Buddhism**. The name appeared first in about 1808 and the society was active in Shandong and also in Henan, Jiangsu, Anhui and **Zhili**, initially as an anti-Qing force, dedicated to restoring the Ming dynasty. The Boxer groups were small, usually 25 or so and under the supreme authority of their leader and assistants. Their targets were the different levels of foreign involvement in their areas. Primary hairy ones (*da maozi* 大毛子) were foreigners themselves, secondary hairy ones (*er maozi* 二毛子) were Chinese Christians or those involved in foreign enterprises, while anyone who used foreign goods was classified as a tertiary hairy one (*san maozi* 三毛子). Members of the Boxer bands were socially marginal individuals with no land or work and tended to be contemptuous of officialdom. Their ideology was millenarian, irrational and theatrical and relied heavily on belief in ritual and magic.

Li Bingheng, Governor of Shandong province, cultivated the Boxers, in particular their branch known as the **Big Sword Society** (*Dadaohui* 大刀會), but he was dismissed in 1897 after the death of German missionaries prompted German forces to occupy the bay of Jiaozhou near Qingdao. His replacement, the Manchu noble Yuxian, also patronised the Boxers and proposed that they train his own forces and ally with him under the slogan *fu Qing mie yang* 扶清滅洋 "support the Qing and exterminate the foreigner". The Boxers were redesignated Yihetuan 義和團, the 'Corps of Righteousness and Harmony ' and began to function as an officially sanctioned militia. Yuxian persuaded the imperial court that they should be supported.

With this official sponsorship, the small Boxer groups coalesced into a major force and, although they still clashed with the armies of the Qing during 1899, by June 1900 they were being called on by the court to support the dynasty against the foreigners. On June 13 Boxer units laid siege to the foreign legation (embassy) quarter in Beijing and foreign troops moved towards Tianjin in response the following day. An expeditionary force of 8,000 Japanese, 4,800 Russian, 3,000 British, 2,100 American and smaller numbers of French, Austrian and Italian troops was mounted to lift the siege and set out for Beijing on August 4. The siege was finally lifted on August 14 and the Empress Dowager **Cixi** and her court fled to Xi'an.

On September 7 1901, **Li Hongzhang**, acting for the court, was forced to sign the Boxer Protocol. China agreed to pay the equivalent of £67 million in reparations over the next forty years and to the punishment of officials deemed guilty of causing the rising, including death sentences. China's defences were also greatly downgraded and foreign troops were to be stationed in China permanently.

Joseph ESHERICK, *The Origins of the Boxer Uprising* (Berkeley: University of California Press, 1987); David BUCK, *Recent Chinese Studies of the Boxer Movement* (M.E. Sharpe, 1987).

BRAUN, OTTO Li De 李德 (1900–1974)

Comintern military adviser who accompanied the CCP on their **Long March**. Braun was a German communist from Munich who escaped from prison and went to Moscow. He was given military training and sent to China and arrived in Ruijin, the capital of the **Jiangxi Soviet** in 1932 with **Bo Gu** and other senior CCP members. He was a forceful advocate of positional warfare and opposed Mao Zedong's guerrilla tactics. Disastrous losses discredited Braun's policy and at the **Zunyi Conference** of January 1935, he was finally defeated.

Otto BRAUN, *A Comintern Agent in China 1932–1939* (Stanford University Press, 1982).

BRONZE AGE

May be dated in China from the early second millennium BC onwards. Argument persists over possible external sources of inspiration from the Eurasian steppe or south-east Asia. Earliest evidence comes from **Erlitou**, and leads directly into the great tradition of bronze craftsmanship associated with north China and the Shang domain. Important regional centres existed in the **Yangzi River** valley (see **Wucheng**) and in modern Sichuan (see **Sanxingdui**) in the late second or early first millennia BC. Bronze was valued as an elite symbol of Shang royal power, and bronzesmiths were respected as important members of society in the Shang domain. It was particularly associated with ritual vessels, but was also used for the manufacture of bells and weaponry. Piece-mould casting seems to have been practised from earliest times, and *cire* *perdue* production developed from around the mid-fifth century BC. Use of bronze spread among lower orders of the nobility through the Zhou period and fine artefacts, including lamps, figurines and Buddhist statues, continued to be made of bronze into the imperial era, but the development of iron technology from around 500 BC put limitations upon its development for further general use. See also ***Taotie***

C. DEYDIER, *Les Bronzes Archaiques Chinois : Archaic Chinese Bronzes, Vol. I, Xia and Shang* (Paris: Les Editions d'Art et d'Histoire, 1995); BAGLEY, Robert W., *The Great Bronze Age of China* (New York, Metropolitan Museum of Art, 1980).

BRONZE INSCRIPTIONS

In the middle Shang period, when importance was attached to the overall aesthetic effect of design and decoration, these were rare and usually limited to a few characters. In the late Shang and Western Zhou, when the range of vessels expanded and some pieces were larger and heavier, longer inscriptions became more frequent and form a major source of documentary information on the history and institutions of the period, complementing the written evidence of the ***Shijing*** and ***Shujing***.

BRONZE MIRRORS *Tongjing* 銅鏡 or *Tongjian* 銅鑒.

Most mirrors are circular but occasionally square or in floral shapes. Early examples of bronze mirrors, from tombs of Qijia culture, late Neolithic period and Shang tombs at **Yinxu,** are small and thin, with a polished reflecting surface and a back either with geometric patterns or plain. Mirrors from the Warring States period were found in many areas, showing their greater popularity, technical advance and richer decorative motifs. For the purpose of carrying or hanging, a small fluted loop is usually on the back for the passage of a cord. The loop was transformed into a round boss by the time of Han dynasty as mirrors became larger and thicker. Auspicious inscriptions appeared on the back of Han mirrors and cosmic designs, such as symbolic animals of the four quarters (***sishen*** 四神), became popular. The artistic characteristics of bronze mirrors changed significantly in the Tang dynasty. Floral and animal motifs became less stylised and stylistic influences from the Middle East countries were evident. Many mirrors were decorated with inlaid mother-of-pearl, gold and silver. Later bronze mirrors had more importance attached to their functional performance than to their decorative appearance. During the Qing dynasty, bronze mirrors were gradually replaced by glass mirrors.

BUCHAREST CONFERENCE (1960)

The Third Congress of the Rumanian Workers' Party held in Bucharest in June 1960. On June 21, Nikita Khrushchev, Prime Minister and First Secretary of the Communist Party of the Soviet Union, made a speech in which he denounced Chinese views on Leninism, war and imperialism. This was an early indication of the looming **Sino-Soviet Dispute** and foreshadowed the break that was to come at the Conference of Representatives of Communist and Workers Parties in November of the same year in Moscow.

BUDDHISM *Fojiao* 佛教
Religion which spread from India to dominate China from the second century AD onwards. Key concepts of Buddhism, like transmigration and *karma*, were derived from the earlier Hinduism. Buddhism differs from Western religions in the sense that it does not include the idea of a supreme being, or God, controlling the universe; all beings, including Buddha himself, are subject to the same impersonal rules. All sentient beings are part of the system so unlike in Western religions man is not seen as occupying a special place in creation and devout Buddhists are vegetarian (plants are not regarded as sentient). The Supreme Buddha was born around 563 BC in present-day Nepal and originally called Siddhartha (Sanskrit version). He came from the Gautama family, part of the Sakya clan and as a result is also known as Gautama Buddha and Sakyamuni 'sage of the Sakyas'. He is not the only buddha: over twenty others had preceded him and **Maitreya**, the future Buddha, was due to follow him. Until the age of 29 Siddhartha enjoyed a life of some luxury, married and had a son but he then left home on a mission to seek truth and enlightenment. He spent the following six years in self-denial as an ascetic but did not achieve enlightenment so he went to sit in meditation under a bodhi tree. After several weeks he attained enlightenment and set out to expound his teaching for the next 45 years, after which he achieved nirvana. His teaching was based on the belief that all sentient beings are bound to a cycle of constant re-birth, *samsara*; the nature of this re-birth is determined by the karma built up over this and previous lifetimes. *Karma* refers to the good or evil intentions behind our deeds and all karma, good or bad, leads to re-birth in a higher or lower state. For Buddha the aim of life was to break the cycle of constant rebirth by not producing *karma*. He taught the four noble truths: that all existence is suffering, that the cause of suffering is the desire for sensual pleasure, that suffering can be brought to an end by the elimination of desire and that this can be achieved by the eight-fold path (perfection in view, resolve, speech, conduct, livelihood, effort, mindfulness and concentration). Through the eight-fold path it is possible, by removing desire, to break the cycle of karmic re-birth and escape from the suffering of existence into extinction, nirvana.

After the death of the historical Buddha, disciples spread his teachings and many different schools developed. In the long run, two main traditions emerged Theravada (also called Hinayana) which came to dominate southern Buddhist areas and Mahayana which came to dominate northern areas, including China. Theravada is more ascetic and emphasises individual effort, whereas Mahayana (literally 'greater vehicle', as opposed to the term Hinayana 'lesser vehicle' used pejoratively by Mahayanans) holds out the promise of assistance from buddhas and bodhisattvas to enable ordinary people leading normal lives to attain nirvana. Bodhisattvas are enlightened beings who voluntarily postpone their own entry to nirvana in order to help others.

Buddhism spread to China around the second century AD and made rapid progress in the period of disunity from the third to the sixth centuries. Chinese thought has traditionally been eclectic and from the beginning Buddhism was explained by reference to existing thought, especially **Daoism**. The main schools which emerged in this period were *Huayan* 華嚴, *Tiantai* 天臺, ***Chan*** 禪 and ***Qingtu*** 清土 (Pure Land). In the long run it was the latter two, especially

Chan, a fusion of Daoist and Buddhist ideas, which predominated. Buddhism reached its peak in the Tang dynasty (618–907) when its influence pervaded society from the emperors downwards and Buddhist monasteries owned vast estates and had enormous economic and political influence. As the Tang reunified China and extended the Chinese empire, it came to view the Buddhist church as a rival to the state, particularly when the church used its tax free status to gather more and more land into its control, depriving the state of tax revenue. After the **An Lushan** rebellion the previously open Tang society became more xenophobic and suspicious of things foreign and monasteries were closed down and monks' licences revoked (there was a major purge in 845). Scholars like **Han Yu** attacked Buddhism and reaffirmed traditional Confucian values, anticipating the revival of the native tradition which, in its **Neo-Confucian** form, replaced Buddhism as the dominant intellectual force in Chinese society. However, Buddhism continued to have a strong influence on popular society into the twentieth century. After the 1949 revolution the Buddhist church suffered restrictions under the Communist authorities, but not as severely as Western-influenced Christian churches. In the **Cultural Revolution** immense damage was done to Buddhist temples, but some have been restored since and recent years have seen an easing of restrictions and a revival of Buddhism.

Kenneth CH'EN, *Buddhism in China: A Historical Survey* (Princeton University Press, 1964); E. ZÜRCHER, *The Buddhist Conquest of China. The Spread and Adaptation of Buddhism in Early Medieval China* (2 vols.) (Leiden: E.J. Brill, 1959); Holmes WELCH, *The Practice of Chinese Buddhism: 1900–1950* (Harvard University Press, 1967); Arthur F. WRIGHT, *Buddhism in Chinese History* (Stanford University Press, 1959).

BUDDHIST SCULPTURE

The most important and most widely discussed body of Chinese sculpture from the fourth century. Buddhism was absorbed alongside other religious beliefs in Han China. Buddhist iconography forms and sculptural types were introduced from the kingdoms of Central Asia, especially Indian styles with Western classical influences.

The practice of cutting cave temples into the rock was also transmitted to China, and a great number of Chinese Buddhist sculptures were carved directly into the rock face. Early cave temples built at sites such as **Dunhuang**, Maijishan and **Yungang** were marked by the quality and richness of their sculpture.

Another type of early Chinese Buddhist sculpture is represented by the stele, which commonly took the form of a rectangular monolith with images in high relief.

It was the rulers of Wei and Liang states in North China who provided substantial imperial patronage and encouraged the making of Buddhist images in stone, clay, wood and metal, including bronze, gold and silver. In this period, the solid and heavy Indian style was gradually modified and refined by the native Chinese predilection for abstract expression in terms of the flowing, rhythmic line.

Tang sculpture represents the classic age of this art form in China. Complete technical mastery of media such as dry lacquer and metal was matched by utter confidence, convincing naturalism, a high sense of drama, and exquisite taste.

Tang sculpture sets the standard against which all earlier and later achievements are measured. Although many of the greatest works in wood, dry lacquer, and clay have perished, major statements still survive in metal and stone. Tang cave temples, such as the **Longmen** site, are encyclopaedias of Buddhist sculpture of the period. Buddhist sculptures served to propagate the faith and, by commissioning religious works of art, its followers attempted to gain favour and salvation.

W. ZWALF, ed., *Buddhism: Art and Faith* (London: British Museum, 1985).

BURNING OF BOOKS

The best known instance of this form of limitation on intellectual freedom is attributed to **Li Si**, who memorialised the First Emperor in 213 BC that in order to destroy the reactionary forces of **Confucianism** and feudalism all those who owned books on literature (such as the ***Shijing*** and the ***Shujing***) and philosophy should burn them within thirty days, on pain of branding and forced labour. Books of practical value on medicine, agriculture, and arboriculture were exempt, as were those on Qin history and on **divination**. Li Si did not share the Emperor's faith in the latter, but may have deemed it expedient not to attack this ancient and widespread art. Only in the court were copies of the proscribed books to be preserved, and the library collection there perished in the conflagration when **Xiang Yu** captured the capital in 206, a far worse loss than seven years before.

The destruction of books was not new in 213, nor would it be the last time that it occurred in Chinese history. **Shang Yang** had persuaded Duke Xiao of Qin on a similar course of action in the fourth century BC, when the *Shi* and the *Shu* were again the principal targets. The great persecution of **Buddhism** in 842–5 saw the destruction of many sutras. Two sets of the *Yongle Dadian* (see **Encyclopaedias**) perished in the Manchu capture of **Beijing** in 1644, and the third was largely lost in the **Boxer Rising** in 1900. In recent times the Great Proletarian **Cultural Revolution** was responsible for the loss of countless ancient and modern volumes.

CADRES *Ganbu* 幹部

General term for officials in either the government of the People's Republic or the Chinese Communist Party.

CAI JING 蔡京 (1046–1126)

Radical reformist Chancellor under Song **Huizong** in 1103–6 and 1107–9, also known as Yuanchang. For the large part of Huizong's reign (1101–1125), Cai Jing was the chief advisor to the much younger emperor. A native of Xianyou, Fujian province, Cai had risen from being Prefect of **Kaifeng** in 1084 to become Finance Minister under Emperor Zhizong in 1094. After a period in provincial government under the anti-reformist Emperor Zhizong he was restored to court in 1102 thanks to the influence of his friend, the **eunuch** Tong Guang. Thereafter they helped to advance each other's careers until they disgreed and became enemies in 1116. Tong's rise continued and from 1117 to 1126 he was supreme army commander, a rare achievement for a eunuch. Cai Jing was responsible for the downfall of the Northern Song empire and was sent into exile by the Qinzong emperor and died in Tanzhou (Changsha today). He was a highly gifted calligrapher, but his artistic talents have been ignored in mainstream Chinese art history because of the taint on his character. However a number of his calligraphic works in *fatie* form survive today.

Herbert FRANKE, ed., *Sung Biographies* (Wiesbaden: Franz Steiner Verlag GmbH, 1976).

CAI YUANPEI 蔡元培 (1868–1940)

Leading figure in the modernisation of China's education in the early 20th century. Cai was chancellor of Beijing University from 1916–26 during which time the university became the leading centre in China for the propagation of new social, literary and political ideas during the May Fourth Movement. He received a traditional education and passed the *jinshi* 進士 examination in 1890 but became disillusioned with the Qing government, especially after its defeat by the Japanese in 1895, and decided to devote himself to educational reform and joined the revolutionary cause. He studied in Germany from 1908–11 and later in France too, where he set up a work-study programme for Chinese. After his period at Beijing University he helped set up in 1928 the leading research institute, **Academia Sinica**. After the Nationalist Government started its terror campaigns against dissidents Cai resigned his posts in protest. He died in Hong Kong in 1940.

William J. DUIKER, *Ts'ai Yuan-p'ei: Educator of Modern China* (Pennsylvania State University Press, 1977).

CAIRO DECLARATION (1943)

Statement issued at the conclusion of the 1943 Cairo Conference at which Roosevelt, Churchill and **Jiang Jieshi** met to discuss war aims and post-war strategy. The declaration made on December 1 1943 called for the unconditional surrender of Japan, the first time this had been demanded, and the complete restoration to China of all Chinese land which had been occupied by Japan, that is Manchuria, Taiwan and the Pescadores archipelago. The future independence of Korea and the return of Sakhalin and the Kurile islands to Russia were also promised. These demands were endorsed by the Potsdam declaration in 1945 and implemented after the surrender of Japan. The **Yalta Conference** modified these terms without Jiang Jieshi's consent.

CALENDAR

The traditional Chinese calendar consists of a number of ways of expressing dates, which enables a cross-check for accuracy to be made for any recorded event. A date could be identified as the specified reign year of a certain emperor, known as *nianhao* 年號 the reign title, and on such a day of a particular moon. The year, month, day and hour could also be designated by the serial numbers (or the animal symbols) of the ten celestial stems and twelve terrestrial branches known as ***ganzhi*** 干支. The traditional method of dating is, in fact, the combination of both *nianhao* and *ganzhi.*

Points in time are also indicated by 24 terms or *jieqi* 節氣, with different names referring to seasonal changes, of the solar year in the farming calendar *nongli* 農歷. The division of terms corresponds to the day on which the sun enters the first and fifteenth degree of the zodiacal signs.

On the other hand, the Chinese lunar year is divided into 12 ordinary months, each of which has either 29 or 30 days. The first day in each month is arranged to correspond to the new moon, and the 15th day to correspond to the full moon. As the 12 lunar months do not equal one solar year, an intercalary month is interposed every third year.
The lunar calendar, *yinli* 陰歷, is still in use side by side with the *nongli* and the Gregorian calendar, *yangli* 陽歷.

CALLIGRAPHY
Calligraphy, the art of writing, was cultivated in its own right as an independent form of visual art in ancient China. An essential characteristic of Chinese writing is the use of a flexible brush which conveys the subtle movements of the writer's hand and so preserves a sense of the person's individuality in the final work.

Writings of the early periods, from the seal scripts on bronzes and stones to the clerical scripts on wooden or bamboo strips (see **Writing System**), provided the foundation of the art of calligraphy. From the third century AD the idea developed that some writing should be regarded as calligraphy – an art form which expressed values, aesthetic and moral, as distinct from text content. The view that writing was aesthetically valuable led to the widespread copying and reproduction of calligraphy by noted masters (see ***Bei tie***) and to the establishment of particular types and styles of calligraphy venerated as the classical tradition. From the Tang dynasty onwards imperial collections of calligraphy were made, which further encouraged its development as a form of high art.

The aesthetics of calligraphy was an important part of education, and the finer points of the art of calligraphy can only be appreciated with long study and training. As a person's writing was regarded as a clue to temperament, moral worth, and learning, emperors of the Tang and Song dynasties often selected their ministers on the basis of the quality of their calligraphy.

The art of calligraphy, with the extravagance of its lines, embodies the sophistication of human sensitivity in every brush movement, in the structure of every character and the spatial relationship of all elements. The life of the calligraphic tradition was sustained by the notion that calligraphy could convey the spontaneous feelings of the truly perceptive individual through an outflowing of spirit at a particular instant. These expressive moments were often compared by scholar-officials with the composition of poetry and associated with retreat from the routines of daily official life.

Appreciation of Chinese calligraphy is also essential to an understanding of Chinese **painting**, as the two are technically very close, sharing identical artistic criteria, and parallel in their developments. From the Song dynasty, literati artists developed forms of painting that exploited calligraphic techniques and also embodied the values of calligraphy.

Y. TSENG, *A History of Chinese Calligraphy* (Hong Kong: Chinese University Press, 1993).

CANTLIE, SIR JAMES (1851-1926)
Scottish doctor and friend of **Sun Yixian** (Sun Yat-sen). Dr Cantlie was Dean of the College of Medicine for Chinese in Hong Kong where Sun was a student

from 1887 to 1892. After the failure of Sun's first attempt at revolution in Guangzhou in 1894 and his subsequent flight to Hong Kong, it was Cantlie's advice that he leave there for London because the British government was planning to comply with a Chinese government order to ban him. On October 11 1896, Sun was kidnapped by the Chinese legation in London and was only saved from deportation and possible execution by the intervention of Dr Cantlie with the British Foreign Office.

CANTON see **GUANGZHOU**

CANTON COMMUNE see **GUANGZHOU COMMUNE**

CANTON COUP see **GUANGZHOU COUP**

CANTON SYSTEM

Strategy adopted by the Qing government to restrict foreign trade during the eighteenth and nineteenth centuries. Guangzhou (Canton) had been open to Western traders since the seventeenth century, but in 1757, it was declared the only legal port for overseas trade. All trade had to be transacted through a member of a small circle of merchants, the ***hongs***, authorised by the government to trade with foreigners, and organised into the **Cohong**. The hongs rented land along the Zhujiang 珠江 (Pearl River) outside the walled city of Guangzhou to foreigners whose warehouses, known as factories, were based there. This restriction, which was anathema to Western traders, was one of the issues which led to the **Opium War** and one of the effects of the Treaty of Nanjing which ended the War was to open other ports to trade. See **Nanjing, Treaty of.**

Louis DERMIGNY, *La Chine et l'Occident: le commerce à Canton au XVIIIe siècle, 1719–1833* (4 vols.) (Paris: SEVPEN, 1964).

CAO CAO 曹操 (d. AD 220)

Military dictator in north China who rose above the warlordism that dominated the reign of the last Han emperor and tried to restore an administrative system based on centralised authority reminiscent of **Legalism**. As part of his emphasis on economy measures he banned the use of **jade** funerary shrouds (see **Liu Sheng**). He introduced official ranks graded on a nine-point scale, which became the commonly used classification for posts in all subsequent dynasties, but his idea of qualification for office rested on local influence rather than intellectual talent. His armies were successful in suppressing the **Yellow Turban** rebels, and he resettled homeless peasants as state tenants on abandoned land. His son **Cao Pi** founded the Wei dynasty (221–265, capital **Luoyang**; see **Three Kingdoms**). The story of Cao Cao is told in the Ming dynasty novel ***Sanguo yanyi*** 三國演義, *Romance of the Three Kingdoms.*

See also **Zhuge Liang.**

CAO PI 曹丕 (187–226)

Second son of **Cao Cao** who became Emperor Wen of the Wei and the first emperor to be a distinguished literary figure. He wrote ***shi*** and ***fu*** poems (around

30 *fu* and 40 *shi* survive), a pioneering poem in seven-syllable lines and one of the earliest works of literary criticism. The latter, the *Dian lun* 典論, of which only the *Lun wen* 論文 'Essay on Literature' chapter survives through its inclusion in the ***Wen xuan***, offers critiques of contemporary poets and leading figures of the past like **Qu Yuan**, discusses literary genres dominant at the time and puts forward the concept of ***qi*** 氣 'breath' or 'vital force', a concept mentioned in **Mencius**. *Qi* for Cao denotes a mystical quality or talent which is manifested as skill in a particular field; literary works produced by writers who possess this talent become imbued with the writer's *qi*. *Qi* became one of the main terms in traditional literary and art criticism.

CAO XUEQIN 曹雪芹 (1715–63) see ***HONGLOUMENG***

CAO YU 曹禺 (1910–96)

Playwright and pioneer of *huaju* 話劇 spoken Western-style drama. *Huaju* developed during the **New Culture Movement** as a medium for social criticism under the influence of works by Western dramatists like Ibsen and Shaw. Cao Yu was the first Chinese dramatist to produce *huaju* which won both critical acclaim and commercial success. His first play *Leiyu* 雷雨 'Thunderstorm' (1934) exposed the hypocrisy of traditional male-dominated Confucian society and explored such forbidden areas as incest and sexual inequality in an outwardly respectable family. *Leiyu* was followed by *Richu* 日出 'Sunrise' in 1936, *Yuanye* 原野 'The Wilderness' in 1937 and *Beijing ren* 北京人 'Peking Man' in 1940.

Joseph LAU, *Ts'ao Yu: The Reluctant Disciple of Chekhov and O'Neill. A Study in Literary Influence* (Hong Kong University Press, 1970); John Y.H. HU, *Ts'ao Yu* (New York: Twayne Publishers, 1972)

CAPITALISM, SPROUTS OF *Zibenzhuyi mengya* 資本主義萌芽

During the 1950s, historians in the People's Republic of China engaged in a concerted attempt to analyse the failure of China to produce a significant capitalist economy in its long history. The enquiry followed a statement by Mao Zedong that feudal China had contained the essential constituents for a capitalist society and would, had it not been for the intervention of the West, have developed into one, in line with orthodox Marxist view of historical development. These "sprouts" or "shoots" *mengya* 萌芽 were found in various aspects of industry and commerce from silk and porcelain production to commercialised agriculture and banking. Although "sprouts" were uncovered in various historical periods, as far back as the Song and even as early as the Tang dynasty, the majority of scholars pointed to the middle years of the Ming dynasty, the sixteenth century, as the time when they were most highly developed. The research carried out under this project varied greatly in quality. At its worst it was the mechanical application of crude Marxist concepts, but some important studies, based on previously little-used primary sources, were written.

CAPITALIST ROADERS

Supporters of **Liu Shaoqi** and **Deng Xiaoping** during the **Cultural Revolution**, who were accused of "following the capitalist road" *zou zibenzhuyi de daolu* 走資本主義的道路 because they favoured wage differentials as incentives and advocated placing economic and technical priorities ahead of political ones. Liu was criticised as the "top party person taking the capitalist road".

CASTIGLIONE, GIUSEPPE (1688–1766)

Italian **Jesuit** priest who arrived in **Beijing** in 1715. He is best known as an artist, particularly for his paintings of horses, but preferred portraits and historical scenes. He was employed at court by the **Yongzheng Emperor**, who never spoke to him, and by the **Qianlong Emperor** whose portrait he painted. He designed and built the Yuanming yuan (see **Summer Palaces**). Despite speaking out bravely to Qianlong against persecutions of Christianity in 1736, 1737 and 1746, he was honoured with gifts from the Emperor on his seventieth birthday.

C. and M. BEURDELEY, *Giuseppe Castiglione: a Jesuit Painter at the Court of the Chinese Emperors* (Rutland: Tuttle, 1972).

CATHAY

Name by which northern China was known to the West in mediaeval times, derived from that of the **Khitan** rulers of the Liao dynasty. See also **Marco Polo.**

Sir Henry YULE and H. CORDIER, *Cathay and the Way Thither* (London: The Hakluyt Society, 1913–6).

CC CLIQUE

Right-wing faction within the Guomindang which refused to countenance the agreements reached by General George C. Marshall in his negotiations with the CCP, the **Marshall Mission**, in 1946. It was named after its two senior members, Chen Lifu 陳立夫 and Chen Guofu 陳果夫.

CENSORATE *Yushi tai* 御史臺

Both **Legalism** and **Confucianism** had stipulated that those in authority should accept remonstration. **Wudi,** the Han dynasty emperor, appointed officers to oversee the work of provincial officials (106 BC), and from the Sui dynasty onwards a body of censorial officers under the command of a Censor in Chief (*Yushi taifu* 御史大夫) formed one of the three principal branches of government, together with the civil and military administration. The task of the censors was to maintain an independent watch on the formation and implementation of policy from the level of the Emperor himself down to that of county **magistrates**. Their brief was to sustain the Confucian principle of government for the good of Heaven's people, to proffer positive advice to the throne, to warn against corruption, and to impeach officials guilty of improper behaviour. This they often did at risk to their own lives, although even censors sometimes found it impossible to avoid being used as agents, rather than critics, of imperial policy and to avoid being sucked into political intrigue.

Charles HUCKER, *The Censorial System of Ming China* (Stanford University Press, 1966).

CENSUS

China has gathered population data either at national or regional level since AD 2, mainly for the purposes of tax gathering and the organisation of labour. Data collection was made easier by the introduction of the ***baojia*** and ***lijia*** systems in the later Middle Ages, but until modern times has been subject to inaccuracies due to both under- and over-reporting of statistics to officialdom, and the exaggeration of figures by writers with particular interests to promote. Official histories, for example, record the death toll in Sichuan during the occupation of **Zhang Xianzhong** as six hundred million, but can scarcely have expected such a figure to be taken literally. Interpretation of contemporary statistics and their use by later historians is therefore problematic, but a sample of estimates of likely population levels at key periods, based on official figures, is shown below. It is accepted that land yields and natural forces helped to maintain a remarkable level of population consistency between the Han and the Northern Song period, when a combination of climatic, agricultural, industrial and social changes sparked off a notable increase. A combination of oppressive political conditions, severe epidemics (including the infamous outbreak of bubonic plague which spread to Europe and became known as the Black Death) and rebellions reduced it through the Yuan and Ming periods, but a long period of social stability and agricultural improvements began its upward curve again in the early Qing. This was reversed in the mid-nineteenth century by the ravages of the **Taiping Rebellion** and again in the Republican era by a combination of warlordism and natural disasters. In modern times the government of the PRC has had to struggle with a further demographic explosion resulting from improvements in living conditions, health care and nutritional levels. The first largely accurate census in the history of China was carried out in 1953 and the collection of reliable data has been a central preoccupation of the state. During the **Great Leap Forward, Mao Zedong** saw a high population level as a source of national strength, but official policy has generally promoted birth control, and strict measures have been taken since 1978 to try and limit the acceptable number of children to one per family.

Date/period	Census data	Modern estimate
AD 2	59,594,978	
157	56,486,856	
755	52,919,309	
1109	46,734,784	
1125–7		100 m.
c.1200		110 m. +
1290	58,834,701	
1393	60,545,812	65 m.
1578	60,692,856	
c.1600		150–160 m.
1741	143,411,599	
1767	209,839,546	
1790	301,487,114	
1830	394,784,681	

Date/period	Census data	Modern estimate
1953	582,603,417	
1957		646.53m.
1970		829.92m.
1982		1015.41m.

Mark ELVIN, *The Pattern of the Chinese Past* (Eyre Methuen, 1973); P.T. HO, *Studies on the Population of China, 1368–1953* (Harvard University Press, 1959); PENG, X.Z., *Demographic Transition in China, Fertility Trends since the 1950s* (Oxford University Press, 1991).

CERAMICS (porcelain)

Pottery and porcelain have long occupied a special place in the arts of China and archaeological finds of pottery dating back to the Neolithic cultures of **Yangshao** and **Longshan** testify to the quality of early wares. By the Han dynasty, techniques of glazing and high temperature firing had already reached a high level and were the basis for the development of porcelain. During the Tang dynasty, fine earthenwares (including the **Tang *sancai*** 唐三彩) and stonewares were produced and many pieces approached the quality of fine porcelain. The precise date of the production of the first true porcelain is unclear, but it had certainly appeared before the end of the Yuan dynasty. Although research and archaeological finds in the 1970s and 1980s have directed the interest of scholars towards the Yuan dynasty it is still the Ming dynasty which is regarded as having produced the finest quality ceramics, particularly those manufactured in the town of **Jingdezhen** 景德鎮, although other centres such as Dehua 德化 in Fujian and Shantou (Swatow) 汕頭 and Foshan 佛山 in Guangdong also produced high quality wares. Simple blue-and-white designs popular in the early Ming were augmented by more highly decorated styles in the 16th century as porcelain was exported to Japan and to Europe where it found a ready market. During the Qing dynasty, the most distinctive wares were *famille rose* and *famille verte* and export porcelain which fed the fashion for *chinoiserie* in eighteenth-century Europe.

Margaret MEDLEY, *The Chinese Potter: a Practical History of Chinese Ceramics* (Oxford: Phaidon, 1976).

CHAHA'ER 察哈爾

Originally the name of one of the most powerful tribes of Mongols during the Ming period, it was reintroduced as a name for an administrative unit in the eastern part of Inner Mongolia in the twentieth century. The Chaha'er Special Region was established in 1914 and it became a province in 1928. It was under Japanese occupation from 1937–1945. Today, the area it covered is included in the north-west of Hebei Province and the Xilingol League of **Inner Mongolia**.

CHAMDO (*Qamdo*)

Eastern region of the ancient kingdom of **Tibet**, now divided between the Tibetan Autonomous Region and Qinghai Province. Chamdo was the scene of some of the fiercest resistance to the People's Liberation Army in 1959.

CHAN 禪 BUDDHISM

An indigenous Chinese form of **Buddhism** which became the dominant sect in China and spread to Japan, where it is known as Zen. This meditative school of Buddhism was strongly influenced by the native Chinese philosophy of **Daoism**. It stems from the Mahayana tradition and was developed by Bodhidharma (c.470–543), a native of south India who travelled to China and became the first patriarch of the Chan school. He chose Hui Ke 慧可(487–593) as his successor, but it is the outstanding sixth (and last) patriarch, Hui Neng 慧能 (638–713) who is often considered the real inspiration for the Chan tradition. He is acknowledged as the author of the *Liuzu tanjing* 六祖壇經 'Platform Sutra', a seminal Chan text. Hui Neng came from a humble background but achieved enlightenment when he heard the Diamond Sutra being recited. He met the fifth patriarch of the Chan school who, realising Hui Neng's ability, made him sixth patriarch instead of his presumed successor, Shen Xiu 神秀 (c. 606–706). This led to a split in Chan between Hui Neng's Southern School and Shen Xiu's Northern School with the Southern School, emphasising immediacy, later predominating.

Chan stresses sudden enlightenment directly perceived. Like Daoism it places little emphasis on intellectual knowledge and, unlike in other schools of Buddhism, ritual is of little importance. It affirms that the Buddha-mind exists in everyone and that the realisation of it can take place directly without intermediary; in this sense the scriptures, the church and the organisation all become redundant. Chan uses Daoist-style meditation and *gong an* (Japanese *koan*) 'cases' to aid enlightenment. The latter take the form of questions and answers, like: "What is Buddha?" "Three pounds of flax.", or short stories, like Hui Neng's coming across two monks arguing whether it was the flag or the wind flapping and his telling them it was their minds flapping.

Followers of Hui Neng set up different traditions; these still exist in Japan, where Zen is vigorous, as the Soto School and the Rinzai School, but in China Chan became amalgamated with other forms of Buddhism and more or less died out as a separate entity.

HUI NENG, *The Platform Sutra of the Sixth Patriarch: the Text of the Tun-huang Manuscript*, trans. Philip B. YAMPOLSKY (Columbia University Press, 1967).

CHANG'AN 長安

Ancient capital of China on a site in southern Shaanxi close to modern Xi'an which had been a centre of political power since the Shang period. Capital city of the Later Han, Sui, and Tang dynasties, and periodically during certain of the Northern and Southern Dynasties' regimes (Jin, 311–6; Zhao, 319–29; Qin, 351–85; Later Qin, 386–417; Northern Zhou, 557–81). It was naturally defended on all sides by mountains but well connected by the Wei River to the **Yellow River** and the Great Plain, and with access to the south-west by mountain passes. Chang'an was often regarded as the sister city of **Luoyang**, with which it periodically alternated as capital, and with which there was usually a sense of rivalry. Han Chang'an occupied c.454 hectares (c.1120 acres) and was laid out around the Weiyang Palace. The Sui emperor **Wendi** redesigned it, but the city reached the peak of its development in the eighth century when it was the world's greatest urban centre of population and civilisation. It then had an area of 8,631 hectares, and housed a population of nearly one million within the walls and nearly twice as many within the metropolitan area overall, including many foreigners. It was built on a rectangular plan, surrounded by 5.3 metre-high walls of packed earth and divided internally by a grid of wide roads, eleven on the north-south axis and fourteen on the east-west. These created an irregular chequerboard pattern of 114 wards which were themselves walled and allocated for residential, religious, commercial, agricultural and recreational purposes. Canals also aided communication and transportation. The main gate was in the south wall, and the eastern half was more well to do than the western. In separate compounds inside the northern wall lay the palace city and the official city of the government. An additional palace area, the Great Luminous Palace (*Daming gong* 大明宮) was begun in 634 above the north-eastern corner of the city by Emperor **Taizong** of the Tang dynasty, and extended by **Gaozong** in 662. It was here that the **Hanlin Academy** was located. The city was ravaged by **Huang Chao** in 880 and suffered further destruction in 904–6, after which it was never again occupied as the capital city. Its layout was imitated in the capitals of other countries in the Chinese Culture Zone, including Kyongju (**Silla**) and Nara (Japan). See also **Xianyang, Zhou dynasty**

Z.X. Zou, trans. S. Whitfield, *The Land within the Passes, a History of Xi'an* (London:Viking Books, 1991).

Changchun 長春 (Qiu Chuji 丘處機) (1148–1227)

Daoist monk who travelled from Shandong to what is now the area around Kabul in Afghanistan at the command of **Chinggis Khan** who was then based there. He journeyed through Mongolia and Central Asia, arriving at the court of Chinggis in 1220 and, on his return to Beijing in 1224, wrote an account of his travels, which is an invaluable source of information on the geography of Inner Asia.

Li Chih-ch'ang, *Travels of an Alchemist,* trans. Arthur Waley (London: Routledge, 1931; reprinted New York: AMS Press, 1979).

Changsha 長沙

Capital city of Hunan province. Situated on the banks of the Xiang River, Changsha has been an important cultural and economic centre of this region. First established as a large prefecture in the Qin dynasty, it was later changed into a state governed by marquises in the Former Han and back to a prefecture again with much shrunk boundaries in the Latter Han period. From the Sui dynasty it had been renamed many times in following dynasties as either Changsha or Tanzhou 潭州 until it finally became the capital of Hunan province in the Qing dynasty. Changsha is known for the important archaeological finds from its Warring States and Han tombs and for its craft trades such as embroidery and porcelain.

Chavannes, Edouard (1865–1918)

Leading French scholar and authority on Chinese history whose pioneering work included the first major translation from the ***Shiji*** into a European language, entitled *Mémoires Historiques de Sseu-ma Tsien* (1895).

CHEN BODA 陳伯達 (1904–89)
Mao Zedong's political secretary, speech writer and adviser in the **Yan'an** period. He joined the Politburo in 1956, edited *Hongqi* (Red Flag) the theoretical journal of the CCP from 1958 to 1966 and became leader of the **Cultural Revolution** Group in 1966, with Jiang Qing as his first deputy. By the 1970 Lushan plenary meeting of the Ninth Central Committee, Chen had become a close ally of **Lin Biao**, with whom Mao was coming into bitter conflict and was purged at the meeting as an ultra-leftist. He disappeared completely in 1970, only to resurface in 1980 as one of the defendants in the trial of the **Gang of Four**. Along with other defendants, he pleaded guilty to having been implicated in a plot directed by Lin Biao to kill Mao in 1971 and was sentenced to 18 years in prison. He was released from prison in 1982 because of poor health and died on September 20 1989.

CHEN CHENG 陳誠 (1897–1965)
Nationalist general and second-in-command to Jiang Jieshi. He was appointed governor of Taiwan in 1948 and set about attempting to improve the bad relations between native Taiwanese and the mainlanders that had resulted in the 1947 **February 28 Incident.**

CHEN DUXIU 陳獨秀 (1879–1942)
Leading figure in the New Culture Movement and the **May Fourth Movement**, founder member of the CCP. Chen was from Huaining in Anhui, had a traditional education in classical Chinese and passed the first level of the civil service examination in 1896. Under the influence of the 1898 Reformers, he began to study Western ideas and from 1900-10 spent periods as an overseas student in Japan and France. In 1915, he founded the journal *Xinqingnian* 新青年 *(New Youth)* sub-titled *La Jeunesse* which was to become the most important forum for cultural and intellectual debate. At this point Chen promoted Western liberal concepts of science and democracy as the key to China's Salvation. He took up an academic post at Beijing University and in 1918, with **Li Dazhao**, created another influential periodical, *Meizhou pinglun* 每周評論 'Weekly Review'. This was much more political in content and contributed to the political protests culminating in the **May Fourth Movement**. He moved gradually towards Marxism and was a member of the Shanghai Communist Group in 1920 and one of the founding members of the CCP. He served as its General Secretary until 1927, when he was stripped of his post for his association with Trotskyist groups and finally expelled from the party in November 1929. He died in Sichuan in 1942.

Lee FEIGON, Chen Duxiu: *Founder of the Chinese Communist Party* (Princeton University Press, 1983).

CHEN DYNASTY 陳 (557–89)
One of the Northern and Southern Dynasties founded by survivors of the massacre of the Liang dynasty aristocracy who initially found shelter in **Chang'an**. Chen forces recaptured the city of Shangyang, which is close to present-day Nanjing, and controlled it until the armies of the Sui dynasty wiped them out.

CHEN RONG 諶容 (1936–)
Prize-winning novelist born Chen Derong in Hankou, Hubei. Chen Rong (often romanised as Shen Rong) graduated in Russian in 1957 and worked as an editor and translator at the Central People's Broadcasting Station. After a break of almost ten years due to illness, she was appointed to teach Russian in Beijing. Chen's writing career began to take off in the early 1970s when two of her novels were published. However, it was not until 1981 when her most famous story *At Middle Age* won a literary prize, that she became widely recognised. Adapted for television and film, *At Middle Age* is emblematic of her work as it reflects the social problems encountered by middle-aged professionals, particularly women, here through the description of opthalmologist Lu Wenting's life and work. Chen Rong became a professional writer employed by the Beijing Branch of the Chinese Writer's Association.
CHEN RONG, *At Middle Age* (Beijing: Panda Books, 1987).

CHEN SHENG 陳勝 (CHEN SHE 陳涉)
Rebel leader at the end of the Qin dynasty. Chen was a farm labourer who led a group of conscript labourers in revolt in 210 BC and established himself as the King of Chu. He was killed after only six months in his new role, but the uprising destabilised the Qin regime and allowed a more successful rebel, **Liu Bang**, to overthrow it and replace it with the Han dynasty.

CHEN YI 陳儀 (1883–1950)
Warlord officer who joined the Guomindang after the **Northern Expedition**. He was governor of Fujian from 1934 to 1941 and was appointed governor of Taiwan in 1945. His repressive policies led to the **February 28 Incident** of 1947 after which he was replaced by Chen Cheng. In 1949, he was accused of having made contact with CCP agents and was executed by the GMD in 1950.

CHEN YI 陳毅 (1901–1972)
CCP officer in the **Workers' and Peasants Red Army** and the **New Fourth Army**. He joined the CCP in Beijing after a period studying in France and served under Zhou Enlai at the **Huangpu Military Academy**. He became Mayor of Shanghai in 1947 and Foreign Minister in 1958.

CHEN YONGGUI 陳永貴 (1913 –1986)
The model peasant politician of the Cultural Revolution period, invariably photographed wearing his north China peasant turban. Chen was party secretary of the **Dazhai** Production Brigade from Shanxi which was Mao Zedong's ideal of a frugal, self-reliant agricultural unit. He became a member of the **National People's Congress** in 1964, and during the **Cultural Revolution** rose to be a member of the CCP Central Committee and Vice-Premier, a post from which he was removed in September 1980, when **Zhao Ziyang** replaced **Hua Guofeng** as Premier.

CHEN YUN 陳雲 (1905–1995)
CCP politician, government minister in the PRC and influential figure in China's economic development. A veteran of the Shanghai **May Thirtieth Incident** and the **Long March**, Chen spent some time in the Soviet Union in

1935–7 and returned to hold key posts in the CCP Central Committee with responsibilities for organisation and economic development. After the foundation of the PRC, he played key roles in the State Planning and State Financial and Economic Commission, which he chaired from 1979–1981. He was a hard-line opponent of the move away from the planned economy and withdrew from his party and government posts in October 1987 as part of the group that stood down when Deng Xiaoping retired.

CHENG HAO 程灝 (1032–85)
Brother of **Cheng Yi**, cousin of **Zhang Zai**, and student of **Zhou Dunyi**. His ideas were developed by Lu Jiuyuan (1139–93) as *xinxue* 心學 "study of mind", and eventually led to the doctrines of **Wang Yangming** and his extreme followers (see **Li Zhi**) in a form that contrasted starkly with those of his brother and **Zhu Xi** (see **Neo-Confucianism).**

CHENG YI 程頤 (1033–1107)
Brother of **Cheng Hao**, cousin of **Zhang Zai**, and student of **Zhou Dunyi**; perhaps the most influential of all eleventh century **Neo-Confucians**. He belonged to the *xuedao* 學道"Study the Way" group which emphasized moral example and self-cultivation over statecraft and political measures as a means of transforming the country. His thought was passed down by his students to **Zhu Xi**, who formulated it into the system known as *lixue* 理學 "study of principle" (see **Neo-Confucianism**). He is credited with being the originator of some of the strictest rules of Neo-Confucian behaviour for both public and family life, such as the condemnation of widow re-marriage (see **marriage**), and appears to have been a dour, unattractive character. Both he and **Su Shi** were tutors to Emperor Zhizong, but Cheng was dismissed when they clashed over whether it was proper to play music during the mourning period for **Sima Guang**. Even Zhu Xi said that Su Shi stood for pleasure (*le* 樂), Cheng for respect (*jing* 敬). The two also disagreed over the relationship between art and the **Dao**: Cheng said that they were incompatible, Su that art inspired the Way.

CHENGDI 成帝, HAN EMPEROR (Liu Ao 劉驁, 51–7, r.32–7 BC)
Son of **Yuandi** by the Empress **Wang**, whose clan was able to seize effective power because of his own lack of interest in government. During his reign the court much enjoyed popular music, dubbed "music of Zheng" by its purist critics who sought to revive ancient forms. This prompted his successor **Aidi** to close down the **Music Bureau**. During his reign and that of his father, scholar officials who advocated a return to what they believed to be classical (Zhou) values and practices generally prevailed over the modernisers who had been reforming the country since the time of **Wudi** (see ***Gu Wen***). One of the most important of these was **Liu Xiang**. See also **Han dynasty, Liu Xin.**

CHENGHUA 成化, MING EMPEROR (r.1465–87)
Zhu Jianshen 朱見深 succeeded his father the Tianshun emperor on February 23 1464, at the age of seventeen. He avoided as many of his imperial duties as he could and his reign became notorious for **eunuch** dominance of the court,

CHENNAULT, CLAIRE LEE (1890–1958)
American General who joined the United States Army Air Force during the First World War and went to China in 1937 as the Guomindang government's aviation adviser. He created a squadron of American volunteer pilots, the Flying Tigers, which operated from its base in Kunming from August 1941. The incorporation of this group into the United States Fourteenth Air Force on July 4 1942 marked a significant increase in American aid to **Jiang Jieshi.**

CHIANG CHING-KUO see **JIANG JINGGUO**

CHIANG KAI-SHEK see **JIANG JIESHI**

CHINA PROPER
The Chinese-speaking heartland of China, excluding the frontier areas of Tibet, Xinjiang and Mongolia

CHINAWARE see **CERAMICS**

CHINESE ACADEMY OF SCIENCES *Zhongguo kexueyuan* 中國科學院
National body for the coordination of research in the natural and social sciences. Established on November 1 1949 under the chairmanship of **Guo Moruo**, it was based on the **Academia Sinica**, which had been founded in 1928 and its organisation and control by the state was modelled on the Academy of Sciences of the USSR. In 1977, social sciences were made the responsibility of a new body, the Chinese Academy of Social Sciences *Zhongguo shehui kexueyuan* 中國社會科學院 with Hu Qiaomu taking up the post of President in 1978.

CHINESE COMMUNIST PARTY *Zhongguo Gongchandang* 中國共產黨
One of the two major political parties in twentieth century China (the other being the **Guomindang**), and the party in control of the government of the People's Republic of China since 1949. Although the name has remained the same since its inception, the party itself has changed much over the decades and has adapted to local conditions to become a distinctively Chinese party.

The Communist Party grew out of the radical nationalism of the **May Fourth Movement**, heavily influenced by reports of the success of the 1917 October Revolution in Russia. The first and founding conference of the CCP took place in the French concession of Shanghai from July 23–31 1921 with fifty delegates from various parts of China. From 1923 until 1927 the CCP, in line with Comintern policy, cooperated with the Guomindang in the First United Front. This included participation in the **Northern Expedition** of 1926–7 which was led by the GMD and Jiang Jieshi, although the party was also organising peasant associations and trades unions on its own account. After the **Shanghai Coup** of April 1927 when GMD units attempted to wipe out communists, the CCP was forced out of the cities and into the countryside, where it remained until after the Second World War, effectively independent although in theory in alliance with the Guomindang in a joint resistance to the Japanese invasion of 1937.

The CCP's experience of rural government began with the establishment of the **Jinggangshan** base in 1929 and the larger **Jiangxi Soviet** which lasted from

1930 to 1934. Forced out by Nationalist military campaigns, the communists embarked on the **Long March** during which Mao Zedong became their most powerful leader. When Mao and his followers reached Yan'an in Shaanxi province and made it their base, Mao set about remodelling the party so that it would be in a postion to take control of the country. The methods he used included a **Rectification Campaign** to centralise and unify the organisation, the creation of a new ideology which became known as Marxism-Leninism **Mao Zedong Thought** and aimed at simplifying Marxism and adapting it to the Chinese environment, and the development of guerrilla campaigns of resistance to the Japanese which brought in thousands of recruits.

Once in power after the **Civil War** of 1946–9, the CCP still felt the need for constant renewal and purges through a series of political campaigns which culminated in the **Cultural Revolution**. Although the CCP is formally separate from the government and from the military, in practice the three are closely interlinked with shared and rotating membership at all levels.

Jacques GUILLERMAZ, *A History of the Chinese Communist Party, 1921–1949*, trans. Anne Destenay (Random House, 1972); Arif DIRLIK, *The origins of Chinese Communism* (New York: Oxford University Press, 1989); Robert NORTH, *Moscow and Chinese Communists* (Stanford University Press, 1953); Edgar SNOW, *Red Star over China* (New York: Random House, 1938).

CHINESE COMMUNIST YOUTH LEAGUE *Zhongguo gongchanzhuyi qingnian tuan* 中國共產主義青年團

Junior branch of the CCP with members between the ages of fourteen and twenty-five. It was created in February 1925 when the Socialist Youth Corps changed to the present name and for a brief period in the 1950s was also known as the New Democratic Youth League. Its newspaper *Zhongguo Qingnianbao* 中國青年報 closed down in August 1966 and the League ceased to function during the most intense period of the Cultural Revolution, not holding a national congress until 1973.

CHINESE EASTERN RAILWAY

In 1896, China granted to Russia a concession to build a railway from Chita to Vladivostok. Two years later, Russia also extracted an agreement allowing the construction of a **South Manchurian Railway** which would link the Chinese Eastern Railway to the ports of Dalian and Port Arthur in the **Liaodong** peninsula.

CHINESE LANGUAGE

It is more appropriate to speak in terms of Chinese languages, both in spoken and written terms. Chinese is usually placed with Tibetan and Burmese languages as part of the Sino-Tibetan group, of which the Chinese languages are by far the largest in terms of the number of speakers. Chinese people usually consider the different languages spoken by Han people as 'dialects', and only those spoken by minority peoples as separate languages. However these 'dialects' are often mutually unintelligible and considerably greater in difference than, for example, Norwegian, Swedish and Danish. Mandarin has the most native speakers, accounting for over 70% of the total of around 1.3 billion Chinese people. It thus has the largest number of native speakers of any language. Since the foundation of the People's Republic, a considerable effort has been made to encourage the use of *putonghua* 普通話, Modern Standard Chinese (MSC), a standard language based on Mandarin which is the medium of instruction at higher level educational institutions and the language of radio and television. One of the most striking features of the spoken language is the use of tones. There are four tones in MSC, high level, rising, falling and rising, and falling. In the standard PRC *pinyin* romanization, these tones are indicated as *1, 2, 3, 4*. There are only around 1,300 possible syllables in MSC, a relatively small number, and the use of tones facilitates the differentiation of words made up of the same sounds. Chinese is often thought of as monosyllabic but, although that may be historically true, in MSC many words are disyllabic or polysyllabic. Syntactically, MSC is similar to English in following a basic sentence structure of Subject-Verb-Object, e.g. *gou chi rou* 狗吃肉 'dogs eat meat', and modifier before modified, *hongche* 紅車 'red vehicle'. There is essentially no inflection: verbs do not change to show tense (cf. 'see', 'saw' in English) and nouns do not change to show number (apart from very limited use of the plural suffix *men* 們). Chinese uses particles like *le* 了, *guo* 過 and *zhe* 著to convey some of the meaning conveyed by verbal inflection in other languages; word order is very important for meaning.

The other striking feature of Chinese is the use of characters in the script. Although *pinyin* is used in a limited way to teach children to read, plans to romanize Chinese completely have never materialized. The PRC authorities in the 1950s introduced a number of simplified forms for characters to make literacy easier to achieve, but these are not used in other Chinese-speaking areas like Hong Kong and Taiwan. The total number of different characters in the standard **Kangxi** dictionary of 1716 is 40,545 but only a small proportion of these is commonly used. Of course, the total number of words, many of which use two or more characters, is much greater than this.

In the West, the nearest equivalent to characters is numerals. The figures 2 or 22 mean the same to speakers of many languages, but all pronounce them differently. Although the origins of characters may be pictures, like 山 *shan* 'mountain', most were formed in more complex ways and, like the numerals, convey a complete idea with no phonetic connotation. There are traditionally reckoned to be six ways of creating characters. Apart from pictographs, others include logical compounds, like 日 *ri* 'sun' and 月 *yue* 'moon' make 明 *ming* 'bright' and the largest category, usually referred to as "radical plus phonetic", where a semantic element is combined with phonetic loan element. An example of this is 心 *xin* 'heart' + 刃 *ren* 'blade', which produces 忍 *ren* 'to bear'. The earliest characters so far known, from oracle bones dating from around 1500 BC, are already quite sophisticated. Classical Chinese *guwen* 古文 or ***wenyan wen*** 文言文, was used as the main written medium until the **New Culture Movement** was successful in its campaign in the early twentieth century to have it replaced by a written form of the spoken language. The classical language was based on language used in the Warring States and Han periods and took a considerable effort to master. From the Song dynasty onwards certain writing, such as religious texts, some records of philosophical discussions and, increasingly, literary texts like the famous novels of the Ming and Qing were written in the vernacular of the time.

Mandarin Chinese, *guanhua* 官話, the language of the civil service, was based on the language of Beijing and was used widely in northern and western China. Modern Standard Chinese *putonghua* is its modern equivalent. The other major 'dialects' are *Wu* 吳, spoken by around 8% of the population, in Jiangsu and Zhejiang; Cantonese or *Yue* 粵(5%) in Guangdong, Guangxi and Hong Kong, *Xiang* 湘(5%) in Hunan; *Min* 閩 in Fujian and *Gan-Hakka* 贛客家 (6%) widely spread over the southern provinces. All areas use a common written language based on Mandarin and the differences between different dialects are mostly in pronunciation and vocabulary rather than grammar. See also **Bai hua**, **Wen yan**.

Jerry NORMAN, *Chinese* (Cambridge University Press, 1988); John DEFRNCIS, *The Chinese Language: Fact and Fantasy* (University of Hawaii Press, 1984); S. Robert RAMSEY, *The Languages of China* (Princeton University Press, 1987).

CHINESE PEOPLE'S POLITICAL CONSULTATIVE CONFERENCE CPPCC *Zhongguo renmin zhengzhi xieshang huiyi* 中國人民政治協商會議)

Broadly-based united front organisation established by the CCP to give greater legitimacy to its rule. The CPPCC first met in Beijing on September 21 1949 and adopted the **Common Programme** and Organic Law of the PRC. Although it has met regularly since 1949, it has had no real power, but has been used to consult non-Party people, including members of ethnic and religious minorities.

CHINESE REVOLUTIONARY PARTY see **ZHONGHUA GEMING DANG**

CHINGGIS KHAN (?1167–1227)

Creator of the **Mongol** empire of the 13th and 14th centuries. Chinggis Khan (Genghis in the Turkic forms of his name) was born Temujin to a noble family but was orphaned as a child. His greatest skill was being able to manipulate the complex system of alliances which existed between the diverse tribes who lived on the grasslands of north-east Asia. By a combination of armed force and diplomacy, he managed to dominate all of the tribes and merge them into a powerful confederacy. His leadership was acknowledged at a great *khuriltai* (conference) held at the Kerulen river in 1206 and the united Mongols set out to conquer most of Eurasia, beginning with the subjugation of the Tangut state of Xi Xia in 1215. Chinggis divided the territory he had conquered among his sons and, on his death in 1227, was succeeded as Great Khan of the Mongols by his third son Ogodei.

Leo DE HARTG, *Genghis Khan, Conqueror of the World* (I.B. Tauris, 1989).

CHONGQING 重慶 (CHUNGKING)

River port on the upper reaches of the Yangzi to which the Guomindang government retreated in 1937 after the invasion by Japan. In the early 1940s as the temporary capital it was a key location for operations in the China-Burma-India theatre of the Second World War.

CHONGZHEN 崇禎, MING EMPEROR (1611–1644, r.1628–1644)

Last emperor of the Ming dynasty and brother to the Tianqi emperor, whom he succeeded at the age of seventeen. The growth of a powerful Manchu state to the north of his capital and internal disorder destabilised his rule and he committed suicide by hanging himself on Coal Hill *Jingshan* 景山 just to the north of the **Forbidden City** when the rebel **Li Zicheng** appeared to be poised to take the capital.

CHU 楚

The heartland of this enormous state covered modern Hubei and Hunan Provinces, stretching along the **Yangzi** valley and bordering the central states at its northern limits. To the west it touched the state of **Ba** in the Han River valley, while in the east its armies campaigned as far away as **Yue**, in modern Zhejiang. To the inhabitants of the conservative northern plains its inhabitants were as different and as fearful as the ruthless people of the state of **Qin**, and indeed they were the last great opponents of Qin in its advance towards total domination. The state had known a long history, being mentioned on **oracle bones** and establishing its military might under King Wu (740–690 BC), and it only succumbed after the capture of its capital Ying in 277 BC. Even then its influence was not finished, for after the overthrow of the Qin dynasty the Chu military commander **Xiang Yu** all but outdid his compatriot **Liu Bang** in the resultant struggle for supremacy.

Chu culture owed much to inspiration from the South as well as from the North, and it was its lack of conformity and presumed wildness that frightened the more conservative inhabitants of the central states. This differentness may be sensed in the shamanistic tone of some of the ***Chuci*** 'songs of Chu', the southern penchant for using incense burners, the unrepentant individuality of the great Daoist writings associated with it (see ***Daodejing***, **Zhuangzi**), and the boldness and bright colouring of the artefacts to be seen in tombs from the Chu region, such as those at **Leigudun** and **Mawangdui**. Most notable is the striking use of red and black **lacquer**. See also **Qu Yuan.**

S.F. SAGE, *Ancient Sichuan and the Unification of China* (State University of New York Press, 1992).

CHUCI 楚辭

Collection of poetry from the state of **Chu** traditionally associated with **Qu Yuan** (c. 340–278 BC), a leading minister until his suicide. The collection was compiled by Wang Yi (d. 158 AD) and consists of seventeen sections each with a single poem or a small group of related works. The early works were traditionally attributed to Qu Yuan, the later ones are from the Han, the last, the *Jiu si* 'Nine Longings', being by the compiler Wang Yi. The *Li sao* 離騷 'Encountering sorrow', the first poem and reputedly by Qu Yuan, encapsulates many features typical of the genre: the writer's feeling of rejection and disillusionment, introspection, a journey, elaborate descriptions of landscapes, birds, animals, plants and natural phenomena, the frequent use of allusion, symbolism and allegory. This epic poem describes how the poet, disillusioned when his loyalty to his lord is doubted, sets out on a mystical journey through the sky to the West. It is usually seen as a political allegory and later *sao* poems tend to degenerate into self-pitying monologues of rejected ministers. Other poems originate in shamanistic rituals; the *Tian wen* 天問 'Heavenly questions' is, exceptionally, a series of cryptic questions on history and legend assumed to be riddles. Most of the works have a pentasyllabic base and fall into either the 'song style' (*tum tum tum xi tum tum* – where the *tum* is a stressed, meaningful syllable and the *xi* is an unstressed, meaningless carrier sound) or the double pentasyllabic '*sao* style' (*tum tum tum tee tum tum xi tum tum tum tee tum tum* – where the additional *tee* is an unstressed particle). The subject matter, the highly embellished style and the prosody, which all differ from the ***Shijing***, have led scholars to speak in terms of northern (*Shijing*) and southern (*Chuci*) traditions in Chinese poetry, but recent scholarship has cast doubts on this and regards the two as different developmental phases of a single tradition.

David HAWKES, *Ch'u Tz'u: The Songs of the South* (Oxford University Press, 1959); Geoffrey R. WATERS, *Three Elegies of Ch'u. An Introduction to the Traditional Interpretation of the Ch'u Tz'u* (University of Wisconsin Press, 1985).

CHUN QIU 春秋 see ***SPRING AND AUTUMN ANNALS***

CHUNGKING see **CHONGQING**

CIVIL SERVICE

For most of Chinese imperial history the administration of the empire was in the hands of a civilian administrative organization responsible to the emperor. The origins of the system can be traced back beyond the unification of China by the Qin dynasty in 221BC. In the early years of the feudal Zhou dynasty a kinship system prevailed: heredity governed status and office. The feudal lords were an aristocracy occupying minsterial posts while members of a lower gentry *shi* 士served as lower level officials. The formation of larger states brought a relative rise in the status of the ruler, the loosening of kinship ties and the development of a civilian bureaucracy based more on merit and with a greater degree of functional specialization. Rulers appointed prime ministers to oversee the administrative system. Hence, courtiers joked with Duke Huan of Qi 齊桓公 (ruled 685–643BC) that after appointing **Guan Zhong** 管仲 as prime minister he had nothing to do. A system of local government based on districts *xian* 縣and commanderies *jun* 郡 governed by centrally appointed magistrates came to replace local hereditary fief holders in these states. The rise of Qin as a major power has been partially attributed to the reforms of **Shang Yang** 商鞅, which included weakening the power of the aristocracy by dividing the state into 31 *xian* and making everyone subject to centrally determined laws. The fact that Shang Yang was from the rival state of Wei testifies to the development of professional administrators.

When **Qin Shi huang** 秦始皇 unified China in 221 BC he abolished what remained of the feudal system and instituted the commandery and district system throughout China, dividing the whole country into around 40 commanderies controlled by centrally appointed officials. This system was basically adopted by the Han and successive dynasties, with many variations in the nomenclature and details, but it was headed by a central administration in the capital with the emperor at the apex. According to the Confucian ideal, below the emperor should be 'three chief ministers and nine ministers' *san gong jiu qing* 三公九卿. In the Han the three chief ministers, nominally just below the emperor and in charge of civil and military affairs, were in practice supplanted by the Secretariat, *Shang shu tai* 尚書臺, as the highest policy making body. Throughout imperial history there was a tendency for the emperor's private office to replace the formal highest civil service body as the real focus of power. Such a body would consist of civil servants or others like relatives (particularly favoured by empress dowagers during periods of regency) or **eunuchs.** The Secretariat developed six specialist branches, the Six Boards *Liubu* 六部, which by the Tang had become the ministries in charge of civil personnel (*Libu* 吏部), revenue (*Hubu* 戶部), rites and education (*Li bu* 禮部), war (*Bing bu* 兵部), justice (*Xing bu* 刑部) and public works (*Gongbu* 工部). After the Secretariat, then called *Shangshusheng* 尚書省, was abolished in the Ming, the Six Boards came directly under the emperor. The other important government body was the **Censorate**, called the *Yushitai* 御史臺 until the Ming when it became the *Duchayuan* 都察院. Its function was supposedly two-fold: to remonstrate with the emperor and to investigate and impeach other officials. Not surprisingly, the second function tended to predominate.

Under the Han system, at local level the head of the commandery, the *taishou* 太守, the district magistrate, *xianling* 縣令, and his two subordinates, the *cheng* 丞, dealing with civil affairs, and the *wei* 尉, dealing with military affairs, were all appointees of the central government. Other lesser officials and officers were local appointees, as were those at the lower levels of administration, the *xiang* 鄉, *ting* 亭 and *li* 里 where local elders and leaders were employed. This system was basically followed throughout imperial history. In the Song dynasty the *jun* was replaced by the prefecture *fu* 府 and in the Yuan, provinces *sheng* 省 were added above the *fu* as an intermediate level between central and local government. The chain of command ran from the emperor, through the Six Boards to the provinces, prefectures and districts. The appointees down to district *xian* level were all civil servants graded according to a scale and paid a salary in piculs *dan* 石 of grain according to grade. There was a tendency to use the 9 grade system which was supposed to have existed in antiquity but these were often subdivided into typically 18 grades (though it varied considerably, with 30 at one point in the Song). Civil servants' performance was regularly assessed by their superiors and by investigating censors; they were then promoted or demoted (or, in extreme cases, dismissed and punished). Civil servants were generalists by training; the district magistrate, for example, was expected to take charge of everything from dispensing justice to organizing militias, public works, tax collection, education and so on. In practice there were specialist assistants to help with areas requiring particular expertise. These included both regular civil servants, like the provincial *buzhengshi* 布政使 and the *anchashi* 按察使, who specialized in fiscal and judicial affairs, and members of the private office of the incumbent. The latter, called *muyou* 幕友, were typically people of gentry status who were supporting themselves and hoping to gain a regular position in the future. Below them was an assortment of officers, clerks, yamen runners, and so on who were not part of the civil service. Civil servants were subject to regular redeployment and to a rule of avoidance which prevented them from being employed in their home area. These anti-corruption measures did not apply to the notoriously venal officers and clerks on whom district magistrates were forced to rely.

In early imperial history, selection for office was mainly by recommendation. Local officials were urged to suggest suitable men to the emperor and were then held responsible for their recommendees. During the Han, aspirants worked in local offices to learn the business before being recommended for higher positions. When they arrived at court they might be tested on their grasp of policy and administration; this was clearly a precursor to the later examination system. The recommendation system was formalised into the *jiupin zhongzheng* 九品中正 system by Emperor Wen of the Wei (r.220–226), under which *zhongzheng* (literally 'impartial and upright') officials appointed in each area assessed candidates, nominally into 9 grades. The **examination system**, introduced progressively from the Sui dynasty, and used exclusively for important offices from the Ming onwards, was clearly more objective than the recommendation system, which had been manipulated by local leading families to reinforce their positions. However, the switch to the examination system also had the effect of increasing the power of the emperor.

Particularly in the later period of imperial history, a civil service post was the principal way to securing social status and financial well-being. The low status accorded to merchants and the consequent limited legal protection meant that although merchants might accumulate large sums of money, they often sought gentry status, by purchase for themselves and through education and examination for their sons, in order to secure the family's future. Although gentry status, which brought social and legal benefits such as exemption from certain punishments, could be purchased, examination success at *jinshi* 進士 level was normally the only avenue to significant civil service office in later imperial times.

The Chinese imperial civil service was one of the wonders of the pre-modern world. Descriptions by Jesuits of a state run by highly educated scholars and based essentially on a humanist philosophy made a deep impression on 17th and 18th century thinkers of the European Enlightenment. This was reflected in the Western vogue for *chinoiserie*. By using a single national syllabus in its selection system and sending officials anywhere in the country, except their home areas, it created an homogenous elite deeply imbued with the state ethos and able to communicate with each other in a common written language, classical Chinese, and a common spoken language, *guan hua* 官話 'mandarin language'. Yet, by the mid-19th century the Chinese civil service was viewed, at best, as arrogant and inefficient and, at worst, as a cesspit of incompetence and corruption. This was partly due to cyclical decline and partly to the nature of the institution. It was not designed to reach deeply into the daily lives of its citizens, as modern governments do, and to mobilize national resources in order to compete with other states. Its aim was to run a universal empire largely through a system of local self-government. In cost terms this made it extraordinarily efficient. However, the civilian nature of the institution, which gave it a very attractive and highly cultural orientation, was a weakness when China was faced with aggressive external forces.

Charles O.HUCKER, *The Censorial System of Ming China* (Stanford University Press, 1966); HO Ping-ti, *The Ladder of Success in Imperial China: Aspects of Social Mobility, 1368–1911* (Columbia University Press,1962); CHANG Chung-li, *The Chinese Gentry* (University of Washington Press, 1955); CH'Ü TUNG-TSU, *Local Government in China under the Ch'ing* (Harvard University Press, 1962 + reprints); Kenneth FOLSOM, *Friends, guests and colleagues: the mu fu system in the late Ch'ing Period* (University of California Press, 1960).

CIVIL WAR (1945–1949)

The war between the military forces of the CCP and GMD after the defeat of Japan in August 1945. The two rivals had fought each other between 1927 and 1937 after a four year alliance collapsed in the **Shanghai Coup** of 1927, but during the Japanese occupation of China they had a nominal alliance. China accepted the surrender of Japanese forces on September 9 1945 and General George C. Marshall attempted to mediate between the Communists and the Nationalists in the hope that a civil war could be avoided and a coalition government created.

On May 1 1946, the CCP formally renamed their armed forces the **People's Liberation Army** (PLA), indicating their intention to take power. CCP forces clashed with GMD troops in Hubei and Hunan in June of the same year. The civil war had begun in earnest. Although GMD forces were able to capture the CCP capital of Yan'an in March 1947, it was the PLA that made the running. **Lin Biao** commanded a major assault on the Nationalists in the north-east in May 1947 and this culminated in the seizure of Shanyang in September 1948. The following November, the **Huai-Hai campaign** in northern China was launched under **Chen Yi** and Lin Biao commanded the Beijing-Tianjin operation that was to bring the CCP to power. Tianjin was taken on January 15 1949, Beijing on January 31, Nanjing, the Nationalist capital fell on April 23 and Shanghai on May 27. The Civil War finally ended with the establishment of the Peoples Republic of China on October 1 1949.

Steven LEVINE, *Anvil of Victory: the Communist Revolution in Manchuria, 1945–48* (Columbia University Press, 1987); A. Doak BARNETT, *China on the Eve of Communist Takeover* (London: Thames and Hudson, 1963); Suzanne PEPPER, *Civil War in China: The Political Struggle, 1945–1949* (Berkeley: University of California Press, 1978).

CIXI 慈禧 (1835–1908)

Empress Dowager during the last years of the Qing dynasty and *de facto* ruler of China from 1861 until her death in 1908. She was concubine to the Xianfeng emperor who ruled from 1851–1861 and bore him a son. The Empress, Ci'an, had no children. On the death of the emperor in 1861, Cixi, Ci'an and Prince **Gong** served as regents during the minority of Cixi's son, the **Tongzhi emperor**, but it was Cixi who exercised real power. The reign of the Tongzhi emperor saw a temporary revival of the fortunes of the Qing dynasty in the **Tongzhi Restoration** and the limited success of the **Self-Strengthening Movement**. However, the final failure of the dynasty and the collapse of the empire is often blamed on Cixi's narrow-minded attitudes and corrupt manipulation of the court. In particular she obstructed the **Hundred Day Reforms** during which **Kang Youwei** proposed a series of measures designed to strengthen the position of the Qing dynasty. On the death of the Tongzhi emperor in 1874, the **Guangxu emperor**, also a minor, was enthroned and Cixi remained as regent. The Guangxu emperor died on November 14 1908, Cixi the following day.

CLAN OR LINEAGE ORGANISATIONS

Clan or lineage (*zu* 族) organisations have played an important role in Chinese society, particularly in rural China. Typically consisting of households sharing the same surname and residing in one village, the lineage would manage the graves of its common ancestors, commemorative tablets, halls and temples and would perform ritual and charitable tasks for the community. In the early Empire their significance was mainly concerned with political and economic power derived from land holding. From the Song dynasty onwards, their role in society and their value to the government as a means of extending its control grew. Their organisation became more complex and more disciplined according to the development of clan rules, which gave clan heads considerable legally-approved powers over their members. Those rules generally reflected the currently approved **Neo-Confucian** principles for communal living, including respect for seniority and authority and maintenance of mourning rites. For the mutual benefit of the whole clan, the richer families were expected to help the deserving poorer ones, perhaps by contributing to a clan chest from which the educational expenses of a promising boy might be drawn. Lineages might also own and farm land and some acquired wealth and power which was seen as a potential threat by the CCP when it came to power in 1949. Lineage organisations were targeted during the **land reform** programme of the early 1950s and **collectivisation** was intended partly to replace the old village structures that they controlled. Since the introduction of the **responsibility system** in 1979, the influence of lineages has resurfaced as opportunities for political and commercial profit have been fostered amongst member families.

Hugh BAKER, *Chinese Family and Kinship* (Macmillan Press Ltd., 1979); H.C.W LIU, *The Traditional Chinese Clan Rules* (New York, Association for Asian Studies, 1959).

CLASSES

The traditional classification of Chinese society, disregarding the imperial clan, was fourfold: according to the *Guanzi* (see **Guan Zhong**) it comprised the scholars (*shi* 士), peasants (*nong* 農), artisans (*gong* 工), and merchants (*shang* 商), with whom soldiers (*bing* 兵) were often deemed to share last place. Scholars were honoured for their intellectual prowess and responsibility for running the country and peasants for their essential role as food producers. As **Mencius** said, there are those who work with their minds and those who work with their hands: they may not occupy equal social positions, but all deserve respect. Merchants, whose service in supplying the wants and needs of the literati earned them no recognition, were condemned by Confucians for profiteering and having no productive activity. Soldiers were despised and feared. Many were convicts, and they were often ill-disciplined and preyed upon the country around their garrisons. They frequently deserted and became vagrants or **bandits**. Though certain occupations were hereditary (see **Hereditary Occupations**) social mobility occurred, upwards as a result of education, wealth and influence (see **Clans**) and downwards as a result of economic misfortune, criminal justice or intrigue, and in practice the relativity of social groupings and occupations was different from and more complex than the theory. Through much of the imperial era the small literati elite were the leaders of society, held in awe by most of the population. Only the educated were qualified for government office, but in economic terms, and in the influence they wielded over local populations, the **gentry** might be just as powerful. They comprised the rich landowners and merchant families. The third class, the artisanate, comprised a great range of occupations and levels, from influential industrialists, multiple workshop-owners, expert craftsmen and prosperous retailers down to single workers selling their daily output of hats, fans or paper lanterns, or humble employees contracted to perform their skills for others through their **guilds**. The peasantry too were in an equivocal position. Able to own land as free men and sometimes even in receipt of grants of land from the government (see **Equal Field System, Land Tenure**), they had the chance of becoming rich in good times. But when natural or man-made disasters struck they might be unable to pay their taxes or resist their predators, and be forced into tenancy or selling their home and family (see **Land Tax, Single Whip Tax System**). In really bad times they might even end up as soldiers or as homeless bandits.

Beneath these four classes of free men was a further band stigmatised as *jianmin* 賤民 "despised people". This comprised members of service and entertainment occupations, such as water-carriers, grave-diggers, prostitutes and actors, the dregs of society. But even they had the right to rise if they had the talent and the opportunity. Slaves did not. Though they never constituted a significant percentage of society, those who were born into slavery or condemned to it by the courts must stay there, with their descendants, unless pardoned by imperial amnesty.

As parts of China came into contact with Western influences and slowly and partially industrialised in the late nineteenth and early twentieth centuries, social classes similar to those in the West began to emerge, particularly in the **Treaty Ports**. A newly-emerging merchant class, the **compradores,** developed to mediate between Chinese officialdom and the Western traders, and a small but influential working class was created by the growth of textile factories, mines, dockyards and railways. Gradually the old military structures declined and a new breed of officers emerged, the forerunners of the warlords of the pre-Second World War period. By the 1920s, cities like **Shanghai** and **Hong Kong** had a flourishing and powerful urban bourgeoisie. After 1949, those wealthy merchants and industrialists who had not collaborated with the Japanese during the Second World War were designated as the National Bourgeoisie and allowed to retain some influence, although this was taken away from them in the **Five-Anti Campaign.**

CLASSIC OF HISTORY see ***SHANGSHU***

CLASSICAL CHINESE see ***WENYAN***

CLASSICS see **FIVE CLASSICS, THIRTEEN CLASSICS**

CLOISONNÉ ENAMEL *Jingtailan* 景泰藍

Cloisonné enamel decoration consists of coloured glass paste applied to metal vessels and contained within enclosures made of copper. The practice of inlaying metalwork with glass had existed in China from the Shang dynasty onwards and was used on bronzes, ceramic and silver. In the Tang dynasty, cloisons (partitioned compartments) filled with precious stones appear on silver jewellery and vessels.

The golden age of cloisonné was during the reign of the Ming Emperor Jingtai 景泰(1450–1457). It was then that some of the best cloisonné was thought to have been made, so much so that the Chinese term for cloisonne is *Jingtailan* (Jingtai blue ware). One reason for this was the arrival, after Constantinople fell to the Turks in 1453, of a large number of Greek artisans skilled in making Byzantine cloisonné. However, the earliest examples of dated Chinese cloisonné occur in the Xuande period (1426–1435). They include incense burners in archaic shapes, dishes and boxes, animals and birds, and pieces for the scholar's desk.

The bodies of early cloisonné pieces are made of heavy cast bronze or brass with cloison wires, made by hammering bronze ingots, soldered on. By the later Qing dynasty, copper replaced bronze and brass as the base material, creating pieces that were much lighter, and vegetable glue was used to attach the cloisonné wires, replacing soldering. A wider variety of colours was also introduced which made a more detailed style of enamel painting possible.

Although in Ming dynasty pieces the cloisons are not perfectly filled and the surface has a certain roughness, the designs are bold, vigorous, and endlessly varied. Gradually technique improved but quality was lost during the Qing period. Cloisonné enamel in traditional shapes and designs have been produced up to the present day, and Beijing has remained as the most important centre for *Jingtailan* production.

Barry TILL, *Antique Chinese Cloisonné* (Art Gallery of Greater Victoria, British Columbia, 1983).

COHONG

Monopoly guild operated by the merchants of Guangzhou who traded with foreign merchants under the **Canton system**. The name is derived from the Cantonese pronunciation of *gonghang*, 公行 "officially authorised firms". It functioned as an intermediary between the foreigners and the Chinese government for which it collected taxes and customs dues.

COLLECTIVISATION

Policy adopted by the CCP of converting family ownership of land and farming into collective ownership. Areas under the control of the CCP before 1949, notably the **Jiangxi Soviet** experienced experimental versions of this policy, but after 1949, it was implemented nationwide. Aware of the catastrophic results of the forced collectivisation in the Soviet Union in the 1930s, the Chinese adopted a gradualist approach, collectivising in stages through **Land Reform**, **Mutual Aid Teams**, **Cooperatives** and finally **People's Communes.**

Vivienne SHUE, *Peasant China in Transition: The Dynamics of Development toward Socialism, 1949–1976* (University of California Press, 1980); Jean C. OI, *State and Peasant in Contemporary China: the Political Economy of Village Government* (University of California Press, 1989).

COLOUR SYMBOLISM

Colour has its appropriate meaning and purpose in Chinese symbolism and may be emblematic of rank, authority, virtues and emotions. The five primary colours have been used since the Chinese **bronze age** to represent the **five**

elements, five directions and four seasons (without yellow): yellow for earth and centre; blue for wood, east and spring; red for fire, south and summer; white for metal, west and autumn; and black for water, north and winter. Red is the emblem of joy and is employed for all festive occasions. ***Duilian*** couplets, written on red paper. are pasted on doors and red paper-cuts on windows in Chinese households at the lunar New Year (see **Traditional Festivals**). Red is also the colour for weddings. It was believed that marriages were arranged by the old man of the moon who connects the future couple's feet with an invisible red silk thread. Yellow was sacred to the emperor and Daoist magic charms and incantations were written on yellow papers which would expel the evil spirits. White was associated with death and used for mourning apparel and funeral decorations. However it also symbolises purity when related to some popular sages and religious deities. Detailed imperial codes on the use of colours were issued in different dynasties for regulating court ranks, especially on costumes and accessories, and for ceremonial purposes.

COMINTERN

Abbreviation for the Communist International, the Moscow-based organisation of Communist and Workers parties which was established in 1919 by Lenin and which played a key role in the establishment of the **Chinese Communist Party** and in directing its policies before its abolition in 1943. It was replaced by the Cominform, Communist Information Bureau which lasted until 1956.

COMMANDERIES *Jun* 郡

Administrative units of the Qin dynasty which replaced the feudal princedoms of the Zhou period and which were also used by the Han dynasty. They were abolished by the Sui emperor **Wendi** and the two-tier system of prefectures and counties, which remains in use today was introduced.

COMMERCE

Trade was anathema to orthodox Confucian thinking: merchants were at the bottom of the social hierarchy, below scholars, peasants and artisans, and traditional writers of the history of China generally ignored the role of commerce in the development of Chinese society. Nevertheless, as in any agricultural society, it took place on a large scale, and there are records of trade that go back to the Qin and Han periods. Certain periods are notable for the rapid expansion of commerce. During the 11th and 12th centuries, there was such a rapid expansion of merchant activity that it has been described as a commercial revolution. The number of markets increased dramatically, market towns emerged and there was a move from barter trade to the greater use of copper coinage and paper money. In the middle period of the Ming dynasty, notably the 16th century, China experienced another tremendous growth in commercial activity and the rise of merchant syndicates based in certain regions, including the Shanxi traders who were particularly active on the northern frontiers of the empire and the Xin'an or **Huizhou merchants** of southern Anhui, who dominated the trade of the Yangzi.

Commercial Press ***Shangwu yinshuguan*** 商務印書館
Influential publishing house founded in Shanghai in February 1897. It published major works on Chinese history and culture, including an important edition of the ***Siku quanshu*** in 1934.

Common Programme ***Gongtong gangling*** 共同綱領
The provisional constitution of the People's Republic of China adopted by the **Chinese People's Political Consultative Conference** on September 29 1949. It outlined the general character of the new regime, which committed itself to the redistribution of land, industrialisation to develop the economy and an alliance with the Soviet Union.

Communes
People's Communes (*renmin gongshe* 人民公社) were the final stage in the **collectivisation** of Chinese agriculture, and were created during the **Great Leap Forward** by merging existing Agricultural Cooperatives. Communes remained the fundamental administrative unit in the Chinese countryside until the **Responsibilty System** was introduced in 1979. In addition to managing agricultural activity and allocating resources, they were responsible for banking, education, child care, retirement homes, medical centres, road and bridge building and maintenance and other public works.

Communist Party see **Chinese Communist Party**

Communist Youth League see **Chinese Communist Youth League**

Compass, magnetic
The principle of magnetic attraction had been known to the Chinese since the Han dynasty, when it was applied for geomantic purposes in conjunction with the diviner's board. During the eleventh century AD its use as a guide to navigation was recognised and is mentioned by **Shen Gua**. It assisted in the rapid commercialisation of the Song economy and the subsequent exploration of the Indian Ocean by Chinese shipping (see **Zheng He**). Its introduction to Europe by the beginning of the thirteenth century seems to have come by way of Arab intermediaries.

Compradores
Derogatory term, derived from the Portuguese word meaning "buyer", for Chinese merchants who acted as middlemen between foreign and Chinese businesses.

Concessions, foreign
Areas in the **Treaty Ports** reserved for foreign residences and businesses. The concessions were administered by the foreigners and the laws of the foreign nations applied under the rules of **extraterritoriality**. Although there were precedents in the allocation of land to **Arab traders** in the Tang and Song dynasties, the privileges that foreigners enjoyed in the concessions and the virtual exclusion of Chinese, apart from those performing menial tasks, were deeply resented by patriotic Chinese.

CONFUCIAN CLASSICS see **FIVE CLASSICS, THIRTEEN CLASSICS**

CONFUCIANISM ***Rujiao*** **儒教**

There are two generally accepted usages of the term Confucianism:

(1) The name given to the political philosophy first espoused by the rulers of China in the early Han period, and the theoretical basis of imperial government until its rejection as outmoded in the early twentieth century (see **May Fourth Movement**). It was the interpretation and crystallisation by scholars and officials such as **Mencius**, **Xunzi**, **Dong Zhongshu** and **Liu Xin** of the principles and ideas attributed to **Confucius** emphasizing the ruler's duty to set a moral example and govern in the interests of the populace. In practice, and as time went by, it developed characteristics going far beyond anything conceived by the Master himself. It defended the right of the people to rebel against an unjust ruler (see **Mandate of Heaven**) and continually recognised the imperative of high moral standards in government (see **Censorate**, ***Dao***) but in its accommodation with law codes and harsh punishments it revealed that imperial Confucianism had learned many lessons from **Legalism**. In particular, it overlooked Confucius' dictum that the moral and political implications of names and titles should be understood and practised and that rites and ceremonies should be simplified for the sake of economy and to draw attention to their underlying meaning. On the contrary, they became complex, costly, and self-justifying. Under the Han emperor **Wudi** Confucian books were selected as the basis of the education and selection system aimed at producing government officials, so that the political fortunes of Confucianism seemed to be guaranteed. The state cult of offering **sacrifices** to Confucius was first begun under Emperor Han Guangwu in AD 37. However, it failed to produce any original thinkers in the Later Han and proved weak at countering Buddhist ideas, and politically it was undermined by the **eunuchs** and the clans belonging to senior court women in the second century AD. During the Northern and Southern Dynasties it was rivalled by **Daoism** and **Buddhism**, until its revival was begun in the Tang by **Li Ao** and **Han Yu** and completed in the guise of **Neo-Confucianism** during the Song.

(2) The social philosophy and system which has shaped the outlook and behaviour of the Chinese people from the **Warring States** period to the present day. Based on concepts of the family and state which predate Confucius (see **Ancestor Worship**), the Confucian Classics defined exact details of social behaviour and particularly exalted **filial piety**, stressing the mutual obligations of superior:inferior enshrined in the **Five Relationships** of father:son, ruler: minister, elder brother:younger brother, husband:wife and friend:friend. These were also extended to the traditional system of inter-state relations (see **Tribute System**). Concepts such as male superiority (see **Marriage**, ***yin-yang***), respect for generational seniority, and mutual responsibility underlay the development of the clan system in the Song period.

Confucianism was not a religion and had no priesthood or liturgy. The statues to be found in its temples were dedicated to a variety of deities, especially those of local heroes, and Confucius himself was not treated as a god. The spiritual side of Confucianism was in the hands of the clan or family head, whose responsibility it was to worship before the memorial tablets of deceased ancestors and to maintain appropriate sacrifices to them. Towards the end of the twentieth century, the adjective Confucian has been used in a vague and general way to describe the traditional societies in those parts of East Asia which have been influenced over the centuries by Chinese thought, including Japan, Korea, Vietnam and Singapore. See also **Son of Heaven.**

William Theodore DE BARY, *The Trouble with Confucianism* (Harvard University Press, 1991); Wei-ming TU, *Confucian Thought, Selfhood as Creative Transformation* (State University of New York Press, 1985); Irene EBER, *Confucianism, the Dynamics of Tradition* (Macmillan, 1986); William Theodore DE BARY, *The Liberal Tradition in China* (Columbia University Press, 1983).

CONFUCIUS Kongzi 孔子 (Kong Qiu 孔丘, Kong Zhongni 孔仲尼, 550–479 BC)

The first political theorist and teacher known by name in Chinese history, though probably not the first of either profession. He lived in the small state of **Lu**, where he criticised the style of government practised by its court, which he regarded as usurping the rightful authority of the Zhou dynasty. He sought a political career with a view to rectifying corrupt institutions but (despite later stories which credit him with holding professional appointments) achieved no prominence in his lifetime, and made his living as a private tutor. By training gentlemen (*junzi* 君子) he hoped that his ideas would permeate court circles and influence the ruler. His teaching materials included the current editions of the ***Shijing***, the ***Shujing*** and the ***Yijing***, which he interpreted and may have indirectly edited, though he was not responsible for writing either these or the ***Spring and Autumn Annals*** as was later claimed by his apologists. His professed aim was to recreate what he believed to have been the golden age of the early Zhou, ruled by the sage Kings **Wen**, **Wu** and the Duke of Zhou (see **Zhou Gong**), but the subjects on which he concentrated inevitably stemmed from and reflected the concerns of his own day, and contributed to the profound social and bureaucratic changes affecting the central states in the fifth century BC. A handful of his disciples are known by name, and it may be they who began the compilation of the book of sayings, the "Analects" later attributed to him (see ***Lunyu***). The emphasis of his teaching lay on the responsibility of the king and ruling elite to set a high moral example which would be followed by their subjects, enabling men of any background to realise their full potential as members of a peaceful and just society. It did not comprise a systematic statement of a comprehensive ethical or political philosophy, and by its refusal to be dogmatic was open to wide variation in interpretation by later generations. Its chief concern was with the following of the Way (***Dao*** 道) and the pursuit of Goodness (***Ren*** **仁).**

H.G. CREEL, *Confucius, the Man and the Myth* (New York: The John Day Co., 1949); D.C. LAU trans. and intr., *Confucius*: *The Analects* (Penguin, 1979).

CONSTITUTION OF THE PEOPLE'S REPUBLIC OF CHINA

The first constitution, which replaced the **Common Programme** as a statement of intent of the CCP-led government, was approved by the National People's Congress on September 20 1954 during its first session. Drafted by a constitutional committee in 1953, it leant heavily on the Soviet Union's 1936

Constitution and included clauses on the structure of central and local government, the legal system, ownership of property and policies towards different categories of citizens. A new constitution which reflected the changes that had taken place during the **Cultural Revolution**, in particular the absence of a State Chairman, was adopted by the National People's Congress on January 17 1975, and two more were approved after the death of Mao Zedong, on March 5 1978 and December 4 1982.

CONSTITUTIONAL MOVEMENT (1901–1911)

An attempt by modern minded Han Chinese gentry to implement constitutional reforms in the crisis after the failure of the **Hundred Days Reform** and the suppression of the **Boxer Rising.** After the Qing court returned from its self-imposed exile in Xi'an in 1901, missions were sent abroad to examine and report on the workings of constitutional government. Proposals for reform of the educational and military systems were made in 1901, but it was the victory of Japan in the 1904–5 **Russo-Japanese War**, a victory which many Chinese students who had studied in Japan attributed to that country's constitutional monarchy, that precipitated the real change. In 1905, the imperial **examination system** was abolished, and Ministries of Education, Police and War were established in 1906.

The principle that China should move to a constitutional government was established by an edict of September 1 1906 and in August 1908, an outline constitution was published. With the death of the Empress Dowager on November 15, a day after the Guangxu emperor died, the main obstacle to reform vanished. Provincial Assemblies met during 1909 and although only a small proportion of the population, principally scholars and rich landowners, were represented, they became a powerful focus of opposition to imperial government. In February 1910, delegates from the assemblies called for the convocation of a parliament and a National Consultative Assembly met the following October. A cabinet of high officials and Manchu nobles on the Japanese model was appointed in April 1911 and a parliament promised for 1913, but these moves were completely superseded by the **Revolution of 1911.**

COUPLETS see ***DUILIAN***

COURT RANK INSIGNIA

Complex regulations of court costumes were established in every dynasty. The designs of court hats and robes were often used to signify the wearer's position in the imperial hierarchy.

Insignia badges, known as *buzi* 補子 or "mandarin squares" on the front and back of a surcoat, were used in Ming and Qing courts to indicate ranks, which fell into three main categories:

1. Imperial insignia: The upper ranks of the imperial nobility were indicated by the dragon roundels on the surcoats, as the dragon symbolised imperial power and the circle symbolised Heaven. The number of roundels, the style in which the dragons were portrayed, and the number of claws on the dragons were all indications of the wearer's rank.
2. Civil officials' insignia: Images of fabulous birds were used to signify civil officials' ranks, and included: (from the first to the ninth rank) crane, golden

pheasant, peacock, wild goose, silver pheasant, egret, mandarin duck, quail, and paradise flycatcher.

3. Military officials' insignia: Images of animals were displayed on the military officials' badges, and included: (from the first to the ninth rank) the Chinese unicorn or *qilin* 麒麟, the lion, the leopard, the tiger, the bear, the panther, two kinds of rhinoceros, and the sea-horse.

Verity WILSON, *Chinese Dress* (London: Bamboo Publishing 1986).

COURTESANS

Professional female entertainers whose culture flourished between the Tang and the mid-Qing and was important in the development of both performing and literary arts. Their role was similar to the more familiar *geisha* of Japan.Trained to stimulate their male admirers with dance, musical and poetic accomplishments, they were particularly associated with the *ci* form of song-poem (see **Musical Entertainment**). Whilst some courtesans earned high reputations for their independence as well as their skills, others inevitably became concubines in literati households. See also **Marriage, Women.**

Dorothy KO, *Teachers of the Inner Chambers: Women and Culture in Seventeenth-Century China* (Stanford University Press, 1994).

CULTURAL REVOLUTION *Wuchanjieji wenhua da geming* 無產階級文化大革命 ('Great Revolution in Proletarian Culture')

Factional struggle within the **Chinese Communist Party** that brought hundreds of thousands of students and other young people onto the streets in demonstrations and pitched battles and which toppled many of the old guard leadership.

The first open sign of the split within the leadership was an attack on **Wu Han** for his play *Hai Rui Dismissed From Office* and on his supporters including Deng Tuo and Liao Mosha, with whom he had collaborated in the satirical "**Evening Talks at Yanshan**" column in *Beijing Daily*. **Yao Wenyuan's** article attacking the play was published November 29 1965 in Shanghai and then in Liberation *Army Daily*, the newspaper under the control of **Lin Biao**, after it was blocked in Beijing by **Peng Zhen**. The article took months to prepare and was revised several times by **Jiang Qing**, **Zhang Chunqiao** and Yao. Mao does not seem to have been involved in writing the article as he is said to have criticised it for not making the parallel with **Peng Dehuai** clear enough, but he was prepared to put his name to the authorization of publication. On February 6 1966, Peng Zhen, in a circular, the "February Outline Report", on problems of socialist culture, attempted to restrict the argument to historical and literary matters and keep it away from political conflicts. He showed the report to **Liu Shaoqi** who advised him to get personal clearance from Mao. He did not do this but set up his own "Group of Five in charge of the Cultural Revolution." On March 26 1966 Peng Zhen was dismissed.

Less than two months later, the Circular of the Central Committee of the CCP known as the "May 16 Circular" condemned Peng Zhen's circular and in explicit class-conflict terms attacked "representatives of the bourgeoisie who have sneaked into the Party", and dissolved Peng's Group of Five. It established a new Cultural Revolution Group directly under the control of the Standing Committee of the Political Bureau. Lin Biao was influential in creating the circular and it was linked with his move to create a cult of Mao's "genius".

On May 25 Nie Yuanzi (a niece of Marshal Nie Rongzhen, who was an old comrade of Lin Biao) and other members of the Department of Philosophy at Beijing University put up ***dazibao*** 大字報 attacking Beijing University Vice-Chancellor Lu Ping in the name of the Cultural Revolution. They were suppressed.

Early in June 1966, work teams under Liu Shaoqi and **Deng Xiaoping** were sent into universities. One theory at the time was that they were to test Liu and Deng's loyalty. Liu probably using them as a means of control after the precedent set during the **Socialist Education Movement**. The sending-in of the work teams polarised the nascent **Red Guard** movement in the universities. Two groups with opposite aims emerged, one determined to denounce the old administration, and the other stubbornly defending it and protecting their relatives who ran it.

In July, Mao left his retreat in Hangzhou, returned to Beijing which was under PLA and Lin Biao's control, ordered the publication of Nie's poster and published his own, "Bombard the Headquarters". On July 16, Mao took a highly publicised swim in the Yangzi, and on the 25 he forced through the withdrawal of the work teams against Liu Shaoqi's wishes. The Central Committee adopted Lin Biao as First Vice-Chairman of the CCP on August 1 (Army Day) and the *Sixteen Points* Document issued on August 11 put forward the idea of the Cultural Revolution as a new stage in socialist revolution in which the masses would rise up and educate. A mass rally of Red Guards (the radicals who opposed the work teams) from all over China took place in Beijing's Tiananmen Square on August 18. Mao gave them his blessing by publicly donning a Red Guard armband.

A mass movement hitting at the existing power structure developed in Shanghai and spread throughout China. On September 9 1966 Beijing Red Guards "liaising" in Shanghai (and including Nie Yuanzi and Kuai Dafu from Qinghua University) attempted to occupy the Shanghai CCP headquarters, but were repulsed by local students and workers opposed to intervention. On November 9 the Shanghai Workers Revolutionary Rebel Headquarters was formed. Scarlet Guards, broadly in support of the existing Party organisation, had initiated a general strike to counter the "Rebel" campaign. Shanghai was paralysed and polarised between Municipal Committee and Workers Headquarters. The power seizure in Shanghai in January 1967 led to "Maoist" groups seizing power with the idea of a Paris Commune type organisation.

On January 23, the PLA was ordered in to "support the left" and ensure the establishment of a **Revolutionary Committee** (composed of 50% cadres from the old Party committee, 25% members of the PLA and 25% mass organisation leaders) rather than a Commune and channelled energies along more moderate or conservative lines. Some regions were effectively under military control. As more Revolutionary Committees were set up in 1967–8, the proportion of mass organisation representatives decreased, although there was a radical revival in 1968 which was answered by the dispersal of Red Guards through *xiafang* 下放 or "sending down", usually to rural areas.

From April – September 1967 there was criticism of Liu Shaoqi, though not at first by name: there were simply denunciations of "China's Khrushchev" or the "Top Party Person taking the Capitalist Road". He was finally removed from the position of State Chairman in October 1968. Deng Xiaoping, Zhu De, Zhou Yang and many others were also purged. At the Ninth Party Congress held from April 1–24 1969, Lin Biao was designated as Mao's successor and Jiang Qing and her supporters made members of the Politburo. After the death of Lin Biao in 1971, the Cultural Revolution gradually petered out, although some commentators maintain that it did not finally come to an end until the death of Mao Zedong in 1976 and the arrest and trial of the **Gang of Four**.

David ZWEIG, *Agrarian Radicalism in China, 1968–1981* (Harvard University Press, 1989); Anita CHAN, *Children of Mao: Personality Development and Political Activism in the Red Guard Generation* (University of Washington Press, 1985); Willaim A. JOSEPH, Christine P.W. WONG and David ZWEIG, eds., *New Perspectives on the Cultural Revolution* (Council on East Asian Studies, Harvard University, 1991); Hong Yung LEE, *The Politics of the Chinese Cultural Revolution: A Case Study* (Berkeley: University of California Press, 1978).

DA XUE 大學 Great Learning

Originally a chapter of the ***Liji***, this became one of the **Four Books** chosen by **Zhu Xi** as a basic syllabus of **Confucianism**. The title refers to learning for the adult, as opposed to children's learning, and the work suggests the steps people should take to develop their moral character in order to become fit for their role in society. It begins with a definition of the three aspects of the Great Learning (manifesting clear character, loving the people and dwelling in the highest good) and then goes on to recommend a multi-stage process of acquiring knowledge and cultivating the mind in order to develop the moral sense and humanity required for correct behaviour in public life. All people from the ruler to the commoner should regard cultivation of the personal life as the foundation. The text had remained in obscurity as part of the *Liji* until **Sima Guang** produced a commentary on it (now lost); **Cheng Yi** and **Cheng Hao** both took it up and Zhu Xi followed with his own elucidation. He affirmed that the brief main text was by **Confucius** and the following commentaries were by his disciples; there is no evidence for this attribution but the origins of the text remain obscure.

Wing-tsit CHAN, *A Sourcebook in Chinese Philosophy* (Princeton University Press, 1963); Daniel K. GARDINER, *Chu Hsi and the Ta-hsueh. Neo-Confucian Reflection on the Confucian Canon* (Harvard University Press, 1986).

DAI WANGSHU 戴望舒 (1905–50)

Poet who began writing 'new poetry' in the early 1920s. He was politically associated with the left and artistically regarded as a modernist writer influenced particularly by French symbolist poetry. His best known poem is *Yuxiang* 雨巷 'Rainy alley' published in 1928. He travelled in France and Spain in the early 1930s and was an accomplished translator and literary editor.

Gregory LEE, *Dai Wangshu: the Life and Poetry of a Chinese Modernist* (Hong Kong: The Chinese University Press, 1989).

Dai Zhen 戴震 (1724–1777)
Scholar whose contribution to Chinese philosophy only came to be fully appreciated in the present century. Dai Zhen was born into a relatively poor family in Anhui. He passed the *xiucai* 秀才(1751) and *juren* 舉人 (1762) examinations but failed numerous attempts at the metropolitan examinations until he was awarded the *jinshi* 進士 degree by special decree in 1775. He acted as tutor to many leading scholarly families and, using evidential research techniques, produced works on astronomy, mathematics, phonology, technology, geography and history. On the basis of his scholarly reputation he was invited to work on the ***Siku quanshu*** 四庫全書 project in 1773 and was highly praised by the **Qianlong Emperor** for his *Shuijing zhu* 水經注 'Notes on the Classic of Waterways' (later the subject of a plagiarism accusation). In philosophical writings like *Yuanshan* 原善 'The origin of goodness' Dai Zhen rejects the **Neo-Confucian** dualism of ***qi*** 氣 'ether' or 'matter' and ***li*** 理 'principle' which he puts down to Buddhist and Daoist influence on Song scholars. According to this theory *li* is a transcendent principle within all physical beings which are composed of *qi*. In humans *li* exists in our *xing* 性 'nature' as our inherent goodness but it is masked by our desires, which are manifestations of our sense organs and belong to the realm of *qi*, our physical being. Our aim should be to recover the *li* immanent within us by overcoming our desires. For idealist Neo-Confucians like Wang Yangming this process was essentially an intuitive one, resembling Buddhist enlightenment. Even for realist Neo-Confucians, who emphasised the utility of knowledge, the scope of their quest for knowledge was largely the Classics and other literary sources; it did not lead them to the kind of objective investigation of the physical environment which fuelled the scientific revolution in the West. Dai Zhen rejected the existence of a separate *li*: it was nothing more than the pattern discernible in *qi*. Man's goodness came from knowledge and was the result of his higher intelligence; desires and emotions were natural and their orderly expression should be encouraged, not repressed. Understanding came from the wide acquisition of knowledge and the application of objective reasoning to it. Although there is scant evidence for Dai Zhen's having transcended the literary heritage in his quest for knowledge, he at least came to appreciate the limitations of the traditional approach and his ideas have been applauded by Marxist scholars in China as anticipating modern materialism.

Dai Zhen, *Tai Chen's Inquiry into Goodness. A Translation of the Yuan Shan, with an Introductory Essay by Chung-ying Cheng* (University of Hawaii Press, 1971).

Dalai Lama 'Ocean of Wisdom'
The title given to the God-kings of Tibet since 1578, when the Mongol leader **Altan Khan** first bestowed it on Sonam Gyantso, Abbot of **Drepung**. He also conferred it posthumously on **Tsong Khapa's** disciple Gedun Truppa as first Dalai Lama and his nephew Gedun Gyatso as second Dalai Lama, and thus confirmed his support for the **Gelugpa** "Yellow Hat" Order. The Great Fifth Dalai Lama created the title of **Panchen Lama**, built the Potala Palace (see **Lhasa**), and established the supreme religio-political authority of the office independent of either Mongol or Chinese sanction or support. As part of his foreign policy he travelled to China to visit the **Shunzhi Emperor** in 1652.

Following a decree by the Great Fifth the Dalai Lama is believed to be a reincarnation of Chenrezi (Avalokitesvara in Sanskrit, **Guan Yin** 觀音 in Chinese). Not all holders of the title have borne evident witness to the fact: the Sixth, being better known for womanising and writing poetry, died on his way to **Beijing** as the **Kangxi** Emperor sought to have him removed from office, and the Ninth to Twelfth all died young in circumstances provoked by rivalry with either the representatives of Qing dynasty China (see **Amban**) or the Panchen Lamas. The Thirteenth proved to be an intelligent and determined politician but was unable to implement his plans for modernisation and independence in the face of reactionary monastic attitudes and Sino-British obduracy (see **Simla Convention**). He had fled to China when the British threatened Lhasa in 1904, returning in 1909, but was again forced into exile, this time in India, by the invasion of the warlord Zhao Erfeng in 1910. This was the first time that Chinese troops had entered Tibet unrequested, something that was to occur again in 1959 as PLA troops reinforced Han Chinese rule over the country, forcing the Fourteenth Dalai Lama to flee to India.

Despite the authority stemming from his divine status the Dalai Lama had no absolutist rights. He governed through a Council of lay nobles and senior clerics; the post of Regent, occupied by a senior lama during a new Dalai Lama's minority, often continued to constitute a controlling influence even after the attainment of his majority; and the Panchen Lama acted as a further brake on his power.

Dalai Lamas:

First	Gedun Truppa	1391–1475
Second	Gedun Gyatso	1475–1572
Third	Sonam Gyatso	1543–1588
Fourth	Yonten Gyatso	1589–1617
Fifth	Ngawang Lobsang Gyatso	1617–1682
Sixth	Tsang-yang Gyatso	1683–1706
Seventh	Kezang Gyatso	1708–1757
Eighth	Jampel Gyatso	1758–1804
Ninth	Luntok Gyatso	1806–1815
Tenth	Tsultrim Gyatso	1816–1837
Eleventh	Khedrup Gyatso	1838–1856
Twelfth	Trinle Gyatso	1856–1875
Thirteenth	Thupten Gyatso	1876–1933
Fourteenth	Tenzin Gyatso	1935–

DALIAN 大連
Port city on the **Liaodong** Peninsula in Liaoning province, also known as Dairen.

DAO 道 'The Way'
(1) The impersonal creative force of the universe; the source of *yin* and *yang* and of all ten-thousand things and their characteristics; the constant principle amid the essential round of life, death and change. Too vast to be contained within

words, no complete definition of Dao is possible. It is being and non-being; knowing and not-knowing; action and quietude; timeless, valueless, impartial. To some the distinction between Dao and Heaven was vague, but unlike Heaven the Dao was non-judgemental: disaster might follow failure to understand and act in accordance with the natural laws, but did not imply cosmological criticism of the ruler. A closer analogy might be with the **Neo-Confucian** conception of the Supreme Ultimate (*taiji* 太極). It was the effort to understand the all-encompassing principles of the Dao that led to early investigation in the fields of natural science. Its recognition of the paradoxical weakness of the hard and ultimate strength of the pliant led to its symbolic representation as water.

(2) The correct form of human behaviour in accordance with the principles of Heaven and the realisation of the full potential of man. Confucian understanding of the true Way implied the observance of socially-based virtues as elaborated in the **Confucian Classics**, and in early imperial times these became codified following the prescriptions in the *Liji, Xiaojing* etc. There was a Way that could be followed by lesser men simply through the observation of rules of etiquette (*li*) alone, but for the true scholar the Way should not be so precisely identifiable. Confucius is quoted as saying "With me there is no inflexible may or may not" (*Lunyu* XVIII/18), and his idea of correctness was identified with appropriate and tactful behaviour according to circumstance. Government too should take account of conditions and not be rigid in its policies. The Confucian Way recognised the ruler's answerability for his people's welfare. **Han Yu**, in *Yuan dao* 'The Origins of the Way', wrote that the true Way was that of the **Former Kings** and involved universal love, righteousness, and the maintenance of Heavenly and ancestral sacrifices. **Liu Zongyuan** challenged the involvement of Heaven in this obligation and **Huang Zongxi** developed the idea of the rulers' accountability to the people, but it was often the **Censors** who bore the practical responsibility for reminding an emperor of the true Way.

See also ***Daodejing***, **Daoism**, **Heaven,** ***Huang-lao*****, Kingship.**

LAO TZU (LAOZI), *Tao Te Ching: The Classic Book of Integrity and the Way, trans. Victor Mair* (Bantam, 1990); Holmes WELCH, *The Parting of the Way: Lao Tzu and the Taoist Movement* (Beacon Press, 1957); John LAGERWEY, *Taoist Ritual in Chinese Society and History* (Collier Macmillan, 1987).

DAO ZANG 道藏

The complete collection of Daoist scriptures, gathered as an equivalent to the corpus of Buddhist scriptures and commentaries found in the *Dazang* 大藏 (*Tripitaka*); first printed in 1019.

DAODEJING 道德經

The principal canonical text associated with philosophical **Daoism**; also known as the *Laozi* 老子 "Old Master". It is attributed to Li Er, a reputed contemporary of **Confucius**, but the present edition dates from around 300–250 BC and the author cannot be identified. The oldest exant version of the text, discovered at **Mawangdui** in 1973, bears the title *Dedaojing* 德道經. The title of Arthur **Waley's** earlier translation, *The Way and its Power* (1934), is apt as an indication of the content of the book, which comprises statements about the ***Dao*** 道 itself and the powers (*de* 德), or qualities or virtues, it invests in each of the ten thousand things to give them their particular nature and function. The book is one of the world's greatest pieces of mystical writing. It teaches the need for an understanding of the natural laws of the universe as a means of achieving communion with the creative and sustaining force, *Dao*, immanent in man. It delights in the paradox, promising enlightenment through the rejection of knowledge, advancement through yielding, the gaining of satisfaction through the renunciation of possessions. The Mawangdui edition opens with the statement, "The highest virtue is not virtuous; therefore it truly has virtue" (tr. R. Henricks). Its author recognises his own inadequacy, insisting that words are too partial to describe the *Dao* in its totality. "The Way that can be spoken of is not the constant Way".

D.C. LAU, trans., *Lao Tzu: Tao Te Ching* (Penguin,1963); R.G. HENRICKS, *Lao-Tzu, Te-Tao Ching* (Bodley Head, 1990).

DAOGUANG 道光, QING EMPEROR (r. 1820–50)

The reign title of the Qing emperor Xuanzong 宣宗 (1782–1850). The Daoguang emperor succeeded to the throne at a time of cyclical decline and, in spite of his endeavours, by the end of his reign the situation had further deteriorated. The reign of the **Qianlong emperor** (1735–96) had been spectacularly successful but expensive military campaigns and his indulgence of a notoriously corrupt favourite, Heshen, left state finances greatly depleted. The succeeding Jiaqing emperor, faced with widespread rebellion in central and west China by the **White Lotus Sect** *Bailian jiao* 白蓮教 from 1796–1804, had limited success in reversing the decline. When the Daoguang emperor took the throne he attempted to follow his predecessor's frugality in court expenditure but similarly lacked the authority to take the radical steps necessary. The failure to carry out large scale public works, repairing dykes on the **Yellow River** and dredging the **Grand Canal** resulted in the latter being unusable for grain transportation after 1849 and the Yellow River shifting course amidst great flooding in the early 1850s, both bringing great economic distress. This was an important factor in the **Taiping Rebellion** which lasted from 1850–64 and nearly destroyed the Qing. The Daoguang emperor was unlucky in that his reign coincided with a deepening crisis over trade with Western powers which resulted in the **Opium War** with Britain from 1839–42. Poor advice from ministers and the Emperor's own vacillation between firmness and compromise contributed to the debacle. The 1842 Treaty of Nanjing with Britain involved substantial financial loss for China as well as great loss of face for the beleaguered emperor, but worse was to come for his unfortunate successor, the Xianfeng emperor.

DAOISM

(1) Naturalistic philosophy originating in **Chu** in the **Warring States** period based on recognition of the laws of the universe and the need for men to accommodate with them. Its principal texts were the ***Zhuangzi, Daodejing*** and ***Huainanzi***. It stressed the importance of non-competitiveness and the artificiality of human institutions, and urged the abandonment of worldly

knowledge and desires in favour of the pursuit of naturalism. The symbolisation of the ***Dao*** 道 as water with curiosity about the mysterious (*yin* 陰) has led to the frequent association of Daoism with the feminine (and by analogy, of **Confucianism** with the male (*yang* 陽), but by definition Daoism, which stressed the need for balance between contradictory forces, was bound to be just as concerned with the nature of human affairs, the city and public business as with that of the natural world, the countryside and the domestic inner quarters. Its key tenet of *wuwei* 無爲 "non-action", was misunderstood by some as an injunction to renounce responsibilities, whereas it meant in fact that man owed a responsibility to the natural world by doing nothing that would compromise its laws and creatures. Some adherents of Daoism were tempted into rural eremitism, to a permanent life of contemplation and chrysanthemum cultivation, but many appreciated it as an antidote to the busy public life of Confucian officialdom, something to which they could turn periodically for spiritual regeneration. Rather than requiring its followers to opt out of human society, it may have been intended as a means of surviving the unpleasant pressures of life in a state at war and undergoing social and economic upheaval.

(2) "Popular", "religious", *xuan* 玄 "dark" Daoism: names given to forms of a popular religion that developed in the Han period, associated around AD 150 with the Celestial Master Sect under Zhang Daoling. Unlike philosophical Daoism, which was individualistic and self-abnegating and which eschewed set forms of liturgy, this was a religion that developed into a church with clerical hierarchies, canonical texts, liturgies, and a pantheon of deities and saints. It offered its adherents the prospect of **immortality**, through faith and worship, through the intercession of deities or Immortals, or through the practice of breathing, dietary or sexual disciplines. It has survived to the present day and is still prominent in **Taiwan** and **Hong Kong**, but it never comprised a homogeneous creed or organisation and local variations sometimes rendered it easily confusable with forms of popular **Buddhism**. See also **Eight Immortals, *Huainanzi*, Ximuwang, Yellow Turbans.**

H.G. CREEL, *What is Taoism?* (University of Chicago Press, 1970); Joseph NEEDHAM, *Science and Civilisation in China, vol.2* (Cambridge University Press, 1956).

DAQING 大慶 OILFIELD

Oilfield in Heilongjiang province. Oil was found in 1959 while there was still technical assistance from the Soviet Union. With the withdrawal of technicians at the beginning of the **Sino-Soviet Dispute**, oil had to be extracted using primitive technology in some of the harshest climatic conditions in China and Daqing became a model of self-sufficiency for the radicals of the **Cultural Revolution** and the industrial parallel of the **Dazhai** agricultural production brigade.

DARWIN

Theories associated with Darwin, particularly social Darwinism, had an important influence on late 19th and early 20th century Chinese intellectuals. On the basis of Darwin's theories on the evolution of species, social Darwinists like Herbert Spencer suggested that social entities, from individuals to nations, were governed by the same rules of natural selection as biological species. Spencer coined the term 'survival of the fittest' to describe this phenomenon. The pseudo-scientific basis of such theories made them chillingly compelling to nations like the Chinese who seemed to be in terminal decline. Social Darwinist works translated into Chinese (see **Yan Fu**) exerted an important influence on both reformers and revolutionaries. Revolutionaries like Zou Rong 鄒容 in his book *Geming jun* 革命軍*Revolutionary Army*, written in 1903, suggested that China's decline was a result of being governed by the racially inferior Manchus.

James PUSEY, *China and Charles Darwin* (Council on East Asian Studies, Harvard University, 1983).

DAWENKOU 大汶口

Early to mid-neolithic culture in eastern China from which the **Longshan** culture developed, named after a site in western Shandong province. It was contemporary with the early **Yangshao** tradition represented at **Banpocun**. Its pottery vessels are less highly decorated than those of Yangshao but more complex in form. They include hollow-legged tripods and pedestal-mounted containers, and have more handles and spouts. The early use of the wheel is evident in their manufacture. Elaboration of burial practices led to the furnishing of tombs with goods that provide evidence of craft specialisation, including jade carving.

DAXI 大溪

A rice-growing neolithic culture on the south bank of the **Yangzi** River in eastern Sichuan, lasting from the sixth millennium BC to c.3300 BC. As in northern and central China, hand-made red pottery gave way to black vessels made on the wheel.

DAZHAI 大寨

Model production brigade on low-yielding land in Shanxi province's Taihang mountain range. In the radical period of the **Cultural Revolution**, it was hailed as a monumental success for having increased crop yields by organising a cooperative and without relying on state aid. As a result, the Dazhai CCP secretary, **Chen Yonggui**, was promoted to the Politburo.

DAZIBAO 大字報

Big character posters or wall newspapers. As in the Soviet Union, it has been customary in the People's Republic of China for official newspapers to be displayed on walls, usually in glass cases, so that those who could not afford to buy them could still read them. A tradition of dissenters posting the equivalent of political pamphlets has grown alongside this and was apparent during the **Hundred Flowers** period. The Big Character Posters are generally associated with the **Cultural Revolution** in which they were used to attack individual CCP members. Mao Zedong's own *dazibao*, "Bombard the Headquarters" was the signal for the Cultural Revolution to start.

De Wang 德王 (Prince De)
Chinese name for Demchukdonggrub, Mongolian aristocrat and the leader of an autonomous Inner Mongolian government, created in October 1933 and formally supported by the Japanese in 1935.

Dee, Judge see **Di Renjie**

Democracy Movement ***Minzhu yundong*** **民主運動**
Student and citizen protest that led to the massacre in and around Tian'anmen Square in June 1989. The **Reform and Opening** policy instituted by Deng Xiaoping in 1979 led to rapid economic development, but also the loss of old certainties and the old value system and confusion about how to deal with the new values coming from the West. In September 1985, there were protests against Japan's new economic aggression and what was seen as the Chinese government's craven attitude. The demonstrations were timed to coincide with the 54th anniversary of the Japanese invasion of Manchuria on September 18 1931. Demonstrators also complained about inflation and price rises and, in particular, corruption and nepotism involving the *gaogan zidi* 高幹子弟, the sons and daughters of senior officials. The government intervened to stop demonstrations at Beijing and Qinghua universities in December 1985.

In December 1986, there were further student demonstrations in 15 major Chinese cities, demanding freedom of speech, freedom of assembly and press and democratic elections. The first demonstration at the key Chinese University of Science and Technology in Hefei, the capital of Anhui province, demanded consultation over nomination of delegates to the NPC by local CCP branches. Fang Lizhi, an astrophysics professor at the university, called for decisive action on political democracy. On December 19 1986 in Shanghai 30,000 students and 100,000 workers marched on municipal government and in Beijing 4,000 students marched to Tian'anmen Square and burned copies of *Beijing Daily*, claiming that it libelled the demonstrators. There was a dispute within the leadership on how to deal with the demonstrations. Conservative hardliners launched a campaign against what they termed "bourgeois liberalisation" *zichanjieji ziyouhua* 資產階級自由化. The CCP Secretary-General **Hu Yaobang** and his supporters favoured leniency. Hu was reluctantly dismissed by Deng Xiaoping in January 1987 under pressure from the hardliners. Significant anniversaries fell in 1989: it was the 40th anniversary of the PRC, the 70th anniversary of the **May Fourth Movement** and the 200th anniversary of the French Revolution. Anti-communist movements in Poland, Hungary and the Baltic states were gaining momentum. The political temperature was high.

On January 6 Fang Lizhi sent a letter to Deng Xiaoping asking for an amnesty for political prisoners, in particular for **Wei Jingsheng,** who had been sentenced to 15 years in prison in 1979. Fang was prevented from attending a reception given by the President of the United States, George Bush, in Beijing. On April 15, Hu Yaobang died and mourning led to student boycotts and demonstrations, with possibly a million participants by mid-May. On May 16, Mikhail Gorbachev, Secretary-General of the Communist Party of the Soviet Union, arrived in Beijing on a state visit which was intended to heal the breach between China and the USSR that had lasted since the **Sino-Soviet Dispute**.

When he was unable to enter the Great Hall of the People by the main door, the CCP leadership was greatly embarrassed. Martial law was declared on May 20 and on May 30, the replica of the Statue of Liberty which became known as the Goddess of Democracy was erected in Tian'anmen Square and this appeared to infuriate the leadership. The Communist Party was divided, with Secretary-General Zhao Ziyang arguing for conciliation and Prime Minister Li Peng determined to put down the demonstrations. On June 4, at 4 a.m. the People's Liberation Army marched into central Beijing. Hundreds of students and other citizens of the capital died at Muxidi 木樨地 in the west of the capital, in the area around Tian'anmen Square and at Qianmen 前門 to the south of the square.

Andrew J. NATHAN, *Chinese Democracy* (New York: Knopf, 1985); FANG Lizhi, *Bringing Down the Great Wall: Writings on Science, Culture and Democracy in China*, ed. and trans. James H. Williams (New York: Knopf, 1991); Tony SAICH, ed., *The Chinese People's Movement: Perspectives on Spring 1989* (M.E. Sharpe, 1990).

DEMOCRACY WALL

Site of dissident posters (***dazibao*** 大字報) which began to appear on a wall in Xidan 西單 Street in central Beijing in November 1978. A variety of political positions were expressed including an attack on Mao for having been a supporter of the **Gang of Four** and **Wei Jingsheng**'s famous demand for the fifth modernisation, democracy for which he was sentenced to fifteen years in prison. Many political poems were also posted. The dissidents of 1978 modelled their wall on a Democracy Wall which had existed at Beijing University during the **Hundred Flowers Movement** .

David GOODMAN, *Beijing Street Voices: The Poetry and Politics of China's Democracy Movement* (London: M. Boyars, 1981).

DEMOCRATIC LEAGUE *Zhongguo minzhu tongmeng* 中國民主同盟

Third force party supported during the 1940s by liberal intellectuals including the poet **Wen Yiduo**. It was created in September 1944 as a coalition of minor parties to provide an alternative to the GMD and CCP. It pledged itself to neutrality, but was outlawed by the GMD in October 1947 and moved its headquarters to Hong Kong in January 1948, where it called for cooperation with the CCP and other democratic groups to overthrow the GMD dictatorship. In May 1948 it supported the **Chinese People's Political Consultative Conference** that the CCP had established and consequently was one of the non-Communist parties permitted to exist at least in name after the creation of the PRC.

DENG MU 鄧牧 (1247–1306)

Daoist scholar and poet who refused to serve under the Mongol conquerors. He was the author of a work on the "Way of the Ruler" (*Boya qin* 伯牙琴) which stressed that government should imply service of the people, and which may have inspired **Huang Zongxi's** *Plan for the Prince.*

DENG TUO 鄧拓 (1912–1966)

CCP journalist. Deng Tuo was editor-in-chief of *People's Daily* from 1950–7 and its managing director from 1957 until his denunciation during the **Cultural Revolution**. He was the author of ***"Evening Chats at Yanshan"***.

DENG XIAOPING 鄧小平 (1904–1997)
Career CCP politician whose reputation changed overnight in 1989 from the hero of the post-Mao reform programme to the villain who had ordered troops of the PLA to attack demonstrators in Tian'anmen Square (See **Democracy Movement**). Deng was born in Guang'an in Sichuan province and studied while working in France for six years with a group of later to be influential Chinese radicals including **Zhou Enlai**. He joined the CCP in 1924 and after a period of training in Moscow was assigned to various CCP units in China before joining **Mao Zedong** and Zhu De in the Jiangxi Soviet. He took part in the **Long March** and was political commissar in several army units, including the **Eighth Route Army** in 1937.

In the early years of the PRC, Deng was based in his native south-west as secretary of the CCP's regional bureau, but he transferred to Beijing in 1952 to be Deputy Prime Minister to Zhou Enlai and Secretary General of the CCP in 1956. In the 1960s, Deng was associated with the pragmatic and bureaucratic policies of Zhou and **Liu Shaoqi**, rather than the revolutionary romantic ones of Mao Zedong. When the two groups clashed in the **Cultural Revolution**, Deng was criticised after Liu had been denounced and he lost his party positions and retired to Sichuan.

As the Cultural Revolution drew to a close, Zhou Enlai resumed his former positions of power but was seriously ill and Deng was brought in, secretly at first, to support him. He returned to the Deputy Premiership and the Politburo but had to step down once more in 1976 after the **April Fifth Incident** in Tian'anmen Square. After Mao's death and the arrest of the **Gang of Four**, he rose to his position of greatest power ever, heading the central military commissions of both the CCP and the government and acting as Chief of the General Staff. He spearheaded the drive for **Reform and Opening** after 1979, both in political meetings in Beijing and in regal tours to the provinces. In 1989 and 1990, he began the process of withdrawing from his senior posts and encouraged others of his generation to stand down as well, in particular those who were opposed to the reform process. Well into his nineties, he remained in a position of pre-eminence in spite of having no formal appointment. He died on February 19th 1997.

Richard EVANS, *Deng Xiaoping and the Making of Modern China* (London: Penguin, 1995)

DENG YINGCHAO 鄧穎超 (1904–1992)
CCP political activist, particularly in women's organisations, and married to Zhou Enlai. In the PRC government, she continued to have responsibility for women's issues and was honorary president of the Association for Friendship with Foreign Countries among many prestigious appointments.

DESPOTISM see **ORIENTAL DESPOTISM**

DI RENJIE 狄仁傑 (d.700)
Outstanding statesman under the Empress **Wu Zetian** and one of the few chief ministers (see **Prime Minister**) whom she trusted. It was partly his advice that

deterred her from nominating **Wu Chengsi** as heir apparent in 691, and in 698 Di led an army to resist the invading force of the Northern Turk Qapaghan. His early success as a county **magistrate** became legendary in later periods and has been fictionalised in modern Western literature as the Judge Dee stories by Robert van Gulik.

Di Xin 帝辛 (Zhou Xin 紂辛)
Last king of the **Shang** dynasty, also known as the Tyrant Zhou, whose overthrow by **King Wu** of **Zhou** is attributed to his neglect of government and his preference for drink and women. One of his senior lords, Ji Zu, was imprisoned for criticizing him and later, when released by King Wu, wrote the 'Great Plan' section now contained in the ***Shujing***.

Dialects see **Chinese language**

Ding Ling 丁玲 (1904–86)
Left-wing woman writer whose career mirrored the vicissitudes of twentieth century artists. Ding Ling, the pen name of Jiang Bingzhi, was born into a declining gentry family in Hunan. Her father died when she was three and her life was dominated by her strong-willed and progressive mother. After studying contemporary May Fourth vernacular literature and foreign writers at school in Changsha in 1919 (where she had two poems published in the local paper) she rejected a marriage arranged by her uncle, moved to Shanghai and entered the *Pingmin nüxiao* 平民女校, a school established by a group of left-wing intellectuals. She went on to a bohemian existence as a member of a group of young intellectuals, attended Shanghai University (where she was taught by **Mao Dun** and **Qu Qiubai**), and in 1924 went to Beijing where she met a young poet, Hu Yepin, whom she married the following year. Her first short story *Mengke* 夢珂, about an aspiring young actress, was published in December 1927 and followed in 1928 by her most famous short story *Shafei nüshi de riji* 莎菲女士的日記 'Miss Sophie's Diary'. Typical of her early writing is its exploration of the psychology of the young, emancipated 'modern woman' and of female sexual desire (she was considered particularly daring in the later). After their return to Shanghai, her husband became a founder member of the **League of Left Wing-Writers** in March 1930; he was arrested by the Guomindang in January 1931 and executed soon afterwards. Ding Ling, left with a two-month old son, was further radicalised by her husband's execution; she turned to more political themes, as in her 1931 story *Shui* 水 'Flood' which describes peasant famine and rebellion following disastrous floods. In 1932 she joined the Communist Party and was herself arrested by the Guomindang in 1933 and imprisoned for three years. After her release she made her way to Yan'an where she spent twelve years writing and carrying out propaganda work. Articles and stories critical of party organisation and the way women were treated even in liberated areas, including *Zai yiyuan zhong* 在醫院中 'In hospital' (1941) and *Sanbajie you gan* 三八節有感 'Thoughts on Women's Day' (1942), made her a target of the first **rectification campaign** in 1942 (see **Yan'an Forum on Literature and Art**). Ding Ling was forced to admit her errors, produce a self-criticism and participate in the virulent campaign against **Wang Shiwei**. Her work on land

reform from 1946 inspired her Stalin prize-winning novel *Taiyang zhao zai Sangganhe shang* 太陽照在桑乾河上 'The sun shines on the Sanggan river' (1948). After 1949 Ding Ling held high positions in official cultural organisations but published very little fiction. Nevertheless her earlier 'sins' made her a prime target: in 1955 she was accused with Chen Qixia of forming the 'Ding-Chen anti-Party clique' which in 1957 became a principal target of the **Anti-rightist Movement**. As a result, she spent twelve years from 1958–70 in exile in Manchuria and the following five years in solitary confinement in Beijing. She was released in 1975, exiled to Shaanxi for a further three years then finally allowed to return to Beijing where she continued her writing career after her rehabilitation in 1979.

DING LING, *Miss Sophie's Diary and Other Stories,* trans. W.F. Jenner (Beijing: Panda Books, 1985); Yi-tse Mei FEUERWERKER, *Ding Ling's Fiction. Ideology and Narrative in Modern Chinese Literature* (Harvard University Press, 1982).

DIVINATION

Methods of interpreting messages from ancestral or other spirits in ancient China, including the use of **oracle bones**, a royal prerogative mostly of the late Shang period, which involved the reading by a specialist of the cracks which resulted when heat was applied to a prepared indentation in a tortoise shell or ox bone; and the rolling of yarrow stalks or throwing of coins as a guide to consulting the correct hexagram in the *Zhouyi* (see ***Yijing***). Both practices concentrated power in the hands of literate specialists, and were significant in the growth of China's early respect for learning and authority.

See also **Omens and Portents.**

R.J. SMITH, *Fortune-tellers and Philosophers: Divination in Traditional Chinese Society* (Boulder, Colorado: Westview Press, 1991).

DIVORCE

Under imperial legal codes a man was allowed to divorce his wife but not *vice versa*. Grounds for divorce comprised failure to bear a son, wantonness, failure to serve her parents-in-law, talking too much, theft, jealousy, and malignant disease. Though divorce is often cited as a major example of male domination of traditional society, it could cause loss of face to both partners and was not resorted to indiscriminately. Equality of divorce was one of the reforms proposed in the PRC **Marriage Law** of 1950. See also **Courtesans, Marriage.**

DIXIE MISSION

The assignment given to the United States Army Observer Group in Yan'an in 1944 to estimate the possible contribution of the CCP and its forces to the war effort against the Japanese. Impressed by the guerrilla tactics they saw, the Americans under their leader Colonel David D. Barrett, urged the genuine incorporation of the CCP into the resistance to Japan. **Jiang Jieshi** was not prepared to countenance this and the Dixie Mission was recalled. Because of the rising tide of anti-communism inteh Unied States during the Macarthy period after the Second World War, many of those associated with the mission lost their jobs.

David BARRETT, *Dixie Mission: the United States Army Observer Group in Yenan, 1944* (Berkeley: University of California Press, 1970).

DOCTRINE OF THE MEAN see ***ZHONG YONG***

DONG QICHANG 董其昌 (1555–1636)
Painter, calligrapher, theorist and connoisseur of the Ming dynasty, also known as Xuanzai 玄宰, born in Huating (today's Songjian). Dong Qichang was the dominant figure of Chinese painting in the late Ming and thereafter. He obtained his *jinshi* in 1589 and served as the Minister of the Board of Rites under Emperor **Wanli**. (see **Six Boards**) and now rates as the most famous late Ming figure of the amateur scholar (*wenren hua* 文人畫) tradition in art and one of the most significant landscape painters of all time. It was he who defined the Northern and Southern School categorisation of artists (see **Landscape Painting**) on which he wrote extensively. According to his theory, **literati painting** should follow the Southern school as the "Orthodox school", relying on brushwork and eschewing excessive detail or painterly effects. He painted with distinguished brushwork and clear compositions and outlines and pursued the aim of restoring the ancient values of the Song and Yuan masters to the painting of his own day. He based his own style on that of **Mi Fei** and **Zhao Mengfu**, the leading literati artists of the Song and Yuan dynasties, yet it was a transformed, novel style with intellectual rather than emotional qualities. His style and concepts were later followed by many other painters who considered themselves to be in this school.

DONG ZHONGSHU 董仲舒 (c.179 – c.104 BC)
Though never achieving a high government post, Dong is closely associated with the establishment of **Confucianism** as the state cult during the Former Han dynasty. In practical terms, he it was who together with Gongsun Hong is said to have been behind the foundation of the **Imperial Academy** in 124 BC. Yet his "Confucianism" was neither that of the Master or **Mencius** themselves, nor of **Xunzi**. It is for his ideas on the nature and functioning of government as a part of the natural order of ***yin-yang*** and the **Five Elements**, and the mutual interaction of Heaven and earth that his reputation has survived the strongest. As a **New Text** scholar his name is linked with the authorship of the *Chunqiu fanlu* 春秋繁露, though three of his memorials recorded in the ***Hanshu*** may give a more precise indication of his political views. He believed that the ruler was an intermediary in relations between Heaven and earth, that **omens and portents** were a warning of Heaven's displeasure with the government, and that it was possible to influence Heaven – and thereby for example the weather – by the performance of proper rites. In common with other early Han political theorists (e.g. the compiler of ***Lushi chunqiu***) he regarded the connection between ritual **music**, good government and the proper balance between Heaven, earth and man as axiomatic. He opposed the unlimited accumulation of large private estates at the expense of the poor. He openly criticised the **Qin** regime and his own Emperor Han **Wudi**, and though sentenced to death was later reprieved.

DONGLIN ACADEMY *Donglin shuyuan* 東林書院
Founded in Wuxi in 1604, this was the most prominent of the independent **academies** which in the late Ming became centres of political discussion.

Members of the Donglin (Eastern Grove) Academy were conservative Confucians alarmed at the extremism of current trends exemplified by **Li Zhi**, but they advocated practical reform action, and the spirit of **Neo-Confucian** idealism inspired them to self-sacrificing outspokenness as corruption grew at the late Ming court. One of its leaders, Huang Zunsu, father of **Huang Zongxi**, died in prison for opposing **Wei Zhongxian**. Wei was responsible for its closure in 1625. It was restored in 1628 and survived into the nineteenth century, but never regained the authority it had under Emperor Xizong.

DORGON (1612–1650)

Fourteenth son of Nurhachi, the founding father of the Manchu empire and commander of the Manchu military units invited by the remnants of the Ming armies to take control of Beijing rather than allow it to fall to the rebel **Li Zicheng**. The new Qing dynasty began with the reign of the **Shunzhi emperor** (r.1644–61) who was seven or eight years of age at the time of his accession to the throne, and it was Dorgon as Imperial Uncle Prince Regent who was the real power in China. He was responsible for the military campaigns which brought most of China under Manchu control, but made himself extremely unpopular with the Han Chinese by ordering that the Manchu **queue** be worn by all.

DOUBLE TAX

Agricultural taxes payable twice a year in summer and autumn. The taxes were originally consolidated in the eighth century under the Tang dynasty and the Summer tax and Autumn grain taxes, the latter always being the larger, were the most important sources of tax revenue for the Ming dynasty.

DOUBLE TENTH *Shuangshi* 雙十

October 10, the tenth day of the tenth month, commemorated, particularly in Taiwan, as the anniversary of the **Wuchang Rising** which began the Revolution of 1911 that brought about the collapse of the Qing dynasty and the beginning of Republican China.

***DOUGONG* 斗栱**

Bracket set used in Chinese buildings. To support the heavy and overhanging ceramic tiled roofs, a complex system of carved wooden brackets was devised whereby the pillar and beam met to increase the surface of contact and reduce the span. The *dougong* system was an outstanding element of the Chinese architectural tradition, as both a structural and decorative feature, being visible from the interior as well as the exterior of the building.

DRAGONS

The dragon is one of the oldest mythical creatures in China. The origin of Chinese dragons is unknown but pre-dates written history. Stylised jade dragons appeared in sites of the Hongshan culture dated to about 4000 BC. Dragons occupy a very significant position in Chinese mythology. They appear in arts, literature, architecture, costumes, and many aspects of the Chinese conscience. In contrast to Western mythology, dragons in China are rarely depicted as malevolent. They may be very fearsome and powerful, flying amid thunder and lightning, but are also considered just and benevolent, and as dispensers of rain and water and the bringers of wealth and good fortune. Dragons also symbolise imperial authority and are therefore associated with every aspect of the **Son of Heaven** and are used as the chief motif for court costumes (see **Dragon Robe**) and decorations. The symbolic meaning of the dragon is however multi-faceted. To a Chan Buddhist, for example,to paint a dragon appearing from the clouds is to depict a cosmic manifestation, symbolising the elusive vision of the truth. And to a Daoist, the dragon is the Dao itself, an all-pervading force only momentarily revealing itself to man. The dragon represents the fifth terrestrial branch in the ***shengxiao*** cycle. The dragon dance was invented to pray for rain and to stop the spread of epidemics,but it later evolved into a folk activity which, together with the lion dance, is an indispensable part of **traditional festivals,** especially the Chinese New Year.

DRAGON BOAT FESTIVAL ***Longzhou jie*** **龍舟節**

A colourful event as a major part of the **Duanwu Festival** *duanwu jie* 端午節 held around the fifth day of the fifth month in the lunar calendar. This festival is originally to commemorate the Chu poet and statesman **Qu Yuan** who drowned himself in the Miluo river. The people set out in boats to find the body, but to no avail. They later set out again with *zongzi* 粽子(rice dumplings) to offer to Qu's spirit. The festival is now an occasion in which boat races are held throughout the Chinese-speaking world on any convenient stretch of water. The boats carry men beating gongs and drums, and waving flags to inspire the excitement of competitors and spectators. The boats are usually long and narrow, decorated in bright colours and with dragon-head prows and high stems shaped like dragons' tails, and this was another means by which people hoped to placate the dragons who are dispensers of the rain and waters. See also **Traditional Festivals.**

DRAGON ROBES ***Longpao*** **龍袍**

A general term for various dragon-decorated robes worn by the emperor, the imperial clansmen and senior officials of the court, on official and state occasions. As the dragon was the principal motif emblazoned on almost all court robes, the differences in the materials, colours and cut of the robes, together with the number, pose and style of the dragon motifs, were very complex and varied in accordance with the imperial codes of successive dynasties. For instance, the Qing emperor's dragon robe was a full-length, side-fastening surcoat decorated with nine five-clawed dragons, worn as part of *jifu* (festive dress). Dragon robes were also worn by the empress, the women of the imperial household and the wives of those officials entitled to them.

Gary DICKINSON and Linda WRIGGLESWORTH, *Imperial Wardrobe* (London: Bamboo Publishing, 1990).

DRAMA

The earliest appearance of drama in China was related to shamanism and religion. Rituals performed in villages and temples included dancing and theatrical elements, such as role playing, for example where a shaman would act as a medium to communicate with the gods. The court dances of the Zhou dynasty also resembled the enacting of a drama and court jesters of the Spring and Autumn Period, wearing make-up and costumes, acted out stories to entertain their masters. By the Han dynasty, palace singers would perform warrior stories.

Emperors of the Tang took a great interest in the stage arts and encouraged the establishment of academies of music, dance and acting. This period saw the development of various features which would be incorporated in the more complex later Chinese drama and several important types of performed literature have been identified in this respect. The first of these is *shuochang wenxue* 說唱文學 or prosimetric literature (composed of alternating prose and sung passages) which included the *bianwen* 變文 of the Tang. The *bianwen* were texts of religious sermons which were sung or chanted to a musical accompaniment. Many features from this were adopted by later drama and these included the mixture of prose and song, the unilinear plot and the way in which characters introduced themselves to the audience. Long passages of scenic description were also used as this negated the need for sets – a lack of scenery is a distinct feature of most traditional Chinese drama. Another important early form was the *Canjun xi* 參軍戲 'Adjutant play' in which the set roles of later drama (as opposed to specific characters) originated. This was a short comic piece with a simple but witty plot. The small cast was often composed of female actresses and this appears to have been typical of most acting troupes of the time. This type of play was popular from the eighth century on, however, by the Song dynasty it was replaced by *zaju* 雜劇.

From the Tang dynasty on huge entertainment quarters had begun to emerge in the developing metropolitan areas i.e. capitals such as Bianliang (modern Kaifeng), Dadu (modern Beijing) and Wulin/Linan (modern Hangzhou). Various performing arts such as the *zaju* were popular in the theatres situated in these entertainment quarters. In the Song *zaju* could refer to an entire variety show in these entertainment quarters. These were composed of a mixture of small plays and coit referred more specifically to the complex northern drama which developed during the Yuan. The *Zhugongdiao* 諸宮調 'All Keys and Modes' was also very popular in these areas during the Song. Another form of prosimetric literature, it mic sketches (also referred to as *zaju*), martial arts, dance and acrobatics. Later, however, s lyrics were a form of *qu* 曲 and these were interspersed with prose dialogue. Northern *zaju* drama subsequently adopted the *qu* for its lyrics. The only entire extant example is the *Xixiang zhugongdiao* 西廂諸宮調 'The Western Wing' by Dong Jieyuan 董解元 (c.1190–1208), an adaptation of the Tang *chuanqi* tale 'The Story of Yingying' which was later developed into the northern *zaju* masterpiece ***Xixiangji*** 西廂記. Also popular in the entertainment areas, particularly in the Jin dynasty were the *yuanben* 院本 'scripts from the entertainers guilds', an entire variety show in four parts composed of jests and comic sketches interspersed with acrobatics, dance and martial arts. It has been suggested that this structure may have been the origin of the four-act structure of northern *zaju*. In the both the *zhugongdiao* and *yuanben* we see the continued development of set roles. Evidence also suggests that costume, make-up and masks were commonly utilised in these forms of drama.

Due to the division of the Song dynasty into Northern and Southern periods the trend for the development of drama continued in two different ways. The northern *zaju*, also known as *Yuanqu* 元曲 or *Beiqu* 北曲, flourished from the 13th century to the mid-15th century, an age referred to as the golden age of Chinese drama. The large number of works produced in this period can be attributed partly to the keen patronisation of drama by the Mongol court. More importantly, however, it was due to the discrimination against native Chinese literati who found their career choices limited by their rulers. Many of them turned to drama and actually found it an ideal vehicle of protest against Mongol rule. The northern *zaju* was not only popular with the literati but it was also enjoyed by commoners as many of the themes were according to popular taste. Love was a prominent theme but tales of spirits and marvels, historical events, religious stories, and social and domestic themes were also common. The *zaju* was highly organised, both in terms of structure and the pattern of its *qu* lyrics. It was composed of four acts with an optional "wedge" and these were interspersed with acrobatics, martial arts and comedy routines. Song sequences were strictly regulated right down to the rhyme scheme and this meant that the main emphasis of the play was on the lyrics as opposed to the prose dialogue. The plot was usually unilinear and was carried by the one character permitted to sing in any act. Examples of northern *zaju* drama include Wang Shifu's ***Xixiangji*** (a reworking of the earlier *zhugongdiao*), and **Guan Hanqing's** *Dou E Yuan* 竇娥冤 'The Injustice to Dou E' and *Wutong yu* 梧桐雨 'Rain on the Wutong Tree' by Bai Pu (1226–post 1306) which traces the love story between the legendary imperial concubine **Yang Guifei** and the **Xuanzong Emperor** (r.712–756). *Pilgrimage to the West* by Yang Ne (late fourteenth-early fifteenth century) is another typical example of *zaju* and is based on the pilgrimage to India of the Tang monk **Xuanzang** and his disciples (a story more fully worked out in the Ming novel ***Xiyouji***).

Nanxi 南戲 'southern plays' developed from the early fourteenth century until the Ming dynasty when they became known as *chuanqi* 傳奇 (*Wenzhou zaju* 溫州雜劇 and *Kunqu* 昆曲 being regional variations). This form of drama flourished until the mid-seventeenth century. The *nanxi* tended to be looked down upon by the literati as lyrics were loosely organised and were set to southern folk tunes. In addition, themes and language often pandered to common taste. However, this all changed with the appearance of the elegant and highly sophisticated *Pipa ji* 琵琶記 by Gao Ming 高明 (c.1305–c.1370) which marked the shift to *chuanqi*. Here was a more refined style of drama which could be appreciated and explored by the literati in their search for an aesthetic ideal. The structure of *chuanqi* was less restricted than the *zaju*. A prologue (*jiamen* 家門) introduced the theme of the play and this was followed by two main sections. This form offered the possibility of a more complex plot and in many cases the different strands of the plot were connected by a leit-motif. In the *Taohua shan* 桃花扇 'Peach Blossom Fan' by Kong Shangren 孔尚任 (1648–1718), for example, a fan is used. This work is considered the greatest historical drama. Based on the events of the Hongguang reign (1644–1650) of the Southern Ming in Nanjing it details the conflict between honest intellectuals and ambitious politicians. At the same time it follows the love story between scholar Hou Fangyu and his mistress Li

Xiangjun. Musical arrangement was also much less rigid in the *chuanqi* and all characters were allowed singing roles which permitted the further development of secondary characters. Other examples of *chuanqi* include *Mudan ting* 牡丹亭 'Peony Pavilion' by **Tang Xianzu,** *Chang sheng dian* 長生殿 'Palace of Eternal Youth' by Hong Sheng (1645–1704) and *Baojian ji* 寶劍記 'The Precious Sword' by Li Kaixian 李開先(1501–68), a political satire against the villainous Yan Song.

Jingju 京劇 or '**Beijing Opera**' is a style of *Pihuang* 皮黃 drama which became popular from the mid-seventeenth century onwards and is, perhaps, the most well-known form of traditional Chinese drama. Themes are derived from well-known stories, novels and drama, and acts are drawn from both *zaju* and *chuanqi*. Unlike the previous two forms of drama the emphasis in *Jingju* is on dramatic spectacle where dance and acrobatics play a significant role. The rhythmic beating of clappers to mark time for movements in *Jingju* is developed from 'clapper opera' *Bangzi qiang* 梆子腔. *Jingju* continues the trend toward characterisation through composed roles, but also makes a more distinct use of make-up and costume. Highly coloured masks identify the particular roles of the characters – black stands for loyalty, white for treachery and red for bravery.

During the twentieth century Chinese drama has undergone many changes. The post-**May Fourth** period saw the introduction of Western style plays and these were known as *huaju* 話劇 or 'spoken plays'. This was the first time plays were not set to musical accompaniment. In addition, Western stage conventions were also adopted. Unlike the bare sets of the traditional drama, scenery was employed thus putting the emphasis on realism as opposed to symbolism. Playwrights such as **Cao Yu** took their cue from writers such as Ibsen, Chekhov and Shaw and introduced social themes into their works. Cao Yu's famous *Leiyu* 雷雨 'Thunderstorm', for example, focused on the hypocrisy in traditional morality, exploitation of the masses, the clashes between generations and the unequal position of women. The rise of Communist power led to a tighter control over culture and a move away from the Western-influenced plays which were deemed to be elitist and urban. They saw the political potential of drama and Mao Zedong encouraged the production of **Revolutionary Opera**, simple stories with political messages and stirring musical accompaniment. These were used to spread propaganda to the masses in the countryside. The post-1978 period has seen a return to a more Western-style drama. Gao Xingjian 高行健 is well-known for his modern, experimental plays. His work *Chezhan* 車站 'Bus Stop' depicted the interaction of people waiting at a bus stop.

J.I. Crump, *Chinese Theater in the Days of Khubilai Khan* (University of Arizona Press, 1980); William Dolby, *A History of Chinese Drama* (London: Elek Books, 1976); Colin MacKerras, *Chinese Theater from its Origins to the Present Day* (University of Hawaii Press, 1983).

Dream of the Red Chamber see ***Hongloumeng***

Drepung
The pre-eminent monastery of **Tibet** and the first of the "Three Pillars of the [Tibetan] State" (see also **Sera, Ganden**). Their three Abbots, together with eight government ministers, presided over the National Assembly. Drepung was founded in 1416 by a disciple of **Tsong Khapa**, extended by the Great Fifth **Dalai Lama**, and at its height had a registered total of 7,700 monks and often as many as 10,000. Its four Colleges were those of Philosophy and Metaphysics; Ritual and Magic; Medicine; and Scripture. It was the home of the State Oracle.

Du Fu 杜甫 (712–770)
One of China's two great national poets and almost always spoken of in the same breath as the other, his contemporary and friend, **Li Bai**. Du Fu was born near the Tang dynasty capital, **Chang'an**, into an elite family, and, in spite of his obvious ability, was unable to pass the **examinations** for the civil service, so minor posts were found for him. Du Fu is considered by many to have been China's greatest poet ever. His poems reflect his character, the serious and humane Confucian moraliser, the polar opposite of Li Bai.

Du Mu 杜牧 (803–852)
Grandson of **Du You**. Official and writer of fine poetry and prose well known for his interest in military theory and affairs. A strong supporter of Confucian values, he became disillusioned by court corruption and continued **Han Yu**'s campaign which led to the development of **Neo-Confucianism**.

Du You 杜佑 (735–812)
Compiler of the *Tongdian* 通典 'Comprehensive Documents', a collection of documents relating to political and administrative affairs.

Duan Qirui 段祺瑞 (1865-1936)
Aide to **Yuan Shikai** and head of military planning in the late Qing modernisation programme. Commander of a **Beiyang army** divison and head of Beiyang military academy 1886–9. In 1912, he served as Minister of War under Yuan Shikai in the newly established Republic and was Provisional Chief Executive *Linshi zongzhizheng* 臨時總執政of the Beijing government from 1924–6.

Dubs, Homer H. (1892–1969)
American sinologist who as Professor of Chinese at Oxford University made a significant contribution to Western appreciation of Chinese history and philosophy through his translations of the ***Hanshu*** (*History of the Former Han Dynasty*, 1944) and Xun Qing (*The Works of Hsuntze*, 1928) (see **Xunzi**).

***Duilian* 對聯**
Couplets, also known as *yinglian* 楹聯 or *duizi* 對子, are a distinctive Chinese form of poetic expression. They consist of two lines, called the "head" and "tail", and the number of characters in each is the same. The form arises out of the satisfying symmetry of antithesis and parallelism in poetic expression, a key feature of Chinese poetry going back to the Classics. In the couplet a balance must

be found between head and tail, between each character in the one and the usually contrasting character in the same position in the other, and in tone, rhyme and meaning. Combined with the capacity for multiple layers of meaning in individual characters and the esoteric allusiveness of Chinese poetic expression, the form provides potential for infinite wit and subtlety of expression – a combination which has always delighted the scholarly Chinese mind.

Couplets are commonly divided and carved symmetrically on both sides of the entrance to a room, pavilion, temple or other building. Sometimes a horizontal inscription or *hengpi* 横披, with a few characters, is added above the entrance, to bring out the theme from the two vertical lines of the couplet. Couplets on buildings first appeared in the early tenth century, though there are records of couplets in literature from the early Tang dynasty. Couplets are still popular today in the form of calligraphy written on red paper, especially at the New Year.

T.C LAI, *Chinese Couplets* (Hong Kong, 1969).

DUKE OF ZHOU see **ZHOU GONG**

DUNGAN see **HUI**

DUNHUANG 敦煌

The site of one of the military garrisons that stretched out across the **Western Regions** in the Han dynasty, and an important staging post for over a thousand years for travellers leaving or arriving in China on the old **Silk Road**. Dunhuang became an important Buddhist centre in the Han dynasty because of its position at the junction of the northern and southern tracks of the Silk Road. It was under Tibetan control between 781 and 847, when there was intense rivalry for control of the trading routes across Central Asia.

The incomparably rich evidence for all aspects of life at Dunhuang, covering civil and military administration, religious beliefs and practices, economic and cultural activities, was first discovered by Aurel **Stein** and much of it brought to the British Museum. Of principal significance are a thousand inscribed bamboo strips from the Han period and the contents of cave 17 in the Caves of the Thousand Buddhas (*Qianfodong* 千佛洞). This had been walled up early in the eleventh century, housing a huge collection of paintings, statues, manuscripts and textiles spanning approximately six centuries. It is one of the several hundred caves, constructed and decorated as shrines from AD 366 to the fourteenth century, which provide matchless evidence for the history and development of Chinese art. The frescoes and clay statues are of particular renown. See also **Dunhuang Grottoes**.

L. GILES, *Descriptive Catalogue of the Chinese Manuscripts from Tun-huang in the British Museum* (London, 1957); M. LOEWE, *Records of Han Administration*, 2 vols., (Cambridge University Press, 1967); R. WHITFIELD and A. FARRER, *Caves of the Thousand Buddhas: Chinese Art from the Silk Route* (London: British Museum, 1990).

DUNHUANG GROTTOES 敦煌石窟

Buddhist cave temples near the town of Dunhuang, in the north-west corner of Gansu province, also known as the *Mogaoku* 莫高窟, Mogao Caves, or

Qianfodong 千佛洞, Caves of the Thousand Buddhas. The caves were excavated between 366 and 1300 from the gravel conglomerate of the cliff and decorated with stucco and painted images. There were originally up to a thousand caves, of which 492 caves still survive together with about 2,400 clay statues and 45,000 square metres of mural paintings. Early mural paintings from the Northern Wei period show the strong influence of Central Asian Buddhist traditions. Unlike **Longmen** and **Yungang,** there are no imperial commissioned cave temples, but some caves dated to the Tang dynasty show a sophistication which reflects close links with Buddhist art at the Tang capital **Chang'an**. The sculpture was modelled in clay on wooden or brushwood armatures. There were extensive explorations in Dunhuang by Western and Japanese archaeologists in the late 19th and early 20th centuries. As a result, collections of antiquities such as paintings, textiles and manuscripts from Dunhuang are now held in major museums around the world, including the British Museum in London and Musée Guimet in Paris. The term Dunhuang grottoes sometimes refers to a larger group of Buddhist cave temples scattered in this region, which, in addition to the Mogao caves, include the western Qianfodong, eastern Qianfodong, and the Yulin caves.

R. WHITFIELD and A. FARRER, *Caves of the Thousand Buddhas: Chinese Art from the Silk Route* (London: British Museum, 1990).

DUTCH EAST INDIA COMPANY see **EAST INDIA COMPANIES**

DUYVENDAK, J.J.L. (1889–1954)

Pioneering Dutch sinologist who published widely on Chinese history and philosophy, including the first analytical study of **Legalism** in his translation of *The Book of Lord Shang* (1928).

DYNASTIC CYCLE

The cornerstone of traditional Chinese historiography. It depicts history as a series of dynasties each of which rises from the ashes of its predecessor, climbs to a peak of splendour and then in turn declines because of corruption, over-ambition or some other moral failing. At this point it loses the **Mandate of Heaven**, which passes to a new dynasty. More sophisticated versions of this analysis have included a refinement to allow for a late flowering before the decline, but the underlying assumption is that there is little real development or social and economic change.

DYNASTIC HISTORIES *Ershiwu shi* 二十五史

Refers to the series of 25 official histories from the ***Shiji,*** written in the early Han, to the History of the Qing, produced in 1928. The *Shiji* was a private venture, though its author, **Sima Qian** (c.145–85 BC), held official post as a record keeper, and it spanned the whole period of history down to his own time. Subsequent histories, starting with **Ban Gu's *Hanshu*** 漢書 History of the Han, covered a single dynasty (the *Hanshu* in fact only covered the Former Han from 206 BC to 23 AD) and the work was gradually made more and more official; the practice developed for dynasties to write up the history of the previous dynasty based on its records. The *Shiji* 史記 pattern of five sections was modified and reduced to four in the *Hanshu* (*biao* 表 tables, *ji* 記 annals, *zhi* 志 treatises and *liezhuan* 列傳 biographies) and this became the standard for later dynasties. An official *Shi guan* 史館 History Office was set up by the Tang in 629 for the purpose of maintaining the history archive. Having history written by the successor dynasty was not necessarily a recipe for an objective approach and, where they were felt to be unsatisfactory, some histories were subsequently re-written, but the overall result was to produce for China an outstanding historical record.

W.G. BEASLEY and E.G. PULLEYBLANK, eds., *Historians of China and Japan* (Oxford University Press, 1961); Denis TWITCHETT, *The Writing of Official History under the T'ang* (Cambridge University Press, 1992).

DYNASTY

Period of rule by members of a single clan. In Chinese history the three earliest known dynasties (*sandai* 三代), Xia, Shang and Zhou, were ruled by kings. The first imperial dynasty was that of Qin and the last that of Qing. Since 1911 no ruler has sought to pass power on to a clansman, though **Yuan Shikai** did make an unsuccessful attempt to revive the monarchy in 1916. In imperial times two non-Chinese dynasties conquered and ruled the whole of China, the Yuan (Mongols) and Qing (Manchus), but in northern China the population also fell under the control of the Toba people (Wei dynasty), the Khitan (Liao dynasty), the Tibetans (Xi Xia dynasty), and the Jurchen (Jin dynasty). See also **Son of Heaven**.

EAST INDIA COMPANIES

In the early seventeenth century, European countries interested in trading with India and East and South-East Asia created companies which were given government authority to trade. The Dutch East India Company, *Vereenigde Oost-Indische Compagnie,* and the French *Compagnie de Chine* were founded in 1604. The earliest was the British East India Company which was created in 1602 when the British Crown granted it a charter entitling it to monopoly on trade with the East Indies. A second charter in 1609 extended this right to China. It became an imperial force in its own right and took control of parts of India which became the basis for the British Raj. The company became interested in the China trade in the mid-eighteenth century and in 1759 sent a Chinese-speaking merchant, James Flint, to negotiate for more open trade. This mission failed but the East India Company continued to be part of the commercial pressure on China that led to the embassy led by Lord **Macartney** and the **Opium War**.

EDUCATED YOUTH GOING TO COUNTRYSIDE see ***XIAFANG***

EDUCATION see **ACADEMIES, EXAMINATIONS SYSTEM, IMPERIAL ACADEMY, SCHOOLS**

EDUCATION THROUGH LABOUR ***Laojiao*** **勞教**
Imprisonment in a rural labour camp, normally for up to three years, a punishment available within the legal system of the People's Republic of China. Sentences can be passed by administrative authorities and the police and it is not necessary for the case to go through the courts. See also **Reform through Labour.**

EIGHT IMMORTALS ***Baxian*** 八仙
Daoist legendary beings. The Eight Immortals, canonised in the twelfth century, were supposed to have had immortality granted to them for the most diverse virtues, and their images symbolised various blessings. The theme of Eight Immortals was and remains one of most popular themes in Chinese decorative art, and the following are the eight celebrated individuals:
Zhongli Quan 鐘離權, who carries a fan with which he revives the souls of the dead.
He Xiangu 何仙姑, a graceful girl carrying a ladle or a long-stalked lotus blossom.
Zhang Guolao 張果老, a beaded figure carrying a tubular drum of bamboo with two rods to beat it.
Lü Dongbin 呂洞賓, a dignified elderly figure with a sword in his hand or slung over his back.
Han Xiangzi 韓湘子, the philosopher Han Xiang, represented as a youthful figure carrying or playing a flute.
Cao Guojiu 曹國舅, the imperial brother-in-law, an elderly bearded figure carrying a pair of castanets.
Li Tieguai 李鐵拐 (Iron Crutch Li), an emaciated, deformed figure, leaning on a crutch and carrying a gourd which contains capsules of the elixir of immortality and devours evil demons.
Lan Caihe 蘭采和, usually represented as a boy, but sometimes as a girl, carrying a basket of flowers.

EIGHT-LEGGED ESSAY ***Baguwen*** 八股文
Highly structured essay prescribed as the standard form of examination answer from the mid-15th century until the beginning of the 20th century. Essays had eight prescribed sections but the name is said to refer to the double four-section pattern. Candidates for civil service examinations were obliged to use this format to produce essays of 300–600 characters commenting on classical phrases set by the examiners. Late nineteenth-century critics argued that it emphasised form above content and had become an empty literary device; it was abolished in 1905 after a vigorous campaign by reformers who targeted it as a symbol of what was wrong with the educational system.

EIGHT TRIGRAMS ***Bagua*** 八卦 **REBELLION**
The Eight Trigrams was a secret society, and a branch of the anti-Qing **White Lotus Sect** and had considerable support in northern China. In 1813, two sect leaders, Lin Qing and Li Wencheng declared themselves respectively the reincarnation of **Maitreya** (the Buddha of Compassion, who is yet to appear) and the King of Men. They launched an attack on the Imperial Palace on

October 8 while the Jiaqing Emperor was on his way back from a hunting trip in Manchuria, but of the 250 rebels sent only a fraction entered the palace and they were rapidly overcome. Uprisings associated with the Eight Trigrams broke out to the south of the capital, based on the city of Huaxian in northern Henan and were finally put down by Qing forces on January 1 1814. The millenarian Buddhist tradition persisted in northern China and resurfaced towards the end of the century in the **Boxer Rising**.

Susan NAQUIN, *Millenarian Rebellion in China: The Eight Trigrams Uprising of 1813* (Yale University Press, 1976).

EIGHTH ROUTE ARMY *Balujun* 八路軍

Reorganised CCP armed forces renamed to indicate their incorporation into the National Revolutionary Army as a result of the agreement between the CCP and the GMD on September 22 1937 to reform the **United Front** in an attempt to resist the Japanese invasion. Eighth Route Army troops were active in resisting the Japanese in North China. The army was later renamed the Eighteenth Route Army but is far better known by its earlier name.

ELDER BROTHER SOCIETY *Gelaohui* 哥老會

Anti-Manchu **secret society** active in northern China since the **Taiping rebellion** and with some influence in the military. Society members took part in the **Revolution of 1911** and the CCP attempted to encourage them into an anti-Japanese alliance with some success.

ELGIN, LORD (James Bruce, 1811–63)

British diplomat and negotiator in the period following the **Arrow War**. He is best known in China for his leadership of the military mission in 1860 during which he ordered his troops to destroy the Yuanmingyuan Summer Palace by burning it to the ground, before dictating the Convention of Beijing. (See **Beijing, Convention of**).

ELLIOT, CAPTAIN CHARLES

British Chief Superintendent of Trade in Guangzhou in 1836 and the man responsible in 1839 for handing over to **Lin Zexu** opium in the hands of British traders in the period immediately before the Opium War. He was second-in-command of the British Expeditionary Force in the war, under his cousin Admiral George Elliot who commanded it, replacing him later when the Admiral fell ill.

EMIGRATION see **OVERSEAS CHINESE**

EMPEROR, see **SON OF HEAVEN**

EMPRESS DOWAGER see **CIXI**

EMPRESS LU see **LU ZHI**

EMPRESS WU see **WU ZETIAN**

ENCIRCLEMENT CAMPAIGNS *Weijiao* 圍剿
Attacks on the Communist-controlled **Jiangxi Soviet** by Nationalist forces. The first and second campaigns in November 1930 and in the spring of 1931 were repulsed by guerrilla warfare. The third campaign of summer 1931 came to an end as the GMD authorities turned to consider the Japanese invasion of Manchuria and the 1932 fourth campaign was also defeated by Communist troops. It was the fifth campaign, launched in October 1933 with the largest number of Nationalist troops, some 800,000 men with air back-up, that was decisive. The CCP felt it necessary to evacuate the Jiangxi base and began its epic journey north on the **Long March**.

ENCYCLOPAEDIAS *Leishu* 類書
Collectaneous works of earlier writings arranged by category. The categories could be topics, such as history, geography, classics or literature, or styles, for example documentary, literary or illustrations, and could be arranged either thematically or phonetically. They were compiled through the initiative of individuals or groups of scholars, or by imperial command. The first *leishu* is generally reckoned to be the *Huanglan* 皇覽 'Imperial compendium', compiled between 220–222 by Liu Shao 劉劭and Wang Xiang 王象 for **Cao Pi** 曹丕, Emperor of Wei, but lost by the time of the Song dynasty. One of the earliest extant *leishu* is the *Beitang shuchao* 北堂書鈔 'Collected writings of the North Hall' compiled by Yu Shinan 虞世南 around 620. This was followed by many examples in the Tang including the *Yiwenlei ju* 藝文類聚 'Literary works arranged by category' and *Chuxueji* 初學記'Record of elementary study'. The number of examples and their scope continued to increase: the numerous Song dynasty *leishu* included the *Taiping yulan* 太平御覽 'Imperial Compendium of the Taiping period' produced in 977–983 and the *Cefu yuangui* 册府元龜'Guide (literally "turtle") to the literary storehouse', compiled 1005–13. The former was an officially compiled work produced by a team of fourteen scholars and amounted to 1000 volumes 卷 *juan* in 55 sections *bu* 部 with 5363 categories *lei* 類; it concentrates on the classics, history and philosophy and is a particularly rich repository of early works. The *Cefu yuangui*, also in 1000 *juan*, was given its title by Emperor Zhenzong in recognition of its role as a guide for government. It is divided into 31 sections *bu* subdivided into 1106 categories *men*門; each *bu* has a general preface and each *men* has its own specific preface. It concentrates on the classics and histories and includes **Veritable Records**, decrees and memorials from the Tang and Five Dynasties periods.

These were dwarfed by some Ming and Qing compilations. The Ming *Yongle dadian* 永樂大典 'Yongle era encyclopaedia' produced by 147 scholars in 1403–4, and revised by 3000 a year later, came to 22,877 *juan* plus an index of 60 *juan* in a total of 11,095 册 *ce*. As a result of its size, it was not printed, but a further copy was later made. The original was mostly destroyed at the end of the Ming and the second copy largely burnt by foreign troops during the Boxer Rebellion; about 800 *juan* remain scattered in libraries throughout the world. The largest extant *leishu* is the *Gujin tushu jicheng* 古今圖書集成 'Ancient and modern collected works', produced in the Qing Kangxi period and subsequently type-set and printed. It consists of 10,000 *juan* plus a 40 *juan* index, divided into 6 *hui* 匯 compendia, 32 *dian* 典 albums and 6109 *bu* sections.

TENG Ssu-yu and Knight BIGGERSTAFF, *An Annotated Bibliography of Selected Chinese Reference Works*, 3rd Edition (Harvard University Press, 1971).

ENNIN

Japanese monk who, together with his student Ensai, left Japan in July 838 and travelled to China in search of the Buddhist Law. During a stay of nine years he spent two months in the **sacred mountain** region of Wutai, modern Shanxi Province, before moving to **Chang'an**. Here he observed **Buddhism** at the peak of its popularity. But here too he was caught up in the greatest **religious persecution** in Chinese history, that instigated by Emperor **Wuzong** in 842–5, as a result of which he returned home to Japan. His diary survived, and has been translated by Edwin Reischauer.

E. O. REISCHAUER, *Ennin's Travels in T'ang China* (New York: Ronald Press, 1955).

EPANG PALACE *Epang Gong* 阿房宮

Palace built by **Qin Shi Huangdi** at Epang, across the Wei River from the capital at **Xianyang**, which he believed would match those of the Zhou Kings **Wen** at Feng and **Wu** at Hao. According to the ***Shiji*** more than 700,000 men slaved over its construction and that of the Emperor's mausoleum at Mount Li (see ***Lishan***), using stone from the mountains to the north and timber from **Shu** and **Chu** to the south. Epang became a byword for the luxurious and self-indulgent lifestyle favoured by the First Emperor.

EQUAL (EQUITABLE) FIELD SYSTEM *Jun tian* 均田

System of land distribution introduced by Emperor Xiaowen of the Northern Wei dynasty in 485, intended to safeguard the livelihood of free peasants against the domination of large estate-owners and enforced tenancy. Sui **Wendi** elaborated and extended it across the whole country in 582. A man and wife were allocated 140 *mu* 畝 of land for use during their working lifetime (17–59 years of age), the greater part (120 *mu*) reverting to the government on their death or retirement and the remainder, known as "mulberry fields" being inheritable. **Taxation** and labour dues were related to land holding. Practical implementation, however, failed to live up to the rather complicated ideal, and large landowners, especially the Buddhist church, continued to accumulate land. Officials were entitled to larger allocations and even merchants and craftsmen had small grants, but the availability of land for distribution varied from one region to another and depended in part on population density, and the whole system was susceptible to corruption. The Tang maintained *jun tian* until the **An Lushan rebellion**, but after 780 loss of control over the owners of big regional estates forced the central government to abandon the distribution of land and to admit purchase as the principal means of land acquisition. See also **Land Reform**, **Land Tax**, **Land Tenure**, **Well-field**.

ERLIGANG 二里崗

An important middle Shang site at modern Zhengzhou showing evidence of craft specialisation and the social importance of skilled bronzesmiths. It may have been within the limits of the Shang capital of **Ao**. Its predominantly grey pottery bears witness to **Longshan** antecedents, but of most significance is its

range of ritual bronzes, which clearly indicate the source of the great vessels later made at Yin. Stratum III has been carbon dated to c.1595 BC.
K.C CHANG, *Shang Civilization* (Yale University Press, 1980).

ERLITOU 二里頭
The site of an early Shang dynasty settlement discovered in 1957 at Yanshi, near modern **Luoyang** in northern Henan. Small pieces of bronze have been found at its lowest stratum, carbon-dated to c.1900 BC. The oldest known Chinese bronze vessels (*jue* 爵) come from its third stratum, in the middle of the second millennium. This phase of early civilisation follows after the Neolithic **Longshan** culture and precedes the **Erligang** stage of the Shang dynasty. Some authorities link it with the location of the shadowy Xia dynasty. Remains of two palace buildings indicate that they were built on packed earth (*hangtu* 夯土) platforms inside walled fortifications. Other remains include ordinary dwellings, bronze foundries, kilns, wells and roads. Around one hundred sites contemporary with this cultural phase are known in southern Shanxi, Henan and northern Hebei, including urban centres at Dongxiafeng, Xia Xian, Shanxi, and Wangchen'gang, Denfeng, Henan.
K.C. CHANG, ed., *Studies of Shang Archaeology* (Yale University Press, 1986).

EUNUCHS
"Everyone has known for thousands of years that eunuchs are like poison and wild beasts" (**Huang Zongxi**). Confucians frequently denounced the political threat from these "non-men", yet they played a significant and often powerful role at court throughout the imperial era. Originally employed to perform duties in the innermost court chambers where they were trusted in the presence of the women of the harem, they frequently felt bitter at their physical deformity and inability to bear sons, and gained revenge by exploiting their opportunities for influence over the emperor, especially when he was a minor. In this way they often rose to positions of high power (see **Inner Court**). They indulged in political intrigue, associated themselves with the Buddhist church and its cliques at court, and were at loggerheads with the Confucian literati who despised them and resented their power. They played a significant part in the factionalism that helped to bring down the Han dynasty and the undermining of imperial authority at the end of the Tang dynasty (especially by Tian Lingzi and Yang Fugong). Blame for their domination of the late Ming court, when they are estimated to have numbered seventy thousand, must lie with the early emperors. The **Hongwu** Emperor weakened the power of the civil administration (see **Prime Minister**) and placed too much authority in the hands of the **Son of Heaven**, and the **Yongle** Emperor trusted too much in his own eunuch spies and advisers. Two factors that particularly assisted their corrupt grasp on power from the **Wanli** period onwards were their rapacious collection of silver, the metal that formed the basis of tax assessment (see **Single Whip Tax System**), and the succession of emperors who came to the throne as minors. Eunuchs in the Inner Court had unrivalled opportunities to dominate a young Son of Heaven. Well known Ming eunuchs included the admiral **Zheng He** and the tyrannical **Wei Zhongxian**, the last of four infamous eunuch dictators (the others being Wang Zhen in the 1440s, Wang Zhi in the 1470s, and Liu Jin in the 1500s).

Mary M. ANDERSON, *Hidden Power: The Palace Eunuchs of Imperial China* (New York: Prometheus, 1990).

EVENING TALKS AT YANSHAN ***Yanshan yehua*** 燕山夜話
Satirical column in the *Beijing Evening News* written by **Deng Tuo** and published between March 1961 and September 1962. It was issued as a book in four volumes and on April 16 1966 came under attack in *Beijing Daily* as the **Cultural Revolution** loomed.

EVER-VICTORIOUS ARMY ***Changsheng jun*** 常勝軍
Foreign-led mercenary forces which fought with the Qing army against the **Taiping Rebellion**. It was commanded at first by the American Frederick Townsend Ward and then by General Charles Gordon. Gordon, later to become known as Gordon of Khartoum, earned the soubriquet of Chinese Gordon for his exploits with this army.

EXAMINATION SYSTEM ***Ke ju zhi*** 科舉制
The system used in imperial China to select candidates for the civil service, a system which also became the criterion for gentry status. Throughout its history only males were eligible to take the examinations. During the early imperial period, from the beginning of the Han in 207 BC to the beginning of the Sui in 581 AD, the normal civil service recruitment system was by recommendation. Social status at that time was based on an hereditary aristocracy.

However, tests were conducted as part of the recruitment procedure as early as the Han. In 178 BC Emperor Wen asked for men who were 'worthy and upright' and 'plain-speaking in remonstrance' to come forward to take the *duice* 對策 tests, where candidates were asked to write answers to questions on government and the classics. These tests were held irregularly. One aim was to gauge public opinion, the other was recruitment. **Dong Zhongshu** was one of the luminaries recruited in this way. The Western Jin used a series of five *duice* to determine who should pass the annual 'flourishing talents' *xiucai* 秀才 tests. The Sui abolished the formal *jiupin zhongzheng* 九品中正 recommendation system but took over the existing *xiucai* and *mingjing* 明經 'classical erudite' examination categories and added the *jin shi* 進士 'advanced scholar' category, which became the gold standard of the examination system. The Tang further refined the system, using special examinations *zhi ke* 制科 and regular examinations *chang ke* 常科. The special examinations were similar to the Han ones, with categories like 'plain speaking in remonstrance' *zhiyan jijian* 直言級諫, 'worthy and upright' *xianliang fangzheng* 賢良方正 and 'widely learned and eloquent' *boxue hongci* 博學宏詞. The regular examinations included *xiucai, mingjing, jinshi, mingfa* 明法 'legal erudite', *mingsuan* 明算 'mathematical erudite' and so on. The *mingjing* and the *jinshi* were the most popular, with the latter always the most highly regarded. The examinations were normally held annually, with 800–2,000 candidates, of whom just over 1% passed. This extremely competitive situation was a feature throughout the history of the examination system, with candidates repeatedly retaking and failing the examinations. The examinations were originally organised by the Board of Civil Office, *Libu* 吏部, but later transferred to the Board of Rites

Libu 禮部, where they remained in subsequent dynasties. Successful candidates had further tests at the Board of Civil Office, but Empress Wu initiated the practice of holding an examination for successful candidates at the palace. In 702 military examinations *wuju* 武舉 were begun, administered by the Board of War *Bingbu* 兵部. They continued through later dynasties but never enjoyed the prestige of the civil examinations.

The Song formalised a three-stage system with candidates first taking a qualifying examination, *jieshi* 解試, in their own locality or at a designated institution. If they passed that, they became a recommended man, *juren* 舉人, eligible to take part in the Secretariat examination, *shengshi* 省試, held over three days in the capital. A list of the successful candidates was sent to the palace for the palace examination, *dianshi* 殿試, which was personally supervised by the emperor after 973. The Song introduced many refinements into the system, like anonymous marking and a prohibition on canvassing, to make it fairer and more effective. Successful candidates were also given other benefits, including tax reductions and exemption from corporal punishment for certain offences. In the Song the system expanded greatly with many more candidates qualifying. However, the succeeding Yuan dynasty initially abandoned the examinations altogether, and when they later re-introduced them they imposed ethnic quotas, holding down the number of Han Chinese to 25% of the total. The effect was to reduce the scale and prestige of the examination system.

This was soon reversed in the Ming, after which the examination system became the main route for personal advancement throughout the rest of imperial history, until its abolition in 1905. The examination system continued the three-tier pattern, with *xiangshi* 鄉試, local examinations, held in the autumn of every third year in provincial capitals and the two metropolitan areas. For successful candidates, these were followed the next spring by the metropolitan examinations, *huishi* 會試, which were in turn closely followed by the palace examinations, *tingshi* 廷試. From the Yuan onwards the Cheng-Zhu School of **Neo-Confucianism** was adopted as the standard interpretation of the classics, hence prominence was given to the **Four Books**. The provincial and metropolitan examinations consisted of three parts at three day intervals. Questions mainly involved knowledge of the classics and histories, but candidates were also asked to write essays designed to test their views on government policy and practice. The highly stylized 'eight-legged essay' ***baguwen*** 八股文 was adopted as the obligatory format for answers. There was originally no fixed quota, but the metropolitan examination was fixed from the year 1475 at 300 candidates. The palace examination was a single examination in the form of essays on topics. During the Ming, the *jinshi* degree became essential for the highest offices. Early in the Ming those who came highest in the *jinshi* rankings were made compilers, revisers and scrutineers in the **Hanlin Academy** 翰林院 (which from the Tang onwards was responsible for drafting high level official documents, decrees, etc.). From 1458 the possession of the *jinshi* degree became a requirement for Hanlin academicians and membership of the Hanlin Academy became a requirement for some of the highest posts in government, including the **Grand Secretariat** *Neige* 內閣.

Additional features introduced by the Qing included the juvenile examination, *tongshi* 童試, a qualifying examination which had to be taken, regardless of age, at district, prefecture and academy levels before candidates could proceed to the provincial *xiangshi*. After the award of *jinshi* degrees to successful candidates in the palace examination, *dianshi*, there followed a further written examination, the court test, *chaokao* 朝考, on topics set by the emperor. This was a job placement test: the highest candidate was made a Hanlin compiler and the second and third revisers; others were ranked according to their performance in the examinations and given appointments.

The examination system provided China with a ruling elite based on merit and with a shared set of common values. It helped to destroy the hereditary aristocracy and create a society with a much greater degree of social mobility. This elite was more dependent on the ruler and the growth of Ming autocracy has been linked to the development of the examination system. Although the examination system was a recruitment method for the civil service, in practice only a tiny fraction of one percent made it through the system to the job at the end. Many spent most of their lives failing the examinations time after time and ended up as disillusioned teachers (the commonest refuge for the failures) or clerks, and in other occupations they felt below their status. The positive side of this was the large pool of educated men available to organize local society on an unpaid basis. The emphasis running through the syllabus on moral rather than technical or scientific knowledge was doubtless beneficial to social harmony but probably contributed to the stunting of China's material progress in the later period, a time when the West was making rapid advances. There is always a conflict between education and examinations: success in the latter comes from orthodoxy not innovation. The examination syllabus lagged further and further behind current scholarship in the Qing. The arrival of the West and the requirement for technical and scientific knowledge meant that even the examination system's monopoly of civil service posts could not save it. It was abolished in 1905 as part of the Qing government's reform programme.

Ichisada MIYAZAKI, *China's Examination Hell: The Civil Service Examinations of Imperial China*, trans. Conrad Schirokauer (New York: Weatherhill, 1976); HO Ping-ti, *The Ladder of Success in Imperial China: Aspects of Social Mobility, 1368–1911* (Columbia University Press, 1962); Benjamin A. ELMAN and Alexander WOODSIDE eds., *Education and Society in Late Imperial China, 1600–1900* (Berkeley: University of California Press, 1994).

EXTRATERRITORIALITY

The principle that foreigners in China had the right to be judged according to their own laws rather than Chinese law. This principle, which extended the rule still commonly associated with embassy compounds to the foreign concessions that grew up in nineteenth century **treaty ports**, became a major source of conflict between China and the West.

EYUWAN SOVIET ***Eyuwan suweiai*** **鄂豫皖蘇維埃**

Area under CCP control during the 1930s, second in size only to the **Jiangxi Soviet**. It included territory on the border area between Henan, Hubei and Anhui to the northeast of Wuhan and was led by **Zhang Guotao**. It fell victim to the fourth **Encirclement Campaign** of May 1932 and had to be evacuated.

FACTORIES
Warehouses and trading depots established by foreigners in Guangzhou in the seventeeth and eighteenth centuries and later in the other treaty ports. They were not manufacturing plants in the European sense.

FAIRBANK, JOHN KING (1907–91)
Leading American historian of modern China and one of the most influential twentieth century writers and teachers on China in the Western world. Among his many authoritative works were *Trade and Diplomacy on the Chinese Coast*, *The United States and China*, and *The Great Chinese Revolution, 1800–1985*. He also contributed to major textbooks on East Asia, notably *East Asia: the Great Tradition* and *East Asia: the Modern Transformation*, and was the principal editor of the modern volumes in *The Cambridge History of China*. His autobiography, *Chinabound*, is also a major contribution to the history of the profession of sinology, particularly in the United States and his final work *China: a New History* was completed two days before his death.

FAN KUAN 范寬 (late 10th-early 11th century)
Outstanding landscape artist whose heavy, monumental style of painting mountain scenery is now known only by one surviving picture, *Travellers among Streams and Mountains*, but who had a profound effect on Song dynasty painters, especially in the Academy tradition (see **Landscape Painting**).
M. LOEHR, *The Great Painters of China* (Phaidon Press, 1980).

FAN PAINTING
Painting on the silk or paper that covered the frame of a fan. There were different types of fans in China such as oval fans, folding fans and large ceremonial fans. Early records of fans are dated to the Former Han and painted fans are known to have existed from at least the fifth century. The folding fan was introduced into China from Korea in the eleventh century. Its convenient shape and size soon made it a popular personal accessory. Painted or inscribed fans were often exchanged or given away as tokens of friendship. Fan painting became a unique genre of literati art in the hands of Song scholars. The fan shape, either round or folding arc-shaped, has gradually detached itself from its functional origin and assumed its independent existence as a form of painting. Painted fans are often removed later from their original supporting frames and mounted as album leaves purely for artistic appreciation.
Christina Chu, *Fan* (Hong Kong, 1994).

FAN WENLAN 范文瀾 (1893–1969)
Member of the Chinese Peoples's Political Consultative Conference, historian and author, among many other works, of *Zhongguo jindaishi* 中國近代史 (*A Modern History of China*), the publication of which began in Yan'an in February 1947.

FAN ZHONGYAN 范仲淹 (989–1052)
Reformist statesman and early **Neo-Confucian** thinker who helped establish the reputation of the ***Yi Jing*** and the ***Zhong Yong*** and tried to instil the spirit of

Confucian self-sacrifice into government recruitment and service. He established the **Imperial Academy** in **Kaifeng** and many prefectural schools, and raised the importance of the **examination system** in the selection of officials. He was made a Councillor at court in 1043 after three years of successful military campaigning against **Xi Xia**. Despite support from **Ouyang Xiu** his political programme of 1043–4 containing the administrative reforms foreshadowed in his Ten-Point Memorial was defeated by conservative opposition, but was shortly reflected in the modernisation programme of **Wang Anshi**.

FANG ZHIMIN 方志敏 (1900–35)
Early CCP martyr. Fang Zhimin was a native of Jiangxi province and educated locally before moving to Shanghai where he joined the Party. On his return to Jiangxi, he became involved in the peasant movement and was head of the North-east Jiangxi or Xin River *Xinjiang* 新江 Soviet and a member of the Central Committee of the CCP. His troops were driven out of Jiangxi in the 1934 **encirclement campaign** and he was captured and imprisoned in Nanjing, where he was executed on July 6 1935.

FA XIAN 法顯 (fl. 399–416)
Famed Buddhist monk who was the first known Chinese pilgrim to return from an epic journey to holy sites in India, Sri Lanka and Java. His travels lasted from 399 to 413, and he brought back scriptures which he subsequently translated into Chinese in Nanjing where he settled. The account of his travels, *Records of Buddhist Kingdoms (Foguoji)* 佛國記 is the oldest surviving travel book in Chinese literature and has been invaluable in establishing the chronology of Indian, and South-east Asian history history and culture. See also **Kumarajiva, Xuanzang.**

FANG LA REBELLION see **HUIZONG, SONG EMPEROR**

FEBRUARY 28 INCIDENT (1947)
Anti-Guomindang uprising in **Taiwan**. Under the terms of the **Cairo Declaration**, Taiwan was to be returned to China after the end of the Japanese occupation. Jiang Jieshi named **Chen Yi** as governor of the island and he arrived there in October 1945. Disquiet at the way in which the interests of the local people were ignored in favour of the mainlanders who had arrived with him and criticisms of corruption erupted into demonstrations. On February 28 1947, Chen Yi's troops fired on a demonstration, killing many people. Demonstrations and armed resistance spread throughout the island, GMD reinforcements from the mainland landed on March 8 and in the months that followed, nearly two thousand Taiwanese were killed. As the GMD lost the Civil War, more mainlanders fled to Taiwan. Supporters of Taiwanese independence now look back to the suppression of the 1947 uprising as the beginning of their grievances against the GMD.

Tse-han LAI, Ramon MYERS and WOU Wei, *A Tragic Beginning: The Taiwan Uprising of February 28, 1947* (Stanford University Press, 1990).

FEI XIAOTONG 費孝通 (1910–)
Pioneer social anthropologist Trained under Bronislaw Malinowski at the London School of Economics. *Peasant Life in China* (1939) was his first work in English and has become a classic. Fei is renowned for having introduced Western methodology, including fieldwork, into Chinese anthropology. He carried out research in the USA and further fieldwork in Yunnan in 1939–43. Publications that resulted from this were *Earthbound China* (1945) on land ownership and tenancy in the rural area around Kunming, and *China's Gentry* (1953). Fei's **Democratic League** activities brought him into conflict with the GMD. He returned to China in 1947 to teach at Qinghua University in Beijing and became a **Democratic League** delegate to the **Chinese People's Political Consultative Conference**. He was attacked as a rightist during the **Anti-Rightist Movement**, but after the Cultural Revolution resumed his academic career with senior posts in the Chinese Academy of Social Sciences Institute of Ethnology.

FENG GUIFEN 馮桂芬 (1809–74)
Official, scholar and proponent of Western reforms. Feng came from Wuxian, Jiangsu and was a pupil of **Lin Zexu** 林則徐, the official whose handling of the Guangzhou opium problem culminated in the first **Opium War**. Fen obtained his *jinshi* degree in 1840 and was appointed a Hanlin compiler. In 1853, when the forces of the **Taiping Rebellion** captured Nanjing, he was ordered to raise a force in Suzhou but was obliged to flee to Shanghai in 1860 when the Taipings attacked Suzhou. There he participated in the setting up of a joint Chinese-Foreign defence organization against the Taipings, the *Huifangju* 會防局 and sought assistance from **Zeng Guofan**, who sent **Li Hongzhang** to Shanghai to defend the city. Feng became one of Li's advisers and proffered many reformist suggestions, all based on the concept of retaining China's traditional values but adopting the Western methods and the technology responsible for the West's wealth and strength *fuqiang* 富強. Apart from setting up factories and arsenals, he advocated limited institutional reform, including encouraging students to take up Western learning by recognising their qualifications as equivalent to the regular civil service examinations. He helped Li Hongzhang establish an interpreters' college in Shanghai, the *Guangfang yanguan* 廣方言館, also known as the Shanghai ***Tongwenguan***. Feng was an accomplished scholar in many fields and taught for over twenty years at academies in Shanghai, Nanjing and Suzhou. He had a much more acute perception of what was necessary than earlier commentators on Western affairs, like **Wei Yuan**, and his proposals formed the theoretical underpinning to the reform process from the modernization movement of the 1860s through to the reform movement of the 1890s. Many of these suggestions were included in his collection of essays *Jiaobinlu kang yi* 校邠廬抗議 'Protests from the Jiaobin Studio', a work which was issued to ministers by order of the **Guangxu Emperor** in 1898.

FENG XUEFENG 馮雪峰 (1903–76)
Poet, translator and literary theorist who suffered severe criticism in the 1950s. Born in Zhejiang, Feng in 1921 joined the *Chenguang she* 晨光社 'Dawn Society', a literary group organised by Zhu Ziqing and Ye Shengtao in

Hangzhou and in 1923 formed with friends the *Hupan shi she* 湖畔詩社 'Lakeside Poetry Society' which published a joint collection of 'new' vernacular poetry *Hupan*. He went to Beijing in 1925 and there began translating works on Soviet Russian literature; in 1927 he joined the Communist Party. In 1928 **Lu Xun** asked him to edit *Mengya* 萌芽 'Shoots' or 'Sprouts', a monthly literary magazine, and they jointly edited *Kexue de yishu lun congshu* 科學的藝術論叢書 'Scientific Theories of Art Series' which introduced Marxist literary theories. In 1929 Feng became a founder member of the *Zhongguo zuoyi zuojia lianmeng* 中國左翼作家聯盟 **League of Left-wing Writers**. In the early 1930s he held a succession of Communist Party literary posts and in 1934 participated in the **Long March**. He was sent back to Shanghai in 1936 to collaborate with Lu Xun. There he worked with **Hu Feng** and both were involved in acrimonious disputes with **Zhou Yang**. In 1941 Feng Xuefeng was arrested by the Guomindang and held in a concentration camp for two years where he wrote the poems in his *Zhenshi zhi ge* 眞實之歌 'Song of truth' collection (1943). He remained in Chongqing, free from the restrictions in Yan'an which followed the **Yan'an Forum on Literature and Art**, until 1946 when he returned to Shanghai. After the Communist victory, he occupied a number of important literary posts including, from 1952, the editorship of the leading literary paper *Wenyi bao* 文藝報 'Literary Gazette' and vice-chairmanship of the Chinese Writers' Union *Zhongguo Zuojia Xiehui* 中國作家協會. Like his friend **Ding Ling**, Feng began by competing with Zhou Yang in demanding conformity to the Party line. However, once securely in post he seems to have been guilty of backsliding to an earlier, more independent line and in 1954 he was the target of a sustained attack by Zhou Yang and his followers for bourgeois thought. This was ostensibly occasioned by his support for Yu Pingbo's analysis of ***Hongloumeng*** and by his rejection of Yu's critics, but seems rather to have been the result of Zhou Yang's determination to settle scores with Feng and his group. Feng immediately confessed and the campaign moved on to its principal target, Hu Feng. Feng Xuefeng was branded a rightist in 1957 and suffered in the **Cultural Revolution**. He was posthumously rehabilitated in 1979

Ba Jin, 'Xuefeng – In Memoriam' in BA JIN, *Random Thoughts* trans. Geremie Barmé (Hong Kong: Joint Publishing Company, 1984); Merle GOLDMAN, *Literary Dissent in Communist China* (Harvard University Press, 1967; Atheneum, 1971).

FENG YOULAN 馮友蘭 (1895–)

Philosopher and scholar of the history of Chinese philosophy, a native of Tanghe in Henan. He graduated from the Philosophy Department of Beijing University in 1918, went to Columbia University in the United States a year later and completed his doctorate in 1923. After returning to China, Feng taught philosophy at several universities including Qinghua, where he was Dean of the Faculty of Letters from 1928–52 and South-west United University during the war against Japan. From 1952, he was appointed professor of philosophy at Beijing University and also a member of the Philosophy and Social Sciences Section of the Chinese Academy of Sciences. In his philosophical writings he sought to integrate traditional Chinese Cheng-Zhu **Neo-Confucian** ideas with modern Western philosophy. His many works included the two volume

Zhongguo zhexue shi 中國哲學史 'History of Chinese Philosophy' (published in 1930 and 1934) which was translated into English and Japanese and has established itself as an international standard work on the subject

FUNG Yu-lan, *A History of Chinese Philosophy* (2 vols.), trans. Derk Bodde (Princeton University Press, 1969).

FENG YUXIANG 馮玉祥 (1882–1948)

Powerful northern **warlord** based in Shaanxi. His forces had taken control of Beijing in 1924 and he proposed discussions with **Sun Yixian** on national unity. After the **Northern Expedition**, he was considered to be one of the "new warlords" who entered into an alliance with the Guomindang while remaining an independent force in the north. He broke away from the GMD in 1929 and cooperated with **Wang Jingwei** but his forces were defeated by Jiang Jieshi's troops in 1930. Feng was known as the "Christian general" as he was a convert, at least in name, to the Protestant church and was photographed baptising his troops with a hosepipe.

***FENGSHUI* 風水**

Literally meaning 'wind and water' and sometimes translated as geomancy, *fengshui* is the art or science of siting graveyards, buildings and other man-made constructions or even whole cities so that they fit in with the forces of nature rather than clash with them. Even in modern Chinese societies such as **Hong Kong**, the services of *fengshui* practitioners are frequently sought before the sites of major buildings are agreed upon.

FENGTIAN 奉天

Former name of the province of Manchuria now known as Liaoning 遼寧.

FENGTIAN CLIQUE

Group of **warlords** from Fengtian led by **Zhang Zuolin** in the 1920s. The Fengtian forces fought a civil war with their Zhili counterparts in 1922. Zhang's Fengtian armies were comprehensively defeated and retreated beyond the Great Wall into Manchuria.

FESTIVALS see **TRADITIONAL FESTIVALS**

FIELD ARMIES

Units of the **People's Liberation Army** which had served in different regions during the **Civil War** of 1946–6. They were designated as Field Armies in February 1949. The five armies were known by their numbers, apart from the fifth, which is usually known as the North China Field Army. The importance of the armies continued beyond the end of the Civil War as political loyalties forged in battle influenced policy decisions in the CCP.

FIGURE PAINTING

The earliest existing figure paintings on silk in China are from the Warring States period and by the Former Han period, large-scale paintings with complicated arrangements of figures were being produced. Many early figure paintings are didactic, such as those which depict idealised images of virtuous rulers and exemplary men, reflecting the hierarchical nature of Confucian attitudes to the world. Other main genres of didactic painting include Buddhist and Daoist iconography and teachings. The introduction of **Buddhism** had a powerful impact on Chinese figure painting. From the models and techniques of India and Central Asia, the Chinese artists gradually devised their distinctive method of rendering receding and protruding forms and, rejecting colour shading, indicating three dimensions with a modulated, thickening-and-thinning brushline.

The value of early portraits, as part of the didactic mode of painting, depended largely on the moral quality they represented. A later type of portrait then relied on symbolic or metaphorical means to represent the subject. For example, the figure could be placed in a setting that presented to the viewer a supposed projection of the subject's mind. Great figure painters in China include **Gu Kaizhi,** who was famous for his fine portraits, and **Wu Daozi**, who was best known for his powerful figures created with impetuous brushwork. See also **Painting**.

T. LAWTON, *Chinese Figure Painting* (Freer Gallery of Art, Washington DC, 1973).

FILIAL PIETY ***Xiao*** **孝**

The cardinal principle of Chinese social ethics, which developed also into the basis for the political philosophy of imperial China (see **Confucianism**) and its traditional world view system (see **tribute system**). It stemmed from the ancient practice of **ancestor worship** and was evidently considered important by **Confucius**, but it was **Mencius** who explained the merits of sons caring for their parents' needs and exalted it into the very root of desirable human behaviour and heavenly approbation. The acme of its cosmic significance was indicated in the *Classic of Filial Piety* (*Xiaojing* 孝經), edited for educational use in the early Han. While stressing the primary obligations of a son to his parents both living and dead (and of a younger brother to an elder, and a subject to his ruler) and pointing to the creative, liberating effect of their observance, it recognises the reciprocal nature of the relationship and the father's responsibility to listen to his son's advice. However, as time went by the spirit of harmonisation which may be seen underlying the original philosophy was commuted more into a system of prescribed rules and attitudes. When thus codified into law, filial piety appeared to support the attempts of heavy-handed fathers and authorities to limit the freedom of the younger generation.

FIRST EMPEROR see **QIN SHI HUANGDI**

FIVE-ANTI CAMPAIGN ***Wufan yundong*** **五反運動 (1952)**

A campaign against bribery, tax evasion, fraud, theft of government property and leakage of state secrets. It was directed against the "national bourgeoisie" who had until then been treated as allies, and was more specific than the earlier **Three-Anti Campaign** and reflected the tension that had developed during the **Korean War**. It was launched in January 1952 at a time when there was an effective stalemate in the Korean War. Like the Three-Anti Campaign, it was an urban movement and affected all major cities. It was a campaign directed explicitly against capitalists, particularly wealthy capitalists, who were considered to be breaking the law and committing a range of economic crimes annd defrauding both the state and the general public, but its long-term target was the national bourgeoisie as a class.

The Five-Anti campaign strengthened CCP control over businesses as activists in workers' organisations were encouraged to examine their employers' finances and uncover evidence of tax evasion or other malpractices. In turn these activists became a new middle management elite to replace cadres and others purged because they were considered corrupt. Businesses also became more dependent on the state as the anti-corruption drive had the effect of weakening them financially, resulting in applications for new loans and government contracts. During the campaign, CCP branches were established in many of the larger businesses with the result that the Party gained a great deal of information and understanding about the workings of the private sector.

In addition to the intrinsic importance of campaigns such as the Five-Anti and the part they played in enabling the CCP to consolidate its control, they were also significant as precedents and many future campaigns were to adopt the methods such as mass meetings and a numerical target for people to be purged that appeared in the Five-Anti campaign.

Gordon BENNETT, *Yundong: Mass Campaigns in Chinese Communist Leadership* (Center for Chinese Studies, University of California, 1976); Frederick C. TEIWES, *Politics and Purges: Rectification and the Decline of Party Norms, 1950–1965* (M.E. Sharpe, 1979).

FIVE CLASSICS *Wu jing* 五經

The five canonical texts, supposedly edited by Confucius, which formed the basis of education in traditional China. They were the: ***Shi***詩'Poetry', ***Shu*** 書 History', *Li* 禮 'Ritual', ***Yi*** 易 'Changes' and ***Chunqiu***春秋 'Spring and Autumn Annals'. According to tradition a sixth classic, the *Yuejing* 樂經 'Classic of Music', was destroyed in the **burning of the books**. For details of the five classics see separate entries under their Chinese names (for *Li* see: ***Liji, Yili, Zhou li***). See also **Thirteen Classics**.

FIVE DYNASTIES AND TEN KINGDOMS *Wudai shiguo* 五代十國 (907–60)

Name given to the period of disunity following the collapse of the Tang dynasty. In the North five dynasties succeeded each other, all claiming by their titles (Later Liang, Tang, Jin, Han and Zhou) to bear the legitimacy of historical antecedence and four of them siting their capital in **Kaifeng** (the exception being Later Tang, which chose **Luoyang**). The North was therefore subject to frequent military upheaval as rivalries, claims and counter-claims were fought out. Of most significance was the acquisition by agreement in 936 of sixteen prefectures by the **Khitan**. These lay inside the **Great Wall** and formed the base from which the intruders would shortly begin to establish their own dynasty, the Liao. In the South, most of the kingdoms were geographically rather than chronologically separate, and the population enjoyed more peaceful conditions. Northern Han, ranked as one of the Ten, was in fact a protectorate of the Khitan in Shanxi Province.

Economic progress was made, encouraging **Korea** to trade with the southern as well as northern states, and the momentum of Tang culture was maintained in both South and North. But many Chinese were traumatised by the destruction of **Chang'an** and the loss of parts of the North to barbarians, and it was no doubt the inspiration of "Great Tang" in its heyday that prompted the swift return to unified rule initiated by Zhao Guangyin. (See **Song dynasty**).

The Five Dynasties:	**The Ten Kingdoms:**
Later Liang, 907–23	Former Shu, 907–25 (Sichuan)
Later Tang, 923–34	Later Shu, 934–65 (Sichuan)
Later Jin, 936–47	Southern Ping, 907–63 (Hubei)
Later Han, 947–51	Chu, 927–56 (Hunan)
Later Zhou, 951–60	Wu, 902–37 (lower Yangzi)
	Southern Tang, 937–75 (Jiangxi, Zhejiang)
	Wu-yue, 907–78 (Zhejiang)
	Min, 907–46 (Fujian)
	Southern Han, 907–71 (Guangzhou, Guangxi)

G.W. Wang, *The Structure of Power in North China during the Five Dynasties* (Stanford University Press, 1963).

Five elements ***Wu xing*** 五行

Also referred to in English as the Five Agents, these five basic substances, *shui* 水 water, *huo* 火 fire, *mu* 木 wood, *jin* 金 metal, and *tu* 土 earth, were traditionally thought to be the elements from which all things were created. They first appear in the *Hongfan* 洪範 chapter of the ***Shangshu*** 尚書 'Book of History'; by the Han they had been combined with the *yin* and *yang* concept to produce a cosmology accounting for the formation of the world and the constantly shifting fortunes of the things in it. Each element was said to overcome another, as water overcomes fire, and the shifting balance of cosmological influence of the elements accounts for the rise and fall of things associated with them.

According to the ***Lüshi Chunqiu***, the power of a dynasty to rule was linked by Heaven to the virtues stemming from its possession of one of the five elements, wood, metal, fire, earth, water. It was a theory associated particularly with the name of **Zou Yan**, a philosopher from the state of **Qi**, where the so-called ***Yin-yang*** and Five Elements School flourished, but the concept of five elements was probably familiar to King **Wen**, and it was nearly a thousand years later, in the Former Han, that the greatest attention was paid to this kind of attempt to find a naturalistic explanation for changes in the political fortunes of the empire. The succession from one element to the next was held to result from conquest, as in the case of the temporal dynasty's power. Xia had possessed wood, Shang metal, and Zhou fire. Qin therefore claimed to rule by virtue of water, but the early Han rulers discounted this temporary usurpation of the sequence and assumed water for themselves. A proposal originating from **Jia Yi** resulted in the change of the dynasty's power to earth in 104 BC, but a debate developed over whether the succession really resulted from one element overcoming another, or whether one generated the next. The latter view was held by **Dong Zhongshu**, **Liu Xiang** and **Wang Mang**, who believed that Zhou had reigned by the virtue of wood and Han by fire. Wang Mang's expectation when he ascended the throne was therefore to gain the support of earth, its colour being yellow, thus fitting in with his claim to be a descendant of the **Yellow Emperor**. Ironically, the fact that his downfall followed the change in course of the **Yellow River** in AD 11 could have been interpreted as a sign of water overcoming earth. In fact, the restorer of the Han dynasty, the new Emperor Guang Wudi, chose to return to the virtue of its earlier element, fire. Thus the victory of Han over Qin was predetermined through its elemental association. The Five Element theory underpins much of traditional Chinese philosophical and scientific thought including, for example, traditional Chinese medicine.

John B. HENDERSON, *The Development and Decline of Chinese Cosmology* (Columbia University Press, 1984); Joseph NEEDHAM, *Science and Civilisation in China, Volume I* (Cambridge University Press, 1956).

FIVE EMPERORS *Wu di* 五帝

There were two different groups of five emperors worshipped in China:

(1) Mythological heavenly emperors worshipped since the Eastern Zhou period, including the Blue Emperor, Ling Weiyang 靈威仰 of the East, the Red Emperor, Chi Biaonu 赤熛怒 of the South, the Yellow Emperor, Han Shuniu 含樞紐 of the Centre, the White Emperor, Bai Zhaoju 白招拒 of the West and the Black Emperor, Zhi Guangji 汁光紀 of the North.

(2) Legendary emperors of the remote ancient periods, of which a number of different groupings exist. See also **Sage Emperors**.

FIVE PRINCIPLES OF PEACEFUL COEXISTENCE

Principles agreed on at the **Bandung Conference**, the Afro-Asian Conference held in Bandung, Indonesia from April 18–24 1955, and based on clauses in an agreement signed between China and India on trade with Tibet in April 1954. The five principles were mutual respect for territorial integrity and sovereignty; mutual non-aggression; non-interference in each others internal affairs; equality and mutual benefit; and peaceful co-existence. They typify the moderate foreign policy associated with **Zhou Enlai** that lasted until the Cultural Revolution.

FIVE RELATIONSHIPS *Wu lun* 五倫

The five basic relationships underpinning Confucian society: father – son (characterised by ***ren*** 仁 'benevolence'), ruler – subject (characterised by *yi* 義 'righteousness'), husband – wife (characterised by *bie* 別 'separateness'), elder brother – younger brother (characterised by *xu* 序 'precedence') and friend – friend (characterised by *xin* 信 'good faith'). All but the last are unequal relationships, reflecting the deeply hierarchical nature of Confucian society, and, with the exception of husband – wife, they are all envisaged as male relationships.

FIVE SACRED MOUNTAINS *Wu yue* 五岳

The five sacred mountains (*yue*) include the Eastern *yue* of **Taishan** in Shandong province, the Southern *yue* of Hengshan 衡山 in Hunan province, the Central *yue* of Chongshan 嵩山 in Henan province, the Western *yue* of Huashan 華山 in Shaanxi province; and the Northern *yue* of Hengshan 恆山 in Shanxi province.

It was believed that the five mountains were the sacred residences of gods and they therefore became the places for successive emperors to go and perform the rituals of worship. *Wu yue*-worship became a state affair after the Han Emperor **Wudi**, and the status of the five mountains was further defined by Emperor **Xuandi**. Later the five sacred mountains were given the titles of "Kings" in the Tang dynasty, "Emperors" in the Song dynasty, and "Gods" in the Ming dynasty. All five mountains have high peaks and temple complexes, and have been famous scenic spots, providing inspiration for emperors, poets and painters for many centuries.

FIVE VIRTUES *Wu chang* 五常

Literally the five constants, refers to the Confucian virtues ***ren*** 仁 'benevolence', *yi* 義 'righteousness', *li* 禮 'propriety', *zhi* 智 'wisdom', and *xin* 信 'good faith'. The ***Hanshu*** biography of **Dong Zhongshu** lists these as what the ruler should cultivate, but development of these was the primary goal of education in general. Of the five only wisdom is personal, the remaining four are all concerned with relationships. *Ren*, also translated as humanity, is defined by Confucius as *ai* 愛 and Mencius as *qin* 親, both implying 'love' and not unlike the Christian concept of love; it is generally seen as the inner primary virtue which underlies the others. *Ren* and *yi* are often paired in early Confucian texts; *yi* is a sense of duty which results in right conduct. *Li*, literally 'ritual', is usually translated as propriety and implies a sense of what is proper in behaviour. *Zhi*, like wisdom, suggests understanding rather than knowledge and *xin* is keeping to your word. There are other versions of the five, which may include *zhong* 忠, often translated as 'loyalty', and *shu* 恕 'reciprocity', but *ren* and *yi* are always present as the two essentials.

FIVE-YEAR PLANS *Wunian jihua* 五年計劃

China followed the Soviet model of economic development – after Mao's decision to "lean to one side" and ally China with the USSR in 1949, there was no choice and it was the only economic and social system of which the CCP leadership had any real understanding. This meant a planned economy and specifically Five-Year Plans. The First Five-Year Plan (1953–1957) is generally regarded as having been a success. Nationwide planning could only begin in 1953 when the mass campaigns in rural and urban areas had assured the CCP of political control. Initial attempts at long-tem planning were delayed by built-in problems of "planning and statistical capabilities", the demands which the **Korean War** made on the Chinese economy and difficulties in negotiating an aid package with the Soviet Union. At first, plans were made only on an annual basis, but by 1983, when the Korean War had finished and aid negotiations with the USSR had been concluded, long-term planning became a possibility. The principles of the First Five-Year Plan were published in 1953, but it was not until April 1955 that a full version was made available. During the Plan, life expectancy increased, as did the number of children in primary schools, urban housing standards, consumption and real wages. There was very little outside help: the USSR supplied capital goods but these were paid for at the time or on short-term credit. Major institutional changes took place in this period: the private sector was virtually eliminated and modern industry came under state control, although handicrafts remained in private hands or were organised in cooperatives. In line with practice in the USSR, the strategy of the government was to emphasise capital construction and heavy industry. To assist in the implementation of the Plan, the State Statistical Bureau and the State Planning Commission were established in 1952. The Second Five-Year Plan was due to run from 1958 to 1962, but by 1955 Mao was already worried that agriculture was lagging behind in the First Five-Year Plan and wanted to increase the pace of economic development. The old slogan of *duo kuai hao sheng* 多快好省"more, quicker, better, cheaper" was revived in November 1956 and Mao announced that China would overtake UK industry in 15 years. This was the prelude to the **Great Leap Forward**. The concept of the plan continued to dominate the thinking of China's economists, and even in the period of Reform and Opening that followed the death of Mao Zedong, economic developments were still expressed in terms of Five-Year Plans.

FLOWERS AND BIRDS PAINTING *Huaniaohua* 花鳥畫

One of the main categories of Chinese painting. The art of flower painting was developed from the Buddhist banner painting brought from India and Central Asia. Tang Buddhist art was rich in this decorative style of flower painting, but by the tenth century it had become an art in its own right. Later painters loved to animate their flower studies with birds, and thus "flowers and birds" became recognised as an independent category in the repertoire.

The Song dynasty was the golden age of *huaniaohua* when two main schools of this art were formed. One school was represented by Huang Quan 黃荃, who worked almost entirely in delicate, transparent washes of colour, a refined decorative style which eventually became more popular with professionals and court painters.

The other school was led by Xu Xi 徐熙, Huang Quan's contemporary and great rival, who had a different and more expressive approach, using his brush swiftly with ink and ink-wash and adding only a little colour. Xu Xi's style, in which a spiritual quality is pre-eminent, found favour among the literati. The techniques from both schools are still popular with flower painters today.

FOOTBINDING

Carried out on girls at around six years of age by the women in a family, this remained a physical reminder throughout a woman's life of her gender difference, and for many a constraint upon their mobility and social freedom. The bones of the feet were broken and tightly bound with cloth to prevent further growth, the ideal length of the so-called "Golden Lotus" being no more than three inches.

Sometimes associated with Yaoniang, a dancer at the tenth century Southern Tang court, the custom spread during the Song. Though it later became a symbol of male sexual domination, its early practice may have been intended as a means of differentiating between masculinity and femininity at a time when men themselves were becoming more refined in appearance, and between upper-class Han women and those of neighbouring races. Male voices were raised against footbinding in the Qing, by, for example, the poet **Yuan Mei** (1716–1797), but its continuation over a thousand years would have been impossible without the collaboration of women themselves. Though primarily practised in upper-class households, it was not unknown in lower-class families ambitious for their daughters. Footbinding was not generally found in non-Han Chinese communities and it was not practised by the Hakka people.

Howard S. LEVY, *Chinese Footbinding: The History of a Curious Erotic Custom* (New York: Walton Rawls, 1966).

FORBIDDEN CITY ***Zijincheng*** 紫禁城 (literally 'the Purple Forbidden City')
The former palace of 24 emperors of the Ming and Qing dynasties. The Forbidden City, located in the centre of **Beijing**, was built in the Ming dynasty but extended and restored many times. It occupies 7.2 square kilometres and is surrounded by a wall of 10 metres high. The palace complex contains over 9,000 rooms. Most of the structures are made of wood in red, sit on large white stone slabs, and are roofed with yellow glazed tiles.

The plan of the complex indicates the hierarchical arrangement of the buildings and demonstrates the order of society. The principle building, the Hall of Supreme Harmony, lies at the centre of the complex and is elevated above all the surrounding buildings, as seen from the south, the direction in which courtiers and ambassadors would have approached. Here major state ceremonies were performed. Behind it the other main halls, the Hall of Central Harmony, the Hall of Preserving Harmony and the Hall of Heavenly Purity, are all erected along a central axis extending from the south to the north. To the east were the emperor's and the male living quarters, while the women lived in the western apartments. Many of the lower side buildings were government offices. The buildings were not only implicitly ranked according to the status of their owners or their uses, but access was also determined by rank.

After the Republic of China was founded in 1911, the last emperor, **Puyi**, continued to live in the Forbidden City until he was ordered to leave by warlord general **Feng Yuxiang** in 1924. A year later, the Palace Museum or *Gugong Bowuyuan* 故宫博物院 was established in the complex. Although an important part of the imperial collection was removed to Taiwan in 1949, the Forbidden City still holds the largest collections of imperial treasures, including some of the best samples of painitng, calligraphy, bronzes and porcelains.

YU, Cho-yun, *Palaces of the Forbidden City* (New York: Viking, 1984).

FOREIGN MATTERS MOVEMENT see **SELF-STRENGTHENING MOVEMENT**

FORMER KINGS ***Xianwang*** 先王
This rather vague title is frequently encountered, especially in early political and historical writing. It applies in particular to two groups of ancient rulers whose merits were held up as paradigmatic, those of Yao 堯, Shun 舜 and Yu 禹, and **Wen**, **Wu** and **Zhou Gong**. The latter are the historical founders of the Zhou dynasty. The former are semi-mythological figures with imaginary dates traditionally ascribed to the third millennium BC. **Confucius** and **Mencius** praised their exemplary virtues, which included their dedication to the service of the people and the fact that each was chosen for the throne on the grounds of ability and not by right of succession. Yao is said to have devised a calendar and encouraged agriculture. Shun, who served him as a minister, was originally a

peasant but demonstrated outstanding qualities as a devoted and self-sacrificing son. Yu was also an official under Yao who later became the founder of the Xia dynasty. His fame included success in controlling a serious flood said to have occurred during Yao's reign, which led to the development of waterways and the administrative division of the country into nine regions based on the quality of their land and the resultant tax yield. This resulted in his being credited with the invention of feudalism: details are given in the ***Shujing*** section entitled ***Yugong***. See also Sage Emperors.

FORMOSA see **TAIWAN**

FOUR BOOKS ***Si shu*** 四書
The four texts, the ***Lunyu*** 'Analects of Confucius', ***Mengzi*** 'Mencius', ***Daxue*** 'Great Learning' and ***Zhongyong*** 'Doctrine of the Mean', selected in the Song dynasty by **Zhu Xi** as the key canonical texts of **Confucianism** in its **Neo-Confucian** form. The Four Books became the most important texts in the curriculum of the **examination system** for the next 800 years. See individual entries for details.

FOUR CLEANUPS CAMPAIGN ***Si qing*** 四清
Part of the **Socialist Education Movement** which was a forerunner to the **Cultural Revolution.**

FOUR GENTLEMEN ***Si junzi*** 四君子
One of the favourite themes in Chinese painting and decorative art. It refers to four plants loved by Chinese scholars: prunus blossom, orchid, bamboo, and chrysanthemum, which are associated with the qualities of a gentleman: purity, integrity and high principles.

FOUR MODERNISATIONS ***Sige xiandaihua*** 四個現代化
Policy aims announced in 1978, marking the return to power of **Deng Xiaoping** after the death of Mao Zedong and the end of the **Cultural Revolution**. The strategy was to develop agriculture, industry, science and technology and defence. Although it is associated with Deng, the original slogan was suggested by Zhou Enlai some years before. The Four Modernisations policy evolved into the **Reform and Opening policy.**

Richard BAUM, ed., *China's Four Modernizations: The New Technological Revolution* (Boulder, Colorado: Westview Press, 1980).

FOUR OLDS ***Si jiu*** 四舊
Old customs, old habits, old culture and old thinking. These were the targets of the **Red Guards** during the **Cultural Revolution**. Although the categories were specified by the leadership of the Cultural Revolution, precisely what was meant was never made clear and Red Guards were able to use the slogan to attack any victims they chose. Consequently, temples, monasteries, churches and mosques were damaged and traditional artefacts in public and private hands were destroyed.

FOUR TREASURES OF THE SCHOLAR'S STUDIO *Wenfang sibao* 文房四寶
A scholar's accoutrements for writing and painting, consisting of brush, ink, paper and inkstone.

Brush. The Chinese *bi* 筆, used for both painting and writing, consists of a carefully structured bundle of graded hairs which are fixed in the end of a holder, usually made of bamboo. The most common types of hair are goat, wolf, badger, deer, fox and hare. The selection of hairs and the details of the construction of a brush are varied according to the taste and purpose of the user. A brush with a highly waxed core would produce a lively and responsive line, while a soft core would produce a more even stroke or be used for applying ink and colour washes in painting. The free movement of the pliable brush has been an important technical factor underlying artistic development.

Ink. *Mo* 墨 is traditionally prepared in dry sticks or cakes which are ground with water on an inkstone to produce a solution of the desired density. Carbon, the main ingredient, was derived from burning pinewood, to which lampblack made from animal, vegetable or mineral oils was added. This was mixed with animal glue, moulded and dried. Other ingredients might be added to improve the lustre, fragrance and consistency. Inksticks are often decorated with moulded designs, enhanced with coloured lacquers or gold leaf. The earliest example of an inkstick was found in a Qin tomb.

Inkstone. *Yan* 硯 is generally made of stone or ceramics, and is used for grinding solid inksticks and preparing liquid ink for writing or painting. Inkstones vary in shape and size but usually have a smooth flat area, or bed, for grinding ink and a depressed area, or well, for holding excess liquid. Highly prized inkstones such as Duan 端 and She 歙 stones (named after the place where they were produced) have been collected by scholars since the Tang dynasty, and much attention was paid to the selection of the inkstone, with colour, marking, smoothness and sound all being taken into consideration.

Paper. *Zhi* 紙 is attributed to an invention of the eunuch Cai Lun 蔡倫 in the early second century AD, though excavations from a tomb near Xian have produced samples of paper dating to the second century BC. Paper was at first used for documents and religious texts and was only regularly employed for painting from the Yuan dynasty. Many different papers were developed for the different requirements of writing and painting, among which *xuan* paper 宣紙produced in Anhui province, using sandalwood bark as the main raw material, has been widely favoured.

THE ORIENTAL CERAMIC SOCIETY OF HONG KONG, *Arts from the Scholar's Studio* (Hong Kong, 1986).

FOUR TREASURIES see ***SI KU QUAN SHU***

FU 賦
A literary genre often called in English 'prose poetry' because it has characteristics of both, although it is more closely identified with the latter. Its debt to the ***Chuci*** is evident in its form, style and subject matter. A well known early example, dating from 174 BC, is **Jia Yi**'s *Funiao fu* '*Fu* on the owl'), a philosophical speculation on the meaning of life occasioned by the arrival of an owl, a bird of ill-omen, in Jia Yi's room. The genre was later developed by Sima

Xiangru 司馬相如 (179–117 BC), regarded as one of its greatest exponents, who produced descriptive *fu* on, for example, royal hunts. These descriptive *fu,* on subjects like cities, ceremonies, musical instruments, animals, rivers and journeys, may run into hundreds of lines and set out both to inform and to act as a vehicle for the writer's literary prowess. The typically long Han *fu* became shorter and more rigid in form in the Six Dynasties, a tendency which culminated in the *lüfu* 律賦 'regulated *fu'* of the Tang with, like *lüshi* 律詩 'regulated verse', a prescribed rhyme pattern and strict parallelism. The ***guwen*** 古文 (ancient style prose) movement of the late Tang reacted against this and Song masters like Ouyang Xiu and Su Shi reemphasised its prose aspect. The *fu* lost popularity after the Song when it was replaced by ***baguwen*** 'eight legged essays' as one of the prescribed examination forms.

XIAO Tong, *Wen Xuan or Selections of Refined Literature, Volume 1: Rhapsodies on Metropolises and Capitals*, translation, annotation and introduction by David R. KNECHTGES (Princeton University Press, 1982).

FU HAO 婦好
Principal consort of the Shang King Wu Ding and an important military and political figure in her own right. She is believed to be the occupant of tomb number 5 unearthed in 1976 at Xiaotun, **Anyang**, the contents of which included an invaluable collection of **bronzes, jades** and bone artefacts. These attest to high artistic standards, ritual and military practices, and feudal intercourse between the royal domain and regional centres.

K.C. CHANG, ed., *Studies of Shang Archaeology* (Yale University Press, 1986).

FU XI 伏羲
The first in the legendary age of Five Rulers (Fu Xi, **Shen Nong**, Huangdi (see **Yellow Emperor**), Yao and Shun (see **Former Kings**)); the so-called "founder of history". He is popularly associated with the invention of writing and **music**, the creation of **marriage** laws, the teaching of fishing and animal husbandry.

FU ZUOYI 傅作義 **(1895–?)**
Military officer in the service of the warlord **Yan Xishan** and governor of **Suiyuan** province from 1931 to 1947. He was the Nationalist General who negotiated the surrender of Beijing to the PLA in 1949 and during the PRC became active in the Chinese Peoples Political Consultative Conference and held the post of Minister of Water Conservation and was a member of the National Defence Council.

FUQIANG 富強 'wealth and strength'
The slogan of 19th century modernizers who sought to introduce Western methods to rectify China's military and economic weakness. It was used as early as the 1860s by commentators like **Feng Guifen**. The Westernizing *Yangwu yundong* 洋務運動 'Foreign Matters Movement', developed in the **Tongzhi Restoration** and continued through the 1870s and 80s but gradually lost momentum and credibility. The defeat in the 1894–5 **Sino-Japanese war** was the catalyst for a more fundamental reappraisal. This resulted in the reform movement, the revolutionary movement and the activities of interpreters of

Western thought like **Yan Fu**. All sought to analyze the real roots of Western power and to introduce political, educational and institutional reforms to enable China to emulate the West in wealth and strength.

FUSHE 復社 'Restoration Society'
Successor body to the **Donglin Academy** 東林書院 group which fought the eunuch faction at the end of the Ming dynasty. Wei Zhongxian 魏忠賢 (1568–1627), eunuch favourite of the Tianqi 天啓 emperor and de facto ruler from 1624–7, carried out a vicious campaign against the reformist Donglin group resulting in the deaths of many members and its effective disbandment. After the death of Wei Zhongxian, a number of scholars from the Jiangnan 江南 area of south-central China who were in sympathy with the Donglin party's ideals brought together a group of small associations and formed the *Fushe* 'Restoration Society' in 1628. Leading figures included Zhang Pu 張溥, Zhang Cai 張采 and Sun Chun 孫淳. It held major assemblies in 1629, 1630 and 1632 attended by several thousand people and spread from Jiangnan into neighbouring provinces, at one stage numbering over 2,000 members. The association had some success in influencing government in the early years of the new Chongzhen emperor but attacks by the eunuch groups and other parties weakened it later. When the Manchus invaded, as a loyalist organization its members naturally supported the Ming and tried to galvanize opposition to the Manchus, hence it was suppressed once the Qing gained control.

GANDEN
Tibetan Buddhist monastery established in 1409 by **Tsong Khapa**, this was the third of the Three Pillars of the Tibetan State, and of prime importance in the formation of **Gelugpa** doctrine. It once had an official maximum registration of 3,300 monks, but has not recovered its former size since being severely damaged by the **Red Guards** in 1966 during the early stages of the **Cultural Revolution**. Tsong Khapa's own magnificent gold and silver *chorten* or shrine was destroyed, and although it has since been replaced by a copy the rebuilt monastery is only a shadow of its former self.

GANG OF FOUR ***Siren bang*** 四人幫
Name given to the most prominent supporters of Mao Zedong's **Cultural Revolution** after the Chairman's death. The four were Mao's widow **Jiang Qing**, **Zhang Chunqiao**, **Yao Wenyuan** and **Wang Hongwen**, all members of the radical faction based in Shanghai. The term was alleged to have originated in a warning given by Mao to Jiang Qing that they should not act as a gang of four. After Mao's death in September 1976, the political struggle between Maoists and Dengists flared up again. The four were arrested on October 1976 and ***People's Daily*** carried an article accusing the Gang of Four of sabotaging production on November 1. The trial of the four and six others accused of treason began on November 20 1980. At the end of the trial on January 25 1981, Jiang Qing and Zhang Chunqiao were sentenced to death with a two-year reprieve, Yao Wenyuan to twenty years in prison and Wang Hongwen to life imprisonment.

GANZHI 干支

A chronological term referring to the combination of *tiangan*天干, the ten celestial stems, and *dizhi* 地支, the twelve terrestrial branches. The system is applied to the numbering of years, months, days and hours. Each of the stems and branches is named with a single character, and in any combination the stem comes first and the branch comes next. Such combinations form the Cycle of Sixty, or *huajia* 花甲. To form such a cycle, the first of the twelve branches is joined to the first of the ten stems until the last or tenth of the latter is reached, when a fresh commencement is made, the eleventh of the series of twelve branches being next appended to the first stem.

The stem correspond to the **five elements**, while the branches are symbolised by different affinities, better known as ***shengxiao*** (the twelve animals). The application of the *ganzhi* system can be dated back to the Shang dynasty, but it was not until the Han dynasty that the practice of using animals to represent the terrestrial branches became customary. Using this system, people in China often indicate their age by referring to the animal appertaining to the year of their birth. Old people also refer to their age as "over a *huajia*".

GAO GANG 高崗 (1905–1955)

Chairman of the North-east People's Government in August 1947 and appointed as Chairman of the key State Planning Commission in 1952. Gao Gang together with **Rao Shushi**, was expelled from the CCP at a national Communist Party conference on March 31 1954, on the grounds that he had tried to divide the party and establish an independent kingdom. It was later reported that Gao had committed suicide.

GAOZONG 高宗, SONG EMPEROR (Zhao Gou 趙構, 1107–87, r.1127–62)

Ninth son of Emperor **Huizong** and first emperor of the Southern Song dynasty. His first capital was at **Nanjing**, from where his armies and navies fought the **Jurchen** for control of the **Yangzi** valley, but after 1138 the court was comfortably established at **Hangzhou**. Despite the efforts of General Yue Fei to continue the campaign, peace was made with the Jin dynasty in 1142 and the Song accepted tributary vassaldom under the barbarian empire in northern China.

H. FRANKE, *Sung Biographies* (Wiesbaden: Franz Steiner Verlag, 1976).

GAOZONG 高宗, TANG EMPEROR (Li Zhi 李治, 628–83, r. 649–83)

Ninth son of Emperor **Taizong**. The history of this period is dominated by the rise to power of Wu Zhao (see **Wu Zetian**), former concubine to his father, and the undermining of court affairs by constant intrigue. But though the Emperor himself was weak-willed his reign, the longest yet of the Tang dynasty, was not without important achievements. In particular, the law code was revised and strengthened and the **examination system** developed as a route into the bureaucracy. Monetary policy, however, was not able to keep up with mounting government expenditure at home or an extravagant foreign policy far across Central Asia and the Korean peninsula. The latter temporarily brought China to the height of its international influence. Against **Koguryo**, for example, Gaozong enjoyed much greater success than **Taizong**, and by assisting **Silla's** unification (668) helped to create China's most loyal tributary ally. But against the Turks and the Tibetans his authority could not be sustained, and when Gaozong died the state was under both economic and military threat from the North-west.

GAOZU 高祖, HAN EMPEROR (Liu Bang 劉邦, 247–195, r. 202–195 BC)
Liu Bang, made King of Han by his rival **Xiang Yu** in 206 BC, assumed the title of Emperor by defeating him four years later. He was the first man of humble origin to rise to such pre-eminence, and the first to acquire it solely by force of arms. Appreciating the resources of the South-west (from where his title of Han was derived) and having seen for himself the successes of Qin in **Shu**, his government maintained its economic reliance on that region and its trust in the law as an essential control system. **Legalism** was the only political system ever to have been adopted by a state, and Gaozu was certainly not confident enough to reject one that had clearly proved its potential. **Confucianism** had not yet established its credentials and received little encouragement from the new emperor. Although feudalism had been abolished in 221 BC Gaozu instituted a modified political system which, while preserving centralized rule as instituted by Qin at the heart of the Empire, nevertheless restored kingdoms in large peripheral areas that were too far away to be within easy communication with the capital. The new kings were eventually limited to members of the imperial clan and the size and significance of their domains whittled down by division on inheritance. As a means of effecting a smooth transition of authority across an unprecedently wide empire it was an inspired concept, even though Gaozu himself immediately began the process of undermining kingly power by fighting against those holders of the title who were not his blood relatives.

Gaozu was the temple name of Liu Bang: he is also known by his posthumous title of Gaodi. See also **Lu Zhi.**

D. TWITCHETT and M. LOEWE eds., *The Cambridge History of China, vol.1: the Ch'in and Han Empires* (Cambridge University Press, 1986).

GAOZU 高祖, TANG EMPEROR (Li Yuan 李淵, 566–635, r. 618–26)
Formerly Duke of Tang and a senior Sui official and military commander at Taiyuan who led the successful revolt against his imperial masters in 617 (see **Yangdi**). He pacified the many areas controlled by other regional warlords and laid the groundwork for the subsequent strength of the Tang dynasty in political, economic and military affairs. He encouraged education, relaxed the harshness of the late Sui law code, and succeeded, albeit with a degree of appeasement, in protecting the new empire from the threats of the Turks on the northern frontier. After the disastrous experience of Sui Yangdi's expeditions to **Koguryo** he promoted friendly relations with the new king there and received tribute in addition to many repatriated Chinese prisoners-of-war. He had twenty two sons, of whom his successor Li Shimin was the second (see **Taizong, Tang Emperor**).

D. McMullen, *State and Scholars in T'ang China* (Cambridge University Press, 1988); W. Bingham, *The Founding of the T'ang Dynasty: The Fall of the Sui and the Rise of the T'ang* (Baltimore: Waverly Press, 1941).

Gardens

The garden was an important part of **gentry** culture in traditional China. Within its walls the city-bound official or merchant could recreate the natural world of the countryside, and escaping the dusty world of his competitive public life find peace and solitude amid reminders of the ***Dao*** – the running water of the stream, rocks on the hillside, gnarled pine trees, fronds of swaying bamboo and sprays of flowering shrubs. In a secluded summerhouse he might find a place to rest, write, paint, or play his *guqin* (see **musical instruments**). The scholar took time and intellectual pleasure in planning and stocking the garden so that every element appeared as casual as possible, at every turn a reminder of some lesson to be learned from nature. Trees and plants were glimpsed through artistically shaped windows, doorways or lattice fences. Each was planted in the most advantageous of settings for its symbolic value as well as the seasonal appearance of its colour, the lotus for purity, orchid for femininity, peony for riches, chrysanthemum for steadfastness, plum for new hope after the winter. The public and palace gardens of **Chang'an** and **Luoyang** were renowned in the Han and Tang dynasties. In later times **Hangzhou** and Suzhou were especially famous for their private gardens, but famous examples survive to the present in other cities as well, including **Shanghai.**

Maggie Keswick, *The Chinese Garden* (London: Academy Editions, 1978); R.S. Johnson, *Scholar Gardens of China* (Cambridge University Press, 1991).

Gazetteers *Fangzhi* 方志

Important sources of local history for the imperial and republican periods. Histories of provinces, prefectures and counties were compiled by local officials and updated from time to time. The standard format, used in most of the gazetteers from the Ming and Qing dynasties, includes prefaces for each subsequent edition discussing the principles of compilation, maps or plans of the area covered, administration, topography, famous sights, official buildings, schools, temples, bridges, canals and irrigation works,, officials and examinations, taxation, markets, crops, local products, local customs, disasters, prominent local people and miscellaneous topics. Most of the extant gazetteers are from the Qing dynasty, although there are several hundred Ming volumes and a smaller number from the Song and the Yuan periods. Gazetteers were also produced in the Republican period, and to a certain extent the tradition has been continued under the People's Republic with the production of new local histories.

Gelaohui see **Elder Brother Society**

Gelugpa

Tibetan monastic order commonly known as the Yellow Hats, a name first given to them by the Chinese to distinguish them from their principal rivals, the Red Hats of the Karmapa Order. Its foundation is attributed to **Tsong Khapa**, though his intention was probably to strengthen rather than to diverge from the Kadampa Order when he founded **Ganden** monastery in 1409. It subsequently became the centre of Gelugpa teaching. Kadampa teaching, brought to **Tibet** by the Indian mystic Atisha in the early eleventh century and based upon the study of the sutras first and tantras second, was too uncompetitive to survive in the increasingly political monastic world of the late middle ages. Tsong Khapa and his disciples emphasized the need for study, but allied to it a strong sense of monastic morality and discipline which developed as the Gelugpa, or Virtuous, school through the fifteenth century. Its growing authority, and association with the capital province by virtue of its great monastic foundations of Ganden, **Drepung** and **Sera** in and near **Lhasa**, brought it into both ecclesiastical and temporal conflict with the Karmapa, the headquarters of which lay in the capital of the province of Tsang, **Shigatse**. Tsong Khapa's nephew and disciple Gedun Truppa (posthumously recognised as the first **Dalai Lama**) founded Tashilumpo monastery in the heart of this alien territory, and all subsequent Dalai Lamas have belonged to the Gelugpa Order, but it was not until 1642, when the Fifth Dalai Lama Lobsang Gyatso called upon assistance from a Mongol army to destroy the power of the King of Tsang, that Gelugpa power was irrefutably established.

R.A. STEIN, *Tibetan Civilisation* (Stanford University Press, 1972).

GENGHIS KHAN see **CHINGGIS KHAN**

GENTRY *Shenshi* 紳士

The educated elite of imperial China. Also known as the Literati or the Scholar-Gentry, the gentry were those who had passed at least the lowest level of the traditional **examination system**. Some would also serve as officials, but there was always a large reservoir of gentry who did not succeed in obtaining an official appointment and these might participate in running local communities on an informal basis or occasionally become the focus of dissent and the leaders of **peasant rebellions**.

GEOMANCY see ***FENGSHUI***

GILES, HERBERT ALLEN (1845–1935)

Giles served in the British consular service in China between 1880 and 1893 and taught in Aberdeen before becoming Professor of Chinese at the University of Cambridge from 1897, succeeding Sir Thomas Wade who took up the first chair there in 1888. Giles compiled the standard *A Chinese-English Dictionary*, which was published in **Shanghai** in 1892. The **Wade-Giles system** of romanising Chinese was completed by Giles on the basis of a scheme devised by Wade.

GINSENG *Renshen* 人參

Although ginseng is most readily associated with Korea, the plant with its forked aromatic roots has also been widely used in Chinese medicine. It was found throughout China but the Manchurian ginseng was considered to be the highest quality. Under the Qing dynasty, trade in the plant was a government monopoly.

Gobi
Chinese transliteration (*gebi* 戈壁) of the Mongolian word for a desert or semi-desert *gov'* and used as the name for the desert plain that stretches throughout the Inner Mongolian Autonomous Region and Mongolia.

God of longevity *Shouxing* 壽星
A popular folk deity in China, usually represented as an old man with a high forehead and long white beard, carrying a peach and a rustic staff, and accompanied by a deer or a crane. He is often included in painting and decorations with the **Eight Immortals**.

God of wealth *Caishen* 財神
A popular folk deity in China, who has been identified with a number of different individuals including Luxing 祿星, the Star God of Rank and Affluence. The original and best known until later times was Zhao Gongming, though several versions of him existed. Zhao was also called "the master of the Black Altar", one of the legendary heroes in Xu Zhilin's novel *Fengshen Yanyi* 封神演義, usually represented in pictures with his attributes: a black tiger, pearls and gold and silver ingots. Another widely-loved icon of Caishen is "the living god of wealth" Shen Wansan with his magic casket of multiplying treasures. Caishen was widely worshipped in China. His images were on display in every household and premises of trade during the New Year festival season. Talismans, trees of which the branches are strings of coins, and the fruits ingots of gold, to be obtained merely by shaking them down, and magic inexhaustible vessels full of gold and silver – these and other spiritual sources of wealth are always associated with this much-adored deity.

Golden Lotus see ***Jinpingmei***

Gong, Prince (*Gong Qinwang* 恭親王)
Younger brother of the Xianfeng emperor of the Qing dynasty. Prince Gong played a prominent role in negotiations with the British at the end of the **Arrow War** and during the settlement of the Convention of Beijing. His position was less secure when his brother died in 1861 but he was co-regent with the **Empress Dowager** during the minority of the **Tongzhi Emperor**. He was an enthusiastic supporter of the **Self-Strengthening Movement** and was responsible for the creation of the **Zongli Yamen.** See **Beijing, Convention of.**

Gongyang zhuan see ***Spring and Autumn Annals***

***Gongbihua* 工筆畫**
Technical category of Chinese painting, referring to works executed in a minute and precise manner, and usually on silk or sized *xuan* paper (see **Four treasures of the scholar's studio).** *Gongbihua* was essentially the continuation of a long tradition of decorative painting of fans, screens and other utensils of court and elite life. *Gongbihua* favours a realistic approach to subject matter, which is contrary to the approach of ***xieyihua*** and is best represented by the works produced in the Song dynasty **Academy of Painting.**

GONGSUN LONGZI 公孫龍子 (fourth – third century BC)
Philosopher associated with the School of Names or **Logicians**; also the text bearing his name. Gongsun Long was said to have been attached to the court of Lord Pingyuan 平原君 who died in 251 BC. He was much concerned with the relationship between language and logic. One of his most famous propositions, that 'a white horse is not a horse' *bai ma fei ma ye* 白馬非馬也, argues that a more restrictive definition like 'white horse' excludes the general one 'horse'. The present text bearing Gongsun Long's name consists of an introductory chapter on his life and five further chapters of philosophical argument. These mostly revolve around perception, as filtered through language, and reality: *Bai ma lun* 白馬論 'On a white horse', *Zhi wu lun* 指物論 'On indications and things', *Tong bian lun* 通變論 'On the understanding of change', *Jian bai lun* 堅白論 'On hardness and whiteness' and *Ming shi lun* 名實論 'On name and reality'.
A.C. GRAHAM, *Studies in Chinese Philosophy and Philosophical Literature* (Albany: State University of New York Press, 1990); Wing-tsit CHAN, *A Source-book in Chinese Philosophy* (Princeton University Press, 1963).

GORDON, GENERAL CHARLES C. see **EVER-VICTORIOUS ARMY**

GOVERNOR *Xunfu* 巡撫
Most senior government official in a province. During the Ming dynasty, what had been a temporary post to co-ordinate the implementation of court policies became established. The Qing dynasty appointed permanent governors to every province apart from Zhili and Sichuan, which were controlled by **Governors-General**.

GOVERNOR-GENERAL, OR VICEROY *Zongdu* 總督
Government official originally appointed to supervise areas larger than one province during times of crisis such as rebellion or natural disasters. Like the post of **governor,** these positions became permanent during the Qing dynasty, with the majority of Governors General being Manchu, overseeing Han Chinese **governors**.

GRAND CANAL
The importance of canals for commercial and military communication and transportation had been recognised since the Warring States period, and Qin had made good use of inland waterways in its unification campaigns in the third century BC. But it was the Sui Emperor **Yangdi** who was responsible for extending the canal network into a system linking south China with the North, a shrewd logistical and psychological move after the divisions of the Northern and Southern Dynasties period. With no consideration for the suffering of the tens of thousands of labouring men and women and convicts set to work on its construction, his civil engineers completed an enormous project in 605–6 connecting the **Yellow River** with the Huai and the **Yangzi River** (the Tongji Canal), which made direct communication possible between the capital **Chang'an, Kaifeng** and Yangzhou. A second canal (the Yongji Canal) was finished in 608 leading north-eastwards from the **Yellow River** towards the Gulf of Bohai, aimed at assisting the military build-up against **Koguryo**; and a third

extension to the system (the Jiangnan Canal) was opened southwards from Yangzhou into the **Hangzhou** region in 610. The network fell into disuse during the Song, but the establishment of the capital at Dadu (modern **Beijing**) by **Khubilai Khan** meant that food had to be transported from the Yangzi valley to the North-east, and in 1289 a connecting link was cut across the base of the Shandong Peninsula between the Tongji and Yongji Canals, thus completing a thousand-plus mile artery between Hangzhou and Beijing. The main benefit of this was reaped in the fifteenth century, when improvements including dredging, widening and the installation of a chain of locks, begun in 1411 ensured that Beijing would benefit fully from the grain tribute system once it became **Yongle**'s splendid but economically isolated capital. See also **Water Control.**

HOSHI AYAO, *The Ming Tribute Grain System*, trans. Mark Elvin (Ann Arbor: University of Michigan Press, 1969).

GRAND COUNCIL *Junjichu* 軍機處

The highest policy-making body from the mid-Qing dynasty onwards. As its Chinese name, which means Military Planning Office, suggests, when it was originally set up in 1729 it was as a military planning body, but its role soon expanded to cover all important matters of state, both civil and military. It was a relatively informal organization composed of a variable number of members who concurrently held substantive posts elsewhere. The status and duties of individual members varied according to the emperor's wishes and members acted individually as imperial advisers. They were also appointed concurrently to other non-substantive but key posts like membership of the **Zongli Yamen**. The Grand Council was serviced by its own secretariat, the *Junji zhangjing* 軍機章京, composed from 1799 of four sections, two Manchu and two Han, each with eight people. The Grand Council continued until 1911 when, as part of the late Qing constitutional reforms, it was replaced by a cabinet. Its role was expanded in the nineteenth century to include the supervision of the Zongli Yamen and it helped the Qing dynasty to endure into the twentieth century. See also Prince **Gong.**

B.S. BARTLETT, *Monarchs and Ministers: The Grand Council in Mid-Ch'ing China* (1723–1820) (Berkeley: University of California Press,1991).

GRAND SECRETARIAT *Neige* 內閣

The highest policy-making body in the Ming dynasty. The Ming initially followed earlier practice and had a Secretariat, *Zhongshusheng* 中書省, with a senior and junior prime minister, *chengxiang* 丞相. Emperor Taizu 太祖 suspected his prime minister of treason and abolished these offices in 1380. This move had the effect of removing a possible alternative focus of power and hence increasing the emperor's own. However, it was still necessary to have a high-level consultative and coordinating body and eventually his successor, Chengzu 成祖, appointed a group of **Hanlin** compilers and others to staff the *Wenyuange* 文淵閣 'Literary Depths Studio'. Since it was located in the inner court it became known as the *Neige* 'Inner Studio'. The members of this were originally of relatively low status and their duties were to provide secretarial assistance to the emperor, but gradually they were encouraged to offer opinions and their status accordingly rose. Documents from the **Six Boards** were channelled though the *Neige*, which would attach a recommended response, *piao ni* 票擬, for submission to the emperor.

In 1658 the Qing set up a *Neige* modelled on the Ming system. There were two Manchu and two Han officials, all Grand Counsellors grade 1, the highest on the civil service scale. However, in order to prevent the *Neige* from becoming too powerful, the policy formulation role and the drafting of responses to memorials were separated and the former was undertaken, for most of the Qing dynasty, by the **Grand Council** *Junjichu*. Thus, although the *Neige* continued nominally to be the highest organ of state below the emperor, in practice its work became largely routine and the Grand Council was the more important body. The two were merged in 1911 to form a Cabinet, also called *Neige*, along Western constitutional monarchy lines. The Cabinet was headed by a Prime Minister, *zongli dachen* 總理大臣, and was once again the highest state body. After the 1911 Revolution ended the Qing dynasty, the *Neige* survived in name for much of the period until 1928, when the Northern Expedition ended warlord rule.

GRAVE ARCHITECTURE

Grave architecture was an important part of the Chinese architectural tradition. Tombs in ancient China were replicas of the outside world and, as in the world, the proper status of the deceased had to be shown. Life was viewed as literally continuing after death, and the dead would, as they had when alive, require all the utensils of daily life and of ritual. The structures both below and above the ground were designed for this purpose. The burial chambers were the sumptuously equipped homes of the deceased. The buildings above ground were the places where descendants offered their respects and cared for the well-being of the dead.

Early tombs from the Neolithic times consisted primarily of structures under the ground, featuring a large vertical pit with a step, or platform on which burial goods were placed. At the bottom of the pit were two coffins of wood: an outer coffin or *guo* 槨 and an inner coffin or *guan* 棺. Over time, tomb structures started to recreate the shape of buildings. In the Western Zhou, subsidiary chambers within the *guo* began to appear, starting the practice of representing the burial chambers as parts of the types of buildings that the person had lived in when alive. Han burials were constructed to resemble the contemporary mansions or palaces. This tradition continued in later centuries. From the Warring States period, mounds were constructed over tombs, preceding the huge mounds over the tombs of later emperors. As time passed more and more complex buildings and sculptures were placed above ground. The complexes of later emperors' tombs consisted of temples, halls, walls, courtyards, gates, stele pavilions, memorial arches and the Spirit Road or *shendao* 神道 where rows of stone sculptures were placed.

GRAVE ARTEFACTS *Mingqi* 明器

The idea that a deceased person would require service and physical comforts in his next life similar to those enjoyed in this is evident from the royal tombs of the Shang dynasty, and has survived in one form or another throughout the history of Chinese society. Human sacrifice, of military defenders and slaves, had been practised in the Shang but had generally been abandoned by the Spring and Autumn period, when **Confucius** even criticised the habit of burying wooden models with the dead, presumably lest it should lead to a return to the earlier practice. This particular habit however continued, as is shown by the fine wooden figures of musicians and attendants from the Warring States tomb of the Marquis of Zeng (see **Leigudun**), and by Han times the tombs of the nobility were richly furnished with top quality examples of useful artefacts, such as the superb bronze lantern in the shape of a serving girl well known from the tomb of Princess Dou Wan (see **Liu Sheng**); with replicas, including pottery models of farmsteads, bronze models of chariots and horses, and fine ornaments in the shape of animals made in jade, metalwork and lacquerware; and sometimes, curiously, with full-size artefacts that had not been fully finished off, such as musical instruments that could not be played – except in the spirit world – because they lacked the strings. **Mozi's** criticism of the excessive cost of lavish funerary practices had gone unheeded. Grave artefacts from many periods provide invaluable evidence of lifestyle, social features, dress and hairstyles, entertainment and architecture, since the dead were often provided with the best quality goods to take into the next life. Best known are perhaps the large numbers of brilliantly modelled pottery figurines from Tang tombs, including polo players, Central Asian caravanserai, troupes of female musicians and dancers, and guardian spirits, but for sheer opulence it would be impossible to outdo the treasures buried with the Ming emperors in their tombs outside **Beijing** (see **Ming tombs**). See also **Immortality, Tomb Architecture.**

Ann PALUDAN, *Chinese Tomb Figurines* (Hong Kong: Oxford University Press, 1994)

GREAT KHAN

The senior tribal chief of the **Mongols**. **Chinggis Khan** was the first Great Khan and his successors who ruled China from their capital at **Karakorum** inherited the title. As Mongol control over China declined, so did the position of the Great Khan.

GREAT LEAP FORWARD ***Dayuejin*** **大躍進**

Reversal of economic policy in 1958 that called for a dramatic rise in industrial production. Chinese economic policy from 1949 had followed the **Five Year Plan** model of the Soviet Union. Mao Zedong was dissatisfied with the speed of development that these Plans permitted, and criticised those who held back from radical change. At a conference in Chengdu in 1958 he put forward the slogan *duo kuai hao sheng* 多快好省 "more, quicker, better, cheaper" which effectively launched the Great Leap Forward. It was approved in February 1958 by the National People's Congress, which called for increases in the production of steel, coal and electricity of almost 20% over three years and for China to pass British industrial production levels within fifteen years. Production quotas throughout the country were raised and the entire population was mobilised. Steel was produced in backyard furnaces, but was of such poor quality as to be unusable, and large-scale public works projects such as road building and bridge construction were undertaken by people temporarily withdrawn from their normal employment, mainly from the farms. By the end of the year, enormous increases in production figures were announced. In Mao's day it was stated that problems encountered in the countryside during the years following the Great Leap were caused by adverse weather conditions. There were both heavy floods and serious drought in 1959. In 1960, drought, typhoons, floods and pests affected more than half of the land under cultivation and the Yellow River in parts had almost dried up. It was said that a serious food shortage had developed, but that famine had been avoided by careful rationing and collective effort and that the newly-created **commune** system had helped to prevent famine, because it had the ability to mobilise large numbers of people.

Historians today, both Western and Chinese, now concede that the 1958 policies were a complete disaster and that there were at least 20 million (and some commentators go as far as 40 million) excess deaths attributable to famine and diseases linked to famine. Such was the dissatisfaction with the GLF policies when their true effects (in particular the famine) were realised, that Mao Zedong's political influence declined markedly and was only regained by his efforts in the **Cultural Revolution.** See also **Peng Dehuai, Lushan Plenum, Second Great Leap Forward.**

Roderick MACFARQUHAR, *The Origins of the Cultural Revolution, vol.2: The Great Leap Forward, 1958–1960* (Columbia University Press, 1983; David BACHMAN, *Bureaucracy, Economy and Leadership in China: The Institutional Origins of the Great Leap Forward* (Cambridge University Press, 1991).

GREAT PROLETARIAN CULTURAL REVOLUTION see **CULTURAL REVOLUTION**

GREAT WALL *Wanli changcheng* 萬里長城

From the Zhou dynasty onwards the heartland of Chinese civilisation, the Great Plain and the Wei River valley, was subject to regular interaction with the nomadic peoples of the Inner Asian steppes. Sometimes they were welcome as pilgrims, merchants and official envoys. Sometimes, as political infiltrators or even invading armies, they were most unwelcome, but in pre-modern times it was impossible to keep them out when they were really determined to come in, and the concept of defined and fixed frontiers was not in any case part of traditional China's view of the world and her place in it. China's efforts to control her Inner Asian neighbours included attempts at peaceful acculturation (see **Tribute system**), pre-emptive military strikes (see Tang **Taizong**), and the creation of defensive walls. The latter expedient was favoured particularly during the Qin, Han, Northern Wei, Northern Qi, Sui and Ming periods. The Qin wall, reputed to have been built between 220 and 210 BC, stretched from modern Gansu province to the eastern end of the Liaodong peninsula, and is inseparably associated with the name of **Qin Shi Huangdi** and his harsh treatment of huge labour gangs, but it incorporated long sections of existing walls built by the states of Qin, Zhao and Yan and may never have formed a single continuous construction. The early Han added sections out as far as Yumen. Military encampments were sited inside the wall, and guard posts built into the watch towers at periodic intervals were defended with large mounted crossbows and could communicate with each other by means of chariots driven along the top of the wall. The cost of maintaining the wall as a defensive measure, and of repairing, rebuilding or adding to it when it fell into decay, was enormous and not always thought to be worthwhile. In the late twentieth century the government of the People's Republic has reconstructed parts of the Ming dynasty wall mainly as a tourist attraction, the most popular section being at Badaling to the north of **Beijing**. The wall has not been exhaustively excavated or mapped. Its total length even today is unknown but is likely to be between three and four thousand miles.

Arthur WALDRON, *The Great Wall of China, from History to Myth* (Cambridge University Press, 1990).

GREEN GANG *Qingbang* 青幫

Most powerful criminal organisation in early twentieth-century **Shanghai** with wealth and influence built on the basis of profits from opium, gambling and prostitution. It had connections with local and national politicians, possibly with **Sun Yixian** and certainly with **Jiang Jieshi**. The Green Gang was used in the 1920s to break strikes and destabilise the newly evolving trades unions. In April 1927, members of the organisation, calling themselves the Society for Common Progress, ran a force of armed men which attacked trades unions in the prelude to the **Shanghai Coup**. After the expulsion of the CCP from the city, the Green Gang set up their own pro-GMD unions.

GREEN STANDARD ARMY

Chinese provincial troops serving the Manchu Qing dynasty as distinct from the Manchu and Mongol banners. They had early successes in their suppression of the **Three Feudatories Revolt**, but by the end of the nineteenth century, they were regarded as an effete and ineffective force incapable of anything but local policing. In 1898, the government in Beijing ordered that the force, which then consisted of 400–500,000 troops, be disbanded so that the funding could be used to train Western-style armies, but local officials were unwilling to do so.

GU CHENG 顧城 (1956–1993)

One of the best known of the 'misty' or ***menglong*** poets who caused a sensation when he brutally murdered his wife and committed suicide. Gu Cheng was the son of a well-known writer Gu Gong 顧工 (b. 1927) and began to write poetry when he was very young. He followed his father to five years' exile in Shandong in 1969 during the **Cultural Revolution** where he continued writing. One of his best known poems and one which is regarded as typifying the *menglong* genre, *Shengming huanxiang qu* 生命幻想曲 'Life Fantasia', was written during this period when he was just 15 years old. His early poetry, which is inspired by nature, accessible, optimistic and fairy-tale like, made him one of the most popular of the *menglong* poets. He was deeply affected by his experiences in the Cultural Revolution and inspired to write works which captured the mood of that time like the two-line *Yi dai ren* 一代人 'A Generation' ('The dark night has given me black eyes, yet I use them to search for the light'). However, his later work became introverted and self-absorbed and in the end increasingly disturbed and violent.

GU CHENG, *Selected Poems – Gu Cheng,* trans. and ed. Sean Golden and Chu Chiyu (Hong Kong: Chinese University Press, 1990).

GU JIEGANG 顧頡剛 (1893–1980)

Modern Chinese historian. Gu Jiegang came from a scholarly family in Suzhou. He was initially family educated, then entered Beijing University (*Beida*) preparatory department in 1913, followed by the Philosophy Department in 1916, from where he graduated in 1920. After graduation he worked initially in the library at *Beida* before going to Shanghai where, as an editor at the Commercial Press, he jointly edited textbooks on Chinese history and the modern language (*guoyu*). He returned to *Beida* in 1924 to edit *Guo xue ji kan* 國學季刊 'Chinese Civilization Quarterly', and *Ge yao zhou kan* 歌謠周刊 'Folk Song Weekly'. From 1926 onwards he was employed successively at a number of universities; after 1949 he was a researcher at the Historical Research Institute of the Chinese Academy of Sciences, and later Social Sciences.

Gu Jiegang devoted himself to rediscovering China's past through building on the work of Qing scholars and using modern Western methodology. Qing *kao zheng* 考證 'evidential research methods' had already cast doubt on the authenticity of classical texts and early Qing scholars like **Gu Yanwu** had used non-textual evidence in their research. Gu Jiegang was particularly indebted to Yao Jiheng姚際恆 (1647–1715), author of a work critical of scholarship on the ***Shijing***, and Cui Shu 崔述(1740–1816), author of an influential evidential research work, the *Kaoxinlu* 考信錄. Contemporaries who particularly influenced him included **Hu Shi**, who studied Western philosophy and research methodology at Columbia University, and **Wang Guowei** 王國維, who pioneered the use of oracle bones and bamboo strip documents as historical evidence. Gu Jiegang began his historical career early: by 1916 he had produced in draft his *Qingdai zhushu kao* 清代著述考 'Study of Qing Dynasty Works'. In 1923, in an exchange of letters with Qian Xuantong 錢玄同, he propounded the view that Chinese ancient history had been built up layer by layer, i.e. he was putting forward the historical truism that when a record becomes more detailed the further it is from the event, there is *prima facie* evidence of myth-making. He pointed out that the geographical boundaries attributed to the time of the early mythical emperors were implausibly those of the Warring States period. This sparked a lively debate; articles by Gu and others from this debate were published in *Gu shi bian* 古史辨 'Verifying Ancient History' and he was recognised as founder of the *Gu shi bian* school of historical research. By casting doubt on the view that the Chinese people shared a common ancestry traceable back to the Yellow Emperor, Gu Jiegang's research had controversial and far-reaching implications. He was a prolific writers and has left numerous works on early history, historical geography, legends and folk songs.

Lawrence A. SCHNEIDER, *Ku Chieh-kang and China's New History: Nationalism and the Quest for an Alternative Tradition* (Berkeley: University of California Press, 1971).

GU KAIZHI 顧愷之 (c. 348–c.409)

Painter of the Eastern Jin period. Born in Wuxi, Jiangsu province, Gu Kaizhi was one of the earliest important painters of antiquity known by name. Although a versatile artist, he is known primarily as a figure painter and the source of one of the two principal styles of figure painting (the source of the other being **Wu Daozi**). By the ninth century, Gu's style was characterised as exhibiting fine continuous line, with a sensitive rendering of character. Some of his recorded works were wall paintings and none of his originals survive. The most famous painting attributed to him is a handscroll entitled *The Admonitions of the Court Instructress (Nüshi zhentu)* 女史箴圖, of which a Tang copy is in the British Museum. Only three of his articles on painting survive, in which he suggests a number of concepts which have been in Chinese painting, such as "using forms to depict the spirit".

CHEN Shih-hsiang, *Biography of Ku K'ai-chih* (Berkeley : University of California Press, 1953); M. SULLIVAN, *The Birth of Landscape Painting in China* (London: Routledge Kegan Paul, 1962); M. LOEHER, *The Great Painters of China* (Phaidon, 1980).

GULIANG ZHUAN see ***SPRING AND AUTUMN ANNALS***

GU YANWU 顧炎武 (1613–1682)

Philosopher, philologist and historian; Ming loyalist who refused to serve the Qing dynasty. He came from Kunshan 昆山 in Jiangsu and in his youth was concerned by the developing political crisis. At the age of 24 *sui* he joined the **Fushe,** a reformist society dedicated to cleaning up political corruption. At the age of 27 *sui* he gave up thoughts of taking the civil service examinations and began a study of China's geography and natural resources which resulted in his *Tianxia junguo libing shu* 天下郡國利病書 'Study of the advantages and disadvantages of the regions of the Empire'. This was an attempt to take scholarship back to serving practical purposes, *jingshi zhiyong* 經世致用. He came to the conclusion that the cause of China's decline in the Ming was the obsession with cosmological speculation, and the neglect of the true meaning of the classics. In his words: "What the ancients called study of principle, was study of the classics; what people now call study of principle, is study of Chan Buddhism" (*Gu zhi suo wei li xue, jing xue ye; jin zhi suo wei li xue, chan xue ye*. 古之所謂理學, 經學也, 今之所謂理學, 禪學也). His solution was to get back to the true meaning of the classics by studying early commentaries; this gave rise to *Hanxue* 漢學, the movement which dominated Qing scholarship. Its methodology was *kaozheng* 考證, painstaking philological research. In the end, rather than rediscovering the true classics, as Gu Yanwu hoped, this process ended up turning them from repositories of eternal truths into, as Zhang Xuecheng put it, works of history.

After the Manchu invasion, Gu Yanwu held a post in the Board of War at the Southern Ming court in Nanjing. He organised a resistance force in Suzhou but was defeated and forced to flee. He continued to work for the Ming cause for ten years or so before giving up, leaving home, in 1657, and travelling around the north. When the Qing arranged to compile the history of the Ming 明史 he was encouraged to participate but adamantly refused. He spent the rest of his life travelling and writing, producing his *Rizhi lu* 日知錄 'Record of daily insights' and works on the classics, philology, and geography, and some poems and essays (the latter, collected as *Tinglin shiwen ji* 亭林詩文集, was included in the *Sibu congkan*, the major modern reprint of classical texts). Gu Yanwu's empirical scholarship and his anti-Manchuism endeared him to late nineteenth-century radicals for whom he became a cult figure.

Willard J. PETERSON, "The Life of Ku Yen-wu (1613–1682)", *Harvard Journal of Asiatic Studies*, no. 28 (1968), pp.114–56 and no. 29 (1969), pp. 201–47.

GUAN HANQING 關漢卿 (c.1240–c.1320)

Leading dramatist of the Yuan Dynasty with sixty-three plays attributed to him. In the 1330 *Register of Ghosts* (a record of Yuan poets and dramatists) he is said to have been a native of Dadu (present-day **Beijing**). Much of his work is no longer extant although he was one of the most prolific writers of the period. The wide range of topics covered by Guan, such as the justice system, courtship and **marriage**, and historical incidents, include all aspects of tragedy, comedy and satire. Many plays focus on female protagonists who embody virtue, morality, integrity, intelligence and courage, traits which are not usually found in the traditional Chinese image of women. His most famous play in the *zaju* style (see **drama**) is *Dou E yuan* 竇娥冤 'Injustice to Dou E'.

SHIH Chung-wen, *Injustice to Tou O* (Cambridge University Press, 1972); YANG Hsien-i and Gladys YANG, *Selected Plays of Kuan Han-ch'ing* (Beijing: Foreign Languages Press, 1958).

GUAN ZHONG 管仲 (d.645 BC)

Minister to **Huan, Duke of Qi** who is credited with making Qi the most powerful state of its time. Though the Duke acquired the title of *ba* 霸, **hegemon**, **Confucius** attributed much of his success to Guan Zhong, who clearly had administrative expertise. The book of *Guanzi*, though bearing his name, was probably compiled by **Liu Xiang** and is a miscellany of Warring States thought that shows the influence of both **Legalism** and **Daoism**.

W. Allyn RICKETT, *Guanzi: Political, Economic and Philosophical Essays from Early China* (Princeton University Press, 1985).

GUANDONG ARMY *Guandong jun* 關東軍 (Japanese *Kantōgun*)

Army that grew out of the **Guandong Leased Territory**. Between 1906 and 1919, the governor-general of the territory was concurrently the commanding officer of the military based there. In 1919, a separate Guandong Army Command was created to defend the territory and Japanese railway interests throughout Manchuria. In 1928 its headquarters were moved from Port Arthur to Shenyang (Mukden) and it became effectively an independent military force with very little control exerted over it by the government in Tokyo. It was the Guandong Army under Colonels Ishiwara and Itagaki that precipitated the crisis of 1931 which provided the excuse for the Japanese occupation of Manchuria and the creation of the state of **Manzhouguo**.

GUANDONG 關東 LEASED TERRITORY

The name given in 1906 by the Japanese (*Kantō* in Japanese) to the southern part of the **Liaodong** peninsula including Dairen and Port Arthur, which Japan acquired as part of the peace settlement that followed the **Russo-Japanese War**. It means "east of the pass", that is the **Shanhaiguan** pass, and should not be confused with **Guangdong** province.

GUANGDONG 廣東

China's southernmost province until Hainan was created a separate administration. The name Canton, applied to the administrative capital city of the province, Guangzhou 廣州, is probably derived from the name of the province.

GUANGMING DAILY *Guangming ribao* 光明日報
The second most important national daily newspaper in the PRC after ***People's Daily*.** It began publishing on June 16 1949 in Beijing and is the newspaper aimed at scientists, engineers, academics, teachers and other educated Chinese.

GUANGXI ZHUANG AUTONOMOUS REGION *Guangxi Zhuangzu zizhiqu* 廣西壯族自治區
Provincial level administrative unit in south-western China named after the Zhuang ethnic minority, created an **autonomous region** on March 5 1958.

GUANGXU 光緒 QING EMPEROR (1871–1908, r. 1875–1908)
Penultimate emperor of the Manchu Qing dynasty. His personal name was Zaitian and he was the son of Prince Jun and of the sister of the Empress Dowager, **Cixi.** When the Tongzhi emperor died on January 12 1875, at the age of only 18 and with no children, Cixi formally adopted Zaitian, the late emperor's cousin, as her son and he was installed as the Guangxu emperor at the age of 4 *sui,* with Cixi and Ci'an acting jointly as regents. He announced his intention to rule in his own right in 1886 when he attained majority but was never able to exercise real power. This was shown clearly in the **Hundred Days Reform** when he supported Kang Youwei and the reformers but was thwarted by Cixi and court conservatives. He died on November 14 1908, aged 37, one day before the death of Cixi.

GUANGZHOU 廣州 (CANTON)
The most important city and seaport in southern China, its name was formerly written Canton in the Post Office system of romanisation. The spoken language of Guangzhou, Cantonese, is the *lingua franca* of many Chinese communities throughout the world. See also **Canton System, Chinese Language.**

GUANGZHOU COMMUNE (1927)
Armed insurrection in Guangzhou city led by Ye Ting 葉挺, Zhang Tailei 張太雷 and other senior Communists. In spite of the failure of the **Autumn Harvest Uprising**, the CCP continued with its strategy of capturing towns. Taking advantage of a dispute between GMD military offficers, the rebels, including workers and Nationalist mutineers, seized control of the city and set up a Soviet Government on December 1. GMD forces counterattacked and the Commune collapsed on December 13. The CCP strategy of working in the cities foundered with it and the peasants became the main focus of their work. See also **Shanghai Coup** and **Jiangxi Soviet**.

GUANGZHOU COUP (1926)
The bloodless coup d'etat by which **Jiang Jieshi** established himself as leader of the Guomindang. Since the death of its founding leader, **Sun Yixian** on March 12 1925, the leadership of the Nationalists had been in disarray, There were claimants to the succession from both the right and left wing of the **Guomindang**, **Hu Hanmin** and **Wang Jingwei** respectively. Jiang Jieshi as director of the **Huangpu Military Academy** was the most important military leader of the Nationalists. On March 20 1926, Jiang ordered the arrest of a gunboat, the

Zhongshan, and took into custody the crew of fifty and the captain, all of whom were members of the CCP, on the assumption that a strike against the GMD was imminent. He declared martial law in Guangzhou and on March 24 expelled all his Soviet advisers. Left-wing GMD members resigned, including Wang Jingwei who left China for France, and Jiang was in effective control of the party and able to launch the **Northern Expedition** to re-unify China.

GUANGZHOU-HONG KONG GENERAL STRIKE (1925)
Strike and boycott of British goods that began in the Shamian area of Hong Kong on June 19 1925 and spread up the Pearl River to Guangzhou on June 21. The strike, which involved as many as 200,000 people, was part of a nationwide wave of protests at the killing of demonstrators in the **May Thirtieth Incident** in Shanghai. When dozens of demonstrators were killed by French and British troops on June 23, disturbances became more widespread. A strike committee was established in Guangzhou on July 6 and received some backing from the Nationalist authorities in the city. The strike persisted for nearly two years.

GUANYIN 觀音 (Sanskrit *Avalokitesvara*)
The most popular Bodhisattva in China. Guanyin was originally represented as a male figure in Indian and early Chinese Buddhism. From the Song period, the giving and saving aspects of Guanyin became the attributes of a gracious female deity who was widely worshipped as the "Goddess of Mercy" or simply as *Pusa* 菩薩 (Bodhisattva). She was the comforter to suffering humanity, the giver of children, the preserver from peril of all those who call upon her name.

Guanyin was usually depicted as holding an ambrosia bottle or the lotus flower, though in later times she was also represented with a fish basket or holding a baby. She was believed to be resident at Putuoshan 普陀山, a small island off the coast of Zhejiang.

GUANZHONG 關中 'Within the Pass'
Name given in classical times to the region upstream of the Hangu Pass and along the Wei River valley into the metropolitan area of **Chang'an** (in modern times, to the west of the Sanmen Gorge and into southern Shaanxi province). The land to the east of the Pass was less commonly referred to as Guanwai 關外 'Outside the Pass'.

GUILDS *Hang* 行
Guilds of merchants originated in the markets of the Tang dynasty and evolved into licensed trading firms, becoming important to the commercial economy in the Song and Ming dynasties. Merchants from one region trading in another area established guild halls *huiguan* 會館 for the support of their fellow provincials, provided lodgings and introductions to local traders, arranged for finance and transport and guaranteed the transactions of their members. See also **Huizhou Merchants.**

GUNPOWDER
Known in China as early as the Six Dynasties period and referred to in a Daoist text of the ninth century, its use was limited to the making of fireworks until the tenth century, when it was developed as a means of projecting incendiary devices. In the

eleventh century its military application extended to the making of grenades and bombs, and the forerunner of the modern barrel gun appeared in the Song defence against the **Jurchen** invaders around 1120. Both defenders and attackers used gunpowder in the Mongol conquest of China. Thereafter its military use was forgotten until **Jesuit** missionaries taught the late Ming defenders to cast cannon for use against the Manchus. Again, however, the long-term significance of firearms went unrecognised, and the antiquated nature of Chinese weaponry contributed to the ease of the British victories in the First Anglo-Chinese War of 1839–42. See **Opium Wars.**

GUO MORUO 郭沫若 (1892–1978)

Leading left-wing literary and political figure. Born Guo Kaizhen 郭開貞 Into a landlord-merchant family of Leshan, Sichuan, he initially had a traditional education and, under the influence of his mother, developed a love of Tang poetry. Encouraged by his elder brother, he began to read **Yan Fu**'s translation of works on Western throught and Lin Shu's translations of Western literature. Guo went to Japan in 1913 and spend most of the next ten years there studying medicine but becoming more and more involved in the new literature which resulted from the **New Culture Movement**. Influenced by Tagore and Whitman, Guo Moruo began to compose lyrical free verse 'new' poetry and had poems published from 1919. Some of his best known poems such as *Fenghuang niepan* 鳳凰涅盤 "Phoenix nirvana", *Diqiu, wode muqin!* 地球, 我的母親 "Earth, my mother!" and *Tiangou* 天狗 "Dog of Heaven" were included in the collection *Nüshen* 女神 *Goddesses* published in August 1921, a work which had considerable influence on the development of new poetry. In July 1921 with **Yu Dafu** and others he started the *Chuangzao she* 創造社 Creation Society with its quarterly magazine, *Chuangzao jikan* 創造季刊, to promote romanticism in literature, in opposition to the Literary Research Society (see **Mao Dun**) with its more realistic and utilitarian approach. In 1924 Guo became a convinced Marxist, returned to China, was even more politicized after the **May 30th Incident** and held a propaganda post in the National Revolutionary Army during the **Northern Expedition**. However, as a leading communist, Guo was forced to flee to escape **Jiang Jieshi**'s bloody purge of left-wingers in April 1927. He spent the next ten years in Japan studying and writing on ancient Chinese history and palaeography. He returned in 1937 to take part in the national defence literature movement, producing anti-Japanese propaganda. He spent most of the war in Chongqing and his writings at this period included several patriotic historical plays, the best known of which is ***Qu Yuan*** 屈原, on the Warring States minister of Chu. After 1949 Guo held a number of important posts in the P.R.C. central government including vice-premier, chairman of the Commission of Culture and Education, president of Academia Sinica and a member of the Central Committee of the 9th, 10th and 11th Party congresses.

GUO MORUO, *Selected Works of Guo Moruo: Five Historical Plays* (Beijing: Foreign Languages Press, 1984); David Tod ROY, Kuo Mo-jo: *The Early Years* (Harvard University Press, 1971).

GUO XI 郭熙 (c.1020–90)

Leading landscape artist, member of the **Academy of Painting** and commentator on the aesthetics of **landscape painting**. His style was in the tradition of the large-scale works of **Fan Kuan** and others but evolved into softer, more abstract design in his later career and was much admired and imitated, especially in **Korea**. He described the need for the artist to be able to convey the mood of a scene under varying weather and seasonal conditions, and taught the viewer that he should not simply survey the entire vista with a quick, all-embracing glance, but mentally enter it, absorb its atmosphere, travel through it, rest and even stay in it.

GUOMINDANG 國民黨 (GMD, formerly Kuomintang, or KMT)
Nationalist party and, with the **Chinese Communist Party**, one of the two leading political forces in twentieth century China. The original GMD was created by **Sun Yixian** and Song Jiaoyuan in 1911 from members of the **Tongmenghui** and other revolutionary organisations, but it and allied parties were outlawed by **Yuan Shikai** in 1913. In 1923, with support from the Comintern adviser, Mikhail **Borodin**, Sun began to rebuild the Guomindang, using the Leninist democratic centralist model employed so effectively by the Communist Party of the Soviet Union. The ideological basis of the party, however, was not Marxism-Leninism, but Sun's published lectures on The **Three People's Principles** *Sanmin zhuyi* 三民主義. Individual members of the CCP were permitted to join the GMD as part of the **United Front** policy. The GMD established the **Huangpu (Whampoa) Military Academy** in 1924 to provide the officer corps of the army they realised was necessary to take control of the whole of China. This army, the National Revolutionary Army, was the backbone of the **Northern Expedition** which the GMD launched in 1926. The party broke with the CCP in 1927 after the **Shanghai Coup** and formed the National Government based in Nanjing from 1928 until the Japanese invasion of 1937 when they were forced out and moved to Chongqing. After losing the **Civil War** to the CCP, the GMD leadership fled to **Taiwan** where the party ruled virtually unchallenged as the continuation of the Republic of China until the 1990s when native Taiwanese opposition parties began to oppose it.
George T. YU, *Party Politics in Republican China: the Kuomintang, 1912–1924* (Berkeley: University of California Press, 1966).

GUQIN see **MUSICAL INSTRUMENTS**

GUWEN 古文 Ancient script
Refers originally to early script existing before standardisation by the Qin but by extension to the old text version of the **Classics** (as opposed to *jinwen* 今文**New Text** versions) and later to a plain classical style of writing rather than the ornate parallel prose style. As a result of the **burning of the books** by the Qin the Classics were destroyed and had to be reconstituted from memory in the Han when they were written down in the new standardised script. Some years later old text versions appeared which had supposedly survived concealed in places like the walls of **Confucius**' old family home. Doubts were later expressed over the authenticity of some of the *guwen* texts and the old text ***Shangshu*** 尚書 'Book of History' was proved by Yan Ruoju 閻若璩 (1636–1704) in the Qing to be a forgery. In the late Tang **Han Yu** and **Liu Zongyuan** 柳宗元 pioneered a movement away from the ornate *pianwen* 駢文 style of the Six Dynasties back to a *guwen* classical style which concentrated more on content than form. This movement can be seen as both political – a rejection of the elitist aristocratic form for a more accessible one – and

nationalistic – a reaffirmation of Confucian values in the face of Buddhist domination of the intellectual sphere. The *guwen* / *jinwen* schism re-emerged in the Qing as an historicist versus theologist debate in which *guwen* scholars saw the Classics as historical documents while *jinwen* scholars revered them as sacred texts.

Jerry NORMAN, *Chinese* (Cambridge University Press, 1988); Benjamin ELMAN, *From Philosophy to Philology: Intellectual and Social Aspects of Change in Late Imperial China* (Harvard University Press, 1984).

GYANTSE

Formerly **Tibet**'s third town, an important crossroads between Tibet, India, Nepal and Bhutan, and a centre for the wool trade. After the battle in January 1904 when the British expedition commanded by Colonel Francis Younghusband killed six hundred Tibetans it became the site of a British trade mission. Its cosmopolitan nature is commemorated in its "Golden Pagoda", Kumbun. Built in 1427 this is the largest stupa in Tibet and the best example of Nepalese Newari art in the world. Its murals show Chinese as well as Nepalese influence and are amongst the finest surviving early Tibetan wall paintings.

HAIGUO TUZHI see **WEI YUAN**

HAI RUI 海瑞 (1513–1587)

Minor official who criticised the Jiajing emperor for neglecting the government of the country while absorbed in the search for longevity through Daoist ceremonies. He was sent to prison and tortured but was released after the death of the emperor and was eventually given a senior post in the Censorate. Hai Rui became the symbol of the incorruptible official.

***HAI RUI DISMISSED FROM OFFICE Hai Rui baguan* 海瑞罷官**

Play written by the dramatist, historian and deputy mayor of Beijing, **Wu Han,** published in the January 1961 edition of *Beijing Literature and Art (Beijing wenyi* 北京文藝*)* and as a book, with Wu Han's preface dated August 8, in November of the same year. **Hai Rui** is portrayed as the honest official not afraid to criticise his emperor. At the **Lushan Plenum** of 1959, **Peng Dehuai**, who clashed bitterly with Mao Zedong over the **Great Leap Forward**, is reported to have said that he was going to play the role of Hai Rui in the conference and when the play was published, the implied criticism of Mao was crystal clear. An attack on the play by **Yao Wenyuan** in the Shanghai daily *Wenhui bao* 文匯報 on November 10 1965 is generally regarded as the first intimation of the political struggles in the run-up to the **Cultural Revolution.**

HAILUFENG see **PENG PAI**

HAKKA *Kejia* 客家

Ethnic group, considered to be part of the **Han Chinese** family, living mainly in Guangxi and Guangdong in southern China, who probably migrated from the north some time during the twelfth century. Their language, which is closer to northern Mandarin than to southern tongues such as Cantonese and their customs, including the fact that they did not bind the feet of women, differentiate them from the other inhabitants of these provinces. Conflict between the Hakka and the *bendi* (often written *punti*) natives of Guangxi and Guangdong played an important part in the **Taiping Rebellion** and Hakkas have been prominent in twentieth century radical movements.

HAN CHINESE *Hanzu* 漢族

The ethnic designation of the majority of the population of China, approximately 94% of the total, leaving 6% designated as **National Minorities**. The use of this one term suggests far greater homogeneity than actually exists and neglects major differences of language and culture that exist between the regions of China. The name derives ultimately from the **Han dynasty** and it is interesting that Han Chinese from southern provinces often prefer to identify themselves as Tang people *Tang ren* 唐人, after the Tang dynasty.

HAN DYNASTY 漢朝 (206 BC – AD 221)

The first great imperial dynasty of Chinese history, founded by **Liu Bang** and divided into two halves (the Former, or Western, 206 BC – AD 9, capital at **Chang'an**; and the Later, or Eastern, AD 23–220, capital at **Luoyang**) by the interregnum of **Wang Mang**. It was a period to which peoples and rulers in subsequent times frequently looked back with nostalgia. Its achievements established patterns for future dynasties, especially with respect to political and legal institutions, social philosophy, and cultural and intellectual experiment and enquiry.

In 141 BC Emperor **Wudi** had dismissed officials maintaining Legalist positions and in 136 established erudite (*bo*) scholars to specialise in the Confucian **Five Classics**, but, although **Confucianism** was adopted as the state ideology, the nature of Han and subsequent government represented a mixture of both philosophies, a recognition of the value of firm law tempered by humanitarian considerations. Neither was **Daoism** without influence in court politics, for officials were not yet confident enough to reject any philosophy that offered a view on the working of the universe and the place of man in it. The perception of a connection between government, cosmology and religion was strong, and the intellectual search for a Heaven-sent pattern or rationale that would embrace history, economics, agriculture and a political order was concentrated by many scholars on numerological theories. Yet innovation could not be justified in its own right: it had to be legitimised by appeal to earlier precedent. The **burning of the books** by the First Emperor of the Qin dynasty (**Qin Shi Huangdi**) necessitated the writing or re-writing of works on almost every subject, from history to **divination**, law to science, **music** to family life. Though the professed aim of many authors and editors was to restore from memory ideas and books which had been destroyed, and which would now help to re-establish an earlier Golden Age, their own works inevitably reflected contemporary concepts and values, and the task of establishing standards for a unified empire on the basis of an idealized past far back in the early Zhou dynasty offered plenty of scope for debate, disagreement, and even deliberate falsification (see **Liu Xin**). Nevertheless education was recognized as essential to a civilized state, and scholars at the **Imperial Academy**, established in 124 BC, studied both Confucian and Daoist Classics. This was the age when bureaucratism became the hallmark of the Chinese state, and recognition of intellectual merit brought office and often financial reward. Feudalism had been abolished, but what has been termed "bureaucratic feudalism" continued to sustain a clearly stratified society in accordance with Confucian principle.

As the frontiers of the empire were pushed outwards across Central Asia as far as Samarkand, eastwards into the Korean peninsula (see **Lelang**), and southwards down into **Annam**, the Han Chinese had to come to terms with foreign practices and pressures (see **Xiongnu**), and as their taste for conquest and trade grew so did their understanding of economic forces become more sophisticated (see **Salt and Iron Debate**). But the expansionist successes between c.140 and c.90 brought challenges which they could not yet handle, and as the first century BC wore on court politics were characterised by the kind of factionalism that would mark many later periods of Chinese history (see **Aidi**).

The return of the house of Liu after the brief attempt by Wang Mang to implement his own interpretation of the ideal standards of the past provided for a period of Confucian-led consolidation rather than further innovation. No emperors of the post-restoration era showed the same degree of personal initiative as **Gaozu, Wendi** and **Wudi** before them, or as Wang Mang, and the conduct of government passed more into the hands of the politicians and their rivals. Internal and external trade flourished and as well as officials and descendants of the old nobility, merchants invested their conspicuous wealth in large estates. The Western Regions of modern Xinjiang remained costly and sometimes difficult to hold, but the Xiongnu were no longer the danger to the Han Empire that they had once been**. Buddhism** had already arrived with merchants from India and taken root, although its ideology did not yet begin to challenge those of Confucianism or popular Daoism. There was, however, a rising mood of rationalist doubt about many of the beliefs relating to Heaven, nature, man, and the afterlife which ranged from the esoteric to the escapist (see **Wang Chong**). Civil unrest linked to a popular religious movement (see **Yellow Turbans**) marked the beginning of the end of the dynasty in the later part of the second century, but its final collapse came as the result of a struggle for power at court between the Confucian literati, **eunuch** factions, imperial consorts hoping to advance the prospects of their own sons and clans, and provincial military commanders.

Emperors:

Former Han		**Later Han**	
Title	*Reigned*	*Title*	*Reigned*
Gaozu	202–195	Guang Wudi	25–57
Huidi	195–188	Mingdi	57–75
Empress **Lu**	188–180	Changdi	75–88
Wendi	180–157	Hedi	88–106
Jingdi	157–141	Shangdi	106–106
Wudi	141–87	Andi	106–185
Zhaodi	87–74	Shaodi	125–125
Xuandi	74–49	Shundi	125–144
Yuandi	49–33	Chongdi	144–145

Former Han		Later Han	
Title	*Reigned*	*Title*	*Reigned*
Chengdi	33–7	Zhidi	145–146
Aidi	7–1	Huandi	146–168
Pingdi	1 BC-AD 6	Lingdi	168–189
		Shaodi	189–189
[Wang Mang 9–23]		Xiandi	189–220

Source: M. LOEWE, *Divination, Mythology and Monarchy in Han China* (Cambridge University Press, 1994).

See also **Ban Chao, Ban Gu, Ban Zhao, Cao Cao, Dong Zhongshu, *Hanshu*, Helingeer, Jia Yi, Liu Sheng, Mawangdui, Sacrifices, Silk Road, Sima Qian.** H. BIELENSTEIN, *The Bureaucracy of Han Times* (Cambridge University Press, 1980); CH'Ü T'ung-tsu, *Han Social Structure* (University of Washington Press, 1972); Michael LOEWE, *Crisis and Conflict in Han China, 104 BC to AD 9* (George Allen and Unwin, 1974); Michele PIRAZZOLI-T'SERSTEVENS, *The Han Dynasty*, trans. Janet Seligman (New York: Rizzoli, 1982); WANG Zhongshu, *Han Civilisation*, trans. K.C. Chang (Yale University Press, 1982).

HAN FEIZI 韓非子 (?280–233 BC)
One of the most influential political thinkers whose ideas played a prominent part in the drive of Qin towards unification. He was a former associate of **Li Si**, whose Legalist convictions he shared after they had both studied under Xun Qing (see **Xunzi**). The book that bears his name, said to have been written for the ruler of the state of **Han**, is the most complete exposition of Legalist doctrine, and develops the ruthless efficiency of **Shang Yang's** reliance on impersonal, practical law. In 234 he was sent as an envoy to **Qin** and seems to have considered staying there out of admiration for the ruthless policies of King Zheng, but he was induced to take poison by Li Si, who perhaps saw him as a potential rival. See also **Legalism.**

HAN, KINGDOM
A new kingdom in the Han River valley created by **Xiang Yu** in 206 BC when he enfeoffed **Liu Bang** as its king. It comprised forty-one former counties incorporating former **Ba** and **Shu** territory, with its capital at Nanzheng. Liu was not content with this attempt to sideline his political ambitions, but after defeating Xiang and establishing his own capital at **Chang'an**, he retained the name Han as the title of his new dynasty. See also **Han Dynasty.**

HAN, STATE
The smallest of the three states, together with **Wei** and **Zhao**, into which **Jin** had broken up in 453 BC. To the South lay the volatile and threatening **Chu**, to the West the even more dangerous **Qin**, with which its relations in the third century were hostile. But though state loyalty was a developing concept in the late Warring States period, men of talent moved around freely and sold their services to the courts of rival leaders. Thus it was a man of Han, Zheng Guo 鄭國, who

was responsible for building the irrigation canal system for Qin which opened in 246 and helped transform the region to the North of **Xianyang**. However, because of the suspicion between the two states and the fear of fifth columnist activity he was at first suspected of ulterior motives, perhaps aimed at distracting Qin attention and military labour away from Han. According to the ***Shiji*** it was this fear that prompted Qin to consider expelling aliens in 237, a move that threatened both **Li Si** and **Lü Buwei.** Perhaps its most famous politician was **Han Feizi**, a member of its ruling house who had espoused and developed Legalist political philosophy. He too seems to have been on the brink of changing sides when he died in Qin. Han surrendered to Qin in 230 BC.

HAN YU 韓愈 (768–824)

Official and scholar known for his outspoken support for traditional literary and philosophical values and one of the foremost scholars of the mid-Tang period. Though no mean poet, he was principally a master of the ***guwen*** style of classical prose writing, which laid stress on purity, clarity, and simplicity. To Han it also reflected ancient Confucian values which were being neglected in an age when **Buddhism** appeared triumphant. A memorial in protest against Emperor **Xuanzong**'s patronage of the foreign religion led to his exile for the second time, but his determination to re-emphasize the values of the ancient Chinese philosophy played a part in the birth of **Neo-Confucianism**. He refuted **Daoism** as well as Buddhism, and laid emphasis on the revival of the humanistic Confucian Way (***Dao***). As a one-time teacher himself at the **Imperial Academy** Han emphasized the role of the teacher in passing on the understanding and practice of the Way. See also **Li Ao, Liu Zongyuan.**

C. HARTMAN, *Han Yu and the T'ang Search for Unity* (Princeton University Press, 1986).

HANGZHOU 杭州

City in Zhejiang province, located at the lower reach of the Qiantang river and the southern end of the Grand Canal. Hangzhou was one of China's ancient capitals. The city had different names in its history: known as Xifu 西府 during the Five Dynasties period when it was the capital of the state of Wuyue; as Qiantang 錢塘 during the Tang dynasty; and as Linan 臨安 when it became the the capital of the Southern Song dynasty in 1138. To the exiled Song rulers it was their Xingzai ("temporary halt"), from which **Marco Polo**'s transliteration of Quinsai was derived. At the western side of the city is the West Lake, a famous scenic resort, known for its elegance and tranquillity for pleasure-seeking house- and boat-parties and for the artistic and literary study groups that congregated there, especially in the late Ming and Qing periods. Many sites in and around the lake district are associated with ancient fairy tales which have inspired many poets and playwrights. Hangzhou has been a centre of the silk industry and is known for its traditional specialities such as Dragon Well tea. Its economy, which also included shipbuilding, boomed during the Song and Yuan periods, when its cosmopolitan population included a community of Genoese merchants. It is estimated to have had a population of two million within its walls and perhaps the same number again outside. It declined after the sixteenth century, though it continued to be attractive as a tourist and cultural centre with its canals, bridges, and **gardens**. The **Grand Canal** starts from Hangzhou and was the main waterway linking the city with other regions up to Beijing, making the city an important trading centre.

L.C. JOHNSON, ed., *Cities of Jiangnan in Late Imperial China* (New York: State University of New York Press, 1993).

HANLIN ACADEMY *Hanlin yuan* 翰林院

Established in 725 by the Tang emperor **Xuanzong** in the Daming Gong (see **Chang'an**) as a meeting place for the most intellectual writers, artists, religious, and astrologers in the land, it spawned a subsidiary but more powerful group of literati in the Hanshi Yuan "Academy of Scholars", established in 738, who assisted the **Son of Heaven** in the preparation of state documents. It retained this vital function within the **Inner Court** until the Qing dynasty. In the Song dynasty it was responsible for the recruitment and training of court artists to the **Academy of Painting**. See also **Academies, Imperial Academy**

F.A. BISCHOFF, *Le Foret des Pinceaux* (Paris, 1964); A.Y.C. LUI *The Hanlin Academy 1644–1850* (Hamden, Connecticut: Archon Books, 1981).

HANSHU* 漢書 *Book of Han

Also known as the *Qian Han Shu* 前漢書, 'History of the Former Han Dynasty', by **Ban Gu** of the Eastern Han dynasty. *Hanshu* is the first work on dynastic history, presented in a biographic series and with a total of 100 sections in 120 *juan*.

This work was started by Ban Gu's father **Ban Biao** who collected historical material in writing a sequel of ***Shiji***, which, after Ban Gu took over Ban Biao's unfinished work, formed a part of *Hanshu*. It took over twenty years for Ban Gu to write up the work of *Hanshu*. He died however before the work was fully completed. His sister **Ban Zhao** and Ma Xu 馬續 were then asked by Emperor **Hedi** to sort out the remaining work, including eight lists, such as the list recording the changes in the system of official positions, and the annal of astronomy.

Hanshu is similar to *Shiji* in style, with only a small number of differences in their approaches, e.g. the format of *shu* 書, book, in *Shiji* was changed to *zhi* 志, annal, in *Hanshu*; a main category in *Shiji*, *shijia* 世家, the sections on aristocratic families, was dropped in *Hanshu* and the materials were included into *liezhuan* 列傳, biographies. Four new categories: the annals of penal codes, the **five elements**, geology and arts were established in *Hanshu*, providing a standard model for later works on dynastic history.

W.G. BEASLEY and E.G. PULLEYBLANK eds., *Historians of China and Japan* (Oxford University Press, 1961); H. DUBS, *The History of the Former Han Dynasty*, 3 vols., (Baltimore: Waverly Press, 1938–1955); Burton WATSON, *Courtier and Commoner in Ancient China: Selections from the "History of the Former Han" by Pan Ku* (Columbia University Press, 1974).

***HANYU PINYIN* 漢語拼音**

System for romanising the **Chinese language** developed in the 1950s in the PRC. It is based on a pre-war system, *Ladinghua* 拉丁話, 'Latin-language', and has the merits of simple spelling and none of the diacritical marks and apostrophes that bedevil the Wade-Giles system. Detractors claim that pronunciation values attached to certain letters have no relationship with their English equivalents (although they have in Eastern European languages). *Pinyin* is the official romanisation in the PRC, although it is not widely understood. It is unpopular in Taiwan. See also **Romanisation.**

HART, ROBERT (1835–1911)
Inspector-General of the Chinese **Imperial Maritime Customs** from 1863 and head of the Imperial Postal Service from 1896 until 1908.
Katharine F. BRUNER, John K. FAIRBANK and Richard J. SMITH, eds., *Entering China's Service: Robert Hart's Journals, 1854–1863* (Council on East Asian Studies, Harvard University, 1986); Richard J. SMITH, John K. FAIRBANK and Katharine F. BRUNER, eds., *Robert Hart and China's Early Modernization: Robert Hart's Journals, 1863–1866* (Harvard University Press, 1991).

HE LONG 賀龍 (1896–1969)
General of the Workers and Peasant Red Army who commanded the 20th Army before and during the **Long March** and a division which fought the Japanese in Shanxi. After 1949, he served in the CCP's Military Affairs Commission.

HE YINGQIN 何應欽 (1890–1987)
Instructor at the **Huangpu Military Academy** in the 1930s and commander of the troops ranged against the CCP in the second **Encirclement Campaign** in 1931. As Minister of War in the Nanjing Government, he and Umetsu Yoshijiro, the Japanese Commander, signed the 1935 He-Umetsu agreement under which the Chinese agreed to withdraw armies and GMD organisations from Hebei. In 1950, he joined the Central Advisory Committee of the GMD, by then relocated to Taiwan and became chairman of the Strategic Advisory Committee.

HE-UMETSU AGREEMENT see **HE YINGQIN**

HEAVEN see **SHANGDI**

HEAVEN AND EARTH SOCIETY *Tiandi hui* 天地會
Anti-Qing Ming loyalist secret society responsible for uprisings in 1786–9 and later in 1849–50 when it became part of the **Taiping Rebellion**. Its name derives from the saying that "heaven should be worshipped as the father and the earth as the mother" *bai tian wei fu, bai di wei mu* 拜天爲父, 拜地爲母. It was also known as the **Triad** *sandianhui* 三點會 or *sanhehui* 三和會 and sometimes as the *Hongmen* 洪門 after the **Hongwu** reign name of the first Ming emperor. Its many branches include the **Small Sword** and the **Elder Brother** societies. After the suppression of the **Taiping Rebellion**, the society persisted as an underground organisation and was involved in the revolutionary movements that continued into the twentieth century.

HEAVENLY STEMS AND EARTHLY BRANCHES
Sexagenary system used for counting years in traditional China. Each year within a sixty-year cycle was named with a bisyllabic combination of one of ten celestial stems and one of twelve earthly branches. Thus, years 1–10 of a cycle

would be designated A1, B2, C3 and so on to J10. Year 11 would be A11, 12 would be B12, 13 C1, and 14 D2. There was no means of distinguishing one cycle from another, so identification of a date in a text using this system depends on the reader knowing from context which century is being referred to. See also **Reign periods, Calendar, *Ganzhi*.**

HEDIN, SVEN (1865–1952)

Swedish explorer whose expeditions between 1895 and 1926 revealed the lost cities of the **Silk Road** around the Taklamakan Desert and evidence for the life of Chinese military garrisons in mediaeval Central Asia.

Sven HEDIN, *My Life as an Explorer* (Cassell and Co., 1926).

HEGEMONS *Ba* 霸

The most powerful leaders of the feudal states in the Spring and Autumn period, during whose rule their own states acted as magnets around which less important states rallied. In particular they headed leagues of northern states against the southern threat from **Chu**, for which the Zhou king granted the title *ba* to Dukes **Huan of Qi** and Wen of **Jin**. However, whilst they theoretically acknowledged Zhou supremacy, they were later denounced by **Mencius** as the very epitome of self-centred, power-hungry autocrats whose policies were the antithesis of true **kingship**. Traditional Chinese writers refer to five hegemons, but are not always consistent in defining them. The most common list comprises Duke Huan of Qi (685–643 BC)(see **Guan Zhong**), Duke Mu of Qin (659–621 BC), Duke Xiang of Song (650–637 BC), Duke Wen of Jin (635–628 BC) and King Zhuang of Chu (631–591 BC).

HELINGEER, Inner Mongolia

The location of an impressive brick-built Han tomb dating from the mid-second century AD, nearly twenty metres in length and up to four metres high. It comprises five chambers with vaulted ceilings, representing a meeting room, the ritual hall, the private quarters, a kitchen and the stables. The walls are richly painted with scenes depicting the estate of the deceased, showing members of the nobility, huntsmen, farmers, entertainers, soldiers, and servants, and providing valuable information on architectural styles.

HELL

The underworld based on the Buddhist concept of *Naraka*, which was governed by the judge and ruler Yanluo 閻羅, or Yanwang 閻王, who was based on the Sanskrit *Yamaraja* in Buddhism. Under Yanluo there were demons who operated the punishment machines in Hell. All the souls of the dead who had committed crimes would be tortured in different ways in Hell. The suffering beings could only be delivered from the torments of Hell later by the Bodhisattva Dizang 地藏 (Sanskrit *Ksitigarbha*).

HEREDITARY OCCUPATIONS

Yuan dynasty system of occupational and status registration (first envisaged by **Guan Zhong**) designed to ensure the adequate provision of manpower concerned with activities essential to the economy and defence of the state. It was continued into the Ming period. Certain categories were very broad, such as *min* 民 (commoners), *ru* 儒 (scholars), *jiang* 匠 (craftsmen); others were more specific, such as *jun* 軍 (soldiers), *yan* 鹽 (salt workers), *kuang* 礦 (miners), *yi* 醫(doctors). The *jiang* category was sub-divided according to trade, e.g. carpenters, textile workers, ink makers. In 1381 the recognised statuses had been reduced to *min* (which also included Confucian scholars), *jiang* and *jun* and it is doubtful how consistently the system was recognised or applied after the fifteenth century. In the early Qing dynasty only the special status of salt worker still existed. See also **Military Farms.**

HEXAGRAMS see ***YIJING***

HIDEYOSHI (Toyotomi Hideyoshi, 1539–98)
One of Japan's greatest military leaders. After uniting the nation in 1590 he harboured ambitions of conquering China, and invaded **Korea** in 1592 with an army of 160,000. A Chinese army under Li Rusong helped to repel him but he returned in 1597, only to die the following year in the midst of the campaign. The cost of the Chinese support for its ally (the so-called *dong zheng* 東征, "eastern pacification") was great, both in economic terms and in terms of the doubt raised in the minds of Korean intellectuals about the value of their tributary relationship with China. See also **Tribute System.**

HIGHER PRODUCERS' COOPERATIVES
The stage of **collectivisation** that followed the **Mutual Aid Teams Agricultural Producers' Cooperatives** . HPCs appeared in 1956 and 1957 and were amalgamations of APCs. No income derived from land ownership was payable as the land was decreed communally owned. In 1958 the HPCs were themselves consolidated into People's **Communes.**

HIGH TIDE OF SOCIALISM IN THE COUNTRYSIDE *Nongcun shehuizhuyi gaochao*. 農村社會主義高潮
The speeding up of the creation of **Agricultural Producers' Cooperatives** in 1955. See also **Collectivisation, Great Leap Forward.**

HONG KONG *Xianggang* 香港
British Crown Colony returned to Chinese rule on July 1 1997. Strictly speaking, Hong Kong is the name of just the island acquired by the British Crown under the terms of the **Treaty of Nanjing** in 1842, but it is commonly used to refer to the whole of the colony, including Kowloon (Jiulong 九龍), which was handed over after the Convention of Beijing, the New Territories to the north of Kowloon, which were leased to Britain for 99 years on June 9 1898, and the many outlying islands. The colony developed rapidly as a trading and manufacturing centre. It was also a safe haven for anti-Qing radicals, and, during the years of the Chinese Republic was the scene of early trades union and CCP activity which culminated in the **Guangzhou-Hong Kong** general strike of 1925 . Hong Kong was occupied by Japanese troops in 1941 and remained under Japanese control until 1945. When the CCP took control of China after the 1946–9 **Civil War**, many families,

particularly the wealthy and educated, fled to Hong Kong. During the 1950s and 1960s, the greater industrialisation of the colony and the collapse of the smallholder economy in the New Territories led to substantial emigration to Britain and elsewhere.

The PRC viewed the continued British control over Hong Kong as a major indignity, but negotiations on the future of the colony after the lease of the New Territories was due to run out in 1997 did not make real progress until September 1982, when the British Prime Minister, Margaret Thatcher, visited Beijing. Long negotiations ended with an agreement between Britain and China signed in December 1984 by the two Prime Ministers, Margaret Thatcher and **Zhao Ziyang**. The basis of the agreement was that Hong Kong would become a Special Administrative Region of China from July 1 1997, but would remain autonomous in certain areas, including the law, education, finance and the economy. Its capitalist system would be retained under a concept described as "one country, two systems", and China agreed that the social structure of Hong Kong could remain untouched for 50 years beyond the handover date. Initial optimism that the handover would proceed sucessfully and peacefully received a severe setback in June 1989 with the crushing of the **Democracy Movement**.

HONGLOUMENG 紅樓夢

Written by Cao Xueqin 曹雪芹 around 1760 and usually known in the West as *The Dream of the Red Chamber*, but also translated into English as *The Story of the Stone*, this is regarded as the greatest of the traditional Chinese novels. Its author was a member of a leading family which fell on hard times after a new emperor ordered the family property to be confiscated in 1728, when Cao Xueqin was a youth. The present version of the novel follows the form of earlier novels: it is divided into 120 chapters and includes typical storyteller features like introductory verses and remarks addressed to the audience. However, in content it marks a considerable advance: it is an intimate account based on the author's personal experience and, like modern novels, concentrates on psychological description of the characters rather than narrative of events. It chronicles the decay of a once great household as the highly cultured family members, victims of their own effeteness and of imperial whim, are powerless to stem the decline.

CAO Xueqin *The Story of the Stone* trans. David Hawkes and John Minford (Penguin Books, 1973 et seq. (total 5 volumes)); C.T. HSIA, *The Classic Chinese Novel: A Critical Introduction* (Columbia University Press, 1968).

HONG MERCHANTS

Owners of trading companies in Guangzhou authorised to do business with foreigners. They originated during the Ming period and became extremely wealthy and powerful under the Qing dynasty. They were organised into the **Cohong** in 1720.

HONG REN'GAN 洪仁玕

Relative and supporter of **Hong Xiuquan** who named him in 1859 as Prime Minister of the regime established after the **Taiping Rebellion**. Hong Ren'gan had lived in Hong Kong and wrote *A New Treatise on Aids to Administration* in which he proposed Western-style reforms including new transport, legal and banking systems. Although Hong Xiuquan is reported to have approved of the reforms, they were never seriously considered.

HONG XIUQUAN 洪秀全 (1814–1864)
Charismatic leader of the **Taiping Rebellion**. Hong was born into a village Hakka family in Guangdong province. Though his family was poor they educated him, but he failed the examination for the *shengyuan* degree twice. He travelled to Guangzhou to study and while there acquired a religious tract, *Good Words for Exhorting the Age,* from a Protestant missionary or one of his Chinese converts. Hong failed the examination again in 1837 and subsequently had some kind of major mental crisis. He dreamed that he had ascended to heaven where he had been provided with a new set of internal organs, was given a sword by an old bearded man and been commanded by a younger man, whom he called Elder Brother, to slay demons. Re-reading the Christian tracts after a fourth examination failure, he understood that he was the younger brother of Jesus Christ. He gathered around him a group of Hakkas in the God Worshippers Society and in the **Taiping Rebellion** was proclaimed Heavenly King. He either commmitted suicide or died of an illness in July 1864 as his Heavenly Kingdom was ended by attacking Qing troops.

HONGQI see ***RED FLAG***

HONGWU 洪武, MING EMPEROR (r. 1368–98)
The reign title of the first Ming Emperor, Zhu Yuanzhang 朱元璋 (1328–98), posthumously known as Ming Taizu. 明太祖. He came of peasant stock and forsook the life of a mendicant monk to play a leading part in the rebellious movement that drove the Mongols out of north China (see **Red Turbans**). His long reign was paradoxical. Despite his Buddhist background he espoused the role of Confucian Son of Heaven with determination. Despite encouraging local education and producing his own edition of the book of Mencius his rule was characterised by autocratic, often cruel measures directed as much against his own officials as against opponents. He created a strongly centralised government over which he exercised strict personal control, but allowed more local autonomy as a check on the excesses of his own regional authorities. He severely limited the international trading system which had prospered under the Mongols and re-emphasized the controls of the tribute system, yet the restoration of Han authority in China brought the return of respect from neighbours such as Korea.
John DARDESS, *Conquerors and Confucians: Aspects of Political Change in Late Yuan China* (New York: Columbia University Press, 1973; E.L. DREYER, *Early Ming China, a Political History 1355–1435* (Stanford University Press, 1982).

HSIEN-PEI see **XIANBI**

HU FENG 胡風 (1902–1985)
Literary theorist and target of a major rectification campaign in 1955. Hu Feng is the pen-name of Zhang Guangren who was born in Hubei. In 1923 he joined

the Communist Youth League. After studying foreign literature at Beijing and Qinghua universities from 1926 he went to Japan in 1929 and studied at Keio University. As a result of his communist activites, including links with leading left-wing Japanese writers, he was deported by the Japanese authorities in 1933. In Shanghai he held posts in the **League of Left-Wing Writers** and worked with **Lu Xun**. At this point he was involved in a series of disputes with **Zhou Yang** over the correct line on various literary issues (paradoxically, at this time the literary figures around Lu Xun sometimes appeared more doctrinaire than commissars like Zhou Yang). In 1937 he launched the literary magazine *Qiyue* 七月 'July'. After the Japanese invasion he moved to the Guomindang capital, Chongqing, where he was able to criticise the Communist Party's evolving art policies with relative impunity. For example, he made clear his opposition to Zhou Yang's, and Mao's, line on national forms; he argued that China's old 'folk' literature was feudal and writers should use modern forms which had evolved in the West. In 1945 Hu Feng started the magazine *Xiwang* 希望 'Hope' to promote the ideas of his group. The most controversial article, *Lun zhuguan* 論主觀 'On subjectivity' by Shu Wu 舒蕪, argued that art was a personal subjective vision, a reflection of reality as the artist sees it, not the artificial product of the refraction of art through Marxist theory, what the Party recognised as objective reality. Hu Feng was attacked in a 1948 campaign orchestrated by Zhou Yang but at that stage he was still beyond direct Party control. In the first five years of the PRC Hu was fairly circumspect in what he said, but sensing he could sway the leadership towards his viewpoint he wrote a report to the Central Committee in 1954 criticizing Zhou Yang and the literary commissars. However, he had misread the situation and from January 1955 brought upon himself the most bitter and widespread rectification campaign to date in which he was accused of counter-revolutionary activities. Hu was imprisoned in July 1955, reportedly until 1979 when he was exonerated and restored to an official position.

HU FENG, 'Realism Today' trans. Paul G. Pickowicz, in Kai-yu HSÜ ed. *Literature of the People's Republic of China* (Indiana University Press, 1980); Merle GOLDMAN, *Literary Dissent in Communist China* (Harvard University Press, 1967; Atheneum, 1971).

HU HANMIN 胡漢民 (1879–1936)

A 1911 revolutionary and subsequently a member of the **Guomindang** leadership. Hu Hanmin was born in present day Guangzhou 廣州, had a traditional education and became a *juren* 舉人, recommended man, at the age of 21 before leaving for Japan in 1902 to enrol on the education course of a college in Tokyo. He joined the ***Tongmenghui*** in 1905 and quickly became a leading figure, acting as secretary of the Secretariat and editor of the party organ, ***Minbao*** 民報 'People's Journal'. He was involved in a number of uprisings and after the revolution held posts in the provisional government, but was forced to flee to Japan with **Sun Yixian** after the unsuccessful Second Revolution against **Yuan Shikai**. He helped organize the **Zhonghua Geming Dang**,' Chinese Revolutionary Party', became head of its Political Bureau and editor of its newpaper, *Minguo* 民國, 'The Republic'. After returning to China in 1917 he was active in the Guomindang organization in Guangdong and Shanghai, where he took part in the founding of *Jianshe* 建設 'Construction', a magazine for which he wrote articles supporting the student **May Fourth Movement**. At the first Guomindang national congress in January 1924, Hu Hanmin was chosen as a member of the five-person presidium. After the death of Sun Yixian in March 1925, he emerged as one of the right-wingers opposing the alliance with the Communists and later collaborated with **Jiang Jieshi** in eliminating Communists from the Guomindang. He later split with Jiang, was involved in a power struggle, detained by Jiang and only released after his supporters set up in Guangzhou a rival to Chiang's Nanjing government. After the Japanese invasion of Manchuria, there was an uneasy truce, but Hu made it clear he still regarded **Jiang Jieshi** as a 'warlord'. He died in Guangzhou on the May 12 1936.

HU QIAOMU 胡喬木 (1911–1992)
CCP historian and ideologue. Hu Qiaomu became editor of ***People's Daily*** in 1949 and in 1951 published *Thirty Years of the Communist Party of China*, an official history which backed Mao Zedong's interpretation of Party history. Out of favour during the **Cultural Revolution**, he returned to the Central Committee in 1978.

HU SHI 胡適 (1891–1962)
Modern Chinese scholar, philosopher and literary theorist. Hu Shi came from an official–merchant family from Jixi 績溪 in Anhui province. After initially receiving a traditional education at home, he went to a new-style school in Shanghai in 1904. From there he won a scholarship to Cornell University in 1910. After graduating from Cornell in philosophy in 1914, he went to Columbia University and completed a doctorate under the supervision of John Dewey. This was an inspired choice. Dewey was not only a leading philosopher and founder of his own pragmatist school, but also a pioneer in educational psychology and an advocate of a progressive, child-centred approach which was the absolute antithesis of traditional Chinese methods. Hu Shi was greatly influenced by Dewey's ideas and remained a life-long advocate of the pragmatic bit-by-bit, try-it-and-see approach, as opposed to the grand solutions offered by the 'isms' like Marxism. In January 1917 ***Xin qingnian*** 新青年 'New Youth' magazine published Hu Shi's essay *Wenxue gailiang chuyi* 文學改良芻議 'Tentative Suggestions for Literary Reform'. In this he made eight proposals, all of which revolved round having something to say and saying it in one's own words, in vernacular rather than classical language. In 1918 he summed up the essence as: *Guoyu de wenxue, wenxue de guoyu* 國語的文學, 文學的國語 'a national-language literature, and a literary national language'. Hu Shi led the way and published some vernacular language poems in the February 1917 edition of *Xin qingnian* and later published his *Changshi ji* 嘗試集 'Experimental collection'. He also wrote a comedy, translated Western works of literature and began a long term study of the great vernacular classics of Chinese fiction, including ***Hongloumeng***, ***Shuihuzhuan*** and ***Xiyouji***.

In 1917 Hu Shi had agreed with other intellectuals not to engage in politics, but to concentrate on reforming China's culture and society. After the Russian Revolution and the **May Fourth Movement**, many intellectuals were drawn back into politics, particularly Marxism. He remained a liberal and, although associated with the **Guomindang**, remained largely non-political. He acted as ambassador in Washington for the Guomindang government from 1938–42 and was appointed head of Beijing University in 1945. He returned to the United States when the People's Republic was established and was appointed as the Taiwanese Guomindang government's representative at the U.N. there in 1957. In the following year, he was made head of the Academia Sinica, Taiwan's leading research institute. He died in Taiwan in 1962

Jerome B. GRIEDER, *Hu Shih and the Chinese Renaissance: Liberalism in the Chinese Revolution, 1917–1937* (Harvard University Press, 1970); CHOW Tse-tsung, *The May Fourth Movement: Intellectual Revolution in Modern China* (Harvard University Press, 1960).

HU YAOBANG 胡耀邦 (1915–1989)
Hu Yaobang's experience of the CCP went back to the **Autumn Harvest Uprising** and the **Jiangxi Soviet**. He took part in the **Long March** and was in the PLA during the **Civil War** and the conquest of Sichuan. In the post-**Cultural Revolution** restructuring of the Party, he held senior positions in the Party School, Organisation Department and Propaganda Department. In 1980 he joined the Standing Committee of the Politburo and was Secretary General of the CCP from 1982 to 1987 when he was dismissed in the wake of a series of student demonstrations. He died on April 15 1989 and the memorial services and demonstrations that followed were the prelude to the **Democracy Movement** that ended with the June 4 massacre.

HUA GUOFENG 華國鋒 (1920–)
Caretaker Chairman of the CCP after the death of Mao Zedong. Hua Guofeng's political base was in Hunan, Mao Zedong's home province and he served as Chairman of the Provincial Revolutionary Committee during the **Cultural Revolution**. He became Minister of Public Security and Acting Prime Minister on the death of Zhou Enlai in January 1976 and in April of that year Prime Minister and First Deputy Chairman of the CCP. When Mao Zedong died on September 6, he took over as Chairman, Mao having apparently told him "With you in charge I am at ease" (*ni banshi wo fangxin* 你辦事我放心). In spite of his links with the leftists, he ordered the arrest and detention of the **Gang of Four**. He exercised little power and was replaced at the top of the CCP hierarchy by Deng Xiaoping who was back in control by 1979.

HUAI ARMY *Huaijun* 淮軍
Army recruited by **Li Hongzhang** on the orders of **Zeng Guofan** to defend Shanghai from the **Taipings**. It was set up in 1862 modelled on Zeng Guofan's **Xiang Army** *Xiang jun* 湘軍 (Hunan Army), a local force recruited after the failure of the Qing Banner forces to deal with the Taiping threat. The Huai army, also called the Huai Braves, *Huaiyong* 淮勇, worked with the foreign forces in Shanghai to fight the Taiping troops in that area, then joined forces with the Xiang Army to capture the Taiping capital at Nanjing. Unlike the Hunan Army, the Huai army was armed with Western weapons and partially trained by Western instructors, although it retained the same *ying* 營, battalion, structure as the Hunan Army. After the defeat of the Taipings, the Huai army was put into service fighting the **Nian** rebels from 1865–8. Thereafter it remained the

principal Qing army in eastern China and Li Hongzhang's power base. After defeats in Guangxi in the 1884 **Sino-French war** and, more ignominiously, in the 1894–5 **Sino-Japanese war**, its prestige declined. With the establishment of **Yuan Shikai's** 'New Army', the Huai Army ceased to be China's elite military force, but it continued in being until the end of the Qing.

Stanley SPECTOR, *Li Hung-chang and the Huai Army: A Study in Nineteenth-Century Chinese Regionalism* (University of Washington Press, 1964).

HUAI-HAI 淮海 CAMPAIGN (October 1948 – January 1949)

After the Liaoxi-Shanyang campaign, the second and decisive military campaign of the **Civil War**. Fought near Xuzhou in the area between the Huai River and the Long-Hai railway by CCP troops under General **Chen Yi**, the operation cost the lives of over 100,000 GMD troops. A further 200,000 were captured and many defected. The victory allowed a direct attack on Nanjing, the GMD capital, which fell on April 21 1949.

***HUAINAN ZI* 淮南子**

A heterogeneous Daoist text containing many quotations from other works and produced by a group of scholars as a result of debates initiated by **Liu An** 劉安(c.179–122 BC), the King of Huainan. This is a long work divided into 21 chapters which begins with a discussion of the nature of the ***Dao*** 道 and other metaphysical questions and goes on to deal with aspects of government and military strategy. Like the *Laozi*, and unlike the ***Zhuangzi***, it offers a Daoist blueprint for government as an alternative to the prevailing Confucian orthodoxy and suggests how the ideal Daoist ruler should behave. The work was presented to the Han emperor **Wudi** in 139 BC.

Roger T. AMES, *The Art of Rulership: A Study in Ancient Chinese Political Thought* (University of Hawaii Press, 1983); John S. MAJOR, *Heaven and Earth in Early Han Thought: Chapters Three, Four and Five of the Huainanzi* (Albany: State University of New York Press, 1993).

HUAN, DUKE OF QI *QI HUANGONG* 齊桓公 (685–643 BC)

One of the **hegemons** of the inter-state system during the Spring and Autumn period. Ably assisted by his minister **Guan Zhong** he pursued economic and military policies that earned him a reputation for wise and successful leadership and prompted other states to seek alliances with Qi. State monopolies over salt and iron, which would become one of the staple sources of income in the imperial era, were created for the first time. Skilful diplomacy balanced the competing pressures from Zhou, **Chu** and **Qin**. Military assistance was sent to allied states of Song, **Lu**, Zheng and Yan in defence against attack from barbarian tribes.

HUANG CHAO 黃巢 (d.884)

Bandits and warlordism became endemic in Tang dynasty China as central administration failed to reestablish control after the **An Lushan** rebellion. Huang Chao, under whose banner other groups joined in a major rebellion from 875 to 884, was a member of the rural gentry engaged in the salt trade and frustrated by his inability to become an official. His armies successfully campaigned across a wide area of central and southern China, reputedly massacring many thousands of foreigners in Guangzhou in 879 and finally capturing **Chang'an** in 880. Emperor Xizong, like **Xuanzong** in 755, fled to Sichuan. Huang emulated An Lushan before him and proclaimed a new dynasty, that of Great Qi, but his "reign" was characterised by such destruction and brutality that his supporters became disillusioned and Tang armies retook the capital with Shato (Turkish) help in 883.

H.S. LEVY, *Biography of Huang Ch'ao* (Berkeley: University of California Press, 1961).

HUANG XING 黃興 (1874 -1916)
One of the founders of the China Revival Society *Huaxinghui*. After a failed uprising in 1904, he fled to Japan. In July 1905, Huang, **Song Jiaoren** and **Sun Yixian** met and agreed to form a merged revolutionary organisation, the ***Tongmenghui***, the 'United League', and Huang's journal, *Twentieth Century China,* became the League's official journal. He became Minister of War in the Republican government under Sun Yixian that emerged after the Revolution of 1911, but when **Yuan Shikai** replaced Sun, Huang took a series of more modest postings.

HUANG ZONGXI 黃宗羲 (1610–1695)
One of the great Ming loyalist scholars of the early Qing period and a major intellectual figure in the **Neo-Confucian** tradition . He came from Yuyao 余姚 in Zhejiang province. His father Huang Zunsu 黃尊素, a censor, was arrested as a result of his attack on the notorious eunuch Wei Zhongxian 魏忠賢 and died in prison when Zongxi was just 17 *sui.* This traumatic experience helped develop his very strong character, particularly his deep sense of justice and of right and wrong. Zongxi spent the next twenty years fighting the eunuchs, becoming a leader of the **Donglin** 東林 group. He ended up imprisoned in Nanjing and was, ironically, freed when the Manchu forces attacked the city. He went to his home village and organised an anti-Manchu militia, but it soon became clear that the Ming cause was hopeless. He retired from official life and boldly remained an avowed Ming loyalist throughout his life. Huang refused all offers from the Qing government and wrote laudatory epitaphs for men who died out of continued loyalty to the Ming.. He became one of the great early Qing polymaths, excelling in a number of fields and producing voluminous writings, analyzing the reasons for the downfall of the Ming dynasty. He was against the laxity, both scholastic and moral, of the late Ming and advocated the rigorous study of history, including modern history; in this he was regarded as the founder of the east Zhejiang school of historical research (which later included such luminaries as Quan Zuwang 全祖望 and Zhang Xuecheng 章學誠).

His major works include the *Mingyi daifang lu* 明夷待訪錄, translated as *A Plan for the Prince*, a swingeing attack on autocracy. In it he describes the ruler as the biggest menace to the world (*wei tianxia zhi da haizhe, jun er yi yi* 爲天下之大害者, 君而已矣). In traditional Confucian style he views history as a decline from a former golden age: in the Three Dynasties rulers emerged from the people as representatives, as guests *ke* 客, of the people who were the hosts *zhu* 主. Later rulers turned this on its head, regarding themselves as the more important entity, setting up laws enshrining this view and subordinating the interests of the people to their own. He advocated the restoration of the post of prime minister as a check on the autocratic power of the ruler and reform of the legal and examination systems. He saw schools as a means of curbing despotism by promoting generally accepted, public standards of right and wrong, something which would check the arbitrariness of rulers. Huang's views were eagerly taken up by late nineteenth century reformers and revolutionaries who regarded him as an early Chinese democrat.

Philosophically Huang was part of the Neo-Confucian tradition; he disagreed with the Cheng-Zhu school over the primacy of principle *li* 理 over matter *qi* 氣 and was inclined towards a monist position like **Zhang Zai**, regarding principle as not having a separate existence from matter. Modern Marxist scholars have applauded his materialism on this point. However, as far as heart, *xin* 心, is concerned, Huang contrarily was drawn to the idealist position of **Wang Yangming**. An interesting feature of his economic thought is his refusal to toe the orthodox Confucian line on the primacy of agriculture and the secondary nature of the artisan and the merchant: he regarded all three as fundamental. His assessment of earlier scholarship, in his *Mingru xuean* 明儒學案 *Accounts of Ming Scholars* and the uncompleted *Song Yuan ruxue an* 宋元儒學案 *Accounts of Song and Yuan Scholars*, set new standards for philosophical evaluation and the former, in particular, is still very highly regarded. **Liang Qichao** called Huang "China's Rousseau" and he was admired by **Sun Yixian**. In modern times his reformist ideas have found favour with Chinese scholars since 1989, and Theodore de Bary has called his book "the most enduring and influential Confucian critique of Chinese despotism through the ages."

HUANG Zongxi, *Waiting for the Dawn . A Plan for the Prince: Huang Tsung-hsi's Ming-i Tai-fang lu*, trans. and introd. by William Theodore DE BARY (Columbia University Press, 1993).

HUANGLAO 黃老

School of thought followed by a number of senior court members during the second and first centuries BC. They included the consort of Emperor **Wendi**, but their beliefs did not conform closely enough with those of the Confucians or the Daoists to ensure their survival, and the school dwindled into insignificance. It was "re-discovered" in 1973 when tomb no. 3 at **Mawangdui** yielded texts known to be associated with it, the *Huangdi sijing* 皇帝四經 "Yellow Emperor's Four Classics". Its philosophy was concerned with a cosmological explanation for human government that indicates its indebtedness to all three major philosophies of the early Han period: it sees the ***Dao*** as the origin of the universe and the creator of man in it. The *Dao* entrusted rule to a sovereign, who established standards of behaviour for man in relation to the universe and his fellow men, and enshrined them in a system of law. The first such sovereign was the **Yellow Emperor.**

HUANGPU 黃浦 (WHAMPOA) MILITARY ACADEMY

Academy for the training of an officer corps for the National Revolutionary Army, which was being prepared for the **Northern Expedition**, and established on the river island of Huangpu, ten miles from Guangzhou in May 1924. Jiang Jieshi was appointed first commandant. Cadets from the Academy were prominent in both the GMD and CCP military forces, the majority of GMD supporters having formed an intense personal devotion to Jiang, which gave him a powerful base for future political struggles. However, because of the **United Front** in operation at the time, many CCP members were trained by the Academy or worked there. They included Zhou Enlai, who was political commissar.

HUI 回

Ethnic minority group of Chinese speaking Muslims who trace their ancestry back to immigration from the Arabian peninsula during the Tang dynasty and from Central Asia during the Mongol conquests when they were brought back to China during the Yuan dynasty. Hui people live throughout China but there are large closely-knit communities in Yunnan in south-west China and in the **Ningxia Hui Autonomous Region** and Gansu province in the north-west. Although they are designated *Huizu* 回族 in contemporary China, they are also known as *Huihui* 回回 and as Dungans to speakers of Turkic languages.

HUI SHI 惠施 (c.380–305 BC)

A native of Song who became minister in the state of **Wei** and who may have had a hand in introducing its written law code. Hui Shi was a philosopher concerned with logic, a member of the School of Names *Ming jia* 名家 or **Logicians** and is best known for his series of ten paradoxes cited by the author of Chapter 33 of the ***Zhuangzi***, a chapter devoted to a critique of extant schools of philosophy. These paradoxes are taken to be explorations of the concepts of time and space. They begin with the assertion that there is nothing beyond the largest thing and nothing within the smallest thing and include the arguments that Heaven is as low as earth, mountains and marshes are on the same level and that one can go to the state of Yue today and arrive yesterday. Hui Shi was a contemporary and friend of Zhuangzi and there are echoes of this relativist position in chapters of the main text of the *Zhuangzi* like *Qiushui* 秋水 'Autumn Floods'.

Burton WATSON trans., *The complete works of Chuang-tzu* (Columbia University Press, 1968).

HUIGUAN **see GUILDS**

HUIZHOU MERCHANTS *Huishang* 徽商

Commercial syndicate operating from the Huizhou (or Xin'an) area in the southern part of Anhui province in the Ming and Qing dynasties. Their rise to success began with imperial licences to allow them to trade in salt in return for supplying grain to the border defence guards. They moved from salt trading into timber and rice and the products of the handicraft centres of southern China, including porcelain, tea, cotton and silk and eventually became wealthy enough to finance small industrial concerns.

HUIZONG 徽宗, SONG EMPEROR (Zhao Ji 趙佶, 1082–1135, r.1110–25)

Eleventh son of Emperor Shenzong, who assumed the throne personally in 1101 after the death of the regent, Empress Dowager Xiang. Though he was not politically inclined and much preferred the kind of self-indulgent and luxurious life style that ran counter to Confucian principles of true **kingship**, he was persuaded to involve himself in court factionalism to the extent of restoring the reform party to power at court (see **Cai Jing, Song dynasty**), and in a disastrous intervention into foreign affairs in 1115 he initiated the policy of collaboration with the Jurchen against the neighbouring **Khitan** Liao empire. At the same time he tried unsuccessfully to persuade the Koryo court in **Korea** to resist Jin. Poor living conditions resulting partly from an inflationary issue of **paper money** led to the Fang La 方臘 rebellion in 1120–1, which weakened the position of the dynasty and hastened its collapse. Having put down the rebels, the military commander Tong Guang turned north to confront the Khitan, but was twice defeated. The Jurchen had little difficulty in overrunning the Liao empire and the northern half of the Song empire. In 1126 Huizong and his son, already invested as Emperor Qinzong 欽宗, fled south into Jiangsu under the protection of Tong Guan 童貫, but the latter was killed by his own countrymen and the Jurchen captured the imperial cortege. The ex-Emperor died in captivity in Manchuria.

Incapable as he was as a politician, Huizong ranks among the greatest of Chinese emperors in the artistic field. He was a ***ci*** poet, a patron of **music**, and famous as a calligrapher and painter in the Academy tradition. He is said to have formed an Academy of Calligraphy and Painting within the **Hanlin Academy**, though this is doubted by some historians. He was an ardent Daoist and sponsored the building of many temples.

HUMAN NATURE

In the late Zhou period the search for a formula that would reunite the land and end the trauma of constant warfare prompted the principal social and political theorists to comment on the basic quality of human nature. **Confucius** had not done so and it was scarcely a question that concerned philosophers after the Han, but during the Warring States opinions were strongly expressed and deeply divided. On the one hand the idealist **Mencius** affirmed that men are born fundamentally good, are led astray from birth by the temptations that surround them, but may recover their original nature (*benxing* 本性) and fulfil their potential through education. The Legalists believed in the inherent badness of human nature and set out to suppress its effects by the imposition of harsh laws and punishments, and by denying ordinary people the right to education. In their view the selfishness of human nature constituted a challenge to the authority of the state. Xun Qing agreed with them on the fundamental evil of mankind, but stated that education as well as law should be used to control and train people (see **Xunzi**). The Daoist view expressed no moral judgement since moral standards are the result of human, partial understanding, and taught that the harmony of the universe could only be achieved if man recognised that he was just one of the myriad creations of the ***Dao,*** that it was his function to live according to the innate qualities and abilities given him by the *Dao* rather than any trained or acquired skills and ambitions, and that he must return to a state of fundamental "non-knowing" (*wuzhi*) in order to harmonise with the rest of the natural world. Fundamental human nature therefore had a priority that it was essential to recognise but which lacked any judgement quality.

D. MUNRO, *The Concept of Man in Early China* (Stanford University Press, 1969).

Hunan peasant movement

Drive by the early CCP to create a network of peasant associations in Hunan province. The movement began in 1925 and Mao Zedong, whose family home was in Hunan, was involved in organising militant peasants. In two articles he wrote around this time, *Analysis of the Classes in Chinese Society* in March 1926 and *Report on an Investigation into the Peasant Movement in Hunan* from March 1927, he developed his ideas on the class structure of the Chinese countryside and the role of peasants in the CCP's revolution. During the PRC, these articles were used to suggest that Mao had been the only CCP member interested in the peasants and the role of other peasant association organisers such as **Peng Pai** was obscured.

Hundred Days Reform ***Wuxu bianfa*** 戊戌變法

The short period between June 11 and September 21 1898 when the **Guangxu Emperor**, under the influence of **Kang Youwei**, issued a flurry of reformist measures only to have them countermanded when the Empress Dowager, **Cixi**, took back power in a coup d'etat. China's defeat in the 1895 **Sino-Japanese war** brought a crisis of confidence in the system on the part of a broad spectrum of Chinese intellectuals, including a group of metropolitan degree candidates mobilised by one of their number, Kang Youwei, to mount a demonstration against signing the treaty. Kang subsequently sent up memorials to the emperor outlining his plans for institutional reform. There was no immediate result but the 'scramble for concessions' by the foreign powers in 1898 appeared to presage the dismemberment of China and brought another crisis to the government in Beijing. Although Kang's proposals, which consisted of wholesale restructuring of the governmental system along Western lines, including constitutional monarchy, reforms to the legal system, the educational system, the military, industry and commerce, were radical, nevertheless the sense of crisis was so great that the young emperor agreed to issue edicts promulgating them. Leading officials initially felt obliged to mute their criticism, though they did not rush to put the reforms into effect, but Kang's ideas threatened so many vested interests that it was not long before the Empress Dowager, officially retired from her regency since 1889, staged a coup, took back power from the emperor and executed six of the leading reformers leaders including **Tan Sitong** (Kang Youwei and **Liang Qichao** escaped to Japan).

Luke S.K Kwong, *A Mosaic of the Hundred Days: Personalities, Politics and Ideas of 1898* (Council on East Asian Studies, Harvard University, 1984).

Hundred Flowers Movement ***Baihua yundong*** 百花運動

Period of intellectual and political debate in the 1950s. Zhou Enlai had proposed reforms to placate the intellectuals, many of whom had returned from abroad to serve "New China" only to find that the independence and initiative that they had cultivated was valued less than loyalty to the CCP. The movement was inaugurated by Mao Zedong in his speech of May 2 1956 to the Supreme State Conference, when he put forward the slogan "let a hundred flowers bloom, let a hundred schools of thought contend", originally suggested by the head of the CCP's propaganda department, Lu Dingyi. The call came during a period of turbulence in the international communist movement. On February 14 1956, at the 20th Congress of the Communist Party of the Soviet Union, Khrushchev denounced Stalin's excesses and later in the year there were violent workers demonstrations in Poland and the Hungarian Rising. Mao's call can be seen either as a genuine attempt to find out what grievances people had or a Machiavellian ruse to smoke out the opposition. People were very slow in coming forward with criticisms and it was not until April and May 1957 that large numbers of articles began to appear in the press complaining about bureaucracy, maladministration, nepotism and corruption. Critical articles appeared in *Renmin wenxue* 人民文學 'People's Literature' and in *Guangming Daily* 光明日報. The movement developed a momentum of its own. Historians and social scientist criticized the whole basis of the regime including the relevance of Mao Zedong Thought to China's problems. Wall posters were displayed in Beijing University, on what was to be the prototype for the **Democracy Wall** of 1978 and unofficial magazines were published. Such was the force of the criticism that terrified CCP leaders launched an **Anti-Rightist Campaign** that effectively stifled dissent for many years. See **Hundred Schools.**

Roderick MACFARQUHAR ed., *The Hundred Flowers Campaign and the Chinese Intellectuals* (Praeger, 1960; Octagon, 1973); Roderick MACFARQUHAR, *The Origins of the Cultural Revolution (vol. 1): Contradictions among the People, 1956–1957* (Columbia University Press, 1974).

HUNDRED SCHOOLS *Bai jia* 百家

Name given to the late Spring and Autumn and Warring States periods by later Chinese writers, referring to the proliferation of political, social and cosmological theories as the old religio-feudal authority of the Zhou dynasty declined. Proponents of ideas as different as **Legalism**, **Confucianism**, Mohism and **Daoism** presented their ideas about the nature of man, the state and the universe, some as would-be political advisers, some as teachers, some as writers. Many travelled from court to court, expounding their views on how the empire might be reunited or serving those whose political system most appealed to them. Some, such as **Mencius**, advocated pacifism in turbulent times. Others, such as **Sun Wu** and **Mozi**, contributed more positively to the conduct of warfare. Sometimes known as philosophers, the majority of these scholars were less concerned with abstract than with practical matters, but among those who were interested in theoretical discussion were the logicians and dialecticians **Hui Shi** and **Gongsun Long**, whilst the writings associated with philosophical Daoism, the ***Zhuangzi*** and the ***Daodejing***, made important contributions to early ideas on spirituality, relativity and the scientific approach. The interests of the Daoists coincided to some extent with those of the so-called Naturalists (e.g. **Zou Yan**), who speculated about the controlling forces and laws of the universe, in particular *yin* and *yang* (see ***Yin-yang***) and the **Five Elements**. Whilst scholars during this period were well aware of the major differences between the followers of **Confucius**, the Legalists, and the more individualistic Daoists, they did not yet see themselves as belonging to schools and were certainly not so organised.

FUNG Yu-lan, *A History of Chinese Philosophy Vol. 1* (Princeton University Press, 1937).

Huo Guang 霍光 (d. 68 BC)
Minister for thirty years under the Han emperor **Wudi** and appointed by him as regent for the young Emperor **Zhaodi**. He maintained his power as effective ruler of the state throughout the boy's brief reign and into that of **Xuandi**, whose accession he influenced. During his lifetime his position was unchallenged and he died to the accompaniment of praise and honour from the Emperor, who accorded him a jade suit for burial (see also **Liu Sheng**). But he had been guilty of nepotism on a grand scale, and after his death his family were unable to survive the intense political rivalry of the **Chang'an** court.

Michael Loewe, *Crisis and Conflict in Han China, 104 BC to AD 9* (George Allen and Unwin, 1974).

Ibn Battuta (1304–68)
The greatest world traveller before the era of European voyages of discovery. A Muslim from Tangier, he spent most of his life travelling throughout the Middle East, India, South-east Asia and China, an account of which is preserved in the most famous *rihla*, "Travelogue" in Arabic literature. Travel in search of knowledge was in obedience to a *hadith* (saying of the Prophet Mohammed) in which he exhorted Muslims to seek knowledge even as far as China. His claims to have visited south-eastern China and **Beijing** have been doubted by some scholars. See also **Islam**.

Ili 伊犁 (Yining 伊寧, Ghulja)
City in the north-west of **Xinjiang** close to the border with Kazakhstan. Taken by Qing forces during the expansion of the eighteenth century, it was occupied by Russia beween 1871 and 1881 when it was returned to China under the terms of the Treaty of St Petersburg. It was the headquarters of the short-lived Eastern Turkestan Republic set up in November 1944.

Ili, Treaty of (1851)
Agreement on trade between Russia and Ili which was signed on July 25 1851 and was the basis for Russia's occupation of the region twenty years later. Under the terms of the treaty, Russia was allowed to trade with and build warehouses and consulates in Ili and the Tarbaghatay, region of northern Xinjiang but not in Kashghar, which it had also requested,

Ilkhans
Khanate of Persia established by the Mongol Khan Hulegu after the capture of Baghdad in 1258. See **Mongols**.

Immortality
There was a widely held belief in ancient China that a person had two souls. When he died one, called *po*魄, went off into Heaven to take its place amongst the feudal hierarchy of spirits. The other, *hun* 魂, remained in the corpse, buried in the soil, and should receive sacrifices to sustain it until it went off to the **Yellow Springs**: otherwise it might arise as a hungry ghost and trouble the local community. Where Heaven was, and what it was like, were imprecisely defined. Two common ideas in the early Han located it either beyond the Kunlun

mountains to the North-west, or in the mysterious islands of Penglai 蓬萊 in the opposite direction. By that time concepts of immortality were already varied. Intellectuals were groping for some understanding of transcendentalism as an escape from the cares of the temporal world through the philosophical tenets of **Daoism**, ordinary people were more interested in the instant promise of a better incarnation in a happier realm as offered either by the rituals and practices of popular Daoism or the millenarian teachings of the Queen Mother of the West (see **Xiwangmu**). Few of the lower classes probably relished the idea of immortality as the continuation of their present life style into eternity, but the privileged might: the First Emperor (see **Qin Shi Huangdi**) engaged many researchers to try and discover for him an elixir of immortality. During the Han dynasty esoteric practices aimed at extending a man's natural life to its uttermost limits included breathing, sexual and dietary exercises. Religious Daoism popularised belief in the *xian* 仙 (Immortals), who were thought to have achieved a kind of immortality and to appear, ready to offer advice to the living, in the guise of an old man or some more unexpected form such as a donkey or a stone by a roadside.

The arrival of **Buddhism** in the Former Han period brought fresh concepts of life after death and of reincarnation. The more philosophically inclined glimpsed Nirvana, while ordinary people might hanker after the **Amithaba** Buddha's Tushita Heaven. This was reminiscent of the Western Paradise and, as depicted in some of the great paintings of the Tang dynasty from **Dunhuang**, perhaps not unlike the imperial courtrooms of **Chang'an**. But for those who dared not aspire to heavenly immortality, the prospect of rebirth and perhaps a happier existence would only follow a period of torturous purging in a series of ten or eighteen hells. See also **Tibetan Book of the Dead, TLV mirrors**.

W. EBERHARD, *Guilt and Sin in Traditional China* (Berkeley: University of California Press, 1967); M. LOEWE, *Ways to Paradise: the Chinese Quest for Immortality* (George Allen and Unwin,1979).

IMPERIAL ACADEMY *Taixue* 太學

Established at **Chang'an** in 124 BC to recruit and train candidates for an official career. Its syllabus was based on the study of the **Five Classics** and was in the hands of newly created "professors" (*boshi* 博士). Students were originally restricted to fifty in number, but this had risen to thirty thousand in the Later Han, when there was a second university in **Luoyang**. The State University (*Guozi Jian* 國子監) of the Tang was set up in 627. Its constituent colleges included three providing specialist training in law, mathematics and calligraphy. Registration was dependent on recommendation and included foreigners (such as Koreans) whose own courts had requested places for sons of their nobility. A special college for imperial scions and the sons of senior officials, the College of Literary Studies (*Wenxue guan* 文學館), was the forerunner of the **Hanlin Academy**.

Intellectual ability was increasingly recognised regardless of social background in the Song. Enrolment at the Imperial Academy rose to 3,800 in 1104 but fell during the Southern Song. Short-lived specialist Colleges under the Northern Song included those of Law, Mathematics, Calligraphy, Painting, and Medicine.

In the Ming enrolment rose to ten thousand, but though its own testing system constituted a possible route to office, graduation from the Academy had never been on a par with the acquisition of degrees available by examination, and by the Qing the number who bothered to seek this route to advancement dwindled to around three hundred. See also **Academies, Examination System, Schools.**

IMPERIAL ERA

The period of Chinese history between 221 BC and AD 1911 during which the rule of China was conducted by emperors. See **Dynasties, Reign Periods, Son of Heaven**

IMPERIAL HOUSEHOLD DEPARTMENT *Neiwu fu* 內務府

An influential branch of Qing government established in 1661 that lay outside the structure of the regular, **Outer Court**, administration. Originally intended to cater for the needs of Forbidden City and **Inner Court** residents and staffed by imperial **bondservants**, it comprised numerous departments covering education, ceremonial, banqueting, medicine etc. During the late seventeenth and eighteenth centuries its staff level grew to nearly sixteen hundred and its activities spread into management of estates, the salt monopoly, the imperial porcelain and textile factories, the imperial printing office, and trading agreements and customs posts. See also **Jingdezhen.**

P.M. TORBERT, *The Ch'ing Imperial Household Department* (Harvard University Press, 1977).

IMPERIAL MARITIME CUSTOMS

New customs and excise administration that resulted from Western domination of the **Treaty Ports** and which succeeded the existing collectorate in 1854 after the **Small Sword Rising** in Shanghai. Although it collected revenue on behalf of the Chinese government, it remained largely independent of it. It was controlled by Inspectors General, the most distinguished being **Robert Hart**, who served from 1863–1908.

John K. FAIRBANK, Katharine Frost BRUNER and Elizabeth MacLeod MATHESON, ed., *The I.G. in Peking: Letters of Robert Hart, Chinese Maritime Customs, 1868–1907* (2 vols.) (Belknap Press of Harvard University Press, 1975).

INFANTICIDE

As practised in China this was usually female infanticide, although disabled sons might also be left to die. It was most common among the lower classes and occurred for two main reasons. First, the economic situation of poor families was often so precarious that, in the absence of effective family planning or abortion methods, the point might be reached when more children simply could not be supported. Girls might be sold into concubinage or prostitution, but many were killed or abandoned. Second, the desire for sons was so strong, both for their economic value and as a means of continuing the family line, that they were supported in preference to daughters. **Census** figures for the eighteenth century show an imbalance of 120:100 in favour of males. Infanticide was against the law and public orphanages existed in the Han, Song and Qing periods to care for abandoned babies. It was also widely regarded as inhuman and sinful, and many a grieving family would prefer to try and sell a child rather than to drown or abandon it.

INNER COURT *Neiting* 内廷

From Han times until the Qing, a bifurcation existed in central government between those servants of the emperor and empress who were allowed into the innermost palace quarters and the majority of officials whose daily business could only be conducted in the "public" offices of the court. The former consisted primarily of **eunuchs** and **Hanlin** Academicians, the latter of the large number of ministers and bureaucrats who were responsible for the running of the nation's affairs. The former was known as the Inner Court, the latter as the **Outer Court**. Members of the Inner Court, though holding fewer regular appointments and nominally of lesser importance than the senior government personnel outside, were neverthless numerous and came to wield great power. They catered for the needs of the emperor and his relatives through twenty-four separate departments in Ming times (see **Imperial Household Department**) under the command of the Director of Ceremonial; they were also the channel through which ministers might have to send and receive communications to and from the emperor. Their opportunities for influence were enormous, especially at times of political disunity such as the late eighth century. Members of the Inner Court could move freely through the Outer Court, but by very definition entry to the Inner Court was much more limited. Some coming and going was inevitable: court musicians, for example, might be called on to play for the separate **sacrifices** conducted in both Courts. But in general, the inability of senior officers to have final access to the **Son of Heaven** was a frequent source of frustration. The **Wanli** Emperor is said to have gone twenty-five years without seeing an Outer Court official.

A. CHAN, *The Glory and Fall of the Ming Dynasty* (University of Oklahoma Press, 1982).

INNER MONGOLIA

The part of Mongolia closest to China, now designated as the Inner Mongolia Autonomous Region *Nei Menggu Zizhiqu* 内蒙古自治區 and having a high proportion of Han Chinese in the population. Outer Mongolia, the Mongolian Peoples Republic from 1921 to 1991, is today known as Mongolia. All of the Mongol lands were under the control of the Qing empire and there is still a perception among many Chinese that both parts of Mongolia belong under Chinese rule. This is not accepted by pro-independence groups within Inner Mongolia and some Mongols prefer to use the term Southern Mongolia.

INVENTIONS AND DISCOVERIES

No single country has such a history as China in terms of its contributions to the scientific progress of world civilisation. Some inventions and discoveries that have had a major impact on western history are well known, and include **paper** and **printing**, **gunpowder**, and the magnetic **compass**. Others are less commonly recognised, such as the wheelbarrow, the continuous driving belt and the treadle-operated loom, whilst there are yet many more which were never transmitted beyond China's boundaries but are just as great an indication of the fertility of the Chinese imagination, such as Zhang Heng's seismograph or Su Song's water-driven armillary sphere and clock at **Kaifeng** (models of which may be seen at the Science Museum in London). State-controlled workshops were the source of some inventions and for the production of machines and commodities required by the court, such as imperial carriages, weapons, **ceramics,** and high quality textiles (see **Silk**). Here too were employed architects and civil engineers, the builders of roads, bridges, locks and dams. Officialdom did much to sponsor progress, but it also controlled the development of new knowledge, and the vested interests of the literary ruling elite prevented the maximum exploitation of the people's ingenuity, whether or not it might have benefited them.

It was the ancient Chinese reliance on the land and the climate, and early attempts to discover and explain the principles of the universe and man's place in it, that led to many discoveries in the natural sciences, including astronomy, physics, biology, chemistry, and botany. The constant search for an alchemical source of gold or for an elixir of **immortality** may have been unsuccessful but it yielded other understanding, and whilst disease and infant mortality kept life expectancy low, anatomical and medical knowledge such as the use of acupuncture did improve the quality of life for some. See also **Needham**, Joseph.

Joseph NEEDHAM, *Science and Civilisation in China* (Cambridge University Press 1953– (series in progress, vols I-VI published to date)); Colin RONAN, *The Shorter Science and Civilisation in China, Vol 1* (Cambridge University Press, 1978 – (series in progress)).

IRON RICE BOWL ***Tie fanwan*** **鐵飯碗**

Guaranteed income for all, particularly in state-run enterprises. "Breaking the iron rice bowl" was one of the phrases used to describe the move towards private enterprise in the 1980s.

ISLAM

Islam appeared in China when it was in transition from the Sui dynasty (581–618 AD) to the Tang Dynasty (618–907). Chinese scholars, searching historical sources to find the earliest record of Muslims in China have arrived at several possible dates, some even pre-dating the foundation of Islam, probably simply referring to travellers from the Middle East. Visitors to Tang dynasty China came overland across Central Asia, along the **Silk Road** and by sea into south-eastern ports, known as the Spice Route as most of its travellers were merchants seeking spices from the islands of South-east Asia. Quanzhou, Changzhou and Guangzhou (Canton) all became celebrated commercial centres. The travellers from the Middle East who traded and later settled in these cities are usually known as Arab merchants, but there were **Jews** and **Nestorian** Christians as well as Muslims. From temporary trading outposts came permanent settlements and these were the first source of the present Muslim population of China. In Quanzhou there are still hundreds of gravestones with inscriptions in Arabic. Persian and Chinese, marking the lives and deaths of Muslims from the Yemen, Persia and Central Asia.

The second source of China's Muslim population was the **Mongol** conquests of the thirteenth century. On their expeditions westward to conquer Central Asia, the armies of **Chinggis Khan** and his successors sacked major Islamic centres including Bukhara and Samarkand and transported sections of the population including skilled armourers, craftsmen and enslaved women and children back to China, where they were settled as servants of Mongol aristocrats. When the Mongols established their Yuan dynasty (1260–1368) to rule China, they used Central Asians as border guards, tax collectors and administrators. Although it is impossible to be certain of the numbers of Central Asians who were moved into China at this time it is clear that they far outnumbered the Muslims settled in China before the Mongol conquests and this was certainly the case in northern China. So the Mongol conquest was probably the single most important factor in the creation of important Muslim communities in China. See also **Hui**.

IVORY

Ivory has been used in China since the Neolithic period. It is a versatile but expensive material and was used in the manufacture of a wide variety of objects. It was mainly imported from other Asian countries and Africa. Ivory was used in the sixteenth century for carving sculptures of Daoist and Buddhist gods and immortals, particularly in Fujian, An elephant tusk was usually cut into sections suitable for particular purposes. Because of the fine surface and dense grain of ivory, delicate designs were commonly carved in either low or high relief. Ivories with open-work, stained or painted decoration also came into fashion in the Qing dynasty. By this period, ivory was also favoured for making scholar's desk items such as brush handles, wrist-rests, wine vessels and seals. Intricately carved ivories from Guangdong, the leading centre for ivory carving since the eighteenth century, were presented to the court as tribute from that area and were also exported to the West.

W. WATSON ed., *Chinese Ivories from the Shang to the Qing* (London: British Museum, 1984).

JADE

Of all materials in the world of Chinese antiquities, jade best exemplifies the essential aspects of Chinese culture and aesthetic appreciation. Jade is viewed as the most valuable of all precious stones and objects made from it are admired for their enduring beauty and moral quality. The metaphorical values ascribed to jade were emphasised in the Confucian Classics, which expounded the importance of jade to the virtues of a perfect gentleman. With time, jade came to be identified as a symbol for everything that is good, pure, noble and sublime. While the living wore jade as a symbol of their moral integrity, jade was also used to accompany the deceased, to comfort the soul and confer immortality to the body in the afterlife.

The art of jade-carving in China had its beginning early in the Neolithic culture. Jade sacrificial and auspicious utensils were commonly used for ritual functions in the early dynasties. The development of jade utensils of later dynasties tended more towards pure craftsmanship and artistry, attributable mainly to their sophisticated aesthetic appeal. Fine ornaments, jewellery, small sculptures and items for the scholar's desk made of jade became popular.

Jade is the name given to two minerals: nephrite and jadeite. Most Chinese archaic jades were nephrite in various colours, which is from the region known today as Xinjiang, but in ancient times it may have come from other sites now worked out or lost. Jadeite, with its emerald green hues, is found in Burma and was unknown in China before the 18th century. Jade is found in mountains and riverbeds, and is considered as "the essence of heaven and earth." The boulders or pebbles of jade are cut into slices with a cord and an abrasive sand and then shaped, a process which requires considerable effort and time.

E. CHILDS-JOHNSON, *Ritual and Power: Jades of Ancient China* (New York: China House Gallery, 1988).

JADE EMPEROR Yuhuang 玉皇 or **Yudi** 玉帝

The chief of all gods, the Lord of Heaven in **Daoism.** He also became a Buddhist deity, being identified with Indra. Despite the antiquity of the myths which surround the Jade Emperor, he was established as the supreme deity in the Northern Song dynasty and became one of the most popular gods worshipped in China. Emperor Zhenzong (reigned 968–1022) claimed to have had a visitation from Heaven in order to put a seal on his own authority, and made the Jade Emperor the principal deity of worship at court. Emperor **Huizong** also exhausted national resources in building magnificent Daoist temples to the Lord of Heaven throughout the country. The Jade Emperor was always presented in art as a majestic figure with a gentle facial expression.

JANUARY STORM

Turbulent phase of the **Cultural Revolution** in Shanghai also known as the January power seizure. In January 1967, Red Guard organisations in Shanghai, backed by the central Cultural Revolution Group in Beijing moved to eject the existing CCP leadership in the city and replace it with a more Maoist administration. **Scarlet Guards** and workers in docks and on the railways opposed this and mounted a general strike so that Shanghai was effectively paralysed. **Zhang Chunqiao**, a confederate of **Jiang Qing** succeeded in defeating the strikers and their political allies by taking over the local press and attacking the CCP leadership at mass meetings. He announced the creation of a new, radical, form of government, the **Shanghai Commune**, later to be replaced by a **Revolutionary Committee**.

JAPANESE PIRATES ***Wokou*** **倭寇**

Pirates ravaged the coast of East Asia from Korea down to Indo-China from the thirteenth to the seventeenth centuries and three missions were sent to Japan from the Chinese court to persuade the government of Japan to help check the problem. The term, more accurately translated as "dwarf pirates", is not only discourteous but also inaccurate. Some of the marauders were probably Japanese, but the name was used indiscriminately and applied also to Chinese smugglers and Portuguese adventurers. The campaign against them in the mid-sixteenth century encouraged the commutation of militia service into a silver assessment (see **Single Whip Taxation System**) from which a volunteer naval defence force could be recruited. See also **Hideyoshi, Koxinga.**

K.W. SO, *Japanese Piracy in Ming China during the 16th Century* (Michigan State University Press, 1975).

JEHOL see **REHE**

JESUITS

Members of the Society of Jesus founded by St. Ignatius Loyola in 1534. Patronised by the Kings of Portugal and given papal right of jurisdiction over the territories they reached by journeying eastwards, they followed in the wake of merchant explorers. St. Francis Xavier founded a mission at Goa in 1542 and reached Japan in 1549. A Portuguese base was acquired on **Macao** in 1557 and a Jesuit training centre established there in 1579. The first **missionaries** to set foot on Chinese soil were Michele Ruggieri and Matteo **Ricci**. Ricci, who obtained permission to open a house in Beijing in 1601, was the greatest and most influential member of the Order to work in China. He was followed by other outstanding leaders in Adam **Schall** von Bell and Ferdinand **Verbiest**, and the foreign presence at the late Ming and early Qing courts was firmly established as a result of their intellectual skills, especially in astronomy. Their contributions to scholarly debate and creativity also included geography and cartography, acoustics and musicology, painting and mechanics (see **Castiglione**), and diplomacy (see **Nerchinsk**), as well as theology and philosophy. Their critics (including members of the Dominican and Franciscan Orders) accused them of compromising their duty of preaching the Gospel by so concentrating on literati activities, and it is true that they made comparatively few converts during the 190 years of their mission to China. Nevertheless they suffered persecution and martyrdom in the name of the Gospel, especially under Emperor **Yongzheng**. When the Order was disbanded in 1773 (see **Rites Controversy**) a total of 456 Jesuit missionaries had worked in China but there may have been no more than 200,000 Chinese Christians in total. Even their scientific teachings were apparently forgotten after their departure. It may be argued that however disappointing their short-term achievements, the foundation they laid for the future development of Christianity in China was crucial.

David MUNGELLO, *Curious Land : Jesuit Accommodation and the origins of Sinology* (Wiesbaden: Franz Steiner Verlag and University of Hawaii Press, 1985); Jonathan SPENCE, *The Memory Palace of Matteo Ricci* (Viking Penguin, 1984); John WITEK, *Controversial Ideas in China and Europe: A Biography of Jean-Francois Foucquet, S.J. (1665–1741)* (Rome: Institutum Historicum, 1982).

JEWS

The small Jewish community in China probably originated with the ethnically mixed traders from the Middle East, generally called Arabs, who took part in the Indian Ocean trade which reached Sui and Tang dynasty China. The best known community was in Kaifeng in Henan province which still had an active synagogue in the nineteenth century. Manuscripts in Hebrew were discovered there but none of the community knew the language. The community appears to have been assimilated into the non-Jewish population over the course of the eighteenth and nineteenth centuries, one theory being that the group of Muslims known as the Blue-capped Hui (*Lanmao hui* 藍帽回) are the descendants of Jews. A more recently arrived community in the north-east of China, especially in Shenyang was made up of refugees from pogroms and the 1917 revolution in Russia.

Donald D. LESLIE, *The Survival of the Chinese Jews: the Jewish community of Kaifeng* (Leiden: E.J. Brill, 1972).

JIA YI 賈誼 (201–169 BC)
Senior official under the Han emperor **Wendi**, well known for his outspoken comments on the principles of good imperial government which was still reeling from the collapse of Qin, the resultant civil wars, and the recent manipulation of power by the Empress **Lu**. Qin had claimed to rule by virtue of the element water. Jia advised Wendi to adopt earth as the patron element of the new dynasty (advice that was not finally taken until 104 BC). Jia criticised the errors of Qin, and in so doing indirectly remonstrated with his own Emperor and stressed the need for government to heed moral principles. He was unafraid to speak up for what he believed were realistic policies, yet tried to define these in accordance with inherited standards: he condemned the currently favoured foreign relations policy of *heqin* 和親 as appeasement, undermining correct hierarchical relations between Han Chinese and barbarians. Instead he put forward proposals for luring **Xiongnu** leaders into Han clutches by appealing and pandering to their base material senses to subvert them.

JIANG JIESHI (CHIANG KAI-SHEK) 蔣介石 (1887–1975)
Statesman, leader of the **Guomindang** and President of the **Republic of China**. Jiang came from Ningbo and entered the military after a normal classical school education. He studied in Japan in 1908–10 and was back in China for the 1911 revolution, taking part in the political turmoil in Shanghai. He joined **Sun Yixian**'s army in Guangdong and in 1924 became commandant of the **Huangpu (Whampoa) Military Academy**, a position from which he was able to launch his political career. On the death of Sun Yixian in 1925, he used his connections within the military to gain political power, effectively taking over the Guomindang in the **Guangzhou coup** of March 1926. He was to remain the unchallenged leader of the GMD until his death. His successful leadership of the **Northern Expedition** to reunify the southern part of China consolidated his position and he formed a National Government in Nanjing which ruled until the Japanese invasion of 1937 forced its evacuation to Chongqing. With limited Allied support, he maintained his government in exile and after the defeat of Japan assumed that he would return to Nanjing to continue the National Government. His forces were defeated by the CCP's People's Liberation Army in the **Civil War** and he was forced to retreat to Taiwan where he presided over a successful economy but was never able to acheive his main aim – the recovery of the mainland.

JIANG JINGGUO (CHIANG CHING-KUO) 蔣經國 (1918–1988)
Son of Jiang Jieshi. Jiang Jingguo was ordered to solve the problems of inflation and black marketeering in post-war Shanghai and did so with great brutality, including the execution of speculators and black marketeers in October 1948. He became Prime Minister in his father's government on Taiwan in 1972 and succeeded C.K.Yen as President in 1978, serving two terms in office. He is credited with having played a positive role in Taiwan's economic development and in particular in the liberalisation and democratisation of the island's political structure. He died on January 13 1988.

JIANG QING 江青 (1914–91)
Wife of **Mao Zedong** and leading member of the **Gang of Four**. Jiang Qing enjoyed a career of limited distinction as an actress in the Shanghai film world of the 1930s under the name of Lan Ping 藍蘋. She moved to Yan'an after the Japanese invasion of China in 1937 along with many other radical young intellectuals and artists. She met Mao and became his third wife. The match did not meet with the approval of others in the CCP leadership who kept her away from direct involvement in politics. She became deeply immersed in artistic circles, film and opera in particular, and built herself a power base in Shanghai. In the early 1960s, she was the guiding light behind a movement to create **Revolutionary Operas**, a cultural battle that was part of the power struggle that culminated in the **Cultural Revolution**, during which she became deputy leader of the Cultural Revolution Group. After Mao's death in 1976, she was arrested with the other members of the Gang of Four and sentenced to death with a two-year stay of execution on January 25 1981. She died in prison.
Roxane WITKE, *Comrade Chiang Ch'ing* (Boston: Little, Brown, 1977).

JIANG ZHAOHE 蔣兆和 (1904–86)
Outstanding figure painter who combined traditional Chinese skills of brush-work with Western concepts of form and mood and portrayed the emotions of his characters in an unprecedented manner. His most successful subjects depicted the toil and suffering of ordinary people during the Republican period and Japanese occupation, especially in his long mural of life-sized figures entitled "Refugees".

JIANG ZILONG 蔣子龍 (1941–)
Short story writer specialising in industrial stories. Jiang Zilong was born into a peasant family in Hebei. Apart from a spell in the navy, he worked at Tianjin Heavy Machinery Plant from 1958. His first published story dates from 1965, but his writing career took off after he published 'Manager Qiao Assumes Office' in 1979, although he continued to work full-time and write on his day off. This story describes how a new manager puts economic reform into practice in his enterprise by cutting out abuses, demoting the lazy and incompetent, promoting the diligent and qualified, tackling back-doorism and the use of connections. Jiang Zilong's writing is characterized by its earthy, unpolished but humorous style. The story was initially criticized in an article in *Tianjin Daily* but it was strongly backed by readers and won first prize in the 1979 National Short Story Competition. He has written a number of other successful stories since, including a novelette, 'All the Colours of the Rainbow' (1981).
JIANG Zilong, *All the Colours of the Rainbow*, trans. Wang Mingjie (Beijing: Panda Books, 1983).

JIANGNAN 江南
Literally meaning south of the river, this refers to south-central China or the area south of the **Yangzi River**. Originally one administrative unit under the Tang dynasty, it is now divided into several provinces including Zhejiang, Anhui and Jiangxi. In Ming and Qing times it was an important agricultural and commercial centre.

JIANGNAN ARSENAL

Factory founded in 1865 by **Zeng Guofan** in Shanghai to build ships and manufacture guns and cannon. It was a key establishment in the **Self-Strengthening Movement** and also had a translation bureau which made key Western works on science, military matters and technology available to China's modernisers.

JIANGXI SOVIET ***Jiangxi Suweiai*** **江西蘇維埃 (1931–1934)**

First significant area under the control of the CCP. After the **Shanghai Coup** and the debacle of 1927, the CCP was compelled to abandon the cities and relocate to the countryside. The first rural base was in Jinggangshan on Jiangxi's south-western border with Hunan, but the Jiangxi Soviet (named after the soviets or councils of the 1917 revolution in Russia), grew around the south-eastern Jiangxi town of Ruijin. Other Soviet bases were added as CCP influence grew and the Central Soviet Government was proclained in November 1931 after the first All-China Soviet Congress (November 1–7). It was defined as a democratic dictatorship of workers and peasants under CCP leadership. Peasant support was won by **Land Reform** and the Soviet government enacted much social legislation, but the regime finally collapsed under GMD military pressure in the Encirclement Campaigns. Lessons learned in the Jiangxi Soviet period affected CCP policies in **Yan'an** and nationwide after the establishment of the PRC.

Ilpyong KIM, *The Politics of Chinese Communism: Kiangsi under the Soviets* (Berkeley: University of California Press, 1973).

JIAOZHOU 膠州

Bay to the west of Qingdao in Shandong province, occupied by Germany in 1897 after the expulsion of the Chinese garrison from Qingdao.

JIE GUI 桀癸

The tyrannical last ruler of the Xia dynasty, whose wickedness was said to have been so extreme that it dried up rivers. Reputed to have been overthrown around 1766 BC by the founder of the Shang dynasty, Tang, who claimed to be descended from the **Yellow Emperor**. See also **Former Kings.**

JIN 晉, STATE

One of the most important feudal states of the Spring and Autumn period, situated across much of the Great Plain in modern Shanxi province. Its Duke Wen (reigned 635–628 BC) was the second great **hegemon** of the seventh century, and was officially invested with the title *ba* by the Zhou king after defeating **Chu** in battle in 632 BC. But the state was too large for a time when control and communications were still insufficiently developed, and it broke up into **Han**, **Wei** and **Zhao** in 453 BC.

LI Hsueh-chin. (trans. K.C. Cheng), *Eastern Zhou and Qin Civilizations* (Yale Universities Press 1985).

JIN 晉 DYNASTY (266–316)

Brief period of reunification after the Three Kingdoms, with rule by scions of the Sima family from the erstwhile state of Wei. Warlordism was rife, and social and political disharmony led to **Xiongnu** invasions which captured both the capital **Luoyang** in 311 and **Chang'an** (316).

JIN 金 DYNASTY (1115–1234)
Jurchen (Ruzhen) dynasty of conquest which first dispossessed the Khitan Liao in north and north-east China before establishing its own rule across the Great Plain in 1127 (see **Aguda, Huizong**). Its capital was moved from Shangjing (modern Harbin) to Yanjing (modern **Beijing**) in 1153. Despite Korean warnings about its barbarism the regime became quite sinicized and favourable relations developed with the Southern Song regime. A peace treaty was signed in 1142, under which **Hangzhou** paid annual tribute to Jin in silver and silk. The dynasty fell victim itself to the third wave of non-Chinese invasion, by the Mongols under **Khubilai Khan**.

Emperors:

Taizu	1115–23
Taizong	1123–35
Xizong	1135–49
Hailingwang	1149–61
Shizong	1161–90
Zhangzong	1190–1209
Feidi	1209–13
Xuanzong	1213–24
Aizong	1224–34

Jing-shen TAO, *The Jurchen in Twelfth Century China: A Study of Sinicization* (University of Washington Press, 1977); Hok-lam CHAN, *Legitimation in Imperial China: Discussions under the Jurchen Chin Dynasty* (University of Washington Press, 1984).

JINGDI 景帝, HAN EMPEROR (Liu Qi 劉啓, 188–141, r. 157–141 BC)
Grandson of Han emperor **Gaozu**. A revolt by seven princes headed by the leader of one of the vassal kingdoms, Wu (modern Jiangsu), was put down in 154 BC. It may be seen as a reaction to the rising political influence of the gentry class, but after its failure the power of the semi-feudal vassal kings was diminished. Under Jingdi the country achieved a new state of political peace and economic welfare. Caution in government spending resulted in the reduction of taxation and unprecedented state wealth. See also **Liu Sheng, Sima Xiangru.**

JIN-CHA-JI BASE see **BASE AREAS**

JIN-JI-LU-YU BASE see **BASE AREAS**

***JIN PING MEI* 金瓶梅**
Written around the late sixteenth century by an anonymous author (known by the pseudonym *Lanling Xiaoxiao Sheng* 蘭陵笑笑生 'The Scoffing Scholar of Lanling') and published in 1618 or thereabouts, the *Jinpingmei* is one of the masterpieces of traditional fiction. A long (100 chapter) and exceedingly complex work of prose fiction considered the predecessor to the great eighteenth century novel ***Hongloumeng***, the novel is filled with quoted material in the form

of poetry, drama and song and retains many features associated with the traditional storyteller. Branded a work of pornography due to its graphic sexual descriptions, the novel was prohibited for long periods. However, it has also been interpreted as a *roman à clef*, a novel of manners, a Buddhist morality tale and, more recently, an inversion of the Confucian cult of self-cultivation. Set in the Song dynasty but demonstrably a satire on Ming government and society, the novel is filled with an unprecedented amount of detail about the life of the Ming. Beginning from the tale of Ximen Qing and Pan Jinlian found in ***Shuihuzhuan***, it details the rise and fall of the household of Ximen Qing, a wealthy merchant who uses his influence and money to seduce women and gain power in official circles. Much of the action centres on the women Ximen Qing collects both inside and outside his household and it is the first Chinese novel to portray women to such an extent. The title can be translated as 'Plum Blossoms in a Golden Vase' but literally consists of three characters from the names of the three main female figures.

David Tod ROY, *The Plum in the Golden Vase or, Chin P'ing Mei Vol.1: The Gathering* (Princeton University Press, 1993); Clement EGERTON, *The Golden Lotus* (4 vols.) (London: Routledge and Kegan Paul, 1972); Andrew H. PLAKS, *The Four Masterworks of the Ming Novel* (Princeton University Press, 1987).

JING TIAN see **WELL-FIELD SYSTEM**

JINGDEZHEN 景德鎮

The pottery town of Jingdezhen in Jiangxi province was one of the first great industrial centres in China and probably one of the earliest in the world. According to local traditions, pottery was made in the area around Jingdezhen – Fuliang *xian* 浮梁縣 – as early as the Han dynasty. The imperial court of the Chen dynasty received pottery from Fuliang in AD 583 and during the Tang, kilns near the town which have since been excavated, supplied porcelain to the emperor on several occasions. Pottery and porcelain were made throughout the Song and Yuan periods, but the kilns and workshops remained scattered around Fuliang, and little, if any, was made in Jingdezhen itself, which functioned primarily as a market and as a government control point for official orders.

During the Ming dynasty, the industry and the town of Jingdezhen underwent radical changes. The quantity of porcelain produced increased dramatically and the quality greatly improved. Jingdezhen was transformed from a market into an industrial centre, so that by the end of the dynasty most kilns outside had closed down and production was concentrated in the town. Although this process of concentration took place throughout the Ming dynasty, the period of most rapid change was in the 16th century in the reigns of the Jiajing (1522–66) and **Wanli** (1573–1620) emperors. A number of factors were involved in this transformation. Among the most important were the interest of the imperial household in porcelain, the availability of raw materials, the technical expertise of the potters, supply of labour, appropriate managment and finance and the great changes taking place in the Chinese economy as a whole in the 16th century. However, two factors which played an important role in the development of the industry, and which have perhaps been underestimated, were the existence of a viable local transport system and Jingdezhen's access to a nationwide marketing network. The complex marketing network revolving around the guilds served the industry well enough in its developing years, but began to fail when Jingdezhen found itself in competition with machine-made foreign pottery in the late 19th and early 20th centuries. The town evolved into a specialised industrial production centre with hundreds of workshops and small kilns and porcelain for the court was ordered through imperial depots established there. The industry and its art flourished in the 15th and 16th centuries under Ming commissioners and again in the eighteenth century under officials including Tang Ying who oversaw production for the palace, but declined in the nineteenth century. By the 1930s control by the guilds was seen as one of the factors preventing the modernisation of the industry, and the combination of this and declining trade brought about the collapse of the system. Post-1949 Jingdezhen received the modern equipment and organisation it needed but the quality of the best Ming and Qing products was never repeated. See also **Ceramics**.

JINGGANGSHAN see **JIANGXI SOVIET**

JINMEN 金門 (QUEMOY)

Island just off the coast of Fujian, which was one of the strongholds of **Koxinga** and his base for plundering China in the 17th century. Jinmen was held by the Guomindang when it retreated to Taiwan in spite of its proximity to the mainland and is very heavily garrisoned. The island and its neighbour Mazu 馬祖 (Matsu), also under GMD control, became the focus of political crises in 1954 and 1958 when the two sides shelled each other.

***JINSHIXUE* 金石學**

The study of bronzes and stones, which was the forerunner of Chinese archaeology. The scholarship of *jinshixue* started from the Northern Song catalogues, such as Nu Daling's *Kaogutu* 考古圖 (*The Illustrated Catalogue of Studied Antiquities*) published in 1092 and Wang Fu's *Xuanhe bogutu* 宣和博古圖 (*Illustrated Record of Ancient Objects in the Xuanhe Palace*) published in 1119–1125. Details of physical appearance, measurement, inscriptional contents, and decorative designs were so carefully recorded and classified in the Song catalogues and other antiquarian writings that the terminology and methods used by Nu Daling and others had a profound influence upon Chinese antiquarianism and, later, archaeology.

Over time, especially during the mid and late Qing dynasty, the scope of *jinshixue* was expanded from bronzes and stones into a variety of subject areas ranging from jades, seals and tiles to coinage and measuring instruments.

This traditional scholarship was further developed early this century by scholars such as **Wang Guowei** and **Guo Moruo** with, for example, their work on the systematic approach to inscriptions on oracle bones, the evolutionary way of viewing stylistic development of bronzes, and the interpretation of historical data in terms of social evolution.

JINWEN see **NEW TEXT SCHOOL**

JIUJIANG 九江
Port on the **Yangzi River** which was added to the list of **Treaty Ports** in the 1858 Treaty of Tianjing. Under the Ming and Qing dynasties it was an entrepot for the porcelain produced in **Jingdezhen.**

JOFFE, ADOLPH
Comintern representative sent to China in 1922 to negotiate the conditions for cooperation between the Soviet Union, the Guomindang and the Chinese Communist Party. The negotiations, conducted with **Sun Yixian** resulted in the Sun-Joffe agreement, announced on January 26 1923, in which it was accepted that China had not yet reached the stage at which a Soviet form of government was appropriate, and the USSR relinquished all rights and privileges over China that could be construed as imperialist. The practical details of the GMD reorganisation were subsequently undertaken by Mikhail **Borodin**.

JOKHANG see **LHASA**

JOHN OF MONTECORVINO (?1246–1328)
Franciscan monk sent by Pope Nicholas IV with letters to **Khubilai Khan**, who reached **Beijing** in 1294. After a successful period of ministry under the Emperor's protection he built his first church in the capital (1299) and was appointed Archbishop of Cambaluc in 1307. Three suffragans arrived in 1308, Andrew of Perugia, Peregrine of Castello, and Gerald. In 1313 Friar Gerald set up a church in Quanzhou under the patronage of a wealthy Armenian lady. This early Western mission, which ministered mainly to European merchants but also made converts among the Chinese, disappeared with the overthrow of the Mongols in the mid-fourteenth century.

JURCHEN (Ruzhen 女眞)
Ancestors of the **Manchus**. The Tungusic-speaking tribespeople of north-eastern China became a powerful nation under **Aguda.** The Jurchen language, related to Manchu, was written in characters similar to those used in Chinese, but which are still largely undeciphered**.** See also **Bohai** and **Jin** Dynasty.
Jing-shen TAO, *The Jurchen in Twelfth-Century China: A Study of Sinicization* (University of Washington Press, 1977); Hok-lam CHAN, *Legitimation in Imperial China: Discussions under the Jurchen Chin Dynasty* (University of Washington Press, 1984).

JUREN see **EXAMINATION SYSTEM**

KAIFENG 開封 (formerly **Bianzhou 汴州**)
Capital of the Later Liang (907–23), Later Jin (947–51) and Later Zhou (951–60) dynasties (see **Five Dynasties and Ten Kingdoms**) and of Song China from 960 to 1127. At that time it became one of the largest conurbations in the world, with a population of around one million. It was a great national and international trading centre and a showplace for the many advanced aspects of Song civilisation, including the porcelain (see **Ceramics**) and printing industries. It was also a manufacturing centre taking advantage of the nearby iron and coalmining

industries. It was here that Su Song's water-driven clock was built in 1088 (see **Inventions and Discoveries**), and that Li Jie wrote his great architectural treatise ***Yingzao fashi***. A contemporary painting by Zhang Zeduan 張擇端 entitled *Qingming shanghe* 清明上河圖 "Going up the river at Qingming", apparently shows the city flourishing on the eve of its capture by the Jurchen invaders (see **Jin** dynasty). It is preserved at the Palace Museum in Beijing, but copies were produced by many other artists in later periods. The post of Metropolitan Prefect held at Kaifeng was not a central government appointment but was valuable as a stepping stone in that direction: it was held, for example, by **Cai Jing**. Kaifeng was the centre for the small community of Chinese **Jews**, whose religion first arrived in the Tang dynasty.

KALGAN Zhangjiakou 張家口

City to the north-west of Beijing in Hebei province, once an important trading post for commerce between the capital and the Mongols. The railway line from Beijing completed in 1909and later extended to Baotou in Inner Mongolia increased its importance as a commercial centre during the Republican period.

KANG SHENG 康生 **(1899–1975)**

Long-term member of the CCP Central Committee on which he first served as secretary in Yan'an in 1937, and connected with Party security matters for much of his career. In 1980 after the trial of the **Gang of Four**, he was posthumously expelled from the CCP after it was revealed that he was implicated with Jiang Qing and Chen Boda in an attack on **Liu Shaoqi** in 1967 during which the State Chairman was injured.

KANGXI 康熙 **(1654–1722) QING EMPEROR (r. 1662–1722)**

Second Qing dynasty ruler of China. He was one of the most impressive and effective rulers of China. His personal name was Xuanye 玄燁 and he was born in Beijing, the third son of the Shunzhi emperor, who died of illness aged only 23. Like his father he ascended the throne as a minor, at the age of eight *sui*, and power was in the hands of regents. The Kangxi emperor became responsible for governmental affairs at the age of 14 *sui*. Two years later he had the powerful senior regent Oboi arrested and took personal control of government. From then on his ability and prodigious energy enabled him to maintain a tight grip on all decision making, large and small. The Kangxi emperor did not flinch from taking hard decisions and his boldness usually paid off. His first concern was that a large part of south China was under the control of the **Three Feudatories**, *san fan*, three Ming generals who had helped the Qing take over China. The Kangxi emperor provoked the leader of the three, Wu Sangui, into revolting and by 1681 had captured his stronghold in Kunming. He dealt at the same time with a revolt among the Mongols, and in 1683 moved to retake Taiwan from the family of Zheng Chenggong (see **Koxinga**). He checked Russian expansion into Manchuria and signed the Treaty of Nerchinsk in September 1689, holding the Russians to the new borders. He later also incorporated Outer Mongolia and Tibet into the Qing empire.

In spite of all these military ventures, the Kangxi emperor managed to ensure that governmental finances were sound by encouraging the resettlement of abandoned land and by his own personal frugality. The area of cultivated land rose from 550 million *mu* to over 800 million and the population similarly increased. He was so successful that he was able to grant a series of tax holidays and in 1711 to fix the poll tax payers at the existing number in perpetuity. Decay in the infrastructure, both a symptom and a cause of Ming decline, was reversed with extensive work on the Yellow River and the Grand Canal, reducing flooding and improving grain transportation from the rich Yangzi rice basket to the north.

Although some notable scholars (see **Ming Loyalists**) refused to compromise with the Qing, the Kangxi emperor's policy of conciliation towards intellectuals and his patronage of scholarly enteprises won over all but a few diehards. His generally tolerant approach to dissidents contrasted with that of the **Qianlong** emperor (see **Literary Inquisition**) and he avoided the opprobrium heaped on the latter. Projects he supported included the writing of the history of the Ming dynasty, the *Mingshi* 明史, the compilation of the *Kangxi zidian* 康熙字典 (still the definitive Chinese character dictionary) and encyclopaedias like the *Peiwen yunfu* 佩文韻府(1711) and the massive *Gujin tushu jicheng* 古今圖書集成 (1706). His strong support for Confucianism, particularly Zhu Xi's brand of **Neo-Confucianism**, was reflected in his 1670 *Shengyu* 'sacred Edict'. This was a series of 16 seven character maxims designed to foster moral values; it was publicly read to the population at large annually throughout the Qing dynasty.

The Kangxi emperor's open-mindedness was reflected in his attitude to the **Jesuits,** whom he employed to pass on Western skills in areas like mathematics, astronomy, horology, calendrical science and military technology. The Jesuits' religious progress in China relied on their taking a relaxed attitude towards aspects of traditional Chinese culture, like ancestor worship and Confucian shrines, which could be deemed to conflict with the Christian's duty to God. Their success encouraged other less broadminded orders to flock to China. The latter's reports back to Rome resulted in the **Rites Controversy** and pope Clement XI's decree of 1704 and bull Ex Illa Die of 1715 banning Chinese Christians from participating in such rites. This resulted in a trial of strength which the Papacy was bound to lose. The Kangxi emperor and his successors banned missionaries who supported the Pope, and the Jesuits' painstakingly constructed edifice crumbled. It was the mid-19th century before Christians, and then largely the rival Protestants, were able to return.

Lawrence D. KESSLER, *K'ang-hsi and the Consolidation of Ch'ing Rule, 1661–1684* (Chicago University Press, 1976); Jonathan D. Spence, *Emperor of China: Self-portrait of K'ang-hsi* (New York: Knopf 1974).

KANG YOUWEI 康有爲 (1858–1927)

Leader of the 1898 **Hundred Days Reform** movement and subsequently exiled supporter of the **Guangxu Emperor**. Kang was from a scholarly family of Nanhai, Guangdong; his early academic promise led to his being accepted as a student of an eminent local scholar, Zhu Ciqi 朱次琦 at the age of 19 *sui*, after which he spent four years in studying by himself. He was firmly committed to the **New Text** school of scholarship which emphasised the central role of Confucius and the transmission of his ideas. During this period he visited Hong Kong and paid his first visit to Shanghai (in 1882) where he was impressed by what he saw and realised that the foreigners could not be dismissed in the traditional way as ignorant barbarians; he began to buy and read books on the West. On a visit to take examinations in Beijing in 1888, in the aftermath of the Sino-French war, Kang submitted a 10,000 character memorial to the throne on the need for reform; this, like most of the subsequent ones, was blocked and never reached the Guangxu Emperor. After his return to Guangdong, he accepted **Liang Qichao** and others from the famous Xuehaitang 學海堂academy as his students and in 1891 formally set up his own Wanmu caotang 萬木草堂 academy. It was at this time that he produced his *Xinxue weijingkao* 新學僞經考 'Study of the forged Xin classics', a work which rocked the scholarly world with its assertion that the old text versions of the classics were all forgeries perpetrated by Liu Xin 劉歆 in an attempt legitimize Wang Mang's usurping Xin dynasty. Kang and Liang's 1895 visit to the to the capital to take part in the metropolitan examinations coincided with **Li Hongzhang**'s negotiations at Shimonoseki following China's defeat in the **Sino-Japanese war**. The treaty conditions included cession of territory to Japan and payment of a heavy indemnity. Kang and Liang organised a protest petition which was signed by 1200 of the metropolitan candidates (known as the *gongche shangshu* 公車上書) asking for the rejection of the peace terms and for China to be put on a war footing, but the petition was rejected on the grounds that the treaty had already been signed and could not be revoked. Kang passed the examination, was awarded the *jinshi* degree and given a post which he did not take up. Instead, he returned to Guangdong to complete an even more provocative work, his *Kongzi gaizhi kao* 孔子改制考 'Study of Confucius as a Reformer'. In this he suggested that Confucius was not merely the transmitter of ancient knowlege, as he himself had claimed, but an innovator who had used the cloak of antiquity to add credence to some of his more radical ideas. This went a step further in creating a quasi-religious cult of Confucius, an image unacceptable to those who saw Confucius as a purely secular figure, at most a *primus inter pares* among the pre-Qin philosophers. Among his many other works he also produced a study of the Meiji reform movement and when, in 1898, a further crisis occurred with the 'scramble for concessions' by Western powers, he headed once again for Beijing and presented a fifth petition urging the Emperor to start a reform movement modelled on those of Russia and Japan. After two more petitions and a meeting at the Zongli Yamen with a group of leading officials, including Li Hongzhang and Weng Tonghe, there followed an audience with the Guangxu Emperor and a heady three months of reform over the summer, the so-called 100 Day Reform Movement, during which the Emperor issued edict after edict ordering a raft of military, economic, political, institutional and educational reforms suggested by Kang. The reforms threatened many vested interests and the Guangxu Emperor's weak power base was not sufficient to push them through; **Cixi,** the Empress Dowager, staged a coup taking back power on September 21. Kang was forewarned by the Emperor and he and Liang Qichao fled via Shanghai and Hong Kong to Japan but six others who refused to flee, including **Tan Sitong**, were executed. Kang travelled as far as Canada and Britain publicising the reformist cause and in July 1899 set up the ***Baohuanghui*** 保皇會 'Protect the Emperor Society' to promote the cause of the Guangxu Emperor. In 1900, during the **Boxer Rebellion**, the reformers attempted a military coup led by Tang Caichang 唐才常 but lack of funds, poor organisation and half-hearted support doomed it to failure. After that Kang would have nothing more to do with armed uprisings and he went to India and wrote his *Datongshu* 大同書 'Book of Great Harmony' in which he expounded an extraordinary vision of the withering away of all institutions and social boundaries leading to a unified world of individuals freely enjoying publicly provided benefits. It was based on the three ages theory (that the world was going from chaos, to lesser peace, to great harmony) of the *Gongyang* 公羊 commentary on the ***Spring and Autumn Annals*** plus elements from Buddhist and Western millenarianism. Kang himself seems to have been apprehensive about the reception the work would receive and it was not published in its entirety until after his death. In 1907 the Protect the Emperor Party was changed into the National Constitution Party and pressed the late Qing authorities for constitutional reform. After the 1911 Revolution Kang returned to China but remained opposed to republicanism and gave his support to Zhang Xun's abortive attempt to restore the monarchy in 1917. He spent his last years in Shanghai promoting traditional scholarship in the face of the May Fourth tide of Western ideas and values. See also ***Qiangxuehui***.

Jung-pang LO ed. and trans., *K'ang Yu-wei A Biography and a Symposium* (University of Arizona Press, 1967); Laurence G. Thompson trans., *Ta T'ung Shu: The One World Philosophy of K'ang Yu-wei* (George Allen and Unwin, 1958); HSIAO Kung-ch'uan, *A Modern China and a New World: K'ang Yu-wei, Reformer and Utopian, 1858–1927* (University of Washington Press, 1975).

KARA KHITAI (Qarakhitai)

Local name for the Western Liao dynasty founded by the **Khitan** in 1124 after it had been driven west by the Jurchen. It was in turn overwhelmed by Mongol forces under **Chinggis Khan** as they moved westwards in 1211.

KARAKORUM

Capital of the Mongol empire constructed on the orders of **Chinggis Khan** but completed by his successor **Ögödei Khan**. Many thousands of craftsmen were brought in from territories conquered by the Mongols in Central Asia to build the capital. The site, known to Mongols today as Harhorin, lies some 400 kilometres south-west of the modern Mongolian capital Ulanbaatar. The ruins of the ancient capital can still be seen, although many of the stones were removed in the sixteenth century to build the monastery of Erdene-zuu which was constructed in 1586

KARLGREN, BERNHARD (1889–1978)

Distinguished Swedish sinologist. In 1925 J.G. Andersson had established the Museum of Far Eastern Antiquities in Stockholm to house his extensive collection of Chinese neolithic antiquities, and it also acquired many bronzes. Karlgren was its Director from 1939 to 1959, and edited its Bulletin from 1959 to 1976. He wrote copiously on his researches, particularly in the fields of ancient bronzes and phonology. He published a well known translation of the *Book of Songs* (1950) and a unique dictionary, *Grammata Serica Recensa* (1957), which combines *kaishu* 楷書 script with **oracle bone** and bronze script forms of characters.

KARMAPA

The so-called "Red Hat" Order of Tibetan Buddhism, founded by a disciple of Milarepa, Dusum Kyempa (1110–93). Its power base was at Tsurpu, in the province of Tsang, but it had no single major monastic headquarters. Dusum Kyempa's reincarnate successors, the second, third, fourth and fifth Karmapas, all visited China during the Yuan and Ming dynasties. Through their services to **Khubilai Khan** and his successors they, like the Sakya Abbot '**Phagspa**, attracted the Mongols to the "patron-priest" relationship. But through the wealth and influence they earned in China they also gained the patronage of the Tsang nobility. This drew them into the struggle between Tsang and Ü, and into rivalry with the **Gelugpa** "Yellow Hat" Order. This was their eventual undoing. In 1642 the tenth Karmapa fled from Gusri Khan's invasion in support of the Great Fifth **Dalai Lama**, and the power of Tsang and the Karmapa Order's challenge for political and ecclesiastical supremacy was broken for ever. The Red Hats themselves survived, however, as befits descendants of the great literary mystic Milarepa.

R.A. STEIN, *Tibetan Civilisation* (Stanford University Press, 1972).

KASHGHAR Kashi 喀什

Main market and garrison town of south-western **Xinjiang**. This predominantly Uyghur-speaking city was the base for the independent khanate ruled by Yakub Beg between 1870 and 1877 and also for the short-lived Turkish-Islamic Republic of Eastern Turkestan in 1933 and 1934. It has the largest mosque on Chinese territory.

KAZAKHS

Turkic-speaking Muslim ethnic group living on both sides of the Tianshan mountains, that is in northern **Xinjiang** and in Kazakhstan, where they make up almost half of the population today, most of the remainder being Russian. Kazakhs were traditionally nomadic pastoralists, closer in culture to the Mongols than the other Turkic groups in Central Asia. After attempts by the Chinese authorities to collectivise the herds of Xinjiang Kazakhs during the **Great Leap Forward**, many fled over the border into what was then the Soviet Union. The sealed border during the **Sino-Soviet Dispute** separated family members who were not reunited until the 1991 collapse of the USSR. Russified Kazakhs in Kazakhstan look to what they perceive as a purer Kazakh culture in Xinjiang for inspiration in seeking their roots.

Linda BENSON and Ingvar SVANBERG eds., *The Kazaks of China: Essays on an Ethnic Minority* (Stockholm: Almquist and Wicksell International, 1988).

KHANBALIGH

Mongol capital of **Khubilai Khan** built in the northern part of present-day **Beijing**. Construction took place between 1267 and 1292, during which time, the Mongols adopted a Chinese dynastic name, the Yuan. In the **Marco Polo** accounts of China it appears as Cambaluc.

KHITAN

Semi-nomadic tribe whose empire, the Liao (947–1125), extended over the vast expanse of land that is today Mongolia and the north-eastern provinces of

China. Khitan tribes each had a military leader and their economy combined steppe pastoralism with agriculture.

KHUBILAI KHAN (1215–94, r. 1260–94)

Grandson of **Chinggis Khan**, and the first non-Chinese ever to rule the whole of China, which he did as Yuan dynasty emperor Shizu 世祖. He established his capital (Dadu, known to **Marco Polo** as Cambaluc) on the site of modern **Beijing** in 1264, and completed his conquest with the capture of **Hangzhou** in 1279. He failed in attempts to extend his empire still further to Japan and into South-east Asia but nevertheless ruled the widest empire the world had ever seen, establishing unprecedently settled conditions across Asia from the Caspian to the Korean peninsula (the so-called *Pax Mongolica*). As **Son of Heaven** his reputation was that of a harsh despot, discriminating against his Chinese subjects, but this may be unfair. Initial attempts to woo the Confucian literati were rejected by many, and he turned to foreigners in his efforts to manage a civilisation very different from his own. Mongols and Central Asians were given greater privileges than northern and southern Chinese, but his continuation of the Song policy of encouraging international commerce benefited many, as Marco Polo's description of Hangzhou illustrates. Members of the Mongol court were converted to **Nestorian** Christianity and Khubilai pursued a policy of religious eclecticism, despite his own patronage of **Buddhism** (see **'Phagspa**).

Morris ROSSABI, *Khubilai Khan: His Life and Times* (University of California Press, 1988).

KIAKHTA, TREATY OF (1727)

Russo-Chinese agreement on the boundary between Outer Mongolia and Siberia, the extension of overland trade and the institution of a religious mission in Beijing. Most of the issues discussed remained unresolved after the **Treaty of Nerchinsk** (1689).

KIAOCHOW see **JIAOZHOU**

KINGSHIP

In the Warring States period the two most extreme definitions of kingship came from the **Legalists** and **Mencius**. According to the former, the king had the right to exercise supreme power but might ideally expect the state to function so smoothly beneath him that he need do nothing – *wu wei* 無爲 – other than indulge his pleasures. He, like his subjects, was bound by the impersonal law once created, but it was he who framed it and it reflected his interests. Ultimately the people were there to serve him. Mencius also accepted the king's position at the top of the political pyramid, but emphasized that his interests were subordinate to those of the people. This distinguished the true king from the **hegemon**, and marked him out as the possessor of Heaven's **mandate**. His personal example and his policies would therefore be devoted to encouraging morality in both private and public life, and to restoring the ideal standards of the **Former Kings.** See also **Son of Heaven.**

KOGURYO

The most northerly of the three kingdoms that ruled much of the Korean peninsula between the first and seventh centuries AD. Said to have been founded in 37 BC in the upper Yalu and Tumen River regions, its inhabitants were toughened by the mountainous terrain and by military confrontation with Chinese armies, even though it paid tribute to China and adopted many aspects of Chinese culture. Its court adopted **Buddhism** in 372 and established a Confucian Academy in the same year. The largest of the three kingdoms, its territory covered much of modern Manchuria and two-thirds of modern North **Korea**, its capital from 427 being near modern P'yongyang. It astutely sent tribute to both northern and southern Chinese courts (see **Northern and Southern Dynasties**). Its armies inflicted heavy defeats on Sui forces in 612–4 and repelled the Tang emperor **Taizong's** determined invasion in 645, but it finally succumbed to a joint Silla-Tang campaign in 668.

KOREA

As a near neighbour showing readiness to adopt many aspects of Chinese civilisation and conform to China's diplomatic expectations, Korea was a prominent partner in the traditional **tribute system** of the **Middle Kingdom**, exchanging missions in every dynasty from the Three Kingdoms (**Koguryo, Paekche, Silla**) period onward. Despite receiving a biography in Chinese official histories under the heading of Eastern Barbarians, it was also favourably referred to as *junzi zhi guo* 君子之國 "Country of Gentlemen", in recognition of the fact that the literati were highly educated in the **Confucian Classics**. Chinese influence was to be seen in upper-class literature, philos ophy, painting, architecture, dress, social customs, state examinations and court rituals, though the nobility as well as the ordinary people also enjoyed Korea's own distinctive culture, and the court showed itself well able to make political and military decisions independently of China when necessary. As in China, **Buddhism** was widely accepted among all levels of society and opened up a second line of learned communication between Korea and China. Commerce was a third source of contact, both by overland routes and by sea via the Shandong Peninsula and the port of Mingzhou (modern Ningbo).

During the Koryo dynasty (935–1392) the court patronised Buddhism, and the **Khitan** (Liao), the **Jurchen** (Jin) and the **Mongols** (Yuan) successively competed with the Song Chinese for its political allegiance. The following Choson dynasty (1392–1910) coincided with the return of a Chinese dynasty on the mainland, the Ming, and saw the triumph of **Zhu Xi's** brand of **Neo-Confucianism** and the strengthening of Chinese influence over the Korean literati. However, the Manchu conquest again prompted a more independent spirit, and by the nineteenth century official ties between the two countries had become quite lax. When the West, and particularly Japan, sought to dominate Korea towards the end of the century, China was stung to try and re-activate her traditional suzerainty. She sent a Resident Director-General to Seoul and endeavoured to influence court policy, especially through the powerful Queen Min. The involvement of both China and Japan in the Tonghak Rebellion (1894–5) led to the outbreak of the **Sino-Japanese War**, bringing humiliation to **Li Hongzhang** whose Korean policy was a failure and who was compelled to sign the Treaty of **Shimonoseki.** Luckier to escape was **Yuan Shikai**, whose career as Chinese Resident in Seoul (1885–95) failed to benefit his country but also failed to diminish his own political ambitions.

After the Japanese colonisation of Korea in 1910 many Koreans used China as a base for resistance movements. The North-east was a focus for military activity, while **Shanghai** became the seat of the Korean Provisional Government in exile. The Korean Communist Party maintained contacts with the **Chinese Communist Party**, and Kim Il-sung trained as a guerilla fighter in Manchuria. China took no part in the political struggle in Korea following the Japanese defeat in 1945, being too much involved in her own Civil War, but Chinese troops, officially described as Chinese People's Volunteers, played a major part in the **Korean War** from October 1950 onwards.

Martina DEUCHLER, *The Confucian Transformation of Korea* (Harvard University Press 1992)

KOREAN WAR (1950–3)

Was brought about (1) by the absence of an agreed plan, either amongst the Koreans themselves or between the Western Allies, for the future of Korea after the ending of the Japanese colonial period (1910–45), and (2) by post-Second World War rivalry between the United States and the Soviet Union for ideological domination of both eastern and western hemispheres. The battle for control of the peninsula must also be seen in the context of the CCP's success in the Chinese **Civil War**, the fear that this prompted in America, and of China's own anxiety for her territorial integrity in the North-east. Finally, the War was a reflection of the weakness of the fledgling United Nations to understand the Korean situation and to rise above national interests of the contending parties.

Korea had been divided since the Japanese surrender in 1945, though all parties had agreed that this should only be a temporary situation. The War began with the Russian-backed North Korean invasion of the South on June 25 1950, which evoked an immediate US-led response. At the beginning of October **Mao Zedong** ordered Chinese "volunteers" to "resist US aggression", and the first clash between Chinese and Republic of Korea forces took place just south of the Yalu River on October 25. China's initial commitment of 130,000 men of the 13th Army Group was led by Marshal **Peng Dehuai**, whose own reputation was enhanced by the overall success of the Chinese armies in this global confrontation which they had not sought and were unprepared for. It was, however, at tremendous cost. Chinese casualties may have totalled half a million men. Most of the fighting involving Chinese forces took place between November 1950 and July 1951, and an uneasy stalemate with occasional skirmishes followed until a ceasefire was signed at Panmunjon in 1953. The economic effect on a country just recovering from the **Anti-Japanese** and **Civil Wars** was crippling. The enforced indebtedness to the USSR was unwelcome but inevitable since China had been branded as an "aggressor" and found herself denied diplomatic recognition and economic aid from America's allies. The conflict put pressure on a leadership already faced with the problems of establishing political unity while carrying out land and industrial reform.

Bruce CUMINGS, *The Origins of the Korean War* (2 vols.) (Princeton University Press, 1981 and 1990); Max HASTINGS, *The Korean War* (London: Michael Joseph, 1987);

Allen Whiting, *China Crosses the Yalu: The Decision to enter the Korean War* (New York: Macmillan, 1960).

KOWTOW *koutou* 叩頭
Ritual kneeling and placing the forehead on the floor which became a diplomatic issue when performed by members of **tribute** missions presenting themselves to the emperor. Although this symbolic submission posed no problems to the tributary embassies from China's less powerful Asian neighbours, it was considered inappropriate by the envoys of Western diplomats attempting to negotiate with the imperial court for trade and diplomatic rights in the eighteenth and nineteenth centuries, in particular Lord **Macartney** in his 1793 mission.

KOXINGA *Guoxingye* 國姓爺
Literally "Lord of the Imperial Surname", a common name for Zheng Chenggong 鄭成功, a Ming loyalist and member of a prominent Fujian trader and privateer family, who was granted the use of the Ming emperors' surname Zhu because of his loyal support for their lost cause after their defeat by the Qing forces in 1644. When the Qing armies attacked his base in Amoy, he moved over to **Taiwan**, taking the Dutch base there by force. He died in 1662 and Taiwan eventually fell to the forces of the Qing in 1683.

KUBILAI KHAN see **KHUBILAI KHAN**

KUMARAJIVA (fl. 385–409)
Indian scholar kidnapped in Central Asia in 385 and taken to north-west China. In 401 he arrived in **Chang'an**, where he became head of the state translation office and one of the most prolific translators of Buddhist scriptures into Chinese. He completed the best known translation of the **Lotus Sutra** (AD 406).

KUOMINTANG see **GUOMINDANG**

KYRGYZ (also **Kirghiz**)
The semi-nomadic Kyrgyz of Xinjiang are spread throughout western and southern Xinjiang, but there is a significant concentration in the Kizilsu Kyrgyz Autonomous Prefecture in the foothills of the Tianshan mountain range which separates them from their relatives in the former Soviet Republic of Kyrgyzstan. Traditionally, the Kyrgyz are herdsmen with flocks of sheep and camels and, like the **Kazakhs** moved their animals across the mountains according to the season until the **Sino-Soviet** dispute closed the border. Their language and customs are closely related to those of their Kazakh neighbours.

LACQUER
Lacquer is the natural sap of the tree *rhus vernicifera*, which becomes highly resistant to chemicals, damp and considerable heat when dried in a humid atmosphere. It may be stained with almost any colouring matter, and applied in thin layers to most surfaces. Coats on a single piece may number 100 or more but each layer must be allowed to dry before the next is applied. This material has been used in China since the Neolithic period, mainly as an

impermeable coating for objects made of delicate materials such as bamboo, wood and silk.

From the Tang dynasty onwards, carved lacquer was made by building up a large number of layers of lacquer on to a base that was generally either wood or textile, and then carving through the various layers to create patterns or landscapes, etc. Different coloured lacquers are sometimes used and the carving technique reveals the underlying different colours. The technique of carved marbled lacquer was developed, in which a multi-coloured marbled effect is achieved along the sides of the cut edges. *Guri* is another form of carved lacquer where alternate layers of different coloured lacquers are carved in schematised special scrolls. The deeply cut lines are often bevelled.

WANG Shih-hsiang, *Ancient Chinese laquerware* (Beijing: Foreign Languages Press, 1987).

LAND REFORM *Tudi gaige* 土地改革

In twentieth century China, the expression Land Reform, or Agrarian Reform *tudi gaige* is usually reserved for the policy of confiscating land from the landlord class and redistributing it to the poorest peasants. Occasionally the meaning is extended to include the process of collectivisation that followed it and led to the formation of the People's **Communes** in 1958. It should also be noted that Land Reform is not purely a Communist Policy. Japan went through a similar process during the American occupation after the Second World War, Taiwan has had a land reform programme and so have right-wing military regimes in Latin America. The earliest experience that the CCP had of rural policies was in 1922–3 when **Peng Pai** organised peasant associations in Guangdong province. He was later ignored in official Communist Party histories so that Mao Zedong could appear as the first senior Party figure to have taken an interest in the peasantry. Serious attempts at Land Reform under the auspices of the Communist Party began in the **Jiangxi Soviet** period (1929–35) when the beleaguered CCP, surrounded by Guomindang armies, carried out a ruthless land redistribution campaign which cost the lives of many landlords. This period can be seen as the laboratory in which many policies were first tested. In their land policies, the CCP tried to copy policies that appeared to have succeeded in the USSR at that time, and, to paraphrase Mao, they relied on the poor peasants and landless labourers as the core of their support while trying to rally the middle peasants to the cause. During the **United Front** period of 1937–1945, attempts at an alliance with the Guomindang to resist the Japanese invasion led the Communist Party to moderate its land policies, and mass redistribution was replaced by an emphasis on the reduction of land rent and interest on loans, the dual burden on poor peasant farmers. Nationalist sentiment meant that, in this phase of the CCP's revolutionary endeavour, even landlords who were prepared to resist the Japanese were brought into the struggle, although the peasants remained the prime interest of the Party. Increased production to support the war effort became a key part of their agrarian policies. When the Japanese were defeated in 1945 and China was dragged into yet another civil war, far harsher land reform policies were set in motion by the CCP, many landlords were killed, excess land was compulsorily purchased and redistributed and a conscious attempt was made to eliminate the rich peasant farmers as a class. The chief motives of the CCP at this time were to increase farm production in the ever expanding rural areas under their control and to expand the already substantial support they enjoyed among the poorer farmers. So, by the time the Communist Party came to power as the government of the People's Republic in October 1949, the Land Reform process was well advanced. The main task of the new government was to codify the practice and in many cases to restrain overzealous activists who were redistributing land and killing landowners with little regard to their status and histories. The legislation designed to do this was the Land Reform Law which was promulgated in 1950. The general principles of the law were outlined in Article 1: "The land ownership system of feudal exploitation by the landlord class shall be abolished and the system of peasant landownership shall be introduced in order to set free the rural productive forces, develop agricultural production and thus pave the way for New China's industrialisation." The CCP had far more experience and better trained personnel for Land Reform than for its urban campaigns. Different approaches were tried, based on the experience the CCP had accumulated in the "liberated areas" of Manchuria and North China and the methods of ensuring compliance were gradually refined. In 1950, Mao's view was that the "agrarian reform in the north was carried out in wartime, with the atmosphere of war prevailing over that of agrarian reform, but now, with the fighting practically over, the agrarian reform stands out in sharp relief and the shock to society will be particularly great". The main difference was that Land Reform was now carried out over a much wider geographical area. Land seizures were "restricted to a small fraction of the population. Although the holdings of the landlords themselves were confiscated and redistributed, in many cases the land of the rich peasants was not touched." This was because the food production of the farms belonging to rich peasants was vital for reconstruction and they were not to be alienated. Land Reform could not begin until an area was firmly under the control of the new regime. PLA units spread across China, first taking the major cities and than fanning out to the rural market towns and the villages. "Bandit Suppression Campaigns" were launched in which potentially hostile groups and individuals were disarmed and new village militia units were organised. The Land Reform campaign was coordinated at county town level, where work teams of from three to thirty people were established. These included local people considered to be reliable, veteran Party and army officials and members of the PLA. but also many students and other politicised urban intellectuals. The first task of the work teams was to organise a system of tax collection and this cost the lives of over three thousand cadres during the first year of land reform, although the resistance lessened once the tax burden was switched from the poor to the less poor. Peasant associations were then set up on the model established by Peng Pai, rent and interest reductions were secured and mass meetings were held to attack those seen as the most oppressive members of the former élite. The objective of these meetings was to shatter the traditional patterns of control and deference that had characterised rural China for centuries. Work teams identi--fied landlords and sought to isolate them from the poorer members of their extended families. "The work teams soon became familiar with the complex deceptions that landlord families followed in the countryside, whether it was dramatically dropping their standard of living to appear poorer than they really were, consuming livestock that could not then be counted as wealth, withholding fertiliser from land about to be confiscated, or failing to perform customary charitable deeds that might brand one as being of the landlord class". Peasants, unsure of the how long the new regime was likely to survive, sometimes secretly gave back the amount by which their rent had been reduced to their landlords with whom they may have had family or other ties. Peasant associations were not always dependable and in some areas as few as forty per cent of peasants were members. The traditional power and influence of the gentry and landlords and bonds of family, clan and local residence were difficult to overcome. The problems work teams encountered were increased by the fact that many of them were cadres from outside the area in which they were working who had little knowledge of local conditions and might not even understand the local dialect. There has been some controversy over whether the Land Reform policies of the early 1950s were ever intended to be an end in themselves, with every peasant owning his own plot of land, or whether it was from the outset conceived as a halfway house on the road to full collectivisation. In a report by **Liu Shaoqi** on the Land Reform Law of June 1950, he outlined the economic rationale as "freeing the rural productive forces and paving the way for industrialisation", echoing the principles enshrined in the preamble to the legislation. In November and December 1950, during the Korean War, more radical policies of Land Reform were again implemented and there was greater emphasis on class struggle and mass mobilisation. Class identification was carried out more rigorously, landlords' holdings were ruthlessly confiscated and work teams from the county town headquarters were sent down to the villages to clean up and reform the **Peasant Associations** considered to be unreliable. A new leadership of poorer peasant emerged in the associations, and "speak bitterness" meetings at which landlords were publicly criticised, accused and humiliated were followed by executions. It is possible that as many as two million landlords were killed during this period. The result of the Land Reform policies was that 60% of the rural population now owned 43% of cultivable land, a substantial redistribution. Although the poorest farmers benefited, it was probably the middle peasants who gained most. There may also have been an overall national improvement in agricultural productivity but it is difficult to determine how much this was due to redistribution and how much simply to having a period without war. The main achievement was clearly political. The old village power structures of clans, temples and secret societies had been replaced by new ones, which took over their educational, mediatory and economic functions. A new élite of village cadres from a poor and middle peasant background had emerged.

LAND TAX

The principal source of income for governments in imperial China, usually collected in grain or cloth in early dynasties but later in coinage also. Based on the extent and estimated yield of an owner's land and a poll-tax on his family, it was levied at a rate equivalent to between one fifteenth and one thirtieth of farm produce in the Han. In 780, as the Twice-a-year Tax, it incorporated the household and labour dues and for the first time was payable in copper cash (see **Equal Field System**). By the eleventh century the use of metal money was widespread and paper money also made its first appearance. By the late Ming the taxation system had again become more complex, and in 1581 a simplified levy was introduced, based on the land tax and known as the **Single Whip system**. In the Qing the assessment of tax dues was still based on the measurement of land, recorded in the "Fish-scale Registers", and the number of taxable adult residents, listed in the Yellow Registers, but by the early nineteenth century the land and poll taxes had once more been generally merged into one. See also ***Lijia***, **Well-field System.**

K. BERNHARDT, *Rents, Taxes and Peasant Resistance* (Stanford University Press, 1992).

LAND TENURE

The formal abolition of feudalism in 221 BC established the right of non-aristocratic individuals to own land, one which, despite coming under threat during the **Land Reform** of the PRC, has been acknowledged throughout Chinese history. Implementation however has not always been successful. Despite attempts to prevent the accumulation of large estates, including periodic steps to prevent their undivided inheritance, they constituted the most enviable symbol of wealth and material success throughout the imperial era. Large landowners included officials, merchants, **clans**, and the Buddhist church. Small landowners often found the struggle to compete and to pay their taxes and labour dues impossible, and were then forced into tenancy. Until the Tang period it was usual for landowners to live on their estates, but widespread social and economic changes in the Northern Song dynasty encouraged landlords to move from the countryside into the towns, leaving bailiffs in charge of rent collection and land management. Some tenants were exploited by harsh agents, but for others absentee landlordism meant a lack of supervision tantamount to freedom. Tenancy was not always synonymous with poverty: some tenants, though technically servants, became both rich and powerful, even employing staff of their own. In the Qing dynasty county **magistrates** often depended on the support of the powerful rural **gentry** to assist in local administration, and if the gentry withdrew their support or were not present to give it, as happened increasingly through the nineteenth century, the result was a breakdown of services and control which led to peasant suffering and an upsurge in **secret society** activity.

Both the psychological and political role of the emperor as father and mother of his people and the economic importance of the **land tax** to the court and government meant that land tenure was a matter of regular concern. Attempts to improve the system were made or proposed by **Wang Mang**, the rulers of the Northern Wei, Sui and early Tang dynasties (see **Equal Field System**), **Wang Anshi**, Ming Taizu (see **Military Farms**), the **Taiping** leadership, and **Sun Yixian**. CCP Land Reform of the 1950s provides a modern example of the same concern.

Mark ELVIN, *The Pattern of the Chinese Past* (Eyre Methuen, 1973); Dwight PERKINS, *Agricultural Development in China, 1368-1968* (Edinburgh University Press, 1969); P.C. PERDUE, *Exhausting the Earth: State & Peasant in Human 1500-1950* (Harvard University Press, 1987)

LANDSCAPE PAINTING *shanshui hua* 山水畫

Early elements of landscape art appear in the decoration of inlaid bronzes from the Warring States period. From the Han dynasty only examples from the painted walls and decorative bricks and tiles of tombs survive (see **Helingeer, Wuliang Shrines**), though contemporary bibliographies suggest the evolution by then of landscape painting on *silk* and this is supported by the evidence of the funerary banner from **Mawangdui**. A copy of **Gu Kaizhi's** painting *The Nymph of the Lo River* indicates that by the fourth century AD the format for the development of the horizontal landscape had already been established, whilst the oldest surviving handscroll of this genre, Zhan Ziqian's *Travellers in Spring*, reveals that a remarkable leap forward towards depth and realism had taken place by the Sui dynasty. Extant Tang paintings are few in number but supplemented by murals from **Dunhuang**. The influence of both **Buddhism** and **Daoism** on art was already strong, and in retrospect it was later claimed that the beginnings of the bifurcation of painters into those who sought their goal through attention to detail and those who preferred to convey atmosphere in a more impressionistic manner could already be seen. In the Song, when landscape art reaches its full maturity, this categorisation is represented by the work of Academicians and literati (*wenren*) artists (see **Academy of Painting, Ma Yuan, Mi Fei**), and in the Ming and Qing by the so-called northern (Zhe[jiang]) and southern (Wu) schools (see **Dong Qichang**). The goal of all landscape artists was, however, the same, to represent the **Dao** through the depiction of nature and to lead man to an appreciation of his place in the universe. To this end a complete and totally realistic depiction of the scene before the artist's eyes was not regarded as essential, and the viewer did not understand it as such. In terms of Northern Song **Neo-Confucian** philosophical traditions, some painted according to their "investigation [and observation] of things", and some according to their appreciation of "principle" and its rather imprecise inspiration.

Michael SULLIVAN, *The Birth of Landscape Painting in China* (London: Routledge Kegan Paul, 1962); Michael SULLIVAN, *Symbols of Eternity: The Art of Landscape Painting in China* (Oxford: Clarendon Press, 1979).

LANGUAGE see **CHINESE LANGUAGE**

LAO SHE 老舍 (1899–1966)

One of the most prolific authors and playwrights of the post-**May Fourth** period. Born Shu Qingchun 舒慶春 in Beijing and of Manchu descent, Lao She followed an early career of teaching, becoming the head of a primary school in 1918. He learnt English and in 1924 went to London to teach Chinese at the School of Oriental and African Studies in the University of London. There he began writing his first, mainly humorous, novels so that by the time he returned to China in 1930 he had gained the reputation of being a comic novelist. However, *Lihun* 離婚 'Divorce' (1933) expressed Lao's despair at the weakness in the Chinese character and China's low status in the world. Perhaps his most famous story in the West is *Luotuo Xiangzi* 駱駝祥子 'Camel Xiangzi', a tragic yet comic portrayal of an individual living in a uncaring society. During the **Anti-Japanese War** he was head of the All-China Anti-Japanese Writers Federation and afterwards visited the United States. After returning to China in 1950, he ceased to write novels but wrote a number of plays, including the famous *Chaguan* 茶館 'Teahouse'. Both his writings and his activities in the 1950s indicated strong support for the new government but he was an early victim of the Cultural Revolution and committed suicide on August 24th 1966.

R. VOHRA, *Lao She and the Chinese Revolution* (Harvard University Press, 1974).

LAOZI see ***DAODEJING***

LAST EMPEROR see **PUYI**

LATTIMORE, OWEN (1900–89)

American scholar whose early career as a wool trader established him as an authority on China's inner Asian frontiers and Mongolian affairs. In the 1930s and 40s he knew both **Mao Zedong** and **Zhou Enlai** and worked as United States government adviser to **Jiang Jieshi** in wartime Chongqing. Back in the USA his sympathy for China brought him persecution in the McCarthy witchhunt of the early 1950s and he moved to the UK to establish the Department of Chinese Studies at the University of Keeds in 1963. His greatest contribution to Chinese studies was his demonstration of the interplay between Chinese and central Asian history and the myth of China's traditional isolation from the wider world.

Owen LATTIMORE, *Inner Asian Frontiers of China* (New York: Capitol, 1951).

LEAGUE OF LEFT WING WRITERS ***Zhongguo zuoyi zuojia lianmeng*** 中國左翼作家聯盟

Organization set up in Shanghai in the early 1930s to advance the **Communist Party's** propaganda efforts among writers. The 1920s had been a period of diversity and relative freedom in literary output. The success of the **Northern Expedition** and the perceived threat from the Communists led the **Guomindang** to crack down on intellectuals in a particularly brutal and mindless way. This polarized and politicized the intellectual world, with many writers leaning towards the Communists. The League of Left Wing Writers was set up under Communist Party auspices at an inaugural meeting on the March 2 1930. Its function was to educate writers in Marxist literary theory, inform them of the Party line and persuade them to follow it, and to produce literature which popularized it. It also organized attacks on non-League liberal literary groups like the Crescent Moon Society ***Xinyueshe*** 新月社. Members included leading literary figures like **Lu Xun** 魯迅, Tian Han 田漢, **Yu Dafu** 郁達夫 and Jiang Guangci 蔣光慈. The Party group within the organization included **Feng Xuefeng** 馮雪峰, Zhou Yang 周揚 and **Ding Ling** 丁玲. Branches and groups were set up in six other major cities in China and in Tokyo. They also formed links with international Marxist literary organizations. The League produced a number of important publications including *Mengya yuekan* 萌芽月刊 'Shoots Monthly', *Wenxue yuekan* 文學月刊 'Literature Monthly' and *Beidou* 北斗'Northern Dipper'. On February 7 1931, five members and associates of the League, including Rou Shi 柔石, were murdered at police headquarters by the Guomindang. The League continued in operation until the spring of 1936 when it was disbanded in order to fit in with the new Party line, which involved creating a united front with the Guomindang against the Japanese.

Wang-Chi WONG, *Politics and Literature in Shanghai: The Chinese League of Left-wing Writers, 1930-1936* (Manchester University Press, 1991).

LEGALISM *Fajia* 法家

The political philosophy, sometimes referred to as "realism" and sometimes less flatteringly as machiavellianism, which stood at the opposite end of the ideological spectrum from the individualism of **Daoism** in the late Zhou era of the **Hundred Schools**. It eschewed what it regarded as the reactionary, constraining effect of past tradition admired by the **Confucians**, and urged that leadership must keep abreast of changing circumstances and retain political control through the use of force (*shi*), modern statecraft (*shu*), and law (*fa*). Believing that **human nature** is basically evil, it stressed the need for the ruler to implement both harsh punishments and effective rewards (through which the selfishness of individuals could be exploited) to achieve his subjects' observance of an amoral system of detailed laws. Its object was a smooth-running society in which every person would work and behave precisely according to the implications and limitations of his or her name, rank or occupation, in which everyone – the ruler included – was subject to the law, no one would dare to think or act in an independent manner, and in which fear of the law would cow opposition into acquiescence. Members of groups, both civil and military, were to be responsible for each other's behaviour and for ensuring they kept the law, or were brought to justice if they did not. When this kind of society was achieved the ruler's prime ambition would be realised, that of being able to sit back and do nothing (*wu wei* 無爲) other than enjoy the pleasures of his supremacy. Human emotions, as a reflection of individual feelings and thought, were to be suppressed, and study was to be strictly confined within state interests. Occupations which might encourage the spread of dissident talk, such as trading and even inn-keeping, were to be proscribed.

Written law codes were known to some of the feudal states by the eighth century BC, and the concept of centralised authoritarianism was elaborated by **Guan Zhong** in the seventh century BC. As political theorists moved around from court to court through the later Zhou period, so did the discussion of radical new political measures spread across the country. It was **Qin** which first implemented Legalism on a comprehensive scale from the fourth century onwards, but it drew upon the ideas of men from **Qi** (**Guan Zhong**), **Zhao** (Shen Dao), **Han** (Shen Buhai, **Han Feizi**), **Wei** (**Shang Yang**), and **Chu** (**Li Si**). It was **Qin Shi Huangdi** who showed how effective Legalism could be in imposing order on the confused political and ideological situation of the late third century, but the fate of his successor the **Second Emperor** also shows how impractical it was to try and maintain rigid totalitarianism in an age which lacked the sophisticated aids of modern despots. It was the shrewd appreciation of the early Han leaders that Legalism could work if tempered by the more humanitarian approach of **Confucianism**. They thus established a syncretic political system which underpinned imperial government for centuries to come. See also **Xunzi.**

Y.N. LI, *Shang Yang's Reforms and State Control Chinese* (New York, 1977); K.C. HSIAO, trans. F.W. MOTE, *A History of Chinese Political Thought, Vol. 1* (Princeton University Press, 1979).

LEE TENG-HUI see **LI DENGHUI**

LEFT GUOMINDANG

GMD faction led by **Wang Jingwei**. After the GMD split with the CCP following the 1927 **Shanghai Coup**, this faction retained links with the CCP and operated as a separate government in Wuhan. An alliance between Wang and the warlord **Feng Yuxiang** brought the Left GMD back into the mainstream in July 1927.

LEGENDARY FIGURES see **FORMER KINGS, FU XI, SHEN NONG, YELLOW EMPEROR**

LEGGE, JAMES (1814 -1897)
Scottish Protestant missionary who moved to **Hong Kong** from Malacca in 1843 as Principal of the Anglo-Chinese College. Working with Chinese collaborators, he published the first of his monumental translations of nine **Confucian Classics** in 1861. These have been the basis for much subsequent research into Chinese history and philosophy, and Legge is renowned as the first great British sinological scholar, the first to give the British public reliable information about Chinese thought. He returned to England in 1870 and held the first Chair of Chinese at Oxford University.

LEI FENG 雷鋒 (1939–1962)
One of a series of model workers, *laodong mofan* 勞動模範 held up for emulation from the early 1960s onwards. Lei Feng came from Changsha in Hunan, Mao Zedong's own home area. In 1957 he joined the **Chinese Communist Youth League** and took part in a number of development projects where he was regularly praised as a model worker and advanced producer, *xianjin shengchanzhe* 先進生產者. In 1960 he joined a PLA sappers transportation corps and in November of that year became a member of the Communist Party. He was praised as a model of economy, *jieyue biaobing* 節約標兵 and received a second class and two third class commendations. He died on duty on August 15 1962. The following year Mao Zedong inscribed the characters 向雷鋒同志學習 *xiang Lei Feng tongzhi xuexi* – Study from Comrade Lei Feng, launching Lei Feng on a posthumous career as one of China's greatest models. With no danger of embarrassing later transgressions, Lei Feng featured in many poems and literary works throughout the 1960s and 70s and became the best known such figure in China. Lei Feng was a paragon of a PLA soldier, simple, loyal and trusting, who recorded in his diary, *Diary of Lei Feng (Lei Feng riji* 雷鋒日記) which appeared after his reported death, his study of Mao Zedong's works. The movement to 'learn from Comrade Lei Feng' began in the PLA in March 1963 and spread throughout the country during the **Socialist Education Movement**. It is widely assumed that the diaries are fakes and written by the PLA propaganda department. His role as a model continues, with a successful film of his life released in 1996.

LEIGUDUN 擂鼓墩 "Beating drum mound"
In the important archaeological region of Suizhou, Hubei province, 180 kms from Wuhan, remains have been found dating from every period from the **Neolithic** to the Tang. Tomb no.1 at Leigudun was unearthed in 1978 and was identified as that of Marquis Yi 乙 of the small state of Zeng, a vassal of **Chu**, who was buried in 433 BC. Its special significance is twofold: unlike the traditional Shang and Zhou tomb style of a single burial pit it anticipated the Han practice of having more than one chamber as if in imitation of

accommodation for the deceased and his attendants (see **Tomb Architecture**). Second, among the burial objects were bronzes of exceptional quality weighing altogether more than ten tonnes, including the best preserved sets of hanging bell-chimes (*bianzhong* 編鐘) and other **musical instruments** to have survived from the Warring States period, more than 125 in total. The tomb confirms the advanced state of Chu culture and gives a particularly detailed understanding of the development and appreciation of **music** at court. It also contained the oldest sets of inscribed bamboo slips yet discovered. See also **Musical Instruments.**

LI X.Q., *Eastern Zhou and Qin Civilizations*, trans. K.C. CHANG (Yale University Press, 1985).

LELANG 樂浪

The principal of three commanderies established by the Former Han dynasty in the Korean peninsula in 108 BC. Its capital, near modern P'yongyang, was inhabited by a governor and a substantial number of Chinese officials and merchants, who helped the spread of Chinese culture beyond the limits of the commandery. Evidence for this survives in Chinese-style decorated tombs from the fourth century AD in the vicinity of P'yongyang. The colony involved itself in the politics of the peninsula, joining in an attack on **Paekche** in 246 to try and halt the spread of the southern kingdom's power along the Han River, but itself fell victim to attack from its powerful northern neighbour of **Koguryo** in AD 313.

LHASA

The Holy City, capital of **Tibet** since the formation of the state in the seventh century AD by King **Songtsen Gampo**. Standing on the north bank of the Kyichu River in south-central Tibet, Lhasa was formerly the centre of the province of Ü. From time to time it was locked in rivalry with its neighbouring province of Tsang, the princes of which were based in **Shigatse** and virtual kings of Tibet until 1642. Since the early seventeenth century Lhasa has been the residence of the **Dalai Lama**, Shigatse that of the **Panchen Lama**. Its principal religious and historic sites are the Jokhang Temple, the Potala Palace, and the Norbulinka **Summer Palace**. The Jokhang Temple is the spiritual centre of Tibetan Lamaism. It was founded by Songtsen Gampo to house statues of Sakyamuni brought by his foreign wives, of which that brought by Princess Wen Cheng 文成 from **Chang'an** still survives and is revered as one of the holiest relics in Tibet. A stone tablet from 823 AD recording the Treaty between Tibet and China may also be seen.

The Potala Palace was begun by the Great Fifth Dalai Lama in 1645, perhaps on the site of an earlier fortress dating back to the time of Songtsen Gampo. It was completed in 1693 after his death, but it had become his official residence around 1650 and has remained the prime architectural symbol of Tibet and its religious leader ever since. In 1755 the Seventh Dalai Lama created a Summer Palace in the Norbulinka Park, after which the Potala was used and known as the Winter Palace. It was extended by the Thirteenth Dalai Lama in the early twentieth century. It has thirteen storeys and over a thousand rooms and is divided into a Red Palace and a White Palace. The former was used for religious purposes, the latter for civil administration and the living accommodation of the Dalai Lama and other high dignitaries. In the Red Palace are housed the tombs and gold stupas of eight Dalai Lamas.

P. HOPKIRK, *Trespassers on the Roof of the World* (John Murray 1982).

LI (rites and ceremonies) see ***LIJI*, SIX BOARDS, XUNZI**

LI (principle) see **NEO-CONFUCIANISM, ZHU XI**

LI AO 李翱 (774–836)

Contemporary of **Liu Zongyuan** and **Han Yu** with whom he is associated as a major critic of **Buddhism** and **Daoism** and initiator of the revival of **Confucianism**, later to become the **Neo-Confucian** movement. In his principal work, *Fuxing shu* 復性書 "Book about Returning to One's [Original] Nature", he echoes **Mencius**' view that man's basic nature is good by arguing that its honesty (*zheng* 正) and inclination towards the Confucian virtues can be revealed if the hindering effect of the emotions (*qing* 情) is controlled. See **Human Nature**.

LI BAI 李白 (Li Po) (701–762)

Tang poet of extraordinary talent praised as the "Fallen Immortal", Li Bai was brought up in Sichuan but was reputedly of Central Asian origin. He served at the Hanlin Academy for a short while and there gained his reputation for drunkenness which became legendary. It was this addiction to drink and his imagination that enabled him to dash off inspired poems. Some poems reflected Li's fondness for alcohol – *Yuexia duzhuo* 月下獨酌 'Drinking Alone by Moonlight' is one such example. He remained outside the Confucian tradition by not sitting the examinations and taking up office but spent most of his life wandering the country looking for patrons. Over one thousand poems have been attributed to Li Bai, however, it is doubtful that they are all his original work. He was best known for his *yuefu* 樂府 and *gexing* 歌行 'songs', which, with their irregular line length and rhythm, were ideal vehicles for Li's spontaneous style of composition. *Shudao nan* 蜀道難 'The Road to Shu is hard' is typical of Li's *yuefu* style with its extremely irregular lines and rhythm. Exclamations in the Sichuan dialect add to the atmosphere of the poem which has descriptions ranging from the surrounding countryside to the supernatural. Individuality, spontaneity and fantasy are the trademarks of the genius poet Li Bai: he and **Du Fu** (712–770) are regarded as the two greatest Chinese poets.

Arthur COOPER, *Li Po and Tu Fu* (Penguin Classics, 1973); Arthur WALEY, *The Poetry and Career of Li Po* (George Allen and Unwin, 1950).

LI BING 李冰 (fl. 250 BC)

Governor of the **Qin** commandery of **Shu** around 277 BC, Li completed one of the greatest hydraulic feats of the ancient world. The Dujiangyan irrigation project divided the Min River with an artificial island as it flowed south across the Chengdu Plain, re-routing half of it in the direction of Chengdu itself and deriving a number of irrigation channels from the new course. The operation required skilled planning and huge earth-moving works, and was an integral part of the success in building Shu up as the economic base for Qin's military expansion. Both the irrigation scheme and one of the suspension bridges which Li Bing is also said to have constructed are tourist attractions in Sichuan today. See also **Water Control.**

LI CHENG 李成 (919–?967)
Distinguished landscape artist who was the inspiration for many painters in later generations. Three disputed attributions of surviving paintings are made to him, *Travellers among Snowy Hills, Mountain Peaks after a Snowfall*, and *Jasper Peaks and Jade Trees*. His style was remarkable for its concern with detail but also for its acknowledgement of space and balance. See also **Landscape Painting.**
M. LOEHR, *The Great Painters of China* (Phaidon, 1980)

LI DAZHAO 李大釗 (1888–1927)
One of the earliest Chinese Marxists. Li was born in Hebei province and studied in Beijing and Japan. He returned to China and became Librarian of the University Library in Beijing in 1918 and then Professor of History at the University. He worked with **Chen Duxiu** to create literary and political journals and was involved in the influential ***Xin Qingnian*** *New Youth*. He became aware of the importance of the 1917 October Revolution in Russia and the significance it might have for China. Li was executed by **Zhang Zuolin**'s police after they raided the Soviet Embassy in Beijing in April 1927.
Maurice MEISNER, *Li Ta-chao and the Origins of Chinese Marxism* (Harvard University Press, 1967).

LI DEYU 李德裕 (787–850)
Senior official whose political career followed a familiar pattern of ups and downs. A brief chief ministership (see **Prime Minister**) in 833 under Emperor Wenzong was followed by a period in exile, but he held the post again and was the paramount political figure under **Wuzong** from 840 to 846. In recognition of his military success in repelling the **Uyghurs** and settling an internal threat to the administration in Zhaoyi province he was created Duke of Wei in 844. Disgraced by Wuzong's successor he died in exile in Hainan Island.

LI DENGHUI 李登輝 (Lee Teng-hui 1923–)
Mayor of Taibei (1979–1981) and Governor of **Taiwan** (1981–1984), Li was elected Vice-President of the Republic of China (Taiwan) to **Jiang Jingguo** on the latter's second term as President. When the President died on January 13 1988, Lee took the oath as President. As a Taiwan-born politician with a Cornell University doctorate, he was seen as one of a new breed of leaders and gained a reputation for liberalising the Taiwanese political structure.

LI HONGZHANG 李鴻章 (1823–1901)
Leading late Qing statesman and diplomat. Li came under the patronage of **Zeng Guofan**, a fellow student of his father, who recommended him for posts in the campaign against the **Taipings**. In 1862, at the age of only 39, Li became acting governor of Jiangsu, one of China's most important provinces but then almost entirely in rebel hands. He assumed control of the Shanghai-based, foreign-trained and commanded **Ever-Victorious Army** and in co-operation with the forces of Zeng Guofan and Zuo Zongtang succeeded, where the Manchu forces had failed, in putting down the Taiping rebellion. This success was followed by a posting to Shandong to help deal with the **Nian** rebels who were finally defeated in 1868. Partly as a result of their military successes

leading provincial officials like Li Hongzhang became much more powerful than their predecessors and less dependent on central government. The Manchu court's reluctance to deal with foreigners left provincial leaders with no choice but to take on a greater diplomatic role and, because they witnessed the effectiveness of Western technology, especially military, at first hand, to introduce modern technology and ideas from the West. Li supported the development of steamship lines, railways, the telegraph, the navy, military academies and industrial enterprises. From the late 1860s he held in succession governor-generalships in Hunan-Hubei, Zhili and Guangdong-Guangxi and for much of the period from then to his death was concurrently a Grand Secretary, Imperial Tutor and Superintendant of Trade for the North. He had a trouble-shooting role, being involved in dealing with both the Muslim uprising and the **Tianjin massacre** in 1870, and in negotiations with Japan over the Ryukyu Islands from 1871, with Britain in 1876 resulting in the Chefoo Convention, with Korea and Japan over the latter's activities in Korea and with France over the Sino-French war. By the early 1890s Li had unparalleled prestige but his downfall came with China's defeat in the 1894–5 **Sino-Japanese** war for which he was, somewhat unfairly, blamed. The ultimate humiliation was being forced to go to Japan to negotiate with Ito Hirobumi the Treaty of **Shimonoseki**, which included the cession of the Liaodong peninsula, Taiwan and the Pescadores, new trading rights for the Japanese and a large indemnity. After Li was wounded by a Japanese assassin and after the intervention of other foreign powers the Japanese were persuaded to limit their demands but Li was still regarded by young reformers like **Kang Youwei** as a traitor. In 1896 Li Hongzhang carried out a round-the-world tour taking in Russia, Germany, France, Britain and the United States where he met monarchs and presidents, but he remained in semi-disgrace in China. During the **Boxer Rising** Li took a leading role in organising the neutrality of the southern provinces, creating the convenient fiction that it was a rebellion rather than a war. He was also forced to negotiate the ensuing peace treaty in which he was again unable to avoid agreeing humiliating and costly concessions to the foreign powers. He died two months later in November 1901.

Stanley SPECTOR, *Li Hung-chang and the Huai Army: A Study in Nineteenth-Century Chinese Regionalism* (University of Washington Press, 1964).

LI KERAN 李可染 (1907–89)

Landscape artist who successfully achieved a synthesis of traditional aesthetic standards and the changing social and political demands of the twentieth century. Though, like **Shi Tao**, he condemned slavish imitation of the ancients and firmly believed in the expression of the artist's subjective feelings, he also, like **Jiang Zhaohe**, recognised the value of Western techniques in the development of a new Chinese style.

LI LISAN 李立三 (1899–1967)

Dominant figure in the CCP in 1929–30. After the defeat by the GMD in 1927, he advocated military offensives on Wuhan and other cities in the expectation of workers' uprisings to support the party. The insurrections did not materialise and Mao Zedong's strategy of withdrawing to the rural areas and building a base among the peasantry was to prove more successful. The 'Li Lisan line' was subsequently atttacked as a major error.

Li Linfu 李林甫 (?–752)
A member of the imperial clan and the chief minister under Emperor **Xuanzong** who so dominated the government between 736 and 752 that he has been described as a virtual dictator. It was his policy of appointing non-Chinese generals to frontier commands that led to the development of **An Lushan's** military power base in the North-west.
E.G. Pulleyblank, *The Background to the Rebellion of An Lu-shan* (Oxford UP Press, 1955).

Li Po see **Li Bai**

Li Qingzhao 李清照 (1084–*c*.1151)
The best known woman poet of the Song dynasty, also known as Yi'an Jushi 易安居士. She was born into a scholar's family in Jinan, Shandong province and her writing was influenced by her own life experience, which can be divided into two periods:

After her marriage to Zhao Mingcheng 趙明誠 (1081–1129), an eminent scholar and connoisseur, she had many years of peaceful and affluent family life. She devoted most of her time with her husband to collecting and studying early painting and calligraphic works, bronzes and other antiques. During this period, her writing reflected her leisurely and carefree life. She wrote of the feelings of young women and articulated her love for life and nature.

The writing of her later years, however, was marked by deep sorrow brought by the national calamity and the loss of home and relatives. In 1126 her family fled from the advancing Jin army and most of their collections were lost on the way to the south. Her life became totally helpless and wretched after Zhao Mingcheng's death. Her writing became more sentimental, often full of grief, loneliness, or nostalgic thoughts about her hometown in the North. She was especially skilled in *ci* 詞, using elegant language to create fresh and charming imagery. She stressed the special aesthetic characteristics of *ci* and opposed the writing of *ci* in the same way as writing poems with unified sentence lengths. Li Qingzhao wrote unremittingly in her life but only about seventy of her poems have survived. Her style of writing, highly refined but unpretentious, has been followed by many later poets.
The Complete Ci-poems of Li Qingzhao: a New English Translation, trans. Wang Jiaosheng (Philadelphia, 1989).

Li Shangyin 李商隱 (c.813–c.858)
Major later Tang poet born into a lower level official family from Zhengzhou, Henan. His father died when Li Shangyin was a child, but his talent attracted the attention of an official, Linghu Chu, who in 829 invited him to join his private office and be a companion for his son. He became a *jinshi* in 837 and gained minor official posts but never the important positions he aspired to. Li Shangyin was an outspoken critic of eunuch power and his political career may have been blighted by this, or by factional infighting in which he unwittingly became involved. He was forced to leave the capital for extended periods and eventually retired to Zhengzhou where he espoused Buddhism before his death at the age of just 45. He was a prolific writer of both prose

and poetry. In his day, his ability to do draft official documents for his patrons and compose pianwen 'parallel prose' seems to have been most appreciated, but it is his poetry for which he is now chiefly remembered. Almost 600 poems attributed to Li Shangyin are sill extant. His poetry is characterised by its intellectuality, individuality and stylistic complexity, with much use of imagery, symbolism and allusion. As a result, there is much debate over the meaning of his poems, for example whether they should be read as declarations of love or political satires.

LIU James J.Y., *The Poetry of Li Shang-yin – Ninth Century Baroque Chinese Poet* (Chicago: University of Chicago Press, 1969).

LI SHIZHEN 李時珍 (1518–1593)

Author of the *Bencao gangmu* 本草綱目, a classic text on Chinese medicines, which took him a quarter of a century to compile. It gives details of over two thousand drugs, which could be made from animal, vegetable and mineral products and the ailments they could be used to treat.

LI SI 李斯 (?280–208 BC)

Chancellor to **Qin Shi Huangdi** and principal architect of the policies which brought success to the state of **Qin** in its drive towards unification. A native of **Chu**, Li had been a student of Xun Qing (see **Xunzi**), but foreseeing greater scope for his radical ideas of statecraft in Qin, had entered the service of **Lü Buwei** and King Zheng in 247. He then followed a successful career as Minister for Aliens and Chief Justice before becoming Chief Minister after the unification of China in 221. Through his skilful manipulation of espionage, control over intellectual activity (see **Burning of Books**), compulsory removal of surviving aristocratic families into the metropolitan region, reform of regional government, standardisation of weights, measures, coinage and the writing system, his exaltation of economically useful activity and condemnation of the potentially subversive business of travel and trade, and above all his emphasis on the strict and impartial application of laws and heavy punishments, he proved the perfect foil to the despotic ambitions of his monarch. He helped plan the Emperor's regional tours and his successful campaigns against the northern barbarians, though he did not share the Emperor's superstitious beliefs which prompted his visits to regional altars (see **Sacrifices).** Li Si was implicated in the plot which set Huhai on the throne (see **Second Emperor**) and incited him to apply the laws even more harshly than before. But the Second Emperor lacked his father's political acumen and was manipulated by **Zhao Gao**. When Li Si warned him against the **eunuch** he was imprisoned, and despite a famous self-defence was executed by being cut in two in the market place of **Xianyang**. See also **Epang Palace, Legalism.**

D. BODDIE, *China's First Unifier* (Leiden: E.J.Brill, 1938).

LI YU 李漁 (1611–1680)

Playwright, novelist and aesthete, reputed author of outrageous semi-erotic novel the ***Rou putuan***, 'Carnal Prayer Mat'. Li Yu received his *xiucai* 秀才 degree around 1635 but failed to gain his *juren* 舉人 and gave up hopes of an official career after the Qing conquest. He came from a wealthy Zhejiang family but gradually became impoverished and had to support himself by his theatrical and literary activities. He maintained a large household which functioned as a peripatetic theatrical troupe as it toured round the country sponsored by wealthy patrons. The plays were written and directed by Li Yu (ten were later published under the title *Li Weng shi zhongqu* 笠翁十種曲) and he also wrote influential critical essays on dramatic art (contained in his *Xianqing ouji* 閑情偶記 collection). Based on his own practical experience, he emphasised the importance of the medium and the audience: plays should be well structured, with a strong plot, simple in style and with clear cut characters so that the actors could perform them and the audience understand and enjoy them. There are two extant collections of short stories and the two novels attributed to him are the *Rouputuan* and *Huiwenzhuan* 回文傳. His links with Ming loyalists and his penchant for the erotic resulted in the banning of a number of his works in the literary inquisitions of the eighteenth century. After moving to Nanjing in the late 1650s he set up a bookshop and press at his home, the *Jiezi yuan* 芥子園 'Mustard Seed Garden' (his ironic reference to its size) which later published the famous *Jiezi yuanhua zhuan* manual on painting (see **Painting Manuals**). Among his essays, works on architecture, landscape gardening, interior design and female charm were influential in Japan and enthusiastically rediscovered in China in the 1920s.

LI YU, *The Carnal Prayer Mat* trans. Patrick Hanan (London: Arrow Books, 1990); Patrick HANAN, *The Invention of Li Yu* (Harvard University Press, 1988); CHANG Chun-shu and Shelley Hsueh-lun CHANG, *Crisis and Transformation in Seventeenth Century China: Society, Culture and Modernity in Li Yu's World* (University of Michigan Press, 1995).

LI ZHI 李贄 (1527–1602)

Li Zhi's career exemplifies the breakdown of intellectual and sometimes moral discipline engendered among the followers of **Wang Yangming**. Once a Confucian official, he later embraced **Chan Buddhism** and taught that **Confucianism**, Buddhism and **Daoism** were in fact one. He rejected the authority of the **Confucian Classics** as repositories of truth, and among his most radical ideas was support for selfish profiteering as the expression of "natural" behaviour. He championed the concept of **marriage** for love and the style of colloquial literature that was growing increasingly popular among non-conformist readers in the late Ming. He was imprisoned and committed suicide. See also **Donglin Academy.**

LI ZICHENG 李自成 (1605–1645)

Rebel leader at the end of the Ming dynasty. His troops attacked the Ming capital of Beijing in 1644, entering the city on April 15 and the last Ming emperor, **Chongzhen**, hanged himself on Jingshan, the hill overlooking the Forbidden City. Li Zicheng's capture of the capital and of the father of Wu Sangui, commander of the Ming armies based at Shanhaiguan at a time when **Manchu** armies were preparing to invade China, presented Wu with a dilemma. Wu chose to allow the Manchus in rather than let Li Zicheng hold the capital and the Qing dynasty was born. Li escaped from Beijing as the Manchu forces advanced and was killed in June or July 1645, apparently by peasants when he was stealing food.

LI-FOURNIER AGREEMENT (1884)

Settlement of dispute between China and France over influence in Annam (Vietnam). On May 11 1884, **Li Hongzhang** and the French representative Captain Fournier signed an agreement that Chinese troops would be withdrawn from Tongkin and that China would recognise treaties signed by China and Vietnam. Failure to implement the agreement led to war between China and France. See **Sino-French War**.

LIANG 梁 DYNASTY (502–557)

One of the Six Dynasties. The Liang ruled from the Nanjing region over a peaceful and prosperous nation in which Buddhism enjoyed considerable success. It collapsed because of the rise of feuding families and was superseded by the Chen dynasty.

LIANG QICHAO 梁啓超 (1873–1929)

Scholar and leading participant in the late 19th century reform movement, from Xinhui in Guangdong province. Liang received a traditional education, passed his *xiucai* 秀才examination in 1884 and went on to the *Xuehaitang*, the most famous academy in Guangdong. He was successful in the *juren* 舉人 examination in 1889 and travelled to the capital in 1890 for the metropolitan examinations. This time he was not successful, but on his return Liang passed through Shanghai where he obtained translations of Western works. He also met **Kang Youwei**, whom he acknowledged as his teacher and who was a major influence on the rest of Liang's life. In 1895 Liang and Kang once again went to Beijing for the examinations. This visit coincided with peace negotiations at Shimonoseki following China's defeat in the Sino-Japanese war. The humiliation of being defeated by Japan was a bitter blow to most Chinese; Kang and Liang organized a petition of the metropolitan candidates, known as *Gongche shangshu* 公車上書 calling for rejection of the treaty terms and a resumption of the fight against Japan. Although their pleas were ignored by the Qing government, the protesters formed the nucleus of the reform movement, with Kang and Liang at its core. Liang became the leading polemicist for the reformers, setting up newspapers and writing innumerable articles. The newspapers included the *Wanguo gongbao* in Beijing and the *Shiwu bao* in Shanghai. In his articles Liang pressed for radical institutional reform and the introduction of a constitutional monarchy. He was invited to audience with the Guangxu emperor in July 1898 when he presented one of his works, *Bianfa tongyi* 變法通議 'Proposals for Reform'. Liang was given a low-level post and participated in the **Hundred Days Reform** movement but fled to Japan with Kang Youwei following the Empress Dowager **Cixi's** coup. There he set up the *Xinmin congbao* which carried on a long running feud with the revolutionaries arguing the reformist cause. In fact his views underwent subtle changes after 1898. Liang was never as fervent as Kang in his commitment to the Guangxu emperor and the Qing and, at one stage in Japan, flirted with the revolutionaries, but was brought to heel by Kang. He supported the late Qing reform movement in the years up to the 1911 Revolution but remained anathema to the Qing government. After the success of the 1911 Revolution, Liang organized reformist groups into the *Jinbudang* 進步黨 Progressive Party, as a political opposition to the revolutionaries' Guomindang. He initially supported **Yuan Shikai** but broke with him over the latter's imperial ambitions and became a vociferous and very effective opponent in the campaign to stop him. After Yuan's death Liang supported **Duan Qirui**, leader of the Northern warlords, in his campaign for political power, and held a post in Duan's government until it was forced from power in November 1917. Thereafter, Liang took no further direct political role. In 1918 he travelled to Europe, was shocked by the moral decline in the aftermath of the First World War and returned to China disillusioned with the West as a role model. He felt traditional Chinese thought held the key to a better world and for the rest of his life devoted his energies to writing works evaluating and promoting it.

Joseph R. LEVENSON, *Liang Ch'i-ch'ao and the Mind of Modern China* (Harvard University Press, 1953); Hao CHANG, *Liang Ch'i-ch'ao and Intellectual Transition in China 1890–1907* (Harvard University Press, 1971); Philip HUANG, *Liang Ch'i-chao and Modern Chinese Liberalism* (University of Washington Press, 1972).

LIAO DYNASTY 遼朝 (907–1125)

Regime established by the Khitan people in Manchuria and northern China under the tribal leadership of the Yelu clan (see **Abaoji**). It had conquered and absorbed the people of **Bohai** and as its territory and influence extended into the Great Plain it made full use of Chinese military and civil leaders willing to serve it. In 938 it gained control of sixteen commanderies inside the **Great Wall**, which gave it a territorial base for its expansion. The empire was divided into five territories, each administered from its own capital. The capital of the Northern (Manchurian) Region was Shangjing (modern Harbin), that of the Southern Region Nanjing (Yanjing, modern **Beijing**). Having adopted the Chinese imperial style its court operated a quasi-Chinese administrative system and took care to practise rites according to current Chinese usage. But its relations with Song were less than amicable in the tenth century, and after periodic warfare it succeeded in exacting annual tribute from the **Middle Kingdom** under the Treaty of **Shanyuan** (1004), a serious blow to Han morale. The Koryo dynasty in **Korea** also acknowledged its suzerainty after suffering military reverses. Triangular trading relations between the three states prospered despite the diplomatic frost and led to an improvement in relations towards the end of the eleventh century. Then, however, another group of Liao vassals, the **Jurchen**, revolted and in 1115 their leader **Aguda** claimed the title of emperor for himself. With ill-advised encouragement from Song **Huizong** they captured the Liao capital and the dynasty quickly collapsed.

Emperors:

Taizu	907–27
Taizong	927–47
Shizong	947–51
Muzong	951–69
Jingzong	969–82
Shengzong	982–1031
Xingzong	1031–55
Daozong	1055–1101
Tianzu	1101–25

Morris ROSSABI, ed., *China among Equals: The Middle Kingdom and its Neighbors, 10th-14th Centuries*, (University of California Press, 1983); K. WITTFOGEL and C.S. FENG, *History of Chinese Society: Liao 907–1125* (American Philosophical Society, 1949); Herbert FRANKE's chapter in Denis Sinor, ed., *The Cambridge History of Early Inner Asia* (Cambridge University Press,1990).

LIAODONG 遼東
Peninsula in eastern Liaoning with Port Arthur and Dalian (Dairen) at its end. Liaodong was the beachhead for Japanese expansion into Manchuria. See also **Guandong**.

***LIAOZHAI ZHIYI* 聊齋志異 *Strange Tales of Liaozhai*,**
Collection of short stories by Pu Songling 蒲松齡 (1640–1715). Pu Songling spent years compiling anecdotes and stories of strange happenings that he had heard and also composed stories of his own creation. The result was *Liaozhai zhiyi*, a collection of four hundred and forty short stories, completed in 1679, according to the date of the author's preface. The tales in *Liaozhai zhiyi* were derived from a variety of sources, especially the Six Dynasties *zhiguai* 志怪 stories and Tang *chuanqi* 傳奇 tales. But Pu's tales differ markedly from earlier stories in that they reflect more clearly the author's state of mind and his world view.

Pu Songling enhances the artistry of the tales by blending reality and idealism with the supernatural. He is best known for his romantic tales of fox fairies and ghosts. He also turned flowers, fish, and bees into lovely maidens, each with a special personality of her own and affecting the fortunes of her human lover in different ways. On occasion, the souls of living human beings entered into the bodies of non-humans, such as a cricket or a parrot. Although the short stories were distinguished for their refined style, which made them accessible mainly to well-educated people, most of them were later converted into a narrative form by numerous street story-tellers in China.

H. GILES trans., *Strange Tales from a Chinese Studio* (New York: Dover Publications (reprint ed.), 1969).

LIBERATED AREAS *Jiefangqu* 解放區
Areas controlled by the CCP and its armies during the Japanese occupation 1937–1945. See also **Base Areas**.

LIBERATION *Jiefang* 解放
CCP victory in 1949 and the establishment of the PRC.

***LIEZI* 列子**
Recognised as the third of the great Daoist classics after the ***Laozi*** and the ***Zhuangzi***, although there have consistently been doubts about its authenticity. The text is named after Lie Yukou 列御寇, a Daoist sage thought to have lived around 400 BC, and consists of eight *pian* 篇, one of which, on the hedonist **Yang Zhu**, bears little relationship to the other seven which are unambiguously Daoist in content. The text shares many passages with other works, especially the ***Zhuangzi***, and the fact that the *Liezi* appears in all cases to be quoting from the other source lends credence to those who argue for a late date of

composition (up to 300AD). However, the fact that a *Liezi* text is listed in early Han sources means the argument is not conclusive and this may be a corrupted version of an early text. The philosophy of the *Liezi* is closer to the *Zhuangzi* than the *Laozi*; its keynote is *ziran* 自然 'spontaneity' or 'naturalness' and from this it argues for the acceptance of death, the rejection of conscious striving in favour of intuitive understanding (like walking down stairs where awareness of the task makes it harder to perform) and the adoption of fatalism. **Confucius** frequently appears in the text (one *pian* is devoted to him) as a man who comes to realise the superiority of the Daoist approach. The style of the *Liezi* is more vernacular and easier to understand than either the *Laozi* or the *Zhuangzi* and, like the latter, relies heavily on anecdotes.

The Book of Lieh-tzu: A Classic of the Tao tr. A.C. Graham, (London: John Murray, 1960; rept. Mandala Press, 1991).

LIFANYUAN 理藩院 Mongol Superintendency

Central government body set up by the Qing to oversee the affairs of the Mongols, Muslims and Tibetans. Earlier dynasties had managed with *ad hoc* arrangements, but the Qing, sensitive over minorities, developed this formal office which gradually grew in the scope of its duties and the seniority of its staff. It was originally set up as the *Menggu yamen* 蒙古衙門 in 1636 and changed into the *Li fan yuan*, under the control of the Board of Rites *Li bu* 禮部, two years later. It was headed by a minister, *shang shu* 尚書, and was the central government office which oversaw all aspects of government in the areas concerned, following the regulations in the *Lifanyuan zeli* 理藩院則例 (laid down by the **Kangxi Emperor** in 1697). By default, it also became the body dealing with Russians and other foreigners arriving in China. However, its procedures, based on assumptions of Chinese superiority and a tribute relationship, exacerbated communications problems with the Western powers in the period up to the second **Opium War** and it was replaced in that role by the **Zongli Yamen** in 1861. It continued in its original role, although renamed the *Li fan bu* 理藩部 in 1907, until the end of the Qing.

John K. FAIRBANK, *The Chinese World Order* (Harvard University Press, 1968).

LIJI **禮記 'Book of Rites'** or **'Book of Rituals'**

One of the ritual texts which make up the *Li* 禮 Classic of Rites, the *Liji* is the least coherent of the three (the others are the ***Zhou li*** and the ***Yili***). It was traditionally associated with **Confucius** and said to be a record of his teachings as written down by his disciples and later followers. Confucius indeed features prominently in the text but this seems to be more the result of Former Han scholars' attempts to build up his sagely image. The text was said to have been edited from court archives by **Liu Xiang** and later re-edited by Dai De 戴德 (also known as Da Dai 'Elder Dai') and subsequently Dai Sheng 戴聖 (Xiao Dai 'Younger Dai') but there is no evidence for its existing in the present 49 *pian* form before the Later Han. Where the other two texts are canonical the *Liji* is more explicatory; significant parts appear to be based on the debates of Han scholars on questions of ritual. Two chapters, the ***Da xue*** 大學 'Great Learning' and ***Zhong yong*** 中庸 'Doctrine of the Mean' were selected by **Zhu Xi** to form part of his **Four Books** and hence became very influential.

James LEGGE trans., *The Li Ki* (2 vols.) (Oxford: the Clarendon Press, Sacred Books of China Series, 1885 (and later reprints)).

***LIJIA* 里甲**

Ming and Qing dynasty system for assessing labour dues which became an important feature of local government. It was originally introduced under the **Hongwu Emperor** in 1381/2. A *li* comprised ten *jia* of ten households, together with a leadership group of the ten richest families, thus making a total of 110 households. The richest households provided village headmen (*lizhang* 里長). Based on **census** returns and the resulting tax registers (known as "Yellow Registers"), the organisation provided the framework for services including education, but its main function was tax collection. After 1740 labour dues were generally merged into **land taxes** and tax registers taken over by the ***baojia*** organisation. Thereafter *lijia* heads were mainly responsible for tax collection. See also **Land Tenure, Single Whip Tax System.**

LIN BIAO 林彪 (1907–71)

People's Liberation Army Commander-in-Chief and Minister of Defence from 1959, and designated as Mao Zedong's "closest comrade in arms" and heir apparent during the **Cultural Revolution**. Lin was a graduate of the **Huangpu Military Academy** and joined the CCP in 1927, serving with **Zhu De** in Jiangxi and commanding the 1st Army Corps on the **Long March**. During the Civil War, his command of the PLA units in Manchuria and in the Beijing-Tianjin campaign was decisive in ensuring CCP victory. He became deputy prime minister in 1954 and a PLA Marshal in 1955 and replaced **Peng Dehuai** as Minister of Defence after the **Lushan Plenum** of 1959.

During the early 1960s, he was responsible for popularising ***Quotations from Chairman Mao***, first in the army and then nationwide, and during the Cultural Revolution, he put the PLA firmly behind Mao. His pamphlet *Long Live the Victory of the People's War* was an attempt at a theoretical extrapolation of the CCP's peasant army victory to a world revolution.

Differences between Mao and Lin culminated in a bizarre and spectacular end for the latter. The first open split came at the Lushan Conference of September 1970, when Lin's supporters tried to rescind Mao's instruction that there be no reference to a PRC Chairman in the Constitution then being drafted. The position had been left vacant since the purge of **Liu Shaoqi** and Lin Biao wished to fill it. Afraid of loss of power at a time when **Zhou Enlai** was becoming more influential and detente with the USA was under discussion, Lin Biao and his followers apparently devised a plan for a coup d'etat to be launched on September 8 1971. When their plot was discovered, Lin Biao, his wife Ye Qun and his son Lin Liguo tried to flee the country. They were all killed when their plane crashed near Undurkhan in Mongolia in the early morning on September 13.

LIN ZEXU 林則徐 (1785–1850)

Governor-General of Hubei and Hunan, ordered in 1838 by the Daoguang emperor to suppress the opium trade at Guangzhou. On March 18 1839, he seized all foreign-owned opium after the traders had refused to surrender it and had it all destroyed with lime or burned and thrown into the sea. The British Expeditionary Force sent in response began the **Opium War**. After the war. the British complained about the way Lin had treated them and he was exiled to Xinjiang. He was subsequently rehabilitated but died on the way to a new posting.

Arthur WALEY, *The Opium War through Chinese Eyes* (George Allen and Unwin, 1958); CHANG Hsin-pao, *Commissioner Lin and the Opium War* (Harvard University Press, 1964).

LINEAGES see **CLAN OR LINEAGE ORGANISATIONS**

LISAO see ***CHUCI***

LISHAN 驪山 Mount Li

Modern Lintong, 25 miles east of Xi'an. Site of the tomb of **Qin Shi Huangdi**. The tumulus is 60 metres high and over 1,640 metres in circumference, and is enclosed by a double wall. The tomb itself has not yet been opened but may be expected to be constructed and furnished on the same grandiose scale as the **Epang Palace**. According to **Sima Qian** its ceiling was decorated with a map of the heavens and its floor with a map of the world, with the rivers of China depicted in mercury.

One mile to the east lies the famous terracotta army, probably intended as one of four to protect each side of the mausoleum. Discovered in 1974 and still not completely unearthed, it occupies three pits (a fourth being unfinished). The first is divided into a series of brick-paved corridors which were once covered by a ceiling of thick wooden beams supported on wooden pillars. This pit houses the main body of approximately 6,000 life-sized figures of infantrymen, chariots and horses. The second pit contains about 1,400 figures. The third appears to have comprised the command post headquarters. The significance of the find relates to the hitherto unsuspected sculptural skills of the potters, the evidence it provides of the size, organisation, and formational deployment of Qin armies, and their equipment, uniforms and armour.

LITERATI see **GENTRY**

LITERARY INQUISITION

The series of trials carried out in the early-mid Qing period against scholars thought to have made insulting references to the Manchus and their predecessors. The early emperor **Kangxi** (reigned 1661–1722), was little involved until the end of his reign, when Dai Mingshi 戴名世 (1653–1713) was indicted and executed for writing seditious material (principally for using **Southern Ming** reign titles instead of Manchu ones). The reigns of the **Yongzheng** and **Qianlong** emperors saw a great increase in inquisitorial activity: for example, an investigation into Lü Liuliang 呂留良 (1629–83) resulted in 1733 in the unearthing and dismemberment of the bodies of Lü himself and one son, the execution of a further son, the banishment of grandsons, enslavement of female relatives and banning of all his writings with similar treatment for two of Lü's students. The Qianlong emperor took a particularly hard line on this question, even executing people specifically pardoned by his father, the Yongzheng emperor. An important aim of the ***Siku quanshu*** project initiated by the Qianlong emperor in 1773 was to root out and destroy subversive works and to punish those involved in their writing and propagation.

Luther Carrington GOODRICH, *The Literary Inquisition of Ch'ien-lung* (Baltimore: Waverly Press, 1935); R. Kent GUY, *The Emperor's Four Treasuries – Scholars and the State in the Late Ch'ien-lung era* (Harvard University Press, 1989).

LITERATI PAINTING

Paintings by scholar-officials, as opposed to professional court painters and folk artisans. In Chinese they are referres to as *wenrenhua* 文人畫 or sometimes as *shifuhua* 士夫畫. The tradition developed from the reactionary attitude of 11th century scholars such as **Su Shi,** who considered himself an amateur painter, to the practices and aims of the professionals in the Song **academy of painting**. The scholar-officials such as Su and his friends, for whom mastery of the brush had always been considered a central requirement, sought a parallel in painting to the ideals in the tradition of calligraphy: to express the ideas and feelings of the cultivated individual. To them, the perfection of forms was the main concern while nature served only as the raw material to be transformed into artistic idiom. They often worked in ink rather than in colour, deliberately interpolated archaisms and other eccentric touches, and specifically painted for themselves and their own circle, refusing any money for their works of art. In the Yuan dynasty, many highly educated officials left their posts under the Mongol rulers to pursue their own interests. They often gathered together to drink wine, exchange ideas, compose poetry and paint. Some of the most innovative literati painters were from those groups.

Literati painting did not emerge as a distinct category until the Ming dynasty. By the time of **Dong Qichang**, a definite view had been formed that literati painting was superior to professional painting, for its emphasis on self-expression, its spontaneous approach, and its lack of interest in realism, which so concerned the professionals.

S. BUSH, *The Chinese Literati on Painting: Su Shih* (1037–1101) *to Tung Chi-chang* (1555–1636) (Harvard Yenching Studies, no. 27, Cambridge, Mass., 1971).

LITERATURE OF THE WOUNDED *Shanghen wenxue* 傷痕文學

This term, taken from the story *Shanghen* 傷痕 'The Wound' by Lu Xinhua, is used to refer to a genre of stories published from the late 1970s dealing with the scars left by the **Cultural Revolution**. In the story a daughter realises too late how badly she treated her mother in denouncing her when she was labelled a rightist and in breaking off all contact with her. The story puts the blame for such things firmly on the **Gang of Four** and the ultra-leftists but looks confidently to the Communist Party to right past wrongs and lead China to a glorious future. The raw emotion expressed in such stories met a deep psychological need in people trying to make sense of their lives after years of political torment. The genre soon lost its vigour as stories became formulaic and hackneyed.

LU Xinhua, Liu Xinwu and others, *The Wounded: New Stories of the Cultural Revolution 77–78* trans. Geremie Barme and Bennett Lee (Hong Kong: Joint Publishing Company, 1979).

LITTLE RED BOOK see ***QUOTATIONS FROM CHAIRMAN MAO***

LIU AN 劉安 (179–122 BC)
Prince of Huainan and grandson of Emperor Han **Gaozu**. He was an intellectual and writer whose work included a commentary on the ***Chuci*** poem, *Lisao*. In 139 **BC** he completed ***Huainanzi***, containing essays by the group of Daoists he had collected round him at his court in what is now Anhui province. Accused of plotting rebellion against the government in 123, he committed suicide after his arrest. Huainan was then incorporated into the central administrative system.

LIU BANG 劉邦 (Liu Ji, 247–195 BC)
One of the leaders of the state of **Chu** who instigated rebellion against the Second Qin Emperor. As Governor of Pei, a minor official in eastern China, he took advantage of **Chen She**'s revolt in 210 BC to raise his own rebel band, which succeeded in taking over the Qin capital **Xianyang** in 207. The more ruthless **Xiang Yu**'s larger force ousted him and attempted to conciliate him with the title of King of Han, based on the territories of **Ba**, **Shu** and the Han River valley and with his capital at Nanzheng. But strengthened by the rich resources of his kingdom Liu Bang made an immediate and successful counter-attack (206), recaptured Xianyang and assumed the title of Emperor of the Han dynasty. The next four years were spent fighting to establish his imperial authority on the central plains. His great rival Xiang Yu was destroyed in 202 after a famous battle between Han and Chu. See also **Gaozu, Second Emperor.**

LIU DE 劉德
Third son of Emperor **Jingdi** and father of **Liu Xiang**. He was an Imperial Counsellor (*zongzheng*), and may have been the compiler of the ***Yueji***. He was associated with the **Huanglao** school of thought.

LIU SHENG 劉勝 (d.113 BC)
Son of Emperor **Jingdi** and holder of the kingship of Zhongshan 中山 (in modern Hebei Province). Under the early Han administrative system parts of the state were divided into commanderies (*jun* 郡) and kingdoms (*guo* 國) as a quasi-feudal means of exerting control over its vast domains. The kings had no real political power, and Liu Sheng's interests were self-indulgently materialistic. His tomb, and that of his wife Princess Dou Wan, were sealed shortly before 100 **BC** and excavated at Mancheng in 1968, and the luxurious lifestyle of the early Han ruling class revealed by their contents provided much political capital during the **Cultural Revolution**. In the manner of the time befitting members of the highest nobility, their bodies had been clad after death in suits made of rectangular pieces of **jade** sewn together with gold thread, a quite astonishing demonstration of craftsmanship as well as of extravagant opulence. Jade was thought to have a preservative effect on the human corpse, and this represented the most outlandish example of using it in the search for some kind of **immortality**. Also found in the

tombs were brilliant examples of **bronze**, gold and silver wares, textiles, ceramics and weaponry. See also **Tomb Architecture.**

Liu Shaoqi 劉少奇 (1898–1969)

Senior CCP figure and Chairman of the People's Republic from 1959–1969. Liu had studied in Moscow and his early political career was in trades union organisation, often working clandestinely during the late 1920s and early 1930s. He also created underground CCP cells in cities occupied by Japanese troops. In the PRC, his power bases were the All-China Federation of Trades Unions and the **National People's Congress**. In 1959, when Mao Zedong relinquished some of his powers after the debacle of the **Great Leap Forward**, Liu became Chairman of the State, that is President of China, but not Chairman of the CCP, Mao retaining that post. Conflict between the pragmatic policies of Liu and the revolutionary romantic ones of Mao led to the **Cultural Revolution**. Liu died in Kaifeng in 1969, broken by ill-treatment.

Lowell Dittmer, *Liu Shao-ch'i and the Chinese Cultural Revolution: The Politics of Mass Criticism* (Berkeley: University of California Press, 1974).

Liu Xiang 劉向 (79 – 8 BC)

Son of **Liu De** and a descendant of **Liu Bang**. He was appointed by Emperor **Chengdi** to head a group of scholars in the compilation of a catalogue of the Imperial Library. The work was completed by his son **Liu Xin** and included in **Ban Gu's *Hanshu*** (chapter 30,*Yiwen zhi*). Father and son were responsible for the categorisation of literature into philosophy, *belles lettres* (including poetry), and history, and they shared the wide-ranging interest of contemporary scholars in many aspects of cosmology, government, and divination. Liu Xiang followed **Dong Zhongshu's** theory that each of the **Five Elements** generated its successor, and argued that Han succeeded directly from the Zhou (element: wood, colour: green) and ruled by virtue of fire and the colour red. Qin was set aside as a temporary interloper in the system. He also wrote on the study of the heavens as a guide to government (*Shuoyuan*說苑), edited the ***Zhanguoce***, and was the author of the *Lienü zhuan* 列女傳, a collection of biographies of 120 **virtuous women** probably inspired by **Sima Qian's** group biographies in the ***Shiji***.

Liu Xin 劉歆 (?46 BC – AD 23)

Son of **Liu Xiang**, and "one of the most highly advanced men of letters of the day" (Loewe). He shared many of his father's intellectual interests, and defended the reputation of the Han Emperor **Wudi** against earlier critics such as **Dong Zhongshu**. He was a close aide to **Wang Mang**, and was deeply imbroiled as a leading protagonist for the Old Text scholars in the dispute over the interpretation of the Confucian Classics (see ***Gu Wen*** and **New Text school**). He promoted the study of the ***Zuozhuan***, the ***Shujing***, the Mao edition of the ***Shijing***, and the ***Zhou li***. The accusation that he forged versions of some of these in order to justify Wang Mang's succession to the throne was first made by **Kang Youwei** in 1891, but notwithstanding his support for Wang he was ultimately executed for plotting against him. See also **Aidi, Liu Xin.**

H. Vaness, *Politik und Gelehrsemkeit in der Zeit der Han* (Wiesbaden: Harrasointz Vlg., 1993).

LIU ZONGYUAN 柳宗元 (d.819)
An admirer and intellectual rival of **Han Yu**, and early architect with him of the mid-Tang Confucian revival that in the wake of the **An Lushan** crisis laid the foundations of **Neo-Confucianism**. Despite being a promising official he was exiled twice, once after taking part in **Wang Shuwen**'s abortive revolt in 805 and again in the last four years of his life. The years in the southern wilderness brought him into contact with nature and the common people and stimulated his political thought. Above all he believed in the responsibility of the government and literati to help the ordinary people, whose servants they should be. He refuted the idea of the heavenly mandate and claimed that true government required the "mandate of the people". For him the "Way", central to his understanding of **Confucianism**, was the human Way. He used the study of the Classics as a means of criticising the government of his day, including its **taxation** policies. See also ***Dao*****, Mandate of Heaven**

J-S CHEN, *Liu Tsung-yuan and Intellectual Change in T'ang China*, 773–819 (Cambridge University Press 1992).

LOCAL HISTORIES see **GAZETTEERS**

LOGICIANS *Ming jia* 名家
Also called Sophists or School of Names, the latter directly from the Chinese title *Ming jia*, these were a group of philosophers of the late Warring States period (fourth to third century BC) who concerned themselves with logic. Representative members of this group are **Gongsun Longzi** and **Hui Shi**. There is an extant text named after the former, the only text of this school to survive, but much of the information we have about members of the school comes from the works of rival philosophers not entirely sympathetic to their ideas. Most Chinese thinkers were concerned with the relationship between the individual and society; their ideas were intended as a practical guide to behaviour. The logicians by contrast were, like many Greek and later Western philosophers, concerned with logic and the relationship between ideas and language. They produced paradoxes like 'the shadow of a flying bird never moves' and 'a brown horse and a dark ox make three' which they argued endlessly over. They were condemned by other Chinese thinkers for being impractical and wasting their time on pointless argument. After their time the pursuit of logic was largely abandoned and never formed part of the mainstream of traditional Chinese thought.

***LOHAN* 羅漢 Disciples of the Buddha.**
The term *lohan* came from the Sanskrit *Arhan*, also known as *Arhat* or the "Worthy one". They are patrons and guardians of Sakyamuni's system of religion and its adherents, both lay and clerical. It was believed that they were able to use their magic powers to remain alive indefinitely and so preserve the Buddha's teachings, even in times of trouble. Usually groups of 18 *lohans* are present in Buddhist paintings or sculptures, 16 are of Hindu origin and 2 more were added by the Tang dynasty, with each one posed in a fixed attitude with his own strongly characterised face and distinctive symbols. Another popular version is the five hundred *lohans* installed in some Buddhist temples in China. See also **Buddhism**.

LONG MARCH *Changzheng* 長征
The retreat of the CCP from the **Jiangxi Soviet** after the last of the GMD **Encirclement Campaigns** in October 1934. Over 100,000 troops, cadres and supporters left Jiangxi on October 15 with no clear idea of their destination. The main body of the marchers headed west and arrivd at Zunyi in Guizhou in January 1935. At the **Zunyi Conference** held there, Mao Zedong emerged as the main leader of the CCP and led the group that marched north through inhospitable areas of China and arrived in Shaanxi province in October 1935. The CCP and the Workers and Peasants Red Army established their base in the town of **Yan'an**, where Mao set about rebuilding the party. The Long March became part of the creation myth of the PRC and the subject of many films, novels and stories.
Dick WILSON, *The Long March of 1935: The Epic of Chinese Communism's Survival* (London: Hamish Hamilton, 1971); Benjamin YANG, *From Revolution to Politics: Chinese Communists on the Long March* (Westview, 1990).

LONGMEN CAVES *Longmen shiku* 龍門石窟 (near present-day **Luoyang** 洛陽, Henan province).
In 494 **AD** the Toba **Wei** court moved south from Datong, in modern Shanxi province, to **Luoyang**, where it continued the practice of carving Buddhist statues in hillside caves. Here Chinese stone sculptural art reached its peak between the early sixth and early eighth centuries, as gigantic but well proportioned and serene figures of Buddhas and Bodhisattvas bore witness to the artistry of the stone masons and the spread of religious fervour among the wealthy aristocracy. The Tang Emperor **Gaozong** and Empress Wu (see **Wu Zetian**) both sponsored major carvings at Longmen. See also **Yungang Caves.**

LONGSHAN 龍山
Named after a site in Shandong Province, this **neolithic** cultural phase developed out of the early **Dawenkou** tradition, and from the middle of the second millennium **BC** went on to supplant **Yangshao** culture in many regions of northern and central China. It then evolved into the civilisation of the **Bronze Age** and early Shang dynasty. Longshan pottery relies mainly on style and form for aesthetic appeal and lacks the painted decoration of Yangshao vessels. It is predominantly monochrome black, grey or white, with some beater or incised patterning, and its finer quality shows the use of the wheel in its manufacture. Its more advanced stylistic features include the appearance of slender drinking vessels, jugs with handles and pouring spouts, and hollow-legged tripods for heating liquids. Agricultural features of this civilisation included the cultivation of millet (as in Yangshao locations) using spades and sickles. An important example of a Longshan cultural site is Hougang.

LOTUS
In Chinese culture, the lotus is a symbol of purity and perfection because it grows out of mud but is not defiled. This sacred flower is an important motif in Buddhist art, associated with the Buddha who is born into the world but lives above the world. The Buddha and Bodhisattva **Guanyin** are usually represented

as enthroned upon lotuses. The Lotus is also much esteemed by the Daoists, and is the emblem of He Xiangu, one of the **Eight Immortals**. In Chinese folk art, the lotus is often used as a symbol for offspring, as indicated by its pod full of seeds when the flower blooms. The lotus is also regarded as an emblem of summer and fruitfulness, often represented in a set with peony (spring), chrysanthemum (autumn) and prunus blossom (winter). A great variety of lotus designs are employed in Chinese painting, architecture, textiles and ceramics.

LOTUS SUTRA 蓮花經

Buddhist scripture, called in Sanskrit *Saddharma Pundarika Sutra*, which is the fundamental text in the teaching of the Mahayana 大乘 school and the key to much of Chinese Buddhist art. The earliest surviving translation into Chinese dates from 406 AD (see **Kumarajiva**). Also known in China as the *Guanyinjing* 觀音經 as the work contains discussions about the nature of the Buddhist bodhisattva, Avalokitesvara in Sanskrit, who was transformed over the centuries into the popular **Guanyin**, Goddess of Mercy. See also **Buddhism.**

LU 魯

Small state at the base of the Shandong peninsula in the capital of which, Qufu, **Confucius** was born. Its "Spring and Autumn" records for the years 722 to 481 BC have survived, thus bestowing this title upon the period. Though dominated by its larger neighbour **Qi** it had managed to preserve Zhou institutions, but Confucius criticised its Duke for exceeding his prerogative and performing rituals appropriate only to the Zhou leadership. It was overthrown by **Chu** in 256 BC.

LU BAN 魯班

Patron deity of carpenters and builders. Lu Ban is the popular name given to the historical figure Gongxu Ban 公輸般, who was a master builder in the Lu state during the Spring-Autumn period. Many legends were attached to him as a genius mechanic whose inventions ranged from war machines such as the scaling ladder to everyday utilities such as the carpenter's horse and the saw. In art and literature Lu Ban is usually depicted as a wandering artisan, mysteriously appearing to offer inspired advice to builders with insurmountable problems.

LÜ BUWEI 呂不韋 **(d.235 BC)**

A merchant from Handan in the state of **Zhao**, who rose to become Grand Councillor at the court of **Qin** in **Xianyang** and a close personal friend and adviser to King Zhuangxiang (250–247 BC). Having friendly relations also with the Queen he was later rumoured to be the father of the young King Zheng, subsequently the First Emperor (see **Qin Shi Huangdi**), but this is probably defamatory invention by his critics. He is credited with the editorship of the ***Lüshi chunqiu*** "Spring and Autumn of Mr Lu", the visible outcome of his policy of encouraging scholarly disputation at court. It is this book that first links the **Five Elements** with the succession of dynasties. One of Lu's protégés who rose to prominence through the implementation of more realistic views was **Li Si**, later Chancellor to the First Emperor.

R. WILHELM (trans), *Frühling und Herbst des Lu Bu We* (Büsseldorf: Eugen Diederichs Vlg., 1971).

LÜSHI CHUNQIU 呂氏春秋 'The Spring and Autumn Annals of Mr. Lu'
Major compilation of thought reflecting Confucian, Mohist and Daoist views on the correct ordering of state affairs in relation to the pattern of natural forces, including the sequence of seasons. Its wide coverage includes important prescriptions on agriculture and music. It appears to have been edited from other works and is associated with the name of the chancellor of the state of **Qin, Lü Buwei** (d.235 BC) who may have commissioned it from a group of scholars.

LU XIANGSHAN 陸象山 **(Lu Jiuyuan** 陸九淵**, 1139–93)**
Neo-Confucian philosopher who believed that mind and principle are one and inherently good (see **Mencius**). Therefore, to act intuitively is in accordance with nature, to investigate things as a means of gaining understanding is unnecessary. His teaching conflicted with the mainstream of Cheng-Zhu **Neo-Confucianism** but was later developed by **Wang Yangming**. See also **Cheng Yi, Zhu Xi**.
W.T. DE BARY, *Self and Society in Ming Thought* (Columbia University Press, 1970).

LU XUN 魯迅 **(1881–1936)**
Earliest practitioner of Western-style fiction and regarded as the greatest modern Chinese writer. Lu Xun is is the pen-name of Zhou Shuren 周樹人, brother of Zhou Zuoren, born in Shaoxing, Zhejiang. He chose to study medicine as a means to help his fellow countrymen and went to Japan in 1902 to study at Sendai University. In 1906 (highly influenced by a slide show he had seen) he began writing didactic essays in Classical Chinese, ***wenyan***, to boost the morale and awareness of the Chinese. A slide showed the execution of a Chinese by the Japanese watched by a crowd of Chinese ignorant of the shame of such an act. He returned to China in 1909 to teach and in 1912 became a counsellor in the Ministry of Education. He first used the pen name Lu Xun when he wrote *Kuangren riji* 狂人日記 'Diary of a Madman' which was published in ***Xinqingnian*** (*New Youth*) magazine in May 1918. The short story displays the hypocrisy and cruelty of traditional Chinese life through the growing awareness of one man that the rest of his countrymen are cannibals. Lu taught at both Beijing University and Beijing Normal University and in 1920 his most famous work ***A Q*** *zhengzhuan* 阿Q正傳 'The True Story of Ah Q' appeared as a serial in the literary supplement to the *Beijing Morning Post*. Both stories were collected in *Nahan* 吶喊 'Outcry'(1923), his first published collection of stories, many of which attacked aspects of traditional Chinese Society. His second collection *Panghuang* 彷徨 'Hesitation' (1926) continued this theme. Typical examples include *Lihun* 離婚 'Divorce' and *Zhufu* 祝福 'Benediction' which examine the horrors of feudalism and superstition respectively and *Feizao* 肥皂 'soap' which is a satire on **Confucianism**. In 1930 Lu co-founded the **League of Left-wing Writers** and edited their leading periodicals. He died of tuberculosis in Shanghai six years later.
LU XUN, *Diary of a Madman and other Stories* tr. William Lyell (University of Hawaii Press, 1990); Leo Ou-fan LEE, *Voices from the Iron House: A Study of Lu Xun* (Indiana University Press, 1987); Leo Ou-fan LEE ed. and introd., *Lu Xun and His Legacy* (Berkeley: University of California Press, 1985).

LU ZHI 陸贄 (754–805)
Eminent politician and essayist who argued for tax reforms to alleviate the people's sufferings. A **Hanlin** Academician and adviser to the Tang emperor Dezong, he was instrumental in establishing the **Inner Court** as a major focus for political influence in the late eighth century. Chief minister from 792–5 (see **Prime Minister**), he was finally exiled for his outspokenness and rivalry with the senior minister Pei Yanling. See also **Tang dynasty.**

LU ZHI 呂雉 (Empress Lu, d.180 BC)
Wife of Han emperor **Gaozu** and mother of Emperor Huidi (194–188), for whom she reigned as regent. Under her tyrannical rule many of her opponents were assassinated as she bid to replace the imperial clan with her own. When she died her entire clan of Lu was wiped out by her late husband's supporters, who chose one of Liu Bang's sons to become the new Emperor, **Wendi**. Lu Zhi raised the status of the empress dowager's role in Chinese court politics and thereby helped to circumscribe the future power of the emperor himself.

LUGOUQIAO INCIDENT see **MARCO POLO BRIDGE INCIDENT**

LUN HENG see **WANG CHONG**

LUN YU* 論語 *ANALECTS
A compilation of sayings attributed to **Confucius** and about him. The current collection dates from the Han dynasty, when the edition extant today was completed by He Yan 何宴 (AD 190–249). Though it was based on earlier books it therefore represents the ideas of Confucians current some five hundred years after the Master's death, and must be interpreted accordingly. Nevertheless, the fact that the content of the twenty constituent books is scrappy and disorganised, fails even to try and present a comprehensive philosophy of Heaven and Earth such as had taxed the minds of earlier Han intellectuals, and ignores their concern for such matters as numerology and the inherent nature of man (see **Mencius**, **Xunzi**) are some of the features that authenticate a pre-Han date for the material. **Arthur Waley** believes that Books III to IX are the oldest and form part of a single unit. D.C.Lau (*The Analects*, Penguin Books 1979) says only that the last five books appear to be of a late date.

The teaching of Confucius reported in the Analects concerns the role of the ideal man (*junzi* 君子) in the world, his duty in advising the ruler, and the kind of social virtues most admired by Confucius, and contains exhortations and anecdotes indicating his desire to restore the standards of an idealised past identified with the early Zhou period (see **Former Kings**). He refuses to speculate on matters to do with Heaven or the spirit world, though he implicitly acknowledges their existence; neither does he comment on the quality of **human nature**. As a teacher, he is concerned with the improvement of humanity both as social organisation and as support for the individual, for whom the goal of ***ren***, however difficult to envisage, represents total perfectibility.

The *Analects* became a subject for **school** study in the Song dynasty and was raised to the level of a principal Classic when **Zhu Xi** defined it as one of the **Four Books**.

D.C. LAU, *The Analects* (Penguin Books, 1979).

LUO RUIQING 羅瑞卿 (1906–1978)
People's Liberation Army Chief-of Staff, who was attacked in the **Cultural Revolution.** Luo was born in Sichuan and educated at the **Huangpu Military Academy**. He joined the CCP during the **Northern Expedition**, trained in security and intelligence work in the USSR and returned to China to put to use this experience, In 1949, he became Minister of Public Security and later a member of the Central Committee of the CCP. In 1959, after the fall of **Peng Dehuai,** he became Chief-of Staff of the PLA and deputy to the Minister of Defence, **Lin Biao**. He was an advocate of military professionalism rather than political loyalty as the first priority of the army and thus came into conflict with Lin.

LUOYANG 洛陽
City in Henan province and one of China's ancient capitals. Luoyang was the capital during the eastern Zhou period and in the later Han dynasty after its relocation eastwards from **Chang'an**. It was also the seat of government of the northern Wei dynasty and the second city of the Tang dynasty.

LUSHAN CONFERENCE *Lushan huiyi* 盧山會議 (JULY 1959)
The Lushan Conference, technically an enlarged meeting of the Political Bureau of the Chinese Communist Party, lasted from July 2 to August 1. (Enlarging or packing a meeting was a way of ensuring that policies which might not be acceptable to the regular membership were endorsed). **Peng Dehuai**, China's defence minister and one of the ten Marshals of the **People's Liberation Army**, attacked the policies of the **Great Leap Forward**, and by implication the leadership of Mao Zedong. By the end of the meeting, Mao had launched a ferocious counter-attack against Peng, and had set in motion the measures necessary to replace Peng with Marshal **Lin Biao**. The revolt in Tibet in March 1959 and the Chinese military suppression of it was fresh in the minds of the participants in the conference.

Peng Dehuai was close in attitudes and sympathies to the older PLA marshals, to PLA members and to the peasants. Peng was in contact with views from the countryside through the military postal service and other sources, as almost all PLA rank and file soldiers were from the villages. He had also travelled in Warsaw Pact countries early in 1959, returning to Beijing on June 12. He had met Khrushchev and probably discussed with him the **communes**, Sino-Soviet relations and the Chinese army. In June Khrushchev cancelled the Soviet nuclear aid agreement with China and publicly attacked the communes. Mao interpreted this as collusion between Khrushchev and Peng. It was an early sign that Sino-Soviet relations were not as amicable as public pronouncements suggested.

There is some evidence that Zhang Wentian 張聞天, deputy minister of foreign affairs and an old rival of Mao, worked closely with Peng at Lushan, and may have prompted him to launch his attack on the Great Leap Forward. Zhang Wentian, who was hardly ever mentioned in China before Mao's death was CCP General Secretary on the **Long March** but was forced out by Mao and had been gradually marginalised since 1949. Peng may also have been involved in the **Gao Gang** and **Rao Shushi** purges in 1954–5. Gao and Rao mounted the only serious challenge to Mao's position in the early years of the People's Republic and Mao probably saw Peng Dehuai's Lushan intervention as a repeat of this and an attempt to put himself in a position to take over the leadership.

Before Lushan, **Liu Shaoqi** had become Chairman of the PRC, the post which Mao had relinquished. He was looked on as Mao's likely successor and his portrait was given equal status to that of Mao in public. Liu's strong position may have pushed Peng into making his challenge. See also **Lushan Plenum**.

LUSHAN PLENUM (1959)

The Eighth Plenum of the Eighth Central Committee in August and Enlarged Military Affairs Committee in September continued the conflict that had begun in the **Lushan Conference**. Peng Dehuai finally lost his post as Minister of Defence in the September meeting and Zhang Wentian and two others (Huang Kecheng and Zhou Xiaozhou) were purged as members of a military clique.

LUSHAN CONFERENCE 1970 see **LIN BIAO**

LYTTON COMMISSION (1932)

Delegation led by Lord Lytton, Acting Viceroy of India, who was charged by the League of Nations with examining the legality of Japan's rule over Manchuria and the nature of the **Manzhouguo** state. The Commission was in Manchuria from April 21 to June 4 1932, and in its report in September, condemned Japan for its aggression in China. The League of Nations rejected claims that Manzhouguo was an independent state and Japan left the League.

MA RONG 馬融 (79–166)

Prominent scholar who was the first to complete commentaries on all five of the Confucian **Five Classics.** He was the teacher of **Zheng Xuan** and an outspoken critic of political intrigue. See also **White Tiger Hall.**

MA YUAN 馬遠 (late 12th-early 13th century)

Leading landscape artist whose forebears had worked at the **Academy of Painting** in **Kaifeng** and whose son Ma Lin 馬麟, like him, served the emperor at the **Hangzhou** Academy. He was renowned as one of the greatest Southern Song artists, whose work showed a precision and attention to detail in the best Academy tradition yet contained a softness and lightness typical of the southern style (see **Landscape Painting**). A surviving picture attributed to him is entitled *Egrets in a snowy landscape*.

MACAO

Peninsula to the South-west of **Hong Kong** with an area of five square kilometres, a Portuguese possession until its reversion to Chinese rule in 1999. It was first awarded to the Portuguese for settlement in 1557 in recognition of their help in driving away **Japanese pirates**, and soon became the principal location for Western residence and commerce in south China at times when **Guangzhou** was closed to them (see **Canton System**). In particular, it was the site of the first **Jesuit** seminary in East Asia, and was an important base for the Order's penetration of China and communication with Japan.

Cesar GUILLEN-NUNEZ, *Macao* (Hong Kong: Oxford University Press, 1984).

MACARTNEY, LORD (1737–1806)
Leader of the 84–member mission sent by King George III to China in 1792 with the hope of opening up trade between Great Britain and China (see **Canton System**) and establishing formal diplomatic relations between the two nations. Macartney himself bore the title of Ambassador Extraordinary and Plenipotentiary to the Emperor of China, but the latter, **Qianlong**, refused to accede to the British requests. The formal audience took place at **Rehe** (Jehol) on the Emperor's birthday, September 14 1793, and is celebrated for Macartney's refusal to **kowtow**, but this was not the only or the real reason for the failure of the embassy. Rather, the occasion marked the first significant clash between two imperial powers and cultures each determined to impress its own world view and inter-state system on the other. The visit was in many ways a flamboyant and colourful expression of two conflicting concepts of empire, and from the British point of view was an apt acknowledgement of the great attraction China had exerted throughout the century, but it marked the beginning of the deterioration of Anglo-Chinese relations which would lead to the **Opium Wars** and the international exploitation of China in the nineteenth century.
See also **East India Companies, Hong Merchants.**

Alain PEYREFITTE, *Collision of Two Civilisations* (Harvill, 1993) J.L. HEVIA, *Cherishing Men from Afar: Ch'ing Guest Ritual and the Macartney Embassy of 1793* (Duke University Press, 1995).

MAGISTRATES
Occupants of the lowest rung of the administrative ladder leading upwards from local to central government. Though of lowly stature in the hierarchy of imperial rule a magistrate (*zhixian* 知縣) had awesome responsibility and enormous status in the eyes of the people. As surrogate for the Emperor, he was "father and mother" of the residents within his county (*xian* 縣). Nothing lay beyond his charge, but he was especially concerned with the maintenance of law and order, provision of services, and collection of taxes. On behalf of his people he submitted memorials and reports on conditions to his superior, the Prefect, and on behalf of the Emperor he was expected to interpret and implement edicts from court. He was thus in the unenviable position of having to serve two masters, local and national interest. In his offices (*yamen* 衙門) he was assisted by locally recruited secretaries and constables: he himself should be a native of a different county and might not expect to stay in an appointment for more than three years, so that initially at least he needed advice on conditions and perhaps even local dialect. In a county where the population might number fifty to one hundred thousand or more, he also relied on the support of the local **gentry**, the ***baojia*** and ***lijia*** heads, and village headmen.

HUANG Liuhong, *A Complete Book Concerning Happiness and Benevolence: a Manual for Local Magistrates in Seventeenth-Century China*, trans. Djang Chu (University of Arizona Press, 1984) ; John R. WATT, *The District Magistrate in Late Imperial China* (Columbia University Press, 1972): Frederic WAKEMAN, Jr. and Carolyn GRANT, eds., *Conflict and Control in Late Imperial China* (Berkeley: University of California Press, 1975).

MAITREYA ***Milefo*** **彌勒佛**

The Buddha or Bodhisattva of the Future, or Buddha yet-to-come and therefore the Buddhist equivalent of the Messiah. His anticipated coming, it was believed, would presage the arrival of paradise on earth, and though properly believed to be in the unimagineably distant future, it was also invoked more imminently by messianic movements and secret society risings from the Northern and Southern Dynasties to the late Qing, especially by the **White Lotus Society**. Sycophantic monks even identified the Empress Wu (see **Wu Zetian**) with the Bodhisattva's appearance in the form of a female ruler.

MANCHUKUO see **MANCHURIA**

MANCHURIA

North-eastern region of China, originally the homeland of the **Manchus** who conquered China in 1644 and founded the Qing dynasty. After initial prohibitions on migration, the north-eastern frontier attracted many Chinese in search of a new life and the mineral resources of the region made it a target for Japanese expansionism in the twentieth century. Japanese troops of the **Guandong Army** occupied Manchuria after the **Mukden Incident** of September 18 1931 and created Manzhouguo (Manchuguo), nominally independent but in fact a puppet state, on February 6 1932. After the creation of the PRC, the name Manchuria became unpopular and the region is normally referred to as the Three North-eastern Provinces *dongbei sansheng* 東北三省, that is Heilongjiang, Jilin and Liaoning. See also **Puyi, Zhang Zuolin**.

MANCHUS

Tungusic tribes of what is today north-eastern China, related to the **Jurchens** of the twelfth and thirteenth centuries. The Manchus established a powerful state on the borders of China in the sixteenth century and under the command of **Nurhachi**, became a unified force that posed a threat to the Ming dynasty. The Manchu language acquired its own script when the Mongol writing system was modified and a **Banner** system was created to hold all the tribes together. The name Manchu emerged in 1635 when **Abahai** decreed that it should replace all previous names for the tribes including Jurchen. The Manchus conquered China after the collapse of Ming rule in 1644 and the invitation by **Wu Sangui** to enter the passes and save the nation. During the eighteenth and nineteenth centuries, the Manchus were transformed from an external ethnic group into the ruling elite of China, acquiring all the cultural characteristics of Chinese rulers, while retaining their Manchu identity. Manchu communities were located throughout China as garrison troops and the Manchu language had almost died out in China by the twentieth century.

Robert H. G. LEE, *The Manchurian Frontier in Ch'ing History* (Harvard University Press, 1970); Pamela Kyle CROSSLEY, *Orphan Warriors: Three Manchu Generations and the End of the Qing World* (Princeton University Press, 1990).

MANDARIN

(1) A Chinese official in the imperial period, deriving from the Portuguese *mandar* 'to govern'. The term refers only to the highest group, known as *guan* 官.

(2) The national standard language of China, based on the Beijing spoken norm of the northern vernacular. *Guanhua* 官話, "official language" emerged as the language of communication between "mandarin" officials who were from different regions of China and spoke different regional languages. When China was searching for a new national identity in the years after the Revolution of 1911, the issue of a national language was crucial. Conferences were held to decide on which variant of Chinese should be used and there was considerable support for the Wu language of the Shanghai region, but the Beijing standard was finally decided upon. Known as *Guoyu* 國語, (the National Language), in the Republic of 1911 to 1949 and in Taiwan today, and as *Putonghua* 普通話 (the Common Language) in the PRC, Mandarin has the greatest prestige of all the forms of Chinese, although other languages in the family such as Cantonese and Fujianese (Hokkien) are more widely understood outside the country. See also **Chinese Language**.

MANDATE OF HEAVEN ***Tianming*** **天命**

The authority by which rulers in traditional China claimed their right of governance. It was first proclaimed by King **Wen** of Zhou, when Heaven supplanted **Shangdi** as the prime source of political legitimation. Early dynastic founders such as **Qin Shi Huangdi** and Han **Gaozu** claimed it by force and understood it mainly as the justification of military supremacy, but in Confucian terms the emphasis was more on the responsibility of the ruler to act in the interests of his people, and King Wen was regarded as the epitome of this. **Mencius** prescribed the people's right to rebel against bad government, when **omens** and portents might signal Heaven's disapproval and removal of its Mandate, and it thus became a warning to despots and an encouragement to their critics. **Liu Zongyuan** denied Heaven any role in the selection of a ruler or response to his performance, arguing that the people alone should have the right to pass judgement, whilst later **Neo-Confucians** such as **Zhu Xi** saw the Mandate less as an expression of Heaven's wishes and more as a description of the smooth operation of the natural world (see also **Deng Mu**). It also became synonymous with moral order, and more loosely in popular understanding with the concept of destiny or fate. But the value of the supposed receipt of the Mandate to new dynasts, even foreign conquerors such as the early Qing rulers, was potentially too vital to ignore, and the great rebellions of the mid-nineteenth century (see **Nian Rebellion, Taiping Rebellion**) showed that the ancient concept was still widely remembered. See also ***Dao***.

MANDARIN DUCK AND BUTTERFLY LITERATURE Yuanyang hudie wenxue 鴛鴦蝴蝶文學

A term first used in the late 1910s to refer critically to classical-style love-stories which used the traditional symbols of the mandarin duck and butterflies for lovers. Later in the 1920s its meaning spread to include many other kinds of novels, for example, 'social' novels, 'knight-errant' novels and 'detective' novels, as writers of the **May Fourth Movement** attacked all kinds of popular old-style fiction. Centred in Shanghai, authors of this literature were usually middle to upper class and included writers such as Li Hanqiu 李涵秋, Cheng Xiaoqing 程小青, Xiang Kairan 向愷然 and Zhang Henshui 張恨水. Conservative in opinion and deprived of their traditional ladder of success, these authors, many of whom created eccentric lifestyles for themselves, wrote stories that were lighthearted in appearance, masking their insecurity and disillusionment with the world. Xu Zhenya's (徐枕亞) *Yuli hun* 玉梨魂 'Jade Pear Spirit' was a popular story of the 1910s. Written in an ornate classical style which became famous as quintessential "Mandarin Duck and Butterfly" language, the story tells of the unrequited love of the talented Mengxia and the chaste widow Li Niang who refuses to remarry and kills herself so Mengxia can marry her sister. Both Mengxia and her sister kill themselves to repay Li Niang's devotion and purity.

Perry LINK, *Mandarin Ducks and Butterflies: Popular Fiction in Early Twentieth Century Chinese Cities* (Berkeley: University of California Press, 1981).

MANICHAEISM

Iranian religion emphasising the struggle between light and darkness, which became popular among the Uyghurs of Turfan, Gansu and Shaanxi from the seventh century onwards and made an appearance, although amalgamated with Buddhist and Daoist beliefs and practices, in the coastal provinces of Fujian and Zhejiang in the eleventh and twelfth centuries. Manichaen beliefs appear to have persisted in secret societies and it is possible that the choice of name for the Ming dynasty – the character chosen 明 *ming* means light or bright – may have been influenced by Manichaeism.

MANZHOUGUO see **MANCHURIA**

MAO DUN 茅盾 (1896–1981)

Leading modern realist novelist. Born Shen Yanbing 沈雁冰 in Tongxiang, Zhejiang, Mao Dun studied at Beijing University before going to work for the Shanghai Commercial Press. Influenced by the **May Fourth Movement** revolution in intellectual thought, he co-founded the Literary Research Association 文學研究會. This supported western reaalism which was seen as promoting social progress. Mao Dun became editor of *Short Story Monthly* 小說月報, a traditional literature magazine which was changed into a forum for the discussion of new literature. He became a Communist supporter and was involved in leftwing educational and literary causes. He took part in the **Northern Expedition** as a propagandist and in 1927 became chief editor of *Republic Daily* in Hankou. Disillusioned with politics after the **Shanghai Coup** and the Communist-Guomindang split, he lived in seclusion for a time in Shanghai and wrote his trilogy *Shi* 蝕 'The Eclipse', published in 1930 under the pen name Mao Dun. Composed of the stories *Huanmie* 幻滅 'Disillusion', *Dongyao* 動搖 'Vacillation' and *Zhuiqiu* 追求 'Pursuit', *Shi* explores the vast differences between revolutionary ardour and revolutionary reality. The first modern Chinese work of fiction to portray reality in contemporary history, it was attacked by the Communists for lacking in revolutionary optimism. In 1930 Mao Dun co-founded the **League of Left Wing Writers** and published *Hong* 虹 'Rainbow', an allegory of contemporary Chinese intellectual history, written whilst he was in Japan (1928–30). His masterpiece *Ziye* 子夜 'Midnight' was published in 1933. A work of tremendous research, it explored all aspects of the Chinese in their endeavour to build national capitalism. He also wrote several short stories which included *Chuncan* 春蠶 'Spring Silkworms' and its sequel *Qiushou* 秋收 'Autumn Harvest', both considered outstanding works of Marxist proletarian fiction in which the bankruptcy of the Chinese peasantry under imperialism and feudalism is portrayed. Mao Dun did not make the transition from realism to socialist realism after 1949 and ceased to produce new creative writings. However, he rose to the position of Minister of Culture and in 1954 became a deputy to the First National People's Congress. In the **Hundred Flowers** campaign he attacked the conformity of the Communist literary product and was subsequently criticised in the **Anti-Rightist Movement** and removed from office in 1964.

CHEN Yu-shih, *Realism and Allegory in the Early Fiction of Mao Tun* (Indiana University Press, 1986).

MAO ZEDONG 毛澤東 (1893–1976)

Chairman of the **Chinese Communist Party** and the one individual most associated with the successes and failures of the Communist Revolution. Mao was born on December 6 1893 in the Hunanese village of Shaoshan into a relatively privileged farming family. He had a traditional classical education and attended a college and a teacher-training college in the provincial capital Changsha from 1911, the year of the revolution that brought down the Qing government and the empire, to 1918. He became actively involved in politics during the **May Fourth Movement** and was at the founding conference of the CCP in Shanghai in 1921. Although he had various duties in the CCP and also the GMD with which it was then cooperating, it was his involvement in the **Hunan Peasant Movement** for creating peasant associations that played a crucial role in shaping his political views. After the collapse of the **United Front** in 1927, his conviction that a Chinese revolution could only occur with the active involvement of the peasantry rather than reliance on the urban working class was initially unpopular with the more conventional Marxists in the CCP who attempted to organise insurrections in the towns, insurrections that failed. It was only in 1935 at the **Zunyi Conference** held during the **Long March** that he began his ascendancy, and this was consolidated in **Yan'an** where he moulded a Party organisation personally loyal to him and designed for victory.

When the People's Republic of China was formed in October 1949, Mao held the posts of Chairman of the Party and of the State, equivalent to President. He did not have the dictatorial power available to Stalin and, after the failure of the **Great Leap Forward** inspired by his radical and romantic policies, he yielded the Presidency to his arch-rival **Liu Shaoqi** whose pragmatic and bureaucratic approach to economic and social change set the tone for the early 1960s. The **Cultural Revolution** was Mao's political comeback, organised with the help of his controversial wife, **Jiang Qing** and only came to a final conclusion with Mao's death in September 1976. He lies in a mausoleum in **Tian'anmen** Square and attracts thousands of visitors, few of whom would welcome a return of his policies. He wrote prodigiously, his authorised *Collected Works* alone amounting to five volumes. Most of his writing was on politics or political philosophy, but he was also a competent, if unoriginal, poet in the classical Chinese tradition.

Stuart SCHRAM, *Mao Tse-tung* (Penguin, 1966); Stuart SCHRAM, *The Thought of Mao Tse-tung* (Cambridge University Press, 1989); Jerome CH'EN, *Mao and the Chinese Revolution* (New York: Oxford University Press,1965); Edgar SNOW, *Red Star over China* (Random House, 1938; Bantam, 1978).

MAO ZEDONG THOUGHT ***Mao Zedong sixiang* 毛澤東思想**
More fully, Marxism-Leninism-Mao Zedong Thought, *Ma Lie zhuyi Mao Zedong sixiang* 馬列主義毛澤東思想, has been the ideology of the CCP since the **Yan'an** period. Mao Zedong Thought is the body of Mao's writings in which he argued that he was adapting Marxism to Chinese conditions.

MARCO POLO
Venetian merchant who according to the account given in his own *Travels* lived and worked in China as an official for **Khubilai Khan** for a period of seventeen years, probably between 1275 and 1292. His reputation as one of the greatest explorers of the mediaeval world is unchallenged, and though the veracity of his tale has raised some doubts amongst modern scholars, just as it did among his contemporaries, he provides valuable contemporary information about the country under Mongol rule, including a detailed description of **Hangzhou**. See also **Ibn Battuta, John of Montecorvino.**
A.C. MOULE and P. PELLIOT, *Marco Polo: The Description of the World* (AMS Press, 1976); Frances WOOD, *Did Marco Polo go to China?* (Secker and Warburg, 1995).

MARCO POLO BRIDGE INCIDENT (*Lugouqiao shijian* 盧溝橋事件)
Confrontation manufactured by officers of the Japanese **Guandong Army** to justify their invasion of China. On July 7 1937, Japanese troops on manoeuvres near the bridge, which is in the southwest of Beijing, bombarded and occupied the small town of Wanping when Chinese officers refused to allow them to search for a missing Japanese soldier. Reinforcements were sent from Manchuria and Japan when Chinese forces resisted and the fighting escalated into a full-scale invasion of China. See **Anti-Japanese War, Mukden Incident.**

MARING, H.
Dutch Comintern agent, also known as Sneevliet, who first urged that CCP members should join the GMD. He met Sun Yixian in China in 1921 and attended the first congress of the CCP. See also Michael **Borodin, Adolf Joffe**.
Anthony SAICH, *The Origins of the First United Front in China: The Role of Sneevliet* (*Alias Maring*) (Leiden E.J. Brill, 1991).

MARRIAGE
From early imperial times a man was allowed one wife, though he was also entitled to take an unlimited number of concubines or **courtesans**. His wife had a greater degree of legal recognition than his concubines, who were ranked as servants. Rather than as an expression of human love marriage was valued for its role in uniting two families for social and economic purposes and the continuance of the line of one of them. It was therefore arranged by professional matchmakers in accordance with family circumstances and auspicious astrological data. Engagements might be arranged at an early age, even at birth. Childhood marriage was illegal but not unknown: girls were usually married in their late teens, men slightly later. It was the bride's duty to leave her natal family and enter the household of her husband and his parents, whom she should serve with **filial piety**. A wife had powerful responsibilities, especially concerning management of family finances and the education of children. Her

intellectual ability might earn the respect and eventually the love of her husband, and in time she might expect to become a matriarch herself. On the other hand a man might prefer to take into his household a woman of his own choice as a concubine, whose children would rank equally with those of his wife. Songs from the *Shijing* and literature from the Han dynasty onwards show an advanced appreciation of sexuality, and many women were constantly affected by pregnancy and child-bearing. For those who were widowed, even when young, **Neo-Confucianism** stressed the desirability of chastity, but this was not always observed. The Marriage Reform Law of 1950 was enacted by the Chinese Communist Party to give full equality to women in marriage and divorce and proscribed forced arranged and child marriages, but evidence shows that these practices still continue in parts of China. See also **Divorce, Virtuous Women.**

Patricia EBREY, *The Inner Quarters: Marriage and the Lives of Chinese Women in the Sung Period* (Berkeley: University of California Press, 1993).

MARSHALL MISSION (1945)

General George C. Marshall, also noted for his role in the Marshall Plan for reconstructing Europe after the Second World War, was sent by President Truman of the United States in December 1945 to assist in the reestablishment of Guomindang control over China. His attempts to broker a GMD-CCP coalition were unsuccessful because of the irreconcilable differences that had developed between them by then and he was recalled on January 8 1947, by which time the **Civil War** had begun.

MASPERO, HENRI (1883–1945)

Distinguished French sinologist whose literary researches on the history of ancient China complemented the archaeological discoveries being made in the 1920s. *La Chine Antique* (1927) is still valuable as a detailed study of the complex political changes of the Zhou period. *Le Taoisme*, published posthumously (1950), is also a classic study.

MASS LINE *Qunzhong luxian* 群衆路線

Policy principle of the PRC. Cadres were instructed to implement CCP policy by drawing ideas from the masses, systematising them in a Marxist form, and representing them to the masses to ensure their support.

MATSU see **JINMEN**

MAWANGDUI 馬王堆

Archaeological site near Changsha in Hunan Province. It is the site of three important tombs discovered in 1972, dating from c.168 BC. Number 1 was that of Lady Dai, wife of Li Cang 利倉, Marquis of Dai. He had died in 186 and was buried in tomb number 2, and tomb number 3 was that of their son, a military commander who also died in or around the year 168. The Marquis, son of the Emperor Huidi and last **Prime Minister** in the Han kingdom of Changsha, and his wife were laid to rest according to the late Zhou rites which entitled those of their rank to a nest of five coffins. These were finely carpentered in catalpa wood using mortise and tenon joints, and richly lacquered and decorated.

Thanks to a combination of her tomb's water- and air-tight construction, its covering layers of charcoal and clay, and the favourable climatic conditions, the body of Lady Dai had been perfectly preserved and a full post mortem examination could be carried out. On top of the innermost coffin lay a T-shaped silk funerary banner elaborately painted with scenes showing the route of her soul on its way to heaven. The grave goods buried with her included 184 lacquered dishes and vessels, 162 wooden figurines of attendants and entertainers, **musical instruments** (including *qin* and *se* zithers and a *yu* mouthorgan), and forty baskets of clay replica coins. In tomb no. 3 was a rich hoard of books written on **silk**, including an edition of the ***Daodejing***, one of the ***Yijing*** with hitherto unknown commentaries, a fuller version of the ***Zhanguoce*** than was previously known, and texts on history, medicine, astronomy and ***yin-yang*** and the **Five Elements**. In addition, this grave contained the earliest extant examples of maps from China, also on silk. This remains one of the most valuable archaeological discoveries of recent times in China. See also ***Huanglao.***

Michael LOEWE, *Ways to Paradise: the Chinese Quest for Immortality* (George Allen and Unwin, 1979).

MAY FOURTH MOVEMENT *Wusi yundong* 五四運動 (1919)

Initially a demonstration by over three thousand students from Beijing University and other colleges in the capital on May 4 1919 against the peace conference at Versailles that was settling the issues left over from the First World War. In particular, the demonstrators called on the Beijing government to reject the clauses in the treaty that handed over to Japan concessions that had been held by Germany in Shandong province. The tumult grew and there were student strikes and demonstrations throughout China, strikes in factories and a widespread boycott of Japanese goods. The term May Fourth Movement is often used to include the political and intellectual ferment of the **New Culture Movement** that followed, during which the nationalist and communist traditions of contemporary Chinese politics emerged.

CHOW Tse-tsung, *The May Fourth Movement: Intellectual Revolution in Modern China* (Harvard University Press, 1960); Vera SCHWARCZ, *The Chinese Enlightenment: Intellectuals and the Legacy of the May Fourth Movement of 1919* (Berkeley: University of California Press, 1986); Wen-hsin YEH, *The Alienated Academy: Culture and Politics in Republican China, 1919–1937* (Council on East Asian Studies, Harvard University, 1990).

MAY 7TH CADRE SCHOOLS

In a letter to Lin Biao on May 7 1966, Mao Zedong called for the PLA to become a "great school" in which soldiers would study politics and culture as well as military matters and farm the land. This May 7 Directive was used as the basis for a Cadre School set up in Liuhe, Heilongjiang on May 7 1968 where Party cadres were sent to take part in manual labour so that they could identify more closely with the masses. After *People's Daily* published an article praising the Liuhe prototype on October 5 1978, May 7th Cadre Schools were set up all over China.

MAY SIXTEENTH GROUP

Cultural Revolution group emanating from the Philosophy and Social Science Institutes of the Academy of Sciences and supported by **Chen Boda**. Named after the radical bulletin, that the group circulated on May 16 1967, it was criticised as an ultra-left organisation and for its support for **Lin Biao** and was blamed for many of the excesses of the Cultural Revolution.

MAY THIRTIETH INCIDENT (1925)
Demonstration in the International Settlement in Shanghai after students were arrested at a memorial service for workers shot during a strike at a Japanese-owned factory. A British police inspector ordered his men to open fire on the demonstrators and at least nine died and many others were seriously injured. There were many arrests. Strikes, boycotts and demonstrations spread in a wave of nationalist agitation which provided support for the **Northern Expedition.**
Richard RIGBY, *The May Thirtieth Movement: Events and Themes* (Australian National University Press, 1980).

MCMAHON LINE see **SIMLA CONVENTION**

MEI LANFANG 梅蘭芳 (1894–1961)
The greatest actor of modern China, who made his reputation in the 1910s playing female roles in the classical theatre tradition (see **Beijing Opera**). Despite a warm reception when he performed in pre-war Japan he, with other famous actors Zhou Xinfang and Tian Han, resisted pressure to collaborate with the Japanese during the occupation of 1937–45.
A.C. SCOTT, *Mei Lan-fang, Leader of the Pear Garden* (Hong Kong University Press, 1949).

MENCIUS *Mengzi* 孟子(Meng Ke 孟柯, 371–289 BC)
Political theorist who offered advice to the Kings of **Wei** and **Qi** in pursuit of peace and unification. He saw himself as a defender of Zhou traditions and the inheritor of the mantle of **Confucius**, but his ideas were more systematic and went beyond those of his master. He described the humanitarian attitudes and measures that he believed to be typical of ideal **kingship** in the tradition of the **Former Kings**, and condemned the policies of the **hegemons** who acted in the interests of self-aggrandisement. As a pacifist, he tried unsuccessfully to persuade Warring States leaders that measures dedicated to economic and cultural development would bring them more success than military expenditure. He raised **filial piety** to an unprecedented level of significance, and his aim was that all men should be sufficiently educated and have enough spare time to care for their parents in their lifetime and their spirits after death. The possession of a mind distinguished man from animals, and Mencius saw filial piety as the ultimate manifestation of the four natural "germs" – the powers of commiseration, shame, deference, and discrimination. When nurtured, they would produce the four distinguishing human characteristics, ***ren*** (sympathy or benevolence), *yi* (righteousness), *li* (propriety) and *zhi* (wisdom). He believed that man was instinctively good, though his innate potential was veiled and only with education could man realise his *benxing* "original nature" (see **Human Nature**).

Internal evidence suggests that the book of *Mengzi* may be by a single person, and it acquired greater influence in later generations than Mencius did in his own lifetime. Though his optimistic idealism was overshadowed in the early Han by the more practical philosophy of the third in the line of great Confucian apologists, Xun Qing (see **Xunzi**), the *Mengzi* was adopted as part of the Confucian canon in the eleventh century and singled out as one of the **Four Books** by **Zhu Xi**, and has continued to form an essential part of the standard educational syllabus ever since.

D.C. LAU, trans., *Mencius* (Penguin Books, 1970).

MENGLONG SHI 朦朧詩 "Misty Poetry"

The name given, originally by opponents, to poetry produced by young poets from the mid-1970s onwards. The poetry followed few recent Chinese poetic conventions, although it drew its inspiration from both traditional Chinese poetry and modern Western poets like Dylan Thomas. It is generally modernist, employs liberal use of symbolism, is in free verse, and often has social or political themes which reflect the cynicism of a generation nurtured during the Cultural Revolution. Representative figures include: **Bei Dao** 北島, **Gu Cheng** 顧城, Shu Ting 舒婷, Duo Duo 多多.

Stephen C. SOONG and John MINFORD, eds., *Trees on the Mountain* (Hong Kong: Chinese University of Hong Kong Press (Renditions) 1984).

MEXICAN DOLLARS

Silver dollars, imported by Spanish and Portuguese traders, which became an important currency in China during the Ming dynasty.

MI FEI 米芾 **(1052–1107)**

Leading artist in the tradition of the amateur ideal (*wenren hua*). No definite examples of his work have survived, though one attributed to him, *Misty Hills*, gives an impression of the simple, atmospheric effect and naturalness he is known to have aimed for. He liked to work in ink and to eschew over-meticulous concern for detail, and when **Guo Xi** complained about those in his own day who "rain down ink carelessly upon the paper" it is likely that he had Mi Fei in mind.

Max LOEHR, *The Great Chinese Painters* (Phaidon, 1980).

MIAO *Miaozu* 苗族

Ethnic minority group living mainly in Yunnan and Guizhou in south-western China. Low level resistance to the Qing which had persisted since the seventeenth century broke out into open rebellion in 1855 in cooperation with units fighting in the **Taiping Rebellion**. The Miao rising was finally suppressed by a unit of **Zeng Guofang's** Hunan-based **Xiang army** in 1872.

MIDDLE KINGDOM *Zhongguo* 中國

The literal translation for the most common name for China, indicating the attitude that China was at the centre of civilisation and that all other countries were inferior but could enjoy association through the **Tribute System**. Other less well-known soubriquets for China that have persisted into modern times include *Shenzhou* 神州, the Sacred Land.

MILITARY COLONIES *Tuntian* 屯田

Self-sufficient border garrisons whose members had the dual roles of farmer and guard; an extensive early Ming dynasty system of farms established for the purpose of supplying soldiers' needs, mostly but not entirely round military encampments in border regions. Under the registered status system (see **Hereditary Occupations**) military households were either allocated to active duty or required to run farms and provide men for army service. Each soldier-farmer received fifty *mou* of land and was supplied with necessities such as animals, seeds and tools, half his produce going to support those on active service. The system declined in the fifteenth century as discipline deteriorated and the distinction between military and non-military farming became blurred. The spirit of the Military Colonies lives on to a certain extent in the **Xinjiang** Production and Construction Corps. See also ***Weisuo* System.**

E.L. DREYER, *Early Ming China* (Stanford University Press, 1982).

MILITIA, DIVISIONAL

A system of units with both military and agricultural duties which first evolved in the north-west border regions during the sixth century AD as an attempt to raise the status of military service and make it more attractive to good families. Groups of six farming households each provided one able-bodied man, who was then exempt from taxation, and supplied him with his provisions as well as his uniform and weapons. A hundred divisional units were said to have comprised 200,000 men under Zhou Wudi (561–77). Sui **Wendi** linked the militia to the **equal field system**. Both he and Tang **Gaozu** drew on soldiers of militia units when they seized the throne, and the efficiency of the system contributed to the military successes of the early Tang. Decline set in, however, in the second half of the seventh century as tax exemption was ended, the elite reputation of the militia was eroded, and households found more difficulty in making their contributions. The system was abolished in 749.

Mark ELVIN, *The Pattern of the Chinese Past* (Eyre Methuen, 1973).

MINBAO* 民報 *People's Journal

Organ of the ***Tongmenghui*** published in Tokyo. The first issue was published on November 26 1905 and it continued publication until the 24th issue in October 1908 when it was banned by the Japanese authorities. Two further issues were published clandestinely in 1910, plus an irregular issue entitled *Tiantao* 天討 *Heaven's Punishment*. It was edited first by **Hu Hanmin** 胡漢民, then by **Zhang Binglin** after his release from prison in Shanghai and subsequently **Wang Jingwei**. Zhang Binglin in particular was able to raise the level of the paper to provide stiff competition for **Liang Qichao**'s reformist rival, the *Xinmin congbao* 新民叢報, which had until then been very successful in attracting young intellectuals. *Minbao* expounded on the *Tongmenghui's* newly developed *Sanmin zhuyi* 三民主義 **Three People's Principles,** attacked the reformers' support for the Guangxu Emperor and constitutional monarchy, and promoted the need for armed revolution. It was widely circulated in China as well as among the Chinese students in Japan, and was effective in promoting the revolutionary cause and in undermining support among intellectuals for the Manchu government.

Mary Clabaugh WRIGHT ed., *China in Revolution: The First Phase 1900–1913* (Yale University Press, 1968).

MING DYNASTY 明朝 (1368–1644)

Dynasty that emerged from the rebellions against **Mongol** rule in the 14th century as the Yuan dynasty collapsed. It is often exalted as a native Chinese dynasty in contrast to the conquest dynasties of the Yuan that preceded it and the Qing that followed it, although the ethnic composition of the elites of all three dynasties were far more complex than that definition suggests. The rebel group in which the Ming emperors originated was the **Red Turban** movement which was active throughout northern China in the early 14th century and which, in addition to traditional Confucian and Daoist beliefs, drew on Buddhism, especially the cult of the Buddha of the future, **Maitreya**, and **Manichaeism**, the Iranian and Central Asian religion which emphasised the struggle between dark and light. The name Ming, which means "bright" or "light", is probably derived from the Manichaen origins of the Red Turbans. It was the name chosen by Zhu Yuanzhang 朱元璋, who took control of the Red Turban rebels in 1355 and captured Nanjing the following year, and with which he proclaimed his new dynasty and himself as the **Hongwu emperor** on January 23 (the first day of the Lunar Year) 1368.

The main concerns of the founding emperor and his successor Yongle were in consolidating their control of China. Yongle moved his capital from Nanjing, from which the Hongwu emperor had ruled, to Beijing, where he was more easily able to respond to the threat posed by the resurgence of Mongol power in the steppes. He was also responsible for commissioning an **encyclopaedia**, the *Yongle Dadian* 永樂大典, a compendium of all the indispensable works of scholarship in Chinese extant at the time.

Revival of the system of **examinations** for the civil service helped to create an elite group, the **gentry**, which controlled rural China on the basis of land ownership and examination success until the mid-twentieth century. In the 16th century, there was a period of remarkable economic growth during which handicraft industries and commerce expanded immensely. The latter part of the dynasty saw the familiar problems of high taxation, **eunuch** abuse of power, factional strife at court and peasant rebellion. The rising of **Li Zicheng** was the most successful and the dynasty ended when **Wu Sangui**, the Ming general in command of Liaodong, decided to allow the **Manchu** armies into China rather than see Li take the throne. The Manchus then established the Qing dynasty.

The Ming dynasty was noted for ceramics, in particular the blue-and-white porcelains from **Jingdezhen**, and for literature in the vernacular such as ***Shuihuzhuan*, *Xiyouji*** and ***Jinpingmei*.**

Reign dates	Temple Names	Reign Titles
1368–1399	Taizu	Hongwu
1399–1402	Huizong	Jianwen
1403–1425	Taizong	Yongle
1426–1436	Xuanzong	Xuande
1436–1450	Yingzong	Zhengtong
1450–1457	Daizong	Jingtai

Reign dates		Temple Names	Reign Titles
1457–1465		Yingzong	Tianshun
1465–1488		Xianzong	Hongzhi
1488–1506		Xiaozong	Hongzhi
1506–1522		Wuzong	Zhengde
1522–1567		Shizong	Jiajing
1567–1573		Muzong	Longqing
1573–1620		Shenzong	Wanli
1620–1621		Guangzong	Taichang
1621–1628		Xizong	Tianqi
1628–1645		Sizong	Chongzhen
1645	Southern Ming	Anzong	Hongguang
1646	Southern Ming	Shaozong	Longwu
1647–1661	Southern Ming		Yongli

Edward DREYER, *Early Ming China: A Political History, 1355–1435* (Stanford University Press, 1982; Edward L. FARMER, *Early Ming Government: The Evolution of Dual Capitals* (East Asian Research Center, Harvard University, 1976); John DARDESS, *Confucianism and Autocracy: Professional Elites and the Founding of the Ming Dynasty* (University of California Press, 1983); Ray HUANG, *1587, a Year of No Significance: The Ming Dynasty in Decline* (Yale University Press, 1981).

MING LOYALISTS

A group of scholars who refused to serve the Qing dynasty out of loyalty to the Ming. The leading figures of this group were **Gu Yanwu**, **Huang Zongxi** and **Wang Fuzhi**. There was widespread contempt for the Manchus, who, in turn, became mistrustful of scholars. This was reflected in the Manchu over-reaction during the **Literary Inquisition** of the Qianlong period.

Lynn STRUVE, *Southern Ming, 1644–1662* (Yale University Press, 1984); Jerry DENNERLINE, *The Chia-ting Loyalists: Confucian Leadership and Social Change in Seventeenth Century China* (Yale University Press, 1981).

MING TOMBS ***Ming shisan ling*** **明十三陵 (Thirteen Ming tombs)**

The first Ming emperor, **Hongwu** (Zhu Yuanzhang), revived the system of building imperial tombs prior to the ruler's death, which had been abolished in the Song dynasty. He also carried out major reforms in the burial system and implemented new features that dominated the Ming and Qing periods. The tomb mounds changed from square to round. The lower Palace compound of Tang and Song was abolished, and the system of palace women in attendance at the spirit's quarters was also eliminated under the Xuande Emperor. The offering hall compound was enlarged to emphasise the importance of such rites. Each necropolis became rectangular rather than square and consisted of three courtyards aligned on an axis. The Ming revisions also enhanced the beauty and solemnity of the site. Thirteen of the total sixteen Ming emperors were buried at one area near Beijing. The tombs were clustered along the valley with each tomb forming an independent unit. Although many treasures came from the excavation of Dingling, the tomb of the **Wanli** Emperor, they do not approach the lavishness of rich Han and Tang burials.

MINORITIES see **NATIONAL MINORITIES**

MISSIONARIES

China has experienced three great ideological "invasions", those of **Buddhism**, Christianity and Marxism. Of these, Christianity was first introduced in the Tang dynasty in the form of **Nestorianism**. Catholic Christianity reached China under the **Mongols** (see **John of Montecorvino**), but the first serious wave of missionary effort was that of the **Jesuits**, Franciscans and Dominicans in the sixteenth to eighteenth centuries. After 1783 the secular Lazarist Mission maintained Catholic interests into the nineteenth century, but this quickly became the century of Protestantism. Beginning with **Robert Morrison** of the London Missionary Society, who reached **Macao** in 1807, all the major Western societies were active on the mainland. They took advantage of the **Treaties of Nanjing** and **Beijing** to establish their presence in the ports and inland, and although they used dubious or even immoral methods to make Chinese converts, they also did excellent work in the fields of education, medicine and social reform, and contributed invaluably to the slow modernisation of China and the mutual exchange of information between East and West. Like the Jesuits, the Protestants may now be seen as representatives of a particular age and religious climate in Western history, but between them both missionary bodies contributed to China's religious, intellectual and institutional development, and it is from their early work, however flawed, that the contemporary Christian church in China has grown. See also **Islam**.

David MUNGELLO, *Curious Land: Jesuit Accommodation and the Origins of Sinology* (Wiesbaden: Franz Steiner Verlag; University of Hawaii Press, 1985*);* Bob WHYTE, *Unfinished Encounter, China and Christianity* (Glasgow: Collins (Fount paperback), 1988); John K. FAIRBANK, ed., *The Missionary Enterprise in China and America* (Harvard University Press, 1974).

MODERN TEXT MOVEMENT see **NEW TEXT SCHOOL**

MONASTICISM

The eremitic tradition in China goes back to the Zhou dynasty, but the organisation of monastic communities, initially for Indian missionaries, accompanied the arrival of **Buddhism** and dates from the Later Han dynasty. The building of the first monastery is traditionally ascribed to Emperor Mingdi (57–75). Criticism of the foreign religion and its Chinese converts arose quickly (see **Mouzi**), particularly on the grounds that monks and nuns were unfilial by leaving home and adopting celibacy and disloyal to the state by evading tax and labour obligations. In the case of a woman, retirement to a nunnery might indicate religious conviction but was sometimes rendered necessary by either social or economic pressures following the death of her husband. It might also provide welcome harbour for a middle-aged woman whose husband had turned to a younger companion. Monastic communities often provided valuable services for local society, such as jumble sales, moneylending, and basic education. The state nevertheless attacked them from time to time, destroying temples and scriptures (446 AD), defrocking monks and nuns (486), limiting ordinations (492), restricting building work (506) (see **Religious Persecution**). Even so, the

census of 516 showed a figure of 13,727 monasteries in northern China, and the entire church benefited from extensive patronage of Buddhism by wealthy believers (see also **Yungang Caves**, **Longmen Caves**). In 735 Emperor **Xuanzong** ordered monasteries to be built in every prefecture, and a total of 5,358 is recorded as the permitted number throughout the whole country. In **Chang'an** alone there were 64 Budddhist monasteries and 27 nunneries, ten Daoist monasteries and six nunneries. Only four survived **Wuzong's** persecution of 842–5, but the figure of 6,030 houses for 955 AD shows that monastic retreat still had a strong appeal in difficult times.

Recorded numbers of monks and nuns vary greatly from one period to another, reaching a peak of an estimated three million in north China and 82,700 in the South around the middle of the sixth century. At the time of the 842–5 persecution the number was said to be around 360,000, including 100,000 in 40,000 small houses and 260,000 in 4,600 larger monasteries and nunneries. A small house consisted of very few members, and the population of a larger one (average around 56 persons) was still modest compared with the great houses in **Tibet** (see **Drepung, Ganden, Sera**). Despite the severity of Wuzong's persecution 458,855 monks and nuns were registered again during the reign of Song Zhenzong (998–1023), and in 1291 a total of 213,148 were recorded as inhabiting 42,318 houses.

Jacques GERNET, *Buddhism in Chinese Society* (Columbia University Press, 1995).

MONGOLS

Pastoral nomads from the Inner Asian steppes who were united under the leadership of **Chinggis Khan** in a series of alliances and conquests that led to a great meeting of all the Mongol tribes at the Kerulen river in 1206. Steppe society until then had been fragmented with the pastoralist Mongols living in groups of families, each family living in its own *ger* (*yurt* in the Turkic languages) and keeping its own sheep and horses. The main unit of social organisation was the patriarchal common descent clan-lineage, the *obogh* and groups of these formed tribes *aimagh* to which their members swore loyalty. Like other nomads, the Mongols migrated according to the season, with summer and winter pastures. In language and culture they were related to earlier steppe peoples, the **Xianbi** and the **Khitan**.

After the unification of the disparate tribes by Chinggis Khan, the Mongols conquered all before them, the Xi Xia empire was vanquished by 1209, then the Western Liao regime of the Kara Khitai. The Mongols subdued lands far west of their steppe base, far into Central Asia, and including in Persia and Turkestan, and Mongol armies within striking distance of Vienna when they were suddenly withdrawn in 1242. China was conquered in a series of campaigns which began with the subjugation of the Jin empire in 1211–15 and ended when the Southern Song capital of **Hangzhou** was captured in 1276. The Mongols ruled China as the Yuan dynasty, having chosen that title in 1271 and the Yuan emperor was also the Great Khan of the Mongols. The other major khanates were the Khanate of Chagadai in Turkestan, the Ilkhanate of Persia and the Khanate of Kipchak, the Golden Horde based on the lower reaches of the Volga river. Mongol beliefs, like those of so many of the other steppe peoples, had been a form of shamanism, but the form of **Buddhism** popular in Tibet spread to Mongolia in the 13th century and became the main religion of the nation. See **'Phagspa**.

The Mongols ruled China until they were driven back to the steppes by the forces under Zhu Yuanzhang, the first Ming emperor, who took the throne as **Hongwu** in 1368. There was conflict between Ming armies and the Mongols from time to time but the unity that had been forged by Chinggis Khan dissolved and the Mongols were absorbed into the Manchu state by military expeditions under **Abahai** between 1629 and 1634. Under the Qing empire of the Manchus, Mongols were organised in their own **banner** systems, although these remained under Manchu control. When the Qing dynasty was overthrown in the **Revolution of 1911**, the Mongols declared independence with the Living Buddha or Jebtsundamba Khutukhtu of Urga as their temporal and spiritual leader. When Urga was occupied by the White Russian Baron Ungern von Sternberg in 1921, a Mongolian resistance under Choibalsan and Suhbaatar fought for independence and with the support of the newly-formed Soviet Union declared the People's Republic of Mongolia on November 26 1924. Urga was renamed Ulaanbaatar, also written Ulan Bator. In 1991, with the collapse of Communist power in the USSR and its allies, the People's Republic of Mongolia was renamed simply Mongolia. The **Inner Mongolian** Autonomous Region is within the People's Republic of China. See also **Yuan Dynasty**.

C.R. BAWDEN, *A Modern History of Mongolia* (2nd. revised edition) (Kegan Paul, 1989); Sechin JAGCHID and Paul HYER, *Mongolia's Culture and Society* (Boulder, Colorado: Westview, 1979); David MORGAN, *The Mongols* (Basil Blackwell, 1986); Herbert FRANKE, *China under Mongol Rule* (Aldershot: Variorum, 1994)

MORRISON, GEORGE ERNEST (1862–1920)

Correspondent of *The Times* of London in Beijing from 1897–1912, who also acted as an adviser to **Yuan Shikai** and his government from 1912 onwards.

MORRISON, ROBERT (1782–1834)

First Protestant **missionary** to work in China, representing the London Missionary Society. He arrived in 1807 and worked in Guangzhou as a translator for the **East India Company**. He also accompanied **Lord Amherst**'s mission to **Beijing** in 1816. As a missionary his greatest achievement was the translation, with the cooperation of William Milne, of the Bible into Chinese and its publication in 1819.

MOSCOW CONFERENCE (1960)

Conference of Communist and Workers Parties held in Moscow in November 1960 prompted by the growing but still camouflaged **Sino-Soviet Split**. The Chinese delegation attacked Khrushchev's policy of peaceful coexistence with the capitalist world and argued bitterly for three weeks in favour of support for wars of national liberation. Although they signed a common statement on peaceful cooexistence which was published on December 6, the extent of the rift was clear.

MOST FAVOURED NATION

In the treaties signed by China and Western nations during the second half of the 19th century, a clause, extending to all the treaty nations any privilege enjoyed by one, was known as the most-favoured nation clause.

MOUZI 牟子
Author of the earliest known Buddhist apologia in Chinese, *Lihuolun* “Discussion for Removing Doubts”, c.192 AD. The book indicates that Indian sutras had already been translated into Chinese, and is evidence of a growing anxiety at the rapid spread of the foreign religion. Presented in the form of a dialogue and disputation in thirty-eight sections between a Confucian critic and a Chinese Buddhist, it expresses the complaints that would be familiar throughout coming centuries, of **Buddhism’s** heterodox ideas and practices, its unfiliality, its followers’ betrayal of their Chinese heritage. In presenting his answers and defence, however, Master Mou reveals that he does not possess the later Buddhist skill of doctrinal exposition, relying mainly on simple refutation rather than logical counter-argument.

P. PELLIOT, trans.,“Meou-tseu, ou les doutes levés”, *T’oung Pao* XIX,1920 (Leiden: E.J.Brill)

MOZI 墨子 (Mo Di 墨翟, ?479–?381 BC)
A philosopher who cannot be linked with any of the other major *baijia* 百家 thinkers (see **Hundred Schools**). Though his followers were disciplined and well organised his theories failed to survive in the early imperial era. He advocated disinterested, impartial love in contradiction to the different levels of love, and hence as he saw it the prejudice, resulting from **Confucius’** ideas on family loyalty and duty. He believed that men could be controlled by spiritual sanctions rather than man-made legal codes. The emotions were dangerous and must be suppressed, along with their sources of encouragement such as funerals and **music**. These he condemned also on the grounds of excessive cost, and archaeological evidence suggests that his concern may not have been unjustified (see **Leigudun**). Economy and utility were his two principal watchwords and he believed that a people under stress would willingly accept the need for sacrifice, but his was a philosophy of retrenchment with no concept of development. He advocated peace, but on economic rather than ethical grounds, and all the while he trained his followers in militaristic style. He is linked with the invention of siege machines, the kite, and principles of mechanical engineering and optics.

Burton WATSON, trans., *Mo Tzu, Basic Writings* (Columbia University Press, 1963).

MUKDEN INCIDENT (1931)
Explosion of a bomb on the lines of the South Manchurian Railway at Shenyang (Mukden) on September 18 1931. There was little damage and not even any disruption of train services, but Japanese troops claimed that they had been fired on and had to shoot back in self-defence and used the incident as an excuse for the **Guandong Army**’s invasion of **Manchuria** that paved the way for the creation of the puppet state of Manzhouguo.

MUSIC
Origins of musical practice in China can be traced to the **neolithic** period. By the Shang dynasty some of its principal features of later times, including its close association with dance and rites and its use of a five-tone system, were

already apparent. Early evidence is also found in the ***Shijing*** for the subsequent practice of singing poetry. Until the Han dynasty the role of ritual and ceremonial music (*yayue* 雅樂) as a bridge between Heaven and earth was regarded as its most important function, but from the Han onwards the scope for the enjoyment of solo instrumental performance and ensemble playing as entertainment increased, and it was a necessary accomplishment of the true Confucian scholar-aesthete. The power of music to stir the emotions was fully recognised. The **Legalist** philosophers condemned this as potentially destabilizing; **Mozi** criticised the waste of money, time and emotional effort that was expended on it. **Daoists** accepted it as one means of reaching a state of equilibrium with the forces of nature. Confucians understood that at its best music had the power to inspire and to control people, but that they could also be led astray and lose their sense of proper values by unrestrained, wild and licentious tunes, which were often associated with the ancient states of Zheng and **Wei**. Musical purists felt they had to battle to prevent court, and especially ritual, music from being adversely influenced by the "improper" tunes of folk music (*suyue* 俗樂). Throughout the imperial era the state took seriously its responsibility for maintaining high standards of musical performance.

Evidence for the theory and practice of music in ancient and pre-modern times comes from archaeological and literary sources. The tomb of Zeng Houyi at **Leigudun** is a unique source of pre-Han instruments. Despite its importance no Classic (*jing*) of music was in use during the Han or later, but an immense number of books were written about it throughout pre-imperial and imperial times. Many were collected into the *Gujin Tushu Jicheng* and the ***Siku Quanshu.*** The section of the *Liji* which deals with music is the oldest surviving source of the ***Yueji.*** The Treatise on Music (chapter 24) from the *Shiji* gives a similar but more thorough view of Han ideas on the subject. Despite the fact that so much was written about music in China, modern research is still at an early stage and comparatively little is known of what it sounded like. Some scores of the Tang period have been found at **Dunhuang** and others of the Tang and Song periods reconstructed, but most surviving performance music which is today referred to as "traditional" dates from the Ming at the earliest, and has been subject to change as it has been passed on from generation to generation.

See also **Beijing Opera, Music Bureau, Musical Entertainment, Musical Instruments, Revolutionary Operas, *Shi*, Zhu Zaiyu.**

K. DEWOSKIN, *A Song for One or Two: Music and the Concept of Art in Early China* (University of Michigan Press, 1982); Rulan PIAN, *Sonq Dynasty Musical Sources and their Interpretation* (Harvard University Press, 1967); Lawrence PICKEN, *Music from the T'ang Court* (Oxford University Press, 1985).

MUSIC BUREAU *Yuefu* 樂府

The principal Han dynasty governmental music institution, traditionally established in approx. 112 BC though there is evidence for an earlier Han or Qin foundation. Its first Director under Han **Wudi**, bearing the title of Master of Harmony, was Li Yannian, who is linked by some modern scholars with the editing of the ***Yueji.*** Its duties were to arrange sacrifical, ceremonial and military music for the court, recruit and train musicians, maintain their instruments, superintend performances, commission new song texts (*yuefu*) for important occasions, and collect folk songs from around the country as a means of monitoring popular opinion. It was abolished by Emperor **Aidi** in 7 BC, at which time it employed nearly 830 musicians and dancers. This was partly an economy measure and partly because it had been associated with the **New Text School**, and the return to prominence of Old Text standards under **Liu Xiang** meant a return to greater simplicity and economies (see ***Gu Wen***). Furthemore, its repertoire was accused of having fallen prey to corrupting influences blamed as the music of Zheng.

The ***Zhou Li*** indicates that music had been taken seriously at the early Zhou court, although the musical establishment of nearly 1,500 officials attributed to the Spring Minister and his Senior Music Controller is too large to be credible for that early date. The Han title of Music Bureau was not revived for a long time, although later governments had influential music departments and institutions which came under the aegis of the Board of Rites. The largest ever complement of court musicians and dancers totalled around 30,000 in the time of Tang **Xuanzong**, when the main musical organisations were the Grand Music Office (*Taiyueshu*), the Ten Branches of Music (*Shibu [yue] zhi*), the Left and Right Academy (*Zuoyou jiaofang*) and the Pear Garden (*Li yuan*). The Song Emperor **Huizong** temporarily revived the title in 1102 when he created the Great Splendour Music Bureau (*Dasheng yuefu*), which numbered 785 musicians and dancers in 1120.

M. LOEWE, *Crisis and Conflict in Han China* (George Allen and Unwin, 1974).

MUSICAL ENTERTAINMENT

The enjoyment of music as a means of expressing feelings and deriving emotional satisfaction is evident from such early sources as the ***Shijing*** and the description of a performance at the court of **Lu** in 543 BC recorded in the ***Zuozhuan***. It is however from the Han dynasty onwards that more systematic information about this aspect of the musical art is to be found, especially from illustrations on the walls of tombs (see **Tomb Art**). Popular forms of entertainment known as *paixi* included **music**, dance, acrobatics, juggling, sword-swallowing and fire-eating.

By the early Tang period court music included the category known as *yanyue* 宴樂 "banquet music", which in turn included *zaxi* 雜戲, dramatic performances comprising music, dance, acrobatics and mime, some performed with masks. The use of colloquial language and dialogue developed as part of *canjunxi* 參軍戲, comic or satirical performances. Popular story-telling may have given rise to *bianwen* 變文, "transformation texts", the earliest vernacular narratives which employed rhythmic speech and songs. A further major literary entertainment form was the *daju*, a suite of pieces using song and dance.

Daju played a part in the development of the ***ci*** poetic songs of the Song period, and both were to be found in *changzhuan*, popular story-telling, along with popular tunes and street cries. This, together with *zhugongdiao*, an epic ballad performed usually by a woman or women to the accompaniment of a single instrument, represented an important stage in the evolution of Yuan dynasty **drama**. So did *zaju* 雜劇, the Song descendant of *canjunxi*, a new feature of which was improvisation on a plot criticizing the target of the satire. *Zaju* were played at court by members of the *Jiaofang* (see **Music Bureau**). As an entertainment category they also comprised song and dance suites revolving around an epic plot, and performances of puppetry, pantomime and dance, juggling and acrobatics. In the Southern Song they were known as *zhengse*, but when the *Jiaofang* was abolished in the Shaoxing reign period (1131–63), redundant players dispersed across the countryside, there to adapt their entertainment skills to popular taste in such a way as to encourage the development of theatrical arts.

It was during the Yuan dynasty that *zaju* matured into an early form of opera (see **Beijing Opera**), with the Southern drama *chuanqi* prominent.

J.I. CRUMP, *Chinese Theater in the Days of Khubilai Khan* (University of Arizona Press, 1980); M. GIMM, *Das Yueh-fu Tsa-lu des Tuan An-chieh* (Wiesbaden: Harrassowitz, 1966).

MUSICAL INSTRUMENTS

The oldest surviving musical instruments in China are bone flutes and pottery whistles dating from Paleolithic times, but by the Shang period bronze bells and stone chimes, soon to assume special importance for ritual performance, had already been added to the range of flutes, ocarinas and drums. **Oracle bone** inscriptions suggest the possible existence then of stringed instruments, though the evidence is unclear. By the Zhou, however, the wide range of the instrumentarium is proved by both literary references and archaeological finds, e.g. from **Leigudun**. It already included the plucked strings *qin* 琴 and *se* 瑟, the mouth organ *sheng* 笙, and the *xiao* 簫 panpipes. The four-stringed lute, *pipa* 琵琶, was introduced from Central Asia during the Han dynasty and quickly became a popular solo and ensemble instrument. Other foreign instruments which the Chinese willingly adopted were the *huqin* family of bowed strings, especially the *erhu* 二胡, which entered China during the period of Mongol rule, and the dulcimer (*yangqin* 揚琴), imported by **Jesuit** missionaries in the seventeenth century. Though Matteo **Ricci** played the dulcimer to the **Wanli** Emperor, keyboard instruments never gained acceptance in China before the twentieth century.

For ease of reference many modern Chinese writers still use the ancient Chinese classification of instruments into eight categories, *bayin* 八音 "eight sounds", each reflecting the particular timbre resulting from its principal sound-producing material. The eight (with representative examples) are: metal (bells), stone (chimes), silk (zithers), bamboo (flutes), gourd (mouthorgans), pottery (ocarinas), wood (clappers), skin (drums).

Instruments feature prominently in Chinese painting, sculpture and literature and provide ample evidence for the richness in both sound and sight of the musical experience in traditional China. Instruments were made of the finest materials and beautifully decorated with **lacquer** and paint, inlaid with ivory and mother of pearl, and hung with **silk** and brocade. Over the centuries many variations of instrumental forms have been tried, such as by increasing and diminishing the number of bells on a stand or the number of strings on a zither. Modern developments have seen a bass *pipa* resembling a plucked version of the double bass added to the lute family, and provision of a bellows for an outsize *sheng* mouthorgan.

R. van GULIK, *The Lore of the Chinese Lute* (Tokyo: Sophia University, 1940).

MUSLIM REBELLIONS

During the Qing dynasty, China's Muslims acquired a reputation among their Han neighbours for ferocious and disorderly behaviour. There was some resistance to the Manchu conquest of Muslim territories in the late 17th century, but it was in the late 19th century during three outbreaks of harsh and brutal communal violence, usually known as the Muslim rebellions, that this reputation was confirmed. From 1856 to 1873, Muslims in Yunnan (known as Panthays, from the Burmese word for Muslim) rose up against their Chinese overlords and their leader, Du Wenxiu, declared himself the ruler of an independent Muslim sultanate. The insurrection in Shaanxi and Gansu which occurred between 1862 and 1878 destroyed whole regions of north-western China, and the **Hui** Muslim population was drastically reduced and faced the real possibility of extinction. From 1873 to 1877, the region around Kashghar and part of northern **Xinjiang** was ruled as an independent state after the rebellion led by Yakub Beg. Finally, conflict between Muslims and local Han landlords and officials led to lawlessness on the Gansu and Qinghai border in 1895. These insurrections devastated the border regions of China and left behind a legacy of mutual suspicion between Muslims and Han Chinese and Chinese officials have ever since feared the possibility of Muslim separatism.

CHU Wen-djang, *The Moslem Rebellion in North-West China, 1862–1878: A Study of Government Minority Policy* (The Hague: Mouton 1966).

MUTUAL AID TEAMS

Stage in the collectivisation of agriculture. After **Land Reform** had been implemented throughout most of China, family and village groups were encouraged to cooperate, seasonally and later more permanently, on appropriate agricultural tasks, pooling their labour and farm tools. Many of these teams were not new but were based on traditional patterns of rural cooperation. **Agricultural Producer Cooperatives** were formed by amalgamating these teams.

NANBEICHAO 南北朝 see **NORTHERN AND SOUTHERN DYNASTIES**

NANCHANG RISING ***Nanchang qiyi*** 南昌起義

CCP insurrection in Nanchang the main city of Jiangxi province on August 1 1927, a date subsequently designated Army Day in the PRC. The newly formed **Workers and Peasants' Red Army**, created in the wake of the collapse of CCP-GMD cooperation which culminated in the **Shanghai Coup**, held the city for several days before it was surrounded by GMD troops. They broke out and retreated to the hills on the borders of Guangdong , Jiangxi and Fujian. It was the failure of urban insurrections like the Nanchang rising that drove the CCP towards the peasants.

NANJING 南京

'Nanking' in the Post Office spelling, Nanjing is the main city in Jiangsu province and a major port on the **Yangzi River** and has a long history as an administrative centre. It was the first capital of the Ming **Hongwu** emperor and it acquired its present name which means southern capital when the **Yongle** emperor made **Beijing** his main capital as part of his strategy to contain the **Mongols**. During the **Taiping Rebellion**, it was captured by the insurgents and renamed Tianjing, 天京

the Heavenly Capital, suffering much damage when it was recaptured by the armies of the Qing. After the **Revolution of 1911**, Nanjing was designated the capital of the **Republic of China**, but the capital moved to Beijing on **Yuan Shikai**'s accession to power. It became the capital of the Republic after the Northern Expedition of 1926–7 and remained so until the GMD government was obliged to escape to Chongqing to avoid the Japanese armies of occupation in 1937. This period is often referred to as the Nanjing Decade.

NANJING ARSENAL

Armaments factory founded in 1865 by **Li Hongzhang** and part of the **Self-Strenghening Movement**.

NANJING, RAPE OF

Wartime atrocity by Japanese troops. Japanese forces invading China occupied Nanjing on December 13 1937. Over 100,000 civilians were killed and women and girls were systematically raped by the Japanese soldiers.

NANJING, TREATY OF (1842)

Treaty signed on August 29 1842 at the end of the **Opium War** between Britain and China and regarded by the Chinese as the first of the **unequal treaties**. The treaty provided for an indemnity of 21 million dollars to be paid to Britain; the abolition of the **Cohong** trade monopoly in Guangzhou; the opening of the ports of Guangzhou, Xiamen (Amoy), Fuzhou, Ningbo and Shanghai to trade; consuls, merchants and their families to be allowed to reside in these ports; custom duty rates to be fixed; and the island of **Hong Kong** to be ceded to Britain in perpetuity.

TENG Ssu-yu, *Chang--Hsi and the Treaty of Nanking, 1842* (University of Chicago Press, 1944).

NANZHAO 南詔

An independent kingdom in modern Yunnan province which developed as a grouping of ethnically related tribes in the seventh century and established its first capital at modern Dali in 739. Though recognised by Emperor **Xuanzong** as a tribute state it was a threat to Sichuan and engaged in tense triangular relations with **Tibet** and China, acknowledging the supremacy of first one and then the other. During an expansionist period in the early ninth century its armies sacked Chengdu (829) and penetrated another Chinese feudatory and trading partner, **Annam**. Costly military campaigns continued until a stalemate was reached around 875. The kingdom broke up into a number of lesser states following an act of infant regicide and usurpation by a senior official in 902.

C. BACKUS, *The Nan-chao Kingdom and T'ang China's Southwestern Frontier* (Cambridge University Press, 1981).

NAPIER MISSION (1834)

Mission by Lord William John Napier on behalf of Great Britain to the Governor-General of Guangzhou in 1834, the year in which the **East India Company's** monopoly of trade in eastern Asia was due to come to an end. The objectives of the visit were essentially the same as those of the **Amherst** and **Macartney** missions. Napier failed to get official permission to base himself in

Guangzhou and was forced to leave for Macao by Chinese troops. The Napier Mission was the last attempt to secure diplomatic and trade relations by peaceful means and the **Opium War** followed.

NATIONAL MINORITIES ***Shaoshu minzu*** **少數民族**

Designation of minority ethnic groups in the PRC, a name based on the Soviet Union's concept of *natsionalnost'* (nationality) created under Stalin. Under this system, national minorities are defined as groups of people with territory, language, economic life and psychological make-up in common. Official policy stresses the fact that 94% of the population of China are Han Chinese and only 6% belong to the ethnic minorities, but in some areas in the border regions of China, ethnic groups other than the Han are in the majority. In addition to the Han, there are 55 officially recognised National Minorities in China. The most populous are the Zhuang, Hui, Uyghur, Yi, Miao, Manchus, Tibetans and Mongols. There is a widespread feeling among both Chinese and Western ethnographers that the official designations do not reflect the actual ethnic make-up of China.

June DREYER, *China's Forty Millions: Minority Nationalities and National Integration in the People's Republic of China* (Harvard University Press, 1976); Donald MCMILLEN, *Chinese Communist Power and Policy in Xinjiang, 1949–1977* (Boulder, Colorado: Westview, 1979); CHANG Chih-yi, *The Party and the National Question in China*, ed. and trans. George Mosely (Cambridge, Mass: MIT Press, 1966).

NATIONAL PEOPLE'S CONGRESS

Supreme Legislative body set up in the PRC and the nearest equivalent in China to a parliament. The NPC was convened in 1954 and has met annually since then with a gap during the **Cultural Revolution**, when it only met once in January 1975. There is a Standing Committee which meets when the NPC is not itself in session. The NPC is entrusted with the adoption of the Constitution of the PRC, and with the election of the President; the Chairman of the Central Military Commission, the President of the Supreme Court and the head of the Supreme People's Procuratorate and with the creation and amendment of legislation. Although delegates are elected indirectly, the NPC has never been able to function as an independent legislature and in general approves decisions made by the CCP.

NATIONAL REVOLUTIONARY ARMY see **NORTHERN EXPEDITION**

NEEDHAM, JOSEPH (1900–94)

Distinguished biochemist and polymath who became the greatest authority on the history of scientific invention and discovery in traditional China and its relatedness to the development of civilisation throughout the world. His personal experience of China began with a four-year stay in Chongqing from 1942–6 following a scientific mission. Realisation of the richness of the scientific tradition in China led him to begin publication in 1954 of his multi-volumed magnum opus, *Science and Civilisation in China*, which in its conception, scope and influence has been likened to Gibbon's *Decline and Fall of the Roman Empire.* (See **Inventions and Discoveries**)

J. NEEDHAM, *Science and Civilisation in China* (Cambridge University Press, vol. 1, 1954 – (continuing)).

NEI TING see **INNER COURT, EUNUCHS**

NEIGHBOURHOOD COMMITTEE see **STREET COMMITTEE**

NEO-CONFUCIANISM *Daoxue* 道學

The form of Confucianism which developed in the Song dynasty and dominated Chinese intellectual life throughout the rest of the imperial period. The Confucianism of **Confucius** and **Mencius** was primarily concerned with practical problems of ethics and statecraft; cosmological speculation played little part (Confucius' overall attitude towards gods and spirits was that there was no point speculating about the unknowable). Nevertheless, the ***Yijing*** 'Book of Changes', a work on divination and one of the five basic Confucian Classics, was associated with Confucius and offered fertile ground for cosmological speculation. It became a key text for Neo-Confucians. Cosmological speculation became significant from the Han onwards and Buddhism, which was introduced from the second century AD, enjoyed important advantages over Confucianism in this respect. Confucianism went into a decline and Buddhism dominated the intellectual world from the fourth to the ninth centuries. However, when the **examination system** was reinstated during the Tang dynasty, owing to Buddhism's lack of concern with statecraft, it was to Confucian texts that the examiners turned. In the late Tang there was a xenophobic reaction against Buddhism by scholars like **Han Yu** which paved the way for a re-evaluation of the native tradition. In the early Song, **Zhou Dunyi** (1017–73) and **Shao Yong** (1011–77) reinterpreted diagrams which Daoists had used in the quest for **immortality** to offer a native cosmology which was grafted on to the existing Confucian philosophy. At the same time **Zhang Zai** 張載 suggested that everything is made of ***qi*** 氣 (matter/energy) which integrates according to an inherent principle (variously referred to as ***dao*** "way", *taiji* 太極 "great ultimate" or *taixu* 太虛 "great void") when the thing comes into being and disintegrates when the thing dies. Zhang Zai has been praised by Marxist philosophers as an early materialist for this rationalist explanation which denies the existence of any external agent. He was teacher to his two nephews, **Cheng Hao** (1032–85) and **Cheng Yi** (1033–1107) who developed their theory of *li* 理 (principle) as a force governing everything, and led Neo-Confucianism firmly back to its Confucian origins with their primary emphasis on man and morality. These five early figures were followed by **Zhu Xi** (1130–1200) who synthesised their theories to form a coherent system, which became the basis of the Rationalist School of Neo-Confucianism. According to this each thing has within it its own *li* "principle" which is part of the *taiji* "great ultimate" principle governing the whole of creation. *Li* subsists eternally and is *xing er shang* 形而上 "beyond form", whereas physical matter *qi*, for which *li* acts as the organising principle, is *xing er xia* 形而下 "within form" and subject to a cycle of birth and death. Zhu Xi suggests that *li* and *qi* depend on each other and cannot be separated, but ultimately *li* must be regarded as having primacy. The nature *xing* 性 of human beings is *li* and as such is good, as Mencius affirmed, but its goodness is obscured to a greater or lesser extent by the *qi* of our physical self. The purpose of education is to gain knowledge of the *li* through investigating things, *ge wu* 格物. Zhu Xi chose the ***Daxue*** as the text best exemplifying these principles. The process was firmly linked to moral goals, and was not the general spirit of scientific enquiry it might superficially appear. Although Zhu Xi was regarded as heterodox in his lifetime, in 1313 his interpretations were accepted as orthodox and became the basis of the civil service examinations. Inevitably there was eventually a reaction against Zhu Xi; this came with **Wang Yangming** (1472–1529) whose idealist approach rejected the rationalism of Zhu Xi. Wang Yangming affirmed the whole of *li* was contained in our minds; there was no need to go investigating external things. This idealistic approach was discredited in the late Ming and the meticulous scholarship of the *kao zheng* 考證 school of the early Qing was very much a reaction to the perceived excesses of Wang Yangming's followers.

Wing-tsit CHAN, ed., *Chu-Hsi and Neo-Confucianism* (University of Hawaii Press, 1986); W.T. DE BARY et al., *The Unfolding of Neo-Confucianism* (Columbia University Press, 1975); Wei-ming TU, *Neo-Confucian Thought in Action: Wang Yang-ming's Youth (1472–1509)* (Berkeley:University of California Press,1976).

NEOLITHIC PERIOD

Thousands of neolithic sites have been found stretching from present-day Gansu Province in the North-west of China to the south coast around Hong Kong. The greatest concentration is in the North, from Gansu through southern Shaanxi, Shanxi, and Henan to Shandong, and from southern Manchuria down to the **Yangzi** delta. Earliest finds may be dated to approximately 7,000 years BC, and whilst central parts of the country witnessed the development of bronze skills during the second half of the second and the first half of the first millennium BC, it must be assumed that neolithic life styles persisted widely in many regional communities until well into the Zhou period. Two dominant cultural patterns are named after the location of typical early sites. These are known as **Yangshao** and **Longshan**. Modern understanding of the relationship between the two has changed in reponse to the growing number of archaeological discoveries. Originally believed to have been roughly contemporary but spatially distinct, then thought to have been chronologically consecutive, they are now known to have each developed contemporaneously from early through late neolithic times, roughly spreading from West to East and from East to West respectively. Longshan, however, developed the more sophisticated characteristics and outlasted, and in some sites (e.g. at **Erligang**) overlaid, Yangshao culture. The two are chiefly distinguished by the characteristics of their pottery, Longshan showing greater technical mastery and perhaps aesthetic appreciation than Yangshao, and clearly indicating the forms that would be imitated in bronze from the middle of the second millennium onwards. Other skills from both cultures include the drilling and carving of **jade** and bone. Neolithic communities already show signs of patterns of social hierarchy, community structure and religious attitudes that typify Shang society, including the importance attached to family and occupational groupings and to the ability to contact spirits of the departed in the next existence.

G.L. BARNES , *China, Korea and Japan: the Rise of Civilization in East Asia* (Thames and Hudson, 1993); K.C. CHANG, *The Archaeology of Ancient China* (Yale University Press, 4th ed., 1986).

NERCHINSK, TREATY OF (1689)

The first treaty between China and a Western state and the first modern treaty signed by China recognising another as its equal, bringing to an end the first wave of border fighting between Russians and Chinese along the Amur River. Two **Jesuit** missionaries, Frs. Pereira and Gerbillon, acted as interpreters and mediators, and the **Kangxi** Emperor's satisfaction at the outcome of the negotiation was a factor contributing to his Edict of Toleration issued in favour of Christianity in 1692. The principal results of the Treaty were actually more advantageous to Russia than to China. Russia gained territory along the Amur and rights for its traders to enter China under conditions that were more generous than those granted to other foreigners under the **tribute system** (see also **Canton System**). China, however, had now eliminated the risk of Russia's becoming involved in its struggle with the Mongol Khan Galdan.

NESTORIANISM

The earliest form of Christianity to enter China, said to have been introduced by a Persian monk named A-lo-ben in 635. In 638 the Emperor Tang **Taizong** favoured it with a decree ordering the building of a monastery in **Chang'an**. In the cosmopolitan atmosphere of the capital Nestorianism enjoyed some recognition among Chinese as well as the Syrian merchants visiting the Tang Empire, and was especially favoured under Emperor **Xuanzong**. In 781 a limestone stele inscribed with the Nestorian creed and an account of the religion's arrival in China was erected in Chang'an. Nestorian documents have been discovered at **Dunhuang**. Nestorianism disappeared following suppression in 842–5 (see **Religious Persecution**), but was patronised by members of the Mongol court during the Yuan dynasty. The discovery of the Chang'an stele in 1625 benefited the **Jesuit** missionaries seeking recognition among the literati, enabling them to point to an earlier precedent for the presence of Christianity in the Middle Kingdom.

NEW ARMY

Modernised military units developed by the Qing government after 1901. The court organised army committees in every province to build the new armies but kept them under strict central control. Western and Japanese techniques were studied and the modernised army units became an important force in the **Revolution of 1911**.

NEW CULTURE MOVEMENT ***Xin wenhua yundong*** **新文化運動**

Predecessor of the **May Fourth Movement** of 1919. Interest in the West and concepts of democracy, science and modernisation were challenged by Marxism as the impact of the October Revolution of 1917 took effect. It was during this movement that the political division between the Nationalists and the Communists was created. See ***Xin Qingnian,*** **John Dewey**, **Chen Duxiu**, **Hu Shi.**

NEW DEMOCRACY ***Xin minzhu zhuyi*** 新民主主義

Designationfor the interim rule of the CCP after 1949, pre-1949 politics being designated Old Democracy. Mao wrote a pamphlet, *On New Democracy*, in which he outlined the principles of the transitional system in which a temporary alliance of workers, peasants, petty bourgeoisie and national bourgeosie would co-exist under CCP leadership, a system borrowed from Stalin's Soviet Union. The period of New Democracy effectively came to an end with the socialist transformation of industry and the drive for collectivisation in 1953.

NEW FOURTH ARMY ***Xinsijun*** **新四軍**
CCP army based in Shandong and Jiangsu renamed as part of the anti-Japanese **United Front**. On January 5 1941, it was attacked by Guomindang forces and virtually wiped out. On January 17 it was formally disbanded by the GMD, but reorganised by the CCP with **Chen Yi** as its commander. This clash, known as the Southern Anhui incident, effectively brought the United Front to an end.

NEW LIFE MOVEMENT
GMD campaign launched on February 19 1934 by Jiang Jieshi at a mass meeting in Nanjing. Jiang called for a renewing of Confucian morality, including the traditional Chinese values of politenes (*li*), righteousness (*yi*), integrity (*lian*) and self-respect (*chi*) and the movement's tracts emphasised cleanliness, truthfulness and courtesy. The campaign mirrored Fascist movements in Europe and Japan and had little success.

NEW TERRITORIES see **HONG KONG**

NEW TEXT SCHOOL
One of the two classical text traditions. In the early Han, after the **burning of the books** by the Qin dynasty when the original classics were thought to be lost, an agreed version was reconstituted by scholars from memory (feasible when rote-learning was the norm) and written down in the current standard 'new' script *jinwen* 今文. Subsequently original pre-Qin 'old' script *guwen* 古文 versions were said to have been discovered; these largely supplanted the new text versions, until doubts began to be expressed about their authenticity from the Song onwards. The breakthrough came in the early Qing when Yan Ruoju 閻若琚 proved by evidential research techniques that the old text version of the ***Shangshu*** (Book of History) was a forgery. This opened the way for a reevaluation of new text classics and a reorientation of scholarship away from the detailed textual exegesis of Han learning to a new emphasis on the ideas contained in the texts. Han learning itself was a late Ming and early Qing reaction to the intuitive approach of Song learning (**Neo-Confucianism**), especially that of **Wang Yangming**, which was criticised for its adulteration by Buddhist and Daoist ideas. Han studies scholars used the evidential research *kaozheng* 考證 techniques associated with Later Han scholars but refined by men like **Gu Yanwu** to establish authentic texts free from Song learning contamination. In the long run this had the unanticipated effect of demystifying the classics, turning them from repositories of eternal truths into historical documents. In the late eighteenth century there was a reaction against the aridity of Han studies; scholars like Zhuang Cunyu 莊存與 (1719–1788), his grandson Liu Fenglu 劉逢祿 (1776–1829) and Gong Zizhen 龔自珍(1792–1841) pioneered the use of a 'new' text, the ***Gongyang*** 公羊commentary, to explain the true meaning of the ***Spring and Autumn Annals*** (*Chunqiu* 春秋), the only text apart from the ***Analects*** (*Lunyu* 論語) conceivably by Confucius. New text scholars believed that Confucius was not simply a transmitter but used these texts to propagate his own ideas. Hence, this school appealed to statecraft practitioners like **Wei Yuan** and **Zeng Guofan**, and ultimately **Kang Youwei** who claimed that Confucius made up these texts, cloaking his own reformist ideas in an historical mantle to give them credibility.

Benjamin A. ELMAN, *From Philosophy to Philology: Intellectual and Social Aspects of Change in Late Imperial China* (Council on East Asian Studies, Harvard University, 1984); Benjamin A.ELMAN, *Classicism, Politics and Kinship: The Ch'ang-chou School of New Text Confucianism in Late Imperial China* (Berkeley: University of California Press, 1990); Jung-pang LO ed. and trans., *Kang Yu-wei: A Biography and a Symposium* (University of Arizona Press, 1967)

NEW YEAR see **TRADITIONAL FESTIVALS**

NEW YOUTH see ***XIN QINGNIAN***

NEW YEAR PRINTS *Nianhua* 年畫,

These represent the popular print tradition in China. The prints usually portrayed subjects of an auspicious nature, often, but not always directly, connected with the New Year, and various deities and divinities such as the gods of wealth, longevity and kitchen. The prints were made from a black key block, often with the addition of five or six colour blocks, though some were wholly or partly coloured by hand. Early examples of such prints appeared in the Song dynasty. The best known centres of production of New Year prints during the Ming and Qing dynasties included Yangliuqing in Tianjin, Taohuawu in Suzhou, Jiangsu province, and Weifang in Shandong province, and such prints are still produced in those regions. Prints of this type served as cheap and colourful adornment for the homes of the ordinary people, especially in the rural areas, and also allowed them to indulge their beliefs and superstitions. See also **Traditional Festivals**.

NIAN REBELLION (1851–1868)

The Nian, 捻軍 (*nianjun*) "Nian Army", were an extraordinary collection of outlaw bands which operated in the area that is the border region between the present day provinces of Anhui, Henan and Jiangsu. They appear to have been the descendants of **White Lotus** bands but did not have a distinctive religious perspective. They emerged during a period of famine as self-defence organisations based in fortified villages but extended their activities to raiding neighbouring villages. The raids were seasonal, mainly taking place in the spring and autumn. In 1851, the Yellow River shifted its course, running into the sea in the north of Shandong rather than the south. Famine and desperation led to increased banditry and the Nian bands gradually coalesced into an organised rebel band. A powerful landlord and salt smuggler from Anhui, Zhang Lexin, gained control of the Nian alliance in 1852 and assumed the title of king. The Nian insurrection was defeated by forces of the Qing government in a campaign that lasted from 1863–1868. The Mongol general **Senggerinchin** took command of the campaign but was killed in battle in 1865 and replaced by **Zeng Guofan** and later **Li Hongzhang**. One Nian group known as the Eastern Band was defeated by Li in 1867 and the Western Band fled north-west to join the **Muslim rebellion** of Gansu and Shaanxi.

CHIANG Siang-tseh, *The Nian Rebellion* (University of Washington Press, 1954); TENG Ssu-yu, *The Nien Army and Their Guerilla Warfare, 1851–1868* (Paris: Mouton 1961); Elizabeth PERRY, *Chinese Perspectives on the Nien Rebellion* (M.E.Sharpe, 1981).

NIE YUANZI 聶元梓 (1920–)
Niece of Nie Rongzhen 聶榮臻, who was a PRC military and political leader who became deputy chief-of-staff of the PLA and a member of the Politburo. Nieh Yuanzi was the author of the first Big Character Poster ***dazibao*** 大字報 of the **Cultural Revolution.** She was a lecturer in Philosophy at Beijing University, and her poster, put up on May 25 1965, criticised the President of the University and its Party Committee. Mao defended her views and later put up his own poster "Bombard the Headquarters" in support.

NINGXIA HUI AUTONOMOUS REGION Ningxia huizu zizhiqu 寧夏回族自治區
Before 1949, Ningxia was the name of the city in Gansu province that became known as Yinchuan under the PRC. In 1958, Yinchuan and the rural counties around it were redesignated as the Ningxia Hui **Autonomous Region**. Approximately one third of the population of Ningxia are **Hui** Muslims, and in the mountainous southern part of the region, there are many areas which are inhabited almost entirely by Hui people.

NIXON VISIT (1972)
Diplomatic breakthrough in Sino-American relations and symbol of China's emergence from **Cultural Revolution** isolation. Henry Kissinger, President Richard Nixon's foreign affairs adviser visited Beijing secretly in 1971 and **Ping-Pong Diplomacy** was the first indication that Americans would be allowed to travel to China again. Nixon arrived in Beijing on February 21 1972, met Zhou Enlai and Mao Zedong and toured China, commenting that the Great Wall was a "great" wall. The irony that the first American president to visit communist China was the man who had ruined the careers of US China specialists in the 1950 McCarthy hearings was lost on the Chinese who regarded him as a hero, even after the Watergate scandal.

NOIN-ULA
Site of aristocratic **Xiongnu** tombs (*kurgan*) approximately 100km north of modern Ulaanbaatar. They date from the early first century AD and are constructed in the Chinese unmodernised, Zhou style of a timber-lined coffin chamber at the bottom of a vertical pit (see **Tomb Architecture**). The furnishing of the tombs, the form of the coffins, and the range and style of the grave goods (including precious metals, **jades**, lacquerware, and **silks**) all indicate the extent to which Chinese influence under the **tribute system** had entered the nomad leaders' life-style.

NORTHERN AND SOUTHERN DYNASTIES *Nanbeichao* 南北朝 (317–589)
Period of disunity during which northern China was ruled principally by a succession of non-Chinese (Toba) regimes and the south by five Chinese dynasties. **Buddhism** was patronised in both north and south and spread rapidly among all classes (see **Yungang Caves, Longmen Caves**), and there were notable developments in literature and painting (see **Xie He, Gu Kaizhi, Landscape Painting**).

Northern Dynasties	capitals at (A) Datong (B) Luoyang (C)Ye, Henan (D) Chang'an	Southern Dynasties	all capitals at Nanjing
Northern Wei	(386–534)(A,B)	Eastern Jin	(317–420)
Eastern Wei	(534–50)(C)	Liu Song	(420–79)
Western Wei	(534–57)(B)	Southern Qi	(479–502)
Northern Qi	(550–77)(C)	Liang	(502–57)
Northern Zhou	(557–81)(D)	Chen	(557–89)

See also **Land Tenure.**

NORTHERN EXPEDITION

GMD campaign to unify China and defeat the provincial **warlords**. **Jiang Jieshi** ordered his National Revolutionary Army to begin the march north from its base in Guangdong on July 1 1926. Changsha, the main city of Hunan was captured on July 11, Wuhan in September, Fuzhou in December and Shanghai and Nanjing in March 1927. This was the extent of the control of the GMD over China until 1928 when Beijing was brought under GMD control. **Nanjing** became the capital of the Republic of China government. The Northern Expedition was carried out with the support of the CCP and CCP activists played a crucial role in preparing the capture of towns and cities, but in April 1927 this cooperation was ended by Jiang Jieshi and the **Shanghai Coup**.

Donald JORDAN, *The Northern Expedition: China's National Revolution of 1926–1928* (University of Hawaii Press, 1976); C. Martin WILBUR, *The Nationalist Revolution in China, 1923–1928* (Cambridge University Press, 1984).

NUMEROLOGY *Shushu* 數術

Theory particularly prevalent in the Han dynasty that numerical correspondences exist between Heaven, earth and man and that human affairs should reflect these. For example, the ***Huainanzi*** (c. 139 BC) says that man's head in its roundness resembles Heaven and his feet in their squareness resemble earth and that the four seasons, five phases, nine sections and 366 days correspond to man's four limbs, five viscera, nine orifices and 366 joints. In order to ensure human harmony the ruler should seek to pattern his government on the natural order by, for example, appointing officials in numbers which corresponded to it e.g. three principal officials for the months in a season or five ministries for the five elements. Commentators have suggested that the use of numerology and the interpretation of natural phenomena as heavenly warnings were attempts by scholars to limit the power of autocratic rulers by claiming the existence of a higher authority whose will scholars were uniquely qualified to interpret. Han numerological theories were the inspiration for Song **Neo-Confucians** like **Shao Yong** who developed a Confucian numerological cosmology based on the ***Yi jing*** Book of Changes.

John B. HENDERSON, *The Development and Decline of Chinese Cosmology* (Columbia University Press, 1984); Joseph NEEDHAM, *Science and Civilisation in China, Vol II* (Cambridge University Press, 1956).

NURHACHI (1559–1626)
Creator of the **Manchu** state. Nurhachi unified the **Jurchen** tribes of the region to the north-east of China by a combination of diplomacy, arranged marriages and political alliances and organised the military into **Banners**, with appointed rather than hereditary commanders. In 1599, Nurhachi directed that Chinese works be translated into Manchu and written using a modified form of the Mongolian alphabet, thus creating the written Manchu language. He moved his capital from the north-east of the Liaodong peninsula to Mukden in 1625, from where his son and successor **Abahai** was able to create the foundations of the Qing dynasty.

OGODEI KHAN (? -1241)
Third son of **Chinggis Khan** and his successor as **Great Khan** of the **Mongols** from 1229 until his death in 1241. He had a reputaton for tolerance and generosity that was not typical of Mongol leaders of his time and was not as enamoured of the death penalty as his predecessors. During his reign, the Khitan adviser to the Mongol court, Yelu Chucai, carried out a programme of administrative reform which drew Chinese into the Mongol system, and the capital city of **Karakorum** was constructed, the wall of the city being built in 1235. His death in 1241 caused the withdrawal of the Golden Horde from Europe to take part in the *khuriltai* (conference) at which his successor was determined.

OIRATS
Mongol group living to the south-west of Lake Baikal who raided northern China during the Ming dynasty.

OLD TEXT see ***GU WEN***

OMENS AND PORTENTS
Have been commonly regarded and officially interpreted as signs of Heaven's will from ancient to modern times. Natural phenomena such as eclipses, unseasonal weather, epidemic illness, or earthquakes could not be foretold but might be used to maximum advantage by those dissatisfied with the government, giving them cause to memorialise or rebel against its conduct. Officials also reported the occurrence of unnatural events, such as chickens born with two heads or water seen running uphill, and of favourable events such as the appearance of a unicorn, as a means of attempting to influence the emperor with their own views. The great Tangshan Earthquake of July 1976 was widely seen as a portent in a year in which the **Chinese Communist Party** lost **Zhou Enlai, Zhu De,** and **Mao Zedong.** See also **Mandate of Heaven, Wang Chong.**

OPIUM WARS ***Yapian zhanzheng*** **鴉片戰爭**
Two wars between Britain and China over rights to trade and diplomatic representation. The second conflict is usually referred to as the **Arrow War**, the first as the Opium War. Although the trade in opium was the factor that precipitated the war, its deeper cause was the failure of the **Macartney** Embassy and other diplomatic missions to open China to trade in the late eightenth and early nineteenth centuries. Opium had probably been introduced into China by the eighth century by Middle Eastern traders and was cultivated in the south of the country.

Increased demand led to imports, first by the Portuguese and then by the British after the East India Company acquired a monopoly of opium production in Bengal. The company shipped opium to China but kept it separate from its legal trade. Imports rose dramatically in the nineteenth century, addiction and crime related to the sale of the drug became a problem and the Chinese government's opposition to its spread was ineffective. In 1839, **Lin Zexu** was appointed commissioner and ordered to halt the traffic in opium and destroyed over 20,000 chests seized from foreign merchants' warehouses. Britain's response was to send an expeditionary force which blockaded Chinese ports, laid siege to Guangzhou and finally occupied Shanghai in 1842, cutting off supplies to the Chinese capital which were delivered via the **Grand Canal**. Under duress, the Qing government acceded to the **Treaty of Nanjing** and China came more and more under the influence of Western powers.

Peter Ward FAY, *The Opium War,* 1840–1842 (University of North Carolina Press. 1975); James M. POLACHEK, *The Inner Opium War* (Council on East Asian Studies, Harvard University, 1992); Michael GREENBERG, *British Trade and the Opening of China, 1800–1842* (New York: Cambridge University Press).

ORACLE BONES ***Jiagu*** 甲骨

Pieces of bone, mostly tortoise carapace and plastron and the scapulae of oxen, used as part of a **divination** process by shamans in the late Shang period. Many were subsequently inscribed with a record of the questions put to the spirits and the eventual outcome of the enquiry, using the earliest known form of the Chinese script. First recognised as invaluable historical records in the early twentieth century, many thousands of oracle bones have been unearthed around Xiaotun, Henan Province. See also **Academia Sinica, Anyang.**

David N. KEIGHTLEY, *Sources of Shang history: The Oracle Bone Inscriptions of Bronze Age China* (Berkeley: University of California Press, 1978).

ORDOS

Region in **Inner Mongolia** between the bend of the **Yellow River** and the **Great Wall**. It is an arid quarter with a Mongolian nomadic population, but with some farming at oases.

ORIENTAL DESPOTISM

Concept developed by Karl Wittfogel to describe the ancient Chinese society and inviting comparisons with other early river-valley civilisations. The theory is based on Marx's views of the Asiatic mode of production and argues that the need for the organisation and employment of large numbers of people in water-conservancy and irrigation projects provided the foundation for despotic states.

Karl Wittfogel's treatise on *Oriental Despotism (*1957) identified China as one of a number of civilisations in the ancient world in which political power grew from the development of an in-group skilled enough to harness the power of a major watercourse (in China's case, the **Yellow River**) and to maximise the organisational and economic skills they learned from doing so. He termed them "hydraulic despotisms". Wolfgang Eberhard's spirited rejection of this as an explanation of the autocratic, stratified nature of traditional Chinese society (*Conquerors and Rulers*, 1965) attributed it instead to the conquest of one ethnic or military group by another. Both theories now appear too simplistic, but they recognise an important feature of the Chinese socio-political system from the earliest times to the present, stressing the overall power of a ruling elite rather than a ruling individual. Although successive eras have all assumed the right of one man to claim supreme authority, vested in him either by the will of Heaven or the will of the people, the recurrent pattern of government from the Zhou to the Communist period has always sought to counter his potential despotism by making him dependent upon and theoretically answerable to a trained and literate government class. Thus although a **Son of Heaven**, or Chairman of the Communist Party, might always endeavour to get his own way with either benevolence or malevolence in mind, the true nature of Chinese government has been and still is autocratic, with power vested more in the specialised class of the literati or the Party leadership than in one person. Those who, like the First Emperor **Qin Shi Huangdi**, the Empress **Wu Zetian** or the Ming Emperor **Hongwu** sought to set themselves too far above the advice and controls of their officials earned themselves reputations as counter-examples rather than examples of true **kingship**.

Karl A. WITTFOGEL, *Oriental Despotism: A Comparative Study of Total Power* (Yale University Press, 1957).

ORTAQ

Turkic name, (the modern Turkish word *ortak* means partner or associate) for merchant organisations authorised by the court of the Khan to trade during the **Mongol** rule over China. The *ortaq* merchants also functioned as tax collectors for the Mongols.

OUTER COURT ***Waiting*** **外廷**

Title used to refer to those offices and officials engaged in the running of the Ming and Qing empire at central government level who were not admitted to the **Inner Court**. It included the highest ministers of state, including members of the **Grand Secretariat**, **Grand Council**, the **Censorate** and the **Six Boards**, and their bureaux and staffs. See also **Prime Minister.**

OUYANG XIU 歐陽修 (1007–1072)

Northern Song statesman, scholar and literary figure. After the early death of his father, Ouyang Xiu studied at home with his mother and became a *jinshi* in 1030. He enjoyed a long and successful official career, but suffered setbacks through his principled support of reformist politicians like Fan Zhongyan. He discovered the writings of the Tang scholar **Han Yu** and became a strong advocate of the ***guwen*** 'ancient' style of writing, pioneered by Han Yu as part of his reaffirmation of traditional Confucian values. For Ouyang Xiu too, opposition to the prevailing highly stylized *pianwen* 'parallel prose' was based on his perception that it emphasised form over substance. He is given much of the credit for the change in literary taste which occurred in the Northern Song and influenced style throughout the rest of dynastic history. Dissatisfied with the existing *History of the Five Dynasties*, he compliled a new version, the *Xin Wu Dai shi* 新五代史, and was also a leading figure in the compilation of a new version of the *History of the Tang*, known as the *Xin Tang shu* 新唐書. In the field of epigraphy he was also a pioneering figure, amassing a large collection of inscriptions from the Zhou to the Tang, published as the *Ji gu lu* 集古錄. Although he was most admired as an essayist, Ouyang Xiu was also an accomplished poet, producing *shi*, *ci* and *fu*, and a scholar of the Classics.

Ronald C. EGAN, *The Literary Works of Ouyang Xiu (1007–72)* (Cambridge University Press, 1984); J.T.C. LIU, *Ou-yang Hsiu: An Eleventh-century Neo-Confucianist* (Standford University Press, 1967).

OVERSEAS CHINESE *Huaqiao* 華僑

People of Chinese descent, the Chinese diaspora, now resident outside China. Large-scale emigration from China began in the middle of the 19th century as a result of the economic problems and social disruption caused as the Qing dynasty collapsed under pressure from rebellion at home and commercial demands from the West. Chinese men went abroad as sailors or traders, first to the neighbouring countries of South-east Asia and later to Europe and the Americas. Settlements were gradually developed in South-east Asia, wives and families were taken there and the Chinese-speaking communities became a fixture, often, as in Malaysia and Indonesia, playing an important role in the business world and often coming into conflict with the indigenous populations. Emigration from Hong Kong increased dramatically in the 1950s as the small farmer economy lost viability and the community of overseas Chinese in Britain has its origins there.

WANG Gongwu, *China and the Chinese Overseas* (Singapore Select Books, 1991); Lynn PAN, *Sons of the Yellow Emperor: A History of the Chinese Diaspora* (Little, Brown, 1990); Michael GODLEY, *The Mandarin-Capitalists from Nanyang: Overseas Chinese Enterprise in the Modernization of China, 1839–1911* (Cambridge University Press, 1982).

PADMA SAMBHAVA (Guru Rimpoche)

A Tantric mystic and the first famous Buddhist monk to come to **Tibet** from India (Udyana, Kashmir). He arrived in 747 at the invitation of King Trisong Detsen, and is renowned as one of the founders of Tibetan Buddhism. He assisted in the building of the first Tibetan monastery at Samye (775–787), and is associated with the founding of the Nyingmapa Order.

PAEKCHE

In the third and fourth centuries AD this kingdom occupied the western half of modern South Korea. It had a tributary relationship with southern Chinese kingdoms in the Nanbei Zhao period, and later with **Chang'an** under Sui and Tang. As a southern coastal power it also had cultural contacts with Japan. As **Koguryo** extended its authority the Paekche capital was forced south from Hansong (near modern Seoul) to Ungjin (modern Kongju) (475), and thence to Sabi (modern Puyo) under King Song (523–554). China, the suzerain of both kingdoms, declined to send help when asked. Nevertheless Chinese culture was appreciated, and **Buddhism** (introduced in 384) had especially widespread intellectual and artistic influence. Paekche society is generally represented as being less warlike than that of Koguryo and more sophisticated than that of **Silla**, yet in the frequent battling for survival it was Paekche, under King Uija (641–660), that attacked Silla and prompted its cry for help to Tang **Gaozong**. This time China did respond, and the Silla-Tang alliance was formed that would unite the peninsula. A seaborne Chinese army approached Sabi from the west and a Silla army from the East, and Paekche was destroyed in 660.

PAGODA

Originally meant a Buddhist stupa or reliquary, a tumulus or mound for the remains of the dead, or for sacred relics or scriptures. The Chinese pagoda, however, is an architectural monument, single or, more often, multi-storied.

PAINTING

Chinese painting differs from Western painting not only in its materials and techniques, but in its concepts and principles. Early Chinese painting was varied and had many functions. Decorative painting in the Eastern Zhou period was used to decorate coffins and boxes, on which were represented the heavens and the underworld. Didactic painting from the Han dynasty onwards reflected the hierarchical nature of Confucian attitudes to the world. Although **figure painting**, mainly with Confucian but also with Buddhist and Daoist themes, had become sophisticated by the Tang period, it never achieved the same degree of importance as it has in the West. It was **landscape painting** which became an expressive medium during the Song period, which eventually dominated the artistic tradition in China.

The realistic approach was much favoured in the Song imperial **academies of painting** and remained a tradition in later court painting. After the Song, Chinese painting depended more heavily on calligraphic expression, especially in ink **literati painting**. Brushes of different flexibility and thickness are applied with differing pressure to achieve a huge number of varieties of stroke types representing form and space, light and shade. Later, a critical theory was evolved which articulated the links between the calligraphic tradition and such painting.

Painting has been considered a source of spiritual values. The ideal of traditional Chinese painting is to capture the spirit of the subject rather than recreate it. A mountain, tree or bird might be suggested by a few broad brush strokes, while the tiny figure of a man crossing a bridge is shown in exquisite detail. It is therefore essential to realise that Chinese paintings are not simple representations of particular places or other objects but the embodiment of philosophical concepts and attitudes towards the natural world.

PAINTING MANUALS *Huapu* 畫譜

The term *huapu* covers two main types of painting manuals. One is an illustrated manual for introducing painting techniques, and the other is a reference work without any illustration, which could be a treatise on painting or a catalogue of masters' works. Early major works in the first category include *Meihua Xishenpu* 梅花喜神譜 (*The Manual of Painting Prunus Blossom*) compiled by Song Boren of the Southern Song dynasty, and *Zhupu Xianglu* 竹譜詳錄 (*The Comprehensive Manual of Bamboo Painting*) by Li Yan of the Yuan dynasty. In the second category, the *Xuanhe Huapu* 宣和畫譜 from the Northern Song was the official catalogue of Emperor **Huizong**'s collection of earlier masters' works.

As the capacity of woodblock printing and the need for illustrated popular literature expanded, numerous painting manuals appeared from the Ming dynasty onwards. Two of the most influential manuals on painting techniques were *Shizhuzhai Shuhuapu* 十竹齋書畫譜 (*Painting Manual of the Ten Bamboo Studio*), compiled and published by Hu Zhengyan in 1627, and *Jieziyuan huazhuan* 芥子園畫傳 (*The Mustard Seed Garden Manual of Painting*) originally compiled by Wang Gai and first published in 1679. Both works were later reproduced in many new editions, including versions printed in colours.

In such manuals, the basic techniques of brushwork and composition were explained with a step-by-step approach and easily understandable text (some in the form of short poems). Different subjects were covered, from depicting rocks, trees and bamboo, to figures and architectural elements. Selected early master paintings are simplified into ink drawings to be used as references. These illustrated manuals also reflected the interest in painting techniques shown by some leading artists of the late Ming and Qing period.

Mai-mai SZE (trans.and ed.), *The Mustard Seed Garden Manual of Painting* (Princeton University Press, 1977).

PAINTING PERSPECTIVES

Chinese painters have avoided the restrictions of the basic (or scientific) perspective from a fixed viewpoint, as they observe and depict objects and landscapes from the angle of totality with a moving-multi-viewpoints approach. In landscape painting the Chinese term for linear perspective is *jinyuan* (near and distant) and this is further subdivided into three "distances", as set forth by the Song painter **Guo Xi**, which describe the types of scenic view distinguished by the position of a main horizon from which the eye instinctively begins exploring the picture surface; it does not define perspective drawing in the Western sense.

PAN GENG 盤庚

Nineteenth Shang king, who moved the royal capital from **Ao** to Yin (modern Anyang, Henan province) where it remained throughout approximately the last three hundred years of the dynasty. His history is recorded in the *Pan Geng* section of the ***Shujing***.

PAN GU 盤古

The first being in the Chinese creation myth. He is said to have spent 18,000 years carving the earth out of chaos, and when he died, the vermin on his body became the human race.

PANCHEN LAMA

A title meaning "Great Scholar", first given by the Great Fifth **Dalai Lama** to his own teacher as a semi-political gesture, reinforcing **Gelugpa** authority in Shigatse, the centre of **Karmapa** territory. He and three of his predecessors as Abbots of Tashilumpo were then posthumously recognised as reincarnations of the **Amitabha** Buddha. This apparently places the Panchen Lama on a higher spiritual plane than the Dalai Lama, and it is sometimes said that the Dalai Lama bears supreme political and ecclesiastical power in **Tibet**, but the Panchen Lama represents spiritual authority. As such he should stand above political intrigue, but the Chinese tried to woo the Fifth, Sixth, Seventh, Ninth and Tenth (1938–1989) in efforts to further their own interests. The Tenth lived in **Beijing** from

1959 until his death and was accused by some Tibetans of siding with the Chinese authorities against the Dalai Lama, but on his last return to Tashilumpo in 1988 his speech suggested an effort to defend his nation's cause. He embodied a modern version of the "patron-priest" relationship.

J. NEEDHAM, *Science and Civilisation in China, Vol. 5 pt. 1* (Cambridge University Press, 1985).

PAPER

Traditionally said to have been invented by Cai Lun 蔡倫, Director of the Imperial Workshops at **Luoyang**, in AD 105. Surviving fragments of earlier materials show that the search for a lighter, more convenient writing surface than bamboo or **silk** had in fact been going on for some centuries, and Cai Lun's brittle offering to the throne was soon improved upon. By the Tang dynasty a wide variety of surfaces and qualities was in circulation, and paper-making techniques were spread to the Muslim and European worlds by way of merchants returning from China. See also **Printing, Writing Systems.**

PAPER MONEY

Evolved out of credit notes used by late Tang merchants drawn upon the money stored in their business centres, and first introduced by the Song government in 1023–4 following an issue in Sichuan province. Excessive production later in the eleventh century led to heavy inflation. Issues by the Yuan and Ming governments proved unpopular and were abandoned after the Zhengde period (1506–1521). The supremacy of silver was recognised when it became the basis for the collection of the **Single Whip** tax. See also **Banking**.

PEASANT ASSOCIATIONS ***Nonghui*** **農會**

Rural organisations first set up in southern China during the 1920s to fight for the rights of peasant farmers against landlords and local officials. Many associations were sponsored by the CCP, including the best-known organised by **Peng Pai** in Guangdong and Mao Zedong in Hunan. (See **Hunan Peasant Movement**). Although the GMD had a National Peasant Movement Institute during its **United Front** period, the party never took peasant organisations as seriously as the CCP. Peasant associations continued to play a vital role in the rise of the CCP to power, particularly in the **Land Reform** programme of the 1940s and 1950s when they were the main grass-roots organisations.

Roy HOFHEINZ, *The Broken Wave: The Chinese Communist Peasant Movement, 1922–1928* (Harvard University Press, 1977).

PEASANT NATIONALISM

The explanation for the success of the CCP in coming to power in 1949, not because the population fundamentally supported its policies, but because it was more successful than its opponents in creating and exploiting a mass anti-Japanese nationalism among the peasantry.

Chalmers JOHNSON, *Peasant Nationalism and Communist Power: The Emergence of Communist China, 1937–1945* (Stanford University Press, 1962).

PEASANT REBELLIONS

Unrest and uprisings in the countryside have been a constant feature of Chinese history. In the view of history represented by the **dynastic cycle,** dynasties typically came to an end because peasant suffering became so great under the burdens of high taxation, debt, forced labour and famine that they had no alternative but to rise against their rulers. There are countless examples of minor revolts, but also many of major uprisings which did succeed in overthrowing a ruling house. To call them all peasant rebellions is an oversimplification, as many were led by dissident scholars, had marginalised groups as their backbones or were connected with secret societies or millenarian religious orders. Examples of significant rebellions are those of **Chen Sheng** and **Liu Bang** in the Qin dynasty, the **Yellow Turbans** in the late Han dynasty, the **Red Turbans** towards the end of the Yuan period and **Li Zicheng's** insurrection which brought about the downfall of the Ming and caused the Manchu invasion. In the 19th century, the **Taiping**, **Nian** and **Muslim rebellions** and the **Boxer Rising** contributed to the collapse of the Qing dynasty. The tradition continued into the 20th century and was taken up by the CCP with its **Peasant Association** and **Land Reform** policies. Modern Chinese Communist historians have emphasised this tradition of rebellion as a corrective to the view of Chinese history handed down through the official histories and to legitimate their rise to power.

Philip A. KUHN, *Rebellion and its Enemies in Late Imperial China: Militarization and Social Structure, 1796–1864* (Harvard University Press, 1970); James PARSONS, *Peasant Rebellions of the Late Ming Dynasty* (University of Arizona Press, 1970)

PELLIOT, PAUL (1878–1945)

Prominent French sinological scholar who distinguished himself in the siege of the Legations in **Beijing** during the **Boxer Rising**, and later made his name as leader of an expedition to Chinese Turkestan. There, like Aurel **Stein**, he discovered and removed many documents from the Caves of the Thousand Buddhas at **Dunhuang** in 1907–8.

Paul PELLIOT, *Les Grottes de Touen-houang*, 6 vols. (Paris: College de France, 1920–4).

PENG DEHUAI 彭德懷 (1898–)

Minister of Defence from 1954 to 1959 and bitter opponent of Mao Zedong over the policies of the **Great Leap Forward**. See **Lushan Plenum.**

PENG PAI 彭湃 (1896–1929)

Early CCP leader whose pioneering work in **Peasant Associations** in Guangdong was virtually ignored by the party for fear that it would overshadow Mao Zedong's involvement with peasants. From 1922 onwards, Peng Pai organised highly successful associations in Haifeng county near Guangzhou, not only succeeding in persuading landlords to agree to substantial rent reductions, but also organising the peasants to provide basic education and medical care. When the Haifeng Federation of Peasant Associations was formally inaugurated on January 1 1923, it had some 20,000 members. During the course of the **Northern Expedition**, Haifeng was taken by GMD troops with Peng Pai's support and in November 1927, his peasant supporters took control of the town and established a short-lived Soviet government there. Peng was captured by Nationalist troops and executed near Shanghai on August 30 1929.

Fernando GALBIATI, *P'eng P'ai and the Hai-lu-feng Soviet* (Stanford University Press, 1985); Robert MARKS, *Rural Revolution in South China: Peasants and the Making of History in Haifeng County, 1570–1930* (University of Wisconsin Press, 1984).

PENG ZHEN 彭眞 (1902–1997)
Peng Zhen was a CCP member from at least 1923 when he helped to organise the party's Shanxi branch and he was imprisoned by the nationalist Guomindang during the 1930s. Mayor of Beijing from 1951 until 1966, he was one of the first senior CCP leaders to be purged during the **Cultural Revolution**. After the Cultural Revolution, Peng Zhen returned to the Politburo and took an increasingly hard line, being opposed to both economic reform and the **Democracy Movement**.

PEOPLE'S DEMOCRATIC DICTATORSHIP
On the Dictatorship of People's Democracy 論人民民主專政 is the title of an article written by Mao Zedong and published on June 30 1949. In the article, Mao accepted that China had to "lean to one side" and favour the USSR over the USA. The "dictatorship" in the title was supposed to be exercised by "the people", which was here very broadly defined to include sections of the middle class, over the reactionaries.

PEOPLE'S LIBERATION ARMY *Renmin jiefangjun* 人民解放軍 (PLA)
Army of the CCP. Initially called the Workers and Peasants Red Army when it was founded in 1927 and called by various names including the Eighth Route Army during the war of resistance to Japan. It was formally renamed the PLA on May 1 1946 and fought the GMD forces under that name during the **Civil War**.

PEOPLE'S REPUBLIC OF CHINA *Zhonghua renmin gongheguo* 中華人民共和國
State created by the CCP on October 1 1949.
Harold C. HINTON, ed., *The People's Republic of China: A Handbook* (Boulder, Colorado: Westview, 1979); Maurice MEISNER, *Mao's China and After: A History of the People's Republic* (New York: Free Press, 1986); John GITTINGS, *China Changes Face: The Road from Revolution, 1949 – 1989* (Oxford University Press, 1989).

PERIOD OF THE PHILOSOPHERS see **HUNDRED SCHOOLS**

'PHAGSPA (1235–80)
Nephew of the Abbot of Sakya Monastery, Pandita, and "one of the most influential persons in the history of medieval Buddhism" (H.Franke). Following a visit to the camp of the **Mongol** Khan Godan in Liangzhou in 1247 he was taken as adviser by Godan's brother **Khubilai** (1253). Having received spiritual authority from **Sakya Pandita** before the latter's death in 1251, he consecrated Khubilai and later developed a theory posthumously attributing universal Buddhist supremacy to **Chinggis Khan**, and through him his grandson Khubilai. Three years after Khubilai had become Great Khan in 1261 'Phagspa, his spiritual guide, was made head of the Buddhist church throughout the Mongol Empire. In the same year Khubilai established the *Shijiao Zongzhiyuan*, Court of General Administration for Buddhism, overseeing Tibetan affairs. This established nominal political authority over **Tibet** in Dadu (**Beijing**). The

concept of the "patron-priest" relationship between China and Tibet derived from 'Phagspa's own relationship with Khubilai and from his exaltation of the Emperor's Buddhist supremacy. The notion of the Mongol theocracy was also his. As Chief Lama, he saw himself as responsible for the religious welfare of the world and his imperial counterpart as guaranteeing the temporal stability of the empire within which religion would flourish. In 1265 he was sent to **Lhasa** with the title of Tisri (*Dishi*, "Imperial Instructor"), representing Khubilai Khan as his Regent. His appointment confirmed the political supremacy of the Sakya Sect in Tibet, and after his death his successors in the post of Tisri continued to be drawn from this Order. 'Phagspa himself now spent little time away from Dadu. In 1270 he introduced an annual Buddhist ritual in which the imperial family participated. An obviously scholarly man, one of his most significant secular achievements was the invention of a script for pre-classical Mongolian which bears his name.

H. FRANKE, *China under Mongol Rule* (Aldershot: Variorum, 1994).

PING-PONG DIPLOMACY

From April 10 to April 17 1971, a table tennis team from the United States visited China after taking part in the world championships in Nagoya, Japan. It was the first semi-official American group to visit China for a long time and was officially received by Prime Minister Zhou Enlai on April 14. The visit helped to thaw relations between China and the USA and was followed by Henry Kissinger and the **Nixon visit** of February 1972.

PINYIN see ***HANYU PINYIN***

POETRY

For much of China's history, dating back to the early Zhou dynasty of the 11th century BC, poetry has been China's premier literary art. Chinese poetry has typically been short and lyrical; it has originated in folk forms closely associated with music, later to be taken over and refined by the literati. Poetry has been able to utilize to the full features of the Chinese language (particularly in its classical form), like its tonality, grammatical flexibility and the highly evocative nature of the character-based script. It is extraordinarily allusive (sometimes elusive too) and very difficult to translate satisfactorily. Poetry became part of the educational syllabus and, in later imperial times, a person with scholarly pretensions was expected to have the ability to extemporize a poem, often in imitation of the style of some great master, to mark an occasion. Even in the twentieth century poetry has been at the forefront of literary and political movements.

The earliest extant poems are the anonymous verses collected in the ***Shijing*** 詩經, Book of Poetry. This collection of 305 poems, dating from around the eleventh to the sixth centuries BC, was later associated with Confucius and was recognised as one of the **Five Classics** in the Han. The poems are typically short and predominantly of four character lines, although this is very variable. Some are concerned with the ruling families, but most are on the daily lives, troubles and loves of the people. The next major collection is the very different ***Chuci*** 楚辭 associated with **Qu Yuan** 屈原 (c.343 BC-c.289 BC). Poems in this collection feature a more ballad-like style with longer line length, more lines and a highly imaginative, descriptive style. This developed into the ***fu*** 賦 rhyme-prose style of the Han and later. The *fu*, an intermediate form between poetry and prose, put a premium on elaborate descriptions and was criticized, both then and later, for lack of content. In the early Han the **Music Bureau**, *Yuefu* 樂府, was set up to collect folk songs and became, during the Han and later, an important repository. Among the *yuefu* poems originating in the Han is 'The Peacock flies south-east', *Kongque dongnan fei* 孔雀東南飛, a ballad about the troubles of a young couple, which in its final version has 353 lines. The Nineteen Old Poems, *Gushi shijiu shou* 古詩十九首, anonymous verses from the Han, exemplify the trend towards a five-character line and the use of folk forms by literati. In the post-Han period this trend towards poetry as a scholarly art becomes much more evident. We have collections by named poets and can see emerging the image of the Daoist recluse communing with nature, in the works of poets like **Tao Yuanming** 陶淵明 (365–427). Of his poems 125 are still extant, the vast majority *shi* of 5 syllable lines.

The following Tang dynasty is the golden age of Chinese poetry. In addition to the old style unregulated poetry, *gushi* 古詩, a new regulated verse, *lüshi* 律詩, developed. This was a poem of eight lines, each of five or seven syllables/characters. There was an elaborate tonal pattern prescribed throughout the poem and the two middle couplets had to consist of antithetical lines. The *jueju* 絕句, 'cut off verse', was a cut-down four-line version of the *lüshi* and since the poet was able to decide which four lines to use, it offered rather more freedom of form than the *lüshi* . The two greatest figures in Tang poetry are usually regarded as **Li Bai** 李白(701–762), representing the Daoist wine-drinking tradition, and **Du Fu** 杜甫(712–770), often viewed as China's greatest poet ever, the more sober, socially concerned scholar. The output of Tang verse was prodigious, with a total of almost 50,000 poems from over 2,000 poets still extant.

New music developed in the Tang through a fusion of Central Asian music with the native Chinese tradition. The *ci* 詞 style of poetry developed as the words to this new music. It was originally sung by singing girls, but by the Song dynasty had developed into the dominant literati form. The form of the *ci* depended on the tune it was based on, so the number of lines and the number of syllables in a line was very variable. During the Five Dynasties, the greatest *ci* poet was Li Yu 李煜 (937–978) and in the Song some of the most highly regarded poets were **Su Dongpo** 蘇東坡(1037–1101), **Ouyang Xiu** 歐陽修 (1007–1072) and one of the few leading female poets **Li Qingzhao** 李清照 (c.1084–1155). In the following Yuan dynasty the *san qu* 散曲 developed through folksong as a version of the *ci*, still music based but freer in form and more popular in language.

There was little innovation in poetry during the Ming and Qing dynasties, but in the twentieth century poetry again led the way in developing new literary forms. Poetry, written by **Hu Shi**, was some of the earliest 'new literature' produced as part of the **New Culture Movement**. During the 1920s and early 1930s the poetry scene was particularly lively as poets like **Wen Yiduo**, Xu Zhimo and **Guo Moruo** experimented with fusions of the Chinese and Western traditions, especially favouring Western romantic poets. In the 1930s, as literature came more under political direction, poets like **Ai Qing** adopted overtly political themes for their work, though some, like the symbolist **Dai Wangshu** rejected this direction. After 1949 there were at various stages vast outpourings of popular paeans to Chairman Mao, but the emphasis was on quantity rather than literary quality. However, after the downfall of the **Gang of Four** and the liberalization in the late 1970s poetry once again led the way, certainly in quality terms, with 'misty', ***menglong***, poets producing highly introspective works inspired by classical Tang masters and Western modernist poets.

James J.Y. LIU, *The Art of Chinese Poetry* (University of Chicago Press, 1962); Wu-chi LIU and Irving Yucheng LO eds., *Sunflower Splendour: Three Thousand Years of Chinese Poetry* (Indiana University Press, 1978); Hans H. FRANKEL, *The Flowering Plum and the Palace Lady: Interpretations of Chinese Poetry* (Yale University Press, 1976); Michelle YEH, *Modern Chinese Poetry: Theory and Practice since 1917* (Yale University Press, 1991).

POLITBURO *Zhengzhiju* 政治局

Abbreviation of the translation Political Bureau in the Russian fashion. It is the decision-making body elected by the Central Committee of the CCP, which agrees on main policy. A small standing committee of the Politburo has been the seat of real power in Beijing for most of the period since 1949.

POLITICAL TUTELAGE *Xunzheng* 訓政

Concept developed by **Sun Yixian** in his **Three People's Principles**. He argued that underdevelopment meant that China was not yet ready for democracy, but would have to go through a period of tutelage while the people learned about democracy.

PORCELAIN see **CERAMICS**

POST STATION SYSTEM Yichuan 驛傳

System used in traditional China for transporting officials and official mail around China. The system had its origins in the Warring States period, but unification in 221 BC created an urgent need for an effective system for the central government to communicate with officials all over the empire and to arrange transportation and lodgings for government employees on official business. There were three basic transportation methods: by cart, called *chuan* in the Han dynasty, by horse-rider, *yi* and by foot, *you*. Detailed regulations governed the operation of the system, the entitlements of officials and the speed and delivery conditions of mail. It is said that in the Han period there were instances of an imperial decree sent at top speed travelling up to 1000 *li* (over 300 miles) in 24 hours, but the specified highest speed was much less. In the Song, for example, the specified speeds for different grades of document ranged from 200 to 500 *li* per day. The land-based system was supplemented by a water-borne system in appropriate areas: at one point in the Tang there were 1,643 post stations throughout China, of which 1,297 were land stations, 260 water stations and 86 combined land and water. The stations were all graded for importance and had an allocation of horses, in the case of provincial land stations, from 8–60, or of 2–4 boats for water stations.

The Qing version of the system was based on the central post station, the *Huanghuayi* in the capital under the control of the Board of War *Bingbu* 兵部There were over 2,000 local post stations, called *yi, zhan, tai* or *tang* according to area. Local stations were under the control of local officials as part of their many duties: there was no separate management structure of specialist officials. Each station had a complement of staff and animals (horses, donkeys, oxen) ranging from 400 staff and 690 animals in the capital to 100–200 staff and 100 animals in busy provincial stations, down to 20–30 staff and 10–20 animals in minor stations. Officials were provided with horses, porters and provisions, according to rank, on production of an official tally. Mail speeds were normally from 300 *li* to 600 *li* per day according to priority. There were abuses of the system and local officials were often tempted to balance their books by cutting down on post-station expenditure to the point where it impaired efficiency. In the late Qing, **Feng Guifen** suggested the establishment of a Western-style post office and this came about following the development of railways and telegraphs, gradually making the old system redundant. A new style Board of Posts and Communications *Youchuanbu* 郵傳部was formally set up as part of the late Qing reforms in 1906.

PORT ARTHUR see **LIAODONG**

POTALA see **LHASA**

PREFECT *Zhifu* 知府
Local government offical in charge of a prefecture which was a group of counties *(xian)*, all of which were under the jurisdiction of a **magistrate.**

PREHISTORIC CHINA
The earliest appearance of *Homo erectus* in China dates from the middle Pleistocene era and is associated with early Palaeolithic sites at Lantian (800–750,000 years ago) and **Zhoukoudian** 周口店 (see **Beijing Man**). In the upper cave at Zhoukoudian remains of *Homo sapiens sapiens* date from the late Palaeolithic era of 32–16,000 years ago, when East Asia was already well into the late Pleistocene age. They include not only bones but evidence related to clothing and decorative art. The earliest examples of **Neolithic** pottery have been radiocarbon dated to 10–9,000 years ago and come from the **Yangzi River** Basin (Pengdoushan). These coincide with the appearance of two types of agricultural development, based on the use of millet in the North and rice in the South-west (see **Daxi**). The two distinctive lines of Neolithic culture are those commonly known as the **Yangshao** and **Longshan** traditions, their earliest sites including **Banpocun** (modern Shaanxi province) and **Dawenkou** (Shandong province).
G.L. BARNES, *China, Korea and Japan: the Rise of Civilization in East Asia* (Thames and Hudson , 1993).

PRIME MINISTER *Chengxiang* 丞相, ***taixiang*** 太相, ***zaixiang*** 宰相, ***zhixiang***之相
Even a **Son of Heaven** needed support, and the relationship between the emperor and his senior government ministers, whose job was to advise him, to curb his potential **despotism** and to ensure smooth transition of rule between one emperor and the next, was always a sensitive one.

In the Han dynasty the chief ministers were the Chancellor, the Imperial Secretary and the Grand Commandant, of whom the Chancellor was the *primus inter pares*. The case of **Huo Guang** shows that a powerful Chancellor could himself effectively become a dictator.

In the Tang the title of Chief Minister existed in addition to and sometimes in plurality with the leadership of specific ministries or Boards (see **Six Boards**). The number of chief ministers was not fixed. At one time in the early eighth century there were seventeen holders of the title, but the number was reduced to two under **Xuanzong** and later in the dynasty was generally four.

Up to three Grand Councillors served the emperor in the early Song court, but their powers were constrained by a return to more centralised rule, and as a counter-balance to the threat of despotism Neo-Confucian scholars defended the role of powerful ministers. However, the example of **Wang Anshi's** radical tendencies as Grand Councillor under Emperor Shenzong gave the conservatives a warning of what even a powerful minister might do if unchecked, and the rest of the Northern Song period witnessed factional struggles between conservatives and reformists which reflected the uncertainty over the predominant political system. (See **Huizong, Song Dynasty**).

Two Chief Ministers or Councillors superintended the Six Boards in the early Ming, but in 1380 the post was abolished by the **Hongwu** emperor, following Hu Weiyong's execution for treason, and replaced two years later by the **Grand Secretariat** (*neige* 內閣). This led to a breakdown of centralised control under later, less capable Ming emperors and allowed the **eunuchs** to exert excessive influence. The early Qing maintained the Grand Secretariat (with four Grand Secretaries and two Assistant Grand Secretaries) until 1729, when it was replaced by the **Grand Council**. Thereafter no individual ministers assumed *ex officio* supremacy. See also **Outer Court.**

W.T. De Bary (trans), *Waiting for the Dawn: A Plan for the Prince* (Columbia University Press, 1993).

Printing

The precise origins of block printing are unknown. The oldest extant document of this kind is a Korean sutra dating from the first half of the eighth century, and the best known early Chinese text a copy of the Diamond Sutra of 868 discovered at **Dunhuang**. Its frontispiece shows the skill of the craftsman, who had carved the hard pearwood with a complex pictorial design as well as fine characters. The **Confucian Classics** began to be printed in quantity in the tenth century as part of the Neo-Confucian revival, and Bi Sheng's invention of moveable type printing between 1041 and 1049 gave a boost to education and the book publishing industry. However, it was the thirteenth century before it was used in significant quantity. See also **Paper, Writing**.

Production Brigades *Shengchan dadui* 生產大隊

Subdivision of People's **Communes,** corresponding to the Higher Producer's Cooperatives, designated as management units when commune administration was decentralised in the early 1960s. Production Teams *shengchandui* 生產隊 were a subdivision of Production Brigades, and tended to correspond to the Agricultural Producers Cooperatives. See also **Collectivisation.**

PROVINCIAL ASSEMBLIES

Elected provincial councils agreed to by the Qing court as part of the package of reforms implemented between 1901 and the fall of the dynasty in 1911, when many of the proposals of the **Hundred Days Reform** which had been rejected by the Empress Dowager **Cixi** became court policy. The assemblies which only had limited suffrage began to elect their delegates on February 5 1909 and convened on October 14. The delegates demanded an immediate calling of a parliament and the court prevaricated and promised that it would be convened in 1913, but this was superseded by the **Revolution of 1911** in which the delegates to many of the provincial assemblies played key roles.

PURE LAND BUDDHISM see ***QINGTU***

PUYI, AISIN GIORO 愛新覺羅溥儀 (1905–67)

Last emperor of the Qing dynasty and of the Chinese empire. He was a member of the royal Aisin Gioro clan and great-nephew of the Empress Dowager **Cixi** and acceded to the throne at the age of three in 1908 when the Xuantong Emperor died, his father functioning as regent. He was deposed after the 1911 revolution, restored briefly to power by warlords of the Beiyang clique in 1917 and finally made Chief Executive of the Japanese puppet state of Manzhouguo in 1932 and restored to his throne as the Kangde emperor on March 1 1934 at Changchun. See **Manchuria**.

PUYI AISIN-GIORO, *From Emperor to Citizen* (The Ex-Emperor's Autobiography), 2 vols., (Beijing:1964).

***QI* 氣**

Metaphysical concept of a cosmic power with creative functions. **Mencius** linked it with the Way (see ***Dao***) of morality and righteousness; in later ages it was morally neutral, but identified with the energy-inspiring processes as diverse as the birth of a landscape through an artist's brush control (see **Xie He**) and the birth of a human being through male and female sexual drive. "When the material forces of Heaven and Earth come together, all things are spontaneously produced, just as when the vital forces (*qi*) of husband and wife unite, children are naturally born" (**Wang Chong**, trans. W.T.Chan). To Neo-Confucians of the Song period it was identified with matter. It was the complement of *shen* 神, "spirit force" and the opposite of ***li*** 理, "principle". **Zhu Xi**, however, recognised that *qi* and *li* were mutually interdependent (see **Neo-Confucianism**).

QI 齊, STATE

One of the most powerful of the feudal states during the Zhou period, situated across the Shandong Peninsula. In the Spring and Autumn period Duke **Huan** (685–643 BC) was one of the dominant leaders known as the five **hegemons**, a position he owed in part to the proto-Legalist policies of his minister **Guan Zhong**. Together they established a centralised administration ruling regional subdivisions. They are credited with introducing forward-looking economic policies, including a uniform tax system, the first state monopolies on salt and iron, and measures to encourage trade. In 651 a confederation of northern states including Zhou, alarmed at the threat from **Chu** and aiming to create a balance of power, elected Duke Huan as their leader. By the fifth century BC, when inter-state politics had degenerated into all-out warfare, Qi was one of the five principal rivals for supremacy. It had a reputation for military strength and respecting military valour, and is said to have employed the strategist Sun Bin (see **Sunzi**). It also preserved a name for scholarship and **Mencius** visited the court of the sensitive and intellectual King Xuan (319–301) to urge him, in vain, to adopt pacifist policies. Xun Qing (see **Xunzi**) was another contributor to the political and philosophical debates at this court in the time of King Xiang (283–265). It was, however, for their interest in the varied and often heterodox ideas of *yin* and *yang* (see ***Yin-yang***) and the **Five Elements** that the men of Qi were known and rather disparaged in ancient times for their gullibility. **Zou Yan** was a native of Qi, and his ideas were also discussed at the court of King Xuan. Qi was the last state to fall to the unifying armies of **Qin** in 221, and was the location for **Chen She's** uprising against the dynasty in 210.

X.Q. LI, trans. K.C. Cheng, *Eastrern Zhen and Qin Civilization* (Yale University Press, 1985).

QI BAISHI 齊白石 (1864–1957)

The most eminent of all early modern Chinese painters who maintained the tradition of the literati artists. He was influenced by the great Qing individualists **Shi Tao** and Bada Shanren, and is particularly associated with paintings of crabs, prawns, insects, birds and flowers, executed with remarkable originality and vitality.

Catherine Woo, *Chinese Aesthetics and Ch'i Pai-shih* (Hong Kong, 1986).

QI JIGUANG 戚繼光 (1522–88)

Ming general from Shandong province renowned for his campaigning against pirates (see **Japanese pirates**). He commanded a force of 3,000 troops raised in Zhejiang, and because of his success and interest in recruitment and training was transferred to a northern garrison in 1567.

QIANLONG 乾隆, QING EMPEROR (r.1736–96)

Hongli 弘歷 (1711–99) was the fourth son of the **Yongzheng** emperor and succeeded his father in 1796. The long reign of the Qianlong emperor saw the boundaries of the Chinese empire extended westwards to Xinjiang and Tibet and the territory governed by Qianlong is today regarded by both the CCP and GMD as the sacred territory of China. The emperor, who ruled over a stable, increasingly populous and prosperous realm, was regarded as upright and competent and gained a reputation as a patron of the arts. However in terms of foreign affairs, he was less successful and the complacency and sarcasm in his reply to the British monarch George III which was sent back with the **Macartney** Embassy left a difficult legacy for his successors. See ***Siku Quanshu*, Literary Inquisition.**

Harold L. KAHN, *Monarchy in the Emperor's Eyes: Image and Reality in the Ch'ien-lung Reign* (Harvard University Press, 1971); Philip A. KUHN, *Soulstealers: The Chinese Sorcery Scare of 1768* (Harvard University Press, 1990); R. Kent GUY, *The Emperor's Four Treasuries: Scholars and the State in the Late Ch'ien-lung Era* (Council on East Asian Studies, Harvard University, 1987).

QIANGXUEHUI 強學會 'Society for the Encouragement of Learning'

Reformist organisation set up in Beijing and Shanghai in 1895. After the authorities' rejected the petition against the Treaty of **Shimonoseki** signed by 1200 metropolitan candidates, **Kang Youwei** and **Liang Qichao** decided on the need to enlighten the public and established the *Wanguo gongbao* 萬國公報(not to be confused with the better known Christian newspaper of the same name) to spread the reformist message on August 17 1895. In November they set up the *Qiangxuehui* and changed the name of the newspaper to *Zhongwai jiwen* 中外紀聞. Supporters of the Society included Weng Tonghe and **Li Hongzhang**. Kang had meantime travelled south, met **Zhang Zhidong** and set up a branch in Shanghai, also in November, with the aim, according to its constitution, of strengthening China. On January 12 1896, they began publishing the *Qiangxuebao* 強學報 to advocate reform and call for the establishment of a parliament but soon afterwards a member of the Censorate memorialised asking for the Society to be banned; the Beijing branch was subsequently closed down and the Shanghai one disbanded.

Luke S.K. Kwong, *A Mosaic of the Hundred Days: Personalities, Politics and Ideas of 1898* (Council on East Asian Studies, Harvard University, 1984

QILIN 麒麟

Fabulous creature of virtue and benevolence, also known as the Chinese unicorn in the West. Variations of *qilin* are numerous. It may be leonine, with scales and horns, or it may be an elegant cloven-footed beast, with or without scales, with a bushy mane and tail, and a horn, or a pair of horns. It is one of the four great mythical animals *siling* 四靈, the others being the tortoise, phoenix and dragon. It is believed that the *qilin* only appears when a sage is to be born or a great emperor sits upon the throne, thus it was represented in many legends about men of virtue, such as **Confucius** and Emperors Yao and Shun. The *qilin* is a popular creature in folk art, especially in embroidery and **New Year prints.** It often appears with a boy mounted on its back, which delivers the auspicious wish "The *qilin* sends sons", a favoured theme in Chinese families.

QIN DYNASTY 秦朝 (221–209 BC)

Contrary to the expectations of its founder that his successors would be numbered and named up to the Ten Thousandth Generation, only two rulers constituted the life of this dynasty, and the **Second Emperor** was a political non-entity. Yet the importance of this period to subsequent Chinese history was out of all proportion to its brevity. Traditionally decried as the epitome of **Legalist** cruelty and an example to later dynasts of how they should not govern, its reputation has improved in recent years in the light of archaeological discoveries and the realisation that the early Han emperors deliberately set out to discredit their predecessors whilst perpetuating many of their policies. No doubt the First Emperor was a despot who ill-treated and tyrannised his people, but he was not unique in this and his achievements – largely made by acting upon the advice of his Chief Minister **Li Si** – were broad and long-lasting. His successors benefited from inheriting centralised government, the written law code, stiff penalties, remonstrating ministers (see **Censors**), control of the aristocracy, and good communications, even though, as the Han dynasty progressed, they also recognised the need for the moderating, humanising influence of **Confucianism**. In fact, the discovery in 1975 of more than six hundred bamboo strips inscribed with part of the Qin law code at a site in Hubei Province shows that harsh though it was, it also provided for the remission (*shu*) of punishment and – in contrast to the complete inflexibility of **Shang Yang's** law – the grading of punishments according to an offender's rank. **Sima Qian**'s ***Shiji*** also refers to the granting of tax and labour exemption to people forcibly moved from their homes as part of the First Emperor's capricious policies.

In accordance with the current theory that linked political power to the supremacy of one of the **Five Elements**, the First Emperor decreed that Qin, having doused the fire of Zhou, ruled by virtue of the power of water. This was not altogether inappropriate in view of its utilisation of the Han and **Yangzi** Rivers in its military campaigns, the role of irrigation and communication canals in establishing a strong economic base in the south-west, and even the First Emperor's reputed search for the isles of **immortality** across the Eastern Sea.

Emperors:

Shi Huangdi	221–210
Ershi Huangdi	210–209

QIN 秦, STATE

Once a loyal vassal state of Zhou situated in the Wei River valley (modern southern Shaanxi) to the north of **Ba** and **Shu** and to the west of Jin; well defended by mountains from the competition that developed to the east over the moribund corpse of Zhou power in the Warring States period. In 364 BC the King of Zhou bestowed the title of **hegemon** (*ba*) on Duke Xian 獻 of Qin in the hope of securing his help against the growing threat from the states of **Wei, Han, Qi,** and **Chu.** Xian's successor, Xiao 孝 (r.361–338), was also made hegemon in 343, but of greater significance was his recruitment of the political adviser **Shang Yang** from neighbouring Wei. Shang Yang's implementation of radical legal and economic methods so strengthened the state that Xiao's successor, Huiwen 惠文, was awarded royal status and insignia in 326 by a King of Zhou who clearly acknowledged the inevitable. Thereafter the efficient, ruthless campaigning of Qin armies aimed to extend the power of their state independently of Zhou suzerainty. The conquest of Shu in 316 was crucial in giving access to the rich agricultural lands of the south-west and a safe province for political experimentation with practical **Legalism**. The Chu capital of Ying was taken in 278, allowing Qin to move eastwards along the **Yangzi** valley while concurrently waging the campaign across the Great Plain to the north. In 256 Zhou failed to appoint a new king and Qin took over its lands. The political acumen of the state's leadership was enhanced by the Legalist ministers **Lu Buwei** and **Li Si**, and its military strength and tactics could not be matched: Han (230), Zhao (228), and Wei (225) were overcome in quick succession; Chu surrendered in 223, and Yan and Qi were the last to fall by 221. Its last king, Zheng, took the title of First Emperor (*shi huangdi*). See also **Li Bing, Qin dynasty, Qin Shi Huangdi.**

X.Q. LI, trans. K.C. Cheng, *Eastern Xzhout Qin Civilizations* (Yale University Press, 1985).

QIN SHI HUANGDI 秦始皇帝 (Zheng 政, 259–210 BC)

Son of King Zhuangxiang (died 247 BC) who inherited the throne of the state of **Qin** at the age of thirteen. As King Zheng he completed the unification of late Warring States China, and as the self-styled First Emperor from 221 until his death in 210 earned the reputation of a megalomaniac. He is popularly associated with the construction of the **Great Wall**, the **burning of books**, the burying alive of 460 scholars, the ostentatious expenditure on the **Epang Palace**, the building of the artificial Mount Li and his own sumptuous mausoleum nearby (see **Lishan**), and the deaths of hundreds of thousands of his subjects as they toiled in his service or infringed details of the state law code. But his vision and achievements in uniting the Empire – inspired as he undoubtedly was by his Chief Minister **Li Si** – are a testament to a brilliant mind and a capable, ruthlessly determined innovator. In abolishing aristocratic feudalism, extending central government control through a new administrative organisation of commanderies and counties, and subordinating the individual to the group and the group to the impartial requirements of the law, he displayed an unhesitating grasp of the autocratic approach without which the road to unification could never have been followed so far. Yet he cannot be said to have reached his goal. He never really enjoyed the ultimate Legalist state of *wuwei* in which the ruler could depend on the sycophantic service of all around him and take his ease while the work of the empire carried on smoothly and according to plan. His efforts to stifle individual, questioning thought and independent behaviour failed. Despite rewarding successful civil and military leaders he was never free from threat. He survived three assassination attempts and employed all sorts of people in the search for a means of gaining his own **immortality**. Court alchemists sought chemical and herbal elixirs; thousands of young people are said to have been sent across the Eastern Sea to look for the land of the immortals, Penglai. The Emperor himself performed the *feng* 封 and *shan* 禪 **sacrifices**, and officials were ordered to maintain the rites to Heaven, Earth, great mountains and rivers, and other sacred places and spirits. In many of these Shi Huangdi took part. When he died, his failure to have achieved the true unification of the country was immediately apparent. The heir apparent, Fu Su, was tricked out of his inheritance and supplanted by the weak Hu Hai 胡亥 as **Second Emperor**. In the political and military struggle that followed, recession into the particularism of the Warring States was half way to reality. Perhaps the true unifier of China was not the First Emperor, but **Liu Bang**.

Qin Shi Huangdi was buried in an underground palace tomb at the foot of Mount Li, 50 km east of **Xianyang**. Legend affirms its unique construction and the riches and secret defensive measures that filled it. So far it has not been opened by archaeologists, but some suggestion of its grandiose nature is provided by the protective armies of pottery soldiers that surrounded it. See also **Han Feizi, Legalism, Zhao Gao**

A. COTTERELL, *The First Emperor of China* (Macmillan and Co., 1981)

QING DYNASTY 清朝 (1644–1911)

The last of the dynasties of imperial China. It followed the Ming dynasty and was a conquest dynasty, like the Yuan which preceded the Ming. The name Qing was adopted by **Abahai**, the leader of the sinicised **Manchu** tribes of what is today north-eastern China in 1636. Manchu and Ming forces clashed on numerous occasions after that and in 1644, after the rebel **Li Zicheng** took control of the capital, Ming generals led by **Wu Sangui** invited the Manchus in to help suppress the uprising. The Manchus did so and stayed to conquer China. The conquest took many years to complete and China proper was not completely under Manchu control until the defeat of the **Three Feudatories** rebellion, which lasted from 1673 to 1681, by the forces of the **Kangxi** emperor. This was the foundation for a great empire which by the reign of the **Qianlong** emperor extended to Tibet and Eastern Turkestan and the borders of which formed the basis for both the Nationalist and Communist concepts of China's "sacred territory" *shenzhou* 神州. This territorial expansion was paralleled by an unprecedented growth in population as Qing control was secured and the social order stabilised. Although there are no reliable census statistics for the period, it is reasonable to assume that Qing China's population had increased from something of the order of 150 million in 1600 to at least 400 million by the middle of the nineteenth century. China was able to survive such an increase because the area under rice was extended and new techniques were developed to increase the yield from existing land. Agriculture became more labour-intensive and highly commercialised, but, in spite of the appearance of various **sprouts of capitalism**, China did not develop an industrial or modern commercial sector under the Qing dynasty. The Manchus ruled through existing Chinese institutions at first, gradually modifiying them into government organisations with joint Manchu, Mongol and Chinese membership. Manchu scholars and officials moved over to the use of Chinese for bureaucratic purposes, but parallel documents in Manchu were produced until late in the dynasty. Spoken Manchu had effectively died out by the nineteenth century.

Traders and missionaries from Portugal, the Netherlands and other Western countries had been regular visitors to the southern ports since the sixteenth century, but in the eighteenth century, China came under constant heavy pressure from Britain and later France to open up permanent trade and diplomatic links, links which the still largely Manchu court thought unnecessary and undesirable. The pressure eventually led to the **Opium War** of 1839–1842 and the **Sino-French War** of 1884–1885. Defeat by the European powers weakened the Qing government and allowed foreigners to own concessions in the **Treaty Ports**, turning China into what some have termed a "semi-colony".

In addition to pressure from the West, the Qing system was weakened further by a series of insurrections including the **Taiping Rebellion** , which had the potential to form a new dynasty, the **Nian** insurgency in northern China and **Muslim rebellions** in the north-west and south-west. The Imperial Court responded by supporting the **Self-Strengthening Movement** during the **Tongzhi Restoration** of the 1860s and although this began the process of modernising China's defences and developing the economic infrastructure needed to support the modernisation, it still left **China** far behind Meiji Japan. This was demonstrated graphically in the **Sino-Japanese War** of 1894–1895 in which China's land and sea forces were thoroughly defeated. In the crisis that followed, scholars and officials proposed reform in the **Hundred Days Reform** movement of 1898, northern Chinese xenophobia flared up in the **Boxer Rising**, revolutionary organisations flourished and the Qing court gradually lost control. Between 1901 and 1909, a series of constitutional and administrative reforms, including the transition to a limited parliamentary system were agreed in what became known as the **Constitutional Movement**, but it was too late for the dynasty. Anti-Qing sentiment had become so intense that after the **Wuchang Rising**, province after province seceded in the **Revolution of 1911** and the empire was replaced by the **Republic of China**.

Jonathan SPENCE and John WILLS, eds., *From Ming to Ch'ing: Conquest. Region and Continuity in Seventeenth-Century China* (Yale University Press, 1979); Frederic WAKEMAN, Jr., *The Great Enterprise: The Manchu Reconstruction of Imperial Order in Seventeenth-Century China* (2 vols.) (Berkeley: University of California Press, 1985); Thomas METZGER, *The Internal Organisation of Ch'ing Bureaucracy: Legal, Normative and Communications Aspects* (Harvard University Press, 1973).

QINGMING FESTIVAL

Festival of grave-sweeping at which families clean the ancestral graves and honour the memory of both recent and long-dead relatives (see **Traditional festivals**). Demonstrations associated with the festival, which takes place in spring, were part of the **Tian'anmen Incident** of 1976 and the **Democracy Movement** of 1989.

QINGTU 清土 ('Pure Land') **BUDDHISM**

The most popular form of **Buddhism** in China, also known as the Lotus School, offering its believers the goal of life in the Pure Land heaven located somewhere above and beyond the Kunlun mountains in the north-west. Salvation might be attained simply through the invocation of the name of its ruler, the **Amitabha** Buddha. Its formation in China is associated with the great scholar Hui Yuan 慧遠 (333–416).

QIU JIN 秋瑾 (1875–1907)

Revolutionary activist and women's rights campaigner executed by the Qing government. She was born in present day Shaoxing in Zhejiang province into a gentry family and received education. At the age of 21 she was married to a traditionalist husband. In 1903 they moved to Beijing where the state of the Qing government in the aftermath of the **Boxer Rising** made her resolve to take action. In 1904 she left her husband and went to Japan to study Japanese. For young Chinese intellectuals Japan was then becoming a major centre for study and an important focus for anti-Qing activity. Qiu enthusiastically joined in these activities, lectured on revolution and male-female equality and wrote articles for the *Baihua bao* 白話報. In 1905 on her return to China to arrange funds for her continued study in Japan she met **Cai Yuanpei** and Xu Xilin 徐錫麟 and joined the revolutionary *Guangfuhui* 光復會. She returned to Japan and embarked on a teacher training course in Tokyo and joined the ***Tongmenghui***. However, incensed by restrictions put on Chinese students by the Japanese Ministry of Education, she returned to China early in 1906. There she found a teaching post, started recruiting for the *Tongmenghui* and embarked on an ambitious plan with Xu Xilin to organize revolutionary uprisings in the lower Yangzi region. In January 1907 she set up the *Zhongguo nübao* 中國女報 in Shanghai with the aim of improving women's status and advocating female education. In July 1907 Xu was obliged through leaks to put forward the date of his part of their planned uprising and, on July 6, he successfully completed the first stage with the assassination of the governor of Anhui, Enming 恩銘. However, their follow-up attack on the arsenal failed and Xu was executed. His brother implicated Qiu Jin but she refused the chance to flee and was arrested on July 14 and executed on the following day. In her poems she had expressed her willingness to sacrifice her life for the cause and did not flinch when faced with the choice. Her early espousal of women's rights and her martyrdom for the cause have given her a special place in the revolutionary pantheon.

QIYING 耆英 (1790–1858)
Manchu official and statesman. Having held various posts in the Imperial Household, he became resident military governor in Mukden (Shenyang), where he was responsible for the defence of China's north-eastern coast. He was charged with negotiating the **Treaty of Nanjing** of 1842 and other **unequal treaties**, and had a better understanding of the position of foreigners than many of his colleagues. On June 29 1858, he took poison after having been ordered by the emperor to commit suicide because of the concessions granted to foreigners.

QU QIUBAI 瞿秋白 (1899–1935)
Communist writer who succeeded **Chen Duxiu** as General Secretary of the CCP in 1927 after the debacle that ended in the **Shanghai Coup**, but was later attacked for his part in the failure and dismissed the following year, re-emerging as a member of the governing body of the **Jiangxi Soviet** in 1931. He remained a member of the League of Left-Wing Writers until his capture and execution in 1935. He was an essayist, critic and translator of Russian writers such as Gorky and Tolstoy and Marxist works into Chinese. Four volumes of his collected works *Qu Qiubai wenji* were published in 1953 and 1954.

QU YUAN 屈原 (c.340–278 BC)
Minister of the state of **Chu** and putative author of important parts of the ***Chuci***. What we know of Qu Yuan comes from his biography in the ***Shiji*** which describes how he was a leading minister of Chu until he lost the confidence of the ruler as a result of the slander of a rival; Qu Yuan was forced to stand by and watch as incompetent officials used deceit to gain the trust of gullible rulers and lead Chu into calamity. The epic poem *Lisao* is regarded as Qu Yuan's bitter lament on this situation. When his loyal remonstrations eventually earned him banishment he drowned himself in the Miluo River on his way to exile. The **Dragon Boat Festival** *Duan wu jie* 端午節 is said to commemorate Qu Yuan's suicide. He is also thought to have written *Nine Elegies* 九章, and *Nine Odes* 九歌, both of which have had a great impact on later Chinese poetry.
David HAWKES, *Ch'u Tz'u The Songs of the South* (Oxford University Press, 1959).

QUEEN MOTHER OF THE WEST see **XIWANGMU**

QUEMOY see **JINMEN**

QUEUE
Long hair worn in a pigtail by the Manchus and imposed on the Chinese when the Manchus conquered them in 1644. For anti-Manchu revolutionaries in the nineteenth century, cutting off the queue was a symbolic act of defiance.

QUINSAI see **HANGZHOU**

QUOTATIONS FROM CHAIRMAN MAO Mao zhuxi yulu 毛主席語錄
The *Quotations*, also known as the *Little Red Book*, was a by-product of **Lin Biao's** efforts in the early 1960s to make the PLA better trained, both militarily and ideologically, after Lin took over from Peng Dehuai as Minister of Defence in 1959. In order to convey the Party's political message to ill-educated recruits he produced a simplified set of quotations from Chairman Mao in a pocket sized, red plastic-covered handbook from which soldiers were encouraged to learn passages by heart. As the army took on the role of teacher of society, the *Little Red Book* became ubiquitous during the **Cultural Revolution**, when everyone learnt it by heart and daily study sessions were organized in work units to discuss it. Ownership of *Quotations* became obligatory and it was carried by all Red Guards. Quotations from Mao's writings were included in and prefaced all articles and books published in that period. With Lin Biao's mysterious death in 1971, following an alleged plot against Chairman Mao, the *Little Red Book* became something of an embarrassment.

RAILWAY PROTECTION MOVEMENT *Sichuan baolu yundong* 四川保路運動
A movement to resist railway nationalisation which was the trigger for the 1911 Revolution. In the mid 1900s a rights recovery movement developed, alongside the constitutional government movement, designed to recover the railway, telegraph, etc. construction rights lost to foreign consortia during the 1897–8 'scramble for concessions'. In 1905 this resulted in the Hankou-Guangzhou railway concession being retrieved from the American China Development Company. In 1904 returned students and others persuaded the Governor-General of Sichuan to set up the Sichuan-Hankou Railway Company in Chengdu; in 1907 this was changed into a limited company with local people holding shares. It proved difficult for the inexperienced local investors to translate their enthusiasm into railway construction activity and, after a period of inactivity, the Qing government decided on a policy of nationalisation of railway trunk lines in May 1911. This included compulsory nationalisation of the Sichuan-Hankou line. The Qing arranged to borrow six million pounds from a consortium of foreign banks to carry out the work on the two railway lines. This was seen as an affront to local pride, an unpatriotic sell-out to foreigners (something the revolutionaries had long accused the Manchus of) and a financial blow to the investors. On the June 17, over 2,000 people converged on the railway company office and set up a Sichuan Railway Protection Supporters Association *Sichuan bao lu tongzhi hui* 四川保路同志會, which rapidly spread throughout the province until branch members numbered hundreds of thousands. By late August the movement was beyond the control of the original constitutionalist leaders as supporters staged strikes, refused to pay taxes, attacked government offices and threatened to declare independence. On September 7 the government ordered the Governor-General, Zhao Erfeng 趙爾豐 to arrest the association leaders and close down the association. At a demonstration following this decision he ordered troops to attack the crowd, killing 30 people. This further inflamed the situation, leading to declarations of independence by ***Tongmenghui*** supporters in some areas. The Qing government ordered troops from Hubei to go to Sichuan, leading to the **Wuchang Rising**.

Mary Clabaugh WRIGHT ed.: *China in Revolution: The First Phase, 1900–1913* (Yale University Press, 1968).

RAO SHUSHI 饒漱石 (1901– 1975)
Prominent Communist leader at the time of **liberation**. Rao became Chairman of the East China Military and Administrative Committee at a rally in Shanghai on January 27 1950 and also served as director of the Organisation Department of the CCP Central Committee. Rao and **Gao Gang** were attacked by Liu Shaoqi in February 1954 for regarding their regions as "individual inheritances" or "independent kingdoms" and were dismissed from their posts and expelled from the party on March 31 1954, accused of anti-party activities, probably for being too sympathetic towards the Soviet Union. Rao was imprisoned. The purge was remarkable at the time as the CCP leadership was generally very stable.

RECTIFICATION CAMPAIGN *Zhengfeng yundong* 整風運動 (1942)
CCP campaign to standardise political and cultural attitudes in the **Yan'an** period. By 1942, the Yan'an base area which had been founded by veterans of the **Long March**, was a magnet for patriotic and disaffected students, intellectuals and others escaping from areas under Japanese or GMD control. The Rectification Campaign was targeted at these new recruits and designed to instill an orthodox attitude to Marxism as defined by Mao Zedong. The process was successful in creating a party loyal to Mao which was in a position to take control of China after the end of the **Civil War**.

RECTIFICATION MOVEMENT (1957) see **ANTI-RIGHTIST CAMPAIGN**

RED ARMY see **WORKERS AND PEASANTS RED ARMY**

RED EYEBROWS PEASANT RISING
Begun in Shandong Province in AD 18 under the leadership of Fan Zhong, so-called because its members painted their eyebrows as a distinguishing mark. The rebellion was the result of economic sufferings and was encouraged by popular **Daoist** beliefs in divine support. Together with the Green Woodsmen rebels from Hubei Province led by Wang Guang and Wang Feng they defeated a superior force of **Wang Mang's** army in Shandong in AD 22 and another in Henan Province in 23. They entered **Chang'an** in 23 and put Wang Mang to death. See also **Bandits.**

RED FLAG *Hongqi* 紅旗
Theoretical journal of the CCP, edited for many years by **Chen Boda**. It stopped publishing in July 1988 and was replaced by *Qiushi* 求是, which means literally 'seek Truth' and takes its name from Deng Xiaoping's injunction to "seek truth from facts" *shishi qiushi* 實事求是, reflecting the new pragmatism of the post-Mao Zedong era.

RED GUARDS *Hongweibing* 紅衛兵
Students, school pupils and young workers organised in support of Mao Zedong in the **Cultural Revolution**. Officially established in August 1966, they were based on radical groups that had sprung up in colleges and universities, the name having been taken from the *krasnaya gvardia*, who protected Lenin after

the October Revolution. On August 18 1966, a million Red Guards attended a rally in Tian'anmen Square in Beijing, presided over by Mao, with all the other leaders of the Cultural Revolution present. Mao appeared and put on a Red Guard armband. This inspired China's teenagers and new Red Guard groups were formed throughout the country. Red Guards were in the vanguard of all the attacks on CCP organisations and although they are sometimes depicted as the mindless tools of Chairman Mao, many of China's leading dissidents learned their political and organisational skills in these organisations.

RED SPEAR SOCIETY ***Hongqianghui*** **紅槍會**

Twentieth century **secret society**, possibly part of the **White Lotus** tradition, who practised ritual boxing and wore amulets of invulnerabilty that would have been familiar to the **Boxers**. They flourished in the Henan, Hebei and Shandong borders in the 1920s and were responsible for organising village self-defence militia. The CCP, and in particular **Li Dazhao**, took an interest in their methods and attempted to win them over to the Party.

RED TURBANS

Rebel group which joined with members of the **White Lotus Society** from 1351 onwards in resistance to forced labour involved in reconstruction work on the **Yellow River** and **Grand Canal** around the base of the Shandong Peninsula. They proclaimed the restoration of the Song dynasty, but though they had won spectacular successes across much of northern China by 1358, including the capture of **Kaifeng**, their anti-Confucian stance denied them literati support. As a nominal vassal of the pretender to the Song throne, Han Lin'er, Zhu Yuanzhang established his own regional power base in the **Yangzi** valley through the mid-1350s, capturing **Nanjing** in 1356. When Han died in 1366, Zhu disassociated himself from the Red Turban movement, disavowed the restoration of the Song dynasty, and claimed the succession for himself as founder of a new dynasty, the Ming. See also **Hongwu Emperor.**

RED VERSUS EXPERT

Debate within the CCP on the priority to be given to technical or professional expertise as opposed to correct political attitudes, which was essentialy a question of loyalty. The issue was particularly important during the **Great Leap Forward** and the **Cultural Revolution** and the two lines of Chinese politics divided on this matter.

REFORM AND OPENING ***Gaige kaifang*** **改革開放**

The official name for the policies introduced by **Deng Xiaoping** from 1978 onwards. They grew out of the **Four Modernisations** but went much further. Essentially, the economy was to to be transformed from planned to market and China was to be opened up to foreign investment and trade on a scale unprecedented since 1949.

REFORM THROUGH LABOUR ***Laogai*** **勞改**

Labour camp imprisonment for people sentenced for criminal and political offences. See also **Education through labour.**

REHE 熱河 (JEHOL)
Province in north-eastern China during the Republican period and named after the city of Rehe, which was later renamed Chengde 承德. The province was absorbed into Manzhouguo in 1933 and, after the establishment of the People's Republic in 1949, was divided between **Inner Mongolia** and Liaoning province. See also **Manchuria**.

REIGN PERIODS
Two systems were commonly used in traditional China for dating years. One was by reference to the year's title within the sixty-year cycle of **stems and branches**. The other was according to the number of the year within an emperor's reign. But use of the emperor's personal name was taboo, and the temple name by which he would later become known to historians, such as Martial Emperor (Wudi), High Progenitor (Gaozu), or Mysterious Ancestor (Xuanzong), was only acquired posthumously. So dating the current year of the present emperor's reign was done by reference to the auspicious title adopted at its beginning, e.g. the first year of Li Shimin's reign (AD 618) was designated Wude "Martial virtue" 1, the next year (619) was then Wude 2, and so on. Between the Han and Yuan dynasties fresh titles were proclaimed from time to time within a single reign, but this practice ceased in the Ming and Qing, when only one title was used throughout each reign. Among Western historians it is convenient and largely customary to use this reign period to refer to the emperor himself, rather than his temple name. Thus the founder of the Ming dynasty is commonly known as the **Hongwu** "Boundless Valour" Emperor rather than as Ming Taizu "Supreme Progenitor".

RELIGION
The common description of China as the "land of three teachings" (**Confucianism, Daoism** and **Buddhism**) is only a partial indication of the spiritual interests of its people in traditional and modern times. Despite its emphasis on **ancestor worship** Confucianism may scarcely be counted as a religion, lacking a common liturgy, priesthood or organised church. Daoism and Buddhism both developed popular churches with all three of these elements from the late Han onwards, and served the needs of literati and commoners alike. Yet the approach to the needs of the human world and the service of the spirit world was pragmatic: the **Son of Heaven** was responsible for the wider issues affecting "all under heaven"; the local shaman might be employed to intercede with the spirits watching over the affairs of the village community; ordinary people prayed for their own well-being and for that of their ancestors. Confucian in their family rites, they found it no problem to worship in Daoist or Buddhist temples (see **Guanyin**), or to offer incense at the shrines of folk deities (see **Ximuwang**), local heroes, or naturalistic spirits inhabiting mountains, rivers, or even trees. They mostly anticipated some kind of afterlife and were concerned about **immortality**, though their ideas were often vague and these were not the subject of scholarly speculation. Whilst ethical and moral systems were of importance to Confucians, only Buddhism linked the prospects for people's next incarnation to their behaviour in this. People's religious views were personal rather than defined according to the exclusive doctrine of a particular church, and no

religious system before the arrival of **Islam** and Christianity claimed to possess the sole route to enlightenment. This eclectic attitude enabled people to embrace a variety of beliefs and assisted the initial acceptance of Christianity in China. It was the tolerance of an individual's right to work out his or her own salvation that helped China to avoid the spectre of religious wars and persecutions (see **religious persecution**). See also **Jesuits, Jews, Missionaries, Nestorianism.**

M.G. GRANET, *The Religion of the Chinese People* (Basil Blackwell, 1975); Ligi THOMPSON, *The Chinese Way in Religion* (Dickenson & Co. Inc., 1973); H. KUNG and J. CHING, *Christianity and Chinese Religions* (New York: Doubleday, 1989).

RELIGIOUS PERSECUTION

The Chinese state has not traditionally been concerned with the fate of its people's souls, and has not interfered in their religious beliefs or practices provided they have not led to behaviour considered detrimental to state interests. However, the absence of any precise definition of 'state interest' has led to periodic persecutions from the Han dynasty to the present day. In the Middle Ages monasteries were swollen by large numbers of men escaping their lawful fiscal and corvée obligations, and the state sometimes resorted to forceful methods to weed out the pretenders (see **monasticism**). The Buddhist church became very rich; it was also barbarian in origin, and at times of general economic decline or of growing anti-foreignism was liable to persecution on both grounds. These, together with the violent Daoist convictions of Emperor Tang **Wuzong**, were the explanation in 842–5 for the greatest laicisation of religious personnel and destruction of religious property in Chinese history before the **Cultural Revolution** (see **Ennin**). Local cults periodically engendered messianic movements which could destabilise society. Religious leaders were also inclined to support people suffering as a result of government policy and **secret societies** might use local temples as a base for their unlawful activities, thus making the authorities suspicious of popular religion. Christianity suffered from this kind of guilt by association and was persecuted frequently in the eighteenth century (see **Jesuits**), just as in modern times the Christian housegroup movement is suspect because of its secrecy. See also **White Lotus Society.**

***REN* 仁**

A key term in Confucian philosophy. In the *Analects* of **Confucius** (see ***Lunyu***) it represents the sum total of all human virtues, the majority of which have social merit. It indicates perfection, or in **Arthur Waley's** translation, 'goodness'. Other translators have used the term 'benevolence'. According to Confucius it is almost unattainable, only those of the stature of Yao or Shun (see **Former Kings**) obviously possessing it, though the effort of striving after it is both beneficial and meritorious. Writers in later ages still treat it with respect but divest it of some of this idealistic quality, interpreting it as human sympathy (**Mencius**), universal love (**Han Yu**), and humanity (Wing-tsit Chan's translation from **Neo-Confucian** texts attempts to define it on an impartial, non-emotional basis). See also **Human Nature.**

RENMIN RIBAO* 人民日報 *People's Daily

Official daily newspaper of the Central Committee of the CCP, modelled on the *Pravda* of the Soviet Union.

RENZONG 仁宗, SONG EMPEROR (Zhao Zhen 趙禎, 1010–63, r. 1022–63)
Sixth son of Emperor Zhenzong and longest reigning emperor of the Northern Song dynasty. His was a period of internal stability, and following the conclusion of a peace treaty with the state of **Xi Xia** in 1044, of good inter-state relations also. But the treaty required the sending of **silk**, silver and tea to the Tangut kingdom and induced the **Khitan** to raise their own tribute payable under the **Shanyuan** Treaty. This loss of face, together with growing upper class affluence and complacency at peaceful conditions, prompted the beginnings of the reform movement. See **Fan Zhongyan, Wang Anshi**.

REPORT ON THE PEASANT MOVEMENT IN HUNAN see **HUNAN PEASANT MOVEMENT**

REPUBLIC OF CHINA *Zhonghua minguo* 中華民國
The Republic of China succeeded the Qing dynasty in 1912 and continued on the mainland until 1949. After the **Civil War**, the GMD administration on Taiwan has considered itself to be the legitimate continuation of that Republic and the name is used for the Taiwan government.

RESIST AMERICA AID KOREA CAMPAIGN *Kangmei yuanchao yundong* 抗美援朝運動
Domestic campaign designed to provide support for the Chinese People's Volunteers who fought in the **Korean War**. It grew out of a speech Mao Zedong made at a meeting of the Chinese People's Consultative Conference on October 23 1951 and it was focused on increasing production and practising economies in aid of the war effort.

RESPONSIBILITY SYSTEM *Baogan daohu* 包干到戶
New system introduced in 1979, which was designed to develop agriculture by removing many of the constraints of collective farming and introducing material incentives, but was in fact destined to bring to an end the **commune** system that had dominated the Chinese countryside for the previous twenty years. Households were given the responsibility for farming a given area of land, although the land itself still remained the property of the commune with which the household had a contract. The contacts were initially for a year, but these were extended to fifteen years in 1984 and under later legislation they could be inherited. In economic terms, the new system was an enormous success, with a dramatic rise in productivity and visible increases in prosperity throughout the rural areas, especially in the south-eastern provinces. The communes were phased out and their political and social functions assumed by city and county administrations.

RETURNED STUDENTS *Liuxuesheng* 留學生
In general, the term refers to Chinese who had studied abroad in Japan or France in the late 19th and early 20th centuries, but in particular it is used to denote the group known as the **Twenty-Eight Bolsheviks**, or Returned Students Faction, within the CCP.

REVOLUTION OF 1911 ***Xinhai geming*** **辛亥革命**
Collapse of the Qing dynasty and the beginning of a Republican government. Slow progress at reforms led to the **Wuchang Rising** and the secession of provinces one by one from the Qing state. The 1911 Revolution was important as it demonstrated the power of social groups that had developed in the last twenty years of the Qing dynasty, the new urban middle class, modern-minded gentry and new regular army. However, the early years of the Republic were beset by factional problems and warlordism and it was not until 1928 that a more or less united Republican government was established.

Mary Clabaugh WRIGHT, ed., *China in Revolution: The First Phase, 1900–1913* (Yale University Press, 1968); Shinkichi ETO and Harold SCHIFFRIN, eds., *The 1911 Revolution: Interpretive Essays* (University of Tokyo Press, 1984); Joseph ESHERICK, *Reform and Revolution in China: The 1911 Revolution in Hunan and Hubei* (Berkeley: University of California Press, 1976).

REVOLUTIONARY COMMITTEE OF THE GUOMINDANG ***Guomindang geming weiyuanhui*** **國民黨革命委員會**
Breakaway group from the GMD formed on January 1 1948 in Hong Kong. It called for the alliance of all opposition parties, including the CCP, to overthrow **Jiang Jieshi**'s dictatorship and to remove American interference in Chinese affairs. On May 5 it telegraphed its support for a CCP Central Committee resolution calling for the establishment of a Political Consultative Conference (see **Chinese People's Political Consultative Conference**) to determine the political future of China. It was one of the small number of non-Communist parties allowed to operate openly in the PRC, albeit with negligible power, and its most prominent member was **Song Qingling**, the widow of Sun Yixian.

REVOLUTIONARY COMMITTEES ***Geming weiyuan hui*** **革命委員會**
Organs of local government that were created in the **Cultural Revolution**. In January 1967, the radicals behind the **January Storm** tried to create the Shanghai Commune which was intended to be the first of many urban communes. However, the Revolutionary Committee model tested in Heilongjiang province was preferred to the Commune as more moderate or conservative policies prevailed at the time and it was adopted across the nation. The committees were created with military support and included a high proportion of military personnel as well as "revolutionary cadres" and representatives of the "revolutionary masses". Some regions were effectively under military control. Membership was eventually standardised at 50% cadres from the old party committee, 25% members of the PLA and 25% mass organisation leaders. As more Revolutionary Committees were set up in 1967–8, the proportion of mass organisation representatives decreased, although there was a radical attempt to reverse this in 1968, which was answered by the dispersal of Red Guards through *xiafang* 下放or "sending down", usually to rural areas. All other provinces followed suit once the model had been given official approval and all units down to factories and schools had their own "revolutionary committees" Although the names remained after the Cultural Revolution they ceased to be radical and became essentially the management.

REVOLUTIONARY OPERA see **YANGBANXI**

RICCI, MATTEO (1552–1610)
Italian Jesuit who in 1582 became the first European Christian to reside on the Chinese mainland since the Friars of the early mediaeval church (see **John of Montecorvino**). In 1601 he was given imperial permission to establish a mission house in **Beijing**, and in the last nine years of his life he laid the groundwork for the remarkable and controversial work of his Order in China throughout the next one and three quarter centuries (see **Jesuits**). His intellectual gifts, covering astronomy, cartography, music, law and philosophy, together with the linguistic prowess that enabled him to compose and translate into Chinese, won him the respect of the Chinese literati and established the tradition of academic cooperation between the Jesuits and court officials. His most important convert to Christianity was the Grand Secretary Xu Guangqi 徐光啓. He was the author of *Tianzhu shengjiao shilu* ("The True Meaning of the Lord of Heaven"), and compiled a world map in Chinese. He attacked **Buddhism** and disputed **Neo-Confucian** cosmology, but he set the precedent for accommodation between the religious beliefs of the Jesuits in China and the Confucian beliefs and practices of their hosts, a policy that led to bitter argument with the Papacy and other missionary Orders (see **Rites Controversy**).
Jonathan SPENCE, *The Memory Palace of Matteo Ricci* (Viking Penguin, 1984).

RITES CONTROVERSY
The name given to the debate in the 17th and 18th centuries between the Papacy, the Franciscan and Dominican Orders, and the **Jesuit** missionaries in China over Christian attitudes towards Confucian ceremonial. One of the main points of contention concerned participation in the rites connected with **ancestor worship**, especially at court. Following the example of **Matteo Ricci** the missionaries accepted and participated in these as social and civil rather than religious observances. When the Vatican forbade such practices as idolatrous the **Kangxi Emperor**, whose Edict of Toleration in 1692 had supported Christianity and who could not accept such presumptuous interference in Chinese affairs, reiterated its necessity. The visit of the papal legate de Tournon (1705–6) ended in his imprisonment in **Macao**, and the result of the Jesuits' refusal to heed the Bulls *Ex Illa Die* (1715) and *Ex Quo Singulari* (1742) was the disbanding of the Order in 1773.

Other elements in the dispute between the Jesuits in China and their superiors in Rome included the choice of an appropriate Chinese translation for God and the emphasis placed on items of Biblical exegesis and doctrinal matters. The so-called Rites Controversy was in fact a broader ideological confrontation between Western and Eastern cultural authorities, neither of which had as yet had real experience of the need for accommodation.
George MINAMIKI, *The Chinese Rites Controversy from its Beginning to Modern Times* (Chicago: Loyola University Press, 1985); D.E. MUNGELLO, ed., *The Chinese Rites Controversy: its History and Meaning* (Nettetal: Steiner Verlag, 1994).

ROMANISATION
System for the transliteration into Roman letters of the sounds represented by Chinese characters. An early example is the **Jesuit** latinisation of *Kong Fuzi*

"Master Kong" as **Confucius**. As more authors wrote about China from the seventeenth century onwards, individual systems were developed in Russia, France, Britain and other Western countries according to their own prevailing phonetic customs. In the nineteenth century the system devised by the British Minister Thomas **Wade** and the British consul at Ningbo, Herbert **Giles**, known as the **Wade-Giles system**, became used world-wide and continued to be so until the third quarter of the twentieth century. Since then, in some cases in deference to Chinese sensitivity over this remnant of the imperialist age, western writers have increasingly abandoned it in favour of the ***Hanyu pinyin*** system used in China itself. See also **Writing Systems.**

I. L. LEGEZA, *Guide to Transliterated Chinese in the Modern Peking Dialect* (Leiden: E.J. Brill, 1968–9).

RONG HONG see **YONG WING**

ROU PUTUAN 肉蒲團

An erotic novel attributed to **Li Yu** and translated into English as 'The Carnal Prayer Mat' or 'The Pillow of Flesh'. This twenty-chapter work, written in 1657, follows the traditional storyteller format but Li Yu, ever the innovator, stamps his irreverent and witty personality on it. The story, scantily clad in Buddhist morality, plots the amorous adventures of a young man who devotes his life to sexual gratification. The young man's philandering ends in retribution, as it inevitably must in a traditional society where adultery poses mortal danger to the social order, but Li Yu tells the story with far too much verve to convince us of his moralising intent.

LI YU , *The Carnal Prayer Mat,* trans. Patrick Hanan (London: Arrow Books, 1990); Patrick HANAN, *The Invention of Li Yu* (Harvard University Press, 1988).

ROY, M.N.

Borodin's successor as Comintern representative in China. A Communist from India, he arrived in 1927, promoted the idea of CCP cooperation with the left-wing of the Guomindang and left China after the failure of the alliance.

RUIZONG 睿宗, TANG EMPEROR (Li Dan 李旦, 662–716, r. 684–90 and 710–2)

Son of Emperor **Gaozong** and Empress **Wu** and brother of Emperor Zhongzong, whom he succeeded when the Empress sent him into exile only six weeks after his accession. Ruizong, however, was only a puppet for the Empress and abdicated in 690. Zhongzong was restored in 705 but murdered by the Empress Wei in 710. Ruizong was then restored to the throne himself by a coup organised by his sister the Princess Taiping, but lacked the character to exert his authority amid the multiple intrigue of the court, and abdicated in 712 in favour of his son Li Longji (see **Xuanzong**).

RU LIN WAISHI 儒林外史

Known in the West as *The Scholars* (or *An Unofficial History of the Literati*), it is a long satirical novel by Wu Jingzi 吳敬梓(1701–1754) and probably written in **Nanjing** between 1739 and 1750. Wu's novel did not include such popular conventions in Chinese fiction as the use of verse and songs for description.

Here, descriptive passages are recorded in parallel prose and integrated within the text. The sophisticated characterisation in this novel distinguishes it from earlier narrative novels where dramatic action often overshadows characterisation. There are some two hundred characters in the novel, many of them portrayed with impressive subtlety. It is often considerd to be a landmark in Chinese fiction as the first full-length fictional satire based on idealistic Confucianism and is also noted for its written style which is closer to the vernacular language. Set in the Ming dynasty, *Rulin waishi* is a series of tenuously linked stories spanning the period 1487 to 1595. The novel begins with an account of the famous artist-recluse Wang Mian of the Yuan dynasty, an exemplar of moral standards, against whom the later scholars, Du Shaoqing and his friends, are measured. It is clear that scholars who commit themselves to gaining wealth and social position never achieve the self-cultivation required of a true Confucian and thus descend into inhumanity and ignorance. The poignancy of this novel also lies in the fact that it fully reflected the social realities of the time (as well as Wu's own life), such as the obsessive dedication of Chinese scholars to passing the imperial **examinations**, the sterile learning that this produced and the incompetence and corruption of the official class.

WU Jingzi. *The Scholars*. trans. Yang Hsien-yi and Gladys Yang. Introd. C.T. Hsia (Columbia University Press, 1992); Paul ROPP, *Dissent in Early Modern China: Ju-lin wai-shih [The Scholars] and Ch'ing Social Criticism* (University of Michigan Press, 1981).

RUSSO-JAPANESE WAR (1904–5)

Russia declared war on Japan on February 9 1904 and the Japanese navy attacked and defeated a Russian fleet off Port Arthur the same day. Japan formally declared war on Russia the following day and the Chinese government issued a statement of its neutrality on the February 12. The causes of the war were competition by Japan and Russia for influence in Korea and Manchuria, issues that arose out of the **Sino-Japanese War** of 1894–5, and were a result of the clash of two expanding empires. Japanese forces took the Russian garrison of Port Arthur and sunk almost the entire Russian fleet at the battle of Tsushima. Intervention by the President of the USA, Theodore Roosevelt, led to a peace agreement, the Treaty of Portsmouth, (New Hampshire) which was signed on September 5 1905. Japan and Russia agreed to remove their troops from Manchuria, but Japan took over the Russian concession of the **Liaodong peninsula** in what was to become the **Guandong Leased Territory** and the **Chinese Eastern Railway** to the south of Changchun. Victory gave the Japanese an unrivalled opportunity to expand their influence in north-eastern China. It also gave them control of **Korea**, which they annexed in 1910.

SACRIFICES

Sacrificial rites were performed in honour of **Shangdi** and the royal ancestors at the Shang court, and to Heaven after the Zhou conquest. Animal and human sacrifices accompanied ancient funerary rites, but human sacrifice had generally been discontinued by the time of **Confucius**. In the **imperial era** religious cults formed a major part of state ceremonial. They occupied much time for large numbers of specialist courtiers and cost huge sums of money. The principal recipients of sacrifices were Heaven, Earth (from 114 BC), Confucius (from AD 58), and the Imperial Ancestors, but a complete list of the powers and spirits that received imperial worship and sacrifices periodically from the Zhou dynasty to the Qing would be very long indeed. It would include the spirits of geographical locations such as rivers and mountains, the Great Unity (*taiyi* 太一, from 130 BC), the Five Powers (*wudi*) and the colours associated with them, the spirits associated with agricultural seasons and activities, and those of historical personages such as the great Yu (see **Former Kings**) and earlier emperors. The role of Heaven was exalted over that of the Five Powers following a simplification of religious observances in 31 BC. Prior to that, hundreds of shrines were erected in the capital and the provinces for the observance of official rites. Not all ceremonies were carried out regularly: **Qin Shi Huangdi** performed the *feng* and *shan* sacrifices as he toured his empire in 219 BC. These great but occasional imperial rites, to which **Sima Qian** devoted a monograph in the ***Shiji***, were linked with the **five sacred mountains**, the chief of which was Mount Tai. Emperor Han **Wudi** performed them here in 110 BC in search of his own **immortality**. They were next performed again in AD 56. When Tang **Gaozong** revived the ceremony in 659 it was after a lapse of centuries. Special events such as the inauguration of a new dynasty or reign called for appropriate sacrifices, and might be followed by signs of imperial largesse such as amnesty.

The **Hongwu Emperor** was the first to build a temple for the performance of indoor sacrifices to Heaven, and in 1420 the **Yongle Emperor's** own Temple of Heaven was completed in **Beijing**. In the late Ming and Qing periods the sacrifice was again moved into the open air. Inside the Forbidden City lay the Temple of Soil and Grain, finished in 1421, and the Imperial Ancestral Temple (*taimiao* 太廟). The Jiajing Emperor had Altars built to the Sun, Moon, Earth and Agriculture outside the east, west, north and south walls of the Inner City (1530), and with the Altar of Heaven these provided the "suburban" (*jiao* 郊) locations for the major rites, elaborate observations that caused disruption to the regular life of the court and capital. The procession to the Altars of Heaven and Earth took place at the winter and summer solstices respectively. Autumn was marked by rites at the Altars of the Moon and Soil and Grain (for harvesting). In spring ceremonies took place at the Altars of Soil and Grain (for planting), Agriculture, and the Moon. On rare occasions the Manchu court made the arduous journey back to their ancestral capital of Shenyang to profess their loyalty to their ancestors. See also **Ancestor Worship.**

SAGE EMPERORS *San huang wu di* 三皇五帝

Earliest legendary rulers of China credited with providing the essentials of existence, like fire, agriculture, writing, houses, etc. There are many versions of the accounts of the legendary early emperors running into several dozen names. The three sovereigns, *san huang*, are clearly originally divinities and have names like *Tian huang* 天皇 Heavenly sovereign, *Di huang* 地皇 Earthly sovereign or *Dong huang* 東皇 Eastern sovereign. Later, beings who were originally *di* emperors, like *Huang di*, the Yellow Emperor (regarded as the founding ancestor of the Chinese race), were elevated to *huang* status. A typical set is: Fu xi 伏羲, Shen nong 神農 and Huang di 黃帝 as the three sovereigns, and Shao hao 少昊, Zhuan xu 顓頊, Di ku 帝嚳, Yao 堯 and Shun 舜 as the five emperors. See also **Former Kings.**

SAKYA PANDITA (1182–1251)
Abbot of the great Tibetan monastery of Sakya founded in 1073; uncle of **'Phagspa**, whom he took with him when he was received by the Mongol Khan Godan in 1247. Author of a collection of moral maxims written in an Indian form of four-line stanzas.

SALT EXCHANGE SYSTEM
Scheme designed to supply border garrisons with grain. Transporting food supplies to remote border regions was not attractive to merchants, so they were repaid in salt certificates, which entitled them to trade in salt, a profitable business as salt had been a govenment monopoly sincwe the Warring States Period. The salt exchange system had been used in the Song dynasty and was revived in 1370 by the Ming court. By the 15th century most of the border garrisons wer supplied by this method.

SALT AND IRON DEBATE see ***YANTIE LUN* 鹽鐵論**

SANCAI see **TANG *SANCAI***

***SANFAN* CAMPAIGN** see **THREE-ANTI CAMPAIGN**

SANGUO YANYI 三國演義
One of the great classic novels often called in English *The Romance of the Three Kingdoms*. This historical novel is attributed to Luo Guanzhong (born c.1315) but may date from the mid or late 15th century. Storytellers' tales of the *Sanguo* go back to at least the Song dynasty and an extant Yuan 'prompt book' version, the *Sanguo zhi pinghua* 三國志平話 dates back to 1321–3. By comparison with the *pinghua* version the 120 chapter *Sanguo yanyi* is much more extensive (over ten times as long), coherent and closer to historical fact. It is a tale of retribution and intrigue which chronicles the break up of the Han empire into three kingdoms and covers the period from 168 AD up to 280 AD, when the Jin reunified China. Incidents recounted in the *Sanguo* have inspired military strategists throughout Chinese history and it remains one of the most popular traditional novels.
LUO Guanzhong, *Three Kingdoms: A Historical Novel*, trans., annotation and afterword by Moss Roberts (Berkeley: University of California Press, 1991); Andrew PLAKS, *Four Masterworks of the Ming Novel* (Princeton University Press, 1987).

SAN LI "Three Rituals"
Name by which the three principal Confucian Classics concerned with rites – ***Zhouli*, *Yili*** and ***Liji*** – were known. See **Confucianism, Five Classics, Thirteen Classics**.

SAN MIN ZHU YI see **THREE PEOPLE'S PRINCIPLES**

SANG HONGYANG 桑弘羊 (152–80 BC)
An expert in mathematics and financial affairs with a practical approach to government and an awareness of the value of trade appointed as Imperial Counsellor (*yushi dafu* 御史大夫) shortly before Han **Wudi's** death in 87 BC.

In the so-called **Salt and Iron Debate** of 81 BC he defended the government's foreign and domestic policies as being in the interests of the people, including its aggressive and expansionist record against the **Xiongnu** and maintenance of state monopolies on salt and iron. He was executed following his implication in a plot against the Chancellor **Huo Guang**.

SANXINGDUI 三星堆
In present-day Guanghan County, Sichuan Province. A centre of early civilisation dating from the **neolithic** era (c.2100 BC) and extending into the Zhou period, when it seems to have been at the heart of the developing **Shu** culture. The neolithic settlement shows signs of influence from the North, such as hollow-legged ceramic tripods, it also exhibits independent features including some attractive ladles shaped in the form of birds' heads. Most remarkable, however, are the contents of two Shang period burials discovered in 1989. They contain hundreds of precious objects, including gold, **jade**, bronze and ivory artefacts. These show signs of contact between Sanxingdui and Shang domains on the Great Plain (e.g. the use of the ***taotie*** pattern), but whereas bronze at **Anyang** was the prerogative of the ruling clan, here in the distant South-west is unique evidence of a contemporary regional industry of great originality and skill. Found in the second pit were over forty bronze human figures, one evidently a king, and fifteen bronze masks. In common with actual royal burials at Anyang, the heads of the king's attendants had been removed, presumably as a symbol of sacrifice. See also **Ba**, **Bronze Age.**
S.F. SAGE, *Ancient Sichuan and the Unification of China* (State University of New York Press, 1992).

SCARLET GUARDS *Chi weidui* 赤衛隊
Youth organisations from **Cultural Revolution** Shanghai formed to support the local CCP which was under attack by **Red Guard** units supporting Mao Zedong. They attracted a strong following in the factories and docks of the city. See also **January Storm**.

SCHALL VON BELL, ADAM (1591–1666)
German **Jesuit** who arrived in China in 1623 and worked on the reform of the calendar with Xu Guangqi (see Matteo **Ricci**) in 1630. In the early years of the Qing dynasty he continued work on the calendar for the Manchus and had close personal ties with the young **Shunzhi** Emperor, who made him court astronomer. His powerful influence, however, earned him enemies at court, notably a rival astronomer Yang Guangxian, who in 1664 instigated a persecution of the Christian church resulting in Schall's imprisonment. See also **Religious Persecution**.
A. VATH, *Johann Adam Schall von Bell S.J., ein Leibens- und Zeitbild* (Nettetal: Steyler Vlg., 1991).

SCHOLAR-GENTRY see **GENTRY**

SCHOLARS, THE see ***RULIN WAISHI***

SCHOOLS

There is no clear evidence for the existence of schools in Zhou China, though respect for teachers such as **Confucius** and the rise of an educated governing elite are an indication that some kind of formal teaching probably existed. From earliest times the spread of writing and the study of prescribed texts were associated with the training and selection of officials. Systematic organisation on a national scale was first introduced in 124 BC with the establishment of a school in each commandery, teaching the **Confucian Classics** and preparing the sons of officials and promising young men nominated by officials for training as future bureaucrats. The best might go on to the **Imperial Academy**. The pattern was thus set for schools as centres where current political orthodoxy would be expounded but critical comment, advantageous to the government, encouraged. Reality did not always match the ideal: Sui **Wendi**, the "Cultured Emperor", closed down prefectural and county schools in 601 because of lack of determination among students. They were reopened by the Tang emperor **Gaozu** in 624 but declined again in the later stages of the dynasty. Elementary education in the Tang was provided either by private tutors or by Buddhist temples.

The growth of **Neo-Confucianism** and the concurrent development of the **printing** industry in the early Song dynasty led to the rise of **private academies** with good libraries. The state system was no longer reserved for the sons of officials, and schools were opened in all prefectures and sub-prefectures. Student recruitment increased, but some schools, with an eye on civil service recruitment through the expanding **examination system**, would only accept those with some prior qualification. Unsuccessful attempts at more widespread provision of schools were made by **Wang Anshi** and especially by **Cai Jing** in the early twelfth century. **Zhu Xi** was active in promoting both private academies and community schools and was the author of *Xiaoxue* "Elementary Education".

Neo-Confucian writers such as **Su Shi** and **Huang Zongxi** referred favourably to the ancient tradition of schools as sources of political criticism, but in late imperial times the emphasis in government was more on conformity. In 1369 the **Hongwu Emperor** ordered the opening of schools in all prefectures and villages and provided quotas for a number of scholars at each to be awarded a grant of rice and exempted from labour dues. The Ming saw a further expansion in number and types of schools. Government schools were primarily concerned with preparation for the civil service examinations, and it was in the academies of the late Ming that the expression of more independent viewpoints was to be found (see **Donglin Academy**).

Under the Qing, state education was supplemented by private schools, clan schools, community colleges, and charitable foundations in rural areas sponsored both by the government and by gentry philanthropists. The popularity of the official examinations was unprecedented. This, together with the growth of urban culture, enhanced the literacy rate among the population as a whole to an estimated 35–40%.

SCRIPT see **ROMANISATION, WRITING SYSTEMS, CHINESE LANGUAGE**

SCROLLS

Traditional mounting forms of Chinese painting and calligraphic works. There are two main formats: hanging scrolls and hand-scrolls. The scroll format originated in early forms of literature written on foldable silk banners or bamboo strips. The hanging scroll, or *lizhou* 立軸, is a vertical form of presentation, which was intended to be hung on the wall. It was often used for large-scale landscapes and figure compositions. By the tenth century, this format was in popular use and was well suited to the monumental style of Song dynasty landscapes. Above the main picture there is often a section called *shitang* 詩塘 ("the poetic pool") for substantial inscriptions about the work, usually by the artist's friends or the collectors.

The handscroll or *shoujuan* 手卷, also called *changjuan* 長卷 "long scroll", is a horizontal form of presentation, beginning from the right-hand rod and ending at the left hand edge. As such scrolls can be very long, usually measuring between one and nine metres in length and 25–40 cm in height, they were never intended to be seen in their entirety at one glance but were to be gradually wound and rewound to show a picture section by section in a continuous sequence. The format therefore forces the viewer to "read" the picture as if viewing a work of calligraphy, or is even close to music in the way that the artist is able to dictate sequence in his communication. Handscrolls often have narratives with text and paintings interspersed., The main picture is preceded by a title panel and followed by a postscript panel for inscriptions, such as poems, and seals.

SEALS

In China seals were symbols used to indicate ownership, to authenticate documents, and to establish political or religious authority from as early as the second millennium BC. Seals were made from a variety of materials that could be carved or moulded. Generally imperial seals were made of gold or jade, official seals of bronze or silver, and private seals made of anything from ivory or porcelain to bamboo and wood. Since the Yuan dynasty, the primary material for seal carving has been soapstone in which there are three most favoured types: Qingtian and Changhua stones from Zhejiang province, and Shoushan stone from Fujian province. By the Ming dynasty, seals were also regarded as aesthetic objects by the elite and seal engraving was regarded as a special form of calligraphy and an important aspect of the literati's cultivated pursuits. Seal images vary from studio or personal names to verses or pictorial motifs. Inscriptions were carved either in intaglio against a solid background or in relief against a background which had been removed. *Zhuanshu* or seal script has been used as the main style for inscriptions on seals. Seals were pressed into vermilion seal paste and then stamped onto paper or silk.

Jason KUO, *Word as Image – The Art of Chinese Seal Engraving* (New York: University of Washington Press 1992).

SECOND EMPEROR Erhuangdi 二皇帝 (210–206)

Title adopted by Hu Hai 胡亥, younger son of **Qin Shi Huangdi**, who succeeded to the throne at the age of 21 thanks to the plotting of **Zhao Gao** and **Li Si**. He executed officials, made laws harsher and continued the extravagant building of the **Epang Palace**, and after only seven months the first rebellion against his regime occurred in **Chu**. By the third year, when Li Si had been executed and Zhao Gao's grip on the Emperor had tightened, widespread revolt had broken out. Finally the Governor of **Xianyang**, Yan Yue, denounced Huhai to his face and he committed suicide.

SECOND GREAT LEAP FORWARD

An attempt by Mao Zedong in late 1959 and 1960 to continue with his **Great Leap Forward** policies in spite of the disputes at the **Lushan Plenum**. A new political trend in early 1960 included the promotion of **communes** and urban communes and a new push to send cadres down to the countryside. It can be argued that it was this "second leap" rather than the original 1958 policy that caused the disastrous failure in agricultural and industrial production and rural famine, probably the worst in the world in the twentieth century. The government insisted that some land be left fallow in 1959 to make sure there were adequate granary facilities to handle the surplus that was expected. Inevitably, there was a major shortage of food. Severe weather problems and the withdrawal of Soviet technicians in 1960 made matters worse and it is estimated that there were some 20 million deaths more than would have been expected between 1959 and 1961.

SECOND NORTHERN EXPEDITION

Completion of the task of unifying China under a Nationalist government that had begun with the 1926 **Northern Expedition**. Beijing had remained under the control of the Manchurian Warlord, **Zhang Zuolin** but Zhang was killed when his train was blown up by Japanese soldiers of the **Guandong Army** on June 4 1928. Nationalist troops of the Northern Expedition were already marching north, Jiang Jieshi having secured the support of two other northern warlords **Feng Yuxiang** and **Yan Xishan**. Yan Xishan's troops occupied Beijing on June 8 1928 and on June 28 its name was formally changed to Beiping 北平 (Northern Peace), the name by which it is still officially known in Taiwan, and the province of Zhili was renamed Hebei.

SECOND REVOLUTION (1913)

Abortive rising of the southern provinces of China against President **Yuan Shikai** in the early years of the **Republic of China**. Yuan had usurped the Presidency in 1912 and after radical nationalists gained substantial support in the first parliamentary elections that followed, tried to suppress them. Jiangxi declared itself independent in July 1913 and was followed by Jiangsu, Anhui, Guangdong and Hunan. Military units backing Yuan Shikai defeated the rebels and the Second Revolution was over by the beginning of September.

SECRET HISTORY OF THE MONGOLS

The only surviving Mongol source about their empire. Although the Mongol language had a script adapted from the Uyghur script and the original was probably written in Mongolian, the copy of the *Secret History* that has survived was transcribed in the 14th century into Chinese characters, used not for their meaning but for their representation of the sounds of the Mongol text. A shorter version in more conventional Chinese also exists. The book is mainly about the life and career of **Chinggis Khan**, his ancestors and his rise to power

SECRET SOCIETIES *JIAO* 教 OR *HUI* 會

Anti-government, clandestine political and religious associations have played an important role in Chinese history since earliest times. They have been linked with **bandit** organisations and with **peasant rebellions** that overthrew dynasties. Among the most significant have been the **White Lotus**, which can be traced back to the twelfth century and even claimed descent from societies that existed in the fourth century, the **Elder Brother Society** and the **Triads.** Although secret societies drew members from all sections of the population, they were particularly attractive to the poor and dispossessed, providing an alternative route through life to those denied an official career or a prosperous farm. Members of any individual society might include peasants forced off their land, failed scholars, boatmen, day labourers, criminals and outlaws. Societies had very different rules and practices, but were always secretive, as the government was constantly on the look-out for potential threats to its rule. In a culture that viewed the world as a ***yin-yang*** 陰陽 dichotomy, secret societies were thoroughly *yin* 陰. Many were egalitarian, in sharp contrast to the rigid hierarchies of Confucian society, or created alternative kinship relationships, which were valuable for those excluded from the normal **clan or lineage** support systems. Women also found a political and social role – denied to them in their everyday lives – in some of the secret societies. Often the impetus was religious, with many groups having links with Daoist or Buddhist sects, in particular Buddhist believers in the **Maitreya** or Buddha of the future. Secret societies were involved in all of the major anti-Qing activities, including the **Taiping Rebellion**, the **Boxer Rising** and the **Revolution of 1911** and frequently professed loyalty to the Ming dynasty, defeated in 1644, and hatred of the **Manchu** conquerors. Both the CCP and the GMD had links with the secret societies but after 1949, the government of the PRC repressed them ruthlessly. Societies like the Triads and their offshoots still exist in Hong Kong and in Overseas Chinese communities, but they are almost purely criminal organisations today. In the PRC since the end of the Cultural Revolution, there have constantly been reports of the revival of old secret societies, but it is not clear whether they are regaining any of the political influence they had before 1949.

***SELECTED WORKS OF MAO ZEDONG Mao Zedong xuanji* 毛澤東選集**

Official and authorised edition of Mao's collected speeches, articles and essays. Volumes 1–4, which contain material written before 1949, were first published in 1965 and Volume 5, published in 1977, includes articles written up to 1957. The texts in the *Selected Works* often differ substantially from the original and there is a minor academic industry dedicated to finding the earliest texts.

SELF-CRITICISM *Ziwo piping* 自我批評

Powerful method used by the CCP to control its membership and ensure conformity. Individuals criticised for a political mistake or holding unorthodox views were required to write criticism of themselves and an analysis of the mistakes they had made. These were used regularly in political campaigns in the PRC, from the **Anti-Rightist Movement** of 1957 up to and including the aftermath of the **Democracy Movement** in 1989.

Self-Strengthening Movement *Ziqiang yundong* 自強運動 (1861–95)
Programme of military modernisation and strengthening embarked on by the Qing government, deeply aware of how far behind the Western powers China had fallen. It was part of a temporary revival in the fortunes of the dynasty that began with the reign of the Tongzhi emperor in 1861, known as the **Tongzhi Restoration**. Humiliated by their defeat in the **Opium Wars**, senior Qing officials made strenuous efforts to acquire Western military technology and scientific knowledge and to train Chinese personnel to make use of it. As part of this first phase, the **Zongli Yamen**, and the Jiangnan and Nanjing arsenals were founded, together with schools and other munitions factories. In the second phase, the emphasis changed to creating a sound economic foundation for defence industries and the Foreign Matters Movement (*yangwu yundong*) 洋務運動, which was devoted to enterprises copied from the West such as shipping, telegraphs, mining and railways, emerged. Although a certain amount of modernisation was accomplished, China was unable to make the progress that Japan was achieving at about the same time during the Meiji restoration. As a result, when it came to the **Sino-Japanese War** of 1894–5, Japan had a military triumph and the weakess of China's defences was clear for all to see.

Se-mu 色目
Usually translated as "coloured eyes", but also meaning "special status", this was an ethnic classification used during the rule of China by the **Mongols** in the Yuan dynasty. The *Semu*, who were of Central Asian origin and brought into China as slaves or indentured craftsmen, were below the Mongols in rank, but above the native Chinese. Many of the Muslim groups living in China today trace their origins back to the *Semu*.

Senggerinchin (*Senggelinqin* 僧格林沁)
Mongol aristocrat who commanded troops of the Qing government in their attempts to suppress the **Taiping Rebellion**. He was killed in a similar action against the **Nian** rebels on May 18 1865.

September 18 Incident *Jiu Yiba Shijian* 九一八事件 see **Mukden Incident**

Sera Monastery
One of the three great monasteries of **Lhasa**, associated with Tantrism and with a reputation for political radicalism which has lasted until the present day. It was founded in 1419 by a disciple of **Tsong Khapa** as part of the initial spread of **Gelugpa** teaching across Tibet and reached a maximum population of 7,000, reduced to around 300 by the end of the 20th century. It was well-known for its highly trained warrior-monks. See also **Drepung, Ganden**.

Seven Sages of the Bamboo Grove
A renowned group of third century AD **Daoist** scholars who opted out of bureaucratic society and met in the countryside outside **Luoyang** to indulge themselves in sensual and intellectual pleasures, especially poetry, music and drink. Their claim was that the pursuit of "natural" human behaviour and the rejection of the artificality of Confucian institutions and mores was a token of

their moral integrity. Their leader was the poet and musician Ji Kang 嵇康 (223–62). One of the Seven, Yuan Xian 阮咸, gave his name to the oldest of the Chinese lute family, also known as the *qin pipa*, on which he was a virtuoso performer.

SHAAN-GAN-NING BORDER REGION ***SHAAN GAN NING BIANQU*** **陝甘寧邊區**
The formal name for the area controlled by the CCP from its **Yan'an** headquarters during the **Anti-Japanese War**.

SHANG 商
(1) The name given to the royal domain that surrounded the capital of Yin (modern Anyang, Henan province) and to the dynasty of the thirteen kings who ruled there from approx. 1384 BC onwards. Their previous capital was at **Ao** (modern Zhengzhou), before which their base area is reputed to have moved a number of times since the founding of the "state" by the mythical sage King Tang some time before 1700 BC. The house fell, probably around 1045 BC and after the vital battle of Muye, to conquerors from the vassal state of Zhou (in the vicinity of modern Xi'an) during the reign of the reputedly tyrannical and corrupt King Jie. A major royal cemetery of enormous shaft tombs was excavated at Xibeigang, near Anyang, between 1928 and 1937, which revealed the practice of human and animal **sacrifice**. Shang was the feudal *primus inter pares* of many tribal statelets against which it was frequently warring. The power of the court was based upon its exclusive control of bronze, with which it made the ritual vessels used in the religious ceremonies which also authenticated its authority, and the newly evolving skill of writing, now extant principally on **oracle bones**. Its military strength included horse-drawn chariots.
(2) The period corresponding to the above in parts of the country not under royal authority from Yin, but already benefiting from the cultural attributes of the **Bronze Age**.

K.C. CHANG, *Shang Civilization* (Yale University Press, 1980); K.C. CHANG, ed., *Studies of Shang Archaeology* (Yale University Press, 1986); K.C. CHANG, *Art, Myth and Ritual: The Path to Political Authority in China* (Harvard University Press, 1983).

SHANGDI 上帝
The name given to the supreme deity worshipped at the court of the Shang dynasty. He was believed to preside over a pantheon of gods and spirits which included those with particular functions, interests and attributes, such as the God of Agriculture, Houji, and the spirits of the deceased ancestors of the royal line, arranged in a hierarchy reflecting the feudal society of the time. After the Zhou conquest **sacrifices** to Shangdi declined and greater official faith was put in an impersonal Heaven (*tian* 天), but popular belief in the existence of the imprecisely defined supreme deity continued. The propriety of using this term as a translation for the Christian God perplexed Western **missionaries** in China from the **Jesuits** to the Protestants of the nineteenth century. See also **Shang, Oracle Bones.**

SHANGHAI 上海
Largest city of the PRC and the main industrial, transport and cultural centre of eastern China. It was an insignificant fishing village and trading centre on the little

Huangpu River which runs off the Yangzi River. Its growth began with Western interest after the formation of **Treaty Ports** in the late 19th century and the architecture of the Bund, the area along the river is remarkably reminiscent of Victorian British cities. In the 1920s it was home to the International Settlement of foreign (mainly Western) traders and diplomats, the scene of the first major trades union disputes in the newly developed textile and other industries and the birthplace of the **Chinese Communist Party** as well as being a radical artistic and cultural centre. Before the Japanese invasion of 1937, it had become the commercial and financial powerhouse of China, a position that Shanghai's leaders hope it will reclaim from **Hong Kong** in the 21st century. During the People's Republic, Shanghai has been noted for its radical politics, especially during the **Cultural Revolution** when it was the base for Mao Zedong's wife **Jiang Qing** and her followers in the **Gang of Four**. See also **January Storm, Shanghai Commune**.

SHANGHAI COMMUNE ***Shanghai gongshe*** 上海公社
Proposed radical administration for Shanghai following the January 1967 power seizure by pro-Mao Zedong groups during the **Cultural Revolution**. It was modelled on the Paris Commune of 1871 and was the brainchild of Zhang Chunqiao and Yao Wenyuan, members of the **Gang of Four.**

SHANGHAI COUP
Coup against the Chinese Communist Party by Jiang Jieshi on April 12 1927 at the end of the **Northern Expedition** in which the CCP and GMD had been partners. Jiang used his own troops and the Shanghai criminal underworld, including the **Green Gang** to destroy the organisations of the CCP and trades unions in Shanghai and subsequently throughout southern China. Thousands of CCP supporters were killed and imprisoned. This was the end of public CCP activity in the cities – some underground operations continued, even in Shanghai – and marked its move towards becoming a peasant party, which it did by establishing itself initially in the **Jiangxi Soviet**. For Jiang Jieshi, it was the opportunity to become sole leader of the GMD and dictator of China in the Nanjing Government.

SHANGJUNSHU **商君書 Book of Lord Shang**
Legalist school work ascribed to **Shang Yang** 商鞅 (died 338 BC), a native of the state of Wei who made his name implementing Legalist-style reforms for Duke Xiao of Qin. This work is listed in the ***Hanshu*** *Yi wen zhi* as having 29 *pian*, but the present version has only 24 extant *pian*. From the dates mentioned in the text of battles which occurred some years after the well-documented death of Shang Yang, it is clear that the work is not all from the hand of Shang Yang. However, the comments of late Zhou and early Han figures like **Han Feizi** and **Sima Qian** make clear that the ideas in the text are representative of Shang Yang's and that the text was probably compiled by his followers on the basis of his writings. The key idea running through the text is making the state rich and its army strong. This is to be accomplished through strict application of laws, the use of rewards and punishments and emphasis on agriculture and warfare. It rejects as outmoded the Confucian approach of using the classics and morality as the basis of society and advocates strengthening the power of the ruler at the

expense of the aristocracy. Chapters vary in style from descriptions of the reforms he carried out in the state of Qin to analyses of historical development.
J.J.L. DUYVENDAK, *The Book of Lord Shang* (London: Probsthain, 1928).

SHANGSHU* 尚書 *Book of Documents
Also known as the *Shujing* 書經 and sometimes refered to in English as the Book or Classic of History, this is one of the core **Five Classics** of the Confucian canon and includes some of the earliest examples of written Chinese. The work consists of documents issued by rulers or ministers in five categories: *mo* 謨 consultations (discussions between ruler and ministers), *xun* 訓 instructions (ministerial advice), *gao* 誥 announcements (proclamations by the ruler), *shi* 誓 oaths (battlefield proclamations) and *ming* 命 commands (royal decrees). Chronologically they divide into four periods: the *Yushu* 虞書 early semi-legendary emperors, *Xiashu* 夏書 Xia dynasty, *Shangshu* 商書 Shang dynasty and *Zhoushu* 周書 Zhou dynasty. The documents purporting to date from the three earliest periods appear in most cases to date from very much later (i.e. late **Warring States**) but some of the Zhou documents may date from the regency of the Duke of Zhou (1042–1035 BC). (See **Zhou Gong**).The *Shangshu* exists in a **new text** version of 28 (or 29) chapters and an **old text** version of 58 chapters; the old text version was considered orthodox but it was long suspected that the additional chapters (i.e. those not included in the new text version) were later forgeries. The new text version is credited to Fu Sheng 伏勝(生) who is said to have secreted a bamboo strip edition in the wall of his home during the **burning of the books**. Of this text, written in the 'new' standard *lishu* 隸書 script of the Qin, only 28 chapters remained readable when it was recovered. It was accepted as the standard text during the reign of Han **Wudi** (179–157 BC) when a 29th chapter was later added from another source. During this same period an old text version in pre-Qin 'tadpole script' was said to have been discovered in the wall of Confucius' old home; this, which contained a different 29th chapter and a further 16 documents in 24 chapters, was presented to the court by Kong Anguo 孔安國, a descendant of Confucius, and accepted into the imperial library. It seems likely that this version was destroyed since the current old text version, presented to the Jin court around 320 by Mei Ze 梅賾, was convincingly demonstrated to be a forgery by Yan Ruoju in the Qing (something which increasingly led to the historicisation of the Classics and their loss of canonical status).
Bernhard KARLGREN trans., *The Book of Documents* (Reprinted from the *Bulletin of the Museum of Far Eastern Antiquities*, 22 (1950) Stockholm).

SHANG YANG 商鞅 (d. 338 BC)
Formerly Gongsun Yang 公孫鞅, also known as Yang of **Wei** 衛 (his first adopted state). Having been dismissed by Wei he entered the service of neighbouring **Qin** in 361, where he was enfeoffed as Lord of Shang by Duke Xiao. He is famed for the Legalistic policies which he persuaded the Duke to adopt, and which helped to transform the rather peripheral, westerly state into the most efficient combatant for power in the late fourth century. The key to his reforms was the application of written laws which, together with their associated code of rewards and strictly applied punishments, would both stimulate and

control people's conduct. Law was advocated as the key to state power, and centralised authority was imposed in 350 through the thirty one counties (*xian*), absorbing the earlier mixture of commanderies (*jun*) and prefectures (*fu*). Law, harshly and impersonally applied to all through a tight security system, also regulated people's behaviour through fear of the penalties for contravention. Social units were organized for purposes of production and mutual responsibility, and strict discipline imposed throughout both civilian and military units. Agriculture was encouraged, **taxation** made more efficient, weights and measures standardised, and commerce restricted as part of a limitation on movement within society. A state monopoly over iron was established and contributed to its growing economic strength. But Shang Yang's success earned him enemies at court who forced him to flee and then trapped him under his own law against travelling. He suffered death and mutilation. The success of his political philosophy, which survived his execution, is based not only upon its ruthlessness but also on his ability to see the need for a consistent, integrated approach to all aspects of state activity. He also stressed the application of modern, realistic methods in place of the unimaginative appeal to the past which typified the political approach of rival states. He is suspectly credited with the authorship of the ***Shangjunshu***, "Book of Lord Shang". See also **Han Feizi, Legalism, Li Si.**

J.J.L. DUYVENDAK, trans., *The Book of Lord Shang* (London: Probsthain, 1928).

SHANHAIGUAN 山海關

"Pass between the Mountains and the Sea". In present day Hebei province close to the border with Liaoning, Shanhaiguan is the point at which the **Great Wall** descends to the coast of the Gulf of Bohai, and the only route between China and Manchuria. It could be sealed relatively easily, so when **Wu Sangui** made the conscious decision to allow the **Manchu** forces through the pass in 1644 to defeat the rebel **Li Zicheng** it inevitably marked the beginning of a new dynasty, the Qing.

SHANXI MERCHANTS

Traders from Shanxi and Shaanxi provinces who were active in northern China in the Ming and Qing dynasties and also traded as far afield as Mongolia. Their rise can be traced back to their manipulation of the **Salt Exchange system**, profits from which were used to create powerful banks. See also **Huizhou Merchants**.

SHANYUAN, TREATY OF (1005)

The first inter-state treaty to be signed in Chinese history, concluding years of warfare between Song China and the **Khitan** Liao state of the northern Great Plain and Manchuria. The Treaty established diplomatic equality between the two states, despite Chinese attempts to interpret it in terms of the traditional tributary relationship between the Middle Kingdom and a feudal vassal (see **tribute system**). The roles were actually reversed, since China agreed to pay substantial annual dues of silver and **silk** to her former enemy, now turned partner. For its part the Liao court, which was served by a significant number of capable Chinese officials, went to substantial pains to ensure that its organisation and rites observed the most correct and up to date models from **Kaifeng**.

M. ROSSABI, ed., *China among Equals: the Middle Kingdom and its Neighbors, 10th-14th Centuries* (Berkeley: University of California Press, 1983).

SHAO YONG 邵雍 (1011–1077)
One of the five great Northern Song Rationalist **Neo-Confucian** scholars. Shao Yong's ancestral home was Fanyang 範陽 in Hebei but he was brought up at Gongcheng 共城 in Henan. He studied the **numerology** of the ***Yijing*** from Li Zhicai 李之才 and used it, like **Zhou Dunyi**, to produce a Neo-Confucian cosmology. It was based essentially on a binary system, which Shao often doubled to produce a 4 base. He believed that the great ultimate *tai ji* 太極 was the source of the universe and produced heaven *tian* 天 and earth *di* 地. With the inception of movement *dong* 動, *yang* 陽 was produced and at its zenith *yin* 陰 was produced; these interacted to form all the heavenly bodies. Similarly on earth with the inception of quietude *jing* 靜, softness *rou* 柔 was produced, and when it reached its zenith hardness, *gang* 剛 was produced; these two interact to form the four elements (water, fire, earth and stone, omitting wood from the normal list of **five elements**). Using the **heavenly stems and earthly branches** *tiangan dizhi* 天干地支 system and based on the divisions of a year, Shao Yong posited a Buddhist style cycle for the universe of 129,600 years (1 year x 30 = 1 generation *shi* 世 x 12 = 1 revolution *yun* 運 x 30 = 1 concurrence *hui* 會 x 12 = 1 aeon *yuan* 元) which was eternally repeated. Each *hui* was associated with one of the 12 earthly branches *dizhi* and in the present cycle the world was already past its peak (this accounted for the supposed decline from the age of the sage rulers). Shao Yong is usually included in the rationalist school, but his insistence that the physical universe is based on a 'numerology which predates heaven' *xiantian xiangshu* 先天象數 and that the latter itself originates in a mind *xin* 心 which is common to man and the universe, is closer to idealism.

Anne D. BIRDWHISTELL, *Transition to Neo-Confucianism: Shao Yung on Knowledge and Symbols of Reality* (Stanford University Press, 1989).

SHEN CONGWEN 沈從文 (1903–1988)
Writer and historian. Born in a **Miao** minority family in Fenghuang county, Hunan province, Shen Congwen spent his early life in the mountains before he went to Beijing to study. He later became a major figure in Beijing literary circles from the 1920s to the 1940s. He was a prolific and versatile writer: among his long list of works are well-known novels like *Biancheng* 邊城 (*The Border Town*) and *Changhe* 長河 (*The Long River*). During the same period, Shen Congwen also lectured at Beijing University and was literary editor for major newspapers such as *Dagongbao* 大公報 and *Jingbao* 京報.

After 1949, however, his life changed due to political campaigns. He felt he had to give up writing, and devoted himself to historical research. First he worked in the Museum of Chinese History and later in the Institute of History, Chinese Academy of Social Sciences. His work in ancient art and material culture, such as bronzes, costumes and symbolism, resulted in a number of influential publications.

Jeffrey KINKLEY, *The Odyssey of Shen Congwen* (Stanford University Press, 1987).

SHEN GUA 沈括 (1030–94)
A senior official whose career in provincial and central government reflected his broad interests in science and technology as well as more traditional literary and artistic fields. These included astronomy, cartography, geology, medicine, painting, **calligraphy** and **music**. He was responsible for **water control** works and border defences, and undertook diplomatic missions to the **Khitan**. He promoted the ***baojia*** system. He kept notes on his observations, published in *Mengxi bitan* 夢溪筆談 "Brush jottings from a dream brook", c.1088, which contains the earliest reference to the **magnetic compass**.

SHEN NONG 神農
One of the legendary founders of Chinese civilisation; renowned as the great agriculturalist and the father of medicine.

SHEN RONG see **CHEN RONG**

***SHENGXIAO* 生肖 or *SHUXIANG* 屬相**
The twelve animals, representing the twelve terrestrial branches, used to denote the year in which a person is born. The twelve animals in *shengxiao* are: rat, ox, tiger, hare, dragon, snake, horse, ram, monkey, cock, dog and pig, each of which is supposed to exercise some influence over the period of time denoted by the special character which the animal represents. The set of twelve animals appeared in the Han dynasty to represent the terrestrial branches (see **heavenly stems and terrestrial branches**). This practice was widely adopted in decorative art in the Sui and Tang dynasties, especially on bronze mirrors, ceramics, memorial tablets, and in sculpture for tombs. *Shengxiao* also became a main theme for the traditional New Year celebration. It is common in China for someone to give his or her age by stating the animal of his or her birth year.

SHI DAKAI 石達開
One of the first disciples of the leader of the **Taiping Rebellion**, Hong Xiuquan. Shi swelled the ranks of Hong's supporters in 1849 by persuading his entire lineage to join him. He was one of the ablest of the Taiping leaders and attempted to set up his own domain in Sichuan after the internal feuding of 1856 but was killed in 1863 by troops loyal to the Qing dynasty.

SHIJING* 詩經 *Book of Poetry
A collection of verses dating from about the twelfth to about the sixth century BC and one of the **Five Classics**. The poems are typically four syllable lines in stanzas with, frequently, a complex rhyme scheme. There are a total of 305 poems, said to have been culled from 3,000 by **Confucius**, in four categories: 160 *feng* 風 or *guofeng* 國風 (national) airs, 74 *xiaoya* 小雅 lesser odes, 31 *daya* 大雅 greater odes and 40 *song* 頌 elegies. The *feng* from 15 states of north China are inspired by the daily lives of the people and include love poems, descriptions of festivals and the natural world; the *ya* are concerned with a higher social stratum, particularly the courts of the states, with the *daya* concentrating on the activities of the Zhou; the *song*, divided into sections for the states of Zhou, **Lu** and Shang but written primarily in praise of the Zhou,

describe religious rites and other court ceremonial. Each poem is preceded by a short preface *xiaoxu* 小序 commenting on its content; the first poem also has a great preface *daxu* 大序 which outlines the traditional Confucian attitude towards the collection. This was that the poems of the common people reflected their attitudes towards their rulers and could be used by rulers as a mirror for good government. The Great Preface introduces the term *liuyi* 六義 six principles to refer to the above three basic types plus *fu* 賦 narrative verses, *bi* 比 direct metaphor and *xing* 興 indirect metaphor; it also describes *feng* and *ya* as being *zheng* 正 proper or *bian* 變 deviant, meaning that they originated at times of good government or times of decline. *Feng* is taken to imply 'verse criticism' and the *feng* and *ya* were both seen as media for the expression of political dissatisfaction at different levels of society. This reading of the poems prevailed until the 20th century when scholars began to take them at face value instead of looking for moral or political guidance. The prefaces, which are later than the poems, have been ascribed to many authors from Confucius onwards. In the Han there existed three new text traditions, named Lu 魯 Qi 齊 and Han 韓 after the states, and the old text Mao 毛 version, named after its promoter. It was the last which was used by the famous Later Han commentator **Zheng Xuan** 鄭玄 as his basic text and as a result the Mao version came to eclipse the other traditions which were largely lost.

Bernhard KARLGREN trans., *The Book of Odes* (Stockholm: The Museum of Far Eastern Antiquities, 1950); Arthur WALEY trans., *The Book of Songs* (George Allen and Unwin, 1969 (reprint)).

SHI TAO 石濤 (Dao Ji 道濟, c.1640–c.1715)

A Ming prince who earned a reputation for painting with great originality and subjectivism, expressing the spirit of nature through form rather than content. He spurned the ancients as a model, yet ironically became himself the source of inspiration for later artists, including the modern painter **Li Keran**. In praising his *Tall Mountains, Long Waters*, Max Loehr says that it "may well set an absolute standard of landscape in the Ch'ing period". He is often associated with his older contemporary Bada Shanren (Zhu Da, 1626–1705/6) for his unconventionality and strength of brushwork.

SHIGATSE

The second city of **Tibet**, formerly the centre of the region of Tsang, and the official seat of the **Panchen Lama** from the seventeenth century. Its great monastery, Tashilumpo, was the most important outside Lhasa. It was founded in 1447 by a disciple of **Tsong Khapa**, Gedun Truppa (died 1475), who was posthumously identified as the first **Dalai Lama** and is the only Dalai Lama not entombed in Lhasa. It had a maximum population of 4,000 monks. It remained a **Gelugpa** house in the midst of Red Hat territory until the Great Fifth Dalai Lama, with **Mongol** support, crushed the political power of Tsang and the associated power of the Karmapa Order. Shigatse was reached by two **Jesuit** missionaries in 1627, the **East India Company**'s representative George Bogle in 1775, and an invading Gurkha force (which was repulsed by Chinese troops) in 1790, but none of these managed to proceed as far as **Lhasa**.

SHIJI* 史記 *Historical Records

Historical work compiled by **Sima Qian** 司馬遷 (c.145– c. 85 BC) which set the standard for all later Chinese historical writing and is counted as the first of the *Ershiwu shi* 二十五史 25 dynastic histories. The work was said to have been initiated by Sima Qian's father, Sima Tan 司馬談, whom Qian succeeded as *Taishi* 太史 Grand Astrologer, but is usually credited to Qian alone. Although there has been some subsequent editing, the authenticity of most of the text is not in doubt. Sima Qian says his father asked him on his death-bed to complete the work, so when he was later condemned for defaming the emperor through his support for a disgraced general, out of filial duty he accepted castration and lived in ignominy rather than choose suicide, the honourable way out. The post of Grand Astrologer involved keeping records of imperial activities and offered the holder access to court archives. On the basis of these and earlier historical works like the ***Shangshu*** and the ***Chunqiu***, Sima Qian set out to write a general history of China from the era of the semi-legendary emperors 2500 years earlier to his own time. Previous works of history were generally annalistic in style, offering a fragmented chronological record. Sima Qian divided his 130 chapter history into five main sections: 12 chapters of *benji* 本紀, basic annals (important events in the governments of rulers from the five early emperors to the Han), 10 chapters of *biao* 表, tables of historical and genealogical information, 8 chapters of *shu* 書, treatises on ritual, **music**, the calendar, waterways and the economy, 30 chapters of *shijia* 世家, hereditary families, describing the ruling families of the various pre-Qin states and some Han leading families, and 70 chapters of *liezhuan* 列傳, biographies of leading figures from all walks of life and accounts of foreign peoples. Although this format broke up the historical narrative it produced a work of high literary merit which offered greater insight into the development of the life of an individual or of a topic. The biographies in particular, with their lively dialogues and exploration of an individual's strengths and weaknesses, stimulated the later development of the historical novel.

SIMA Qian, *The Grand Scribe's Records,* (9 vols) ed., William H. Nienhauser (Indiana University Press, 1994); SIMA Qian, *Records of the Grand Historian (Vols I and II),* trans. and introd. by Burton Watson (Columbia University Press, 1961); Burton WASON, *Ssu-ma Ch'ien, Grand Historian of China* (Columbia University Press, 1958).

SHIMONOSEKI, TREATY OF (1895)

Peace treaty that ended the **Sino-Japanese** War of 1894–5, signed on April 17 and exchanged at Yantai in Shandong province on May 8. Under the terms of the settlement, **Taiwan**, the Pescadores (Penghu) islands and the **Liaodong Peninsula** were transferred to Japanese control, Japanese citizens were allowed to enter China to trade and an indemnity of 200 million silver *taels* was paid to Japan. China also agreed to recognise the independence of **Korea**, although this was in fact the beginning of Japanese control over the country.

SHIZU, YUAN EMPEROR see **KHUBILAI KHAN**

SHU 蜀

Remote behind the Qinling Mountain range, the Min River-based agricultural state of Shu, the inheritor of the **Sanxingdui** culture, developed independently of contemporary civilisation in the central states from the Shang until the Warring States period. Then, through the expansionist plans of **Qin** to the north and **Chu** to the east, Shu was drawn more frequently into diplomatic, military and commercial contact with the world outside Sichuan. Its culture shared common features with its immediate eastern neighbours in **Ba**, including sericulture, a primitive writing system, metallurgy, and a variety of weapons. But it was military conquest by Qin in 316 BC that first brought the South-west into the mainstream of central states politics and transformed it. It was here that Qin politicians were able to try out aspects of the Legalist-inspired application of the law, the new administrative concept of regional commanderies, and to develop agricultural and hydraulic systems to feed their armies as they advanced eastwards into Chu. See also **Li Bing.**

S.F. SAGE, *Ancient Sichuan and the Unification of China* (State University of New York, 1992).

SHUIHUZHUAN 水滸傳

Ming dynasty novel translated as *Water Margin* and also as *All Men are Brothers.* It is the story of the exploits of a bandit group led by Song Jiang in the western part of what is now Shandong province and is a Chinese equivalent of the Robin Hood saga. It is loosely based on historical events and was probably embroidered by professional story-tellers in the market places before it reached its printed form, the authorship of which has been attributed to both Shi Nai'an, a retired official of the late Yuan dynasty and the writer Luo Guanzhong, but recent scholarship has cast serious doubt on this.

Richard G. IRWIN, *The Evolution of a Chinese Novel* (Harvard University Press, 1953).

SHUJING see ***SHANGSHU***

SHUNZHI 順治 QING EMPEROR (r. 1644–1662)

First Emperor of the Manchu Qing dynasty. Born Fulin, he was the son of **Abahai** and ascended to the throne at the age of six with his uncle **Dorgon** acting as regent. During his reign the remaining supporters of the Ming dynasty were eliminated and Qing rule was firmly established. He attained his majority in 1651 and began to rule in his own right, continuing the policy of recruiting Chinese administrators that Dorgon had initiated. His interest in religion led him to contacts with the Jesuit missionary Adam **Schall von Bell** and with **Chan Buddhism**. He died at the age of 22, but had already sired 14 children, the third of whom succeeded him as the **Kangxi Emperor**.

SIKU QUANSHU* 四庫全書 *Complete Works of the Four Treasuries

Massive collectaneous work compiled by order of the Qianlong Emperor beginning in 1773. The *Siku* (Four Treasuries) refers to the traditional classification of works into four categories: *jing* 經 classics, *shi* 史 histories, *zi* 子 philosophers and *ji* 集 *belles lettres*. The project was initiated to enhance the prestige of the Manchu Qing dynasty and win over the hearts of Chinese scholars, but included a more insidious aspect in its search for subversive literature and the punishment of those connected with it. Ji Yun 紀昀 (1724–1805) and Lu Xixiong 陸錫熊 (1734–92) were appointed chief editors in 1773 and chose works from the Imperial Library, from the Ming **encyclopaedia** *Yongle dadian* 永樂大典, from provincial official and private sources and in addition specially commissioned works for inclusion in the *Siku quanshu*. In total they assessed over 10,000 titles of which around 3,500 in 36,000 *juan* were chosen for inclusion. These were copied into four manuscript sets of the *Siku quanshu* to be housed in four imperial libraries (three further sets were later added to be available for scholarly reference); one set was destroyed by the Anglo-French expeditionary force when they attacked the Yuanmingyuan Summer Palace in 1860. The titles of the works which had been considered for inclusion were listed in the *Siku quanshu zongmu tiyao* 四庫全書總目提要 together with critical comments on them; this became in its own right one of the most important bibliographic reference tools for traditional Chinese literary works. The search for seditious material resulted in orders that over 2,000 titles be destroyed, along with their printing blocks, and a further 400–500 be revised or modified to excise references deemed insulting to the Manchus.

R. Kent GUY, *The Emperor's Four Treasuries – Scholars and the State in the Late Ch'ien-lung era* (Harvard University Press, 1989); Luther Carrington GOODRICH, *The Literary Inquisition of Ch'ien-lung* (Baltimore: Waverly Press, 1935).

SILK

Filament of the cocoon of a silkworm. Sericulture, which involved the gathering of mulberry leaves, tending of silkworms, reeling silk from cocoons and silk weaving, was an important economic activity in ancient China. The history of sericulture extends back to the Neolithic period. Weaving implements and dyed silk gauze excavated from Hemudu in Zhejiang province are dated to 3600 BC. Fragments of silk damask and strips of woven silk with mat pattern dating back to 2700 BC have been found at the Qianshanyang site in Zhejiang province. Silk processing was brought to an advanced state during the Shang and Zhou dynasties when woven silk fabrics of various types were established as valuable commodities in China.

Silk fabrics produced in the Han dynasty were very fine and durable with high tensile strength, and were later exported along the **Silk Road**, and treasured in distant lands including Persia and Rome. Traditionally silk was used for various purposes in China, from making clothes and furnishings to materials for painting and writing. The silk industry has always been an important sector in China's state economy from early periods up to the present day.

Lillian M. LI, *China's Silk Trade: Traditional Industry in the Modern World, 1842–1937* (Council on East Asian Studies, Harvard University , 1981).

SILK ROAD *SICHOU ZHI LU* 絲綢之路

Name given to the overland trade route that connected the north-western frontiers of the Chinese Empire with the Middle East from the Han dynasty onwards. Silk 'route' would be a better translation as there was no single road across Central Asia. From **Dunhuang** its northern branch led to either Turfan or Loulan, around the edge of the Tarim Basin to Kashghar, then across the Pamirs to Samarkand, Bokhara and Merv. The alternative route skirted the southern side of the Tarim Basin to Yarkand and crossed the mountains to Balkh, where one branch turned south down the Indus River valley to the coast of north-west India while the main road continued to Merv.

Much of the archaeological work revealing life in the oases and in staging posts at the eastern end of the Road was done in the early twentieth century by **Hedin, Stein** and **Pelliot**, and later at the western end by Sir Mortimer Wheeler. Trade along the Silk Road was in the hands of middlemen, including Central Asian tribes, Persians and Indians. In the Han period the Roman Empire's craving for Chinese **silk** contributed to its economic decline, and at the same time the opening up of this route for the exchange of commodities first brought **Buddhism** into China. In later centuries Dunhuang developed as an important frontier post through which camel trains brought merchants from as far away as Turkey, Syria, Armenia, and Persia. It was along the Silk Road that the first Christian **missionaries** reached China (see **Nestorianism**), and Europeans such as **Marco Polo** discovered the fabled land of **Cathay**. See also **Zhang Qian.**

SILLA

Being the most remote from direct Chinese influence in the south-east corner of the Korean peninsula, Silla was slowest of the three kingdoms there to develop its civilisation along Chinese lines and had the reputation of being the most backward. Its territory was the smallest of the three, and centralised government was only established in the late fifth century. **Buddhism** arrived from southern China and was adopted as the state philosophy in 535. Like **Koguryo** and **Paekche** Silla paid tribute to China, and having combined against Paekche in 660, Silla and Tang together mounted a successful campaign against Koguryo and destroyed it in 668.

Silla thus became, with Chinese help, the first united dynasty to rule the whole of **Korea**. This was not the Chinese intention, however, and the Tang government first endeavoured to create commanderies along the lines of the former **Lelang** to establish its own authority across the country. But Silla drove the Chinese armies out in 676, and thereafter China accepted the inevitability of unified Silla rule with a remarkably good grace, and concentrated on exerting its influence through peaceful channels. Silla, the most sinicised of China's neighbouring vassals, sent 63 missions to **Chang'an** in the eighth century, 45 of them before the **An Lushan Rebellion** in 755. The capital, Kyongju, was laid out along the lines of Chang'an; the government was organised into **Six Boards**; the Chinese calendar and the Chinese script were used; the **Confucian Classics** were studied and practised; Chinese dress was adopted. Koreans in China studied at the **Imperial Academy** in Chang'an; played **music** and danced at court as members of the *Shibu zhi* musical équipe (see **Music Bureau**); studied the Buddhist law in their own monastic communities; loaded cargoes to carry across the seas in Korean ships. Chinese emperors and Korean kings exchanged warm fraternal messages.

The decline of Silla was not unlike that of Tang, as warlordism severely undermined both governments' authority in the second half of the ninth century. By 935 Silla was unable to hold out any longer, and surrendered to Koryo, descendants of Koguryo, in 935.

SIMA GUANG 司馬光 (1019–86)

Prominent statesman and Neo-Confucian historian; author of the ***Zizhi tongjian*** "Comprehensive Mirror for Aid to Government" (1084), which was perhaps the most influential general history of China after **Sima Qian's *Shiji*** and covered the period from 403 BC to AD 959. Its Neo-Confucian purpose is revealed by its title, and it reflects well the current belief in the accumulation of knowledge through investigation as a guide to ideal behaviour. Sima Guang was a conservative politician who stressed the importance of governmental authority and ritual, and argued for a reduction of expenditure on armies and a tighter fiscal administration. He stressed the value of education in the **Confucian Classics** as qualification for office but also believed that more use should be made of the ***yin*** sponsorship system, allowing leading officials to nominate three persons per annum as candidates for the examinations. His comments on foreign policy reveal his suspicion of barbarian motives at a time when relations with **Liao** and **Xi Xia** were generally good. As a leading opponent of **Wang Anshi**'s reforms which had ended his first period of court service, he unilaterally revoked them when he became **Prime Minister** in 1085 and rejected **Su Shi**'s attempted defence of them, but died less than a year later. See also **Neo-Confucianism, Song Dynasty.**

W.G. BEASLEY and E.G. PULLEYBLANK, *Historians of China and Japan* (Oxford University Press, 1961).

SIMA QIAN 司馬遷 (145–c. 86 BC)

Son of Sima Tan 司馬談 (died 110 BC), from whom he inherited the post of Grand Astrologer at the court of the Han Emperor **Wudi**, and author of the greatest of all China's historical works, the ***Shiji*** (Historical Records). He was responsible for the reform of the calendar in 104. The interpretation of signs from heavenly **omens and portents** and from records of past events was envisaged as a guide for current rulers, so the post of Grand Astrologer was concurrently that of Historian. In keeping with the intellectual curiosity implied by this combination of responsibilities and with the scholarly atmosphere of the early Han, Qian showed himself eclectic in his attitude to the materials to be used in his history, drawing not only on written records but on oral tradition. The work was begun by his father, from whom he took it over on his death. It reveals Qian as a typical product of his age, convinced of Heaven's involvement in the affairs of the empire, interested in both **Confucianism** and **Daoism,** critical of **Legalism** and of rulers – such as his own, **Wudi** – who behaved in a despotic manner reminiscent of the First Emperor (see **Qin Shi Huangdi**). If, on the other hand, the *Shiji* shows that his understanding of history was unlike that of anyone before him or among his contemporaries, its exaltation of Chinese tradition and prowess was nevertheless in keeping with the spirit of his age. As a loyal minister of the Martial Emperor Qian was nevertheless unafraid to express the worries that his ruler's policies sometimes stirred in him, and his principled outspokenness brought him imprisonment and castration. His legacy was to have laid down historiographical principles which would form the basis for official history writing in China for two thousand years.

W.B. BEASLEY and E.G. PULLEYBLANK, *Historians of China and Japan* (Oxford University Press, 1961).

SIMA XIANGRU 司馬相如 (c.179–117 BC)

A man of Chengdu who first joined the court of Emperor Han **Jingdi** but soon returned to his native **Shu**. There he eloped with Zhao Wenjun, the widowed daughter of a rich industrialist. Disowned by her family the couple survived by opening a tavern, further sullying their reputation in their parents' eyes but ensuring a place in history as true lovers. Having returned to the court at **Chang'an** to serve under Han **Wudi,** Xiangru acquired special responsibility for the Emperor's policy in the South-west. It is, however, as a poet specialising in the ***fu*** style rather than as a politician that he is now known.

Y. HERVOUET, *Un poète de cour sous les Han: Sseu-ma Siang-jou* (Paris: Presses Universitaires de France, 1964).

SIMLA CONVENTION (1913–14)

Tripartite conference of representatives from China (Ivan Chen), **Tibet** (Lonchen Shatra) and Great Britain (Sir Henry McMahon) principally concerned with the question of Tibetan claims to independence and definition of its frontiers with China. McMahon emerged as mediator betweeen China and Tibet. The most significant clauses to the proposed agreement were (1) the definition of Inner Tibet (the eastern and northern border areas inside the Sichuan and Gansu provincial boundaries) and Outer Tibet (remaining central, western and southern areas); (2) the acknowledgement of China's suzerainty over Tibet concurrently with the recognition of Outer Tibetan autonomy and the refusal to allow China to make a province of Inner Tibet; (3) the barring of Chinese and British troops and agents from Outer Tibet except for an **Amban** with 300 Chinese troops and a British Trade Agent stationed in **Lhasa**. The Chinese government refused to accept the agreement, which was signed by Tibet and Great Britain in July 1914, and by so doing denied itself the opportunity of gaining foreign recognition for its claim to suzerainty over Tibet. In March 1914 Chen and McMahon also agreed the demarcation of the south-western Indo-Tibetan border along the so-called McMahon Line. See also **Anglo-Chinese Convention, Anglo-Russian Convention, Anglo-Tibetan Convention.**

H. RICHARDSON, *Tibet and its History*, 2nd edition (London: Shambhala, 1984); A. LAMB, *The McMakon Line*, 2 volumes (Routledge & Kegan Paul, 1966).

SINGLE WHIP TAX SYSTEM *Yi tiao bian fa* 一條鞭法

The consolidation into one payment of an accumulating variety of taxes, mainly in the second half of the sixteenth century; the first tax to be generally payable in silver. The movement reached a peak in the 1580s and 1590s. Both land and labour dues were to be assessed on the basis of land area, but as the implementation of tax collection was dependent on local **gentry** many ordinary people failed to realise any reduction in their commitments. Implementation of the reforms was also resisted by the **eunuchs**. The tax was continued under the Qing dynasty and from 1687 its collection was the responsibility of the ***lijia*** authorities, an irony since *lijia* was one of the service dues it was originally intended to supplant.

R. HUANG, *Taxation and Governmental Finance in Sixteenth-Century Ming China* (Cambridge University Press, 1974).

SINO-FRENCH WAR (1883–5)

The war of 1883–5 in which China contested the rise of French influence in Annam (Vietnam), hitherto under Chinese suzerainty. France sent forces to Vietnam in the late 1850s ostensibly to protect French and other foreign

Catholic priests and their native converts. Gradually France expanded its sphere of influence to include most of Laos, Cambodia and Vietnam. Vietnam recognised Chinese suzerainty through its regular tribute missions and the Chinese were unwilling to concede the loss of this influence and the encroachment of France into south-west China. French victories led to the **Li-Fournier convention** of May 1884 agreeing to the withdrawal of Chinese forces and acknowledging France's position in Vietnam. Chinese conservatives successfully pressed the court to reject **Li Hongzhang**'s negotiated settlement and the war continued for a further year in which France scored notable naval victories (destroying Zuo Zongtang's Fuzhou shipyard) but were less overwhelmingly successful on land. The Chinese court recognised the need to settle and Li Hongzhang signed a peace treaty on the basis of his earlier convention in June 1885. The war exposed China's continued military weakness, in spite of the Self-Strengthening Movement, and the inability of the central government to act effectively and decisively.

SINO-JAPANESE WAR (1894–5)

Conflict over influence in **Korea**, a tributary state of China, and a country in which the rulers of Meiji Japan had taken an interest since 1873. Japan attempted to open Korean ports to trade in 1876 and in 1879 annexed the Liuqiu (Ryukyu) archipelago which runs from Kyushu to Taiwan, as part of its imperial expansion. Japanese influence in Korea continued to increase and by 1884, it was almost a joint protectorate of China and Japan. Chinese troops were called in by the Korean King Kojong to suppress an anti-government rising by the Tonghak rebels that had broken out on March 17 1894. On June 2, the Japanese cabinet also ordered their troops into Korea and set up an encampment near Seoul on June 5. On July 23, Japanese troops captured the imperial palace in Seoul, kidnapped the Queen and her family and attacked Chinese positions. A formal declaration of war was made on August 1. China was comprehensively defeated at sea and on land and after Japan broke through the fortifications at Weihaiwei, China agreed to sign the **Treaty of Shimonoseki**.

SINO-JAPANESE WAR (1937–1945) see **ANTI-JAPANESE WAR**

SINO-SOVIET DISPUTE

Friction between the Communist Parties of the USSR and China in the 1960s. Stalin's lukewarm support for the CCP in the 1920s and 1930s provided a weak basis for the alliance established in 1949 and the problems were exacerbated by tensions over Soviet influence in Manchuria and Xinjiang. After Stalin's death in 1953, relations became more friendly, but when Khrushchev denounced Stalin in his closed-session speech to the twentieth congress of the CPSU in February 1956, the CCP were not prepared to accept an attack on the leader on whom Mao had modelled himself. Policy disagreements became more and more pronounced and culminated in 1958 in the failure of the USSR to support China in the **Great Leap Forward** or the crisis over Jinmen. The disagreements were open by the **Moscow Conference** of 1960 and Soviet specialist advisers were withdrawn from China in the same year. China and the USSR attacked each other in print in code, China referring to Yugoslavia and the USSR to Albania instead of their opponents. China attacked the USSR as "new tsars", "social imperialists" and "revisionists" and these denunciations became even more vitriolic during the **Cultural Revolution**. Tensions on the Sino-Soviet border spilled over into violence in clashes on the Ussuri river island of Zhebao (Damanskiy) in March 1969.

O. Edmund CLUBB, *China and Russia: The Great Game* (Columbia University Press, 1971); Donald ZAGORIA, *The Sino-Soviet Conflict, 1956 – 1961* (Princeton University Press, 1962); G.F. HUDSON, Richard LOWETHAL and Roderick MACFARQUHAR, *The Sino-Soviet Dispute* (New York: Praeger, 1961).

SINO-SOVIET TREATY OF FRIENDSHIP, ALLIANCE AND MUTUAL ASSISTANCE

Diplomatic basis for the apparent unity of China and the USSR signed on February 14 1950. An aid programme was agreed and China agreed to accept the independence of Mongolia and the continued involvement of the USSR in Manchuria and Xinjiang. Tensions over these issues led to the **Sino-Soviet Dispute**.

SISHEN 四神 "Four deities"

The four supernatural beings symbolising the four quadrants of the sky and the earth, and the four seasons. They are: *qinglong* 青龍, the blue dragon, symbolising the East and spring; *baihu* 白虎, the white tiger, symbolising the West and autumn; *zhuque* 朱雀, the vermilion bird, symbolising the South and summer; *xuanwu* 玄武, the black warrior in the form of a turtle and a serpent, symbolising the North and winter. With its mystical reference to eternity and its supernatural power to exorcise evil spirits, the theme of *sishen* prevailed in the Han period, especially in the decoration of mirrors, buildings and gravestones. *Sishen* were also used at many royal burials of the later dynasties. The fabulous creatures of *sishen* were originally associated with the constellations of ancient astronomy. It appears that they did not come into existence simultaneously: the dragon and tiger were used in Neolithic burials, but the black warrior did not appear until the Zhou period.

SIX BOARDS *Liubu* 六部

Principal government ministries constituting the heart of civil administration from the Sui dynasty to the Qing, comprising (1) Civil Appointments (*libu* 吏部), dealing with all staffing matters related to central and provincial government; (2) Finance and Revenue (*minbu* 民部 or *hubu* 戶部), responsible for official salaries, population registration, taxation, state monopolies, commerce and transportation; (3) Rites (*libu* 禮部), covering not only important details of imperial ceremonial and music but also the operation of the **tribute system** and **examination system**; (4) the Army (*bingbu* 兵部), handling military staffing, ceremonial, communications, and having a say in military policy formation; (5) Justice (*xingbu* 刑部), including the entire process from legal drafting to organisation of the courts and the implementation of justice and the running of gaols; (6) Public Works (*gongbu* 工部), dealing with the essential business of building and maintaining imperial temples, tombs and shrines; city walls and official buildings; roads, bridges and canals; state granaries; dams, dykes, locks and irrigation works. The Office of Transmission handled communication between the Six Boards and their respective provincial offices through which

business was carried on. See also **Censorate, Grand Council, Grand Secretariat, Outer Court.**
P.C. HSIEH, *The Government of China (1644 – 1911)* (New York: Octagon, 1966)

SIX DYNASTIES
Name given to the period between the fall of the Han dynasty in AD 220 and the reunification of the country by the Sui dynasty in 589. It comprises the Three Kingdoms (220–263/266/280), the Jin dynasty (266–316), and in northern China the period of the Sixteen Kingdoms (304–86), the Northern Wei (386–534), the Eastern Wei (534–50) and the Northern Zhou (557–81) dynasties. See also **Northern and Southern Dynasties.**

SIYI 四藝 "four arts"
A popular theme in decorative art, made up of the lute *qin*, the game of *weiqi* 圍棋, and scrolls of **painting** and **calligraphy**, referring to the four arts to be mastered by a well-educated gentleman. The same theme is also represented, especially in painting, as *siyi yaju* 四藝雅聚 "the gathering of the four arts", with the images of the most celebrated masters of the four arts: Yu Boya 俞伯牙 playing the *qin*, Wang Yi 王奕 playing *weiqi*, **Wang Xizhi** doing calligraphy and **Wang Wei** painting.

SMALL SWORD SOCIETY ***Xiaodaohui*** 小刀會
Triad branch which took control of the walled Chinese section of Shanghai from September 1853 until it was retaken by French and local Jiangsu troops on February 17 1855. The insurrection ran in parallel with the **Taiping Rebellion** but did not receive Taiping support as Hong Xiuquan was concerned about the influence other **secret societies** might have in his crusade.

SNEEVLIET see **MARING**

SNOW, EDGAR (1905–1972)
American journalist. Snow's *Red Star over China*, published in 1937, was the first first-hand account of life in the **Yan'an** base of the CCP. His writing after the formation of the PRC was broadly sympathetic to the efforts of the CCP to create a New China.

SOCIAL IMPERIALISM ***Shehui diguo zhuyi*** 社會帝國主義
Chinese term for Soviet policies during the Cultural Revolution. See **Sino-Soviet Dispute**.

SOCIALIST EDUCATION MOVEMENT ***Shehuizhuyi jiaoyu yundong*** 社會主義教育運動
Preamble to the **Cultural Revolution**. Although Chinese politics from 1962–5 appeared stable under the compromise coalition that had emerged from the conflict at the **Lushan Plenum**, there was a new polarisation below the surface. The initial aim of the Socialist Education Movement was to restore collectivisation and reverse the decentralisation of commune management that had followed the famines, but it rapidly became refocussed on grassroots corruption in the countryside. At the Tenth

Plenum of the Central Committee of the Chinese Communist Party of September 1962 there was a call for the party to focus on the shortcomings of cadres and the need for class struggle. In December 1962 the ***Si qing*** 四清 (Four Cleanups) campaign was launched on an experimental basis to investigate corruption in the administration of collective accounts, communal granaries, public property and work points. The campaign concentrated on reforming the rural leadership and using *Xiafang* 下放, the sending down of experienced urban cadres to replace or reinforce the existing leaders.

R. BAUM and Frederic C. TEIWES, *Ssu-ch'ing: The Socialist Education Movement of 1962–66* (Berkeley: University of California Press, *1968).*

SON OF HEAVEN Tianzi 天子

Title first attributed to the supreme state ruler in the Western Zhou dynasty and cited in the ***Shijing*** and on **bronze inscriptions**, reflecting the Zhou belief that Heaven took an active interest in the government of its people on earth. As its delegate, the Son of Heaven was theoretically responsible for the well-being of the people of the whole world (*tianxia* 天下), though in practice the Chinese emperor never tried to assume such a duty or right. In the **imperial era** Confucian political philosophy maintained both the concept of the **Mandate of Heaven** and the view that Heaven's reaction to the emperor's rule might be judged by the occurrence of favourable or unfavourable **omens and portents**. The Son of Heaven had no divine status, and despite the implications of his title had no claim to be omniscient or omnipotent. He had no constitution to guide him other than the contents of the Confucian Classics and the accumulated weight of precedent from own imperial ancestors and other previous dynasts. He possessed supreme legislative, executive and military powers, but was expected to take decisions and issue edicts in conjunction with the advice of senior courtiers and officials. Though expected to maintain **sacrifices** to Heaven, Earth, and Confucius he was not forbidden to profess belief in religions such as **Daoism** or **Buddhism**.

Inheritance of the throne was normally according to primogeniture, though it was not uncommon for an emperor to nominate a younger and more suitable son as his heir apparent. Since emperors often sired many sons, rivalry to obtain the nomination was common and often intense. Many a candidate died young or in suspicious circumstances. Not infrequently did emperors succeed as minors, when they might find themselves prey to unscrupulous and contending advisors, especially **eunuchs**, and even to physical danger. The boy Emperors Gongdi and Shundi both died violent deaths in 420 and 479. Even in their majority emperors might find themselves dominated by over-mighty courtiers (see **Huo Guang**) or relatives (see **Guangxu Emperor**). The Tang Emperor Ruizong was forced to abdicate in favour of his own mother (see **Wu Zetian**), and the last Ming Son of Heaven, Zhuang Liedi (**Chongzhen**), committed suicide. Of course, emperors sometimes proved to be forceful characters and autocratic rulers. Examples include Wu Zetian and Ming Taizu (see **Hongwu**). And sometimes the capacity to blend principle and statecraft produced a great emperor who almost lived up to the example of King **Wen**. One such was a foreign Son of Heaven, the Manchu **Kangxi Emperor**. See also **Grand Council, Inner Court, Outer Court, Prime Minister, Six Boards.**

F.W. HOUN, *Chinese Political Traditions* (Washington, 1985); H. KAHN, *Monarchy in the Emperor's Eyes : Image and Reality in the Ch'ien-lung Reign* (Harvard University Press, 1971); Jonathan SPENCE, *Emperor of China: Self-Portrait of Kang-hsi* (New York: Knopf, 1974); H.J. WECHSLER, *Mirror to the Son of Heaven: Wei Cheng at the Court of Tang T'ai-tsung* (Yale University Press, 1974).

SONG DYNASTY 宋朝 (Northern Song 960–1125; Southern Song 1125–1279) The chronological profile of the Song dynasty is divided, like those of the Zhou (by the removal of the capital in 771 BC), the Han (by **Wang Mang**) and the Tang (by **An Lushan**), into two halves. Under the Northern Song the whole country – reunited under **Taizu** and his brother **Taizong** – was ruled from **Kaifeng**. After the loss of North China to the **Jurchen** invaders in 1125–7 (see **Aguda, Huizong**) the court fled to the **Yangzi** valley, where it reestablished its regime in **Hangzhou** and continued to reign throughout the period known as the Southern Song.

Neither in political nor military terms was the Song a strong dynasty. Autocratic as they inevitably were, the early emperors succeeded in creating the efficient administration and growing economy of a newly united empire after a period of division. But the traumatic collapse of the Tang bequeathed a new and unsettling spirit of debate which questioned the very foundations of the traditional imperial order. It was symbolised by the radical reform measures attempted by **Wang Anshi** and the bitter conservative backlash against them, and by the **Neo-Confucian** reevaluation of history, government, society, and culture as scholars struggled to understand where the Tang had gone wrong, and how the ideal principles of the universe could be applied to life in the new era. Political factionalism rent the court for much of the eleventh and early twelfth centuries, and even patriots of mighty intellectual powers such as **Su Shi** were more than once subjected to periods of exile. The debate took place against growing foreign pressure. The **Khitan** threatened north China, the Tibetans the north-west (see **Xi Xia**). To both the Middle Kingdom had to pay tribute in the eleventh century (see **Shanyuan**), whilst even the usually loyal vassal **Korea** diverted its tribute to Liao and Jin. The Chinese world order was being challenged, and the Jurchen capture of Emperor Qinzong and his father Huizong confirmed it.

Yet such important developments took place against this unpromising backdrop that some historians have dubbed this the beginning of the modern age in China. An industrial revolution based on mining, **porcelain** and textile manufacture, **paper** and **printing** went hand in hand with urbanisation and developments in the building and entertainment industries (see **Musical Entertainment**). Consumer demand encouraged diversification of output, while official encouragement of domestic and overseas commerce stimulated shipbuilding and brought increased tax revenues. The countryside benefited too, from improved crops and better equipment, though it was generally the landlords rather than their tenant farmers who reaped the profits.

In scholarship and the arts the effects of both the Neo-Confucian enquiry and social changes are apparent. Major **encyclopaedias** were compiled and comprehensive histories were written (see **Sima Guang, *Zizhi tongjian***). The expansion of education was accompanied by the canonisation of the book of **Mencius** as the last of the **Thirteen Classics** of Confucianism, and the composition of numerous commentaries on all aspects of cosmological and human philosophy culminated in **Zhu Xi's** synthesis of the practical and the abstract. Artists conveyed their sense of man's relationship with nature in outstanding paintings of landscape and flower and bird subjects (see **Landscape Painting**). **Poetry** and the performing arts responded to the taste of the new class of city dwellers, as did the manufacturers of fine porcelain (see **Ceramics**). The effects of numerous scientific and technological **inventions and discoveries** were felt, including movable type printing, the **compass**, textile machinery, **gunpowder** and paddle-wheel ships. What is remarkable, however, is the failure to realise the potential of these advances, either economically or scientifically. For this the conservative self-interest of the literati elite, fearing the effects of unforeseeable change on a society which they only understood in traditional terms, is to blame. They sought to recreate the greatness of Tang rather than to look into the future. It was the Chinese, therefore, who stifled their own enterprise in the long term. In the short term they had all they needed to resist the **Mongol** invaders: greater manpower, technological superiority, and "home ground" advantage, but though their armies fought bravely in the final campaigns, it was the deeper failure of the leadership to realise that times were changing and that diplomatic and military strategy had to change too that lost them their country.

Emperors:

Northern Song:

Taizu	960–76
Taizong	976–97
Zhenzong	997–1022
Renzong	1022–63
Yingzong	1063–7
Shenzong	1067–85
Zhizong	1085–1100
Huizong	1100–26

Southern Song:

Gaozong	1127–62
Xiaozong	1162–89
Guangzong	1189–94
Ningzong	1194–1224
Lizong	1224–1264
Duzong	1264–74
Gongzong	1274–75
Duanzong	1275–7
Dibing	1278–9

R.P HYMES and C. SCHIROKAUER, eds., *Ordering the World: Approaches to State and Society in Sung Dynasty China* (Berkeley: University of California Press, 1993); Dieter KUHN, *Die Song-Dynastie (960 bis 1279)* (Weinheim: Acta Humanista, 1987); Brian E. MCKNIGHT, *Village and Bureaucracy in Southern Sung China* (University of Chicago Press, 1972; Jacques GERNET, *Daily Life in China on the Eve of the Mongol Invasion, 1250–1276*, trans. H.M. Wright (Stanford University Press, 1962).

SONG JIAOREN 宋教仁 (1882–1913)
Founder member of the ***Tongmenghui*** in 1905 with Sun Yixian. He was influential in the Revolution of 1911 and became the leader of the Guomindang which was formed when the *Tongmenghui* absorbed other nationalist groups in 1912. He was a trenchant critic of **Yuan Shikai**, whose supporters assassinated him during the **Second Revolution**.

K.S. LIEW, *Struggle for Democracy: Sung Chiao-jen and the 1911 Chinese Revolution* (Berkeley: University of California Press, 1971).

SONG MEILING 宋美齡 (1897–)
Wife of **Jiang Jieshi** and younger sister of **Song Qingling** and Song Ailing. Educated in the USA, a fluent English speaker and a professed Methodist, Song Meiling played an important role in Nationalist China's propaganda effort during the Anti-Japanese War.

SONG QI 宋祈 (998–1061)
Co-compiler with **Ouyang Xiu** of the *Xintangshu (New Tang History)*, who urged reform of the **examination system** during the chancellorship of **Fan Zhongyan**.

SONG QINGLING 宋慶齡 (1892–)
Wife of Sun Yixian and after his death a leading member of the left wing of the Guomindang, who supported the call for an alliance with the CCP in 1949 and played a prominent role in PRC politics.

SONG YINGXING 宋應星 (c.1615–c.1660)
Author of **Tiangong kaiwu** 'Creations of Nature and Man', the 17th century compendium on technology.

SUNG Ying-hsing, *T'ien-kung K'ai-wu: Chinese Technology in the Seventeenth Century*, trans. E-tu Zen Sun and Shiou-chuan Sun (Pennsylvania University Press, 1966).

SONGTSEN GAMPO (608–649, r. 618–641 and 646–9)
King of **Tibet** who consolidated control over the territories of the preceding Yarlung valley kingdom, central **Tibet** and the northern plateau which he had inherited from his father. He established **Lhasa** as the capital of the new state and built up international recognition for its military strength across Central Asia. Embassies had been sent to the Sui emperor **Yangdi's** court in 607 and 608. Songtsen Gampo's first mission was sent to Tang **Taizong** in 634, and was followed up by a request for a Chinese princess in marriage. In 641 Princess Wen Cheng arrived in Lhasa to join the King's Nepalese wife Princess Bhrikuti. Under their influence he became a convinced Buddhist. He introduced laws reflecting Buddhist values, propagated educational measures including the introduction of the Tibetan script, and the Chinese Emperor **Gaozong** bestowed upon him the title of Bao Wang, "Precious King". This was also an epithet applied to the **Amitabha** Buddha, and the King has subsequently been recognised as this deity's reincarnation. He was succeeded by his son in 641, but resumed the throne on the latter's premature death in 646. He was the founder of

the Tubo dynasty, which later included another outstanding patron of **Buddhism**, King Trisong Detsen (755–797).

SOONG DYNASTY

Nickname for the influential Song (Soong) family in Nationalist China during the 1920s and 1930s. T.V. Soong (Song) was a financier who helped to underwrite the **Northern Expedition** and became Finance Minister in the GMD government. His sisters were Song Ailing who married the industrialist H.H.Kong, **Song Qingling** and **Song Meiling**.

SPIRIT AVENUES

Two parallel lines of stone statues leading to a tumulus and underground tomb, through which the coffin of a deceased emperor was carried to its resting place. The figures might comprise civil (*wen*) and military (*wu*) officials, or, as in the case of the **Ming Tombs** to the north of **Beijing** where a single avenue serves the tombs of the entire valley, a combination of human beings, animals and mythological beasts. Their purpose was to guard and bless the departing spirit.
Ann PALUDAN, *The Chinese Spirit Road* (Yale University Press, 1991).

SOUTH MANCHURIAN RAILWAY

Line linking the **Chinese Eastern Railway** with Port Arthur and Dalian. It was built in 1898 by Russia but taken over by Japan after the **Sino-Japanese War** and played a decisive role in the expansion of Japan's power in China. The South Manchurian Railway Company, which managed the line, became a colonial power in its own right, with its own police and a research department that published useful studies of economic and social conditions in Manchuria and north China. Under the terms of the Potsdam Treaty signed by the UK, the USA and the USSR in July 1945, the railway was to remain under joint Russian and Chinese control for thirty years and this was also a condition of the **Sino-Soviet Treaty of Friendship, Alliance and Mutual Assistance** concluded in 1950, although the railway was returned to China in 1953.

SOVIET TECHNICIAN WITHDRAWAL see **SINO-SOVIET DISPUTE**

SPECIAL ECONOMIC ZONES *Jingji tequ* 經濟特區

Designated regions of the PRC allowed to receive foreign investment as part of Deng Xiaoping's **Reform and Opening** policy. The first zones were Shenzhen, Zhuhai and Shantou in Guangdong province and Xiamen in Fujian which were chosen in 1979; fourteen other areas and Hainan island were added in 1986.

***SPRING AND AUTUMN ANNALS* *Chunqiu* 春秋**

Annalistic text covering the history of the state of **Lu** and one of the **Five Classics** of Confucianism. The brief basic text describes laconically events in the reigns of twelve Dukes of Lu in the period from 722–481 BC (hence this time is known as the Spring and Autumn period). However, the text is now always transmitted with one of its commentaries: the *Gongyang* 公羊, *Guliang* 谷梁 or ***Zuozhuan*** 左傳, the former two being based on new text versions, of the *Chunqiu* and the latter on an old text version. Since the text deals with the state of Lu, **Confucius**' home state, and ends around the time of his death it has traditionally been closely associated with him. The commentaries, which in the case of the *Gongyang* and *Guliang* take the form of questions and answers, were believed to be written versions of the oral comments Confucius made on the text to his disciples elucidating the praise and blame methodology said to have been incorporated into the text of the classic. **Mencius** suggested that Confucius wrote the *Chunqiu* in order to condemn through his subtle use of language the decadence of his age. To regard the *Zuozhuan* as a commentary is more problemmatical: this text is much longer than the other two, it covers a further 18 years down to 463 BC and the text and 'commentary' do not always coincide. The *Zuozhuan* may have been originally an independent work but it does provide much additional historical information on events described in the classic.

Burton WATSON trans., *The Tso Chuan. Selections from China's Oldest Narrative History* (Columbia University Press, 1989).

SPRING AND AUTUMN PERIOD

Title popularly ascribed to the years 722 to 481 BC, the period covered by the extant historical records of the state of **Lu** which bear the name ***Spring and Autumn Annals*** (*Chunqiu*). It was an era when Zhou authority was fast declining and the pattern of relationships between the separate states, all but independent though still nominally recognising Zhou feudal overlordship, had not settled down. It is characterised by shifting alliances resulting from marriage, battle, and perceived political advantage, by the growth of bureaucracy, trade and towns, and the development of the concept of loyalty to the state rather than to the feudal suzerain. The art of diplomacy and new concepts of inter-state relations helped give rise to the **Hundred Schools** of thought, representing men's attempts to explain and control the new world in which they recognised themselves to be. The most important states were those of **Qi, Jin, Chu, Qin, Wu,** Yan, **Lu,** Song, and Yue. By the end of the period the old ideas of a balance of power and of the accepted hegemony of one or other mighty state over its lesser neighbours had gone, and in the succeeding Warring States period overall domination became the goal. See also **Hegemons.**

R.L. WALKER, *The Multi-state System of Ancient China* (Hamsden, Conn.: The Shoe-String Press, 1953); Cho-yun HSU, *Ancient China in Transition* (Stanford University Press, 1965).

SPROUTS OF CAPITALISM see **CAPITALISM, SPROUTS OF**

STATE COUNCIL ***Guowu yuan*** 國務院

The highest administrative body in the PRC, created under the 1954 Constitution, and responsible for supervising the various ministries. It is chaired by the Prime Minister and the deputy Prime Ministers and Ministers are members. It normally has a full meeting on a monthly basis and a Standing Committee meets weekly. The State Economic Commission and State Planning Commission which oversaw annual economic plans and long-range planning respectively were Commissions of the State Council as are the State Commission for Restructuring the economy and the State Education Commission created during the **reform and Opening Period**.

STEIN, SIR AUREL (1862–1943)
Hungarian-born, naturalised British explorer whose expeditions between 1900 and 1915 did most to open up the **Silk Road** to modern archaeologists and historians. He is particularly associated with the discovery of the walled-up caves at **Dunhuang** in 1907, and the despatch of many of their treasures to the British Museum.
A. WALKER, *Aurel Stein: Pioneer of the Silk Road* (London: John Murray, 1995).

STILWELL, GEN. JOSEPH (1883–1946)
American adviser to **Jiang Jieshi**, sent to Chongqing by President Roosevelt after Pearl Harbour as Commander-in-Chief of Allied forces in the China-Burma-India theatre of the war. He was universally known as "Vinegar Joe". Although he knew China well and spoke Chinese, his poor working relationship with Jiang, for whom he had little respect, caused much conflict. In particular, he was critical of Jiang's reluctance to commit troops against the Japanese, preferring to save them for the coming battles with the CCP. In 1944, he was relieved of his command at the request of Jiang Jieshi and replaced by General Albert Wedemeyer.

STORY OF THE STONE see ***HONGLOUMENG***

STREET COMMITTEE or **Neighbourhood committee *Juweihui*** 居委會
Lowest level of administration in towns and cities in the PRC, operating from a neighbourhood office and run by selected local residents. It has been used to control both crime and dissent and has had an important role in enforcing major campaigns such as the one-child policy.

SOUTHERN MING (NANMING) 南明
Regime established in southern China, based on Nanjing, by **Ming loyalists** after the **Manchu** Qing conquests of 1644. It was ineffective and collapsed under pressure from the Manchu and Chinese collaborators and the only effective resistance was carried out by **Koxinga.**

SU CHE 蘇轍 **(1039–1112)**
Younger son of **Su Xun**, brother of **Su Shi**. A **Hanlin** Academician and one of the Eight Masters of [Tang and Song] Prose. His political career was greatly affected by the factionalism of the eleventh century. He himself opposed **Wang Anshi**'s New Policies and in the wake of their repeal rose to high office between 1092 and 1094. Disgraced again when Emperor Zhizong restored the reformers, he was restored to favour in 1100, only to lose it after 1103 as **Huizong** patronised **Cai Jing** and his radicalism.

SU DONGPO 蘇東坡 **(1037–1101)**
Leading statesman and aesthete; outstanding poet, painter and calligrapher. Born Su Shi 蘇軾 into a distinguished scholarly family in Sichuan, Su Dongpo was renowned, alongside his father Su Xun and his brother Su Che, as one of the Eight Great Prose Masters of the Tang and Song. Su Dongpu gained his *jinshi* degree in 1057, but his official career was punctuated by periods of demotion and exile, resulting from his unrestrained criticism. He was an accomplished and

prolific writer and artist in many different genres. He is particularly renowned for his *shi* poems (over 2700 are still extant) and his contribution to the development of *ci* poetry. His literary and artistic production is epitomised by its spontaneity, but nevertheless noted for being substantial in content and not showy in style.

H. FRANKE, ed., *Sung Biographies* (Wiesbaden: Franz Steiner Verlag GmbH, 1976); Burton WATSON, *Su Tung-p'o: Selections from a Sung Dynasty Poet* (Columbia University Press, 1965); LIN Yutang, *The Gay Genius* (New York: J. Day Co., 1947).

SU SHI see **SU DONGPO**

SU XUN 蘇洵 (1009–66)

An independent and stylish writer of political essays whose reputation was boosted by the support of **Ouyang Xiu**. One of the Eight Masters of [Tang and Song] Prose. Father of **Su Shi** and **Su Che.**

SUFAN MOVEMENT Movement for the Suppression of Counter Revolutionaries (1951) *Sufan yundong* 肅反運動

Major campaign launched by the CCP in 1949 after **Liberation** to remove all opposition to the new regime. Between January and October 1950, there were 13,812 arrests of people accused of being counter-revolutionary agents. Zhou Enlai signed a Cabinet order on July 23 ordering the more active pursuit of counter-revolutionaries. The movement explicitly followed the example of Stalin's purges in the USSR during the 1930s with *Peoples Daily* quoting from his 1937 speech in an editorial on December 29 1950. The *Regulation on Suppression of Counter-Revolutionaries* was published on February 21 1951 and set out severe penalties, including death sentences, even for those deemed to have opposed the Communist Party before it came to power. The movement was aimed primarily at spies and those who were actively resisting the new government, particularly former members of the Guomindang and organisations associated with it and leaders of secret societies. The campaign was carried out in part through the courts but it was also a mass movement which is said to have involved eighty per cent of the population. There were mass meetings where alleged counter-revolutionaries were denounced and executed, individuals were forced to denounce people they knew and factories, schools, government offices and street organisations established their own Cleansing of Counter-Revolutionaries Committees to supply names to the security forces and the police. One concrete example of how a mass meeting was organised was described in the edition of *Xinhua Monthly* published in April 1951. The meeting was led by **Peng Zhen**, Mayor of Beijing and Secretary of the Beijing City Party Committee who was also first Deputy Chairman of the Cabinet's Political Legal Commission. Peng reportedly called enthusiastically for the executions of those accused who included workers, peasants, secondary school students and members of Daoist secret societies, or rather he persuaded the assembled crowd of 5,000 to call for the executions. A second mass meeting in May 1951 was organised by Peng Zhen and Luo Ruiqing, Security Minister and in charge of security in the capital and a number of "counter-revolutionaries" were sentenced to death or life imprisonment (technically a death sentence suspended for two years). Luo Ruiqing, addressing the meeting announced that 199 counter-revolutionaries had been executed in Beijing since the March meeting. He continued:

"A great number of people have denounced counter-revolutionaries. Wives have denounced their counter-revolutionary husbands; children have denounced their fathers. Young students have caught counter-revolutionaries and brought them to the security offices. This shows that the great propaganda has moved the masses to struggle against the counter-revolutionaries and that the People's Government and the People struggle together. Accusation meetings have been held in many quarters of Beijing, and a total of 200,000 people have taken part in them. Many have written letters to the police. Many, however, have not dared to sign their letters in fear of revenge. The masses have nothing to fear. The government will eradicate the counter-revolutionaries totally. In recent days we have examined the cases of 500 persons. Most of them were denounced by others; 221 will be executed"

Daoist secret society members were also among the 277 killed and 56 sentenced to life imprisonment on July 10 1951 during the campaign in Tianjin, along with members of a **Buddhist** organisation known as the New Buddhist World Association.

It is difficult to get any precise idea of the scale of the campaign and particularly the number of people killed. A figure of 500,000 to 800,000 deaths based on a statement by Mao in 1957 is often quoted but it is impossible to say whether this referred to the campaign specifically or whether it also included deaths in the last stages of the Civil War and land reform. The psychological pressures of forced confessions in small groups and mass meetings are also said to have led to hundreds of thousands of suicides.

SUI DYNASTY 隋朝 (581–618)

Short-lived regime of two emperors whose combined efforts achieved much success in reuniting the country after the long divisions of the Northern and Southern Dynasties. The story of their uncompromising methods and grandiose ambitions and the inevitable popular reaction against them invites comparisons with the Qin dynasty. But as in the case of the Qin they fulfilled an essential role in laying the groundwork for the great dynasty that was to follow (see **Tang).** The main achievements that contributed to the restoration of single imperial authority included improved administration, economic reforms (see **Equal Field System**), and territorial aggrandisement. A unified and simplified law code was introduced. A series of relief granaries were built to supplement the five principal repositories for tax grain, stored in case of future hard times. Immense labour and cost were expended on palace and city construction, especially in **Chang'an, Luoyang** and Yangzhou. The rebuilding of the **Great Wall** was linked to a military and diplomatic programme that removed the threat from the Eastern Turks. The **Yangzi** and **Yellow River** valleys were linked by newly dug canals with a further extension up to the North-east. The borders of the Empire were pushed southwards into northern **Annam** and expeditions sent against southern Annam and **Taiwan,** though in the North-east the costly but unsuccessful invasion of **Koguryo** in 612 pushed the sufferings of the people beyond further endurance. It precipitated revolt at home and when followed by defeat at the hands of the Eastern Turks proved fatal to the dynasty's fortunes. See also**Wendi, Yangdi.**

Arthur F. WRIGHT, *The Sui Dynasty: The Unification of China, AD 581–617* (New York: Knopf, 1978).

SUIYUAN 綏遠
Provincial administrative unit in Northern China in the Republican period. It was formally abolished on March 6 1954 and the land it had controlled was assimilated into the Inner Mongolian Autonomous Region.

SUMMER PALACES
Emperors and their courts would retreat from the heat and dust of their city palaces in summer and seek cooler air in the hills outside. The early Qing emperors built an imitation of the Great Fifth **Dalai Lama's** Potala Palace (see **Lhasa**) at **Rehe** (now Chengde) north of **Beijing**. The Dalai Lamas themselves left the Potala for the Norbulinka Palace in a grand annual procession. In the mid-eighteenth century the **Qianlong Emperor** commissioned the Jesuit Fr **Castiglione** to design the Yuanmingyuan close to the Fragrant Hills, five miles to the North-west of Beijing. Its buildings were in italianate and neo-classical style and its gardens decorated with lakes and mechanical fountains. All were destroyed in 1860 when the Anglo-French expeditionary force attacked Beijing (see **Arrow War**). The Palace was reconstructed as the Yiheyuan late in the nineteenth century by the Empress Dowager **Cixi**, misappropriating funds intended for the Board of Admiralty.

SUN WU 孫武
Military strategist of the fourth century BC who according to the ***Shiji*** had been punished by the amputation of his feet in his native state of **Wei**, thus earning the nickname Sun Bin 孫臏 "Sun the cripple". He then served successfully as a commander in neighbouring **Qi** and later in **Wu**. He is credited with the authorship of the ***Sunzi Bingfa*** "Sunzi's Art of War".

SUN YAT-SEN see **SUN YIXIAN**

SUN YIXIAN 孫逸仙 (1866–1925)
Twentieth-century Republican leader respected by both CCP and GMD politicians as founding father of modern China. Sun Yat-sen is the Cantonese version of his formal given name or style, Yixian. He was also known as Sun Wen 孫文, Wen being his personal name, but in China he is always Sun Zhongshan 孫中山, Zhongshan being the Chinese pronunciation of Nakayama, the surname he used while in Japan. Sun was born to a farming family in Guangdong in the county of Xiangshan (now renamed Zhongshan in his honour) near the Portuguese possession of Macao. Like many from that province, he emigrated and in 1879, joined his elder brother in Honolulu. Sun was educated at various Anglican schools and studied medicine in Hong Kong. He practised in Macao briefly but moved to Guangzhou in 1893, where he rapidly transformed himself into a professional radical politician. After a failed insurrection in 1894, he was forced to flee and went to Japan, the USA and eventually to London where he was kidnapped and briefly imprisoned in the Chinese Legation. (See **Cantlie, Dr. James**). In 1897, he returned to Japan, where he developed his political ideas in a series of lectures later to be

published as the *Three Peoples Principles*. In 1905, he became head of a radical alliance, the ***Tongmenghui***, with **Huang Xing** and **Song Jiaoren** as his main lieutenants. When the imperial system came to an abrupt end after the **Revolution of 1911**, Sun was the clear favourite among radical politicians to serve as President of the new republic and was elected on October 29 1911, but he resigned in favour of **Yuan Shikai** on April 1 1912, after Yuan had threatend to split the newly reunified country. Sun tried to construct a new Chinese Revolutionary Party and made alliances with warlords in Guangzhou, as well as cultivating the newly formed Communist International, which led to the agreement on cooperation with the CCP that he signed with Adolph **Joffe**. He died in 1925 and was succeeded by **Jiang Jieshi**.

C. Martin WILBUR, *Sun Yat-sen, Frustrated Patriot* (Columbia University Press, 1976).

SUN-JOFFE MANIFESTO see **Joffe, Adolph**

SUNZI BINGFA *孫子兵法 Sunzi's Art of War*

The most celebrated work in Chinese history on military strategy. This work is traditionally ascribed to **Sun Wu** 孫武, said to have lived around 500 BC, and has been enormously influential throughout Chinese history right up to the present day (it was extravagantly praised by **Mao Zedong** and is the subject of a recent interpretative study by a PLA general, Tao Hanzhang). The brief text is divided into 13 *pian* each discussing an aspect of the topic: for example, the first *pian, Ji* 計, is on preparatory planning and the following two *pian* are on economic, political and diplomatic stratagems. The key factors Sunzi stresses are good intelligence and the use of deception. The book is the only extant example of a handbook on military tactics compiled during the Warring States era. It is a comprehensive analysis of the principles and conduct of warfare, emphasizing the importance of sound information about the enemy, a detailed knowledge of battleground topography, the advantages of psychological offensive, and the value of tactical withdrawals and redeployment of forces. All of these may be summed up under the heading of guerilla warfare, and the book has continued to be used as a practical manual to the present day. It contributed to **Mao Zedong's** success in the Chinese **Civil War** and Ho Chi Minh's during the Vietnam War (1956–72). The text was believed by many scholars to date from the later Warring States or even later (the traditional version was edited by **Cao Cao**) but a recently excavated version confirms its authenticity and early date (now estimated as early fifth century BC).

SUNZI, Sun Tzu, *The Art of War trans. Ralph D. Sawyer* (Boulder, Colorado: Westview Press, 1994); Roger T. AMES, *Sun-tzu: the Art of Warfare. A New Translation Incorporating the Recently Discovered Yin-chüe-shan Texts* (New York: Ballantine Books, 1993); TAO Hanzhang, *Sun Tzu The Art of War* (Ware, Herts.: Wordsworth Reference, 1993)

SYMBOLS

People in ancient China had great faith in the power of magical symbols. A complicated and diverse system of symbolism has existed throughout the history of Chinese civilisation from the Neolithic cultures to today. Symbolism can be found everywhere in China, from natural phenomena such as clouds and mist to celestial bodies such as the Sun and Moon, from materials such as **jade** and gold to abstract designs such as the ***yin-yang*** symbol and eight diagrams, from mythical animals such as **dragon** and ***qilin*** to real creatures such as carp and bat, and from trees such as pine and bamboo to flowers such as lotus and chrysanthemum. Symbolism also exists in every aspect of social life. From the ceremonies in the imperial court to the birth, marriage and death of the ordinary citizen, every occasion has its symbolic emblems and procedures. There are rich religious elements in Chinese symbolism. Although **Buddhism** had already become a complicated system of ritual and idol worship before it reached China, the Chinese further elaborated its iconography and symbolism, making changes to **Guanyin** and the **lohans** for example, thus echoing their attitudes and their way of life. Chinese symbolism also relies heavily on the mythology of **Daoism** with its numerous divinities of health, wealth, stars, rivers, mountains and rocks. One of the unique features of Chinese symbolism is the wide use of homophonic images. There are numerous homophones in the Chinese language, which enable people to present visual symbols with different verbal connections. The use of homophonic symbolism reached its peak in the Qing dynasty when the techniques of visual-verbal conversion became more sophisticated and their application was evident at all layers of society from the imperial court to the countryside. There are geographical variations in the meaning of identical symbols, due to the diversity of cultures and languages in different regions. Most of the popular symbols in China express auspicious blessings for numerous offspring and a peaceful and prosperous future. Today many of the traditional symbols still influence people's thinking and behaviour in their everyday life.

C.A.S. WILLIAMS, *Outlines of Chinese Symbolism and Art Motives* (Rutland:, 1974); W. EBERHARD, *A Dictionary of Chinese Symbols*, trans. G.L. Campbell (Routledge, 1986).

TAIPING REBELLION (1851–1864)

Rebellion by the founders of the Heavenly Kingdom of Great Peace *Taiping tianguo* 太平天國 which, of all the rebellions, posed the most serious threat to the authority of the Qing dynasty during the nineteenth century. It originated in the south-western province of Guangxi where piracy and **secret societies**, including the **Heaven and Earth Society**, were particularly rife and where the opium trade was a major part of the local economy. The development of the **Treaty Ports** after the **Opium War** shifted the economic centre of gravity to the south-east coast and the Yangzi valley and the economy of the south and south-west suffered badly. Amid growing poverty and unemployment, outlaw and bandit gangs flourished and multiplied. Ethnic conflict between the *Bendi* 本地 (often written *Punti*) and the **Hakka** *kejia* 客家people who had migrated to the region in the twelfth or thirteenth century ripened into vendettas and both sides raised defensive militias. The *Bendi* farmers had strong lineage organisations and fortified villages, and to counter this the Hakka miners, peasants, charcoal burners and boatmen formed themselves into a quasi-religious organisation which eventually became the God Worshippers Society *Bai shangdi hui* 拜上帝會 and was organised by Feng Yunshan. Feng's cousin, **Hong Xiuquan**, visionary, shaman and failed candidate in the imperial examinations was the inspiration for the Taiping rising. He presented himself as the younger brother of Jesus and became the leader of the God

Worshippers. Famine in 1849 and 1850 precipitated a crisis in Guangxi and the vendettas became more intense. God Worshippers from the whole of Guangxi were summoned to the town of Jintian where they fought with government troops. On January 11 1851, Hong Xiuquan's thirty-eighth birthday, the Heavenly Kingdom of Great Peace was proclaimed. Taiping forces marched north on a crusade to bring the whole of China under the Heavenly Kingdom. At first the enterprise was successful. The Taiping armies attracted enormous numbers of followers en route and were able to capture **Nanjing**, the secondary capital of China in March 1853. Nanjing was renamed Tianjing (Heavenly Capital) and a military official system was developed in which the leaders of the rebellion became kings in a hierarchy with Hong Xiuquan as Heavenly King at the apex. The success in establishing control over Nanjing and its region was interpreted as the arrival of the kingdom of heaven on earth. Utopian regulations on land reform and the equality of women were proclaimed and new examination and civil service systems were established, although the structure was the same as that of the Qing authorities. Rivalries and dissension among the kingly leadership rapidly led to internecine strife with the slaughter of tens of thousands of Taiping followers. The subsequent weakening of the Taiping court enabled the reorganised armies of **Zeng Guofan** and other Qing officials to suppress the rebellion in 1864. Hong Xiuquan committed suicide. In spite of the flawed practice of the Taiping leadership, the egalitarian aspirations inspired political thinkers including the founders of the **Chinese Communist Party.** See also **Peasant Rebellions, Nian, Muslim Rebellions.**

JEN Yuwen, *The Taiping Revolutionary Movement* (Yale University Press, 1973); Franz MICHAEL and CHANG Chung-li, *The Taiping Rebellion: History and Documents* (3 vols.), (University of Washington Press, 1966–71); Vincent SHIH, *The Taiping Ideology, Its Sources, Interpretations and Influences* (University of Washington Press, 1967).

TAISHAN 泰山 (MOUNT TAI)

Taishan is also known as Dai 岱 (*Daishan* 岱山 or *Daiyue* 岱岳), and is located at the centre of Shandong province. It is about 200 kilometres long and its highest peak, Yuhuanding, is 1,524 metres above sea level. Among the **five sacred mountains**, Taishan is the Eastern *yue* 岳 (*Dongyue* 東岳) and the most important one for imperial ceremonies. The state ceremony of *feng shan* (Worshipping Heaven and Earth) at Taishan was performed by kings and emperors from the Zhou period. This was considered an urgent matter to be carried out after taking over the throne, in order to get the approval of Heaven, Earth and the gods. Emperor **Qin Shi Huangdi**'s extravagant *feng shan*, with the monumental rock inscriptions at Taishan recording this event, is the best known example of such a practice. Later emperors' *feng shan* were performed in the temple complex known as Daimiao 岱廟, at the foot of Taishan. Daimiao was first built in the Han but rebuilt in the Song, and is one of the few well-preserved palace-style complexes in China. Taishan has inspired many ancient philosophers and poets, from **Confucius** to **Li Bai**, and maintained a unique place in Chinese culture. See also **Sacrifices.**

TAIWAN 台灣

Island lying off the south-eastern coast of China, opposite the coast of Fujian Province. Previously known as Formosa from its Portuguese name of *Ilha*

Formosa, "Beautiful Island", it has since 1949 been the base for the Nationalist-administered Republic of China, with its capital in Taibei (Taipei). The Penghu (Pescadores) archipelago and the islands of **Jinmen** and Mazu are also under its control. It has an areas of 36,000 sq. km. and a population of 21 million, including a number of non-Han aboriginal groups. The aboriginal population, now largely restricted to the central highlands, is related to the people of Malaysia and Polynesia and was driven into the mountains by waves of Han Chinese migrants, mainly from Fujian, in the 16th and 17th centuries. The island became an important trading post for the Portuguese and Dutch traders from the 15th to the 17th century and between 1661 and 1683 was the base for the rebel **Koxinga**, who defied the Manchu armies of the Qing dynasty. It was formally put under Chinese administration in 1683 as a prefecture under the jurisdiction of Fujian province and it became a province in its own right in 1887.After coming under attack by the Japanese in 1874 and France in 1884, it was ceded to Japan under the terms of the Treaty of **Shimonoseki** that concluded the **Sino-Japanese War** of 1894–5, becoming Japan's first colony, or second if the Ryukyu Islands are counted as a colony. The Japanese carried out a wide range of economic and social developments during the 50 years in which they occupied the island. The cultivation of rice, sugar, and tea (largely for export to Japan) was particularly emphasised. Taiwan remained under Japanese colonial rule until the end of the Second World War, by which time there had been considerable Japanese migration to the island and the Japanese language was widely used. Japanese culture has had a lasting effect on the island and the term "Little Japan", by which the island is sometimes known is as much a reflection of that as a reference to its post-war economic success.

Under the terms of the **Cairo Declaration**, Taiwan was due to be returned to Chinese control, and **Chen Yi** was sent by the Guomindang government-in-exile in Chongqing to take over as governor in October 1945. He took with him a sizeable number of mainlanders and established them as a new elite, largely ignoring the wishes of the native Taiwanese. Popular resentment at this mistreatment sparked off an uprising on February 28 1947, which Chen's forces suppressed ruthlessly. (See **February 28 Incident**). When it became clear that the Guomindang were going to lose the **Civil War** against the CCP, Taiwan was chosen as the safest retreat and throughout 1948 and 1949, hundreds of thousands of mainland soldiers and civilians fled to Taiwan. On December 8 1949, the GMD formally installed its government in Taibei. It retained the Chinese seat in the United Nations until 1971, when the PRC was finally selected in its place.

In the immediate post-war years, Taiwan benefited from its alliance with the United States in the Cold War and American investment was the key factor in the spectacular economic growth that followed. Political and social development was restricted and Taiwan remained a one-party state, ruled by the Guomindang. Many of its political leaders owed their positions to military rank and the island was under martial law as late as 1987**. Jiang Jieshi** (Chiang Kai-shek), the wartime leader of the Guomindang, was President until his death in 1975, when he was succeeded by his son **Jiang Jingguo** (Chiang Ching-kuo). On Jiang Jingguo's death in 1988, **Li Denghui** (Lee Teng-hui), a Taiwanese rather than a mainlander, took over as president and a period of transition began. The formal announcement of the end of the Communist Rebellion came in 1991, and in 1991–2 the old guard of GMD politicians who had been elected on the mainland before 1949 finally retired. A new Legislative Yuan (Parliament) took control of the budget legislation and appointment of the Prime Minister, and in 1992 the General Election was won by the GMD, but the pro-independence Democratic Progressive Party won 50 seats.The China New Party formed in 1993 by the defection of members of the mainlander elite who wished to retain their claim to all China further weakened the GMD.

Politically, as the United States grew less hostile to the People's Republic of China, eventually giving it diplomatic recognition in 1979, so Taiwan became more isolated. However, the strength of its economy means that this tendency has now been reversed, and even links with mainland China, although officially prohibited, are very widespread. Both the CCP and the GMD have consistently maintained that China and Taiwan are indissolubly linked and will inevitably be reunited, but the emergence of a new Taiwanese elite and a Taiwan independence movement suggest that this may not necessarily be the case. Taiwan's history has kept it apart from the mainland for centuries and its future may also be as a separate identity.

Simon LONG, *Taiwan: China's last frontier* (Basingstoke: Macmillan, 1991); Mark A. ALLEE, *Law and local society in late imperial China: northern Taiwan in the nineteenth century* (Stanford University Press, 1994); The Republic of China Yearbook (Government Information Office, Republic of China); John COOPER, *A Quiet Revolution: Political Development in the Republic of China* (Washington D.C., 1988).

TAIZONG 太宗, SONG EMPEROR (Zhao Guangyi 趙光義, 949–97, r. 976–97)
Brother of the Song emperor **Taizu**. He completed the reunification of the Empire by recovering Wu-Yue in the south-east (978) and capturing Northern Han from the **Khitan** (979). (See **Five Dynasties and Ten Kingdoms**). He failed, however, to retake the Sixteen Border Prefectures (see **Liao Dynasty**.)

TAIZONG 太宗, TANG EMPEROR (Li Shimin 李世民, c.599–649, r. 626–49)
Second son of Li Yuan, Tang **Gaozu**, whom he helped to capture **Chang'an** in 617. After an unpromising beginning, when he had his brother the heir apparent killed and his father pressured into retirement, his reign is counted as one of the greatest in Tang history. His policies largely continued those of the Sui emperors and his father, concentrating on the strengthening of centralised authority and the law code, the promotion of educated bureaucrats, the improvement of the canal system, the proclamation of power in the building of lavish palaces, the organisation of militia, and above all the pursuit of an aggressive foreign policy. His armies achieved great successes against the Turks in 630, 639–40 and 647–8, giving Tang control of the Tarim Basin and beyond. Peace was achieved with the newly established kingdom of **Tibet** through the marriage of Princess Wencheng to King **Songtsen Gampo** (641). He received tribute from countries as far away as Persia and Syria. In northern **Korea**, however, disaster befell. In 645 and 647 Taizong personally initiated a foolhardy repetition by land and sea of Sui **Yangdi's** attempt at the conquest of **Koguryo**, with like results.

C.P. FITZGERALD, *Son of Heaven, a Biography of Li Shih-min* (Cambridge University Press, 1933).

TAIZU 太祖, SONG EMPEROR (Zhao Kuangyin 趙匡胤, 928–76, r. 960–76)
A former military commander of the Later Zhou dynasty (see **Five Dynasties and Ten Kingdoms**) who usurped the throne and reunited most of the country by diminishing the power of regional military rulers and strengthening centralised government with scholar-officials. He set an example of cautious expenditure and heeding advice, and believing that the state must resist corruption spoke out strongly against **eunuchs**. He wisely decided that it was more important to establish firm control over central and southern China rather than to challenge the **Khitan** or Tangut empires in the north and north-west (see **Liao, Xi Xia**), and the creation of the intendant system based on the division of the country into fifteen circuits was vital to this process. The law code was introduced in 962 for implementation by judicial intendants (*tidian xingyu shi*) and was strict in its use of penalties both as deterrent and punishment.
Brian MCKNIGHT, *Law and Order in Sung China* (Cambridge University Press, 1992).

TALAS RIVER
Site of battle in *AD* 751 in which an Arab army defeated that of Chinese general Gao Xianzhi. Their success provided them with a base from which to extend Arab influence in central Asia as Chinese authority declined after the **An Lushan** rebellion, but **Tibet** also sought to control the lucrative trade routes across what was a very unstable political region.

TAN SITONG 譚嗣同 (1865–1898)
Follower of **Kang Youwei** and one of the six martyrs executed following the failure of the **Hundred Days Reform Movement**. Tan was born into a leading gentry family in Liuyang 瀏陽, Hunan and had a traditional education, but was attracted to knight errant ideals and travelled very extensively throughout China. After China's defeat in the 1894–5 war with Japan, Tan was shocked and began reading works on Western science and technology; he also contacted Kang Youwei and began to study **Buddhism** under Yang Wenhui 揚文會. He began to write his best known work *Renxue* 仁學 *On Benevolence*, an attempt to synthesise **Confucianism**, **Buddhism** and western science into a single world view. Based on his view that ***ren*** 'benevolence' was the source of everything, he saw the inequality of traditional society, the 'three bonds and five relationships' and the autocratic system of government as being in basic conflict with *ren*. His views are among the most extreme of the reformist group and it is probably no coincidence that one of his close associates was the only reformer to attempt an uprising, Tang Caichang 唐才常. **Tan Sitong** returned to Hunan at the invitation of the governor Chen Baozhen 陳寶箴 to take part in a reform programme. He cooperated with Tang Caichang in setting up a current affairs academy, a military academy, the *Nanxuehui* 南學會 Southern Study Society, and a newspaper, *Xiangbao* 湘報 *Hunan News*. After the **Guangxu** Emperor began his reform movement in the summer of 1898, **Tan Sitong** was invited to Beijing and given a governmental post. However, when the Empress Dowager **Cixi** staged her counter coup on the September 21, bringing to an end the **Hundred Days of Reform**, Tan Sitong refused to flee, was arrested three days later with five other reformers and executed on the September 28. He was said to have declared that no foreign reforms

movements had succeeded without shedding blood, and that the shedding of blood in China's reform movement should start with his.

CHAN Sin-wai, *Buddhism in Late Ch'ing Political Thought* (Hong Kong: Chinese University Press, 1985).

TANAKA MEMORIAL

Notorious document revealing Japanese plans to encroach on Chinese territory, on the basis of discussions that had taken place at the Eastern Conference. The Eastern Conference, held from June 27 to July 7 1927 was convened by Japan's Prime Minister Tanaka Giichi and attended by representatives from the Foreign Ministry, the Ministries of War and the Navy, the **Guandong Army**, and other interested parties. The announcement that came after the meeting made it clear that Japan would defend its interests in China and might intervene militarily in the north if necessary. The Tanaka Memorial was apparently presented to the Japanese Emperor after the meeting although doubts were cast on its authenticity in Japan. As it first came to light in China, it is possible that it was of Chinese rather than Japanese origin, but the Pan-Asian, expansionist perspective and the detailed plans for colonising East Asia that it contained were very close to the views of Japan's military leaders at the time. More significantly, when Japan did invade China between 1931 and 1945, many of the plans outlined in the Memorial were followed.

TANG DYNASTY 唐朝 (618–906)

The Tang marked the coming of age of China as the Middle Kingdom, the period when its civilisation unquestionably defined it as the greatest empire in Asia and acted as a magnet drawing peoples from the rest of the continent. Famed abroad for its early military prowess, its efficient administration, the sophistication of its urban culture (see **Chang'an**), its receptiveness to religious practices (the imperial clan sometimes claimed descent from **Laozi** and periodically patronised **Daoism**, **Buddhism** and **Nestorianism**), and its encouragement of scholarship and the arts, it became the cosmopolitan heart of the region, destination for foreign embassies, scholars, merchants, pilgrims, and sometimes attacking armies. Turks, Persians, Arabs, Tibetans, Koreans, Japanese, and South-east Asians were amongst those who stimulated the interest of the Chinese in foreign geography, culture and languages.

Founded by Li Yuan, a Sui military commander of part-Turkic origin driven to rebellion by the harsh autocracy of Emperor **Yangdi's** rule (see Tang **Gaozu**), Tang consolidated its power during the seventh century by a combination of successful foreign policy in Central Asia (see **Tibet**) and domestic measures which included land reform, canal building (see **Grand Canal**), the creation of new central and provincial government structures, and the selection of officials on the grounds of education as well as personal connections (see ***yin***). Though court politics were never free from rivalry and intrigue, the first half of the dynasty benefited from the strong personal authority of four outstanding figures, **Taizong**, **Gaozong**, the Empress Wu (see **Wu Zetian**), and **Xuanzong**. Yet at the very pinnacle of its glory the dynasty showed its frailty to both human and institutional limitations, and the **An Lushan rebellion** did psychological as well as political and economic damage from which the Li court never fully recovered. It was not a swift collapse and there were still cultural achievements to come, but none of its later emperors boasted the stature or the ability of their four great predecessors, and in the ninth century the familiar pattern developed of provincial leaders rivalling each other as regional warlords, and of court surrender to **eunuch** domination. Both Buddhism and overseas trade were made scapegoats for the economic decline, which owed as much to official corruption and incompetence, frightening foreigners away in a reversal of the seventh century trend. After the suppression of **Huang Chao**'s rebellion in 884 the court had no more authority, and succumbed in 907 to Zhu Quanchong, a warlord who turned against his imperial masters just as he had done previously against his former leader Huang Chao.

The Tang marked the full fruition and the end of the early imperial age. Its world view, symbolised by its string of military protectorates stretching across Central Asia (the "Western Regions") and its efforts to command the political evolution of the Korean peninsula (see **Korea**), was still based on the old-fashioned Mencian theory that *de* "virtue" and *wen* "culture" could control the barbarians, and its splendid but costly court ceremonial was designed to prove it. Its socio-economic system had not fully broken the privileges of the old feudal aristocracy, as the landed estates of the gentry and the recommendation system for official advancement showed. And the court's patronage of men of letters, musicians and artists at the twin capitals of **Chang'an** and **Luoyang** was deliberately reminiscent of the flourishing days of Han culture. But in the rich soil of the early imperial seedbed sprouts of fresh growth were already visible. **Neo-Confucianism** was arising from the cross-fertilisation of Buddhism and Confucianism (see **Han Yu, Li Ao, Li Zhongxian**). Forerunners of the Song encyclopaedic movement had appeared. **Landscape painting** and porcelain technology had made sufficient growth to support their full flowering in the Five Dynasties and Song. If there was an autumnal feel about the Tang after An Lushan, the signs of the fresh, reinvigorated spring to come in the Northern Song were already present.

Emperors:

Gaozu	618–26	
Taizong	626–49	
Gaozong	649–83	
Zhongzong	684	(real power exercised by Wu Zetian)
Ruizong	684–90	(real power exercised by Wu Zetian)
Wu Zetian	690–705	(the "Zhou dynasty")
Zhongzong	705–10	(restoration)
Shaodi	710	(real power exercised by Empress Wei)
Ruizong	710–2	(restoration)
Xuanzong	712–56	
Suzong	752–62	
Daizong	762–79	
Dezong	779–805	
Shunzong	805	(abdicated)
Xianzong	805–20	
Muzong	820–4	

Jingzong	824–7
Wenzong	827–40
Wuzong	840–6
Xuanzong	846–59
Yizong	859–73
Xizong	873–88
Zhaozong	888–904
Aidi	904–7

D.G. JOHNSON, *The Medieval Chinese Oligarchy* (Boulder, Colorado: Westview, 1977); David MCMULLEN, *State and Scholars in T'ang China* (Cambridge University Press, 1988); E.H. SCHAFER, *The Golden Peaches of Samarkand* (Berkeley: University of California Press, 1963); John C. PERRY and Bardwell L. SMITH, eds., *Essays on T'ang Society: The Interplay of Social, Political and Economic Forces* (Leiden: E.S. Brill, 1976).

TANG *SANCAI* 唐三彩 Tang tricolours

One of the main glazing techniques used on **ceramics** during the Tang dynasty (618–907). The three main colours of such lead glaze are green, amber and cream, though black and blue were also part of the palette. The glaze was in most cases applied over a white slip which serves to disguise the pinkish buff earthenware body of various Tang tomb figures, horses, camels and vessels. One distinctive way of using *sancai* glaze made use of the fact that it had a low viscosity and so tended to run down vertical shapes, which gives a particularly pleasing contract between the rather casual glaze effect and the perfectly moulded vessels or realistically shaped figures and horses. Wax was sometimes added to the surface of the wares to prevent a particular colour of glaze adhering to that area of the body and so create a batik-like effect.

Margaret MEDLEY, *Tang Pottery and Porcelain* (London: Faber, 1981).

TANG TOMBS

The imperial tombs of the Tang dynasty were created on an unprecedented scale that expressed the heroic spirit of this golden age. The Tang tombs were of two types: those placed inside mountains and those with man-made earthen mounds. The former were the most common and extremely impressive. The tomb sites included impressive architecture, broad spirit paths, and consummately carved stone figures and animals, including emissaries from the subject peoples of the greater empire. Accompanying burials near the imperial tombs also had mounds, and the sites were oriented along a north-south axis. The paintings covering the walls of these tombs, some of which have been excavated, were recreations of the life in the palaces. Judging from the furnishings of these accompanying tombs, imperial grave goods were more sumptuous than ever before and comprised large amounts of gold, silver, and glazed stoneware as well as glass, agate, foreign coinage, and other rarities. ***Sancai*** ware and figures were at their peak during this time and are justly famous for their colour and fine sculpture. It is believed that most of the Tang imperial tombs were robbed, except the Qianling, the joint burial complex of Tang **Gaozong** and Empress **Wu Zetian**. The most important change in the Tang burial system was the separation of the offering hall for sacrifices and the retiring hall where the spirit of the deceased was maintained. The latter was moved to a lower position on the mountain and hence called the Lower Palace. The offering hall became known as the Upper Palace in the Song period. See also **Grave Architecture**.

TANG XIANZU 湯顯祖 (1550–1616)
Playwright of the Ming dynasty. Tang, also known as Tang Yiren, was born in Linchuan, Jiangxi province. He began his official career after he obtained his *jinshi* title in the imperial examination in 1583. Years later he left his post after bitter disputes with senior court officials, and devoted his last years to reading and writing. Tang Xianzu was best known for his *chuanqi* 傳奇 plays, which included *The Story of the Revived Soul* 還魂記 (also known as *The Peony Pavilion* 牡丹亭), *The Story of the Purple Flute* 紫簫記, *The Story of Purple Hairpin* 紫釵記, *The Dream at Nanke* 南柯記 and *The Story of Handan* 邯鄲記. In his play-writing, he broke away from the restrictions of classic rules and forms, such as those of tonal patterns and rhyme schemes. He expressed in his work some Buddhist and Daoist ideas, such as keeping aloof from worldly affairs, and some views critical of the current social establishment. A number of Ming and Qing playwrights followed Tang Xianzu's style and called themselves "the *Yumintang* (Tang's studio name) school" or "the Linchuan school".

TANGSHAN EARTHQUAKE
Earthquake which demolished the industrial city of Tangshan, which is about a hundred miles from Beijing, in July 1976. Superstitious observers took it as an omen and their forebodings were confirmed when Mao Zedong died on September 9. See also **Omens and Portents**.

TANGUTS
Tribes related to the Tibetans who built a powerful state, known in Chinese as the **Xi Xia,** in the Gansu and Ningxia region in the 10th and 11th centuries. Tangut script is similar to Chinese characters, but is still largely undeciphered. The Qiang ethnic group in western China claim descent from the Tanguts.

TAO YUANMING 陶淵明 (c.365–427)
Also known as Tao Qian 陶潛. Tao Yuanming was a poet of the Eastern Jin period, and was born in Xunyang, Jiangxi province. He came from a scholar-official family which had fallen on hard times. As a result he was well-educated, yet used to physical labour. Living in a period of great instability, he was equivocal in his attitude towards official life and in his middle years held a number of government posts. However, he turned his back on this and lived in retirement farming and writing, for the last twenty years of his life. A total of 125 poems, mainly lyrics and idylls, and 12 prose pieces by Tao still survive. His introspective works on the meaning of life show Daoist and Buddhist influence. *Taohuayuan ji* 桃花源記 (*Notes on the Land of Peach Blossoms*) is one of his most celebrated pieces in which he created a Utopia-type of dream land. In his later years he refused offers from the court and died in poverty.

A.R. DAVIS, *Tao Yuan-ming (AD 365–427): His Works and Their Meaning*, 2 vols. (Cambridge University Press, 1983); J.R. HIGHTOWER, *The Poetry of T'ao Ch'ien* (Oxford: Clarendon Press, 1970).

TAO ZHU 陶鑄 (1908–1969)
Senior CCP leader with a power-base in southern China. Tao was governor of Guangdong province from 1955 onwards and rose to become Vice-Premier. He lost all his posts during the Cultural Revolution.

TAOISM see **DAOISM**

***TAOTIE* 饕餮**
Style of decoration first found in the earliest phase of Shang bronzes from **Erlitou**, possibly derived from the ritual **jade** carvings associated with the Liangzhu culture of the Shanghai delta in the third millennium BC. It is commonplace by the mid-Shang and continues into the Zhou period. It comprises the stylised, often abstract representation of a face, sometimes accompanied by the fuller features of a creature's claws, back quills and tail. The face is divided into two mirror-image halves, and may include horns, ears, eyebrows and eyes, nostrils, cheeks, mouth and jaw. These elements may be embedded in complex incised patterns which obscure their presence and hide their physical form, giving rise to the frequent description of *taotie* as monster or mask. It is known that animals were used in Shang rites, but whether the *taotie* was a stylised representation of an actual physical creature or an imaginary supernatural being is unknown. See also **Bronze Age.**

C. DEYDIER, *Les Bronzes Archaiques Chinois*: *Archaic Chinese Bronzes* (Paris: Les Editions d'Art et d'Histoire, 1995).

TASHILUMPO see **SHIGATSE**

TAXATION
Throughout Chinese history the principal means of raising resources needed by the state was by a combination of **land tax**, poll tax, labour dues and military conscription. Both **census** registration and communal organisation such as ***baojia*** and ***lijia*** were relevant to tax assessment and collection, but at no period did a system exist which could cope with the complexity resulting from the size and diversity of the empire and its far-flung regions, or the inherent corruption of officialdom and difficulty of transporting taxes to the capital. It was sometimes accepted that by allowing commutation of labour or military dues by purchase the state could afford to buy the services required for its armies or canal diggers, though this might also mean that an undue burden fell on those who could not afford to buy their release. At no time was fiscal thinking sophisticated enough to design a system based on an assessment of actual or projected needs of both regional and central government. Taxes gathered in the provinces were regarded no differently from the tribute received irregularly from neighbouring or distant states (see **Tribute System**), and might or might not reach the treasury on a reliable basis. Before the monetary revolution of the Northern Song period the collection of taxes in kind implied mainly grain or silk tribute, welcome contributions to life in the northern capital region from the richer economies of the **Yangzi** valley and Jiangnan region, but of restricted financial use. Still less valuable monetarily were some other forms of provincial tribute, such as the quotas of young boys and girls contributed by southern regions for court purposes in the Tang. In view of the constant shortage of fiscal income, it

was inevitable that additional taxes should be imposed and accumulate over periods of time, and attempts had to be made at simplification, as in 780 and again in the late sixteenth century (see **Single Whip System**). Inevitably too, the burden of extra taxation tended to fall on those least able to pay, being passed on by landowners to their tenants or merchants to their customers. Consequently, certain sections of society such as the merchants were regularly penalised, but still enjoyed such conspicuous wealth that they could have tolerated heavier rates of tax in almost every period. Monks and nuns of the Buddhist church, too, were generally tax-exempt, thereby encouraging many false vocations and the loss of income and labour dues from liable adults, yet the riches of the church itself were only limited by non-fiscal means such as the great persecution of 842–5 (see **Religious Persecution**). Meanwhile, small farmers were periodically driven into servitude or **banditry** by their inability to pay heavy tax demands.

Tax collection was in the hands of local officials or of delegates from central government, such as the **eunuchs** who terrorised local communities in the late sixteenth century with their insatiable greed as they exploited opportunities to collect the silver taxes. In the Qing local officials relied increasingly on assistance from members of the gentry with tax collection as the rural population grew rapidly. On the other hand the gentry might act as a buffer against excessive and improper demands. In the early twentieth century, however, even they were in no position to challenge the excessive demands of warlords such as Liu Xiang in Sichuan, where taxes were sometimes levied for fifty years ahead.

Ray HUANG, *Taxation and Governmental Finance in Sixteenth-Century Ming China* (Cambridge University Press 1974); Denis TWITCHETT, *Financial Administration under the T'ang* (Cambridge University Press, 1963).

TEA

Tea was probably introduced to China from India or South-east Asia some time in the Six Dynasties period. By the Tang dynasty it had become widely used although it was valued at first as a medicine rather than an everyday beverage and its capacity to help the drinker keep awake was noted. As a luxury item it was extremely expensive and in the eighth century tax on tea was an important source of government revenue. Demand for tea allowed the development of a nationwide market in the commodity and also stimulated ceramic production as special sets of porcelain tea bowls and tea-pots, notably tea-pots from Yixing in Jiangsu province, were produced for the connoisseur. By the Ming dynasty, it had become an important export, much in demand by Portuguese and Dutch traders. By the 19th century, China tea had become a fashionable beverage in Europe, although it faced stiff competition from the stronger blends produced by India and Ceylon (now Sri Lanka) which were more popular. Tea is grown in many areas of south-central China, particularly in the provinces of Fujian, Anhui, Jiangxi and Zhejiang. The standard Chinese name for tea is *cha* 茶, which is close to the name used in Hindi and Urdu *chai*, but the English word is probably derived from the Fujian pronunciation of 茶, *the*. Even in late twentieth-century China, tea is an expensive product and by far the commonest fluids taken by most of the population are soup and plain boiled water.

TEMÜR (r1294–1307)
Successor to **Khubilai Khan** as Great Khan of the Mongols in 1294. Temür maintained a strong central administration which declined on his death. See also **Toghon Temür.**

TERRACOTTA ARMY see **LISHAN**

THIRD FRONT *Disan zhanxian* 第三戰線
Strategic redistribution of resources for a self-reliant interior economy between 1964 and 1971 with the aim of creating a self-sufficient industrial complex to act as a strategic reserve if China were to find itself at war. As an operation with a military purpose, it remained secret for years. It was closely associated with **Lin Biao**, who first raised the idea at the "7,000 cadre conference" held in January 1962. Lin feared that Guomindang forces on Taiwan might take advantage of the post-**Great Leap Forward** crisis to launch an attack on mainland cities, and suggested that such an attack could not be successfully resisted in the coastal cities especially if Guomindang forces were backed by American naval power. An attack on Shanghai should therefore be met by withdrawal and resistance at a "second front" around Suzhou; if necessary withdrawal to a "third front" in the Huang Shan region of Anhui would take place, and protracted war begin. The Third Front may have had a profound effect on China's economic modernisation. It was an extremely expensive programme carried out for strategic rather than economic considerations. From the point of view of the post-1979 reform programme, it has left many enterprises non-viable and uneconomic to convert into private businesses.
Barry NAUGHTON, "The Third Front: Defence Industrialisation in the Chinese Interior", *China Quarterly* 115, September 1988, pp. 351–386, and "Industrial Policy during the Cultural Revolution: Military Preparation, Decentralisation and Leaps Forward", in William A. Joseph, Christine P.W. Wong and David Zweig , eds., *New Perspectives on the Cultural Revolution* (Harvard University Press, 1991).

THIRTEEN CLASSICS *Shi san jing* 十三經
The biggest of the groupings of the Classics, which vary from five to thirteen in number according to definition. All sets include the ***Shi*** 詩'Book of Poetry', ***Shu*** 書 'Book of History' and ***Yi*** 易 'Book of Changes'; in the group of thirteen the *Li* 禮 'Book of Ritual ' is divided into its three component works, the ***Liji*** 禮記, ***Yili*** 儀禮 and ***Zhouli*** 周禮, and similarly the ***Chunqiu*** 春秋 becomes the ***Zuozhuan*** 左傳, ***Gongyang zhuan*** 公羊傳 and ***Guliang zhuan*** 谷梁傳; in addition there are the: ***Lunyu*** 論語 'Analects of Confucius', the ***Erya*** 爾雅, the ***Xiaojing*** 孝經 'Classic of Filial Piety' and ***Mengzi*** 孟子, Mencius. For details of each work see under separate headings.

THOUGHT REFORM *Sixiang gaizao* 思想改造
Group psychology used to pressurise members of the CCP and others into conformity, termed "brainwashing" by Westerners who encountered its effects among Chinese troops captured during the Korean War.

THREE FEUDATORIES REVOLT
Three fiefdoms in Yunnan, Guangdong and Fujian were granted to the Ming princes, Wu Sangui, Shang Kexi and Geng Jingzhong respectively, by the new Qing

dynasty in return for their help in the Manchu conquest of China. The **Kangxi Emperor**, alarmed at the threat they posed to Qing power, decided to abolish the fiefdoms in 1673 and tried to transfer the three lords to Manchuria. They rose against the emperor but were defeated. See **Green Standard Army.**

THREE KINGDOMS *SANGUO* 三國

The period of division immediately following the fall of the Han dynasty. In the north **Cao Pi** ruled over the kingdom of Wei 魏 from his capital of **Luoyang**. In the south-west Liu Bei established the capital of Shu Han 蜀漢 at Chengdu, while from **Nanjing** Sun Quan ruled the south and south-east. Their rivalry was immortalised in the Ming dynasty novel ***Sanguo yanyi*** "Romance of the Three Kingdoms". The northern kingdom absorbed Shu Han in 263 and Wu 吳 in 280, but in 265 Cao Pi had himself been usurped by a rival clan, the Sima, who renamed the dynasty the Jin. See also **Cao Cao, Zhuge Liang.**

THREE PEOPLE'S PRINCIPLES *SANMIN ZHUYI* 三民主義

The main theoretical ideas of **Sun Yixian**, developed towards the end of the nineteenth century and at the time considered to be revolutionary. They were originally a series of lectures, later published as a book, and became the official ideology of the **Guomindang.** The three principles were Nationalism *minzu* 民族, the assertion of Chinese self-interest against both Westerners and the Manchu ruling elite of the Qing dynasty; Democracy or 'people's rights' *minquan* 民權, which was principally a call for the establishment of a parliamentary system, and People's Livelihood *minsheng* 民生, the vaguest of the three ideas, which was a call for economic reform with control over capital and redistribution of land. Both supporters and detractors of this policy have equated it with socialism. The Three People's Principles were adopted by the ***Tongmenghui*** as their basic policy and then taken over by the Guomindang and included in its manifesto of January 1 1923.

THREE RED BANNERS CAMPAIGN

The collective name for the core policies of the CCP given at the **Lushan plenum** in 1959. The three were the **Great Leap Forward**, the **Communes**, and the General Line for Building Socialism.

THREE-ANTI CAMPAIGN, *Sanfan yundong* 三反運動 (1951–2)

This was publicised as a mass movement to counter corruption, waste and bureaucratism in the early years of the People's Republic and was an urban campaign running parallel to **land reform**. It was aimed primarily against urban cadres "especially those in financial and economic departments, who had become involved in corruption as a result of their dealings with the bourgeoisie" and was carried out on a trial basis in the north-east by **Gao Gang** before being launched nationally. A report published in 1957 stated quite clearly that the Three-Anti campaign was aiming at a quota of 25 per cent of Party members to be purged and this figure was almost certainly reached. See also **Five-Anti Campaign.**

Gordon BENNETT, *Yundong: Mass Campaigns in Chinese Communist Leadership* (Center for Chinese Studies, University of California, 1976); Frederick C. TEIWES, *Politics and Purges: Rectification and the Decline of Party Norms, 1950–1965* (M.E. Sharpe, 1979).

***Tian gong kai wu* 天工開物**

Song Yingxing's 1637 encyclopaedia of agricultural and industrial technology which is copiously illustrated with woodblock prints. It describes the means of producing rice, silk, salt, pottery and porcelain, metals, coal, paper, weapons and many other commodities.

Tian'anmen 天安門 (Gate of Heavenly Peace)

Gate on the southern wall of the **Forbidden City**. It gave its name to Tian'amen Square *Tiananmen guangchang* 天安門廣場 which was constructed in front of the gate in the 1950s on the lines of Red Square in Moscow. The gate was the scene of the protests that led to the **May Fourth Movement** in 1919 and the square was the arena for the Red Guard rallies during the **Cultural Revolution** and for the dramatic **April Fifth Incident** of 1976 and the crushing of the **Democracy Movement** in 1989.

Tian'an men incident (1976) see **April Fifth Incident**

Tian'anmen Square Massacre (1989) see **Democracy Movement**

Tianjin massacre (1870)

The murder of ten nuns, two priests, two French officials and three Russian traders in Tianjin on June 21 1870 after mobs attacked a French Catholic church accused of kidnapping children for its orphanage. Thirty Chinese converts were also killed during the attack. **Zeng Guofan** went to Tianjin on July 4 to negotiate with the substantial foreign community in the city who were demanding compensation and an apology from the Chinese government.

Tianjin, Treaty of (1858)

Series of treaties with Russia, the USA, Britain and France signed in June 1858 after the **Arrow** (or Second **Opium) War** and conceding demands for the opening of further **treaty ports** and the right of diplomats to reside in Beijing and free access to China's interior by missionaries and traders. The Chinese authorities attempted to renege on these agreements and they were only finally imposed in the Conventions of Beijing of 1860. See **Beijing, Conventions of.**

Tibet

The state of Tibet (known in traditional China as Tufan 吐蕃, and in Tibetan as Bod) was formed in the early seventh century AD. Its first King, **Songtsen Gampo** (618–641), established the capital in **Lhasa** and promoted the spread of **Buddhism** after marrying Princess Tritsun of Nepal and Princess Wen Cheng of China. This signified an appreciation of inter-state politics which was important in early mediaeval Asia, and between the seventh and ninth centuries Tibet continued to acknowledge religious affiliations with both countries, although its political ambitions were more definitely concentrated northwards. It competed powerfully with Tang dynasty China and the Uyghur, Turkic and Arab peoples for control of Central Asia, especially the oases along the southern **Silk Road**, and controlled the **Dunhuang** oasis between 781 and 847.

Peace treaties were concluded with China in 714, 783 and 821–2. Tibetan armies withdrew after entering **Chang'an** in 763, but contacts with China ceased after the decline of centralised rule in both countries through the ninth century, and were not significantly restored until the **Mongol** period. By the thirteenth century great land-owning monastic orders had established both civil and religious authority over the country. The most active political orders were the Kagya and the Sakya, both founded in the eleventh century. It was a Sakya scholar, **Sakya Pandita**, who took his nephew **'Phagspa** with him to the Mongol base at Liangzhou in 1247 and initiated the events leading up to the boy's personal partnership with **Khubilai Khan** in Dadu (present day **Beijing**). This established the so-called "priest-patron" relationship between Tibet and China, the exchange of religious services for military support. But not all Tibetan Orders accepted Mongol authority, and although it was temporarily enforced by invasion in 1268 the decline of Mongol fortunes in China weakened their grip on Tibet. There followed another period of disunion, with religious rivalry developing between the **Karmapa** (the Red Hats) and the **Gelugpa** (the Yellow Hats) and political tension between the ancient provinces of Tsang (see **Shigatse**), and U (see **Lhasa**). The Karmapa provided support for the Kings of Tibet, whose power base was in Tsang, but eventually the Gelugpa attained supremacy in both spheres and were wooed by both Ming China and the Mongols: the **Yongle Emperor** awarded the title of "King of Religion" to a disciple of Tsong Khapa in 1419 and Altan Khan created that of **"Dalai Lama"** in 1587. In 1642 the Great Fifth Dalai Lama invoked an invasion by Gusri Khan and thereby suppressed once and for all the political activities of the Karmapa. Gusri took for himself the title of King, which remained in Mongol hands until 1717. Meanwhile the Great Fifth Dalai Lama, displaying shrewd political acumen, consulted Manchus as well as Mongols. He journeyed to Beijing to meet the **Shunzhi Emperor** in 1652, and Manchu monarchs continued to play an active role in Tibetan politics into the next century. Full-scale military invasions in 1718 and 1720 confirmed Qing authority, which remained unchallenged though not always effectively implemented until 1912. In 1720 the political office of regent, created in 1624 as senior adviser to the king, was abolished, as was that of king itself in 1751. Civil as well as religious authority now rested unchallenged in the persons of the Dalai and **Panchen Lamas**, the regents who ruled for them during the minority of their incarnate successors, and the Council of four ministers. But China's interest in Tibetan affairs continued strong through the eighteenth century and was not slow to exploit political opportunities by intrigue. In 1723 the Qing court created the post of **Amban** to represent it in Lhasa. These agents, though claiming no formal administrative power in the government of Tibet, were nevertheless often in sympathetic contact with the regents, who enjoyed a long period of political supremacy from 1757 to 1876 as a result of the sequence of young Dalai Lamas who failed to reach their majority.

Only a handful of individual Westerners were able to penetrate the mountain barriers which preserved Tibet's secrecy through the late eighteenth and early nineteenth centuries. The British, however, seeking trading outlets for their Indian Empire and fearful of possible Russian influence to the north, obtained limited rights of entry to Tibet from the Chinese government in 1893. When local Tibetan authorities refused to sanction them, an expeditionary force under Colonel Younghusband crossed the border in 1904, attacked **Gyantse** and threatened Lhasa. Neither the **Anglo-Tibetan Convention** (September 1904) nor the **Simla Convention** (1913–4) resolved either territorial or sovereignty issues, but thereafter Republican China was too concerned with other matters to reassert its claim. Britain had gained minor diplomatic rights in Lhasa and no longer feared Russian influence, and the result was that de facto Tibetan independence was preserved.

The revolutionary fervour which swept the Communists to power in 1949 revived a sense of Chinese nationalism which again laid claim to supremacy over Tibet. Chinese armies entered the country in 1950 and established Beijing's authority against stiff resistance. A wave of rebellion led to a second military invasion in 1959, whereat the Dalai Lama fled with many of his people to India. During the **Cultural Revolution** (1966–76) Tibet suffered badly from the iconoclasm of the **Red Guards**, and although the Chinese government has subsequently made efforts to repair and rebuild some of the destruction, relations between local people and Han migrants have remained tense.

Tibet was created an **Autonomous Region** of the People's Republic of China in 1965. See also **Anglo-Chinese Convention, Anglo-Russian Convention, Bön, Drepung, Ganden, Padma Sambhava, Sera, Tibetan Book of the Dead, Xi Xia.**

H. RICHARSON, *Tibet and its History* (London: Shambhala, 1984); D. SNELLGROVE and H. RICHARDSON, *A Cultural History of Tibet* (London: Shambhala, 1986); R.A. STEIN, *Tibetan Civilisation* (Stanford University Press, 1972); Melvyn GOLDSTEIN, *A History of Modern Tibet: The Demise of the Lamaist State* (Berkeley: University of California Press, 1989).

TIBETAN BOOK OF THE DEAD ***Bardo Thodol***

Mystical work said to date from the eighth century AD, associated with the introduction of Tantric Buddhism into **Tibet** by **Padma Sambhava**. It prepares the living for the experience of death, and recited as a breviary accompanying the funerary and mourning rites after death it guides the departing soul on its path to enlightenment or rebirth. It treats death as "solemn joyousness", and stresses it as a natural stage in the progression from one level of consciousness to the next.

W.Y. EVANS-WENTZ, ed., *The Tibetan Book of the Dead* (Oxford University Press, 1960).

TI -YONG 體用

Literally 'body' and 'use'; the concept that a thing exists in both its essence and its external manifestations. The two terms are juxtaposed in texts as early as the ***Zhouli*** and were used from the Warring States period onwards as a philosophical concept. The term was adapted by late nineteenth century modernisers, like Zhang Zhidong in his *Quanxuepian* 勸學篇, to suggest primary and secondary, as in the slogan *Zhongxue wei ti, xi xue wei yong* 中學爲體, 西學爲用 'Chinese learning as the essence, Western learning as the practical application'. Their aim was to oppose what they saw as the out-and-out westernization of the reformers and to maintain an essential core of Chinese cultural tradition. As more astute observers pointed out at the time, according to the original philosophical concept the two were aspects of one entity: it was not possible to have the essence of one thing and the practical application of another. The radical institutional reform proposed by the reformers 1898 and carried out by the Qing government after the Boxers dealt this concept a mortal blow.

Joseph R. LEVENSON, *Confucian China and its Modern Fate*, Vol 1 (London: Routledge & Kegan Paul, 1958).

TLV MIRRORS

A class of **bronze mirrors** produced in Han times decorated on the reverse with patterns incorporating geometrical shapes similar to the letters T, L and V. The decorations are often complex and symbolic, and refer to cosmological beliefs related to the school of *yin* and *yang* (see ***yin-yang***) and the **Five Elements**. Typically, they contain a square, representing the earth, set within the circle of the heavens, mounted around a central boss. Some bear inscriptions. They were intended to be used as a guide to lead man to his destination in paradise. A link is also apparent with the board of the diviner's compass.

Michael LOEWE, *Ways to Paradise* (George Allen and Unwin, 1979).

TOBA see **WEI DYNASTY, NORTHERN**

TOGH TEMÜR (r. 1320–3)

Successor to Temür who had followed **Khubilai Khan** as Yuan emperor of the Mongols His interest in Chinese poetry, calligraphy and painting rather than the martial values of traditional Mongol society is seen as a symbol of the degeneration and collapse of Mongol rule in China.

TOGHAN TEMÜR (r. 1333–68)

The last of the Yuan dynasty emperors. He had been educated almost entirely in Chinese and ascended the throne in 1333 at the age of 13. His reign was marked by factional in-fighting between tribal leaders and he lost the throne to the first Ming emperor, **Hongwu** in 1368 and spent the next two years unsuccessfully trying to recover his throne. He died in 1370.

TOMB ARCHITECTURE

Two styles of tomb construction were practised in traditional China. The first, used from the Shang until the late Zhou and early Han, consisted of a vertical shaft at the foot of which rested the coffin or nest of coffins in a timbered chamber (see **Mawangdui**). The floor of the pit might be approached by a descending ramp, as it was in many of the royal Shang tombs outside **Anyang** and Qin tombs at Fengxiang. During the early Han, perhaps in conjunction with the elaboration of funerary rites which required participants to be able to enter the tombs more easily, the second style was widely adopted. This comprised a set of rooms around the coffin chamber, again entered down a sloping corridor. It had already been anticipated at **Leigudun** and remained the norm throughout later imperial times. Walls of tombs had been timber-clad since the Shang, but the Han introduced brick architecture and stone lintels and doors. The side chambers were either extensions to the central coffin chamber or a more elaborate series of rooms connected by passages. The style reached its apogée in the underground palaces of the Ming Emperors (see **Ming tombs**), but even in the Han the construction of these underground "dwellings" was impressive both in size and architectural complexity (see **Helingol, Wuliang Shrines**). Earth tumuli often surmounted noble and royal tombs, and temple buildings were located in the vicinity. See also **Spirit Avenues.**

R. THORP, *The Quest for Eternity* (Los Angeles Museum Service, 1987).

TOMB DECORATION

Decoration of a tomb might be defined according to its contents as well as its adornment. Under the first heading it can be seen from that of Marquis Yi at **Leigudun** that coffins were already richly painted and lacquered in Warring States times, and that the furnishing of a tomb with grave goods of the highest standard of craftsmanship must have contributed to its aesthetic completeness. From the Han onwards, when the entrance ramp and interior chambers assumed the character of halls, reception rooms and even kitchens and stables, they were clad with decorated bricks or tiles (see **Wuliang Shrines**), or painted on the walls and ceilings with elaborate scenes of processions, rituals, entertainments, and domestic and agricultural situations. Mythical figures and beasts were common and included the guardian animals of the four directions, and the arrival of **Buddhism** led to the appearance of lotus decorations, flying deva musicians and other religious symbolism. On the wall of a Chinese-style tomb of 357 AD in modern North Korea is preserved perhaps the earliest surviving example of portraiture, that of the Chinese official Dong Shou and his wife who were interred there. The tombs of the Tang royalty outside **Chang'an** are especially famous for their well-preserved and colourful depiction of court ladies, musicians, soldiers, and scenes of hunting and polo playing (see **Tang Tombs**, Prince **Yide**). See also **Grave Artefacts, Ming Tombs.**

R.C. RUDOLPH and Y. WEN, *Han Tomb Art of West China* (Los Angeles: University of California Press, 1951); Z.W. LO, *China's Imperial Tombs and Mausoleums* (Beijing: Foreign Languages Press, 1993); Ann PALUDAN, *Chinese Tomb Figurines* (Hong Kong: Oxford University Press, 1994).

***TONGMENGHUI* 同盟會 'United League'**

Republican revolutionary alliance founded at a conference convened by **Sun Yixian** and revolutionaries from seventeen different provinces in Tokyo on January 30 1905. The league was formally constituted on August 20 and Sun was named its president, with **Huang Xing** as his deputy and **Song Jiaoren** a member of the league's legal department. The *Tongmenghui* became the nucleus of modern Chinese nationalism and in 1912 absorbed four smaller parties to become the **Guomindang**.

***TONGWENGUAN* 同文館**

Language school of the Zongli Yamen (see **Tongzhi Restoration**), established in 1862 and a major conduit for ideas from the West in the declining years of the Qing dynasty. It was known to Westerners as the College of Foreign Languages or the Interpreters' College.

TONGZHI 同治, QING EMPEROR (r.1862–75)

Zaichun 載淳, late Qing emperor remembered mainly for the **Tongzhi Restoration** which took place during his reign, but in which he played no part.

He was designated heir in **Rehe** on August 21 1861 at the age of five by his father, the Xianfeng emperor, who died the following day. Eight regents were appointed, including the two Empresses Dowager, Ci'an and **Cixi**. The Tongzhi emperor was never able to rule in his own right and his reign marked the beginning of Cixi's *de facto* rule over China.

TONGZHI RESTORATION ***Tongzhi zhongxing*** **同治中興**
Refers to the revival in Qing dynasty fortunes which broadly coincided with the reign of the Tongzhi Emperor. The concept of a *zhongxing* 中興 was based on examples such as the revival of the Han after **Wang Mang**'s usurpation and the Tang after the **An Lushan** Rebellion. Although dynasties were doomed to a cycle of decline, they could arrest this and temporarily revive their fortunes by, typically, defeating insurgent forces and taking appropriate fiscal and economic measures to reduce expenditure and raise tax yields. The Qing in 1860 looked to be on the verge of collapse: Beijing was attacked by Anglo-French forces in the Second **Opium War,** the **Taiping** rebels controlled much of southern China, the **Nian** rebels were active in the north and there was widespread social unrest and economic distress as a result of major floods in the 1850s. Improbably, the Qing survived. The foreigners decided their interests would be better served by supporting the Qing than the rebels, the Qing gave carte-blanche to governors-general in the south to set up their own armies in place of the discredited **Banner** forces and the governors-general, having seen the effectiveness of Western military technology and training, began to set up a military-industrial infrastructure by using receipts from their new tax, the *lijin* (likin) 厘金 transit and sales tax on merchants' goods.

Some measures were largely forced on the government by the foreigners. These included the establishment of a new, equal 'Foreign Ministry' style organ, the *Zongli geguo shiwu yamen* 總理各國事務衙門 (***Zongli yamen***) to replace the ***Lifanyuan***, a part of the tribute system and based on the assumption of Chinese superiority, for dealing with Westerners. The (*Jing shi*) *Tongwenguan* (京師) 同文館 (Capital) Interpreters' College was set up in 1861 to provide a supply of qualified interpreters trained in Western languages so that the government no longer had to rely on untrained merchants. **Zeng Guofan** set up the first rudimentary Western armaments factory in Anqing in 1861. After seeing Western forces in Shanghai in 1862, **Li Hongzhang** bought large quantities of Western armaments and hired a British instructor; he also sent **Yong Wing** to America to buy equipment and in 1865 set up the **Jiangnan Arsenal**, the *Jiangnan zhizao jiqi zongju* 江南制造機器總局. Others included the Fuzhou Shipyard set up by **Zuo Zongtang** in 1866 and the Tianjin Arsenal, also established in 1866.

During the 1860s there was a feeling among foreigners that China was making real progress but gradually this honeymoon period passed with the missionary riots in the early 1870s and the Tianjin massacre. There was no deep institutional change and commitment to reform was half-hearted at the real centre of power. The *Zongli yamen* was composed of seconded officials whose seniority declined; the *Tongwenguan* graduates discovered they, and other foreign affairs experts, were debarred from influential civil service posts and the provincial ventures were too reliant on the incumbent governor general for their long term success.

Mary Clabaugh WRIGHT, *The Last Stand of Chinese Conservatism: The T'ung-chih Restoration in China 1862–1874* (Stanford University Press, 1957); Masataka BANNO, *China and the West, 1858–61: The Origins of the Tsungli Yamen* (Harvard University Press, 1964).

TRADITIONAL FESTIVALS

Most Chinese festivals, whether based on the changing of the seasons according to the Chinese lunar calendar or myths about gods and ghosts, are the occasions for family reunions and for worshipping the gods in order to obtain their blessings and prevent misfortune. Chinese (or lunar) New Year, known as the Spring Festival 春節, is the longest and most important festival in China. Customs include dragon and lion dances, thoroughly cleaning the house, enjoying sumptuous family feasts, offering sacrifices to the gods, and giving friends and relatives "red envelopes" containing "lucky money." Firecrackers explode throughout the night on New year's Eve and sporadically on the following days. New Year's Eve and the first three days of the New Year are usually observed as a public holiday, though the holiday atmosphere may last through the Lantern Festival.

The Lantern Festival 燈節 is held on the fifteenth day of the first month, which was also known as the Yuanxiao Festival 元霄節. The people of ancient China believed that celestial spirits could be seen flying about in the light of the first full moon of the new lunar year. Over time, their torch-lit search for spirits evolved into the Lantern Festival, when temples and streets are decorated with lanterns of various colours and shapes. Chinese parents also prepared lanterns for their children to symbolise the hope that the children would have bright futures.

Qingming Festival 清明節 is for the remembrance of departed spirits, and falls on the first day of the Qingming term (in early April) of the farming **calendar**. Early on this day, people visit the graves of their loved ones and worship their ancestors, usually bringing some sort of offering, burning incense-sticks or paper money and sweeping the tombs.

The Duanwu Festival 端午節 (or 端陽節), also known as **Dragon Boat Festival**, is held around the fifth day of the fifth lunar month. The festival, originally for commemorating the poet **Qu Yuan,** is now an occasion for holding colourful boat races as well as for eating *zongzi* (rice dumplings wrapped in bamboo leaves or reeds) at home. The fifth lunar month is also believed to be a pestilential, danger-fraught period. Hygiene is therefore emphasised, with herbs added to food, and aromatic branches hung above doors. Protective sachets, colourfully embroidered and containing spices or medicines, are fastened to the clothing of young children.

The Moon or Mid-Autumn Festival, 中秋節, on the fifteenth day of the eighth lunar month, is when people observe the biggest and brightest full moon of the year, the harvest moon. The Festival is marked by family reunions, moon-gazing, and the eating of moon cakes – round pastries stuffed with red bean paste and an egg yolk, or fruit preserves.

Chongyang Festival 重陽節, on the ninth day of the ninth month, is the time when people go on outings with their family up into the hills and enjoy the autumn colours and, especially, the chrysanthemums.

TREATIES see place of signature. Eg., for **TREATY OF NANJING** see **NANJING, TREATY OF**

TREATY PORTS

Ports in which foreigners acquired the right to trade and live by virtue of the Treaty of **Nanjing** in 1842 and subsequent **unequal treaties**, where previously only Guangzhou had been open to foreign trade. They became the bases for foreign economic activities in China and many developed large European quarters where life was modelled closely on life in the home country. Treaty Ports were hotbeds of social change. A newly-emerging merchant class, the **compradores,** grew up to serve the needs of the Western traders, and industrialisation created China's modern working class. The first five opened after 1842 were Guangzhou, Xiamen (Amoy), Fuzhou, Ningbo and Shanghai. Ten new ports along the south-eastern coast and up the Yangzi River were added by the Treaty of **Tianjin**.

Rhoads MURPHEY, *The Outsiders: The Western Experience in India and China* (University of Michigan Press, 1977); J.K. FAIRBANK, *Trade and Diplomacy on the China Coast: The Opening of the Treaty Ports 1842–1854* (Harvard University Press, 1953); P.D. COATES, *The China Consuls: British Consular Officers, 1843–1943* (Oxford University Press, 1988).

TRIAD SOCIETY *Sanhehui* 三和會 *sandianhui* 三點會

Group of **Secret Societies**, whose origins lie with the clandestine successors to the Ming loyalist movement after it was suppressed on Taiwan in 1683. The name triad signifies the society's emphasis on the harmony of Heaven, Earth and Man. Branches of the Triad group included the **Heaven and Earth**, the **Small Sword** and **Elder Brother** and they participated in revolutionary movements, including the **Taiping Rebellion**. In modern times, the political aspect of their policies has ceased to be important and Triads are part of the criminal underworld with interests in drugs, prostitution and protection.

TRIBUTE SYSTEM

Formalisation of the Chinese world view that prevailed throughout most of the **imperial era**, based on the superiority of Chinese civilisation over that of foreign countries, which were often referred to as *hu* 胡, "barbarian". The concept may have stemmed from the *ba* **hegemon** system of the early Eastern Zhou period, representing shared cultural standards among different partners under a suzerain head. It was developed during the Han dynasty as part of the earliest attempt to establish a pattern for foreign relations, when the court both received gifts from the **Xiongnu** and sent its own demonstrations of largesse to their leader the Shanyu. The policy known as *heqin* 和親 "harmonious relationship" accepted coexistence on the basis of assumed superiority and inferiority. Though politicians sometimes argued in favour of military confrontation and barbarians themselves often failed to abide by the rules of the tribute system, the concept of *heqin* remained generally preferred. Its economic value was questionable, since the cost of entertaining foreign missions and sending back ostentatious gifts to their rulers outweighed the worth of the foreign 'luxuries' or curiosities accepted as tribute. Imperial gifts included textiles, gold and silver artefacts, porcelain and many other manufactured goods in addition to the seals, robes and official calendar that marked the investiture of a vassal leader. The frequency with which tribute states could send missions was prescribed according to their status within the system and their proximity to the Middle Kingdom, but the rules were unenforceable and rarely invoked. At times it suited officialdom to interpret any foreigners arriving in Chinese ports or markets with rare goods as tribute bearers and to present them as such at court. The system allowed members of tribute missions to trade for limited periods as part of their visit to China, so the dividing line between diplomatic exchange and commerce was often blurred.

It was implicit that a vassal might call upon China for help, but just as a father might chastise a son or refuse his request, so too would China put its own interests first when deciding policy towards a neighbour. Intervening in the politics of the Korean peninsula, both Sui and Tang courts sent armies to attack **Koguryo** (see Sui **Yangdi,** Tang **Taizong**). A plea for help from the Koryo court against the **Khitan** was ignored in 994, but when **Hideyoshi's** armies threatened the Flowery Kingdom in 1592 the Ming court sent troops to **Korea** to assist in defence.

The **Yongle** Emperor sought to expand the tribute system as the basis for an enlarged diplomatic network (see **Zheng He**), and his court at **Nanjing** and **Beijing** received frequent embassies, especially from the countries of south-east Asia, but his less flamboyant successors failed to attract so many. The Qing court tried to maintain the system and preserve the image of superiority it represented even as the growth of foreign commerce around its shores proved it less and less relevant. The **Qianlong** Emperor's famous letter to George III (see **Macartney**, Lord) indicates the unreality of the court's position as it vainly tried to make vassals of the European countries.

J.K. FAIRBANK, ed., *The Chinese World Order* (Harvard University Press, 1968).

TRIGRAMS see ***YIJING***

TSONG KHAPA (1357–1419)

Founder of **Ganden** monastery and the **Gelugpa** (Yellow Hat) Order. Born in Amdo (Xining) he had gone to **Tibet** to study at the age of seventeen under the aegis of the Kadampa Order, but had also received instruction from Kagya and Sakya scholars. His own philosophy, contained within the comprehensive *Lamrim Chempo*, "Stages of the Path", was based on the need to master Exoteric (scriptural) doctrine thoroughly before becoming expert in Esoteric practices (yoga and meditation) and teachings, and was the focus of Gelugpa doctrine and commentary.

TSUNGLI YAMEN see **ZONGLI YAMEN**

TU FU see **DU FU**

TWENTY-EIGHT BOLSHEVIKS

CCP students, also known as the Returned Students Faction, who had studied together in Moscow between 1926 and 1930. They controlled the CCP after the downfall of **Li Lisan** in 1930, and **Wang Ming** and **Bo Gu** were among the most powerful. They favoured orthodox Stalinist policies and did not support Mao Zedong's advocacy of guerilla warfare. By the **Zunyi Conference**, Mao's case was accepted and the Twenty-Eight were removed.

TWENTY-ONE DEMANDS
Japanese demands presented to the Chinese President, **Yuan Shikai** on January 18 1915. They called for Japanese control of Shandong, Manchuria, Inner Mongolia, parts of China's south-east coast and the Yangzi valley and these were accepted by Yuan Shikai on May19. A separate group of demands called for the employment of Japanese political, economic, military and police advisers and for China to buy half her armaments from Japan. Even Yuan Shikai was not prepared to accept these. The resentment at these demands and their acceptance created the climate of opinion which would erupt into nationalist passions in the **May Fourth Movement.**

TWO CHINAS POLICY
Policy, rejected by both Beijing and Taibei, that the PRC and **Taiwan** should be accepted as two separate sovereign states. The idea gained some currency in Taiwan during the 1980s as Taiwan independence became a legitimate topic for political discussion.

TWO LINES
The conflicting factional policies within the CCP in the 1960s. The "line" associated with Mao Zedong was radical, revolutionary-romantic and emphasised ideology and continuing revolution. Liu Shaqi's "line" stressed technical and professional expertise and gradual change. The "struggle between the two lines" was the cause of the **Cultural Revolution**.

UIGHURS see **UYGHURS**

ULANFU (1906–1988)
Inner Mongolian member of the CCP and Politburo and key figure in **United Front** and CPPCC work with ethnic minorities.

UNEQUAL TREATIES
Treaties signed by China after military defeats by Western powers in the nineteenth century, giving foreigners commercial and diplomatic privileges in the **treaty ports**. They included the Treaty of **Nanjing**, the Treaty of **Tianjin** and the Convention of **Beijing**. Both the GMD and the CCP repudiated the treaties. Treaties signed with the USA and Britain in January 1943 provided for the end to extraterritoriality and the return of foreign concessions to the Chinese government, but it was not until after the foundation of the PRC in 1949 that the treaties became ineffective.

UNITED FRONT, FIRST AND SECOND
Periods of cooperation between the GMD and the CCP. The First United Front lasted from the **Sun-Joffe Agreement** of 1923 until the **Shanghai Coup** of

1927 and its greatest success was the **Northern Expedition**. The Second United Front was less tangible and was an expedient during the **Anti-Japanese** War. The GMD was forced into the alliance after the **Xi'an Incident** of 1936. Technically the cooperation lasted from 1937 to 1945, but in practice, such collaboration as there was came to an end in January 1941 after the **New Fourth Army** Incident when GMD and CCP units clashed in Anhui.

Kui-kwong SHUM, *The Chinese Communists' Road to Power: The Anti-Japanese National United Front, 1935–1945* (Oxford University Press, 1988); Tetsuya KATAOKA, *Resistance and Revolution in China: The Communists and the Second United Front* (Berkeley: University of California Press, 1974); Lyman VAN SLYKE, *Enemies and Friends: The United Front in Chinese Communist History* (Stanford University Press, 1967).

URUMQI

Capital of the **Xinjiang** Uyghur Autonomous Region.

USSURI INCIDENT

Clashes between Russian and Chinese border guards in March 1969 on the island known to the Chinese as Zhenbao and the Russians as Damanskiy on the Ussuri river which marks China's north-eastern border with Russia. It was the most serious military incident in the **Sino-Soviet Dispute.**

UYGHURS

The Uyghurs, *Weiwuerzu* 維吾爾族 in Chinese, consider themselves to be the indigenous people of Xinjiang, where the majority of them live, although there are also Uyghurs in Kazakhstan and other parts of the former Soviet Union and small emigré communities in Turkey and Germany. They probably arrived in Xinjiang as part of the great westward migration of Turkic-speaking peoples from what is now Mongolia in the eighth and ninth centuries. The total Uyghur population of Xinjiang today is approximately seven million and their language is related to Turkish, but is sufficiently different to make the two mutually incomprehensible. In addition to their identity as Uyghurs, most tend to identify themselves by the oasis town from which they originate such as Kashghar, Yarkand, Karghalik or Turpan. Uyghurs became highly skilled at oasis agriculture and at making the most effective use of the meagre supply of water available to them. This involvement in settled agriculture distinguished them from most of the other Turkic-speaking peoples of the region like the Kazakhs and Kyrgyz who were still nomadic pastoralists. Indeed they are often known by the name *taranchi*, cultivator, after the eighteenth century Uyghurs sent from southern Xinjiang to Ili (Ghulja) near the border with Kazakhstan to work as farmers and border guards. Uyghur oases in southern Xinjiang and the grape-growing Turpan region east of Urumqi are irrigated by a complex system of *kariz* wells supplied by underground watercourses which channel the melting snow from the mountains and bring it to the fields with the minimum of evaporation.

A group of Uyghurs who migrated into Gansu in the ninth century speak a variety of Uyghur, influenced by Mongolian and Chinese and not now intelligible to the Uyghurs of Xinjiang. They are known as Yellow Uyghurs and have remained Buddhists, being far enough east to have avoided Islamisation.

VERBIEST, FERDINAND (1623–88)
Belgian **Jesuit** who became leader of the Order in China in succession to Adam **Schall** von Bell, and with him and Matteo **Ricci** is renowned as one of the three great founding fathers of Catholic mission work in China. At court he held the post of Director of the Astronomical Bureau under the **Kangxi Emperor**, with whom he maintained close personal relations. His career in China lasted from 1658 until his death in 1688.
J.W. WITEK, ed., *Ferdinand Verbiest, S.J. (1623–1688): Jesuit Missionary, Scientist, Engineer and Diplomat* (Nettetal: Steyler Vlg., 1994).

VERITABLE RECORDS *Shi lu* 實錄
A detailed chronological record of government activities based on the daily diaries of emperors kept by the History Office (known as *qijuzhu* 'notes of activity and repose') and on other central government archives. The *shilu* date from the Liang dynasty but only exist in fragmentary form until the Ming. The *Ming shilu* 明實錄 covering 13 emperors runs to around 3,000 *juan* 卷 and forms a rich source of material on political, military, economic, educational and social matters, natural calamities and court ceremonies. The *shilu* were produced for the previous emperor on the accession of a new emperor so they were not as much affected by the passage of time as the Dynastic Histories, nor did they suffer from dynastic rewriting. However, since the events they recorded were frequently of contemporary relevance they suffered from pressures to produce a record favourable to those in power. The similar *Qing shilu* 清實錄 covers 11 emperors in over 4,300 *juan*.
Charles GARDNER, *Chinese Traditional Historiography* (Harvard University Press, 1961); W.G. BEASLEY and E.G. PULLEYBLANK, *Historians of China and Japan* (Oxford University Press, 1961).

VERSAILLES, TREATY OF (1919)
Peace agreement intended to settle questions arising out of the First World War in Europe, but with significant consequences for China. The conference agreed to Japan's demands that all German interests in Shandong should be transferred to her rather than be returned to China. The weak government in China was unable to resist this and mass demonstrations against this failure by students in Beijing on May 4 1919 precipitated a surge of nationalism, the **May Fourth Movement**, during which both the GMD and the CCP were founded.

VIRTUOUS WOMEN
Ban Zhao is famous for her writing in the *Nüjie* "Women's prescriptions" on female virtue, speech, deportment and work, but after the Neo-Confucian revival established **Zhu Xi's** interpretation of the ***Liji*** as the orthodoxy for literati behaviour it was obedience to the *sancong* (see **marriage**), and especially widow chastity, that were most praised. Outstanding examples of self-sacrificing female virtue were posthumously rewarded and held up as exemplary by the publication of honorific obituaries or the erection of memorial arches.

VOITINSKY, GREGOR
Comintern agent who arrived in Shanghai in May 1920 for talks with **Chen Duxiu** and **Li Dazhao** which led to the drafting of a **Chinese Communist Party** constitution. The party was not officially formed until July 1921.

WADE, THOMAS FRANCIS (1818–1895)
Assistant to Lord Elgin and British Minister in Beijing 1873–4. He became Professor of Chinese at the University of Cambridge in 1888 and devised the system of romanising Chinese that was later modified by **Herbert Giles**, who succeeded him in the chair, and became known as the **Wade-Giles system**.

WADE-GILES SYSTEM see **ROMANISATION**

WAI TING see **OUTER COURT**

WALEY, ARTHUR (1889–1968)
Translator and writer who played a leading part in popularising Chinese culture in the West in the mid-twentieth century. Though he never went to East Asia himself his deep understanding and appreciation of Chinese civilisation helped him to convey a sense of the mood of Chinese society and its thought in a way that attracted specialist and non-academic readers alike. Among his many translations were the Analects, ***Lunyu,*** of **Confucius**, *One Hundred and Seventy Chinese Poems*, and *Monkey* (a version of ***Xiyouji***). As a corollary to the latter he also wrote *The Real Tripitaka*, the true story of the life and times of **Xuanzang**. He also translated works from other cultures, including the Ainu of Japan.
F.A. JOHNS, *A Bibliography of Arthur Waley* (London: Athlone Press, 1988); Ivan MORRIS, ed., *Madly Singing in the Mountains* (New York: Walker and Co., 1970; reprinted by Harper and Row, 1972).

WALKING ON TWO LEGS
Great Leap Forward policy of using traditional methods alongside modern science, in medicine and in other fields

WANG ANSHI 王安石 (1021–86)
The most radical and subsequently infamous would-be political and social reformer in Chinese history since **Wang Mang**. His intellectual attainments as a poet, prosodist and historian were undoubted, but he saw himself as a proponent of the government's duty to act on behalf of the common people in the **Confucian** tradition, and his critics, who ultimately included many Confucian statesmen and bureaucrats such as **Ouyang Xiu**, **Su Shi** and **Sima Guang**, evidently feared him as a neo-Legalist. Even in the 1970s, debate raged over the philosophical basis for the "Ten thousand word memorial" of 1058 in which he set out his programme and the fifteen New Laws he proposed as Chief Minister (see **Prime Minister**) to Emperor Shenzong between 1069 and 1073. These included plans for market intervention and price stabilisation, cheap loans to farmers, **water control** works, tax reforms in favour of the poor (see **taxation**), the extension of state **schools**, reform of the **examination system** in a practical direction, improved military defences based on the distribution of horses to

peasant families in return for cavalry service, and the revival of the ***baojia*** organisation of social units for defence and fiscal purposes. In conventional manner he justified his reforms by appeal to the past. He argued that new talent must be trained to help re-interpret the intentions of the **Former Kings**, requiring more education, better selection methods and more appointments to official posts, all dependent upon economic support for the people. The simplest explanation for the failure of the reforms is that they attacked the vested interests of too many powerful sections of society, in government, commerce and the military. Wang himself resigned in 1076, but the controversy over his policies continued and affected court politics well into the twelfth century (see **Cai Jing, Su Che**). See also **Song Dynasty.**

J.T.C. LIU, *Reform in Sung China* (Harvard University Press, 1959).

WANG CHONG 王充 (27–?100)

Author of *Lunheng* 論衡 'Balanced discussions', an unprecedented book in which he demonstrated his scepticism at the widespread beliefs in the interpretation of either history or of **omens and portents** as a guide to Heaven's will. He did not accept that Heaven intervened in the human world, did not believe in ghosts, and tried to promote a rationalist understanding of natural phenomena such as thunderstorms (or the appearance of dragons). He had some sympathy for the metaphysics of **Daoism** and a proto-scientific acceptance of the interaction of *yin* and *yang* (see ***yin-yang***), but he was a true individualist who cannot be categorised under the heading of any school.

A. FORKE, trans., *Lun-Heng, Philosophical Essays of Wang Ch'ung*, 2 vols. (London 1907, Berlin 1911).

WANG, EMPRESS (Wang Zhengjun 71 BC-AD 13)

After entering the court at the age of seventeen, she became empress to the Han emperor **Yuandi,** mother of **Chengdi**, and Empress Dowager during his reign and that of **Aidi** and Pingdi. During her son's reign she advanced the political fortunes of her clan, in particular laying the groundwork for the later accession of her nephew **Wang Mang** by making him *de facto* ruler for the boy Pingdi, and regent when he died in AD 5.

WANG FUZHI 王夫之 (1619–1692)

Philosopher and scholar who followed **Mencius** in affirming the importance of economic well-being as the basis for good **kingship** and social progress, but rejected the value of past institutions as a guide to the present and denied any supernatural power in the shaping of human progress. To him "the Way is the Way of concrete things" (see ***Dao***) and he is known as a materialist with an evolutionary view of history. He was a stern opponent of the Manchu conquerors of China, and was an example to the late Qing dynasty reformers seeking to rescue China from foreign domination. He emphasized the significance of human desire in the identification of orderly principle in nature (see **Dai Zhen**).

Wang was the most implacable of the three famous Ming loyalist scholars who refused to serve the Qing dynasty but lived out their lives in seclusion. He came from a scholarly background and passed the *juren* 舉人 examination in 1642, raised a local force in his home area (Hengyang, Hunan) and fought the

Qing in 1648 but was defeated. He joined the Ming loyalist forces of Prince Gui but returned to Hunan in 1652 and lived the rest of his life as a reclusive scholar. He was an eclectic scholar who included **Daoism** and **Buddhism** in his studies but principally followed the **Zhu Xi** school of **Neo-Confucianism** and particularly favoured the monist philosophy of Zhang Zai. He was very strongly opposed to **Wang Yangming**, whose discredited intuitive approach was seen as contributing to the downfall of the Ming, and in his classical studies Wang Fuzhi concentrated on the use of philology to elucidate the meaning of texts. In his historical studies he rejected the 'past golden age' concept prevalent in Confucianism and recognised historical progress (for which he has been praised by scholars in the PRC); he also emphasised the primacy of the people in the state. His voluminous writings, which cover a wide field, are suffused with opposition to foreign domination of China and were not generally available until his collective works were published as the *Chuanshan yishu* 船山遺書 in the mid-19th century (the definitive edition in 358 *juan* was published in 1933). They provided fertile ground for the anti-Manchu revolutionaries among whom he became a cult figure.

Alison Harley BLACK, *Man and Nature in the Philosophical Thought of Wang Fu-chih* (University of Washington Press, 1989).

WANG GUOWEI 王國維 (1877–1927)

Historian and ***jinshixue*** 金石學 scholar, also known as Jingan 靜安. Born in Haining, Zhejiang province, he studied in Shanghai under Luo Zhenyu 羅振玉 before travelling to Japan to study with Luo's sponsorship in 1901. After returning to China, Wang Guowei taught at a number of colleges and universities, and served the abdicated emperor **Puyi** as a literature tutor. In the summer of 1927, Wang Guowei drowned himself in the Kunming Lake of the Summer Palace in Beijing.

Wang Guowei was known for his scholarship in classic literature, including *ci* poetry, novels and Song and Yuan plays. His *Renjian Cihua* 人間詞話 (*Notes and Comments on Ci Poetry*), published in 1908, was an influential work on the aesthetics of *ci* poetry. He successfully combined Western scientific methods with traditional Chinese textual research methods in his study of inscriptions on oracle bones, bronzes and wooden slips. For example, he pioneered the method of using textual information from oracle bones in checking the geography, genealogy and ritual systems of the Shang dynasty, and this shed new light on the history of this period. Wang Guowei's other contributions include published work on early measurements, architecture and costumes.

Joey BONNER, *Wang Kuo-wei: An Intellectual Biography* (Harvard University Press, 1986).

WANG HONGWEN 王洪文 (1935–1992)

One of the **Gang of Four**, Wang worked in a cotton mill in Shanghai and was the founder of the **Cultural Revolution** mass organisation, the Shanghai Workers Revolutionary General Headquarters in 1967. He became deputy chairman of the Shanghai **Revolutionary Committee** in 1968 and deputy prime minister of the PRC in 1975. He was sentenced to life imprisonment on January 25 1981 at the end of the trial of the Gang of Four.

WANG JIAN 王建 (847–907)
A former petty criminal and opportunist who, having become a member of Tang Xizong's bodyguard, helped his flight into Sichuan (see **Huang Chao**). Having become a military commander after the Emperor's return, he was again exiled to western Sichuan as a result of **eunuch** intrigue in 886. There he established his own power base. He set up the capital of his quasi-independent but pro-Tang kingdom at Chengdu in 901, named it the Former Shu (see **Five Dynasties and Ten Kingdoms**), and took the title of Gaozu. His rule, unlike that of Huang Chao in **Chang'an**, proved to be remarkably benevolent, and he is renowned for his patronage of writers and musicians. His stone tomb is decorated with a remarkable frieze depicting instrumentalists and dancers.

WANG JINGWEI 汪精衛 (1883–1944)
Founder member of the ***Tongmenghui*** while a student in Japan in 1905, Wang Jingwei joined the GMD Praesidium in 1924 during the alliance with the CCP. He belonged to the left wing of the Party and dominated the **Left Guomindang** government that ruled briefly from Wuhan in 1927. He had cooperated with the CCP but finally expelled them from his administration in August 1927. He served in Jiang Jieshi's Nanjing government, but after the Japanese invasion of 1937, agreed to a Japanese initiative and ran a puppet government based in Nanjing in March 1940. He died in Japan in November 1944.

Gerald BUNKER, *The Peace Conspiracy: Wang Ching-wei and the China War, 1937–1941* (Harvard University Press, 1972).

WANG MANG 王莽 (45 BC – AD 23, r. AD 9–23)
Traditionally excoriated by Chinese historians as a usurper who interrupted the legitimate rule of the Han dynasty and divided it into two halves. Though his *Xin* 新, "New", dynasty failed to survive, his memorial may be seen in the greater acceptance of Confucian principle in subsequent government. Seeing himself in the role of a new "Duke of Zhou" (see **Zhou Gong**) with the heaven-given task of rescuing the country from the economic and bureaucratic ills into which it had fallen, he worked with **Liu Xin** on the production and interpretation of new versions of ancient texts which would justify his claims to power (see **Old** and **New Texts**). His principal reform attempts were concerned with the abolition of large estates and redistribution of land, the freeing of slaves, the introduction of agricultural loans, the debasement of the currency, the "levelling" of production and supply by buying up surplus goods for sale in time of need, and the transfer of administration from the provinces to central government. They made a direct appeal to the ordinary populace but after only three years, long before their long-term benefits could be evaluated, Wang's opponents, including surviving members of the Liu clan, stirred up criticism from all levels of society. The disastrous effects of a change in direction by the **Yellow River** in AD 11 were interpreted as an omen of Heaven's displeasure, and a serious peasant rebellion known as the revolt of the **Red Eyebrows** (AD 18) provoked wider outbreaks of fighting with heavy loss of life, and led to his death.

H. BIELENSTEIN, *The Restoration of the Han Dynasty*, 4 vols. (Stockholm: Bulletin of the Museum of Far Eastern Antiquities, 26 (1954), 31 (1959), 39 (1967), 51 (1979)).

WANG MENG 王蒙 (1934–)
Writer, literary critic and one time Minister of Culture. Wang Meng began to work for the CP underground in 1948 when he was just 14 years old and his commitment to his Communist ideals has never wavered, although his criticism of aspects of the system has brought him into conflict with the authorities. He began writing the novel *Qingchun wansui* 青春萬歲 'Long Live Youth' when he was 19, and since that time has published prolifically on many subjects and in various styles. However, the typical Wang Meng story follows the pattern of his famous 1956 story *Zuzhibu laile ge nianqing ren* 組織部來了個年輕人 'The Young Newcomer to the Organisation Department' which describes the trials and tribulations of a committed young cadre trying to correct what he sees as abuses in the way his department is run. Wang Meng attempted to get away from Yan'an period stereotypes of squeaky-clean Communist heroes versus blackhearted landlord and Guomindang villains, and offers us less than perfect Communist Party members struggling with real life problems. That story brought him a rightist cap in 1958 when he was expelled from the Party after the **Anti-Rightist Movement** and sent to the countryside; he spent most of the next twenty years in exile in Xinjiang until he was re-admitted to the Party in 1979 and allowed to return to Beijing as a professional writer. Prize-winning stories from this time include *Ye de yan* 夜的眼 'Eyes of the Night', a story of corruption and decadence, and *Hudie* 蝴蝶 'Butterfly', a semi-autobiographical novelette about the changing fortunes of a Communist official told in flashback mode (hence the title's reference to **Zhuangzi**'s butterfly). He advanced up the Party hierarchy as a cultural official until he was made Minister of Culture in July 1986, a post he held until September 1989 (he was reportedly opposed to government policy over the **Tian'an men Massacre** in 1989). Since then he has continued to hold official posts, to write and to travel widely abroad. His collected works, *Wang Meng wenji* 王蒙文集, were published in 10 volumes in 1993.

WANG Meng: *Selected Works of Wang Meng I: The Strain of Meeting*, trans. Denis C. MAIR; *Selected Works of Wang Meng II: Snowball*, trans. Cathy SILBER and Deirdre HUANG (Beijing: Foreign Languages Press, 1989).

WANG MING 王明 (1904–74)
The pseudonym of Chen Shaoyu 陳紹禹, the leader of the **Twenty-Eight Bolsheviks**. Wang joined the **Chinese Communist Party** in 1925, studied in Moscow and returned to China in 1930. He was acting General Secretary of the CCP from 1931–2 and a member of the executive committee of the **Jiangxi Soviet**. He was replaced at the head of the CCP after the power struggle at the **Zunyi Conference** in 1935. He moved back to Moscow and took part in the polemics of the **Sino-Soviet dispute** on the side of the Soviet Union.

WANG SHIWEI 王實味 (1906–47)
Translator and writer who became a principal target of the Yan'an **rectification campaigns**. Wang was born into a scholarly but poor Henan family. He attended Beijing University for two years from 1926, was forced to curtail his studies and took a succession of jobs before becoming a translator in 1930. He went to **Yan'an** in 1937 and was given a post in the Marxist-Leninist Academy. In

March 1942 he published an essay, *Ye baihehua* 野百合花 'Wild Lily', which criticised Communist Party cadres for forming a new self-serving elite, like the one they had fought against and replaced. He claimed that artists had a role, developing man's soul, which gave them a duty to criticise and expose even in Yan'an. The fundamental nature of his conflict with the developing party line and his relative obscurity compared to other party critics like **Ding Ling** and **Ai Qing** made him the prime target of the rectification campaign which followed the **Yan'an Forum** in 1942. He refused to recant, even when the others did so and were forced by the Party to attack him. He was condemned as Trotskyite and anti-Party and executed in 1947.

DAI Qing: *Wang Shiwei and Wild Lilies: rectifications and purges in the Chinese Communist Party 1942–1944* (New York: M.E. Sharpe, 1993); Merle GOLDMAN, *Literary Dissent in Communist China* (Harvard University Press, 1967; Atheneum, 1971).

WANG SHUWEN 王叔文 (d.806)

Member of the **Hanlin Academy** and confidant to Crown Prince Li Song, who despite sickness ascended the throne as Tang Emperor Shunzong early in 805. Wang thereupon led a group of officials, including **Liu Zongyuan**, in an attempt to gain power at court and command of the palace armies. His intended policies were aimed at reducing court corruption and reviving the proper Way (see ***Dao***). But his attempted coup was blocked by the **eunuchs** at court and the Emperor abdicated by the middle of the same year, whereupon Wang's defeat and execution were assured.

WANG WEI 王維 (699?-761)

Distinguished Tang poet, painter and musician also known as Mojie 摩詰. Born in Shanxi, Wang Wei experienced several setbacks on the road to official success. He was briefly exiled to Shandong and, shortly after his return, his mother died. During the **An Lushan Rebellion** (755–757) he was forced to serve under the puppet government but received a pardon and rose to the post of Right Assistant Director of the Department of State Affairs. From then on he divided his time between the Court and his retreat on the Wang River at Lantian, south of Chang'an, a place which inspired his *Wang chuan ji* 輞川集 'Wang River Collection'. The author of four hundred poems, Wang Wei was a close observer of the natural order. A practising Buddhist, he relished solitude and his appreciation of the nature that surrounded him is reflected in his poetry. Although none of his paintings survive, he was revered as the father of the Southern School of painting, an archetypal scholar-painter (as opposed to a professional painter). It is believed that he originated the idea of painting a horizontal scroll, having depicted the scene evoked by his Wang River sequence of poems. Whenever he was on holiday or out of office, Wang Wei retreated to his Lantian villa, where the tranquil landscape was the source of some of his best poems and paintings. Wang Wei's typical mood in his poetry is that of tranquillity, solitude, a retreat into nature and **Buddhism** (he became a devout Buddhist after his wife's death in 730). His landscapes, like his poetry, are said to have embodied a sense of distance and "emptiness". His works were described by **Su Shi** as: "In (his) painting there is poetry; in (his) poetry there is painting". Both his landscape painting and poetry had profound influence on later generations.

None of his paintings has survived in the original, but a number of Song copies still exist in China and Japan. He apparently painted both Buddhist and Daoist subjects, but was best known for his landscapes using the technical innovation of breaking ink, *pomo*. All scholar-painters, from the Song onward, shared Wang Wei's belief that the purpose of painting was to express, not the artist's skill with the brush, but his quality as a man.

WANG Wei, *Poems of Wang Wei*, trans. and introd. G.W. Robinson (Penguin, 1973); WANG Wei, *Laughing Lost in the Mountains: Poems of Wang Wei* trans. Tony Barnstone, Willis Barnstone and Xu Haixun (Hanover, New Hampshire: University Press of New England, 1991); Pauline YU, *The Poetry of Wang Wei: New Translations and Commentary* (Indiana University Press, 1980).

WANG XIZHI 王羲之 (307–365)

Also known as Yishao and Wang Youjun (from his official title). Master of **calligraphy** in the Eastern Jin period. Born in Linyi, Shandong province, but later lived in Zhejiang, Southern China. Wang occupied various official positions until he resigned in 355, spending the last years of his life with his circle of literary friends, discussing Buddhist and Daoist topics and cultivating the arts. He is highly praised for the perfection of his writing in standard, running and draft scripts. Due to the spiritual and personal qualities in his works, Wang was much revered under imperial patronage in later dynasties. A number of Tang copies of his works in the *tie* format (see ***bei tie***) still survive in China and Japan. *Lanting xu* 蘭亭序 'Preface at the Orchid Pavilion', written in running script, is one of the most celebrated pieces of calligraphy in China and set a standard for centuries afterwards. His youngest son Wang Xianzhi 王獻之 (344–388) was also a celebrated calligrapher. He and his father are usually referred to as the two Wangs in the history of Chinese calligraphy.

L.L. CHANG and others, *Four Thousand Years of Chinese Calligraphy* (University of Chicago Press, 1990)

WANG YANGMING 王陽明 (1472–1529)

Scholar who developed the idealist *xin xue* 心學 school of **Neo-Confucianism.** Idealist Neo-Confucianism had been promoted by Lu Jiuyuan 陸九淵 (Lu Xiangshan) 1139–93, a contemporary of Zhu Xi in the Southern Song, but had been eclipsed by the Cheng-Zhu rationalist school. Idealism is sometimes called the Lu-Wang school.

Generally known in China as Wang Shouren 王守仁, Wang Yangming came from Yuyao 余姚 in Zhejiang. He obtained his *jinshi* 進士 degree in 1499 and was appointed as secretary *zhu shi* 主事 in the Board of Punishments *Xing bu* 刑部, later transfering to the Board of War *Bing bu* 兵部. In 1506. as a result of his defence of the censor Dai Xian 戴銑, he incurred the enmity of the powerful eunuch Liu Jin 劉瑾 and was sentenced to be flogged and banished to Guizhou as a post station officer. In 1510 he became a magistrate in Jiangxi and for the next twelve years led a very active life as a central and local official; particularly noteworthy was his success as Governor of Jiangxi in eradicating long standing rebellions there in 1517–18. After the death of his father in 1522 he withdrew for five years of mourning and teaching; his *Chuanxilu* 傳習錄 (translated as *Instructions for Practical Living*) is a record of his teachings at this time. He was recalled in 1527 to deal with a rebellion in Guangxi, which he successfully suppressed, but he died on the way back from there.

It was in the solitude of his banishment to Guizhou that Wang, in a sudden **Chan Buddhist** style enlightenment, realised that the universal principle was in his own mind all along. For years he had tried to follow the method of the rationalist Cheng-Zhu school of Neo-Confucianism, which involved building up a composite picture of the universal principle, *taiji* 太極 or *tianli* 天理, by studying the separate principles, *li* 理, of individual objects. He relates how he had once spent seven days studying some bamboo but the only result was that he felt ill. Zhu Xi had affirmed that the mind *xin* 心 and principle *li* were different, Wang Yangming realized that they were the same, and what he had been seeking externally was inside him all along, it was his *liangzhi* 良知 innate knowledge, literally 'knowledge of goodness'. This had a number of important ramifications: for Zhu Xi the ultimate step was 'the extension of knowledge though the investigation of things' *ge wu zhi zhi* 格物致知 and 'making the will sincere' *chengyi* 誠意 was an intermediate stage, for Wang Yangming the latter was the key (see ***Daxue,*** the Great Learning); book learning was less important, contemplation more important; the indivisibility of the mind of man and the principle of the universe meant that true knowledge and right action were inseparable, hence his theory of the unity of knowledge and action *zhi xing he yi* 知行合一. This kind of knowledge is always presented in moral terms: true understanding of, for example, filial piety will automatically result in appropriate action.

Wang Yangming was revered in China from soon after his death until the late seventeenth century. He was also highly regarded in Japan. He was one of the most successful figures in Chinese history at combining the roles of philosopher and practical official (something even Confucius failed to achieve). He saw that Cheng-Zhu rationalism had got itself into a rut of scholasticism and was ignoring the purpose of education, moral cultivation. However, the emphasis on looking inwards inevitably led to greater subjectivism and, among some of his wilder followers, a moral relativism which early Qing scholars blamed for the decadence and collapse of the Ming.

WANG Yang-ming, *Instructions for Practical Living and other Neo-Confucian Writing,* trans. Wing-tsit Chan (Columbia University Press, 1963); TU Wei-ming, *Neo-Confucian thought in action: Wang Yang-ming's youth (1472–1509)* (Berkeley: University of California Press, 1976).

WANLI 萬歷, MING EMPEROR (1573–1620)

Longest reigning emperor of the Ming dynasty. In the early years of his reign, he was assisted by an able Grand Secretary **Zhang Juzheng**, but when Zhang died in 1582, Wanli withdrew from affairs of state and avoided contact with officials wherever possible, relying on the palace **eunuchs** to communicate with them. The court suffered a severe crisis towards the end of the reign, because of the cost of military expeditions to Mongolia and Korea and the **Donglin Academy** founded in 1604 was worsened factional disputes among officials and by the time of Wanli's death in 1620, the dynasty was in terminal decline. Nevertheless, the Wanli reign is remembered as a high point of Ming culture. The porcelain centre of **Jingdezhen** was at its most productive, novels such as ***Jinpingmei*** and ***Xiyouji*** became popular and there was a commercial revolution second only to that of the Song period.

War of Resistance against Japan see **Anti-Japanese War**

Ward, Frederick Townsend

American adventurer who led the **Ever-Victorious Army** and was succeeded on his death by Charles Gordon.

Warlords

Local military rulers in the period between the **Revolution of 1911** and 1949 and in particular after 1916, when **Yuan Shikai** died There was no single government during this period that had control over the whole of the country although this was the aim of the Nanjing government of **Jiang Jieshi** established in 1928. Consequently, power in the regions, especially those most distant from the capital fell into the hands of strong leaders who could muster sufficient military force. **Yan Xishan** in Shanxi, **Feng Yuxiang** in Shaanxi, Tang Jiyao in Yunnan and **Zhang Zuolin** in Manchuria were among the best-known warlords of the era and they and other groups of minor warlords negotiated deals and alliances with the National Government, while retaining a considerable degree of independence.

Ch'i Hsi-sheng, *Warlord Politics in China, 1916–1928* (Stanford University Press, 1976); Lucian Pye, *Warlord Politics: Conflict and Coalition in the Modernization of Republican China* (New York: Praeger, 1971); James Sheridan, *Chinese Warlord: The Career of Feng Yu-hsiang* (Stanford University Press, 1966).

Warring States *Zhanguo* 戰國

Name given to the period of the Eastern Zhou dynasty from the end of the Spring and Autumn to the triumph of the Qin reunification. It is not a precisely dateable era. Some historians speak of it as beginning in 481 BC, when the chronicles of Lu come to an end, others as late as 403 BC, when the Zhou court officially recognised the three separate states (**Han**, **Wei** and **Zhao**) into which Jin had broken up fifty years before. By the beginning of the fourth century there were seven major states, Yan, **Qi**, **Chu**, Han, Wei, Zhao and **Qin**. Ideas of peaceful coexistence had gone; acknowledgement of Zhou authority had also ceased to matter and state rulers took the title of king for themselves. (Ironically in view of what was to come, or perhaps appropriately in view of its own imperial pretensions, Qin continued to defend Zhou interests longer than other states, in recognition of which the Zhou king rewarded Duke Xin with the old-fashioned title of **hegemon** *ba* 霸 in 364.) The aim of each now became the expansion of his own state's power at the expense of its neighbours, until the goal of overall supremacy was reached. Warfare turned from the chivalrous nature of short-lived spring and autumn battles to all-out, ruthless campaigning conducted by enormous armies using cavalry and deadly crossbows, and in which spies as well as military tacticians came into their own. Eventually it was Qin, taking full advantage of its strong economic base in the south-west and the determinedly efficient political organisation developed by **Legalism**, that overcame its last remaining enemies Chu in 278 BC and Qi in 221 BC. It thus achieved what all had been striving for and talking about, yet what nobody had ever known in China on such a scale – the establishment of a united empire.

The Warring States period was one of constant suffering for the multitudes caught up in the backward and forward march of battling armies. Yet the battling for a new political order was but a symptom of the deep intellectual search that was going on to understand more about mankind and his world. The philosophers strove to explain the relationship between man and Heaven and to offer guidance and solace to those caught up in the turmoil of the age (see **Hundred Schools**). Writers discovered the skills of parable, allegory, and humour as subtle means of advancing their case. The growing mastery of tools and materials led to the first use of iron, and enabled craftsmen and artists to produce bold and outstanding works in bronze, wood, **jade**, and **lacquer**. The pain of the Warring States represented the birth-pangs of imperial China. See also **Leigudun,** ***Zhanguoce.***

Mark Edward LEWIS, *Sanctioned Violence in Early China* (State University of New York Press, 1990).

WASHINGTON CONFERENCE (1921–1922)

Deliberations on arms limitation and East Asian matters in general, attended by representatives from Britain, the United States, France, Portugal, Italy, Japan, China, Belgium and the Netherlands and held in Washington D.C. from November 1921 to February 1922. A Nine-Power Pact signed at the end of the conference guaranteed the territorial integrity of China, including the return of **Jiaozhou** and agreed on an open-door policy for foreign relations with China. The Washington Naval Limitation Treaty, agreed at the same time, banned the building of capital ships for ten years, limited the size of other ships and weapons and fixed the ratio of capital ships between the great powers. The agreements proved impossible to enforce as there was substantial opposition to it in Japan and the Japanese government formally renounced them in 1934.

WATER CONTROL

Ever since the great Yu 禹 (see **Former Kings**) rescued the country from a terrible flood the rulers of China have appreciated water as a means of irrigation, communication and transportation. Two known examples of pre-imperial canals are those built by Zheng Guo to irrigate the region to the North of the Wei River in 246 BC and by **Li Bing** as part of his hydraulic scheme for the Chengdu plain. Both benefited **Qin**, where the concept of the "key economic area" and the function of water in the development of a strong agricultural centre were recognised as means of extending military and political control. But too much water could also be a threat. The flooding of the **Yellow River** in 132 BC prompted a debate between Confucians and Daoists about the most appropriate means of remedying its unpredictability, whether by trying to constrain it within newly built dykes along its original course or by letting it find its own preferred route. The dykes were eventually rebuilt in 109, but the River proved that it still had the ultimate power when it changed its course in AD 11 (see **Wang Mang**). Civil engineers developed flash locks by the first century BC and pound locks by the tenth century AD. Major projects called for the deployment of massive labour gangs organised by central government, but more routine maintenance was the responsibility of local officials: as Prefect of **Hangzhou, Su Shi** instituted an effective programme for cleaning up the shores and tributaries of the West Lake in 1089–91. See also **Oriental Despotism, Grand Canal.**

C.T. Chi, *Key Economic Areas in Chinese History* (New York, 1963); L-S. Yang, *Les Aspects Economiques des Travaux Publics dans la Chine Impériale* (Paris, 1964).

Water Margin see ***Shuihuzhuan***

Wei dynasty 魏朝, Northern (386–534)

Regime of the Toba people who had been extending their control over the North China Plain since the mid-fourth century and achieved total domination of the North in 489. The capital was moved from Pingcheng (modern Datong) to **Luoyang** in 494 during the reign of Emperor Xiaowen 孝文帝 (471–99), by which time the dynasty had become almost completely sinicised. Striking evidence of its patronage of **Buddhism** is still to be seen in the huge stone statues in the **Yungang** Caves outside Datong and the **Longmen** Caves near Luoyang. Eventually the more conservative elements among its leadership rebelled against the loss of their tribal identity and broke away. In the north-east the Gao clan formed the Eastern Wei in 534, later taking the dynastic title Northern Qi (550–77). In the north-west the Yuwen clan established the Western Wei (535) and renamed it Northern Zhou in 557 (–581). See also **Northern and Southern Dynasties.**

Wei, Empress 韋后 (d.710)

Wife of Emperor **Zhongzong**, sister of Emperor **Ruizong** and daughter-in-law of Empress Wu (**Wu Zetian**). A lascivious woman who with her daughter the Taiping Princess was deeply involved in court intrigue after her recall from exile in 698. Having failed in her attempt to manipulate the succession to her husband as she wished in 710, she was killed in a palace coup organised by her daughter.

Wei Jingsheng 魏京生 (1949–)

Dissident electrician and editor sentenced to fifteen years' imprisonment on October 16 1979 for allegedly passing military secrets to a foreign national and counter-revolutionary activities. Wei had been active in the **Democracy Wall** protests of 1978 and edited the journal *Beijing Spring* (*Beijing zhi chun* 北京之春). He called for a fifth modernisation, democracy to be added to the **Four Modernisations** called for by Deng Xiaoping. Wei served fourteen and a half years of his sentence and was released in 1993. He was tried again for counter-revolutionary crimes in December 1995 and sentenced to another fourteen years in prison. In 1995 and 1996, he was unsuccessfully nominated for the Nobel Prize for Peace.

Wei 魏, state

The most powerful of the three states (together with Han and Zhao) into which **Jin** broke up in 453 BC. Though its territory crossed the **Yellow River** into the northern part of modern Shaanxi (known as Hexi), its heartland was situated in the most fertile areas of the southern Great Plain. It was sometimes known by the name of its capital, Liang (modern **Kaifeng**). An extension of **Han** protruding northwards across the Yellow River separated parts of eastern Wei from its western regions and made communication and control problematic, which may help to account for its early interest in **Legalism** as a political theory. Among its ministers were **Shang Yang** (prior to his dismissal and departure for **Qin**) and Hui Shi. King Hui (370–19) discussed the difficulties of ruling this awkwardly-shaped state, threatened by Qin to the west and **Qi** to the east, with **Mencius** (*Mengzi* Book 1a). It was finally absorbed by Qin in 225.

WEI YUAN 魏源 (1794–1856)

Scholar and official, specialist in statecraft, author of the *Haiguo tuzhi* 海國圖志 'Illustrated treatise on the maritime kingdoms'. Wei was born into an official family in Hunan. In 1814 he moved to Beijing where he met scholars like Liu Fenglu and Gong Zizhen whose **New Text** ideas, with their emphasis on statecraft and the need for institutional change, had an important influence on Wei Yuan's future intellectual development. After success in the *juren* 舉人 examinations in 1822 he was commissioned to edit a series on statecraft, the *Huangchao jingshi wenbian* 皇朝經世文編 'Collected writings on the dynasty's statecraft', a major collection of theoretical and practical works on the subject. During the following thirty years he produced a large number of works on institutions (he was a specialist on waterways), New Text classical studies, history (a new history of the Yuan dynasty), military affairs and geography. These included his *Shengwuji* 聖武記 'Imperial Military Campaigns' (1842) and the *Haiguo tuzhi* (1844). The former was a history of Qing military campaigns and the latter, based on materials collected by his friend **Lin Zexu**, was an introduction to the geography, history and institutions of Western countries. Although Wei Yuan never held a high official post, his influence was considerable. He was one of the earliest to appreciate the danger posed by the West, he called for institutional reform to create wealth and power (*fu* 富 and *qiang* 強) and advocated learning from the West in order to combat the West: "using barbarian methods to attack barbarians" (以夷攻夷). His works had enormous impact even beyond China – the *Shengwuji* and *Haiguo tuzhi* were both translated into Japanese.

Jane Kate LEONARD, *Wei Yuan and China's Rediscovery of the Maritime World* (Harvard University Press, 1984).

WEI ZHENG 魏徵 (580–643)

Former rebel at the end of the Sui dynasty who became imperial counsellor under the Tang Emperor **Taizong**. His reputation is as a strict and outspoken Confucian critic of the Emperor and the concept of imperial power.

H.J. WECHSLER, *Mirror to the Son of Heaven: Wei Cheng at the Court of Tang T'ai-tsung* (Yale University Press, 1974).

WEI ZHONGXIAN 魏忠賢 (1568–1627)

Notorious **eunuch** leader who dominated the late Ming court, especially during the Tianzhi period (1621–7). He was responsible for the persecution of large numbers of officials, but was driven from court and made to commit suicide at the beginning of the last emperor's reign. See also **Donglin Academy**.

A.W. HUMMEL, *Eminent Chinese of the Ch'ing Period* (Washington, 1944).

WEIHAIWEI 威海衛

Sea port and naval base on the Shandong coast. It was taken by the Japanese in 1895 during the **Sino-Japanese war** and in the scramble for concessions that followed China's defeat in the war, Britain acquired a lease on the port for twenty-five years. It was returned to China on October 1 1930.

***WEISUO* SYSTEM**

Military system introduced under the **Hongwu Emperor**. A *wei* 衛 (garrison) comprised five *suo* 所 (stations) of 1,020 men each, provided by hereditary military households (see **hereditary occupations**). *Wei* were responsible to the military authorities of a province and so were identified with prefectures. Their duties included guarding the capital and border regions in the North and protecting tax grain convoys in the South. They were intended to contribute troops when required for campaign service, but poor pay and service conditions led to frequent desertion and made the use of mercenaries and special mobilisation necessary.

WELL-FIELD SYSTEM ***Jingtian*** 井田

An ancient system of land allocation and tillage discussed from **Mencius** onwards in the context of **land reform** and with reference to the Sage Kings (see **Former Kings**). Land was said to have been laid out in a geometrical pattern comprising eight peripheral squares of 100 *mu* around a ninth, central plot. Eight families worked each of the squares and supported themselves from the produce, sharing their labour on the ninth and delivering its produce to their lord as tax. The well-field system is described as an ancient ideal by classical commentators. The term *jingtian* first appears in the *Guliang Commentary* on the ***Spring and Autumn Annals*** but **Zheng Xuan** suggests that the system of land holding described in the *Zhou li* is the *jingtian* system. Both the characters concerned occur on Shang dynasty **oracle bones**, one of which shows *tian*, field, as a square with the *jing* character in the middle rather than its usual cross. The *Tong dian* 通典 (AD 801) credits the **Yellow Emperor** with the development of well-making technology and the establishment of the well-field system. This suggests that the significance of the *jing* character goes further than just its shape and that there was an actual well which provided water for the families cultivating the land and that this arrangement became a basic social grouping in early Chinese society. Present day Chinese scholars envisage the possibility of this system existing from the Xia dynasty onwards but there is, so far, little reliable evidence for this.

There is no evidence to show that the system ever existed, though **Shang Yang** was said in the ***Hanshu*** to have destroyed it and political theorists from the late Warring States onwards discussed the pros and cons of attempting to "restore" it. Mencius advocated it as a part of his detailed economic reform proposals; **Dong Zhongshu** and **Su Xun** both believed that, however effective it had been in ancient times, conditions were no longer appropriate for its restoration. **Zhu Xi** did not favour it, even if it had ever been universally practised which he doubted. The Ming official Hu Han (1307–1381) argued for it and **Huang Zongxi** saw it as a way devised by the Sage Kings for giving peasants equal allocations of land, but the principal objective of later reformers was not so much a return to a past ideal as the institution in their own time of a system that would guarantee each household sufficient land for its self-support. However, the concept of 'fair shares for all' inherent in the *jingtian* ideal exerted a powerful influence on later Chinese political and economic thought and inspired many later attempts at land reform, including the Sui and Tang *juntian* 均田 **equal field system**. See also **land tax, land tenure.**

J.R. LEVENSON: 'Ill wind in the well-field' in *The Confucian Persuasion,* A.F. Wright ed., (Stanford University Press, 1960)

WEN WANG 文王 King Wen of Zhou

Son of Ji Li and last king of the pre-dynastic state of Zhou, located in the Wei river valley with its capital at Feng 豐, near modern Qishan, Xi'an. Zhou was one of the feudal states under the suzerainty of Shang, but in contrast to the cruel leadership of the last Shang ruler **Di Xin**, the long reign (perhaps fifty years) of King Wen was idealised by later politicians and historians, especially when it became fashionable to look to the past for examples of benevolent and peaceful government. Thus **Mencius**, at a time when state leaders behaved in an autocratic manner, praised King Wen for the way he was said to have shared his pleasures with his people: having employed them as designers and labourers in the construction of the beautiful gardens and terraces around his palace, he then invited them to enjoy the sight of them so that they harboured no resentment at his privileged position and power. Wen became known as a paragon of virtue, so that according to later Confucian ideals he could not appropriately have revolted against his overlord. That was left to his son Wu, the "Martial" (see **Wu Wang**). According to the ***Shiji***, however, it was the contrast between the benevolent rule of Wen and that of his suzerain king that led to his period of imprisonment at Youli, near the Shang capital Yin. Wen is nominally regarded as founder of the Zhou dynasty and probably planned the overthrow of Shang, which took place about five years after his death. See also **Former Kings.**

H.G. CREEL, *The Origins of Statecraft in China, vol.1, The Western Chou Empire* (University of Chicago Press, 1970).

***WEN XUAN* 文選 Anthology of Literature**

One of the earliest Chinese anthologies of literature arranged by genre. It was compiled by Xiao Tong 蕭統 (501–531), crown prince of the Liang dynasty, and includes 761 pieces by 130 writers arranged under 37 genres of poetry and prose, covering the period from the late Zhou to the Liang. It concentrates on literary writing and excludes the classics, philosophers and histories but includes some categories of non-literary works like edicts, memorials, epitaphs, historical treatises and judgments. From the Sui dynasty onwards it was adopted as part of the examination syllabus and became one of the most important texts in traditional China for studying the art of writing. A Song dynasty saying '*Wenxuan* done, *xiucai* half won' attests to its importance.

XIAO Tong, *Wen Xuan or Selections of Refined Literature, Volume 1: Rhapsodies on Metropolises and Capitals*, trans., annotation and introd. by David R. Knechtges. (Princeton University Press, 1982).

Wen Yiduo 聞一多 (1899–1946)

Leading poet of 1920s and developer of modern vernacular poetry. Born in Xishui, Hubei, Wen Yiduo gained expert knowledge of classical Chinese poetry and studied Western literature at college. Prior to the **May Fourth Movement** he was opposed to the use of ***baihua*** or vernacular language but his views changed and he began composing poems in *baihua* in the early 1920s. In 1922 he went to study at the Art Institute in Chicago and while there he encountered much racial discrimination. His feelings are expressed in the well-known poem *The Laundryman's Song*. His first poetry collection, *Hongzhu* 紅燭 'Red Candle' (1923) demonstrated his artistic maturity in the poetic medium. He criticised fellow poets like Guo Moruo for their over-dependence on Western models. In 1925 he returned to China and in the following year wrote the article *Shi de ge lü Form and Rhyme in Poetry* in which he called for poetry to embody the beautiful aspects of music, painting and architecture in having rhythm, verbal ornateness and a well structured form. His attempts at this new style of poetry are displayed in *Si shui* 死水 'Dead Water' (1928), his second poetry collection. In 1928 he co-founded the literary monthly *Xinyue* 新月 'Crescent Moon' with Xu Zhimo and others but their collaboration ended the following year. During the **Anti-Japanese War** Wen worked as a professor in Kunming, and concentrated on researching the Chinese Classics. He joined the China Democratic League in 1944, becoming a member of the league's central committee before being assassinated in Kunming in 1946.

Catherine Yi-yu Cho Woo, ed., *Wen Yiduo, Selected Poetry and Prose* (Beijing: Panda Books, 1990); Wen Yiduo, *Red Candle*, trans. Tao Tao Liu Saunders (London: Cape 1972).

***Wenxin diao long* 文心雕龍 The Literary Mind and the Carving of Dragons**

One of the best known traditional works of literary criticism, written in 50 chapters by Liu Xie 劉勰 (c. 465 – c. 520). Early Confucian emphasis had been on the utility of written works, particularly their moral influence; this did not mean that scholars from Confucius onwards failed to appreciate literary merit, but rather that the writer's technical skill was not separately recognised until works of literary criticism began to appear from the late Han (see **Cao Pi**). The period of disunity from the third to the sixth centuries saw enormous advances in this area, with the Liang dynasty as a particularly productive period. Liu Xie's work is divided into four main parts: chapters 1 – 5 deal with what he sees as the basics (the ***Dao*** 道 as the source, the sages, the Classics and other seminal texts) chapters 6 – 24 are an analysis of different genres and 25 – 49 are on style, theme and other aspects of the art of the writer and of the critic; chapter 50 is in effect Liu Xie's personal preface to the work. Liu's emphasis on the primacy of the Classics as a source of literary inspiration and on Confucius and the sages as mentors mark him as orthodox Confucian in philosophy; however the chapters on technique and style show how far these areas had advanced from the late Han and how the influence of Buddhism was infusing new ideas into scholarship. Liu edited Buddhist texts and became a monk late in life.

Liu Hsieh, *The Literary Mind and the Carving of Dragons,* trans., introd. and notes by Vincent Yu-chung Shih (Columbia University Press, 1959).

WENDI 漢文帝 , HAN EMPEROR (Liu Heng 劉恆, 202–157, r.180–157 BC)
Eldest son of Han **Gaozu** and renowned as one of the greatest and most benevolent Han dynasty emperors. Under his rule government expenditure was reduced and corruption limited, agriculture flourished and the economy expanded. Freeing the minting of copper coinage benefited the **gentry** class whose growing wealth and culture underpinned a number of reforms. Punishments were lightened, and the recommendation of men of talent to serve in the government encouraged: it was Wendi (the "Cultured Emperor") who first created *boshi*, court scholars in various philosophical traditions. He even made peace with the **Xiongnu** in 162, but only after many invasions and not with permanent effect. See also **Mawangdui.**

WENDI 隋文帝, SUI EMPEROR (Yang Jian 楊堅, 541–601, r. 581–601)
Military commander with a power base in Guanzhong (between **Chang'an** and **Luoyang**) who, having been involved in the fierce rivalry of the northern dynasties from the mid-sixth century (see **Northern and Southern Dynasties**), succeeded in uniting the Northern Plain under the name of his father's fiefdom of Sui in 581 and completing the conquest of the South by 589. As Emperor he created the conditions for the preservation of unity, centralising government under firm personal leadership, integrating North and South with a programme of road and canal building, and building up the economic base of the empire. A policy of land distribution (see **equal field system**) was defined with accompanying reforms to the taxation and labour dues. The revised (*Kaihuang*) law code of 581 was strict but its penalties less harsh than those of the northern dynasties, and it formed the basis for the subsequent Tang code. Compared to that of his successor the later reputation of the "Cultured Emperor" stands higher. Official recruitment policies gave initial support to Confucian scholars, and he personally supported the Buddhist church and encouraged the Daoists. Yet by the end of his reign **schools** were being closed down, and his approach to government and the treatment of his own officials has been described as autocratic and in keeping with Legalist tradition rather than that of the **Confucianism**. Historians credit him with raising popular morale, yet it is doubtful whether the peasantry felt the benefit of his land and tax reforms. He certainly deserves credit for achieving unity and stability, but the wide gulf between his reputation and that of his son is undeserved.

***WENYAN* 文言**
Classical Chinese, the literary language which was the main form of written Chinese until the 20th century. See **Chinese Language**.

WEN TIANXIANG 文天祥 (1236–1283)
Scholar and official of the Southern Song dynasty. Born in Luling, Jiangxi province, he began his official career in 1256 after passing the imperial examination as the highest ranked *jinshi* 進士. He served the Song court and spent most of his official life in fighting the incursions of the Mongol army, persistently advising the emperor not to move the capital but to resist the invaders. He was sent as an envoy in 1276 to negotiate with the **Mongols**, then detained as a hostage but managed to escape. He called on local forces in the southern

provinces to oppose surrender and fought against the Mongols in a series of losing battles on the coast of Zhejiang and Fujian provinces until his ultimate capture and execution by **Khubilai Khan**.

Wen wrote poems throughout these turbulent years and most of his poems are powerful, tragic and heroic. He was best known as the author of *Zhengqi Ge* 正氣歌, the "Song of the Upright Spirit", composed just before his death. Wen, as a man of integrity, and his poems became a source of inspiration to patriotic movements in national crises in later periods of Chinese history.

WHAMPOA MILITARY ACADEMY see **HUANGPU MILITARY ACADEMY**

WHITE LOTUS SECT *Bailianjiao* 白蓮教

Religious secret society which had its origins in the thirteenth century. It is often described as a sect of **Buddhism**, but Daoist ideas were also imported to secure popular support. Connected with the cult of **Maitreya** Buddha and the promise of a new social order it already existed by the Tang dynasty and was again in evidence around 1250. Its first period of widespread military activity was in the mid-fourteenth century as part of the movement to overthrow the Mongol regime (see **Red Turbans**). During the Mongol Yuan dynasty the White Lotus resisted what was seen as alien rule and struggled for the restoration of the Song court. It persisted when the Mongol conquest came to an end and was resurrected in the Manchu Qing dynasty when it was committed to restoring the Ming. Persecution by the Qing authorities drove the White Lotus to insurrection between 1793 and 1796, affecting large areas of north and central China including the present day provinces of Sichuan, Hebei, Shaanxi, Gansu, Henan and Hubei. The rising was finally suppressed in 1804, mainly by militia organised by local landlords and officials, but White Lotus ideas endured and found a new expression in the **Boxer** movement of the late nineteenth century.

WHITE TIGER HALL *Baihu guan* 白虎觀

Name given to the location for the scholarly debate on the **Five Classics** held under imperial auspices in 79 AD. The book recording it is a rich source of quotations from the Classics (*jing* 經) and the Apocrypha (*wei* 緯). Its authorship is unknown but it is sometimes attributed to **Ban Gu.** The present edition is corrupt and was probably edited in the fourth century. See also ***Gu Wen*** and **New Text School.**

WHITE-HAIRED GIRL see ***BAIMAO NÜ***

WOKOU see **JAPANESE PIRATES**

WOMEN

The position of women in traditional China was inferior to that of men, though the essential complementarity of *yin* to *yang* (see ***yin-yang***) did afford their status some theoretical respect. They were subject to the *sancong*, "three followings", which subordinated a woman firstly to her father, then to her husband, and then, if widowed, to her son, and which could imply physical ill-treatment as well as social segregation. In the lower classes women shared the physical toil necessary to keep the family together; when times were bad they were liable to be forced into prostitution and might find themselves abused by landlords as part of their husbands' tenancy. In the upper classes they were brought up according to **Ban Zhao's** approved definition of appropriate virtue, speech, deportment and work, and confined to the inner quarters of the household in pursuance of the prescriptions of the ***Liji*** and the later Neo-Confucian authorities (see **Cheng Yi, Zhu Xi**). Their freedom of movement was tightly constrained. The oppression of many women during the late Qing and first half of the twentieth century has been well documented, but recent studies have balanced this picture by showing that in earlier periods women did not necessarily see themselves as suffering discrimination, and that they had various opportunities for self-fulfilment in terms of their own cultural expectations. The **Chinese Communist Party** claimed to have emancipated women after 1949, but while many women now have greater opportunities for education and career development, sexual equality is far from having been achieved in the People's Republic. See **Courtesans, Divorce, Footbinding, Infanticide, Marriage, Virtuous Women.**

Patricia EBREY, *The Inner Quarters: Marriage and the Lives of Chinese Women in the Sung Period* (Berkeley: University of California Press, 1993); Dorothy KO, *Teachers of the Inner Chambers: Women and Culture in Seventeenth Century China* (Stanford University Press, 1994); Margery WOLF, *Revolution postponed: Women in Contemporary China* (Stanford University Press, 1985).

WOODCUTS ***Muke*** **木刻**

A print made from a block of wood of medium hardness, cut along the grain. Parts of the block surface are cut away, leaving the design standing proud to receive the ink. The technique was invented in China during the early Tang dynasty. Colour prints are produced with a number of wooden blocks, each carrying a separate colour and fitted together to make the complete design, with one colour sometimes overlapping another to give greater variety of hue. The process, known as *taoban* 套版, appeared in the Yuan but was fully developed in the late Ming. The best examples of this type of woodcut print are **New Year prints,** reproductions of painting albums and **painting manuals** from the late Ming and Qing period. A new departure in woodcut print making has occurred in this century, in terms of the development of the print as a medium of individual artistic creativity in its own right, rather than a craft produced by anonymous artisans. This change came about with the Modern Woodcut movement of the late 1920s, in which **Lu Xun** revived print making and introduced European and Russian styles as a new popular form of graphic art. The style of fine art printing, including woodcuts, which is taught in art schools in contemporary China, grew out of this movement.

WORK-STUDY

The programme begun in 1915 which enable Chinese students to study in France. It was the means by which **Zhou Enlai, Deng Xiaoping** and many others were able to travel abroad. The Chinese Socialist Youth League evolved from it in 1921 and a year later it became the French branch of the CCP.

WORKERS AND PEASANTS RED ARMY *Gongnong hongjun* 工農紅軍

Also known as just the Red Army, these were the armed forces of the Chinese Communist Party in its early days. The army began with the armed revolutionaries under **Mao Zedong**, **Zhu De** and **Peng Dehuai** that came together in **Jinggangshan** after the defeat in the 1927 Shanghai Coup. August 1 1927, the occasion of the failed **Nanchang Rising,** is commemorated as the date of foundation of the Army. The army grew in size during the **Jiangxi Soviet** period and on the **Long March** and during the second United Front from 1937 to 1941, its main units were redesignated the Eighth Route Army and the New Fourth Army and nominally included within the command structure of the GMD army under Jiang Jieshi. On May 1 1946 at the start of the **Civil War** CCP-led units were renamed the People's Liberation Army.

WRITING SYSTEMS

The earliest known form of the Chinese script is that used on late Shang **oracle bones**, by which time it had evidently gone through earlier stages of development. It was already written with brush and ink, and in later centuries the literati became connoisseurs of these fine implements and materials (see also **Paper, Silk**). The use of bronze encouraged the evolution of heavier forms of seal script, which existed in several regional varieties until **Li Si** unified them as part of the political unification of the country under the Qin dynasty. The newly standardised script was the earliest form of *kaishu* 楷書 which has remained largely unchanged to the present day, partly due to the invention of block and moveable- type **printing** processes. Scholars valued fine **calligraphy**, however, and continued to develop a multitude of handwritten styles on **silk**, paper, and stone. These ranged from the deliberate elegance of the Song Emperor **Huizong**'s "golden script" to the smooth panache with which a poet might dash off his work in flowing "grass" script (*caoshu* 草書). See also **Romanisation Systems.**

C. LINDQVIST, *China: Empire of the Written Symbol* (Harvill Press, 1991).

WU 吳

South-eastern state in modern Jiangsu province which rose to power in the sixth century BC. A canal was built connecting the **Yangzi** to the Huai River valleys, and the waterways of the region assisted its development as a trading state. The *Yugong* chapter of the ***Shujing***, probably dating from the Warring States period, refers to the natural products of the South-east as including precious metals, **jade**, ivory, bamboo, fabrics and fruit. In 482 BC King Fu Chai was recognised by other state leaders as **hegemon** at a conference held near modern **Kaifeng**, but only nine years later his state was overrun by **Yue**.

WU CHENGSI 武承嗣 (d.698)

Nephew of the Tang dynasty Empress **Wu Zetian** who supported her usurpation of the throne and tried in vain to achieve his own succession. See also **Di Renjie.**

WU DAOZI 吳道子 (c.689–c.758)

A landscape and figure painter whose reputation earned at the Tang emperor **Xuanzong's** court ranked him as possibly the greatest Tang dynasty painter.

Much of his work was done as mural painting on the walls of court buildings and in monasteries and temples around **Chang'an**. None survives.

Wu Han 吳晗 (1909–1969)
Historian, member of the Democratic League and Deputy Mayor of Beijing before the **Cultural Revolution**. Wu Han had written an acclaimed biography of the **Hongwu emperor** *Zhu Yuanzhang zhuan* 朱元璋傳 and had collaborated with **Deng Tuo** and Liao Mosha on articles critical of the CCP leadership between 1961 and 1964, but it was his play ***Hai Rui Dismissed*** that brought him to prominence. It was criticised by **Yao Wenyuan** and Wu Han was attacked for lacking a class standpoint, as was his colleague the Mayor of Beijing, **Peng Zhen.**
Clive Ansley, *The Heresy of Wu Han: His Play "Hai Rui's Dismissal" and its Role in China's Cultural Revolution* (University of Toronto Press, 1971).

Wu Wang 武王 King Wu of Zhou
Son of King **Wen** and leader of the campaign which overthrew the last Shang king. The armies involved in the campaign included Zhou soldiers from the Wei river valley as well as representatives of their own subordinate statelets, including **Shu** to the south and Qiang, possibly proto-Tibetans, to the west. The military victory was achieved at Muye, near the Shang capital of Yin. Following it, Wu founded a new capital at Hao, near modern Xi'an. Though he is known as a strict and efficient administrator the nature of his rule emphasised conciliation and moral and religious justification for his usurpation. Survivors of the last Shang house were not ill-treated and some Shang rites were initially maintained. Eventually, however, they were superseded by those connected with the principal Zhou spiritual power, Heaven. Wu's early death only three years after the conquest precipitated the regency of his brother, **Zhou Gong**. See also **Former Kings, Zhou Dynasty.**
H.G. Creel, *The Origins of Statecraft in China, vol.1: The Western Chou Empire* (University of Chicago Press, 1970).

Wu Zetian 武則天 (Wu Zhao 武曌, Empress Wu, 623 (or 625) -705, commonly known as Wu Hou 武后)
Concubine of Emperor **Taizong** who was taken from the nunnery which she entered after his death in 649 and became concubine to his son, Emperor **Gaozong**. In 655 she was made his empress, and on his death in 683 she became regent for her son **Zhongzong**. Resenting the challenge from his wife's clan she had him replaced by his elder brother **Ruizong**, and in 690 deposed him too and assumed the throne herself. Taking the title of Emperor she proclaimed a new dynasty, the Zhou, and established its court at **Luoyang**.

Despite the Buddhist faith proclaimed by the huge statues sculpted under her patronage in the **Longmen** caves, her ruthless personal ambition led her to reign with unscrupulous determination. She was by no means unsuccessful in either domestic or foreign policy, and is remembered for the enlargement of the bureaucracy through the expansion of the examination selection procedure, yet she ruled despotically and with terror, ordering the assassination not only of opponents but of relatives too (see **Yide**). Like many despots she practised favouritism and sexual indulgence, even into old age. Eventually, the fall of her secret service chief Lai Junchen and widespread revulsion against her young favourites Zhang Yizhi and Zhang Changzong forced her to recall Zhongzong to court as heir apparent and to accept the return of the Tang dynasty. See also **Di Renjie, Wu Chengsi.**

Nghiem TOAN and Louis RICAUD, *Wou Tso-t'ien* (Saigon, 1958–9).

WUCHANG RISING

The revolt that precipitated the **Revolution of 1911**. On the evening of October 10 1911, units of the New Army based in Wuchang 武昌 (a part, together with Hanyang and Hankou, of the modern city of Wuhan) mutinied and took over their munitions depot. The following day they took control of the whole city. Units in Hanyang and Hankou followed suit and a new military government declared itself independent of the Qing dynasty. The date of the initial rising, the Double Tenth (the tenth day of the tenth month), became the National Day of the Republic which was established in 1912.

WUCHENG 吳城

Site near Qingjian, Jiangxi Province, first excavated in 1973–5, which has given its name to a regional variant of Shang culture contemporary with the Yin phase. No bronzes have been found at Wucheng, but in a tomb at nearby Xing'an, excavated in 1979, 486 bronzes were discovered. Only fifty of these were ritual vessels, and they show that this centre of bronze manufacture was independent of **Anyang** both in terms of style and function of its artefacts.

C. DEYDIER, *Les Bronzes Archaiques Chinois: Archaic Chinese Bronzes, Vol. I, Xia and Shang* (Paris: Les Editions d'Art et d'Histoire, 1995).

WUDI 武帝, HAN EMPEROR (Liu Che 劉徹, 155–87, r.141–87 BC)

Eldest son of Emperor **Jingdi**, Wudi came to the throne at the early age of sixteen. His reign proved to be one of the most significant half-centuries in the whole of Chinese history. No doubt the great achievements of this period owe much to the practical and intellectual skills of the able men who served him at court and in the empire, but they were surely stimulated by his own drive and interest in politics, cosmology, foreign and military affairs, scholarship, and **music**. Among the famous names who advanced the boundaries of the Han Empire and the scope of its civilisation during his reign were Sima Tan and his son **Sima Qian** (historians), **Dong Zhongshu** (cosmologist, political theorist), **Sang Hongyang** (politician in the modernist trend), Gongsun He (Chancellor), Gongsun Hong (official and interpreter of portents), **Jia Yi** (politician and poet), **Sima Xiangru** (poet), **Zhang Qian** (explorer), Wei Qing (military commander), **Liu An** (philosopher), and Li Yannian (musician, see **Music Bureau**). It was a time of intense discussion, ranging over matters from military and economic policy to religion, from the workings of the universe to the nature of court music. Wudi showed his authoritarian capacity by curtailing the rights of the feudal aristocracy, yet could not prevent the occurrence of argument and intrigue at his own court. Indeed it was encouraged, on the one hand by his susceptibility to the persuasive arguments of Daoist magicians offering him **immortality**, and on the other by the imaginative speculation of scholars interested in linking Confucian ideas on government and society with cosmology and proto-scientific ideas: debate raged over the function of the **Five Elements**, the interpretation of **omens and portents**, the management of the economy (see **Salt and Iron Debate**), the best way to control the **Xiongnu**, and how to tame the **Yellow River**. In such an atmosphere the Emperor, who selected men of literary talent to serve him and whose establishment of the **Imperial Academy** in 124 gave them the incentive to study the past as a means of improving the present, found that he was certainly not immune from criticism. Though his armies helped to establish Chinese protectorates as far west as Samarkand, extended the Empire into the North-west of the Korean peninsula (see **Lelang**), and tried to force a way through the south-western jungles of modern Yunnan towards South-east Asia; though they stimulated the taste for rarities and luxuries from new regions and encouraged commerce; though they threatened the Xiongnu in their steppe homelands and spread the reputation of Han across Asia: yet it was at too great a price. Sima Qian was one of those who was not afraid to question his master's policies, and when he did so on behalf of the disgraced general Li Ling in 99 BC he paid the price of castration as a result. See also **Liu Sheng.**

WULIANG SHRINES

The funerary shrines from the Han dynasty Wu family cemetery in modern Yinan, Shandong Province, the best known being that of the Confucian official Wu Liang 武梁 (78–151). His comprised one of three stone-built chambers (see tomb architecture), the other two being those of Wu Rong 武榮 (died 167) and possibly Wu Kaiming 武開明 (died 148). Its significance lies in its remarkable series of bas-relief decorations, the most complete pictorial document in carved stone surviving from the Han period. It comprises three sections, the ceiling dedicated to the **Mandate of Heaven,** two gables illustrating the realms of the **Immortals**, and a comprehensive history of the human world from earliest times to AD 151. The wide scope of the subject matter depicted, especially in the latter scenes, and the evidence of great artistic skill make this a unique historical resource.

WU Hung, *The Wu Liang Shrine: the Ideology of Early Chinese Pictorial Art* (Stanford University Press, 1989).

WUZONG 武宗, TANG EMPEROR (Li Yan 李炎, 814–46, r. 840–846)

Fifth son of Emperor Muzong (r. 820–4) and younger brother of Wenzong. Best known for his inordinate commitment to **Daoism** and for ordering the greatest persecution of **Buddhism** in Chinese history (842–5, see **Religious Persecution**), but the combination of Emperor and chief minister **Li Deyu** deserves better recognition for its success in the face of political factionalism, **eunuch** intrigue, and territorial challenge from **Nanzhao** in the South-west and the Uyghurs in the North. Even the much criticised persecution, quickly rescinded by his uncle **Xuanzong** who succeeded him, must have made good sense to many contemporaries on economic and political grounds. His premature death was probably due to insanity brought on by drugs.

XI XIA 西夏

Tangut dynasty in north-western China during the eleventh century. In 1038 the kingdom established by Tibetan Tangut tribes in the region that is now Ningxia, Gansu and Inner Mongolia, adopted the Chinese dynastic name of Xia and has since been known in China as the Xi Xia (Western Xia). They attempted to conquer China but were defeated in 1044 and became part of a triangular balance of power which included the Liao dynasty in northern China. The Xi Xia capital was near Yinchuan, the capital of the **Ningxia Hui Autonomous Region**, and the beehive-shaped tombs of the Xi Xia emperors can still be seen at the foot of the Helanshan mountain range outside Yinchuan. The economy of the state was based on irrigated agriculture and pastoralism and trade with Central Asia and its religion was Buddhist. The Xi Xia state came under the influence of **Chinggis Khan** in the early years of the thirteenth century and was annihilated by the **Mongols** in 1227.

XI'AN INCIDENT

The arrest of **Jiang Jieshi** on December 12 1936 by **Zhang Xueliang**, warlord of **Manchuria** and son of **Zhang Zuolin** who had been assassinated by the Japanese in 1928, and Yang Hucheng, Pacification Commissioner of Shaanxi province. Jiang was in Xi'an to direct operations against the **Chinese Communist Party** who had established themselves in their **Yan'an** base to the north of Xi'an. He was staying at the Huaqing hot springs resort just outside the city and apparently fled up the hill in his nightwear when Zhang's troops arrived and was later captured in a hut. Zhang presented him with a list of eight demands, which essentially called for the end to civil conflict between the CCP and GMD and a combined resistance against Japan. Zhou Enlai, who had served with Jiang Jieshi at the **Huangpu Military Academy,** made his way to Xi'an to mediate and an agreement was signed that led to the second **United Front.** Jiang Jieshi was set free. Zhang Xueliang was arrested and spent the rest of his life in prison or under house arrest.

Tien-wei WU, *The Sian Incident: A Pivotal Point in Modern Chinese History* (Center for Chinese Studies, University of Michigan, 1976).

XIA 夏, DYNASTY

The first of what the ancient Chinese often referred to as the Three Dynasties (Xia, Shang, Zhou), Xia has traditionally been regarded by Western historians as "mythical". It was supposed to have been founded by the sagely Yu (see **Former Kings**) and to have succumbed to the Shang King Tang after the reign of the tyrant Jie. Modern archaeologists, noting evidence for some kind of political organisation at the early **Bronze Age** site at **Erlitou**, debate whether this might represent historical justification for the existence of a Xia state or a stage of early Shang authority.

XIAFANG 下放

Variously translated as "rustication", "downward transfer" or "going to the countryside", *xiafang* was the policy of sending school leavers, graduates, cadres and intellectuals to the countryside to bring them into closer touch with the peasant population, who were regarded as the backbone of Chinese society, and convince them of the dignity of manual labour. It functioned as a control mechanism and dissidents often found themselves removed from the cities to the more remote rural areas.

Thomas P. BERNSTEIN, *Up to the Mountains and Down to the Villages: The Transfer of Youth from Urban to Rural China* (Yale University Press, 1977).

***XIAN* 縣**

District or county, the lowest level of local government in China and the seat of the **magistrate**. It was subordinate to the *fu* 府 prefecture.

CH'Ü T'ung-tsu, *Local Government in China under the Ch'ing* (Harvard University Press, 1962).

XIANBI PEOPLE

Northern tribe who invaded China in the fourth century and controlled various small dynasties in northern China. Their descendants in the Toba clan founded the Northern Wei dynasty.

XIANG ARMY *Xiangjun* 湘軍

Provincial Army raised in Hunan (the traditional name for which is Xiang Ïæ) by **Zeng Guofan** in 1852 to fight against the **Taiping Rebellion**. Together with the **Huai Army**, it succeeded in suppressing the rebellion but was less successful in its operations against the **Nian** uprising and was partially demobilised in 1864.

XIANG YU 項羽 (Xiang Ji 項籍, 233–202 BC)

General commanding the main **Chu** army which led the uprising against Qin in 207–6 BC. After capturing **Xianyang** from his rival **Liu Bang** he enfeoffed him as King of the Han River valley and took the title King of Chu for himself. Liu Bang, however, recaptured the city. Xiang Yu defeated him at Pancheng in 205, but was in turn vanquished in 202, after which he committed suicide.

R. DAWSON, trans., *Sima Qian: Historical Records* (Oxford University Press, 1994).

XIANYANG 咸陽

Capital of the state of **Qin** from 350 BC, created by Duke Xiao and **Shang Yang** as part of their policy of consolidation and expansion. It was situated in the Wei River valley to the East of the former Qin capital of Yong, and close to the subsequent site of Han dynasty **Chang'an** and modern Xi'an. Under the two Qin emperors it became the first imperial capital of China and was renowned for the ostentatiously luxurious **Epang Palace**. In 207 it was captured by the rebel **Liu Bang**, having already been ruined during **Xiang Yu's** brief but merciless occupation.

XIAOJING* 孝經 *Classic of Filial Piety

One of the **Thirteen Classics** of the Confucian tradition, the *Xiaojing* takes the form of a dialogue between **Confucius** and his disciple Zengzi 曾子 on the subject of proper behaviour towards superiors, particularly one's parents and one's ruler. The work existed in old text and new text versions (see ***Gu Wen*, New Text School**); the version currently used is based on the new text one. The text's brevity (around 2,000 characters in 9 *juan* 卷) and clear, didactic content made it an ideal early text in the educational curriculum. In the Ming and Qing there were compulsory questions on the *Xiaojing* in the provincial and metropolitan examinations and it was recommended as one of the two basic texts for primary **schools**, though some educators complained that it was too difficult for ordinary pupils and preferred instead to concentrate on rhythmic primers. The provenance of the text is unclear: the traditional attribution to **Confucius** seems unlikely but it possibly originated from versions written down by disciples of Zengzi of orally transmitted accounts of their master's conversations with Confucius. Like most early works many doubts have been expressed about its provenance but internal evidence suggests that it predates the **Lüshi chunqiu** (circa 239 BC).

Mary Lelia MAKRA, trans., *The Hsiao ching* ed. Paul K.T. Sih (New York: St John's University Press, 1961); Michael LOEWE, ed., *Early Chinese Texts: A Bibliographical Guide* (Berkeley: The Society for the Study of Early China, 1993).

XIAO JUN 蕭軍 (1908-88)

The pen-name of Liu Honglin, a Manchurian left-wing writer of proletarian origins. Born in Liaoning province, he trained at a military academy but moved to Harbin after the **Mukden Incident** and began a career as a writer. There he met, and started living with, the female writer Xiao Hong 蕭紅. In 1934 they moved to Shanghai where they were befriended by **Lu Xun**. The following year Xiao Jun published his most famous work, *Bayue de xiangcun* 八月的鄉村 'Village in August', a description of the patriotic activities of an army formed by dissident groups in Manchuria to fight the Japanese. At the time this was widely praised by Communist Party officials, but later (1948) attacked for its weak class stand. Xiao Jun moved to Yan'an in 1940, and although he was criticised in the 1942 **rectification campaign** he was nevertheless sent to Manchuria in 1947 to carry out propaganda work. There he edited *Wenhua bao* 文化報 'Cultural Gazette' but the Party was dissatisfied with the views expressed in it, particularly his lack of enthusiasm for class struggle, his attacks on the Russians and on the land reform programme, the importance he placed on the role of intellectuals and his support for an accommodation with Jiang Jieshi. It used him as a target in a rectification campaign carried out from mid-1948, in order to stamp Party authority on Manchuria. He was sent to the Fushun coal mines for reform through labour; this experience formed the basis for his novel *Wuyue de kuangshan* 五月的礦山 'Coalmines in May' (1954) written after he moved to Beijing in 1951. This was criticised during the **Anti-rightist** movement for its attitude to the workers and for Xiao Jun's "reactionary" ideas, as was his *Guoqu de shidai* 過去的時代 'The Past Generation' (1957), and he did not re-emerge in public until 1977.

T'IEN CHUN (previous pen-name) *Village in August*, trans. Evan King (New York: Smith and Durrell, 1942); Leo Ou-fan LEE, *The Romantic Generation of Modern Chinese Writers* (Harvard University Press, 1973).

XIE HE 謝赫 (fl. c.AD500)

Art critic and aesthete whose *Guhua pinlu* 古畫品錄 'Graded record of old painters' compared the works of 43 painters, and contained in its Introduction Xie's own Six Rules which became the guidelines for artists throughout later centuries. They were:

(i) the spiritual essence (***qi***) of the work must be awoken;
(ii) brushwork should display the structural elements of the subject;
(iii) form should be faithful to the reality of the subject;
(iv) the use of colour should be appropriate to the nature of the subject;
(v) the composition of the work should be carefully planned;
(vi) the artist should pass on the experience of old masters by copying their works as part of his training.

XIEYIHUA **寫意畫**

Category of Chinese painting with bold landscapes, birds and flowers, or figure paintings expressed by rapid freehand brushwork. The essential demand of the art of *xieyihua* is not to represent details realistically but to capture the inner spirit of the object, which is different from the approach in ***gongbihua***. *Xieyihua* is best represented by **Chan Buddhist** sect painting and the works of such artists as Liang Kai 梁楷 of the Song, Xu Wei 徐渭 of the Ming and Zhu Da 朱耷 (Bada Shanren 八大山人) of the Qing dynasty.

XIMUWANG 西母王 (Queen Mother of the West)

The leading popular deity in China by the Tang dynasty, widely revered for her role in promoting **immortality** and worshipped especially by the devotees of the Shangqing school of **Daoism**. The origins of her authority can be traced back to the Warring States period and by the Han dynasty her cult was well established among high and low classes of society. In the Tang she was worshipped by the literati, who expressed their beliefs about her in poetry, hagiography and prescriptions for spiritual development. As the personification of *yin* she was the supreme champion of **women**, yet her function was also to maintain the essential balance between **yin** and **yang** (see **yin-yang**). She was the patron deity of prostitutes and female musicians, associated with **jade** and sexuality as well as the search for **immortality**, to which she might guide both men and women.

CAHILL, S.E., *Transcendence and Divine Passion: the Queen Mother of the West in Mediaeval China* (Stanford University Press 1993).

XIN'AN MERCHANTS see **HUIZHOU MERCHANTS**

XIN QINGNIAN **新青年 New Youth**

Trail-blazing literary journal of the **New Culture Movement**, known in English as *New Youth* but using the French subtitle of *La jeunesse*. It began publication in Shanghai as a monthly on September 15 1915 under the editorship of **Chen Duxiu**. The original title *Qingnian zazhi* 青年雜志 *Youth Magazine* was used for the first series of six issues. After Chen moved to Beijing University, it was produced in Beijing until 1920, when it reverted to Shanghai. Initially the magazine concentrated on promoting democracy and science against the background of attempts by **Yuan Shikai** and the conservatives to revive the monarchy and reinforce Confucian values. The editorial article of the founding issue, *Jinggao qingnian* 敬告青年 'Respectful advice to young people', set the tone with a call to "be independent and not servile, be scientific and not rely on your imagination". From early 1917, with the publication of **Hu Shi's** *Wenxue gailiang chuyi* 文學改良芻議 'Tentative suggestions for literary reform' and Chen Duxiu's *Wenxue geming lun* 文學革命論 'On literary revolution', the focus shifted to the nature and function of literature and the use of vernacular rather than classical language. Both Hu and Chen pressed for a revolution in form and content, throwing out the rigid, stylized, allusion-laden literary forms and replacing them with freer, every-day language forms which emphasised content – having something worth saying. Poetry, whose classical form exemplified some of the worst excesses in their eyes, came under the spotlight with the publication in *Xinqingnian* at the beginning of 1918 of a selection of 'new poetry' *xinshi* 新詩 by Hu Shi and others. The magazine became completely *baihua* vernacular in language from the May issue of 1918, which included **Lu Xun's** well-known short story *Kuangren riji* 狂人日記 'Diary of a Madman', regarded as the first modern vernacular short story. Although literature remained important, the focus gradually shifted to politics after the success of the October Revolution in Russia. **Li Dazhao** published 'The Victory of Bolshevism' and 'The Victory of the Masses' in the October 1918 issue and after May 1919 articles on Marxism predominated. The magazine ceased publication in June 1919 after the arrest of Chen Duxiu; it resumed the following December, then in September 1920 moved back to Shanghai where it became a mouthpiece for the fledgling Communist Party. It finally ceased publication in October 1921. A magazine of the same name was produced from 1923–6 as a Communist Party organ edited by **Qu Qiubai**.

CHOW Tse-tsung, *The May Fourth Movement: Intellectual Revolution in Modern China* (Harvard University Press, 1960).

***XINYUESHE* 新月社 Crescent Moon Society**

A 1920s literary assocation with a Western liberal approach. It began around 1923 as a loosely-organised dining assocation whose members included Xu Zhimo, **Liang Qichao**, **Hu Shi** and Ding Xilin. In October 1925 Xu Zhimo took over editorship of the *Chenbao fukan* 晨報副刊 *Morning News Supplement*, a literary supplement spun off from the *Chenbao*, and he added a poetry supplement (*Shijuan* 詩鐫) and a drama supplement (*Jukan* 劇刊). The former published poems by **Wen Yiduo**, including *Sishui* 死水 'Dead Water'. In early 1927 Hu Shi, Xu Zhimo and others decided to set up a bookshop, which started publishing *Xinyue* 新月 as a monthly magazine from March 1928. The Crescent Moon Society was primarily a literary association; many of its members had studied in the West and typically took a Western liberal approach, emphasising the importance of literature for its own sake. They were socially aware and patriotic but were not politically committed and broadly opposed both the Communists and the Guomindang. Xu Zhimo was the focal point of the group and after his death in an air crash in November 1931 the Society went into a decline. *Xinyue* magazine ceased publication in June 1933 and the bookshop was taken over by the Commercial Press.

Leo Ou-fan LEE, *The Romantic Generation of Chinese Writers* (Harvard University Press, 1973).

***XING ZHONGHUI* 興中會 Revive China Society**

The earliest revolutionary organisation set up by **Sun Yixian**. After Sun's failure to persuade **Li Hongzhang** of the need for reform in the wake of losses in the war with Japan, he decided more direct methods were required and headed for Honolulu. There he established the *XingZhonghui* with around twenty sympathetic Overseas Chinese on November 24 1894. The aim of the society was to "revitalise China and save her from her predicament" (振興中華, 挽救中局). Sun soon moved to Hong Kong and set up the headquarters of the *Xing Zhonghui* there in February 1895. They set up a branch in Guangzhou (Canton) and planned an uprising there for the double ninth (ninth day of the ninth lunar month – October 26) but news was leaked, over 70 conspirators were arrested and the leaders were executed. Sun fled to Japan where he set up a branch in Yokohama. After the failure of the 1898 **Hundred days reform**, when **Kang Youwei** and **Liang Qichao** also fled to Japan, Sun tried to cooperate with the reformers but was ultimately rebuffed. In August 1900 *XingZhonghui* branches in central China were caught up in the clampdown after the failure of the Tang Caichang uprising; in October and November of the same year a failed uprising in Huizhou and a failed assassination in Guangzhou left the organisation severely depleted. A new Henei branch was set up in 1902 and a San Francisco one in 1904 but Sun Yixian had already concluded that a wider revolutionary alliance was needed and the *XingZhonghui* was merged into this, the ***Tongmenghui***, in August 1905.

Harold Z. SCHIFFRIN, *Sun Yat-sen and the Origins of the Chinese Revolution* (Berkeley: University of California Press, 1968.

XINHAI REVOLUTION see **REVOLUTION OF 1911**

XINJIANG 新疆 UYGHUR AUTONOMOUS REGION

The Xinjiang Uyghur Autonomous Region is on the north-western border of China, stretches 2000 kilometres east to west and 1650 kilometres north to south, has an area of over 1,600,000 square kilometres and is the largest administrative unit in the PRC. It has common borders with Mongolia, Afghanistan, Pakistan and India and with three Central Asian states, Kazakhstan, Kyrgyzstan and Tajikistan, and is close to Uzbekistan and Turkmenistan. Its nearest neighbours within China are Gansu and Ningxia, both of which have substantial Muslim communities, **Tibet** which constitutes Beijing's main separatist problem and Qinghai, which is part of old Tibet, and has Tibetan Buddhist and Muslim communities. The spelling "Uighur" has been replaced in English language publications in China with "Uygur" as this is closer to the spelling of the name in the Uyghur language, when written in the modified Latin script that was used during the 1960s and 70s. Reinhard Hahn, in *Spoken Uyghur*, (Seattle,1991), suggests the spelling Uyghur as the closest to the local pronunciation and that has been used in this book. The language is also referred to as Taranchi, Turki or Eastern Turki in late nineteenth and early twentieth century writings.

Xinjiang, although a provincial-level administrative unit, is not considered to be a province but an Autonomous Region in deference to the non-Han majority of the population. Non-Han people in the region and emigré communities in Kazakhstan, Turkey and Germany do not use the name "Xinjiang" because of its imperial Chinese connotations, and refer to the region instead as Eastern Turkestan, *Sharqi Turkistan*. Earlier studies of the region often use the spelling Sinkiang or the term Chinese Turkestan.

Xinjiang is divided by the Tianshan Mountains, with the Zhungar Basin to the north and the Taklamakan Desert and the settled *Altıshahr* (Six Cities) region in the Tarim Basin to the south: the two regions have different histories and cultural identities. There is no definite agreement on which six cities comprise the Altıshahr. Sometimes eight are listed. The region is known in Chinese as Nanjiang 南疆 (Southern Xinjiang).

The original inhabitants of Xinjiang were Turkic migrants from Mongolia from whom the Uyghurs claim descent. The ethnic make-up of the Turkic peoples is complex and names have changed thoughout history, the ethonym Uyghur being one of the most problematic. Chinese influence in the region was consolidated in the eighteenth century, the name Xinjiang (New Frontier) being used first in 1768. The Qing dynasty's military administration encountered constant nationalist and religious resistance, allied to Islamic forces in neighbouring Khokand, but in 1831 the first Han immigrants from China were allowed to move into southern Xinjiang to cultivate reclaimable land. A Muslim insurrection under **Yakub Beg** led to an independent khanate based on Kashghar until it was overthrown by Qing forces in 1878, and Xinjiang was formally incorporated into the Chinese empire as a province in 1884 at a time of intense British and Russian imperial rivalry in Central Asia.

After the 1911 Revolution, Xinjiang, under a warlord government, experienced civil wars and armed risings involving Turkic-speaking Muslims, the **Hui** (or Dungan) Chinese-speaking Muslims and Han Chinese until Sheng Shicai took power after clashes with Hui troops under Ma Zhongying, ruling from 1937 to 1942 with support from the USSR. Turkic Muslims rose against Sheng in southern Xinjiang in 1937, and an independent Kazakh and Uyghur Eastern Turkestan Republic controlled the northwestern **Ili** region from 1944 to 1946.

In 1949, troops of the Communist PLA took control of Xinjiang and a Han immigration programme was announced in 1950. The campaign against counter-revolutionaries and land reform, which included the confiscation and redistribution of mosque-owned *waqf* land (land owned by mosques or other religious foundations), were used to break down the traditional social structure and political and religious authority. The death of eight of the leaders of the East Turkestan Republic in an air crash when they were on their way to Beijing to negotiate with the Communist Party leadership early in 1950 is still seen by some Uyghurs as the deliberate elimination by the Chinese authorities of the pro-autonomy leadership in Xinjiang. On October 1 1955 the Xinjiang Uyghur Autonomous Region was created, with autonomous Mongol, Kyrgyz, Kazakh and Hui counties. Burhan Shahidi, a Tatar, and Seypidin Aziz (Saifudin), an Uyghur, headed the regional government, although real power rested with Wang Zhen, commander of the PLA units which took control in 1949, and the regional Communist Party Secretary, Wang Enmao, both ethnic Hans. The quasi-military Xinjiang Production and Construction Corps, "a predominantly Han organisation of demobilised PLA men, former Guomindang soldiers and resettled Han people" was central in establishing control.

After the 1958 **Great Leap Forward**, radical policies, less sensitive to local feelings replaced the cautious approach of the early 1950s. "Local nationalism" and Han and Muslim leaders sympathetic to the USSR were systematically criticised and bazaars and Islamic organisations closed down. Wang Enmao moderated policies in 1962 after the exodus of 60,000 Kazakhs to Kazakhstan, but the 1966 **Cultural Revolution**, during which he was dismissed caused chaos until the imposition of direct military control in 1971.

Burhan Shahidi, honorary president of the China Islamic Association, died in August 1989. His body was flown from Beijing to Urumqi for burial, accompanied by officials of the United Front Work Department of the Chinese Communist Party Central Committee, the Chinese People's Political Comsultative Conference and the China Islamic Association. Wang Zhen died in 1993.

Joseph FLETCHER, 'The Heyday of the Ch'ing Order in Mongolia, Sinkiang and Tibet', in Denis Twitchett and John K. Fairbank (general editors) *The Cambridge History of China Volume 10: Late Ch'ing, 1800–1911, Part 1;* Andrew D.W. FORBES, *Warlords and Muslims in Chinese Central Asia: a Political History of Republican Sinkiang 1911–1949* (Cambridge University Press, 1986); Donald H. MCMILLEN, *Chinese Communist Power and Policy in Xinjiang 1949–1977* (Boulder, Colorado: Westview, 1979) and "Xinjiang and Wang Enmao: New Directions in Power, Policy and Integration" in *China Quarterly*, September 1984; Stanley TOOPS, "Recent Uyg[h]ur Leaders in Xinjiang", *Central Asian Survey*, Volume 11, No 2, 1992.

XIONGNU 匈奴

Loosely translated into English as "Huns", the name was also applied imprecisely by the early Chinese to the nomadic shepherd peoples of eastern Central Asia who regularly caused trouble to China's north-western frontiers in the Ordos region. The response from the leaders of feudal states and the First Emperor (see **Qin Shi Huangdi**) was to send armies to try and crush them, but the early Han emperors, recognising the impossibility of this, adopted instead a policy of *heqin*, "harmonious relationship", aiming at control through trade and diplomatic relations. In 198 BC, two years after almost capturing Han **Gaozu** in battle, the Xiongnu leader, the Shanyu, was offered a Han princess in marriage. Yet *heqin*, expensive though it was, also failed to achieve its purpose, and rulers throughout the Former and Later Han dynasties continually struggled with both the theory and practice of keeping the Xiongnu in check. Officials such as **Jia Yi** refuted what they saw as appeasement. Han **Wudi** returned to offensive campaigning between 129 and 90 BC, and sent **Zhang Qian** half way across Asia in search of allies. But the argument of how to deal with these foes who could neither be driven away nor bought off continued to be unresolved, and the construction of defensive walls was adopted as another, physical means of trying to live with a problem that was apparently unsusceptible to political solution (see **Great Wall**).

In the second century BC the Xiongnu dominated other nomadic peoples of Inner Asia, including the Wuhuan and the Wusun. But weakened by Wudi's warfare they were defeated by the Wusun in 71 BC, and after internal feuding over leadership they submitted to Han suzerainty in 53 and entered the **tribute system**. The Later Han saw a similar pattern of events. After successes in north China in AD 39 and 44 and the restoration of their authority across the Tarim Basin the Xiongnu again divided, into those in southern Mongolia who preferred to pursue a more peaceful, sinicised way of life and those to the north who remained loyal to their nomadic origins. In 49 they lost control of the Wuhuan and Xianbei tribes, and **Ban Chao** soon wrested back control over the Western Regions. See also **Noin-Ula.**

YU Ying-shih, *Trade and Expansion in Han China: a Study in the Structure of Sino-barbarian Economic Relations* (Berkeley and Los Angeles: University of California Press, 1967).

***XIXIANGJI* 西厢記 Romance of the Western Chamber**

Yuan dynasty masterpiece of northern *zaju* drama (see **Drama**) usually known in the West as *The Romance of the Western Chamber*. Attributed to Wang Shifu

王實甫 (fl. late thirteenth century) and based on the Tang dynasty *chuanqi, Yingying zhuan* 鶯鶯傳 'The Story of Yingying', by Yuan Zhen and the Jim dynasty drama *Xixiangji zhugongdiao* 西廂記諸宮調 by Dong Jieyuan. The play is unusually long, consisting of some twenty acts. The tightly knit plot, interspersed with skilfully composed dramatic lyrics, combines tension and comedy as it details the story of student Zhang Junrui and his sweetheart Cui Yingying. These two lovers overcome the many obstacles that come between them, including a previous engagement, an unwilling mother and a military revolt, and eventually marry and live happily ever after (a change to the original Tang story in which Zhang leaves Yingying). Wang's superb characterisation is most memorable in the role of Hongniang, Yingying's resourceful maid, who contrives to bring the two lovers together.

WANG Shifu, *The Story of the Western Wing,* ed. and trans. Stephen H. West and Walt L. Idema (Berkeley: University of California Press, 1995).

XIYOUJI 西游記 Journey to the West

One of the great traditional Chinese novels, known in **English** as *The Journey to the West* or *Monkey*. This vernacular novel is attributed to the late Ming writer and official Wu Cheng'en 吳承恩 (c.1500–1582), however, there is still debate over authorship. The earliest extant edition was published in 1592 and is based on the epic pilgrimage of the Tang priest Xuanzang 玄奘, also known as Tripitaka or Tang Sancang 唐三藏, to collect Buddhist scriptures from India. The pilgrimage tale was popular with storytellers and the earliest extant prompt book dates from the Southern Song. The novel begins with the background of Sun Wukong, an ambitious monkey king who is forced to accompany Xuanzang on his pilgrimage to make Amends for his disrespectful behaviour towards Buddha. Tales of the monkey king were also popular with the storytellers and there is debate whether the source for these tales is the Indian *Ramayana* or whether it is indigenous to Chinese culture. Mischievous Sun Wukong is the hero of the story, as he protects the timid monk from the numerous demons on the way, with the help of Zhu Bajie (Pigsy) a half-man, half-pig figure addicted to food and sex, mild-mannered Sha Wujing (Sandy) and the white horse. *Xiyouji*'s lively, vernacular style, great humour, imaginative combination of the fantastic and suprnatural with the mundane and ts jaunty irreverence, have ensured its contuinuing popularity throughout Chinese society.

Anthony C. YU, *The Journey to the West* (4 vols.) (Chicago University Press, 1977–1983); C.T. HSIA, *The Classic Chinese Novel: A Critical Introduction* (Columbia University Press, 1968).

XU BEIHONG 徐悲鴻 (1895–1953)

Born in Yixing, Jiangsu province, Xu was a major figure in the modernisation of Chinese art. From 1916 to 1927 he visited Japan and Europe, and studied academic painting in Paris for eight years, where he was known as Ju Peon. After returning to China, he held a series of key teaching positions where he advocated the study of realism. Xu was a prolific painter in both oil and ink. His favourite themes include historic events, the human nude (rare for a Chinese artist) and animals, in which he is best known for his horses, whose spirited movements he captured through rapid and abbreviated brushwork and ink washes. In China, his horses became a symbol of the indomitable national spirit. His home in Beijing is now a museum holding over 1,200 of his works.

The Art of Xu Beihong (Hong Kong Museum of Art, 1988).

XUANDI 宣帝, HAN EMPEROR (Liu Bingyi 劉病已 or Liu Xun 劉詢, 91–49, r.74–49 BC)

Descended from Emperor **Wudi** and the Empress Wei, he succeeded to the throne following the deposition of Zhaodi's successor Liu He for improper behaviour and proved to be a conscientious ruler. During the quarter century of his reign the political emphasis began to shift away from the pragmatic, quasi-Legalist, character of Wudi's period and to take account of the Confucian concern for the common people. Discussion of the **Confucian Classics** was stimulated – in their New Text versions since the discovery of the so-called Old Texts had not yet had its eventual impact – and the interpretation of **omens and portents** revealed an awareness of Heaven's judgement on dynastic government. A conference at the Shiqu Pavilion in 53–1 debated the significance of the Confucian Classics for educational and political purposes and underlined the authority of the scholar-officials. See also ***Gu Wen***, **New Text School**, ***Yantielun***.

XUANTONG 宣統 (1908–11)

The last emperor of the Qing dynasty. See **Puyi**.

XUANZANG 玄奘 (600–64)

Distinguished Buddhist pilgrim and explorer who completed a round trip to India by way of Central Asia lasting fifteen years (629–645) . He returned to **Chang'an** with a collection of relics and Sanskrit scriptures for which Emperor **Taizong** built the Great Wild Goose Pagoda in 652 which still stands. His subsequent translation project of 74 texts, supported by Emperor **Gaozong**, established the Faxiang Sect of **Buddhism** in China. The story of Xuanzang's travels was immortalised in the allegorical sixteenth century novel ***Xiyouji*** *Journey to the West*.

XUANZONG 玄宗, TANG EMPEROR (Li Longji 李隆基, 685–761, r. 712–56)

Third son of Emperor **Ruizong**. Despite the tragic end to his famous love affair with **Yang Guifei** his long reign may be epitomised as being as close to the Mencian ideal of true **kingship** as that of any **Son of Heaven**. He promoted efficient administration at both central and provincial level, reducing the number of chief ministers (see **Prime Minister**), purging corrupt officials and strengthening the **Censorate**. Relations with his senior ministers were harmonious, and though the recurrent problem of **eunuch** influence was in evidence it did not have the undermining effect that it did in later reigns. He reduced court expenditure, and, faced with serious economic difficulties, his administration, notably the former censor promoted Chief Minister **Li Linfu**, endeavoured to reform the **tax system** as a source of regular government income. Li also revised the law code (737) and the system for recruiting and commanding the military units that defended China's long northern frontiers. In general Xuanzong's reign was a peaceful one and included an unprecedented treaty with **Tibet** (714), but inter-state politics were so volatile in the Tang period that it was immediately broken and the need for defensive readiness was ever apparent, not only against the Tibetans but against the many other peoples confronting the Empire from **Korea** in the East to the Tarim Basin in the West. It was the employment of foreigners as professional commanders that led to the rise of **An Lushan** and the rebellion that brought a disastrous end to a brilliant reign. All three major religious teachings and even Christianity (see **Nestorianism**) received encouragement from Emperor Xuanzong. Though strongly Daoist by inclination he developed an interest in Tantric **Buddhism** later in his reign, having at first moved to suppress the Indian religion. As a conscientious Son of Heaven he strengthened the role of Confucian literati at court by the development of the **Hanlin Academy**. Both literary and performing arts flourished at court under his patronage (see **Du Fu, Li Bo, Music, Wang Wei).**

L.T. LIN, trans. Robert des Rotours, *Le Regne de l'Empereur Hiuan-tsong (713–756*) (Paris: Presses Universitaires de France, 1981).

XUNZI 荀子 (c.298–238 BC)

Confucian school philosopher from the state of **Zhao** 趙 called Xun Qing荀卿. Popular during the Han, he was later eclipsed by **Mencius**. Xunzi represents a more rationalist approach than the idealist Mencius and was influential in the development of legalist thinking in the third century BC (**Hanfeizi** and **Li Si** were both his students). Xunzi is best known for his rejection of Mencius' assertion that human nature *xing* 性 is good, arguing that our inherent tendency is towards evil and any goodness is externally imposed. Although he and Mencius may appear as polar opposites, in this respect what they advocated was very similar. Both believed in the perfectibility of people through education, emphasising the role of the traditional Confucian virtues (see **Five Virtues**) and supporting the same paternalistic, hierarchical social structure. However, Xunzi's rationalism emerges in his greater emphasis on the virtue *zhi* 智 wisdom and his more naturalistic concept of Heaven. This rejects even the limited role of a purposeful supreme force envisaged in Mencius' "mandate of Heaven" and is consistent with Xunzi's affirmation of the badness of human nature. This badness of human nature is not, as in the Christian tradition, the result of the existence of a force for evil, but rather that blindly satisfying the desires of our sense organs leads to social conflict. Xunzi's view of Heaven has parallels with that of the **Daoists** but his view of man and society puts him firmly in the Confucian camp. Xunzi's writings are much admired and mark a considerable advance on the dialogue form of earlier works. The 32 *pian* text takes the form of a series of essays in which the ideas are developed in a systematic and logical way. There are doubts about some of the later *pian* but most of the work is accepted as authentic. Although Xunzi was very influential in the Han, he was not regarded by later scholars, especially the Neo-Confucians, as part of the orthodox line of transmission of Confucian thought, and the text remained in relative obscurity until the nineteenth century when a reappraisal began to take place.

XUNZI: *A Translation and Study of the Complete Works*, (3 Vols.) trans. John Knoblock (Stanford University Press, 1988, 1990, 1994).

Yakub Beg (1820–1877)
Uyghur leader from Khokand who rose against the Chinese in 1862 and founded an independent khanate which controlled the area around Kashghar and part of what is now northern Xinjiang. He was supported by the British as his nation provided a buffer between Russia and India which suited their perception of the Great Game of nineteenth century Asia. Russia occupied Yining in 1871, concerned that Yakub Beg would invade first. Yakub Beg's khanate was destroyed by **Zuo Zongtang** in 1877 and he committed suicide on May 29 of that year. See also **Xinjiang.**

Yalta conference (1945)
Meeting of the leaders of Britain (Churchill), the USA (Roosevelt) and the USSR (Stalin) from February 4–11 in the town of Yalta in the Crimea to discuss Germany's unconditional surrender. Although **Jiang Jieshi** was not at the conference, an agreement was signed that in return for the USSR's declaration of war on Japan after the defeat of Germany, railway and harbour facilities in Manchuria would be made available to them. This compelled China to sign an agreement with the USSR, which led to the Soviet occupation of Manchuria in 1945 and looting of military and industrial equipment and plant.

Yan tie lun **鹽鐵論 Salt and Iron Debate**
The record of a celebrated debate held at the Han court in 81 BC to examine popular grievances over economic conditions. Confucian scholars took the side of the ordinary people in protesting against government monopolies in salt, iron and fermented liquor and against price fixing through the Office of Equalisation and Standards, which they said constituted unfair commercial competition. The practically-minded ministers, headed by **Sang Hongyang**, represented the political outlook which has variously been described as "realist" and "Legalist". They defended monopolies on the grounds that they produced government revenues essential to the defence of the country and refused to give way. The debate was recorded and later written up by Huan Kuan.
E.M. Gale, *Discourses on Salt and Iron* (Leiden: E.J. Brill, 1931); N.L. Swann, *Food and Money in Ancient China* (Princeton University Press, 1950).

Yan Fu 嚴復 (1854–1921)
Scholar, educator and translator into Chinese of Western works on sociology, economics, law, etc. Yan Fu was born in Houguan (now Fuzhou city), in Fujian province. After his father, a doctor, died when he was aged 14 *sui*, straitened family circumstances forced Yan Fu to apply to the naval academy attached to the Fuzhou Shipyard rather than pursue the civil service **examinations**. There he studied naval technology and science before graduating at the age of 19 *sui* and going on to practical training on naval vessels at sea. In 1877 he was sent to England to study naval seamanship, first at Portsmouth and later at the Greenwich Naval Academy. This gave him the chance to observe a Western society at close quarters (he went to the law courts and watched trials); he was also befriended by the Qing envoy to Britain, Guo Songtao 郭嵩燾. Yan returned to China in 1879 and in the following year was invited by **Li Hongzhang** to become chief instructor at his newly established *Beiyang shuishi*

xuetang 北洋水師學堂 (Northern Fleet Naval Academy) where he remained for the following twenty years, rising to the post of director. He escaped from Beijing to Shanghai during the **Boxer Rebellion**. He made several unsuccessful attempts to escape from the backwater of *yangwu* 洋務 'Foreign affairs' into the regular civil service, where real power and influence lay. The defeat of the navy in the 1894–5 war with Japan was a particularly bitter blow to Yan Fu and he published a series of essays in the Tianjin newspaper *Zhibao* 直報 caustically attacking aspects of China's political and social system, advocating reform and calling for the abolition of the civil service examination system and the detested **eight-legged essays**. His targets included: traditional scholarship, variously described as 'insubstantial', 'opinionated' and 'useless', China's autocratic monarchy whose rulers were the 'biggest cheats and robbers', China's love of antiquity and cyclical view of history, which he unfavourably compared with the Western belief in progress, and China's hierarchical society which he contrasted with the equality, individuality and personal freedom of the West. Over the next dozen years he published a series of translations of Western social science classics, including T.H. Huxley's *Evolution and Ethics* (1896–8), Adam Smith's *Wealth of Nations* (1901), Herbert Spencer's *The Study of Sociology* (1903), John Stuart Mill's *On Liberty* and *A System of Logic* (1903) and Montesquieu's *L'Esprit des Lois* (1904–9). These were tremendously influential and provided both reformers and revolutionaries with the ammunition they needed for their assault on existing political and social institutions. During this time Yan Fu was associated with a number of educational institutions, including the *Jingshi daxue tang* 京師大學堂 which was renamed *Beijing Daxue* 北京大學, (Beijing University) in 1912 when he became its first principal. After the revolution, he became increasingly conservative, supporting **Yuan Shikai's** attempted restoration and opposing student activities in the **May Fourth Movement**. It was left to his erstwhile admirer, **Cai Yuanpei**, to encourage at Beijing University the spirit of enquiry for which Yan Fu had called.

Benjamin SCHWARTZ, *In Search of Wealth and Power: Yen Fu and the West* (Belknap Press of Harvard University Press, 1964).

YAN XISHAN 閻錫山 (1883–1960)

Warlord who ruled Shanxi province from his base in Taiyuan from 1912 to 1949. Although independent, he was sympathetic to the Guomindang and cooperated with **Jiang Jieshi** in the **Second Northern Expedition** to retake Beijing.

YAN'AN 延安

Town in Shaanxi province that became the headquarters of the CCP at the end of the **Long March** in December 1936 until it was seized by Guomindang troops on March 19 1947. The Yan'an period, as this is known, has become part of the founding myth of the PRC and the leadership in post-1949 China would often invoke the nostalgia of the poor, comradely spirit of the cave houses of Yan'an. Through **Rectification Campaigns**, the CCP was reorganised and strengthened and the diverse range of people who had joined it during the **Anti-Japanese War** was integrated. a series of campaigns established the new CCP policies on a variety of issues, including nationalism, revolution, peasant power and art and literature.

Mark SELDON, *The Yenan Way in Revolutionary China* (Harvard University Press, 1971).

YAN'AN FORUM ON LITERATURE AND ART *Yanan wenyi zuotanhui* 延安文藝座談會

Part of the Rectification Campaigns of the **Yan'an** period and held between May 2 and May 23 1942. Mao spoke at the forum and insisted that literature and art should reflect the views of workers, peasants and soldiers, rejecting the idea of art for art's sake. This speech set the tone of Communist Party attitudes towards writing and art which were put into practice after 1949.

Bonnie MCDOUGALL, *Mao Zedong's "Talks at the Yan'an Conference on Literature and Art": A Translation of the 1943 Text with Commentary* (University of Michigan Press, 1980).

YANG GUIFEI 楊貴妃 (Yang Yuhuan 楊玉環, d.756)

The greatest *femme fatale* in Chinese history, whose tragic love affair with Emperor **Xuanzong** forms the subject of innumerable works of literature, theatre and art. Having deserted her husband Prince Shou and entered a Daoist convent she was chosen as a courtesan by Xuanzong and became his favourite consort. Given the name Guifei 貴妃 "Valued companion" by the obsessed Emperor she exploited her position and acquired political powers, and it was she who persuaded him to adopt **An Lushan** as their son. Members of the Yang clan, such as **Yang Guozhong** and Yang Xian, also benefited from her position of influence. An Lushan's rebellion, however, made her fall inevitable, and as the court fled to exile in **Shu** the grief-stricken Emperor could no longer resist demands for her execution .

H.S. LEVY, "The Career of Yang Kuei-fei", *Toung Pao* XLV (1957) pp 451–89 (Leiden: E.J. Brill).

YANG GUOZHONG 楊國忠 (Yang Zhao 楊釗, ? -756)

A distant relative of **Yang Guifei** who had accumulated positions of power under his rival **Li Linfu** and succeeded him as chief minister (see **Prime Minister**) on his death in 752. Like Li he exercised enormous personal authority, but the Emperor failed to heed his warnings about the threat posed by **An Lushan**, and as the court fled to the South-west he was executed.

YANG SU 楊素 (d.606)

Senior official and military commander who played a leading and ruthless part in the reunification of China in 580 and the consolidation of Sui power.

YANG XIONG 揚雄 (53 BC – AD 18)

Outstanding intellectual of the Han dynasty, a member of the Old Text school and commentator on the *Yijing* and the *Analects* of **Confucius** (see ***Lun Yu***). He was an admirer of **Sima Xiangru** and like him was famous for his *fu* poetry.

YANG ZHU 楊朱 (c. 440–360 BC)

Warring States period thinker associated with egoism *wei wo* 爲我. Since death faces us all, not differentiating between good and bad, Yang Zhu reasoned that we might as well live for ourselves and enjoy the moment, taking pleasure in whatever good things, beauty, music and sexual opportunities come our way. He was charged with hedonism and condemned by other thinkers. For example,

Mencius complained that Yang Zhu was not willing to pluck out one of his hairs to benefit the world, but also said that his thought was very prevalent at the time. There is no authoritative text for him but Chapter Seven of the ***Liezi*** entitled 'Yang Zhu' probably reflects his ideas and may include some early material by him.

LIEZI: *The Book of Lieh-tzu A Classic of the Tao,* trans. A.C. Graham (London: John Murray, 1960; rept. Mandala Press, 1991).

***YANGBANXI* 様板戯**

Model theatrical productions or revolutionary operas which dominated the stage all over China during the **Cultural Revolution**, and were under the control of **Jiang Qing**. *Yangbanxi* included several Beijing operas such as *The Red Lantern, Hongdengji* 紅燈記 and *Taking Tiger Mountain by Strategy, Zhiqu weihushan* 智取威虎山, ballets such as *The Red Detatchment of Women, Hongse niangzijun* 紅色娘子軍 and *The White-haired Girl,* ***Baimao nü*** 白毛女, and musical compositions. They were originally eight in number but gradually increased to ten and more. During the period between 1966 to 1976, *yangbanxi* were used to represent the limits of acceptable thought and the ideological conformity imposed. Mass entertainment was essentially reduced to *yangbanxi* and the songs, films, and local dramas that could be derived therefrom. Expression of thoughts and feelings by individual artists was totally prohibited – only a narrowly orthodox conception of "truth" should prevail.

In Jiang Qing's reductionist mode, as exemplified by *yangbanxi*, revolutionary heroes were magnified and all "middle characters" were eliminated. Ambiguity was not tolerated in the arts, as the slightest indication of sympathy toward a villain was thought to confuse people and lead them astray. The radical guidelines and standards derived from *yangbanxi* were also applied to other arts, including painting, sculpture and literature, during the Cultural Revolution.

YANGDI 煬帝, SUI EMPEROR (Yang Guang 楊廣, r.604–17)

Son of Emperor **Wendi** and his **Xiongnu** empress who sought to consolidate his father's unification of the empire and to revive the glories of Han. He travelled widely and frequently on imperial progresses around his empire and was intent on integrating the South into the northern heartland. He maintained three capitals, in Daxing, **Luoyang** and Jiangdu on the **Yangzi**. His engineers completed the building of the **Grand Canal** and other major engineering works, including roads, grain storage depots, the rebuilding of the **Great Wall**, and the building of a new palace at **Luoyang**. His foreign policy was equally grandiose and included campaigns as far afield as Inner Asia, **Korea** and South-east Asia. It was the repeated failure of strategically unwise attacks on **Koguryo** in 612–4 that began to undermine his position, and following a series of rebellions between 613 and 617 he was murdered by the son of one of his generals in 618. Among later writers his reign became the epitome of tyranny, corruption and immorality, but as in the case of the First Emperor **Qin Shi Huangdi** this probably represents a degree of unfair exaggeration. His policies had indeed been excessively costly in both economic and human terms, but his vision and ambitions were in the tradition of the greatest builders of the Chinese empire.

See also **Yang Su, Yuwen Kai.**

YANGSHAO 仰韶

The earliest phase of the oldest distinctive cultural tradition in China's **neolithic** history. It is named after the village of Yangshaocun in Shaanxi Province, where finds were first made in 1922. Over a period of some five thousand years, from approximately 6,000 BC, Yangshao civilisation spread across northern and central China, until it was gradually superseded by the more advanced **Longshan** culture and early **Bronze Age**. It is typified by its decorated pottery. In earliest times this was frequently surface-textured with patterns made by the application of pieces of cord or textiles. Wares were usually hand-made. As they became finer, painted red and black whirls and geometric patterns came to predominate, often of considerable complexity and aesthetic ingenuity. Animal and human designs appeared, some showing the importance of the fish to Yangshao communities, others providing evidence for the use of dance in ritual. Vessels were used for storage, carrying liquids, and cooking. Shapes were generally plain and functional, showed an appreciation of style and form, and were typically flat or round-bottomed. Sometimes they had two ring handles through which a carrying cord could be attached; a flask with a pointed bottom which righted itself when filled could thus be lifted from the water. Yangshao people were agriculturalists, fishermen, and hunters living in organised village communities. Burial practices indicate belief in spiritual matters. Important sites include **Banpocun**.

K.C. CHANG, *The Archaeology of Ancient China*, 4th. edition (Yale University Press, 1986).

YANGTSE RIVER see **YANGZI RIVER**

YANGWU YUNDONG 洋務運動 (Foreign Matters Movement) see **SELF-STRENGTHENING MOVEMENT**

YANGZHOU 揚州

City in Jiangsu province at the point where the **Grand Canal** runs into the Yangzi River. Its position and the salt trade of which it was the main centre made it a prosperous commercial city and the merchants of Yangzhou were a byword for wealth and lavish living.

YANGZI RIVER

The longest and one of the two most important rivers in China's history. (See also **Yellow River**). It runs for some 3,500 miles from its source on the Tibetan plateau and flows into the sea near Shanghai. It had been a formidable natural boundary between north and south China and there was no bridge over the eastern section of the river until the construction of the bridge at Nanjing in 1969. The Yangzi also marks the boundary between the northern forms of the Chinese language and the southern languages such as Wu, Gan and Cantonese (see **Chinese Language**). Although it is almost always called Yangzi 揚子 (Yangtse) 'son of the Ocean', in English, in Chinese it is always known as the *Changjiang* 長江, 'Long River'.

L.P. VAN SLYKE, *Yangtse: Nature, History and the River* (New York, 1988).

YANJING 燕京

An old name for **Beijing,** derived originally from the Warring State of Yan. It was the southern capital of the Liao dynasty and from 1153, the capital of the Jin dyasty. It was sacked in the Mongol campaigns of 1211–15. The name continued to be used for Yanjing (Yenching) University, a combination of colleges founded by different missionary denominations.

YAO see **FORMER KINGS**

YAO WENYUAN 姚文元 (1931–)

Shanghai journalist and one of the **Gang of Four**. Yao was editor-in-chief of the *Liberation Daily* in Shanghai and came to public attention with his attack on **Wu Han's** play *Hai Rui Dismissed*. Yao rose in the CCP and held posts on the Central Committee, Politburo and the Cultural Revolution Group and continued to serve as Zhang Chunqiao's deputy secretary on the Shanghai CCP Committee. He was sentenced to twenty years imprisonment on January 25 1981 and was released from prison in October 1996, aged 65.

YEARS, ANIMAL NAMES FOR see **SHENGXIAO**

YELLOW EMPEROR *Huangdi* 黄帝

One of the legendary rulers and founders of Chinese civilisation, traditionally credited with the invention of wheeled vehicles, ships, the calendar and the compass. **Zou Yan** identified his supposed period of rule as the first to benefit from the virtue of one of the **Five Elements**, earth. In the early Han he was worshipped by a religious cult associated with popular **Daoism**. **Zhuangzi** linked him with **Ximuwang**, and some devotees believed he would lead them towards **immortality**. Han **Wudi** had state ceremonies performed in his honour in 110 BC. See also **Ban Gu, Fu Xi, *Huanglao,* Shen Nong.**

YELLOW RIVER *Huanghe* 黄河

Popularly known as "China's sorrow" because of the devastation caused by its recurrent flooding and changes of course, the great river of northern China has in fact been of positive significance in the evolution of Chinese civilisation. It rises in **Tibet** and flows over three thousand miles to the Gulf of Bohai. Since prehistoric times it has carried fertile alluvial soil from the Central Asian deserts down onto the Great Plain, assisting the creation of an economic base area which has underpinned political and cultural expansion (see **Grand Canal, Water Control**). It was the experience of understanding and coping with the opportunities and threats of this enigmatic "dragon" that first helped to establish the early centralised and bureaucratic state in China (see **Oriental Despotism**). Despite its unpredictability it formed a major communication artery between West and East and has stimulated the imagination of hydraulic experts, from the builders of dykes and irrigation canals in ancient times to those of dams and hydro-electric plants in the modern era. Major changes of direction by the River in eastern Henan caused great loss of life in AD 11 (see **Wang Mang**), 1194, 1344 (see **White Lotus**) and 1852, and again in 1938 when **Jiang Jieshi** deliberately broke the dykes in an ill-fated attempt to hold up advancing Japanese troops. See also **Hangu Pass.**

YELLOW SPRINGS

Imaginary subterranean dwelling of spirits awaiting rebirth. It was popularly believed to be located somewhere under the yellow earth of the far North, where the waters froze in winter at the ascendence of *yin* and melted at the resurgence of *yang* in the spring. See also **Immortality, *Yin-yang*.**

YELLOW TURBANS

The best known of the late Han millenarian and rebellious movements which developed after AD 140 and from 184 marked the effective end of the Liu clan's dynastic authority; so-called because of the yellow headgear worn by its supporters to indicate the hoped-for succession of the element earth over the Later Han dynasty's guiding element of fire. The religious origins of the movement have been linked with the **Bön** religion of ancient **Tibet**, and in the inquisitive and superstitious climate of Han spiritual practices it was one of many cults associated with popular **Daoism** that enjoyed transient popularity among people gripped by differing ideas of **immortality**. The Yellow Turban religion had more success than most. In eastern China its leader Zhang Jue built up a strong following dedicated to the attainment of Great Peace (*taiping* 太平), but when it turned into a military insurrection against the Han authorities in 184 it was quickly suppressed with great bloodshed and Zhang Jue himself was killed. In eastern Sichuan province **Zhang Daoling** and his successor Zhang Lu were less militaristic and more successful, running a small quasi-independent state until its suppression by **Cao Cao** in 215. This sect attracted the title "Five Pecks of Rice" (*wudoumi* 五斗米) by virtue of the contribution required of its members. The movement is noteworthy for its religious organisation and developed liturgy (using the *Taipingjing* 太平經 'Classic of Great Peace'), for its opposition to sexual and class discrimination, and for its promotion of social services including medicine and famine relief. See also **Five Elements.**

YIJING* 易經 *Book of Changes

This work on divination, also known as the *Zhou yi* 周易, is one of the **five classics** and an extremely influential text in the development of Chinese thought. The text is traditionally associated with Fu Xi 伏羲, who is said to have drawn the eight trigrams *ba gua* 八卦, King Wen (**Wen Wang**) 文王, who is said to have arranged them as 64 hexagrams and written the statements which go with each, and **Confucius,** who is said to have written the commentaries. The trigrams consists of three horizontal broken or unbroken lines (broken lines are associated with *yin*, the female force, and unbroken lines with *yang*, the male force) vertically arranged on top of each other; the hexagrams consist of six lines and are made by combinations of two trigrams. It now seems likely that it is a late 9th century BC text and because it was a useful work, its transmission was not seriously affected by the **'burning of the books'** in the Qin. The work is made up of the classic and a series of seven commentaries (traditionally counted as ten and known as the 'ten wings' *shiyi* 十翼). The classic consists of the 64 hexagrams with names and explanatory statements for each hexagram and each line. The appropriate hexagram was determined during the divination process (for example, short and long yarrow stalks have been used to determine the lines of hexagrams) and the hexagram statement was interpreted by the diviner. The commentaries, which betray late Warring States cosmological theories (i.e. ***yin-yang*** and **five element** school ideas), seek to extend the significance of the text from a practical divination manual to an all-encompassing explanation of the workings of the cosmos. The *Yijing* in this way became one of the principal sources of Confucian thought and Song **Neo-Confucians** eagerly plundered it in their quest for a Confucian cosmology to stand against Buddhism and Daoism. The *Yijing* is one of the most studied, commented upon and translated of all Chinese texts and has enjoyed cult status in the modern West too.

Richard John LYNN, trans., *The Classic of Changes: A New Translation of the I Ching as Interpreted by Wang Bi* (Columbia University Press, 1994).

YILI 儀禮 *Book of Ceremonies and Rites*

The ritual text called, in the Han dynasty, the Classic of Rites, but which now shares that status with the ***Zhouli*** and the ***Liji***. In contrast with the *Zhouli*, which is about the offices of state, the *Yili* is concerned with the daily rituals appropriate to a member of the *shi* 士 lower gentry and hence was an important text for a relatively big group in society. It seems likely that it may originally have been part of a larger work detailing the rituals appropriate to various classes of gentry, but is now the only the section remaining. It consists in total of seventeen *pian* each dealing with a specific situation, e.g. capping rites, marriage rites, banquet rites and so on. However, the section from *pian* 11 to 17 is devoted to mourning rites, the most important area of all, and parts of this have at times been treated as a separate work. This work, like the *Zhouli*, is traditionally ascribed to **Zhou Gong** 周公, the Duke of Zhou, but there is no clear provenance for the text before the Han. In the Han the various **new text** versions and an old text version were edited by Zheng Xuan鄭玄; the current text is based on his work.

Michael LOEWE, ed., *Early Chinese Texts: A Bibliographical Guide* (Berkeley: The Society for the Study of Early China and The Institute of East Asian Studies, University of California, 1993).

YIDE懿德, PRINCE (d.701)

Son of Tang **Zhongzong** and brother of Princess Yongtai, both of whom were assassinated as teenagers by the Empress Wu (see **Wu Zetian**) and reburied by their guilt-ridden father in 706. Their tombs, outside Xi'an, are famous for the high quality of their mural decorations (now preserved in Shaanxi Provincial Museum) of which Yide's alone contained forty, one showing a guard of honour comprising 24 *qiji* halberdiers. The tomb measured 108.8 metres from the top of the ramp to the back of the coffin chamber. Four wall niches opened off the ramp for the location of the grave artefacts, and a series of seven vertical shafts led from the roof of the passage to ground level. Although the tomb had been robbed, when excavated it still contained hundreds of pottery figurines of soldiers, huntsmen and horses painted in polychrome and the current ***sancai*** style.

YIHETUAN see BOXER RISING

*YIN*蔭

System which permitted members of the aristocracy to enter directly into officialdom without the need to qualify by examination, their level of entry being dependent upon their father, relative or sponsor's rank. In the Tang dynasty, when the **examination system** was still in a relatively early stage of development, they were in the majority. In the Song they were still numerous but outnumbered by those with examination success or university education (see **Imperial Academy**). The **Mongols** made more use of *yin*, but in the Ming-Qing period it was used sparingly. The son of a first-rank official could directly enter at fifth-grade level, a son of a third-grade official at seventh-grade level.

HO Ping-ti, *The Ladder of Success in Imperial China: Aspects of Social Mobility, 1368–1911* (Columbia University Press, 1962); J.M. MENZEL, *The Chinese Civil Service, Career open to Talent?* (Boston: Heath & Co., 1963).

YINGZAO FASHI 營造法式 'Treatise on Architectural Methods'

A building manual compiled by Li Jie 李誡 (1035–1110), a Song official in charge of building projects. The work was presented to the emperor in 1100 and published in 1103. Although the erection of buildings has been subject to official regulations from the earliest time, few documentary records exist before Li Jie's compendium of Chinese traditional architecture. The manual has 34 *juan*, with chapters devoted to technical terms, and sets out the rules concerning building methods, workmanship, and the relative measurements and proportions of various architectural elements. It also gives the sizes and costs of the different materials appropriate to various grades of building, prescribing a standard system for the wooden parts of a building, enabling officials efficiently to oversee, organise and cost building projects.

YINXU 殷墟, 'The Ruins of Yin.'

Site of late Shang dynasty city (c. 1300–1027 BC), as Yin was the ancient name for both the city and the Shang dynasty. Yinxu is an area of over 24 square kilometres centred at Xiaotun Village in **Anyang** county, Henan province. Excavations started from 1928 and have revealed tombs, foundations of palaces and temples, bronzes, jade carvings, lacquer, inlaid items, white carved ceramics and high-fired green-glazed wares, as well as inscribed oracle bones of which over 100,000 pieces have been found. Sites with major tombs, including chariot burials, have been discovered at many of the surrounding villages. Large cruciform tombs of the Shang period, all of which had been robbed at an early date, were found north of the Huan River at Xibeigang.

K. C. CHANG, *Shang Civilization* (Yale University Press, 1980).

YIN-YANG 陰陽

Ancient theory of dialectics which attempted to define the nature and workings of the universe on a rational, non-supernatural basis. It was first mentioned in the *Guoyu* and the ***Zuozhuan*** in reference to speeches of the eighth and seventh centuries BC. A Yin-yang school may be identified in the Period of the Philosophers (see **Zou Yan**), and in the Former Han period it combined with the **Five Elements** school as scholars such as **Dong Zhongshu** strove to base government policy on something more precise than subjective moralism but less mechanistic than the absolute rule of man-made law. Attempts to understand and comply with *yin-yang* are particularly associated with **Daoism** but as a simplistic interpretation of the universe the theory found such widespread acceptance that it has survived even to the present as a form of popular cosmology.

Acceptance of the principle of *yin-yang* interaction did not preclude belief in Heaven but reduced its power to act arbitrarily. Its Will might be influenced and determined by the correct balancing of *yin* and *yang*. The two forces were associated with natural phenomena, e.g. sun and moon, summer and winter, and are commonly characterised as male (*yang*) and female (*yin*), though they were not primarily thought of in sexual terms. Rather, they symbolised the contrasting qualities which men in an already patriarchal society might have conceived as corresponding to male and female characteristics, e.g. hard and soft, forceful and submissive, dry and wet, level and curved, military and civil. The balance was unequal, *yang* always being the predominant element, but it respected the essential nature of *yin*. Correct balance was seen to have creative properties, resulting in the bearing of offspring, the ripening of crops, and the prevalence of social harmony. The results of imbalance appeared in undesirable situations as diverse as political disorder, unseasonal climatic conditions, and physical illness. See also **Hundred Schools, Mandate of Heaven, Omens and Portents.**

Joseph NEEDHAM et al, *Science and Civilisation in China, Vol. 2* (Cambridge University Press, 1956).

YONG WING 容閎 (1828–1912)

The first Chinese graduate of an American university, Yong Wing (Rong Hong in Mandarin) came from a poor family from Xiangshan, Guangdong. He studied at the Morrison Academy, first in Macao and later in Hong Kong, before going to America in 1847. After three years of study he gained admission to Yale University, from where he graduated in 1854. After returning to China in 1855 he was employed in a number of foreign institutions before becoming involved in the reformist ***yangwu*** 洋務 movement. In 1863 he persuaded **Zeng Guofan** to set up the **Jiangnan Arsenal** and was entrusted with going to America to purchase equipment for it. In 1868, he suggested setting up a scheme to send young people to America to study. This was accepted and he accompanied the first group to America in 1870. Although the scheme was ended in 1881, Yong Wing remained in America until 1894 when he returned to China. He became involved in reformist activities, culminating in his role as chairman of Tang Caichang's *Zhongguo guohui* 中國國會 (China's Parliament) in Shanghai in 1900. Following Tang's unsuccessful armed uprising, Yong Wing was forced to flee to back to America. From there, he continued to contribute to political activity in China, transferring his support to **Sun Yixian's** revolutionaries. He died in Hartford, Conneticut in April 1912. His life is described in his autobiographical *My Life in China and America* (New York, 1909).

YONGLE 永樂, MING EMPEROR (r. 1403–1424)

Third emperor of the Ming dynasty, uncle of the second Jianwen emperor, whose throne he seized, and second son of the founder of the Ming, the Hongwu emperor. The Jianwen emperor succeeded to the throne because his father, Hongwu's eldest son, had predeceased him. He is regarded as a strong emperor who encouraged scholarship, including the *Yongle dadian* 永樂大典 *Yongle* ***encyclopaedia.*** He expanded the area under Ming control by extending the **tribute system** and was the sponsor of the voyages of **Zheng He**, which brought South-east Asia into that system. In 1421, he moved the capital from Nanjing to Beijing, largely because it would be easier to control the threat of a further **Mongol** invasion from there. He died on an expedition against the Mongols in 1424.

YONGLE DADIAN **永樂大典** ***YONGLE ENCYCLOPAEDIA*** see **ENCYCLOPAEDIAS**

YONGZHENG 雍正, QING EMPEROR (R.1723–1736)

Successor, although in controversial circumstances, to the **Kangxi** emperor and remembered for his reconstruction of the Qing govenrment. He established the Grand Council over the Grand Secretariat as the highest policy-making body, thus consolidating power in his own hands.

Madeline ZELIN, *The Magistrate's Tael: Rationalizing Fiscal Reform in Eighteenth Century Ch'ing China* (Berkeley: University of California Press, 1984).

YU DAFU 郁達夫 (1896–1945).

Born Yu Wen in Fuyang, Zhejiang, Yu Dafu is best known for his short stories, essays, criticism and poetry. Having studied literature in Tokyo, he set up the Creation Society with **Guo Moruo** and others in 1921. It was in this year that he first came to fame with the short story 'Sinking' *Chenlun* 沉淪 which was published in a collection of the same name. It was among the first collections of short stories in the history of modern Chinese literature. In common with many of his later stories, the hero of 'Sinking' is a melancholic young intellectual like Yu Dafu himself. The story chronicles the feelings of humiliation, resentment, loneliness and sexual frustration of a young Chinese student in Japan. Influenced by the **New Culture Movement**, many of Yu's writings at this time reflected anti-imperialist and anti-feudalist trends. 'Nights of Spring Fever' (1923), one of Yan Dafu's best known stories, again has an intellectual made 'hero', rather pathetic in his importance, and an exploited young female factory worker who is, by contrast, much more capable and determined. Throughout the 20s and 30s Yu was a prominent member of the group of left-wing writers and a founding member of the league of left-wing writers. Later be became involved in anti-Japanese propaganda work and went to Singapore, writing articles urging the Chinese to resist the Japanese. After the fall of Singapore, he went to Sumatra, only to be killed by the Japanese military police in 1945.

Leo Ou-fan LEE, *The Romantic Generation of Chinese Writers* (Harvard University Press, 1973); YU Dafu, *Nights Of Spring Fever and Other Writings* (Beijing: Panda Books, 1984).

YUAN DYNASTY 元朝 (1276–1368)

The dynastic title, meaning "origin", used by the **Mongols** for their conquest regime of China. **Chinggis Khan** (Genghis) was the leader who brought together all the Mongol tribes so that they were in a position to take control of China, but it was **Khubilai Khan** who completed the conquest in 1276–79. The dynastic name was first officially used in 1271, five years before the capture of the Southern Song capital Hangzhou confirmed the Mongols' rule over all China. It was not easy for a nomadic people organised on tribal lines to control a sedentary agrarian population and sophisticated urban centres, but an administration based on the civil service system of the Tang and Song dynasties and the assistance of non-Chinese subjects of the empire such as the **Jurchen** and **Khitan** (including Yelü Chucai) and Central Asian Turks made it possible.

The Yuan capital was moved south from the Mongolian steppes to China. The main capital used in the winter was Dadu on the site of present day Beijing and the summer residence was Shangdu in what is now Inner Mongolia. Under Mongol adminstration there were four categories of people. The Mongols were the highest in rank; second came the ***Semu*** 色目 people of "special regard", who were mainly speakers of Turkic languages from Central Asia; below them came the *Hanren* 漢人,from northern China a group which included both ethnic Chinese and other northern peoples such as the Jurchen and Khitan; finally there were the *Nanren* 南人, the southerners who had been under the rule of the Song empire.

There was an increase in commerce, in particular with Central Asia as Chinese contacts with the great Asian land mass were strengthened, but also between north and south China where links had been severed by the conquest of the northern part of the Song empire by the Jurchen Jin dynasty. Maritime trade between China, South-east Asia and Indian Ocean seaports flourished. During the 13th century, the **Grand Canal** was extended northwards to Dadu (Beijing) so that the court could be supplied with grain. The link that the Mongols created between China and the Islamic world led to a number of technologial advances including the development of gunpowder, the construction of astronomical apparatus, and irrigation works based on Persian models.

Literature in a written form of Chinese closer to the vernacular than the traditional genres written in Classical Chinese thrived in the cities under the Yuan dynasty. Novels and short stories were produced in quantity, but it was in drama that the Yuan period excelled.

The Mongol rule of China came to an end amid famine, flood and peasant risings of which the most successful was the rebellion of Zhu Yuanchang, who was to become the first emperor (**Hongwu**) of the Ming dynasty. However, factional disputes among the Mongol leadership were a significant factor. Khubilai was powerful enough to resist rival claimants, but internal dissension wracked the courts of his successors.

Yuan Emperors

Reign dates	**Temple Names**	**Reign Title**	**Mongol name**
1271–1295	Shizu	Zhiyuan	Khubilai
1295–1308	Chengzong	Yuanzhen	Temur
1308–1312	Wuzong	Zhida	Haishan
1312–1314	Renzong	Huangqing	Ayurbarwada
1314–1321		Yanyou	
1321–1324	Yingzong	Zhizhi	Shidebala
1324–1328	Taidingdi	Taiding	Yesun Temur
1328		Zhihe	
1328	Youzhu	Tianshun	Aragibag
1328–1330	Wenzong	Tianli	Togh Temur
1330–1332		Zhishun	
1332–1333	Ningzong		Irinjabal
1333–1368	Huizong	Tongyuan	Toghon Temur

David MORGAN, *The Mongols* (Basil Blackwell, 1986; Herbert FRANKE, *China under Mongol Rule* (Aldershot: Variorum, 1994); Elizabeth ENDICOTT-WEST, *Mongolian Rule in China: Local Administration in the Yuan Dynasty* (Council on East Asian Studies, Harvard University, 1989); John D. LANGLOIS Jr., ed., *China under Mongol Rule* (Princeton University Press, 1981).

YUAN MEI 袁枚 (1716–1797)
Poet, aesthete and advocate of women's literacy. Born into a cultured Hangzhou family, Yuan passed the *jinshi* 進士 examination in 1739 at the young age of twenty-three. After a brief official career he resigned and spent the rest of his life studying, writing poetry and teaching. Yuan was famed and criticised for his Sui Garden 隨園 where women, in particular, would gather to compose and recite poetry. Two of Yuan's sisters were in fact praised for their literary talent. His *Suiyuan shihua* 隨園詩話 'Sui Garden Talks on Poetry' set out his views on literature. He was opposed to the imposition of rigid moral or aesthetic norms, and in favour of originality and self-expression. He is best known as a poet and earned substantial sums for his poems. His interests are also extended to literary criticism, history, ghost stories and cookery.
Arthur WALEY, *Yuan Mei, Eighteenth Century Chinese Poet* (George Allen and Unwin, 1956).

YUAN SHIKAI 袁世凱 (1859–1916)
Late Qing military official turned President of the Republic, who wanted to be Emperor. Yuan was not successful in the civil service examinations, but became a military official and was sent to Korea where he became adviser to the Korean army. He returned to China and was an active reformer in the period before the **Hundred Days Reform** period. However, he eventually betrayed **Kang Youwei** and the other reformers and supported The Empress Dowager **Cixi**, as he believed that she would emerge victorious. His Beiyang army fought on the side of the court during the **Boxer Rising** but also became involved with the **Constitutional Movement** in the early years of the 20th century. In November 1911, he was organising a cabinet for the Qing court, but by February 1912, he had thrown in his lot with the new Republic and was declared President on March 10, ousting **Sun Yixian**, who had withdrawn in the hope that this would ensure national unity. In 1913, Yuan suppressed the **Second Revolution** of southern republicans and by 1915 was sure enough of his position to have himself declared Hongxian emperor. He died on June 6 1916, before he could be formally enthroned, and China slid into a period of rule by **warlords.**
Stephen MACKINNON, *Power and Politics in Late Imperial China: Yuan Shi-kai in Beijing and Tianjin, 1901– 1908* (Berkeley: University of California Press, 1980); Ernest YOUNG, *The Presidency of Yuan Shih-kai: Liberalism and Dictatorship in Early Republican China* (University of Michigan Press, 1977).

YUAN XIAN see **SEVEN SAGES OF THE BAMBOO GROVE**

YUANDI 元帝, HAN EMPEROR (Liu Shi 劉奭, 75–33, r. 48–33 BC)
Son of Emperor Xuandi during whose reign imperial authority was surrendered to **eunuchs** (notably Shi Xian), Confucian literati (notably Kuang Heng), and maternal relatives, notably his Empress **Wang**, mother of his successor **Chengdi** and aunt of **Wang Mang**).

YUANMING YUAN see **SUMMER PALACES**

YUE 越

Ancient state along the lower **Yangzi** in the region of modern Zhejiang. It had assumed the role of inter-state **hegemon** by its defeat of neighbouring **Wu** in 473 BC but was conquered by **Chu** in 334–3 BC. Its inhabitants continued to resist **Qin** rule with guerilla tactics, and its name was preserved both in the name given to the pottery produced in this area in the late Tang period and in the title of the kingdom that ruled the South-east between 907 and 978. See **Five Dynasties and Ten Kingdoms, Taizong.**

YUE LING see **LÜSHI CHUNQIU**

YUEJI 樂記 'Musical record'

Musical treatise probably dating from the second century BC and derived from an earlier work, which survived thanks to its inclusion in the ***Liji*** during the Han dynasty. The name of its editor is disputed but may have been **Liu De**. It shows considerable similarity with sections on **music** contained in the ***Xunzi***, the ***Lüshi Chunqiu*** and the ***Shiji***. It is a didactic rather than descriptive text, the purpose of which is to emphasize the value of music in establishing a bridge between earth and Heaven. It does this by promoting the proper balance between *yin* and *yang* within the universe (see ***Yin-yang***). The beneficial influence resulting from the perfect performance of music, presumably in the context of court ritual, may be observed *inter alia* in the orderly sequence of the four seasons, the flourishing of vegetation, and the timely birth of young creatures. See also **Music Bureau.**

W. KAUFMANN, *Manorial References in the Chinese Classics* (Detroit: Information Coordinates, 1976).

YUNGANG GROTTOES ***YUNGANG SHIKU*** 雲崗石窟

A series of more than twenty large Buddhist cave temples on the south cliff of Wuzhou mountain near Datong, Shanxi province. Datong was the location of the capital of the Toba Northern Wei dynasty between 398 and 494. The major Yungang caves were built from 460 to 494 and a number of small ones were built afterwards, construction stopping in 524. There are a total of 53 caves with about 51,000 Buddhist images carved from rocks. These represent the middle phase of Northern Wei style begun by Emperor Wencheng (reign 452–465) in 460 to compensate for his predecessor's persecution of **Buddhism**. Here were carved from the sandstone cliffs in the second half of the fifth century AD intricately decorated shrines and enormous statues of Buddhist deities, evidence of the imperial worship and patronage of the Indian religion which was then sweeping the empires of both **Northern and Southern Dynasties**. The largest figure is a monumental fifteen metres high.The site was named Lingyansi 靈岩寺 (Temples of Spirit Cliffs) after the grottoes were built but changed to its present name in the Ming dynasty. As most of the images in major caves were executed by imperial order and supervised by the court they are of impressive size against a sumptuous relief background. The early images show strong Central Asian influence particularly in the treatment of facial details and the mantles with their flattened folds. By the end of the fifth century the imported styles had been absorbed and a distinctively Chinese style had emerged, which was perpetuated at **Longmen**.

YUWEN KAI 宇文愷 (d.612)
Outstanding engineer of the Sui period who became President of the Board of Works. Among many impressive projects he was responsible for building Emperor **Wendi's** new capital at **Chang'an** and the important Guangtong Canal linking it with the **Yellow River** (see **Grand Canal**), **Yangdi's** capital at **Luoyang**, the rebuilding of the **Great Wall**, and the construction of a bridge over the Liao River as part of the campaign against **Koguryo** in 612. See also **Water Control.**

ZENG GUOFAN 曾國藩 (1811–72)
Scholar, general and loyal statesman of the late Qing dynasty. Born in Hunan (the older name of which is *Xiang* 湘), Zeng had a successful official career, rising to posts in the **Hanlin Academy** and the Board of Rites and in 1853 he was ordered by the imperial court to raise troops, the **Xiang Army,** in his home province to suppress the **Taiping Rebellion.** He was the inspiration for Li Hongzhang's **Huai Army** and backed the construction of the **Jiangnan Arsenal** and other **Self-Strengthening Movement** enterprises.

ZHANGUO see **WARRING STATES**

***ZHANGUOCE* 戰國策 Intrigues of the Warring States**
A compilation of anecdotes on the stratagems employed in the **Warring States** period (403–221 BC). The work was edited from at least six existing works found in the imperial archives by **Liu Xiang** (c.79–6 BC) to produce a book of 33 *pian* with anecdotes on the Zhou imperial house, seven major states and three minor states. These anecdotes describe principally the methods suggested by strategists and employed by ministers and rulers to try to ensure their survival and the downfall of their enemies. Although the *Zhanguoce* is not necessarily a very accurate record, it is greatly esteemed for its literary merit and features prominently in anthologies. Its lack of a clear moral line denied it canonical status and the text had become very defective by the Song, when it was re-edited by Zeng Gong 曾鞏 (1019–83) and a number of later scholars. This resulted in the two main extant versions, arranged by state and chronologically. Many of the stories are paralleled by similar accounts in the ***Shiji***; **Mawangdui** versions of the text and its sources contain both parts of the existing text, confirming its authenticity, and new material providing a valuable supplement, particularly for the later period.

Chan-kuo Ts'e trans. J.I. CRUMP (Oxford: Clarendon Press, 1970); J.I. CRUMP: *Intrigues: Studies of the Chan-kuo Ts'e* (University of Michigan Press, 1964.).

ZHANG BINGLIN 章炳麟 (1869–1936)
Classical scholar and fervent anti-**Manchu** revolutionary, also known as Zhang Taiyan 章太炎. Chang was born into a lower gentry family from Yuhang, Zhejiang. The family had been seriously affected by the **Taiping Rebellion**, and he was educated at the home of his maternal grandfather. Later, he became a

student of the renowned scholar Yu Yueh 俞樾 at the *Gujing jingshe* academy 詁經精舍 in Hangzhou where he specialised in philology. Although his ***guwen*** training left him diametrically opposed to the views of **Kang Youwei** and **Liang Qichao** on scholarship, he too was indignant at China's humiliation in the **Sino-Japanese War** and joined the ***Qiangxuehui*** 強學會 'Society for the Encouragement of Learning' set up by Kang in Shanghai. In December 1896 Zhang abandoned his studies and went to work at the *Shiwubao* 時務報 newspaper, successor to the Society's banned *Qiangxuebao*. After the failure of the 1898 reform movement Zhang felt impelled to flee to Taiwan, then under Japanese control; from there he went to Japan where he met **Sun Yixian** and the revolutionaries before returning to Shanghai. By social and educational background he was much closer to the reformers, but family tradition was anti-Manchu and after his brief flirtation with the reformers he threw in his lot with the revolutionaries, taking an uncompromisingly anti-Manchu line. In a typically flamboyant gesture he rejected the support of the **Guangxu Emperor**, announced his defection and cut off his **queue** at Tang Caichang's *Guohui* 國會 'parliament' in Shanghai in July 1900. In June 1903 Zhang published *Bo Kang Youwei lun geming shu* 駁康有爲論革命書 'Essay in refutation of Kang Youwei and on revolution' is which he said: "Zaitian (the Emperor's personal name) is a little clown who can't tell beans from wheat" and contributed the preface to Zou Rong's 鄒容 scurrilously anti-Manchu *Geming jun* 革命軍 'Revolutionary Army'. The resulting trial at the Shanghai International Settlement Court, known as the '*Subao* 蘇報 case' from the name of the newspaper in which the article appeared, brought fame to Zhang and publicity to the revolutionaries. He was sentenced to three years and Zou Rong to two, but Zou died in prison. Zhang emerged in 1906 to a hero's welcome in Tokyo and was offered the editorship of the *Minbao* 民報 *People's Journal*, the organ of the ***Tongmenghui*** 同盟會 Revolutionary Alliance. His scholarly prowess contributed greatly to the effectiveness of the revolutionaries' attacks on the reformers but his relations with Sun Yixian, both ideological and personal, deteriorated. After *Minbao* was closed down in 1908 by the Japanese authorities at Manchu request, Zhang concentrated on teaching**; Lu Xun** was at this point one of his students and wrote an essay on how the young Chinese students in Japan all wanted to go and hear the the words of the great man but could scarcely understand their meaning. In 1910 he helped re-establish the *Guangfuhui* 光復會 'Restoration of Light Society' as a separate revolutionary group. After the revolution he supported **Yuan Shikai**'s presidency and the retention of Beijing as the capital and served as an adviser to the new government. He realised after the assassination of Song Jiaoren that he had been duped by Yuan and his attempted remonstrances earned him three years of house arrest. After the death of Yuan, Zhang attempted to work for the revolutionaries in liaising with the warlords but became increasingly estranged from Sun Yixian and grew more conservative politically and academically. He was strongly opposed to the May Fourth movement's rejection of the classical language and of traditional thought and values. He spent his final years teaching and writing.

SHIMADA Kenji, *Pioneer of the Chinese Revolution: Zhang Binglin and Confucianism,* trans. Joshua A. FOGEL (Stanford University Press, 1990); Kauko LAITINEN, *Chinese Nationalism in the late Qing Dynasty: Zhang Binglin as an Anti-Manchu Propagandist*

(Copenhagen: Nordic Institute of Asian Studies in association with Curzon Press, London, 1990).

ZHANG CHUNQIAO 張春橋 (1935–92)
Secretary of the Shanghai CCP Committee during the **Cultural Revolution** and member of the **Gang of Four**. He was the inspiration behind the **Shanghai Commune** and was sentenced to death with a two year reprieve on January 25 1981.

ZHANG DAOLING 張道陵 (34–156)
Also known as Zhang Tianshi 張天師 (Celestial Master Zhang), who converted the philosophical ideas of **Daoism** into a popular religion. Zhang Daoling was the governor of Jiangzhou under the Eastern Han court before he went into the Heming mountains (in Sichuan province) with his disciples and established the first sect of Daoist religion in AD 142. The sect was known as the "Zhengyi Sect" 正一道 ("the Orthodox sect"), "Tianshi Sect" after Zhang's title, or the "Five Pecks (*dou* 斗) of Rice Sect", as to become a member everyone had to donate five pecks of rice. In this sect, **Laozi** was deified as Taishang Laojun 太上老君; members did not forsake home or family; they could marry and were lay followers of the Daoist faith. In later life, Zhang wrote some 24 works of Daoist scripture, cured sick people by incantation, and taught people to confess their wrong deeds and devote themselves to Daoism. The portrait of Zhang Tianshi, in full Daoist priest costume and riding a tiger, became a popular picture to be hung in every household, especially during the **Dragonboat Festival**, to expel poisonous insects, cure diseases and protect the family from calamities.

ZHANG GUOTAO 張國燾 (1897–?)
Founder member of the CCP from Jiangxi province. Zhang went up to Beijing University in 1916, met other radicals and took part in the **May Fourth Movement**. He spent two periods in Moscow and became political commissar in the CCP base on the Hubei-Henan-Anhui borders. His units left for the **Long March** before the main contingent from Jiangxi and he lost many people on the way to **Yan'an**. His old rivalry with Mao Zedong was rekindled and he left Yan'an and the CCP in 1938.
CHANG Kuo-t'ao (ZHANG Guotao), *The Rise of the Chinese Communist Party 1921–1927: The Autobiography of Chang Kuo-t'ao, Vol. 1: 1921–1927; Vol. 2: 1928–1938* (University Press of Kansas, 1971–72).

ZHANG HENG 張衡 (78–139)
Celebrated polymath of the Later Han court at **Luoyang**, holding the post of Grand Astrologer under Emperors Andi and Shundi; author of a treatise on astronomy which identified the sun as the source of the moon's light, and a renowned poet whose best known surviving work is his *fu* on the capital city, modelled on **Ban Gu's** *Liangdu fu*. He was also a painter and calligrapher, but it is as an inventor that his reputation is most individual. His seismograph was capable not only of recording earthquakes far from Luoyang, but of determining the direction of the epicentre, thus enabling the swift despatch of relief supplies. See **Inventions and Discoveries**.

ZHANG JUZHENG 張居正 (1525–1582)
Ming dynasty Grand Secretary from 1567–82, having overthrown his predecessor Gao Gong (1512–78). He earned a reputation as a strict disciplinarian and reformer with a determination to strengthen central authority. His economic policies had begun to improve the country's finances when he died but were subsequently subverted by the **Wanli Emperor's** personal assumption of power. He tightened up on standards of officialdom, established controls over excessive expenditure at court and in the provinces, checked corruption, increased income from land tax, and through military reforms achieved respite from Mongol pressure on the northern frontiers and pirates along the south-east coast. He was ruthless in criticising his opponents, especially among the **censors**, and after his death his detractors brought disgrace to his name and family. His efficiency cannot be reproached, but the fallibility of concentrating too much power in the hands of one man was proven by the collapse of standards in government after his death.

R. HUANG, *1587, A Year of No Significance* (Yale University Press, 1981).

ZHANG QIAN 張騫 (?–114BC)
Envoy sent across Central Asia by Han **Wudi** in 138 BC to seek the Yuezhi people as potential allies against the **Xiongnu**. After being captured *en route* and detained for ten years he eventually escaped and continued westwards as far as Ferghana and Bactria. The Yuezhi, now well established in the Indus Valley, would not cooperate with the Chinese plan and Zhang returned to **Chang'an** in 126 BC. In 115 BC he was sent out again in search of the superior "blood-sweating heavenly horses" believed to come from Ferghana and the Wusun people of the Ili Valley. Horses were highly valued in Han China and Wudi's military campaigns were costly in terms of them. Zhang's missions were valuable for the improvement of geographical knowledge, the opening up of trade routes, and the introduction to China of new seeds which he brought back. See also **Silk Road.**

ZHANG WENTIAN see **LUSHAN CONFERENCE**

ZHANG XIANZHONG 張獻忠 (1605–1647)
One of the two major rebel leaders who contributed to the downfall of the Ming dynasty (see also **Li Zicheng**). Between 1630 and 1643 he was involved in uprisings as far apart as modern Shaanxi and Jiangsu, and in 1641 he captured Wuchang and Changsha. In 1643 he proclaimed himself King of the Great West (*daxi wang* 大西王), and his armies entered Sichuan the following year. In Chengdu he established a government along regular imperial lines, but despite the institution of examinations and the minting of money it was an administration based on ruthless intimidation and even massacre of its opponents, including Confucians and members of the **gentry** class. The death toll is reputed to have been enormous, possibly one million out of a total provincial population of three million, before he was eventually killed by the Manchus.

J.B. PARSONS, *The Peasant Rebellions of the Late Ming Dynasty* (University of Arizona Press, 1970).

ZHANG XUELIANG 張學良 (1898 –)
Known as the Young Marshal and son of the Old Marshal **Zhang Zuolin**. He succeeded his father as Manchurian warlord in 1928, when Zhang Zuolin was assassinated with a Japanese bomb and had control of the north-east until the Japanese invasion of 1931. Although he had sworn allegiance to **Jiang Jieshi** in1926, in 1936 he had him kidnapped in the **Xi'an Incident** to try to force him to organise a united resistance to the Japanese. He released Jiang after intervention by Zhou Enlai and was imprisoned, remaining in prison on Taiwan until 1962.

ZHANG ZAI 張載 (1020–77)
An important **Neo-Confucian** philosopher whose systematic thought shows a strong influence from his years of studying **Buddhism**, though he saw his mission firmly in terms of reviving the Way of **Confucius** and **Zhou Gong** (see ***Dao***). He believed in the inherent goodness of man, and his theories on good and evil, and of a cosmological system based on a polarity of Heaven and earth stemming from the interaction of *yin* and *yang* (see ***Yin-yang***) and taking form through the materialisation of ***qi*** 氣, are contained in the *Zheng Meng* 正蒙 (1076). He was a cousin of the Cheng brothers (see **Cheng Hao, Cheng Yi**), whose reputation has since overshadowed his.
Ira E. KASOFF, *The Thought of Chang Tsai* (Cambridge University Press, 1984).

ZHANG ZUOLIN 張作霖 (1875–1928)
Warlord of Manchuria from the Revolution of 1911 whose power later extended in to Mongolia and to Beijing in 1924. He was a zealous anti-Communist and was responsible for ordering the execution of **Li Dazhao** after his troops raided and seized the Soviet Embasy in Beijing in 1927. He was killed on June 4 1928 by a bomb planted under his train on the orders of an officer of the **Guandong Army**.
Gavan MCCORMACK, *Chang Tso-lin in Northeast China, 1911–1928 : China, Japan and the Manchurian Idea* (Stanford University Press, 1977).

ZHAO 趙, STATE
One of the three states (together with **Han** and **Wei**) created by the break-up of **Jin** in 453 BC. Its territory covered the northern part of the Great Plain and was bounded by **Wei** to the south and west, Yan to the east, and the steppe lands of the barbarian **Xiongnu** tribes to the north. It surrendered to **Qin** in 228. See **Warring States.**

ZHAODI 昭帝, HAN EMPEROR (Liu Fuling 劉弗陵, 95–74, r. 86–74 BC)
Son of Emperor **Wudi** by a favourite concubine, Lady Zhao. His reign was a period of retrenchment after the expensive and even dangerous expansionism of the previous decades. An extensive debate on economic issues, stimulated by concern for the suffering of the common people, took place in 81 BC. See ***Yantielun***.

ZHAO GAO 趙高 (d.207 BC)
Eunuch minister under **Qin Shi Huangdi**, who on the latter's death collaborated with **Li Si**, subverted the rightful succession of Fu Su, caused his suicide and that of General Meng Tian, and put the weakling Hu Hai on the

throne. At his instigation Li Si was impeached and executed and Gao himself became Chief Minister. Still not content, he forced the **Second Emperor** to commit suicide and took the imperial seal for himself, but finding that no officials would accept him he presented it to Zi Ying, younger brother of the First Emperor. Zi Ying, however, had him killed by the eunuch Han Tan, only to suffer execution himself at the hands of **Liu Bang**.

ZHAO MENGFU 趙孟頫 (1257–1322)
Also known as Zi'ang 子昂, scholar-official, painter and calligrapher of the Song to Yuan period. He was a descendant of the first Song emperor and had served the Song court before **Khubilai Khan** appointed him to write memorials and proclamations for the Yuan administration. Later he became the advisor to the emperor and secretary to the **Hanlin Academy**. Though he often regretted his decision to collaborate with the Mongol rulers, it was men like him who bridged the gulf that lay between the regime and the Chinese educated class. Zhao Mengfu was an eminent calligrapher and well known for his legendary skill in painting horses, the animal so dear to the **Mongols**' hearts. His most important contribution however was in **landscape painting**, in which he united a direct, spontaneous expression of feeling with a deep reverence for the antique, thus opened the way not only for the next generation of Yuan literati painters but for almost all subsequent scholarly landscape painters. See also **Literati Painting**.

ZHAO ZIYANG 趙紫陽 (1919–)
Native of Henan who joined the CCP in 1938 and served in the Guangdong CCP in various capacities in the 1950s. He was denounced in the **Cultural Revolution**, but came back into political life with the return of Deng Xiaoping in the 1970s and was Secretary of the CCP in Sichuan from 1975–80. In 1977 he was elected to the Politburo and he became CCP Secretary-General in 1987 when **Hu Yaobang** was dismissed. In the **Democracy Movement** and the massacre of June 4 1989, Zhao tried to mediate between the demonstrators and hard-liners such as **Li Peng**, but he lost the argument. After the massacre, he was dismissed from all his posts but not from the CCP.

ZHENG CHENGGONG see **KOXINGA**

ZHENG HE 鄭和 (1371–1433)
Eunuch Muslim admiral from Guangxi known as China's greatest explorer. On the instructions of the **Yongle Emperor** he led seven large fleets of ships on diplomatic expeditions between 1405 and 1433. Sailing round the Malay Archipelago and through the Straits of Malacca they reached destinations along the Indian coast and as far away as the Persian Gulf and the east coast of Africa. Their main purpose was to extend the Chinese **tribute system** as the basis for a world-wide international order. They are often described as treasure-seeking, but though they brought back cargoes of goods gathered *en route* and prompted the sending of many tribute missions to the Chinese court in Yongle's lifetime, the cost of the gifts they themselves took abroad outweighed the economic value of their returns, and after the Emperor's death the number of incoming missions sharply declined.

J.V.G. MILLS, *Ma Yuan: Ying-yai shenglan, "The Overall Survey of the Ocean's Shores" (1433)* (Cambridge University Press, 1970).

ZHENG XUAN 鄭玄 (127–200)
Leading scholar and commentator on the **Confucian Classics**, ritual and the ***Sanli***. His understanding of the phrase *ge wu* from the *Daxue* "Great Learning", that [good] things (*wu*) will come (*ge*) from an understanding of goodness, was commonly accepted until it became the subject of intense scrutiny by **Neo-Confucians**.

ZHILI 直隸 (Chihli)
Ming and Qing dynasty province around the capital Beijing, and directly administered (which is what Zhili means) by the capital. Its name was changed to Hebei during the Republic. Nan Zhili (Southern Directly Administered) was the equivalent area directly governed from Nanjing and corresponded roughly to present-day Jiangsu and Anhui.

ZHILI CLIQUE see **BEIYANG WARLORDS**

***ZHONG* 中 "Centre"**
A key term in Chinese philosophy and psychology. The cosmic significance of the centre was already established by the Shang, and may suggest a link with the performance of archery for ritual purposes. The centre was defined as the key one of the five directions, the hub around which the other four were balanced. By Warring States times it had also acquired a qualitative appeal, as the "Central States" (*zhongguo*) on the flood-plain of the **Yellow River** came to represent civilised orthodoxy. Before long, China became the "**Middle Kingdom**", the heart of the cultured world around which lesser states were ranged. To **Confucius**, the thin central dividing line between partiality to one side or the other had a strong moral appeal. To the Daoists, *zhong* represented the point of balance between contradictory and constantly shifting forces. They recognised the paradox that the dialectic of opposing elements, *yin* and *yang*, was necessary (see ***Yin-yang***) but that the search for a median point was desirable and must constantly be pursued. The Buddhist Song Zhao, in his *Zhaolun*, said that the Middle Way consisted of a combination of antitheses and syntheses. It summed up in one term all the connotations of the never-ending Chinese search for harmony between Heaven and earth, and for stability amid "all under heaven". See also ***Zhongyong***.

ZHONG KUI 鐘馗
Legendary demon chaser. According to legend, Tang emperor **Xuanzong** (712–755) was tormented in his dream by a petty demon. Then a tall, fearsome figure in a ragged cloak appeared and caught the demon. He introduced himself as Zhong Kui. So the emperor ordered a famous artist, **Wu Daozi**, to paint a portrait of Zhong Kui. The legend later became a popular theme in Chinese painting and **New Year prints**. It was a custom in old China to hang pictures of Zhong Kui in households to chase away demons.

ZHONGHUA GEMINGDANG 中華革命黨 Chinese Revolutionary Party
The name of the revolutionary party set up by **Sun Yixian** in Tokyo in July 1914. After the success of the 1911 revolution, the revolutionary groups were organised into an open political party, the Guomindang 國民黨, to fight elections. Although successful in the elections, the party was outmanoeuvred by **Yuan Shikai** and forced into the abortive 1913 **Second Revolution**. After fleeing to Japan, Sun Yixian in 1913 began reorganising a group of members from the former Guomindang into a tighter revolutionary group with an oath of loyalty devised by him; this was the origin of the Zhonghua Gemingdang. It had branches in a number of overseas locations and was dedicated to armed resistance to Yuan Shikai. From then until Yuan's death in 1916, it carried out a substantial number of armed uprisings and assassination attempts. In October 1919 it was reorganised as the Zhongguo **Guomindang** 中國國民黨.
Edward FRIEDMAN, *Backward toward Revolution: The Chinese Revolutionary Party* (Berkeley: University of California Press, 1974).

ZHONGSHAN INCIDENT see **GUANGZHOU COUP**

ZHONGYONG 中庸 Doctrine of the Mean
Like the ***Daxue*** 'Great Learning', this was originally a chapter of the ***Liji*** selected by **Zhu Xi** as one of his **Four Books**, a set of works which became part of the basic curriculum of **Confucianism**. *Zhong* is defined as centrality, not deviating from equilibrium, and describes our basic nature before it is disturbed by our emotions. *Yong* 'ordinariness' implies that which is unchanging and is the state of harmony resulting from the appropriate interplay of our emotions with things. The *Zhongyong* is one of the most mystical of Confucian works and follows **Mencius** in its emphasis on *xing* 性 human nature and on the interrelationship between man and Heaven (or nature *tian* 天). Its constant references to the **Dao** 道 Way also made the text popular with Daoists but the Way it describes is the moral Way of Confucianism to be attained through *cheng* 誠 sincerity, not the amoral Way of **Daoism**. The basic doctrines of Confucius lacked the mystical and spiritual dimension, relating the individual to the cosmic order, which **Buddhism** and Daoism offered. By developing ideas in texts like the *Zhongyong*, Zhu Xi and other Song scholars were able to offer a renewed version, Neo-Confucianism, which displaced Buddhism and put the native tradition back at the centre of the intellectual world.
Wing-tsit CHAN, *A Sourcebook in Chinese Philosophy* (Princeton University Press, 1963); TU Wei-ming, *Centrality and Commonality* (State University of New York, 1976).

ZHONGZONG 中宗, TANG EMPEROR (Li Xian 李顯, 656–710, r. 684 and 705–10)
Son of Emperor **Gaozong** and Empress Wu (see **Wu Zetian**). Within two months of his accession his mother exiled him and his powerful wife, the Empress Wei, and he was not recalled until 698. His subsequent reign was a constant struggle for supremacy between senior officials, members of the imperial family, and maternal relatives. Prominent among the latter were Empress Wei, her daughter Princess Anle and the Empress Wu's daughter Princess Taiping. On his death he was succeeded by his 15–year old son, who was quickly removed by a coup arranged by Taiping and supplanted by her brother **Ruizong**.

ZHOU DUNYI 周敦頤 (1017–1073)
Early Song scholar credited with being one of the originators of **Neo-Confucianism**. Zhou's studies of the ***Yijing*** 'Book of Changes' led him to construct a schema of existence which may have been inspired by Daoist models but which became the basis for a new Confucian metaphysics. His *Taiji tushuo* 太極圖說 'Explanation of the Plan of the Great Ultimate' provides a description of the process of creation from the formless *wuji* 無極 'ultimateless' to the all-encompassing first principle *taiji* 'great ultimate' which gave rise in repose and activity to ***yin*** and ***yang***, which in turn produced the **five elements** leading to the creation of the myriad phenomena of existence. In his *Tongshu* 通書 'Explication' he provides Confucian glosses on the *Yijing* stressing the primacy of *cheng* 誠, sincerity, in the development of sagehood by associating it with *qian*, the first **hexagram**. Zhou Dunyi and **Shao Yong** provided a basis for the Neo-Confucian claim that Confucian morality and social structure were not only practical and beneficial to society, they were also a reflection of the cosmic order. This paved the way for a regeneration of the native tradition and its domination of intellectual life until the twentieth century.

FENG Yu-lan, *A History of Chinese Philosophy Volume II* trans. Derk BODDE (Princeton University Press, 1953); Wing-tsit CHAN, *A Sourcebook in Chinese Philosophy* (Princeton University Press, 1963); H. FRANKE, ed., *Sung Biographies* (Wiesbaden: Franz Steiner Verlag, 1976).

ZHOU 周 DYNASTY
Zhou had been a feudal tributary of the Shang kingdom, its territory centred on the capital at Feng, near modern Xi'an. Its rise to power had been planned by **Wen Wang** as the moral and political authority of the Shang court dwindled (see **Di Xin**) and was carried out by his son **Wu Wang**. The date of the culmination of their campaign and the inauguration of the new dynasty has long been uncertain, but recent research suggests 1045 BC, after the battle of Muye. By this time much of northern and central China was well into the **Bronze Age** and Zhou extended the Shang feudal system as a means of applying its control. By the time its long claim to possess the Mandate of Heaven was disproved by its own erstwhile tributary of **Qin**, the country had seen enormous changes both in its level of material civilisation and its intellectual and political sophistication. The Zhou dynasty is divided into the following chronological phases:

(1) The Western or Former Zhou; capital at Hao 鎬 (near modern Xi'an). During this period the empire was extended both by military campaign and tributary agreement. Military strength and communications were inadequate to rule by force alone, and the concept of the Heavenly Mandate was developed as a reinforcement of the dynasts' legitimacy (see **Mandate of Heaven**). A cultural revolution took place in the tenth century under Kings Mu and Gong which assisted the spread of bronze culture.

(2) The Eastern or Later Zhou; capital at Luo 洛 (near modern **Luoyang**). The capital was moved in 771 under King You. By this time Zhou had already created 71 feudal states but was increasingly unable to control even those ruled by its own royal kinsmen, and the leaders of the states became virtually independent, arrogating rites and powers and eventually even the title of king that properly belonged to Zhou alone. A succession of **hegemons** attempted to effect

a political system based on a balance of power, but the lust for state aggrandisement and the obvious inefficiency of numerous small units soon made a struggle for supremacy inevitable. The period witnessed enormous economic and social changes, including the development of iron, the growth of commerce, increases in the size of armies and improvements to their weaponry and tactical powers, the extension of writing, and the appearance of non-aristocratic elites. The sense of empire implemented by Qin in 221 BC was totally different from that of the early Eastern Zhou monarchs.

Two sub-periods are often identified within the Eastern Zhou:

(a) The *Chunqiu* "**Spring and Autumn**" period, 722–481 BC;

(b) The *Zhanguo* "**Warring States**" period, 481–221 BC

Throughout the Warring States period the kings of Zhou saw the extent of their territorial domain and their royal authority whittled away by their over-mighty vassals. Through the Period of the Philosophers (see **Hundred Schools**) political theorists argued over means of accommodation with changed circumstances. **Confucius** and **Mencius** tried to restore Zhou fortunes, albeit in modernised form, by glamourising the achievements of the **Former Kings** and re-emphasizing the virtues they associated with the golden past. Others, notably the **Legalists**, saw that a clean break with the past was necessary in order to adapt to modern conditions. The last Zhou king was deposed in 256 BC, and the first act of the new First Emperor (see **Qin Shi Huangdi**) in 221 was to abolish the Shang and Zhou feudal system of aristocratic rank and **land tenure**, clearly signalling the radical difference that should characterise the new imperial age.

H.G. Creel, *The Origins of Statecraft in China, vol. 1, The Western Chou Empire* (University of Chicago Press, 1970); C.Y. Hsu, *Ancient China in Transition* (Stanford University Press, 1965); C.Y. Hsu and K.M. Linduff, *Western Chou Civilisation* (Yale University Press, 1988.

Zhou Enlai 周恩來 (1898–1976)

CCP leader, Prime Minister of the PRC and statesman. Zhou Enlai was born in Jiangsu and studies at Nankai University in Tianjin and in Paris where he joined the Socialist Youth League. He went back to China in 1923 and became director of the political office of the **Huangpu Military Academy**, where he worked with, among others, **Jiang Jieshi**, whose release he was later able to help secure during the **Xi'an incident.** He became Prime Minister of the Government Administrative Council in 1949 and continued to head the State Council that succeeded it. He remained in power until his death with surprisingly little criticism, even managing to survive the **Cultural Revolution** without being denounced. He was an enigmatic and cultured figure and probably the most capable political diplomat in the PRC.

Zhou Gong 周公, The Duke of Zhou

Son of **Wen Wang** and brother of **Wu Wang**, whom he served as a councillor and succeeded as regent for the first seven years of King Cheng's reign. His fame in later Chinese eyes was due not only to his success as a military leader in putting down a revolt by Shang clansmen, nor to his political skill at building a second capital near **Luoyang** where he confined them, nor even to the undoubted administrative success in welding together the newly conquered empire, but to the demonstration of the potential efficacy of regency, a frequent occurence in imperial history, and his exemplification of filial service by a minister who yet held effective political power. See also **Former Kings, Zhou Dynasty.**

H.G. CREEL, *The Origins of Statecraft in China, vol.1, The Western Chou Empire* (University of Chicago Press, 1970).

ZHOU LI* 周禮 *Rites of Zhou

Originally called the *Zhou guan*, 'Officials of Zhou', this is one of three texts on rites which make up the ***Li*** Book of Rites. The *Zhou li* describes the governmental system of the Zhou with a chapter for each of six main ministries of state. These were the ministries of: *Tian* 天 'Heaven' in charge of governmental affairs and presided over by a *Dazai* 大宰 'Prime minister', *Di* 地 'Earth' in charge of education and presided over by a *Dasitu* 大司徒, *Chun* 春 'Spring' in charge of rites and presided over by a *Dasibo* 大司伯, *Xia* 夏 'Summer' in charge of military affairs and presided over by a *Dasima* 大司馬, *Qiu* 秋 'Autumn' in charge of penal affairs and presided over by a *Dasikou* 大司寇 and *Dong* 冬 'Winter' in charge of crafts and presided over by a *Dasikong* 大司空. The final chapter was lost, to be replaced in the Han by a separate text, the *Kaogongji* 考工記 'Record of a study of artisanship'. This old text classic has always been controversial; it was traditionally associated with **Zhou Gong** 周公 the Duke of Zhou, and was said as a result to have suffered particularly in the Qin **burning of the books**, hence all mention of it was excised before the ***Shiji***. It was one of the works edited by **Liu Xin** and was used by the revivalist **Wang Mang** as a blueprint for his Xin dynasty state structure; this naturally did not endear it to the Later Han rulers although **Zheng Xuan** nevertheless considered it an important work and wrote a commentary on it. Doubts about the authenticity of the text were expressed from at least the Song onwards and **Kang Youwei** in the late ninteeenth century declared it to be a work forged by Liu Xin in the service of Wang Mang. Modern scholars tend to regard it as a Warring States period work providing valuable insights into late Zhou institutions.

Michael LOEWE, ed., *Early Chinese Texts: A Bibliographical Guide* (Berkeley: The Society for the Study of Early China and The Institute of East Asian Studies, University of California, 1993).

ZHOU XIN, "the tyrant Zhou" see **DI XIN**

ZHOU YANG 周揚 (1908–)

Literary bureaucrat and translator of Tolstoy and other Russian writers into Chinese. He had been a member of the **League of Left-Wing Writers** and was in charge of education in the CCP base at Yan'an and after 1949 was active in the CCP Propaganda Department.

ZHOUKOUDIAN 周口店

Site in Hebei Province of the first discoveries of Palaeolithic man (*Homo sapiens sapiens* and *Homo erectus*) on Chinese soil by Johan Gunnar Andersson in 1921. Remains of **Beijing Man** were lost during World War Two, but evidence from the cave inhabited by around forty men, women and children suggests that they used fire and ate meat from the changing variety of animals available to them during successive climatic periods (including hyenas, wild cat, elephant, and water buffalo). Scientific analysis indicates a possible occupation period from 500,000 to 230,000 years ago for *Homo erectus* at Zhoukoudian.

Gina L. BARNES, *China, Korea and Japan: The Rise of Civilization in East Asia* (Thames and Hudson, 1993).

ZHU DE 朱德 (1886–1976)

Sichuan-born CCP military leader who led the **Nanchang Rising** in 1927 and organised the **Workers and Peasants Red Army** with Mao Zedong, the two being so close that it was thought they were one person – Zhu Mao. Zhu took part in the **Long March,** was Commander-in-Chief of the People's Liberation Army and a member of the Politburo after 1949.

ZHU WEN 朱溫 (852–912)

A former bandit associate of **Huang Chao** who later recanted and served the Tang court. In 904, however, he assassinated the Emperor Zhaozong, and two years later overturned the last of the Tang imperial incumbents and assumed the throne himself as Emperor Liang Taizu. See **Five Dynasties and Ten Kingdoms**.

ZHU XI 朱熹 (Zhu Yuanhui 朱元晦, 1130–1200)

Leading Neo-Confucian philosopher and reinterpreter of the Confucian tradition whose influence on its implementation through the Song to Qing periods, and in **Korea** as well as China, qualifies him to stand him in succession to **Confucius**, **Mencius**, and **Han Yu** as a recognised definer of the true Way (***Dao***). He obtained his *jinshi* in 1148 before spending much of his career as a provincial official in modern Fujian and Jiangxi provinces. There he introduced measures aimed at improving the living conditions of the people in his care, such as the establishment of a community granary. He unsuccessfully proposed a reform of the land survey and tax system (see also **Well-field System**). He took a firm stand against corruption and lawlessness and in favour of education and rites (see **Schools**). He stressed the importance of moral training, and honoured the memory of worthy men and women, both by the erection of shrines and tablets and the composition of obituaries (see **Virtuous Women**). In this way he paid homage to the early leaders of the Neo-Confucian movement **Zhou Dunyi**, **Cheng Hao** and **Cheng Yi**. His outspoken criticism of maladministration earned him enemies and he died in political disgrace but popular esteem. He was a prolific author and editor, being responsible for the selection of the ***Lunyu, Mengzi, Daxue*** "Great Learning" and the ***Zhongyong*** as the **Four Books**. His compilation of Neo-Confucian thought under the title of *Jinsilu* 'A record of everyday observations' has been called "unquestionably the most important single work of philosophy produced in the Far East during the second millennium A.D." (Wing-tsit Chan), and his edited condensation of **Sima Guang**'s **Zizhi Tongjian**, under the title of *Zizhi Tongjian Gangmu*, presented a moralistic view of Chinese history which, because of his authority, was better known to later historians than Sima's more complete and objective original work. See **Neo-Confucianism.**

Wing-tsit CHAN, *Chu Hsi, Life and Thought* (St. Martin's Press, 1987);Wing-tsit CHAN, ed., *Chu Hsi and Neo-Confucianism* (University of Hawaii Press, 1986); D.J. MUNRO,

Images of Human Nature, a Sung Portrait (Princeton University Press, 1988); Daniel K. GARDNER, *Chu Hsi and the Ta-hsueh: Neo-Confucian Reflection on the Confucian Canon* (Council on East Asian Studies, Harvard University, 1986).

ZHU YUANZHANG see **HONGWU EMPEROR**

ZHU ZAIYU 朱載堉 (1536–1611)
A descendant of the Hongxi Emperor (reigned 1424–5) and the best known musical theorist in Chinese history. Trying to identify the perfect level of the fundamental pitch *huang zhong* and to use it in the recreation of ancient (Zhou dynasty) ritual **music** had been a preoccupation of musicologists through the ages. Zhu Zaiyu wrote widely on musical matters between 1581 and 1606, when he presented to the throne his collected works *Yuelü quanshu* 樂律全書 "Complete work on music and pitchpipes". This included the book that now constitutes his claim to modern fame, *Lulü jingyi* 律呂精義 'The essential meaning of the standard pitchpipe' (1596), which presents his discovery of equal temperament tuning. It was not, however, recognised either at the late Ming or the Qing court, when the emphasis on classical scholarship was too strong for the acceptance of a radical theory based more on empirical observation and argument than on textual interpretation.
Kenneth ROBINSON, *A Critical Study of Chu Tsai-yu's Contribution to the Theory of Equal Temperament in Chinese Music* (Wiesbaden: Franz Steiner Verlag, 1980).

ZHUANGZI 莊子 (fourth century BC)
Refers both to the philosopher Zhuang Zhou 莊周 and to the later text bearing his name. Zhuangzi, along with **Laozi**, is the archetypal Daoist philosopher. Whereas Laozi has much in common with the **Legalists** in his preoccupation with government, Zhuangzi champions a more anarchistic, naturalistic approach which spurns participation in politics in favour of developing one's individual understanding. His main themes concern the quest for enlightenment about the nature of the ***Dao*** 道. This results in the individual's liberation from the bonds of the material world and the realisation of the relativity of all things, including life and death, and hence the limited significance of mankind in the universal scheme (Zhuangzi is one of the least homocentric of all Chinese philosophers). Throughout later history these ideas have been a source of inspiration and comfort to Chinese scholars, especially those feeling their talents were unappreciated. Apart from its philosophical content the text's literary qualities, imagination and vitality have inspired generations of artists and writers. The 33 *pian* text is traditionally divided into three sections: 7 'inner' chapters ascribed to Zhuangzi himself, 15 'outer' chapters by later followers and 11 'mixed' chapters of heterogenous material, including a final chapter consisting of a critical survey of the Chinese philosophical schools. The text may have been compiled around 130 BC; the present version was edited and annotated by Guo Xiang 郭象 (d. 312).
The complete works of Chuang-tzu trans. Burton WATSON (Columbia University Press, 1968); *Chuang-tzu, The Seven Inner Chapters and other writings from the book of Chuang-tzu, trans.* A.C. GRAHAM (George Allen and Unwin, 1981).

ZHUGE LIANG 諸葛亮 (181–234)
Chief councillor to Liu Bei, ruler of the south-western kingdom of Shu Han at Chengdu in the aftermath of the Han dynasty's collapse. Liu Bei had been one of **Cao Cao's** officers before becoming one of his principal opponents in the **Three Kingdoms** period. 'The Romance of the Three Kingdoms' (***Sanguo yanyi***) enhances Zhuge Liang's reputation as an outstanding military strategist. He was a self-avowed Legalist who often compared himself with **Guan Zhong**.

ZIZHI TONGJIAN **資治通鑒**
After the ***Shiji***, the second great multi-dynasty historical work produced as a result of individual initiative. The *Zizhi tongjian* was created by the Song dynasty scholar **Sima Guang** (1019–86) to offer scholars guidance to the mass of historical documentation by presenting a chronological broad sweep of history. The work covers the period from the Warring States, from 403 BC, to the end of Later Zhou, in AD 959, in 296 *juan* plus 30 *juan* of indices and 30 *juan* of *kao yi* 考異 'examination of discrepancies'. Sima Guang started compiling an early draft around 1064; this covered the period from the Warring States to the Qin in 8 *juan* 卷 and was submitted to the throne under the title *Tongzhi* 通志 'Comprehensive Record'. The Yingzong Emperor ordered that an office be established in 1066 for the compilation and after Sima Guang's resignation from office in 1070 (in opposition to **Wang Anshi's** reforms), he was able to concentrate on the work until its completion in 1084. In practice, Sima Guang was assisted by a team of historians who compiled the materials and produced a long draft which Sima Guang then edited into the final version. A feature of the work is the wide range of sources used and their careful evaluation, indicated in the *kao yi*. The title *Zizhi tongjian*, literally "Comprehensive mirror assisting government", was conferred on it by the Shenzong Emperor and reflects the work's preoccupation with political and military history. Lest the lessons still be lost on the reader, Sima Guang provides 118 *pian* of comments giving his own views on the events described, under the byline *chen Guang yue* 臣光曰 'Your servant Guang says'. Apart from its historical value, the work is highly esteemed as literature and some of the battle descriptions are regarded as literary pieces in their own right. This high literary evaluation is a further reflection of Sima Guang's role in its production.

W.G. BEASLEY and E.G. PULLEYBLANK eds., *Historians of China and Japan* (Oxford University Press, 1961).

ZODIAC see ***SHENGXIAO***

ZONGLI YAMEN 總理衙門
Foreign Ministry, in full the *Zongli geguo shiwu yamen* 各國事務總理衙門 (*Zongli yamen*) "General Office for the Affairs of Various Countries" established during the **Tongzhi Restoration** for dealing with Westerners. It was designed to replace the ***Lifanyuan***, which was a part of the **tribute system** and was based on the assumption of Chinese superiority.

ZOROASTRIANISM
Pre-Islamic religion of Iran which became influential in the court of the Tang dynasty in **Chang'an** and survives as the Parsi faith in India.

ZOU YAN 鄒衍 (305–?240 BC)

Philosopher from the state of **Qi** who no doubt reflected earlier attempts, and certainly inspired later ones, to identify the role of the **Five Elements** *wuxing* in the creation and continued workings of the universe. His biography is found in the ***Shiji*** and his ideas on the *wuxing* in the ***Lüshi Chunqiu***. He postulated a cyclical connection between political developments associated with dynastic rise and fall and the successive supremacy of the elements earth (which he identified with the power of the **Yellow Emperor**), wood (the Xia dynasty, colour green), metal (the Shang dynasty, colour white), fire (the Zhou dynasty, colour red), and water, which he believed would inevitably be the next power in the ascendant (colour black). (The question of whether or not Qin had merited the claim to rule with the virtue of water, or whether the Han had inherited its power, much exercised the minds of Han officials. See **Dong Zhongshu.**) Zou Yan may also have been the one to link the theories of *yin* and *yang* with those of the five elements and is sometimes credited with being the leader of a so-called School of ***Yin-yang*** and the Five Elements, though this assumes a greater degree of standardisation and organisation than is probably justified for the third century BC.

ZUNYI CONFERENCE *Zunyi huiyi* 遵義會議

CCP meeting held from January 6–8 1935 in the early stages of the **Long March**. During the conference, Mao attacked the **Twenty-Eight Bolsheviks** for their failures which had led to the loss of the **Jiangxi Soviet**. Mao emerged as the single unchallenged leader of the CCP, a position he consolidated in **Yan'an**.

ZUOZHUAN 左傳 Mr Zuo's Commentary

Historical account of the state of Lu from 722–463 BC associated with the *Chunqiu, **Spring and Autumn Annals***. It was traditionally regarded as one of the three commentaries on the *Spring and Autumn Annals* and believed to have been written by Zuo Qiuming 左丘明, a contemporary of Confucius. Liu Xin (46 BC – AD 23) claimed the credit for putting together an old text version of the *Chunqiu* found in the imperial archives with the *Zuoshi* 左氏 'Mr Zuo text'. Liu's association with the usurpation by **Wang Mang** of the Han throne made his claims deeply suspect to later scholars, some of whom believed that he had forged the *Zuozhuan* using material from an earlier collection, the *Guoyu* 國語, to bolster Wang's position. The general consensus is that this is not the case but it is still not clear if the *Zuozhuan* was originally a commentary or a separate historical text subsequently combined with the *Chunqiu*.

Burton WATSON trans., *The Tso Chuan. Selections from China's Oldest Narrative History* (Columbia University Press, 1989).

ZUO ZONGTANG 左宗棠 (1812–85)

Zeng Guofan's lieutenant and charged by Zeng with suppressing the **Taiping Rebellion** in Zhejiang. He was appointed governor of Zhejiang and governor-general of Zhejiang and Fujian and was sent to Gansu and Shaanxi where he helped **Li Hongzhang** defeat the Hui **Muslim rebellion** in 1867–80. He was responsible for the creation of the province of Xinjiang in 1884 and was a supporter of the **Self-Strengthening Movement** and contributed to it by building the Fuzhou Dockyard.

SELECT BIBLIOGRAPHY

Jacques Gernet	*A History of Chinese Civilisation* (Cambridge 1982)
John K. Fairbank & Edwin O. Reischauer	*China: Tradition and Transformation* (Sydney 1989)
Jonathan Spence	*The Search for Modern China* (New York 1990)
Immanuel Hsu	*The Rise of Modern China* (Oxford 1995)
Joseph Needham	*Science and Civilisation in China* (Cambridge 1954–) continuing
John K. Fairbank & Denis Twitchett (ed)	*Cambridge History of China* (Cambridge 1978–) Fifteen volumes planned
Brian Hook & Denis Twitchett (ed)	*Cambridge Encyclopedia of China* (Cambridge 1991)

*

Victor H Mair (ed)	*Columbia Anthology of Traditional Chinese Literature* (New York 1994)
K.Y. Hsu	*Literature of the Peoples Republic of China* (1980)

*

H. Franke (ed)	*Sung Biographies* (Wiesbaden 1976)
L.C. Goodrich Fang Chaoying (ed)	*Dictionary of Ming Biography* (New York 1976)
A.W. Hummel (ed)	*Eminent Chinese of the Ch'ing Period* (Washington 1944)
Howard L Boorman Janet Krompart (ed)	*Biographical Dictionary of Republic of China* (New York 1976–79)